Baghdad and Isfahan

Baghdad and Isfahan

A Dialogue of Two Cities in an Age of Science ca. 750–1750

Elaheh Kheirandish

I.B.TAURIS
LONDON • NEW YORK • OXFORD • NEW DELHI • SYDNEY

I.B. TAURIS
Bloomsbury Publishing Plc
50 Bedford Square, London, WC1B 3DP, UK
1385 Broadway, New York, NY 10018, USA
29 Earlsfort Terrace, Dublin 2, Ireland

First published in Great Britain 2021
Reprinted 2021
This paperback edition published 2024

Cover image: Shaykh Wafā', *Calendar of Timekeeping: Rūz-nāma...mīqāt*. Harvard University, Houghton Library. MS Arab 397.

A catalogue record for this book is available from the British Library.

A catalog record for this book is available from the Library of Congress.

ISBN: HB: 978-1-7807-6833-5
PB: 978-0-7556-3510-8
ePDF: 978-0-7556-3507-8
eBook: 978-0-7556-3508-5

Typeset by RefineCatch Limited, Bungay, Suffolk

To our two 'Suns'
Leo by *Name* and Leo by *Sign*

Contents

List of Plates viii
Preface x
Notes on Conventions xiii

Introduction 1
Chapter Summaries 9
Chart: Names and Dates 13
0 Cast and Stage 15
1 Time and Place 17
2 Moon and Sun 43
3 Round and Square 77
4 Word and Line 99
5 East and West 125
6 Old and New 151
7 Plan and Chance 181
Postscript 209
Now and Then 209
Moon and Sun 210

Bibliography 213
Name Index 239
Subject Index 259
General Index 263

List of Plates

1. *Dialogues of Baghdad and Isfahan*: *Munāẓirāt-i Baghdād va Iṣfahān*
   © The British Library Board. MS Add 18, 411, fol. 166a
2. *Pseudo-Galen Book of Antidotes: Kitāb al-Diryāq*
   Nationalbibliothek, Vienna. MS AF. 10 fol. 157
3. Jazarī, *Compendium of Theory and Useful Practice in the Mechanical Arts*
   Boston Museum of Fine Arts. MS 15.114
4. Frontispiece. Alhazen and Galileo: *Selenographia*, Johannes Hevelius, 1647
   Harvard University. Houghton Library. Typ 620.47.452F
5. Sagitarrius, Bīrūnī, *Book of Instructions*: *Kitāb al-Tafhīm* (adaptation)
   © The British Library Board. MS Sup 7697
6. ʿĀmilī, *Summary of Arithmetic*: *Khulāṣat al-ḥisāb*
   Harvard University, Houghton Library. MS Arab SM4284 (above)
   Manuscript display: 'Windows into early science', Virtual Gallery (below)
7. *Timekeeping Calendar* (centre): Plate 9 Close up. Other: Private Collection
   © Elaheh Kheirandish https://www.scholar.harvard.edu/ekheirandish/exhibits
8. '*First Small Shahnama*: *Buzurgmihr masters the game of chess*'
   Metropolitan Museum of Art, New York. MS 34.24.1b
9. Shaykh Wafāʾ, *Calendar of Timekeeping*: *Rūz-nāma . . . mīqāt*
   Harvard University, Houghton Library. MS Arab 397, opening folio
10. *Panoramas of Baghdad and Isfahan: Travels and Journal of Ambrosio Bembo*
    The James Ford Bell Library, University of Minnesota. 1676 fBe
11. Maps from Tübingen Atlas of the Near East: ca. 750–1750
    Harvard University, Pusey Library
12. Map from a treatise on Determining the Direction of the Qibla
    Bibliothèque nationale de France. BNF Paris: MS Persan 169, 6, fol. 42a
13. Frontispiece: Alhazen, *Opticae Thesaurus,* Risner, Friedrich (ed), 1572
    Harvard University, Houghton Library. f GC5 R4947 572i
14. Zodiac Constellations, *Compendium of Knowledge* (Jung)
    Harvard Art Museums/Arthur M. Sackler Museum, Gift of
    Philip Hofer. Photo: © President and Fellows of Harvard College.
    MS 1984.463, fol. 131b

15. Photo: Book Camera Obscura, France about 1750
Getty Library and Research Institute, Los Angeles, Nekes collection 93.R.118

16. Shaykh Wafā', *Calendar of Timekeeping*: *Rūz-nāma . . . mīqāt*
Harvard University, Houghton Library. MS Arab 397, opening folio, close up (centre). Other: Moon, Sun and Star icons © Adele Karimian

Preface

This book could not have been written without a chance encounter with a text that I refer to as a *Dialogue of Baghdad and Isfahan*, a text whose discovery would have been improbable, if not impossible, in an age where online searches have changed the nature of surprise finds. Ever since I encountered a printed manuscript catalogue with an entry on a *munazara* (literally eye-to-eye dialogue) between those two historic cities – an incident prompted by my searches under the term's orthographic twin, *manazir* (optics) from the same verbal root *nazar* (view) – I found it irresistible to publish something on it, despite instant challenges, starting with dating. A project involving Baghdad and Isfahan, cities with such historic prominence and timely interest, meant publishing something beyond the text of the *Dialogue* itself from day one. Getting further and further into the project then led to deeper and deeper reconstructions of the parallel stories of these and other related cities from an angle somehow missing from the text itself – that of science.

With all the historical reconstructions and conceptual recreations involved, there is still nothing imaginary in this book. Historically, it captures sources and events traceable to exact times and places. Conceptually, it highlights characters and episodes mirroring real beings and settings. There is no single line in the book without some form of actual correspondence; and there are no random choices made anywhere in it, starting with the title and subtitle: 'Baghdad and Isfahan' represent two age-old cities whose outstanding pasts in a once-visible 'age of science' are reconstructed, chapter by chapter, and century by century. The two modern characters, one textual, one human, evolving side by side in an increasingly rapid age of technology, are added to capture living traces of a more recent past whose own lasting presence is recreated, city by city, and library by library.

The resulting work has taken the book far beyond what seems to have come down from a period after the seventh/thirteenth century, curiously from an interval *after* Baghdad was 'Baghdad', but *before* Isfahan was to become 'Isfahan'. The years that mark the highs and lows of these two ancient cities take the story outside the time when Baghdad and Isfahan were shining, mostly past one another, as the respective capitals of the ʿAbbasid caliphate (ca. 750–1258) and Safavid dynasty (ca. 1501–1722). In these periods, and those in between, the two capitals – represented here as Moon and Sun icons to match the lunar and solar calendars of their respective Arab and Persian lands – stand out, not as the two boasts of Islamic civilization as in the original *Dialogue*, but as two notable seats of patronage (caliphate and dynastic), two prominent voices of culture (Arabic and Persian), two sectarian poles of institutions (Sunni and Shiʿi), and most relevant here, two focal points of science, with 'ups and downs' beyond a linear 'rise and set'.

Other historical *Dialogues*, in languages from Pahlavi, Arabic and Persian to Hebrew, Turkish, and Latin, and in genre from prose and poetry to several comparable forms, could extend all such themes and images still further. But here, the book's focus remains on Arab and Persian lands of the Islamic Middle Ages, and their story of science, with a message for understanding history as a sum of unique moments and events; and if sums are larger than their parts, then the story the book tells is larger than the history it records.

On the evolvement of the book itself, while its conception was occasioned by my chance encounter with an early *Dialogue* between Baghdad and Isfahan, its composition has coincided with the increasingly louder rings of the names of those two cities in successive years – cities sitting across from one another in modern-day Iraq and Iran, within lands whose own names have long crossed over from the ancient Near East to the modern Middle East. Timely crossings of so many other lines in the course of the book's composition, between East and West, science and technology, and humanities and humanity, have further placed both the historic and modern characters in various casts and stages throughout the book. Parallel 'tales' are accordingly presented in each chapter in successive months and years to trace the outstanding lives of two cities other than those immortalised through Charles Dickens's London and Paris of another unforgettable age. Closer to Dickens's original *All Year Round* installments of the same work, the present chapters are filled with their own corresponding actors and settings: the first cast on stage is the physical text of the *Dialogue of Baghdad and Isfahan* in the form of an old manuscript whose many lives, from a composed and transcribed copy all the way to a virtual and multimedia entity, draws the first storyline of the book. The second cast is the observer and handler of the *Dialogue* manuscript, shadowing its multiple forms through the evolving technologies of the time in the person of a young character who embodies generations beyond his own age and gender. The third and fourth casts are representations of the historic cities of Baghdad and Isfahan, brought to life through the distinct narrative voice and signature of that young symbol of the future in their successive passages through time. What emerges are two cities in an age of science next to many others, from Basra, Cairo and Damascus to Kashan, Cordoba, and Istanbul, those whose eventful pasts and vital lives throughout the ages can no longer be assumed isolated or irrelevant.

The completion of the book is owed to all those who have had a share in its continuous evolvement. The days, months, by now years, of accumulation in the course of the book's preparation call for acknowledging those who have variously left marks on it over time, as reflected in the chapter notes and name index: students and colleagues, featured throughout the book in different forms and capacities; students, too many to name here, those not merely participating in my related courses, but contributing to course-based historical plays and manuscript exhibits; and colleagues acting as sources of inspiration and direction: Roy Mottahedeh of Harvard University, encouraging the book's publication, suggesting its publisher and reading its drafts; Anne Davenport of Boston College and Liba Taub of Cambridge University insightfully reviewing it from their respective specialty perspectives; the book's editorial support raising the bar of the project differently: the publisher's own team at London's I.B. Tauris, Bloomsbury, Iradj Bagherzade, seeing the book's publication, Lester Crook, Rory Gormley and Yasmin Garcha overseeing it, and the production team, project management and copyeditors finalising it; outside contributors lending their skills to the project on my own request: Corydon Ireland, science editor at Harvard News Office at the time, Alicia Kennedy of Lasell University and Kennedy Editorial, Maera Siddiqi, a student turned colleague with multiple roles in this and related projects, and Adele Karimian, for Sun and Moon designs; and finally, mentors and supporters: Asadollah Kheirandish of *A Verse Amongst Thousands*, transcribing the manuscript of the *Munazara* and composing verses on its two cities in dialogue, Parvin-Dokht Molavi, acting as our joint 'Pleiades' of inspiration, Hormoz Goodarzy, fully present throughout the book's long production, reading its manuscript, and drafting its Names and Dates Chart; and others, with roles becoming more transparent, and voices more recognisable, in the unfolding chapters.

The threads that at once weave and unravel age-old knots around historic cities as intricate as Baghdad and Isfahan are far from lying in the texture of any one text or object; and for the thousand and one years covered here, more than one thousand and one sources intertwine – sources living physically at libraries and museums around the world, and digitally at the refining spaces of the worldwide web. With the opening of the 'book of life' of the main characters of this work in what follows, it is hoped that what has gone into their creation lives on: whether a book in hand or a page on screen, this book is meant as a 'novel reader': novel in the sense of a new form of historical work, not just a storytelling genre; and reader, as a selective guide to sources, not just a book audience.

Elaheh Kheirandish
Harvard University
Cambridge, Massachusetts
Fall 2019

Notes on Conventions

For section headings, regular fonts are used for modern narratives, italic fonts for historical narratives.

Additions by the present author are placed within square brackets.

For date conversions, Hijri dates are followed by the corresponding Western dates placed within square brackets (e.g. lunar: 672 [1274]; solar: 1396 [2017]); 672/1274 if in the original; otherwise BCE, CE or year only.

Diacritical marks for transliterations appear only in footnotes and indices (Baghdād).

Original pronunciations and transcriptions are observed (Shāh-nāmih for Shahnama).

Footnotes include all sources, bibliography only printed sources. Order: chronological.

Book titles: italics within text, underlined in footnotes; other: within quotes.

Name Index: historical and modern; Subject Index: disciplinary. Order: alphabetical.

Introduction

Why This Book?

There is no shortage of works involving the historical periods, geographical areas, disciplinary fields and classical languages covered in this book. So why write – or indeed read – yet another book on such subjects: periods like the Middle Ages, areas like Islamic lands, fields like early sciences, and languages like Arabic and Persian?

My chance discovery of the seemingly unique manuscript of an unusual historical 'dialogue' between two cities as rich, yet little known, as Baghdad and Isfahan, presented a fitting opportunity to capture through them important and understudied subjects all in a single book, subjects from Arabic and Persian languages and Sunni and Shiʿi distinctions, to highs and lows of early sciences and their developments. This book, while aimed at offering a broad treatment of these and related subjects, has the more focused target of acting as a self-standing source on subjects of wide interest – from scientific concepts to non-scientific contexts – to variously serve students, specialists, and the interested public; a work that is, cautiously, not compromised by misleading labels like 'Islamic Science' long applied to largely secular entities, or the 'Islamic World', often mis-applied to intellectual traditions with more geographical than religious contexts. But above all, this is a book that in words as timely now as a century ago is meant to 'humanise' the subject of not just science, but the much newer 'history of science'.[1] Besides a wealth of published works by various expert authors, the book distinctively draws from a range of unpublished material, from interviews with mentors and teachers, and communications with colleagues and students, to other direct personal experiences. Through such multiple channels, the narrative presents – and at times extends – voices of inspiration, most otherwise unheard, some by now long silent: voices finding full expression beyond this introduction for inspirations and lessons to be followed 'anywhere around the globe', as well put by the poet in timeless terms about 'him or her who speaks in the right voice'.[2]

1 Sarton, George, 'An institute for the history of science and civilization', Science, 45, 1160 (1917), pp. 284–6, p. 286; Kuhn, Thomas S., 'Science: The history of science', International Encyclopedia of the History of the Social Sciences, 14 (New York, 1968), pp. 74–82.

2 Whitman, Walt, The Complete Poems, Murphy, Francis (ed) (London, 1975), p. 404–5, 'Vocalism': 'Surely, whoever speaks to me in the right voice, him or her I shall follow . . . anywhere around the globe'. Of the voices inspiring this book, only those now silent are named within the text.

Voices of inspiration, many transmitted here firsthand, echo throughout the book for both immediate resonances and long-term effects: voices speaking of 'big inspirations, fires of imagination, and being sent to the seventh heaven';[3] of history and science both 'becoming alive' in the history of science, and of the 'Arabic-Islamic period' as a 'continuing living tradition';[4] of being 'happily immersed in manuscript collections . . . more and more engaged in a world of mostly forgotten scientists',[5] and of 'breaking new ground very fast, and exciting new discoveries being made all the time'.[6] Other voices transmit lessons, from interpretation of a manuscript gloss about a 'scribe dancing at the end of a transcription' as evidence for the job's tediousness,[7] to teaching that 'every time we open our eyes, we have glasses on, coloured with ideological belief, past, present, hope, epistemological ideas';[8] and timeless visions themselves, from the very description of the writing of books as 'not for our time but for the ages',[9] to conceiving of historical characters as 'the light of distant stars that left in their lifetimes, but their names reach to us today while others have faded'.[10]

Inspiring voices transmitted directly from leading scholars combine with unique personal experiences, capturing outstanding moments related to the still largely unknown times and places covered in this book: what could be more inspiring to today's prospective students and tomorrow's specialists and contributors than the experience of holding a manuscript like that of a mysterious 'dialogue' between cities like Baghdad and Isfahan;[11] of viewing the earliest copy of the influential *Optics* of Ibn al-Haytham transcribed not far from Baghdad;[12] of being present in the Azhar mosque

[3] Kheirandish, Elaheh, 'Interview: A. I. Sabra', Harvard University, August 1993: Kheirandish, Elaheh, 'Eloge: A. I. Sabra (8 June 1924–18 December 2013)', Early Science and Medicine, 19, 3 (2014), pp. 281–6, p. 284: 'big inspiration . . . '.

[4] Kheirandish, Elaheh, 'Interview: I. Bernard Cohen', Harvard University, August 1993 (unpublished): 'Arabic-Islamic period as a continuing living tradition'; at Cohen's memorial, his inspiration from 'roses of Isphahan' was transmitted by Carla Carlsfield by singing a Fauré piece so titled (private communication).

[5] Ragep, F. Jamil (ed), Naṣīr al-Dīn al-Ṭūsī's Memoir on Astronomy: Al-Tadhkira fī ʿilm al-hayʾa, 2 vols. in Toomer, G. J. (ed), Sources in the History of Mathematics and Physical Sciences, Vol. 12 (New York, 1993), Preface: 'happily immersed in the manuscript collections . . . '.

[6] Kheirandish, Elaheh, 'Interview: David A. King', Zaragoza, Spain, August 1993 (unpublished): 'breaking new ground. . .'.

[7] Murdoch, John E., in Cohen, I. Bernard (ed), Album of Science: Antiquity and the Middle Ages (New York, 1984), p. 5: 'The book finished, this scribe is going to dance'.

[8] Kheirandish, Elaheh, 'Interview: Pietro Corsi', Harvard University, June 1992 (unpublished): 'Every time we open our eyes. . .'.

[9] Greco Josefowicz, Diane, 'Into the blue: Through the years with Jed Buchwald' in Cormos-Buchwald, Diana et al. (eds), Looking Back As We Move Forward: The Past, Present and Future of the History of Science, (New York, 2019), pp. 167–73, p. 170: 'With every book we write, Jed reminds me: This is not for our time, but for the ages'.

[10] Swerdlow, Noel M., 'Preface', in The Renaissance of Astronomy. Regiomontanus, Copernicus, Tycho, Kepler, Galileo (forthcoming): 'like the light of distant stars. . .' (private communication).

[11] Kamāl-i Iṣfahānī, Munāẓirāt-i Baghdād va Iahān [Dialogues of Baghdad and Isfahan], British Library Manuscript Add 18, 411, fols. 166a–178b (unpublished); Kheirandish, Elaheh (tr, excerpts): Chapter One.

[12] Ibn al-Haytham, Ḥasan, Kitāb al-Manāẓir, Books I–III: On Direct Vision; Books IV–V: On Reflection, Sabra, A. I. (ed), 2 vols. (Kuwait, 1983–2002); (tr, comm) The Optics of Ibn al-Haytham, Books I–III: On Direct Vision, 2 vols. in Trapp, J. B. (ed), Studies of the Warburg Institute (London, 1989), Vol. 2, p. lxxx: earliest manuscripts, Basra.

in Cairo where that author copied manuscripts for a living, pretending madness to master pieces of masterpieces away from the eyes of his imbalanced patron;[13] of seeing the same geometric patterns in a manuscript codex in Paris and on the exquisite tiling of old monuments in Isfahan;[14] of discovering constellations representing birth signs of cities, of a single constellation like Sagittarius representing both Baghdad and Isfahan,[15] and of locating illustrations of matching 'Archer' signs in early Arabic and Persian manuscripts.[16] Similarly inviting to onlookers and future enthusiasts are the shared moments of being next to an instrument as old as one from the Maragha observatory,[17] a newly found letter from the Samarqand observatory,[18] and a royal library catalogue from an Istanbul inventory;[19] and to move further west, what may be a more moving experience than facing the self-made telescope of Galileo in Florence,[20] the observation deck of Newton in London or the transported walls of his home in Boston.[21]

Several other occasions are highlighted throughout the book for advancing historical understanding and inspiring lifelong learning through combinations of living examples and creative expressions: the occasion of a historical play performed in and beyond the classroom,[22] of reconstructing a historical experiment in a sun-filled class balcony,[23] of selecting and beautifying items for exhibit showcases and captions,[24]

13 Sabra, Optics of Ibn al-Haytham, Vol. 2, p. xxxi and n. 30.

14 Necipoğlu, Gülru (ed), The Arts of Ornamental Geometry: A Persian Compendium on Similar and Complementary Interlocking Figures (facs) (Leiden, 2017), pp. 145–61; Hogendijk, Jan P., 'A mathematical classification of the contents of an anonymous Persian Compendium on decorative patterns', p. 153 (image).

15 Bīrūnī, Abū Rayḥān, Kitāb al-Tafhīm li-awāʾil ṣināʿat al-tanjīm, Wright, R. Ramsay (Arabic facs, tr) (The Book of Instruction in the Elements of the Art of Astrology) (London, 1934), p. 220.

16 Ṣūfī, ʿAbd al-Raḥmān, Kitāb Ṣuwar al-kawākib [Book of Constellations] (Frankfurt, 1986); Ṭūsī, Naṣīr al-Dīn, Tarjamah-i Ṣuwar al-kawākib [Translation of Book of Constellations] (facs) (Tehran, 1351 [1972]).

17 Sayılı, Aydın, The Observatory in Islam and its Place in the General History of the Observatory (Ankara, 1960; 1988); Varjavand, Parviz, Kāvush-i raṣad-khānah-i Marāgha (Tehran, 1366 [1987]).

18 Kāshānī, Ghīyāth al-Dīn Jamshīd, Bagheri, Mohammad (ed), Az Samarqand bih Kāshān: Nāmih-hā-yi Ghīyāth al-Dīn Jamshīd Kāshānī bih pidar-ash (Tehran, 1375 [1996]); 'A newly found letter of al-Kāshī on scientific life in Samarqand', Historia Mathematica, 24 (1997), pp. 241–56.

19 Kheirandish, Elaheh, 'Books on mathematical and mixed-mathematical sciences: Arithmetic, geometry, optics and mechanics', in Necipoğlu, Gülru, Kafadar, Cemal, and Fleischer, Cornell H. (eds), Treasures of Knowledge: An Inventory of the Ottoman Palace Library Commissioned by Sultan Bayezid II from his Librarian ʿAtufi (Leiden, 2019), Supplements to Muqarnas, Vol. 14/1, pp. 857–68.

20 Telescope made by Galileo: inventory 2428. www.museogalileo.it

21 Westminster House, Westminster Arts Library: 'Meet up' roof-deck observation, September 2018. http://salonforthecity.blogspot.com/p/the-westminster-arts-reference-library.html. Babson College: Newtonia Collection includes the Fore-Parlour of Newton's last London residence. www.babson.edu.

22 Borges, Jorge Luis, 'Averroes' search' in Irby, James E. and Yates, Donald A. (tr), Labyrinth: Selected Stories (New York, 1962); performances, 2005: Harvard University, Quincy House; 'Entertaining Science/Science Cabaret', New York City, host: Roald Hoffman. www.roaldhoffmann.com/entertaining-science

23 Kheirandish, Elaheh, 'From Alexandria to Baghdad: Classical sciences in Islamic lands', 'From Baghdad to Isfahan: Classical sciences in Persian lands', Harvard University, Departments of the Classics, and Near Eastern Languages and Civilization, Fall 2005, 2007 respectively. https://www.scholar.harvard.edu/ekheirandish/teaching

24 Kheirandish, Elaheh, 'Windows into early science', Harvard University, Houghton Library, Spring 2008. Ireland, Corydon, 'Houghton exhibit features Islamic sciences', Harvard Gazette, 22 April 2008: http://news.harvard.edu/gazette/story/2008/04/houghton-exhibit-features-islamic-sciences/ Kheirandish, Elaheh. 'Windows into early science', Iranian Studies, 41, 4 (2008), pp. 581–91. 'Windows into early science and craft', Brown University, John Hay Library, Spring, 2010. https://blogs.brown.edu/libnews/27/. https://www.scholar.harvard.edu/ekheirandish/exhibits

and of preparing collective class assignments to create evidence-based historical narratives and poems:[25] standing out among many scenes filling the book are those featuring a female Averroes performing in a historical play,[26] an unexpected host in a memorable visit,[27] a quoted participant in a historical exhibit,[28] and an insightful composer of a historical poem.[29]

What Age of Science?

There is a reason why the closing title of this book is 'an' age rather than 'the' age of science: the age of science which is the focus of this book is a premodern age covering a long historical period and vast geographical area in and beyond Baghdad and Isfahan of ca. 750–1750 of the 'common era'.[30] The extensive stretches of time and place covered here are partly based on material gathered for courses, exhibits, and lectures presented during two seven-year periods between 2005 and 2019, with self-explanatory opening titles: for courses, 'From Alexandria to Baghdad', 'From Baghdad to Isfahan', 'Science in the Islamic Middle Ages', and 'Historical Dialogues from the Near East';[31] for exhibits 'Windows into early science' and 'Windows into early science and craft';[32] and for lectures, 'From Baghdad to Cordoba', and more recently, 'From Maragha to Samarqand'.[33]

The times and places themselves extend inevitably beyond what I refer to as the 'Islamic Middle Ages': in time, to what are typically labeled 'Ancient Greek and Roman' periods, all the way to 'Early Modern' times; and in place, as far as premodern China and India to Europe and North America. The temporal and regional coordinates that define the 'age of science' presented here are not entirely different from other periods and areas in being determined by coordinates that naturally change positions, relations and combinations. What is distinctive in this age of science, during what may be described as '1001 years in the lands of 1001 nights', is the diversity, continuity and

[25] Kheirandish, Elaheh, 'Science in the Islamic Middle Ages', Harvard University, Extension School: Fall 2004, 2006, 2009. https://www.scholar.harvard.edu/ekheirandish/teaching

[26] Kheirandish, 'From Alexandria to Baghdad'; Historical play 'Averroes' search', Daniela Helbig: Averroes; John Mathew: director, PhD students at the time at Harvard University, Department of History of Science.

[27] Kheirandish, Elaheh, 'The age of Rūmī: Knowledge and patronage through period pieces', Harvard University, Summer School, 2012: Science Center Observatory visit facilitated by the late Yan Yang, Harvard University graduate student and student astronomer, 30 July 2012; memory honoured: 30 July 2019. www.hcs.harvard.edu/~stahr/

[28] Kheirandish, Elaheh, 'Historical dialogues from the Near East', Harvard University, Freshman Seminar, Spring 2008; Ireland, 'Houghton exhibit features Islamic sciences': Patrick Brennan quoted. http://news.harvard.edu/gazette/story/2008/04/houghton-exhibit-features-islamic-sciences/

[29] Kheirandish, 'Science in the Islamic Middle Ages', Fall 2006; Michael Rutter poem: Chapter Six.

[30] Bacharach, Jere L., A Near East Studies Handbook (Seattle and London, 1974, 1976): date conversions.

[31] Above, and https://www.scholar.harvard.edu/ekheirandish/teaching

[32] Above, and https://www.scholar.harvard.edu/ekheirandish/exhibits

[33] 'From Baghdad to Cordoba': 'Entertaining Science/Science Cabaret', above; 'From Maragha to Samarqand', SOAS, 2017; Kheirandish, Elaheh, 'From Maragha to Samarqand and beyond: Revisiting a quartet of scientific traditions in Greater Persia (ca.1300s–1500s)', in Melville, Charles (ed), The Timurid Century: Idea of Iran, Vol. 9 (London, 2020), pp. 161–87. https://www.scholar.harvard.edu/ekheirandish/publications

universality that distinguishes it from ages before and after it. Diversity in 3rd/9th-century Baghdad as a multi-cultural centre of scientific and translation movements;[34] of 5th/11th-century Cordoba as a multi-faith centre of engagement and tolerance;[35] of 7th/13th-century Maragha as a transnational centre of interaction and collaboration;[36] of 9th/15th-century Samarqand as a secular, and non-secular, centre of education;[37] of 10th/16th century Istanbul as an East-West, Asia-Europe centre of exchange;[38] and of 11th/17th-century Isfahan, as the latest of the multi-dimensional centres of diversity.[39] In terms of continuity, not only is the tradition of science during the Islamic Middle Ages continuous with the earlier Greek antiquity and later early modern Europe, despite obvious distinctions; the continuities call for occasional considerations of the whole enterprise as a 'Western' intellectual tradition in 'non-Western' settings. As for universality, an age of science where Baghdad and Isfahan are only two of many other cities with fluctuating profiles at different times and places is one beyond scientific knowledge itself being defined by universal characterisations like 'puzzle solving'; this is an age of the transmission and transformation of knowledge in its first major phases of cross-lingual, cross-regional and cross-cultural transfer and exchange. Our dialogue of two cities in such an age of science translates into following the paths and crosses of scientific knowledge through times and places like the Arab and Persian lands of the Islamic Middle Ages, here with a focus on Baghdad and Isfahan.

Which Baghdad and Isfahan?

Like all historical entities, the history of cities can hardly be reduced to single times and places; and while those like Baghdad and Isfahan may be associated with respective Arab and Persian lands, Sunni and Shiʿi sects, and caliphal and dynastic rules, the nature and relation of all such associations are far from fixed through time. While the peaks of scientific activity and inactivity may be respectively placed within the early centuries of Baghdad as the capital of the ʿAbbasid Caliphate (r. ca. 750–1258), and the much later centuries of Isfahan as the capital of the Safavid Dynasty (r. 1501–1722),[40] the various highs, lows, twists and turns involved, or those in between, cannot follow any precise curves or merges. So which Baghdad and Isfahan were the subjects of the historical 'dialogue' that forms the basis of this book? And which Baghdad and Isfahan are those that inform its chapters?

34 Gutas, Dimitri, Greek Thought, Arabic Culture: The Graeco-Arabic Translation Movement in Baghdad and Early 'Abbāsid Society (2nd–4th/8th–10th centuries) (London, 1998).
35 Menocal, María Rosa, The Ornament of the World: How Muslims, Jews, and Christians Created a Culture of Tolerance in Medieval Spain (Boston, 2002).
36 Sayılı, Aydın, Observatory in Islam.
37 Bagheri, Az Samarqand bih Kāshān; 'Newly found letter'.
38 Hughes, Bettany, Istanbul: A Tale of Three Cities (London, 2017).
39 Melville, Charles, 'New light on Shah ʿAbbas and the construction of Isfahan', in Necipoğlu, Gülru (ed), Muqarnas: An Annual of the Visual Culture of the Islamic World (Leiden, 2016), pp. 155–76.
40 Bosworth, Clifford Edmund, The Islamic Dynasties: A Chronological and Genealogical Handbook (Edinburgh, 1967), pp. 7–10 and pp. 172–4 respectively.

The answer to the first question may only be approximated, not necessarily reached, since the text of the *Dialogue* is undated. Hints at the respective times and places of that text's composition and transcription are, however, given by the single extant copy of it known to date. Its composition date is hinted at as post-7/13th century through the mention of a scholar named there as 'Awhad al-Din Kirmani', datable to 'd. 697' [1297]; and the transcription date as pre-1120 [1708] through its codex's owner stamp so dated, next to the name 'Pad-Shah Ghazi', identifiable as Awrangzib of Mughal India (r. ca. 1658–1707).[41] My reconstructions of the Baghdad and Isfahan of the time of the text's composition and transcription, and of the 'historical' Baghdad and Isfahan of other centuries, are based on such informed approximations for deriving the changing profiles of these and related cities.

The profiles of the text's composor and transciber are differently derivable. The name of the text's author is given with the title of 'Kamal-i Isfahani', a name distinguished by the observant cataloguer from a contemporary poet named as such but with the first name Isma'il.[42] The longer name of the copyist, ending with 'Shakh Jamal', while given next to the day, month, and even time of day, still misses the much more valuable year of transcription.

The present book opens with the dialogue's composer and transcriber in Baghdad and Isfahan of 'post-1250s' and 'pre-1750s' respectively: the named composer is placed in Baghdad of 'sometime after 1250', 'wandering from place to place', according to the text; and the transcriber in Isfahan of 'sometime before the year 1750', given the likelihood of a late copy associated with that city.[43] The next chapters follow with Baghdad and Isfahan of other centuries next to other cities, all represented by actual historical figures and settings; the chapter's 'historical' sections are, in turn, placed in the hands of a 'modern' narrator who follows the historical figures and events from 'place' to 'place', and the contextual settings and details, from 'time' to 'time'.

Whose 'Dialogue'?

The character writing the historical sections of this book, those of Baghdad, as 'an Arab city with a lunar calendar', and Isfahan, as a 'Persian city with a solar calendar', is one who shadows the text of the 'dialogue' as 'an old manuscript with many lives' of its own. This young author of a fast-changing Baghdad and Isfahan, while signing the chapters' historical sections with a specific pen name, is a generic character: it is a 'young' character to speak to both present and future audiences; and it is one 'with many gifts' for the privileges it can both represent and extend.

41 British Library Manuscript Add 18,411, codex folio: 'Pād-Shāh Ghāzī', 1120' [H]; Rieu, Charles, Catalogue of the Persian Manuscripts in the British Museum, 3 vols., Vol. 2 (London, 1881), p. 601: 'Ālamgīr stamps: 1069, 1113 [1658, 1701]; Bosworth, Islamic Dynasties, pp. 210–11: Mughals: Chapter One.

42 Rieu, Catalogue of Persian Manuscripts, Vol. 2, p. 601: 'Ismā'īl'.

43 Rieu, Catalogue of Persian Manuscripts, Vol. 2, p. 601: 'wandering ... in pursuit of knowledge'; Bosworth, Islamic Dynasties, p. 11: 'friendly relations between Mughals and Safavids'.

As the main modern character of the book, 'Leo' has – much like the classic 'hero with a thousand faces' – [44] various manifestations in representing, besides changing times and places, evolving stages with which readers of different ages and profiles may identify: in age, evolving from a young student to a growing adult; and in profile, embodying actual figures in successive stages.[45] There is more to the many faces of Leo, a name picked for the companion of the book's readers as fitting for not just its historical variations,[46] from Arabic, Persian and Turkish to Greek, Sanskrit, Hebrew and Latin, but also as one of the zodiac constellations in a book where cosmological numbers like seven and twelve enumerating these have prominent representations and combinations.

Lastly, the historical dialogue that is the subject of this book is not merely one between two cities like Baghdad and Isfahan, or counterparts with other distinctive features opening the book's historical sections – pairs like Day and Night, Muslim and Zoroastrian, Arab and Persian, and Sky and Earth, all by one author;[47]or Pen and Sword[48], Chess and Backgammon,[49] and Moon and Sun,[50] by different authors. This is also a dialogue between a book and its readers, one offered to a versatile and ageless audience with the hope that the diversity, continuity and universality that form the finest marks of the premodern age of science covered here extend to our own age – one in which we are all still the children of Baghdad's Mesopotamia and Isfahan's Persia that we once were, one way or another.

44 Campbell, Joseph, The Hero with a Thousand Faces (New York, 1949; Princeton, 1968; Novato, 2003).

45 Asad Goodarzy (2005–2006), Kristine Isberg (2006–2007), Patrick Brennan (2007–2008), Daniela Helbig (2008–2009), John Mathew (2009–2010), Maera Siddiqi (2010–2011), Esam Goodarzy (2011–2012) . . .

46 Corresponding terms: Asad, Shīr, Aṣlān, Léon, Ari, Simha, Leo . . .

47 'Munāẓirih-i Shab va Rūz', 'Musalmān va Gabr', ''Arab va 'Ajam', 'Āsmān va Zamīn'; Asadī Ṭūsī, Munāẓirāt (attribution), ca. 1000, in Khaleghi-Motlagh, Djalal (ed), 'Asadī Ṭūsī', Journal of the Department of Literature and Humanities, Firduwsī University, Mashhad, 1, 4 (1978), pp. 68–130, Kheirandish, Elaheh (tr, excerpts): Chapters Two, Three Four, and Five respectively.

48 Jurjānī, Mīr Siyyid Sharīf 'Allāmah, 'Munāẓarah al-Sayf va al-Qalam', post-1350 (attribution), Dastgirdi, Vahid (ed), Armaghan, 15, 1 (1312 [1934]), pp. 702–3, Kheirandish, Elaheh (tr, excerpts): Chapter Six.

49 Khwārazmī, Ḥisām Ṣarrāf, 'Munāẓirih-i Shaṭranj va Nard', ca. 1300s (attribution), Pourjavady, Nasrollah (ed), Nāmih-i Farhangistān, 6, 1 (1383 [2004]), pp. 16–29, Kheirandish, Elaheh (tr, excerpts): Chapter Seven.

50 Sijzī, Zayn al-Dīn, 'Munāẓirih-i Khurshīd va Māh', ca. 1200s (attribution), in Pourjavady, Nasrollah (ed), Zabān-i Ḥāl dar 'Irfān va Adabīyāt-i Fārsī (Tehran, 1385 [2006]), pp. 421–9, 'Moon and Sun' variations: Kheirandish, Elaheh (tr, excerpts): Chapter Seven and Postscript.

Chapter Summaries

Chapter Zero: Cast and Stage

The chapter titled zero introduces the casts and stages of the sections of this book's chapters. Every chapter has a modern and historical division, each with their own sections, characters and settings. Chapters have distinct subjects and messages, with a view of transmitting knowledge about transmission of knowledge, and an eye on the multi-layered and open-ended nature of knowledge itself. The sections of each chapter, narrate, through the casts of an 'old manuscript', a 'young narrator', and an 'Arab' and 'Persian' city on a chronological stage, the unfolding of time's embrace beyond the bounds of any one land or age.

0.1 An Old Manuscript with Many Lives
0.2 A Young Narrator with Many Gifts
0.3 *An Arab City with a Lunar Calendar*
0.4 *A Persian City with a Solar Calendar*

Chapter One: Time and Place

1001 Years (ca. 750–1750)

The first chapter opens with the subject of history and the message that historical knowledge involves understanding history as a combination of various historical players, from sources and figures to developments and outcomes; history as a combined entity which is, significantly, unique as something neither reducible to expected or repeatable cases, nor extendable to all times and places. Key players in this thousand-year story of science are identified in this chapter as 'roots' for foundations, followed in the next chapters by 'routes' for transmissions, 'rules' for directions, 'books' for conceptions, 'schools' for instructions, 'tools' for manipulations, and 'loops' for communications.

1.1 An Old Manuscript with a Special Day
1.2 A Young Student with a Special Year

1.3 *An Arab City with Eastern Links*
1.4 *A Persian City with Western Links*

Chapter Two: Moon and Sun

500 Hundred Years (ca. 750–1250; 1250–1750)

The second chapter extends the subject of history to science, and the message that the methods of history apply to the history of science in identifying, besides key players in scientific developments and outcomes, the occurrence and recurrence of light and dark moments, and their coincidence. In this chapter, the historical sources are more than one old manuscript, the historical figures are practitioners of various fields historically called 'science', and historical developments and outcomes are presented in terms of the nature and role of another key player in the story of early science, here highlighted as the 'routes' of transmission.

2.1 An Old Manuscript with Gold Illuminations
2.2 A Young Viewer with Rich Inspirations
2.3 *An Arab City with a Growing Moon*
2.4 *A Persian City with a Glowing Sun*
2.5 *An Arab City with a 'Westerner'*
2.6 *A Persian City with a 'Falconer'*

Chapter Three: Round and Square

100 Years: A Crescent Phase (ca. 750–850)

The third chapter turns to the subject of geometry, the earliest subject transmitted to and through Islamic lands, and continues with the message that besides roots through ancient Greek sources like Euclid's *Elements*, and routes through classical languages like Arabic, another component critical to developments and outcomes is 'rules'. In this chapter, rules are highlighted in the form of political rules, here early ʿAbbasid patrons, as well as geometrical rules like laws of proportion. Sources, figures, developments and outcomes are all from the first century of scientific translations and transmissions, here termed a 'Crescent Phase'.

3.1 An Old Manuscript with a Microfilm
3.2 A Young Reader with a 'Micromap'
3.3 *An Arab City with a 'House of Wisdom'*
3.4 *A Persian City with an Ancient Kingdom*

Chapter Four: Word and Line

200 Years: A Quarter Phase (ca. 850–1050)

The fourth chapter is focused on optics, a subject with major breakthroughs associated with Islamic lands. Here, the corresponding message is that besides roots through ancient Greek sources, routes through transmissions to Europe, and rules through Arab and Persian patrons, another component critical to both developments and non-developments is 'books'. In this chapter, books are highlighted through an Arabic optical work with more outstanding impacts in Europe than its own native lands. Developments, non-developments, and partial developments are all from the two centuries following the initial scientific translations and transmissions, here termed a 'Quarter Phase'.

4.1 An Old Manuscript with Colour Scans
4.2 A Young Visitor with Secret Plans
4.3 *An Arab City with a 'Critical' Mind*
4.4 *A Persian City Left Behind*

Chapter Five: East and West

300 Years: A Half Phase (ca. 1050–1350)

The fifth chapter treats astronomy as a subject with outstanding developments in both Islamic and Europeans lands. The underlying message here is that besides roots through early Greek, Persian and Indian sources, routes through transmissions to Europe, rules through Arab and Persian patrons, and books through non-Ptolemaic and pre-Copernican models, another component critical to developments and outcomes is 'schools'. In this chapter, schools are highlighted through cases from Cordoba, Maragha and Samarqand to those comparable in Europe, all during the three centuries that are central to the period's full coverage, here termed a 'Half Phase'.

5.1 An Old Manuscript in a Virtual Space
5.2 A Young Traveller with Paths to Trace
5.3 *An Arab City with a Western Court*
5.4 *A Persian City with an Eastern Fort*

Chapter Six: Old and New

400 Years (ca. 1350–1750): Three-Quarter Phase

The sixth chapter continues with mechanics, a subject with its own distinct developments including transmissions to Europe. The so-called 'science of devices' brings in the related message that, besides roots through ancient Greek sources, routes through European transmissions, rules through local patrons, books through teachings on both knowledge and practice, and schools through institutions and communities, another component critical to developments is 'tools'. In this chapter, tools are highlighted through applications in places from mosques and schools to observatories and courts during the four centuries involving various exchanges with Europe, here termed a 'Three-Quarter Phase'.

6.1 An Old Manuscript in a Digital Age
6.2 A Young Curator with a 'Future' Stage
6.3 *An Arab City with a Treasure Box*
6.4 *A Persian City with a Tower Clock*
6.5 *An Eastern City and an 'End of Time'*
6.6 *A Western City with a Turn of Tides*

Chapter Seven: Plan and Chance

1000 Years (ca. 750–1750): Full Phase

The seventh chapter returns to the subject of history through historiography, with a central message about the path of science having involved, besides players highlighted in earlier chapters, the 'loops' of communication as a critical component relevant to all others. Highlighting 'outlooks' as another key component for understanding the past, representing the present, and projecting the future, the chapter turns full circle to the book's own transmission of knowledge about transmission of knowledge, closing with a treatment of elements of chance as relevant players in the mix during a period extended to a thousand years, here termed a 'Full Phase'.

7.1 An Old Manuscript in a Game of Chance
7.2 A Young Player with a Change of Plans
7.3 *An Arab City with Living Traces*
7.4 *A Persian City with Lasting Places*

Chart: Names and Dates

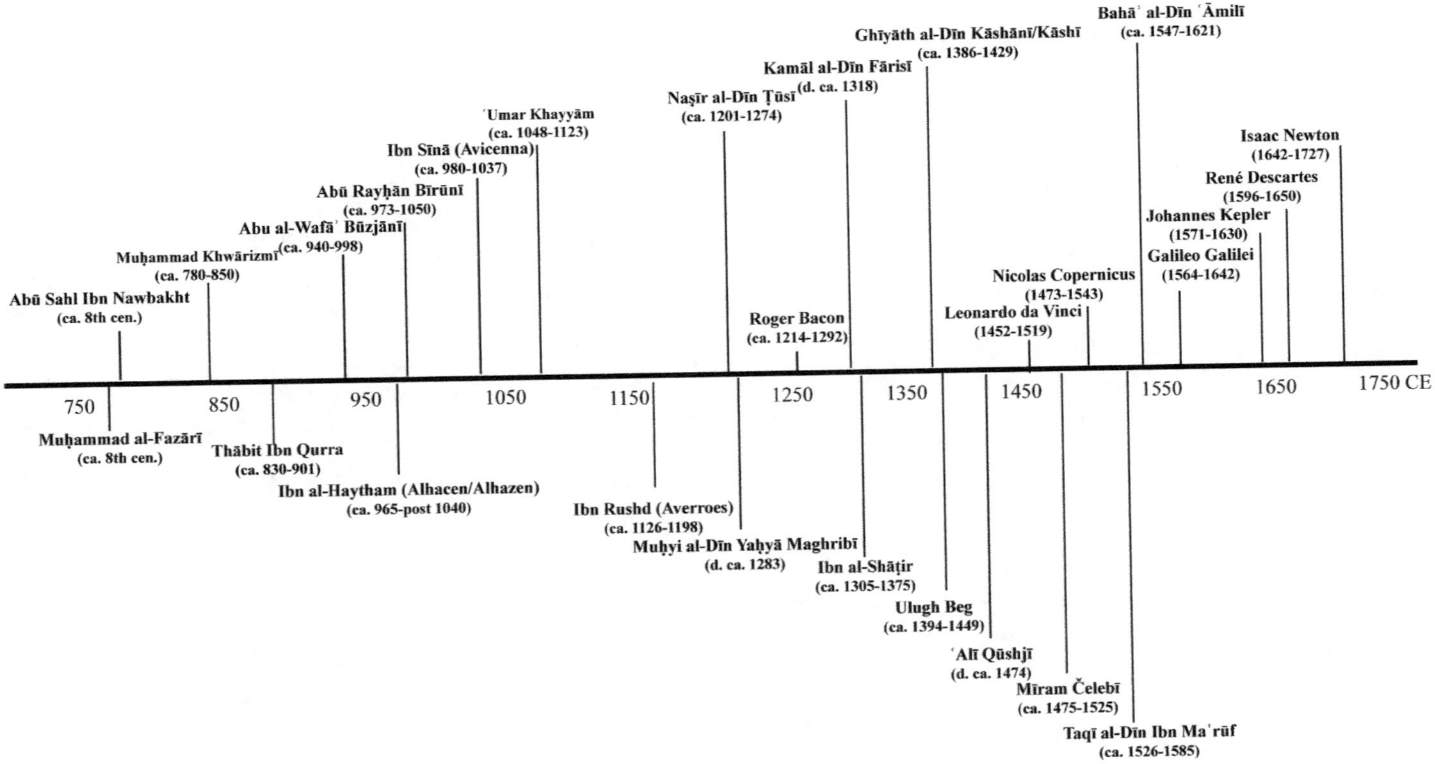

0

Cast and Stage

Zero stands not for the closing of a ring: it is rather a gateway.

Richard Kaplan, The Nothing That Is, 2000, 'Introduction'[0]

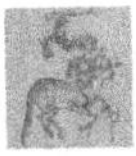

0.1 An Old Manuscript with Many Lives

What matters in life is a lasting trace
When life itself shows no permanence.

Anonymous: inscription[1]

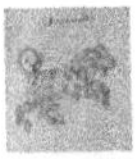

0.2 A Young Narrator with Many Gifts

His genius cast its shadow o'er the world,
And in brief time, he much achieved and wrought:
The Age's Sun was he, and ageing suns
Cast lengthy shadows, though their time be short.

Pāshā-zādah, Kemāl (d. ca. 1534): Turkish poem[2]

0 Kaplan, Robert, The Nothing That Is: A Natural History of Zero (Oxford, New York, 2000), 'Introduction', p. 3.

1 *'Gharaḍ naqsh-īst k-az mā bāz mān-ad*
Kih hastī rā nimībīn-am baqā-yī'.
Anonymous: inscription. Old (ʿAtīq), Congregational (Jāmiʿ)
Friday (Jumʿa) Mosque, Isfahan.
English adaptation: Elaheh Kheirandish.

2 *'Az zemān içre çok iş itmiş idi, sāyesi olmus idi ʿālemgīr,*
Şems-i ʿasr idi 'asırda şemsiñ, Ẓilli memdūd olur zemānı kasīr'.
Pāşā-zāde, Kemāl (d. ca. 1534), Gibb Memorial Series (London, 1915–),
Turkish: cover; Transliteration: Himmet Taskomur; English translation: opening.

0.3 *An Arab City with a Lunar Calendar*

These are our works which prove what we have done;
Look, therefore, at our works when we are gone.

Anonymous, Arabic poem[3]

0.4 *A Persian City with a Solar Calendar*

When we are dead, seek for our resting-place
Not in the earth, but in the mystics' hearts.

Rūmī, Muwlānā Jalāl al-Dīn (d. ca. 1273): Persian poem[4]

[3] *'Tilka āthāru-nā tadullu ʿalay-nā,*
Fa anẓarū baʿda-nā ila al-āthār'.
Anonymous, Gibb Memorial Series, Arabic: cover; English translation: opening.

[4] *'Baʿd az vafāt, turbat-i mā dar zamīn majūy,*
Dar sīnih-hā-yi mardum-i ʿārif qarār-i mā-st'.
Rūmī, Muwlānā Jalāl al-Dīn (d. ca. 1273), Gibb Memorial Series, Persian: cover; English adaptation: Elaheh Kheirandish.

1

Time and Place

1001 Years (ca. 750–1750): Through the Lands of 1001 Nights

He had long been ... wandering from place to place in pursuit of knowledge, and having found Baghdad and Isfahan fairer than all other cities, was at a loss to which he should give the preference, when a friend helped him out of his perplexity by communicating... a dialogue in which each of the contending cities boasts in turn, its glories, privileges, and attractions ...

Charles Rieu, *Catalogue of Persian Manuscripts*, Vol. 2, 1881, p. 601[1]

1.1 An Old Manuscript with a Special Day

It was March 2005, and up to that day a set of emerald-coloured catalogues of oriental manuscripts, shelved next to hundreds of thousands of volumes on the top floor of one of the greatest libraries on earth,[2] had rarely been opened on the page they were open now. For the manuscript of the *Dialogue of Baghdad and Isfahan* (Plate 1) earning a marginal entry on page 600 of the catalogues' second volume, this was a very special day. Its life before that had been quite uneventful. The *Dialogue*'s first life had been lived as an early text on a piece of parchment, a life starting rather unremarkably as a single composition by a little-known author; and its second life, this time as a handwritten copy atypically bound in a volume with a different genre of literature altogether, had become even more discrete as an odd 'joker in the pack'.[3] But that day marked a turning point in the *Dialogue*'s old book of life: its third life as a manuscript entry in a printed catalogue, handled many more times and by many more hands, was to take it very far. In the right hands, the *Dialogue* was to change form, from autographed and transcribed texts to manuscript copies and microfilm rolls, and from colour scans and digital posts

1 Rieu, Catalogue of Persian Manuscripts, Vol. 2, pp. 600, 601. www.archive.org/stream/catalogueofpersi02brituoft#page/600/mode/2up
2 Harvard University, Harry Elkins Widener Memorial Library [Widener], Cambridge MA. https://library.harvard.edu/libraries/widener
3 Walker, Stephen, 'Joker in the Pack', Harvard University Seminar 'Aristotle's Posterior Analytics', Department of the History of Science, Fall 1982 (unpublished essay on PA: 2.19).

to virtual worlds and multimedia platforms. Through the 'charm' of its third life as an entry in a printed catalogue, the *Dialogue*'s old manuscript would end up having many lives, and through them, crossing many paths.

Without the fateful encounter of that special day, however, the printed *Dialogue* entry would have continued a long and static shelf life among three million plus volumes in hundreds of odd languages scattered through ten floors and hundreds of paces across the remote corners of the library's impressive oriental wing. But as it was, the volume in which the *Dialogue*'s entry lived was to have a different fate from so many other volumes hardly ever opened. It would also have a different fate from duplicate volumes in other mega libraries of the world. The difference was not so much the effect of a special library described as the 'heart and soul' of a university, an 'Archimedes bathtub', or the 'first modern book-stack', a library with its very own 'biography'.[4] The big difference was the mere fact of the library's 'open' stacks, meaning anyone with a library pass could browse any book-stacks, and come across new finds, anytime. The key moment was still not when an emerald-green volume was pulled out of its shelf that day from among many others, but when it came to land in the right hands, among so many others, all at the same time.

The catalogue that housed the *Dialogue* entry was only one of many items on a course list in those fateful hands, and the path from this to other items on that list was a long one. Not physically: one would simply cross the aisles of the oriental wing a few blocks across and below, with some stops in between; but intellectually, to get to the other side of the oriental blocks alone meant walking past oceans of knowledge coming from places and continents far and wide, and cultures and languages old and new, all neatly set into mnemonic letters on each stack shelf with labels: OL and Ind for Oriental and Indo-European, ME and Ott for Mid-East and Ottoman, Heb and Jud for Hebrew and Judaic, and so on. This was a space where minds and voices from all times, places, races, and sexes filled it from lower to upper levels, where a domed penthouse next to specialty libraries once hosted a treasure room;[5] a place impressing its once director by the 'physical presence of that much knowledge' on a student visit, and its once university president by features from its 'most compelling voices in history' to the 'matchless power of the book to change the life of a reader, a nation, and the world'.[6] Not only was this a well-named living treasure; as a physical magnet it outmatched the power of any digital versions, even at a *time* calling itself an electronic age.

As a world wide 'web' of a different kind, the majestic library that housed all the items on the *Dialogue* list carried from stack to stack that day was truly timeless. Not

4 Ireland, Corydon, '100 years of Widener', Harvard Gazette, 22 May 2015: quotes: Robert Darnton and Barbara Tuckman. https://news.harvard.edu/gazette/story/2015/05/100-years-of-widener/. Widener tablet, 1916: 'on this spot stood Gore Hall . . . first use of modern book-stacks was in this library'. Battles, Matthew, Widener: Biography of a Library (Cambridge, MA, 2004).

5 'Treasure Room' once on Widener Library's sixth floor formed part of Houghton Rare Book Library. Source: James Capobianco. Specialty libraries: Smythe, Gibb, Judaica: Classics, Middle Eastern and Hebrew Studies.

6 Verba, Sydny, 'Speaking volumes: Professor Sydney Verba champions the university library', Harvard Gazette, 26 February 1998, p. 3. Summers, Lawrence, 'Remarks of Harvard University President Lawrence H. Summers, Widener Library Celebration Dinner', 1 October 2004 (President, 2001–2006). www.harvard.edu/president/speech/2004/remarks-harvard-university-president-lawrence-h-summers-widener-library

just verbally, in the sense of a priceless treasure-house with endless functions, but literally, in the sense of an entity not subject to expected changes through time itself. Among the many oddities of the place was an imposed permanence that was not merely physical but also legal: nothing, including the massive renovations of the year before to make the place 'future-ready', could touch the footprints of a structure that followed the mandates of a will: not to add or remove anything from the library's original foundation was the 'will' of its donor who dictated its fate, as repeated among the many 'facts and fables'[7] of various library tours. A bridge from the library to an adjacent site, the closest of about 100 libraries within the host university, was a clever way out that was pointed to in many tours of the library to amplify its touching history. Its wider geography was no less impressive. With a Science Center to one side, a Humanities Center to the other, and specialised Schools all around it, the extended library was more than a bridge, forming as it did the crucial side of a quadrangular 'Yard' with a capital Y; it was much more like a 'city upon a hill', one with the 'eyes of all people upon' it, as inscribed under a fountain next to a nearby School,[8] aptly named after a president setting such visions literally in stone, for the much wider campus of the country at large.

It was after the name of a young student called Harry Elkins Widener a century before, however, that a monument with a capital M was to be immortalised as a Memorial library, upon his tragic death with the sinking of the Titanic: in the Memorial room[9] of a library long celebrated as Widener, after the name of Harry's father, not Elkins, his donating mother, stood the portrait of the son; and the glass shelves of valuable books all around it, weekly fresh flowers across it, and display cases in an octagonal entrance leading to it, evoked a sense of the touch, taste, script and fate of a young student whose untimely passing at the far too young age of 27 meant an end to his passionate book-collecting. In some years, the four display cases filled with his memorabilia, and final letters were to reduce to one of four displays: featured as 'The Student' next to his Memorial library as 'The Legacy', his funding mother as 'The Inspiration', and the building's architect as 'Out of the Shadows', he would be gradually 'overshadowed' from then on. But long before that would happen, the hosting university, named Harvard after its own donor, and founded in a 'Newtowne' renamed later as the city of Cambridge,[10] was to become part of another lasting story: the library, the university and the city were to be part of the story of a 'dialogue' closely linked to them all.

7 Beach, Denison, 'Everyone's wild about Harry', Harvard Library Bulletin, 13, 1 (2002), pp. 3–4, p. 4: 'outward appearance of the library not being altered'; among fables: fresh flower deliveries to the memorial room daily. Source: Rachael Howarth. https://blogs.harvard.edu/houghton/youve-got-mail-widener/

8 Galbraith, John Kenneth, A Tenured Professor (Boston, 1990), p. 1: 'Harvard Yard . . .' Kennedy, John F., 'City Upon a Hill' speech, Boston, State House, 9 January 1961, quoting John Winthrop, 'we shall be as a city upon a hill – the eyes of all people are upon us'.

9 Walsh, Colleen, 'Harry's books: At the center of Widener Library, a miniature museum', Harvard Gazette, 15 April 2014. https://news.harvard.edu/gazette/story/2014/04/harrys-books/

10 Harvard University is named after John Harvard, whose death in 1638 left his library and half his estate to it. His campus statue is a landmark. www.harvard.edu/about-harvard/harvard-glance/history. The founding of 'Newtowne' is on a bulletin board in Harvard square, Cambridge MA, with the subtitle: 'This is the Place 1630'. www.cambridgema.gov/historic/cambridgehistory

It was in that spring, and within the trio of that 'library, university and city', that the story of an old manuscript with many lives, and of an early science with many paths, was assigned to a young student with many gifts: one whose own life was to be irreversibly changed by the many 'wander's and 'wonder's ahead.

1.2 A Young Student with a Special Year

It was March 2005, and for a young student in whose hands a list with a *Dialogue* entry had just fallen, this was a special day for its own reasons. He was 'Charles Leo', and the curious rhyme of his name with the *Dialogue*'s cataloguer, 'Charles Rieu', was not the only thing that would mean something special to him that day. That morning, Leo, who went by his middle name, had walked along the river 'Charles', a place inspiring the first part of his name. He had long been waiting for that day to deliver his 'senior thesis', a fancy term for a year's work packed into a bound volume. The day itself was special, not just as the first day of spring closing the earth's yearly orbit around the Sun, but as a 'Sun' day, that ruler of the astrological world bound to Leo, the birth sign. But that was not all. Earlier that day, Leo had observed the rising of spring at 'vernal equinox',[11] the split second when winter turns into spring, that year at 7.33am; and later that day, at 6.40pm, he was to chase the Sun's path in a flight across the ocean. Somewhere in between, the path of Leo's own life was to change: chasing the catalogue of an assigned *Dialogue* through the maze of a library at its closing hours entered him into a world that became one of the greatest gifts of his young and privileged life.

Privileged he was, starting with the luxury of skipping the year between high school and college, taking a 'gap year' when everyone Leo knew his age was headed in a different direction. His post high-school, pre-college experience was to be as different from their's as he was from them. He was to open and close the gap of that year with the ocean, spending its second half travelling from his hometown of Cambridge in New England to its namesake in old England. As for its first half, he felt especially lucky to be given a taste of the famous university on his side of the ocean through course work with a faculty advisor, who having acted as the 'outside reader' of his high-school thesis, had offered him some post-thesis work. This involved much more than his part-time job at a library in that university with a 'Middle Eastern Division' where he had worked on Arabic and Persian titles in an online catalogue. A soon-graduating Leo had welcomed the idea of his advisor, soon mentor, to work on a historical 'dialogue' between two cities whose languages he could read and whose old manuscript he was offered a chance to see. This was an offer he could hardly refuse for the boost it could give his college application; and the gap year which followed that life-changing offer was to fill the best year of his life, for which this was the very first day.

It had all started with Leo walking along the Charles river, which besides sharing his first name, connected two iconic universes, universities world-famous as 'Harvard' and 'MIT' with the respective mottos of 'Truth' and 'Mind and Hand', standing out at the

[11] Encyclopedia Britannica, 'Vernal Equinox'. www.britannica.com/topic/vernal-equinox In 2005: 20 March, 7.33am in North America. www.space.com/881-date-changed-start-spring.html

two ends of his path. But that day Leo had left Cambridge towards Boston for a university named after that city, one with a pre-college academy, and the motto of 'Scholarship' added to 'Learning'.[12] At the entrance to his academy, where Leo was to drop off his senior thesis, he had taken a last look at it before opening the after-hour locks with the newly-installed, shape-sensitive technology of 'hand geometry'. He had then returned to the banks of the river that seemed 'ceaseless', in the words of a little-known poem about Cambridge by a well-known 'crafter of verse' named 'Borges', once a scholar in residence.[13] As Leo walked towards a library in that city that hardly ever slept, that Sunday seemed all the more special not only for beating a deadline by one day, but for jump-starting new work before a Monday, a day with 'the illusion of beginnings', as worded in that same Cambridge poem. Of the flying hours between walking back along the river and flying over the ocean to the Cambridge 'across the pond', as the endearing reference to the Atlantic Ocean coasts had it, he spent its first minutes looking up in the library's database the name of Charles Rieu. As weighty as that name stood next to the credentials of a multi-lingual keeper of oriental manuscripts and chair of oriental studies in the other Cambridge, it didn't readily turn up anything but Rieu's 'obituary notice'; then, it only took a moment to notice that the date of his passing fell on the coming of spring for years to come.[14]

On that first day of spring over a century later, the young Charles Leo, while in transit between two cities with a shared name on the two coasts of the Atlantic Ocean, was mindful of two other historic cities as he quickly leafed through Rieu's rich manuscript catalogue now open on the *Dialogue* page before him. Leo was not so studious, but he was interested in classical subjects. In the first three years of high-school, he had elected classical Greek, not Latin; and in his last year of access to courses at the university, not just the academy, he had added his own ancestral, and lately popular, languages of Arabic and Persian. It was these classical languages, not any scholarly tendencies, that had occasioned him to opt for an 'honours thesis', and through it, a bilingual *Dialogue of Baghdad and Isfahan* for its good dose of such classical languages. Another 'tale of two cities',[15] Leo had thought, recalling the title of a book by a 'Charles' he had long admired for his 'tale' of the London and Paris he knew so well. Naturally drawn to two cities whose names had echoes as loud as Baghdad and Isfahan in his own days, he could not wait for a glimpse at the manuscript of their

[12] Harvard University, Cambridge, MA: Motto: VERITAS ('Verity' or 'Truth'). www.harvard.edu. Massachusetts Institute of Technology, Cambridge, MA: Motto: Mens et Manus (Mind and Hand). www.mit.edu. Boston University, Boston, MA: Motto: 'Learning, Virtue, Piety'. www.bu.edu. Boston University Academy: Motto: 'Nil Doctis Arduum': Nothing daunts a scholar. www.buacademy.org

[13] Borges, Jorge Luis, 'Cambridge', in In Praise of Darkness, di Giovanni, Norman Thomas (ed, tr) (New York, 1974), pp. 21–2; Rogers, Hoyt (tr). http://krinndnz.livejournal.com/129602.html. This Craft of Verse: Borges lectures at Harvard University in late 1960s. www.poetryfoundation.org/poets/jorge-luis-borges

[14] Browne, Edward G., 'Obituary notices: Professor Charles Rieu Ph.D. M.A', The Journal of the Royal Asiatic Society of Great Britain and Ireland, June 1902, pp. 718–21, p. 718: on 'Wednesday, March 19, of this year (1902) . . . there passed away from us, one of the greatest oriental scholars of all time. . .'

[15] Dickens, Charles, A Tale of Two Cities (London, 1859). https://www.sparknotes.com/lit/a-tale-of-two-cities/

'dialogue', especially with a line in Rieu's catalogue entry about its author, 'wandering from place to place'.

Hours later, in his flight across the ocean, Leo was formally launching a new project assigned to him. No better time to start something new than the 'new day' of a new year; and no better place than mid-air to set its course, right along the path of a rich sunset, his own eastward stretch cutting short the life of that special day. The assigned project amounted to a thousand and one years of science in the land of 'thousand and one nights', the number inspired by the famous collection of old stories fittingly passing under the titles *Arabian Nights* and *Persian Tales*,[16] with all the diversities and mysteries treasured in them. But the project was to be not just historical, but also cosmological, in line with the spirit of any age-old and far-away land. The course syllabus shared with Leo by his former advisor, now supervisor, had seven themes on its twelve-week term, playing a rhythmic 'music of the spheres' as science pairing with history, locality, authority, methodology, academy, utility, and universality; themes that carved in Leo's mind single-syllabi memory aids as roots for history, routes for locality, rules for authority, books for methodology, schools for academy, tools for utility, and loops for universality. These, in turn, set the terms for charting the best and worst times of his assigned cities in a millennium-long age of science with all its ups, downs, crosses and bends: together these were to 'reconstruct' – whatever that meant – centuries of historical narratives in the language of a tale.

For Baghdad and Isfahan marking the start and end of science beyond their native lands, the tale needed to have a start and an end. What seemed like a good start was a quotation on the course supplement taken from an 'Inaugural Lecture'[17] delivered at a place none other than Greece where Leo had learned it all began: that one should 'not be content to ask questions only of the kind "what happened" and "when" and "how"'; that 'it is necessary also to enquire into the reasons why'; that 'historical explanation, as Herodotus and Thucydides' – the ancient Greek historians Leo had actually read – 'were the first to make clear, is concerned with the causes of events'. In this case, the whens, whats and hows of the story were clear: the years selected for the historical maps[18] on the course website accessible to Leo well covered the whens and whats: 750 was the year of the rise of the ruling Caliphate that made Baghdad a capital city in 762; and 1750 capped the falling years of Isfahan, as a city in 1722 and as a capital in 1736, making the years 750 and 1750 rough turning points in their stories of science: the website's interactive maps with colour-coded links to Arab and Persian cities like Baghdad and Isfahan, zooming in and out of red and green 'hot spots' as distinct from the blue and purple of Greek and European cities, further pointed to the hows, starting with how not to lump together items as individual as cities under a blanket of labels,

16 Pellat, Charles, 'Alf layla wa-layla', Encyclopedia Iranica (EIr), 1, 8 (1985), pp. 831–5. www.iranicaonline.org/articles/alf-layla-wa-layla

17 Huxley, George L., Why did the Byzantine Empire not fall to the Arabs? An Inaugural Lecture: American School of Classical Studies at Athens (Athens, 1986).

18 Kheirandish, 'Science in the Islamic Middle Ages', included Interactive and Color-coded Time and Place Maps. Hotspots: red and green, Arab and Persian cities; blue and purple, Greek and European cities. https://www. scholar.harvard.edu/ekheirandish/multimedia

from Islamic, Arabic and Persian, to Middle Eastern, Near Eastern and South Asian. The challenge here was not even putting any spotlight on the 'whys', but especially the 'why-not' questions, including the highly problematic yet frequently raised question of why modern, Western advances had not occurred in pre-modern times or non-Western places. This was something that, even if well formulated, could hardly be captured through a single cause or agent, let alone linear measures such as maps, without fairly complex and targeted maneuvers.

Some sample formulations were assigned as course readings with their very titles opening with the terms why, when, how and what: the catchiest formulations started with the whys, ranging from 'why the Scientific Revolution did not take place' outside of Europe, and 'why did modern science . . . take its meteoric rise only in the West',[19] to 'why Tycho Brahe', the Danish astronomer before the European Scientific Revolution, did not have a 'Turkish name';[20] those for when and how ranged from 'when and how did the impetus of science in Islam come to an end?', to 'how Islam won and lost the lead in science';[21] and those for what ranged from 'what went wrong', to 'what is wrong with what went wrong'.[22] For Leo, who knew little about the Far East, old *or* new, and little of peripheral Europe, Danish *or* Turk, clues had to come from elsewhere. He would next read that what is wrong with historical explanations in terms of 'preset mentalities, tendencies, or other generalities' is their 'essentialist chataracter', and learn about the alarming tag of 'essentialism' as distinct from 'reductionism' and 'precursorism' with their own problems of seeing everything as a 'reflection of earlier examples', and 'reading the future into the past'.[23] Then there were the unpublished 'ice-box' and 'oven theories' of the same author against viewing science in the Middle Ages as mere preservers, transmitters, a so-called 'intermediate civilization',[24] in intellectual, besides historical or geographical terms; or a mimeographed work on 'Muslim Scholarship'[25] by an author with his own ideals of scholarship against various 'essentialist' treatments

19 Sivin, Nathan, 'Why the Scientific Revolution did not take place in China – or didn't it', Chinese Science, 5 (1982), pp. 45–66; and 'Why did modern science . . . take its meteoric rise only in the West at the time of Galileo?', 2005 (revised), with reference to Needham, Joseph, Science and Civilization in China (Cambridge, MA, 1954–), http://ccat.sas.upenn.edu/~nsivin/writ.html

20 Sabra, A. I., 'The appropriation and subsequent naturalization of Greek Science in Medieval Islam: A preliminary statement', History of Science, 25, 3 (1987), pp. 223–43, p. 238. The author cites E. S. Kennedy's remark: 'no essential reason why Tycho Brahe could not have had a Turkish name'.

21 Hartner, Willy, 'When and how did the Impetus of Science in Islam come to an end?' Introduction to the History of Science: Course Source Book, compiled by A. I. Sabra (Cambridge, MA, 1966, 1978), pp. 99–120. Overbye, Dennis, 'How Islam won and lost the lead in science', The New York Times, 30 Oct 2001. www.nytimes.com/2001/10/30/science/how-islam-won-and-lost-the-lead-in-science.html

22 Lewis, Bernard, What Went Wrong: Western Impact and Middle Eastern Response (Oxford, New York, 2002). https://global.oup.com/academic/product/what-went-wrong-9780195144208?cc=us&lang=en&. Sabra, Adam, 'What is wrong with What Went Wrong', Middle East Research and Information Project, 2003. https://www.merip.org/2003/08/what-is-wrong-with-what-went-wrong

23 Sabra, A. I., 'Situating Arabic science: Locality versus essence', Isis, 87 (1996), pp. 654–70, p. 657; and 'Appropriation and subsequent naturalization', p. 224 respectively.

24 Goitein, S. D., 'Between Hellenism and Renaissance-Islam: The intermediate civilization', Islamic Studies, Journal of the Central Institute of Islamic Research, 2, 3 (1963), pp. 217–33.

25 Rosenthal, Franz, The Technique and Approach of Muslim Scholarship (Rome, 1947), pp. 2–5: quotes.

without uttering the word itself; one with a 'technique and approach' of his own and multiple lessons: historical lessons for sources 'speaking for themselves', individual lessons for 'taking into account irreducible factors', and overall lessons against generalisations, including periodising human cultural development as 'before the invention of writing (prehistoric), of handwriting (manuscript), and . . . of mechanically reproduced writing (printing).

There were other methodological essays, some with titles opening with 'Science and Technology',[26] and placing 'Western' and 'Eastern' views side by side, views as far back as the 1880s, and as far east as Japan. But what stood out more were the words of the named 'father of the history of science', George Sarton, the Belgian émigré to a country as far 'west' as the 'new world': this was the holder of the personal office Leo had visited that day, and the author of the multi-volume 'Introduction' to the history of science' who had applied the words 'decadence and fall' to 'Arabic science and learning in the fifteenth century';[27] the term 'miracle' was given to the 'astounding developments' in the East with the exact dates 'from the second half of the eighth century to the end of the eleventh', while the terms 'decline and fall' described 'three other centuries almost equally astounding', followed by the dates 'thirteenth to fifteenth centuries': the linear formulations ended with 'what was their cause?' But question marks also came through formulations like one on 'cultural orientation':[28] what, Leo wondered, could be more culturally disorienting than quoting a modern Western poet giving ancient Greeks the exclusive gift of an 'insatiable curiosity . . . to follow knowledge like a sinking star', when all evidence went against such exclusivities.

Finally, the closing lines of an obituary notice for Charles Rieu by a succeeding 'orientalist' called Edward Granville Browne, one whose own name would soon become much too familiar to Leo, had brought him the 'last word' on the subject, so much so that it was typed by him word for word: that 'in the realms of science at least we see some dim foreshadowing of that universal brotherhood of mankind which elsewhere is but dreamed of and hoped for wherein the limitations of nationalities and tongues vanish away'; and that 'even East and West, so widely separated by custom, feeling and belief, are reconciled'.[29] That rich passage inspired the spirit of a journey that he was about to begin, both physically and intellectually.

Leo's physical flight did not lose the magic of that day when the day itself turned into the next one on the soon-to-be outdated electronic gadgets that stored some of his material. He began by transporting images from his pocket device into a book-size laptop. The first few were scans of emerald-coloured catalogue covers, followed by the

[26] Daiber, Hans, 'Science and technology versus Islam: A controversy from Renan and Afghani to Nasr and Needham and its historical background', JAMES: Annals of Japan Association for Middle East Studies, 8 (1993), pp. 169–87.

[27] Sarton, George, Introduction to the History of Science, 3 vols. (Baltimore, 1927–48, 1962); 'Arabic science and learning in the fifteenth century, their decadence and fall', Homenaje a Millas-Vallicrosa (Barcelona, 1956), 303–24, p. 318.

[28] von Grunebaum, Gustave E., Medieval Islam: A Study in Cultural Orientation (Chicago, 1946), p. 344: quoted in Saunders, J. J., 'Problem of Islamic decadence', Journal of World History, 7 (1968), pp. 701–20, 719; verses: Alfred Lord Tennyson's Ulysses.

[29] Browne, 'Obituary notices', pp. 718–21, p. 721.

entry of the manuscript of the *Dialogue of Baghdad and Isfahan*. Then came detailed encyclopedia entries on 'Baghdad' and 'Isfahan',[30] each with images on some aspects of the two cities: a map of Baghdad, the 'round city', the time of its rise as a capital when it was also called the 'city of peace';[31] and images of Isfahan, from historical maps of its quadrangular 'square' in a book titled *Half the World*, to the portrait of a native poet-physician with nostalgic verses about that city, following its 'fall' in an Afghan siege;[32] next were texts and images of Baghdad and Isfahan through 'European visitors',[33] both portrayed in their brighter days and vivid colours, even when in black and white: and their highlight came from a travelogue, that of an Italian 'wanderer' with whom Leo shared more than a very young age. Regarding the world as 'a great book', he was accompanied by a French sketcher,[34] who brought to life panoramas of Baghdad and Isfahan that Leo would later 'animate' through the advancing technologies.

The next images transported from Leo's ageing hand-held device were more inspirational than instructional, coming from books he had pulled out hastily from different shelves of that Memorial library for inspiring approaches, mediums and visions for his launching project. Outside a fenced cube housing the private collection of the founder of the history of science as a field,[35] a book titled *The Nothing That Is*[36] inspired open-ended approaches through its 'chapter zero', defining zero as an open 'gateway' not a 'closed ring'; one titled *Weaving the Web*[37] by the inventor of the World Wide Web spoke of unimaginable mediums for 'anything being potentially connected with anything', and a 'new freedom to grow faster than we ever could'; and *A Wonderful Life Book*, orginially titled *The Greatest Gift*,[38] awakened more than one new vision: the

30 Duri, A. A., 'Baghdād', Encyclopedia of Islam (EI^2), 1, 11–22 (1958), pp. 894–909. Lambton, A. K. S., 'Iṣfahān: History', Encyclopedia of Islam (EI^2), 4, 61–2 (1973), pp. 97–105. Sourdel-Thomine, 'Iṣfahān: Monuments', Encyclopedia of Islam (EI^2), 4, 61–2 (1973), pp. 105–7; also, Streck, M., 'Baghdād', Encyclopedia of Islam (EI^1), 2, 1987, pp. 563–6; Huart, Cl. 'Iṣfahān: Sipāhān', Encyclopedia of Islam (EI^1), 3, 1987, pp. 528–30.

31 Le Strange, Guy, Baghdad During the Abbasid Caliphate from Contemporary Arabic and Persian Sources, with Eight Plans (London, 1924): maps of the round city as inner leaves including 150–300AD, (also in Duri, 'Baghdād', p. 909). The quote 'no other round city is known in all the regions of the world', p. 46, is followed by 'numerous references in Islamic literature to other round cities': p. 232, n. 6. Coke, Richard, Baghdad, the City of Peace (London, 1927): Madīnat al-Salām.

32 Blake, Stephen P., Half the World: The Social Architecture of Safavid Isfahan, 1590–1722 (Costa Mesa, 1999), p. 42: 'Map 4. Isfahan in 1135' [1722] (Afghan takeover). Browne, Edward G., A Literary History of Persia, 4 vols. (London, 1902–), Vol. 4, pp. 256–7: Portrait of Ḥakīm Shifā'ī, British Museum. Gilanentz, Petros di Sarkis, Suqūt-i Iṣfahān [Fall of Isfahan] (Isfahan, 1344 [1965]).

33 Stevens, Sir Roger, 'European visitors to the Safavid court', Iranian Studies, 7, Special Issue: Renata Holod (ed), Studies on Isfahan, Proceedings of The Isfahan Colloquium, Harvard University (1974), pp. 421–49.

34 Welch, Anthony, 'Safavid Iran as seen through Venetian eyes', in Newman, Andrew J. (ed), Society and Culture in the Early Modern Middle East (Leiden, Boston, 2003), pp. 97–119; Welch, Anthony (ed), The Travels and Journal of Ambrosio Bembo (1671–1675), Bargellini, Clara (tr) (Berkeley, 2007), pp. 119 and 322: G. J. Grélot panoramas.

35 Harvard's History of Science Library, Widener Library: Room 91 is the former office of George Sarton.

36 Kaplan, Robert, The Nothing That Is, pp. 1–3: quotes.

37 Berners-Lee, Tim with Fischetti, Mark, Weaving the Web: The Original Design and Ultimate Destiny of the World Wide Web by its Inventor (San Francisco, 1999): quotes. www.w3.org/People/Berners-Lee/Weaving/Overview.html

38 Basinger, Jeanine, in Collaboration with the Trustees of the Frank Capra Archives, The It's A Wonderful Life Book, interviews by Leonard Maltin (New York, 1986), p. 94: 'The Greatest Gift'.

'Wonderful Life', highlighting the wonderful effect on life of every single element and event in it through the story of someone given a chance to relive life without himself in it; and the 'Greatest Gift', through the story itself coming to life 'all at once' and 'complete from start to finish – a most unusual occurrence'. Leo recalled his would-be mentor talking about the book's two versions summing up between them history as the combined sum of mostly unique instances and events in ways that no teacher in his own academy and its affiliated university had driven home to him; that one story captured a powerful message about historical understanding, and the other about the magic of storytelling itself. The moments of leisure with images rolling on Leo's screen brought him closer not just to the opening pages of his own story in a single day, but also to the greatest gift of learning about creative works through single blinks. Deeply engaged in view mode on his laptop, his eyes stayed wide open for the rest of the overnight flight.

When Leo's plane landed in London at 6.40am – the exact numerical time it had taken off from Boston the night before in a literal 'coincidence' of flight time and time lag between those two cities – it was still too early for anything to be open. When he reached the library housing the *Dialogue* manuscript, the terms 'Last Word' in its forecourt beamed above some crossed out words to name a transit café stand: this was a sharp contrast to the timeless stand in the lobby offering classic books for 'Adoption', among them 'A Tale of Two Cities' jumping out in gold script on its cover. When Leo reached the third floor reading room of 'Asian and African Studies' to view the *Dialogue* manuscript his eyes popped open at the sight of a much older handwritten volume: inside that cover opened a tale of two other cities from 'Eastern' lands of a good five hundred years before, under the watchful eyes of library guards. For the beautifully transcribed gold-illuminated folio leaves of the *Dialogues of Baghdad and Isfahan* (Plate 1),[39] elegantly bound in languages its young requester could read, the quiet life of that manuscript was now changed; and for its eager reader, being amongst the first to open the volume's fragile pages made everything else more than worthwhile. His only disappointment was being denied taking any pictures of the finely crafted scripts within multi-colour frames of what was the first old 'production' he had laid his eyes on. Ordering a black and white microfilm of its leaves was the best he could hope for.

The delicately executed scripts on the bound manuscript of the *Dialogue*, which Leo examined for the rest of that day, instantly told him that the manuscript did not belong strictly to the Persian catalogue from which he had copied its entry. The text was not only composed in both Arabic and Persian, but as a generous mix of prose and poetry in alternate text and margin forms. Having to circle his eyes around the tiny scripts, some with unclear orders or dotted letters, interfered with the geometry of straight and slanted lines and shapes dancing on each folio, in a way that needed much more time; and as he read and read through the boasts of two cities on trivial matters from climates to resources, he knew their tale of 'science' had to be invented from an angle not in the text itself. To start that tale from a tangible angle, he first placed Baghdad and Isfahan in the days of the *Dialogue*'s own author and transcriber, on the same month of March

[39] Kamāl-i Iṣfahānī, Munāẓirāt-i Baghdād va Iṣfahān.

with years rounded up to post-1250s and pre-1750s, exact dates for the work's composition and transcription nowhere found in the manuscript itself. Setting Baghdad and Isfahan next to Moon and Sun icons after the respective lunar and solar calendars of their Arab and Persian cities, historical entries on each would follow in Leo's own words: piles of notes would turn into typed scripts, complete with chapter number, title and date, above the young author's 'pen name' as a narrator of a reconstructed *Dialogue*; using 'Charles Leo' of his first and middle names, he picked for his last name 'Scribner', not only after the name of fine publishers in the field,[40] but also a name starting a new life through its own meaning as scribe.

Leo's historical narrative, while reflecting old times and outdated scripts, would venture into new ways of historical thinking and writing: it would start with the subject of history, and historical figures and events as transmitters of key elements and moments affecting the various processes involved, from conceptions and interpretations to compositions and transcriptions.

Chapter 1: 'Dialogue' of Baghdad and Isfahan
'Navel of the World', 'Half of the World' – Roots
By Charles Leo Scribner, March 2005

> [*Baghdad:*] *O' Isfahan . . .*
> *Clear as a day, if cities were all bodies,*
> *I'd be the soul running through each one . . .*
> [*Isfahan:*] *O' Baghdad . . .*
> *Not the whole of Baghdad, in all fairness,*
> *Is a fist of my soil in the palm of one's hand . . .*
>
> Kamāl-i Iṣfahānī, *Munāẓirāt-i Baghdād va Iṣfahān* [*Dialogues of Baghdad and Isfahan*], undated; unpublished manuscript: folios 167a–167b; Kheirandish, Elaheh (tr, excerpts)[41]

1.3 *An Arab City with Eastern Links*

It was the month of March in a lunar year corresponding to sometime after the year 1250 of the 'common era'. Post-1250 was a time when Baghdad, a capital once called a 'round city' and 'city of peace',[42] was at a different place from where it long stood. This

40 Gillispie, Charles (ed), Dictionary of Scientific Biography (DSB), 18 vols. (New York, 1970–1990).

41 Kamāl-i Iṣfahānī, Munāẓirāt-i Baghdād va Iṣfahān, Kheirandish, Elaheh (tr) (rhymes preserved):
[*Baghdad*] fol. 167b:
'Chun rūz ruwshan ast kih īn shahr-hā hamih,
Ham-chun tan-and u man zih miyān-i hamih ravān. . .'
[*Isfahan*] fol. 167a: / *'Kih az rū-yi inṣāf u az dād u dih,*
Kaf-ī khāk-am az jumlih Baghdād bih. . .'

42 Khaṭīb al-Baghdādī, Tārīkh Baghdād, Lassner, Jacob (tr) (The Topography f Baghdad in the Early Middle Ages, Text and Studies) (Detroit, 1970), pp. 31 and 228, nn. 28–9; Le Strange, Baghdad During the Abbasid Caliphate, p. 14; Duri, 'Baghdād', p. 909; Coke, Baghdad, The City of Peace; Levy, Reuben, A Baghdad Chronicle (Studies in Islamic History, No. 17) (Cambridge, MA, 1929, 2011), p. xi: '. . . the only sounds that ever issued from the "City of Peace" were those of strife and battle'.

was an Arab city long known for its various eastern links, from the name 'Baghdad' and its possible Persian roots, to Persian cities acting as its prototype models.[43] But this was still a time not far from the heights of the glories of Baghdad close to 500 years after its fateful foundation by the ʿAbbasid Caliphs (r. ca. 750–1258), quite early into their reign.

On this March day of a new Moon rising in an Arab city with a lunar calendar, a young 'wanderer' named Kamal was sitting cross-legged on the floor of an exquisite courtyard in his new city of residence; his pen was dancing clockwise to the curves of a name on a manuscript that would one day make him known outside of his own small world. His title, Kamal-i Isfahani, said he was from Isfahan, a Persian city known as 'half the world', long after he was gone; but he also belonged to Baghdad, an Arab city known as the 'navel of the universe',[44] long before he was born. The first was the city of his fate by birth and name, the second, the city of his choice, in heart and soul. On this first day of a spring in a lunar year followed by the term Hijra[45] to mark the 'migration' of the Prophet of his faith from Arabian Mecca to Medina as the Hijri year zero, Kamal felt doubly exalted by the conjunction of a particularly special date and time. The date was that of the Persian New Year, Nowruz, the literal New Day[46] of his native ancestors, the astronomical moment when winter turned into spring; and the time was the start of a new day, the moment of dusk when a day turned, not just into night, but also into the next day, in the less familiar ritual of his Arab neighbours. The first was the date he observed year after year to the instant when goldfish were said to stand still to mark the turn of a new year in the solar sphere; the second was the moment he longed for, day after day, to the last minute and second when the Moon replaced the Sun in the sky, to mark what on that March day was still a crescent in the lunar sphere.[47]

To Kamal, whose first name meant perfection in Arabic and Persian, nothing was closer to it that day than the place he was sitting, at a moment when the sound of his reed pen on paper was all that broke the deep silence around him. Curving his body to reach a box with inlaid patterns, one that he carried around his waistband, he dipped his pen far into the inkwell.[48] He then transcribed the title *Munazirat-i Baghdad va Isfahan* from right to left to open a contesting 'dialogue' between those two cities. The pen name that followed as Kamal-i Isfahani, translating into 'Perfection from Isfahan', was a name carried by a near contemporary poet with the distinct middle name of Ismaʿil. But without that or a date next to Kamal's name passing through future copyists of his 'autograph' manuscript, what would later claim him as the author of that *Dialogue* rested on one small detail: his mention of a single scholar laying buried in Baghdad as

43 Duri, 'Baghdād', p. 894; Le Strange, Baghdad During the Abbasid Caliphate, p. 10; and Bayani, Shirin, Tīsfūn [Ctesphon] va Baghdād (Tehran, 1377 [1998]), p. 122, respectively.

44 Irving, Clive, 'Half of the world: 1450–1750', Crossroads of Civilization: 3000 Years of Persian History (London, 1979), pp. 147–81, p. 47; Blake, Half the World; Lassner, Topography of Baghdad, p. 17.

45 Bacharach, Near East Studies Handbook, p. 85–6: Islamic Calendar.

46 Levy, R., Bosworth, C. E., and Freeman-Greenville, G. S. P, 'Nawrūz (P.), New (Year's) Day', Encyclopedia of Islam (EI²), 7, 129–30 (1992), p. 1047.

47 van Dalen, Benno, 'Al-Shams (A.), the sun (f.), 2. In Astronomy', Encyclopedia of Islam (EI²), 9, 151–2 (1996), pp. 291–4; Pingree, David, 'Al-Kamar (A.), the moon, I. Astronomy', Encyclopedia of Islam (EI²), 4, 69–70 (1975), pp. 517–18.

48 Pedersen, Johannes, The Arabic Book, Geoffrey French (tr), Robert Hillenbrand (ed) (Princeton, 1984), p. 70.

one of the prides of that city, a figure whose death date was late enough for the modern cataloguer[49] to rule out the authorship of an earlier Kamal of Isfahan.

To the readers of Kamal's *Dialogue* after his own time, the dating of his piece to sometime after the 1250s, given the approximations, could still seem perfect – a perfect snapshot of a time after Baghdad was 'Baghdad' and before Isfahan was to become 'Isfahan'. But to Kamal himself, the time in which he was writing only meant a few centuries after the glorious rise of the capital city, Baghdad, one hardly imaginable as just a few centuries away from the disastrous fall of his native city, Isfahan: about halfway between Baghdad rising as the capital of the ʿAbbasid Caliphate in 762, and Isfahan falling as the capital of Safavid Dynasty to Afghan invaders[50] in 1722, was most dramatic. Soon devastated by the 'Mongol Invasion'[51] from further east in the 1220s, the face of the continent was changed with 'no sharper dividing-line' than between the times before and after. The fast-changing pace of the times was well captured by the poet Kamal of Isfahan, who himself brutally perished at the hands of the Mongols. A 'Creator of Ideas', according to his title, he put into words the idea of having the 'inhabitants' of his native city increase in number by being cut 'into a hundred pieces' even before it happened, and created verses as powerful as:

Last night for one that died a thousand wept,
At dawn not one to weep a thousand slain.[52]

Not far from such charged times, poets raved about Baghdad and Isfahan both before and after their respective falls by Mongol takeovers in 1258 and 1237.

About two centuries before, had said one poet:

A city such as Baghdad, indeed, it is paradise on earth . . .
Its Lord has decided that no Caliph shall die in it.[53]

And about a century before the last Caliph died, another poet had followed with:

Blessed be the site of Baghdad, seat of learning and art,
None can point in the world to a city her equal.[54]

Isfahan had no fewer gems thrown at it, in both Arabic and Persian: in Arabic, it was a 'second Baghdad' before the first was an earthly paradise, with a perfect balance of the

49 Rieu, Catalogue of Persian Manuscripts, Vol. 2, pp. 600–1.

50 Duri, 'Baghdād'; Lambton, 'Iṣfahān'; Bosworth, Islamic Dynasties, pp. 7–10: ʿAbbāsids, 132–656/749–1258, pp. 172–4: Ṣafavids, 907–1145/1501–1732, pp. 174–5: Afghan rule, 1135–45/1722–32; Invasion of Persia, 1135/1722.

51 Browne, Literary History, Vol. 2, p. 542: 'dividing-line'; Bosworth, 'The Mongols', in Islamic Dynasties, pp. 141–3, p. 142: set at 616–17/1219–20; Woods, John E., 'A note on the Mongol capture of Iṣfahān', Journal of Near Eastern Studies, 36, 1 (1977), pp. 49–51, p. 49: Mongols' first assault of Iṣfahān, 625/1228; Spuler, Bertold, The Mongol Period, Bagley, F. R. C. (tr) (Princeton, 1994).

52 Kamāl Ismāʿīl-i Iṣfahānī, Browne, Literary History, Vol. 2, pp. 540–1: 'Khallāq al-Maʿānī', and quotes; Grant, Ethel Watts Mumford, The Hundred Songs of Kamal Ad-Din Isfahan (New York, 1904), p. 14.

53 Lassner, Topography of Baghdad, p. 47, p. 234, n. 14, quoting Ibn ʿAqīl (ca. 798–853). Snir, Reuven (ed, tr), Baghdad: The City in Verse (Cambridge, MA, 2013), p. 93, n. 29, has:
'Have you seen in any corner of the world, a tranquil abode like Baghdad?
. . . God commanded that no caliph will pass away there. . .'

54 Coke, Baghdad, the City of Peace, p. 64: quoting Anvarī (ca. 1126–89).

moist, dry, cold and heat of its four corners, one later drawn to the 'center of the fourth climate, the noblest of the seven'.[55] And in Persian, Isfahan was not only 'life of the world' and 'the world of life' at once, and a city where 'the mind is stunned at, which title to give it by way of logic';[56] it was also 'half the world' becoming 'the whole world' in verses like:

> *Isfahan which was considered half the world became the whole world . . .*
> *because of this new world [Chihil Sutun] created at Naqsh-i Jahan [Square].*[57]

If the Arabic verses were before Baghdad, the city blessed with 'no equals' was to bury not one but many Caliphs, the verses in Persian were before Isfahan, the city 'founded by the Architect of Creation'[58] was to be far from the 'blessed day' of its descriptions. Much more than just Caliphs were to 'die in Baghdad' even before the fall of that city into Mongol hands, when 'nature and man joined hands to eclipse Baghdad' in the 1250s; as was much more needed to keep Isfahan from becoming a 'shadow of itself' in the 1750s: so sharp were the paradoxes of Baghdad and Isfahan that modern authors would continue to write about them in the most extreme terms: about Baghdad, in terms of a 'city of peace' and of 'continuous war', with 'so many and so violent changes of fortune' compared to other 'cities of first rank . . . Athens, Rome, Constantinople, or even London'; and of its 'long succession of ups and downs, from insignificance to wealth and power, and back again to poverty'; and in contrast to depictions of Baghdad as so 'little known' that 'for one who has seen Baghdad, thousands have seen Rome, hundreds Athens, dozens Constantinople',[59] writings about Isfahan would go to extremes in terms of the city's 'rise and decline', from European visitors ranking it as the 'greatest and most beautiful in the whole orient' in the 1600s, to those reporting of landscapes and buildings 'red with blood' within a single century.[60]

[55] Ibn al-Faqīh al-Hamadhānī, Mukhtaṣar Kitāb al-buldān, de Goeje, M. J. (ed) (Leiden, 1967, 2014); and Māfarrūkhī, al-Mufaḍḍal, Kitāb Maḥāsin Iṣfahān, Ṭihrānī, Jalāl al-Dīn al-Ḥusaynī (ed) (Tehran, 1933), pp. 4–5: respective quotes.

[56] Āvī, Ḥusayn ibn Muḥammad, Maḥāsin Iṣfahān (Persian), ca. 729 [1328], copied, 884 [1479], Iqbāl Āshtiyānī, ʿAbbās (ed) (Isfahan, 1385 [2006]), p. 9; Browne, Edward G., 'Account of a rare manuscript [of] history of Iṣfahán, presented to the Royal Asiatic Society on May 19, 1827' in John Malcolm and Edward G. Browne (eds), The Journal of the Royal Asiatic Society of Great Britain and Ireland (Jul., 1901), pp. 411–46, pp. 412–15 (has the author as ʿAlawī, and the year as 1329), p. 415: Persian verse:
'Shahr-ī kih ʿaql khīra shav-ad az rah-i qiyās,
Jān-i jahān laqab dahad-ash yā jahān-i jān'.

[57] Amīrī Fīrūz-kūhī (ed), Kulliyāt-i Ṣāʾib-i Tabrīzī (Tehran, 1333 [1954]), pp. 834–7, Kheirandish, Elaheh (tr, excerpt):
'Iṣfahān shud ghayrat afzā-yi bihisht-i jāvdān, Z-īn jahān-i nu kih shud ibdāʿ dar Naqsh-i Jahān, Gasht az īn manzil bi tashrīf-i tamām-ī sar-farāz, Bud agar zīn pīsh shahr-i Iṣfahān niṣf-i Jahān. . .'.
Citation: Babaie, Sussan, Safavid Palaces at Isfahan: Continuity and Change (1590–1666) (New York, 1993, p. 321, translation, p. 324: *'The creation of this new world [Chihil Sutūn] at the Naqsh-i Jahān [garden] made Isfahan the envy of the eternal paradise, Because of this abode, Isfahan, which was previously [considered as] half of the world, became the whole [world]'.*

[58] Āvī, Maḥāsin Iṣfahān, p. 9; Browne, 'Account of a rare manuscript', p. 415: '*Miʿmār-i āfarinish*':
'Yā rabb kudām rūz-i mubārak banā nah-ād,
Miʿmār-i āfarīnish u bānī-yi kunn fa-kānn'.

[59] Duri, 'Baghdad', p. 902: 'shadow of itself'; Coke, Baghdad, the City of Peace, pp. 13–15, p. 15: 'continuous war'; Browne, Edward G., 'Baghdad During the ʿAbbásid Caliphate from Contemporary Arabic and Persian Sources by Guy Le Strange', The Journal of the Royal Asiatic Society of Great Britain and Ireland, April (Notice of Books), 1901, pp. 349–51, p. 349: 'little known'.

[60] Lambton, 'Iṣfahān', p. 103; and Stevens, 'European visitors', p. 429 respectively.

The historical ups and downs of the cities of Baghdad and Isfahan were many, both before and after the time of the composition of a *Dialogue* between them; but direct relationships between the two did not consume as many pens, either before or after that time. With the limited nature of communications at large, whatever people may have known about one city did not mean they knew much about the other, despite the relatively short distance between them. Kamal was no different. He knew much about Isfahan going as far back as centuries, but not about Baghdad as recently as decades. He naturally knew about an Isfahan of his own time, even its status as the 'highest of cities' by the scholar, Ibn ʿArabī, the scholar from Andalusia, later known as 'southern Spain'. Kamal knew about that 'superlative' compliment through Arabic verses by that mystic in praise of a Persian poetess-princess from Isfahan, bearing his own last name *Isfahani*, with the first name, *Nizam*, meaning order. The verses began with a reverenced bow to an articulate daughter of Persia, before rising up to the peaks of the 'highest city' of her native land:

Long have I yearned for a tender maiden,
Endowed with prose and verse, having a pulpit, eloquent
One of the princesses from the land of Persia,
From the highest of cities, from Isfahan . . . .[61]

Verses that could not have been known to someone living before the 1250s were high applauds of Baghdad and Isfahan in poems that were yet to be written.

A poem in a regional geography composed before 1350 would place Baghdad at the centre of the world above:

Cast your eyes from all sides like a Sun towards Baghdad,
Then rise like a heaven around it until you see it.[62]

And a poem in a regional history with a close composition date would raise Isfahan to the peaks of the world below:

The Land of Iran, finer than all the world's whereabouts,
If thought as a person, overflowing with the arts
Then, Isfahan would be its [ruling] head,
Shiraz and Kerman its legs, Ray and Azarbaijan, its arms.[63]

61 Ibn al-ʿArabī, Tarjumān al-Ashwāq, in Nicholson, Reynold A. (ed, tr), A Collection of Mystical Odes by Muhyiʾddīn ibn al-ʿArabī (London, 1911), p. 8, 24: 'ajall al-bilād' is translated there as 'most glorious cities'; Arabic term is 'Iṣbahān'
'Min banāt-i al-mulūk, min dār-i al-Furs
Min ajall al-bilād, min Iṣbahān'.

62 Mustuwfī, Ḥamd Allāh, Nuzhat al-qulūb (Tehran, 1362 [1983]), pp. 37–8: quoted in Bayani, Tīsfūn va Baghdād, p. 279, Kheirandish, Elaheh (tr, excerpt).

63 Āvī, Maḥāsin Iṣfahān (Persian), pp. 29–30, quoting Fāḍil Saʿd al-Dīn Saʿīd Haravī, ca. 1323, date of composition, 724 [1323–24], Kheirandish, Elaheh (tr, excerpt)
'Mulk-i Īrān rā kih az aṭrāf-i ʿālam khush-tar ast,
Ham chu shakṣ-ī dān kih bāshad az hunar ū rā ravān
Iṣfahān ū rā sar u Kirmān u Shirāz-ash du pāy,
Ray yik-ī dast-ast u dīgar dast-ash Āzarbāygān'.

What Kamal may not have known when writing his *Dialogue of Baghdad and Isfahan*, was not only the specific ethnic conflicts of eastern cities at the time, but also the competition of western Islamic lands with those in the east, places in Andalusia like Cordoba, the so-called 'ornament of the world'[64] in the words of a medieval nun. These were key centres for Islamic, Christian and Jewish exchanges in ways that his two city subjects were to have, then lose, in different times. Kamal could not imagine Baghdad and Isfahan to be anything other than the crossroads for scientific, philosophical and artistic works at the courts of the ʿAbbasids and Seljuqs, as the respective capital cities of a few centuries before; but never as the fallen cities of a few centuries later under the Ottomans or Afghans.[65]

While the fall to the Mongols came for Isfahan before Baghdad in the mid 1200s, the opposite was the case for the Ottomans and Afghans of the 1400s and 1700s. But in all cases, the political and natural went hand in hand in their respective blows. Just before the 1258 Mongol takeover of Baghdad major floods hit the area. But no such signs were visible to Kamal at the time, and no knowledge of the city otherwise. The little he knew about Baghdad included some facts: that it became a capital city under a caliphate named ʿAbbasids, replacing another named Umayyads centuries before; that a reputable ʿAbbasid Caliph with the powerful name of Mansur, meaning 'Victor',[66] moved the capital from Damascus shortly after this change; and that Baghdad had two, not one famous river running through it as was the case in Kamal's native Isfahan. The trivia that stood in his way of composing a sophisticated or even-handed exchange between the two cities hardly rose from the level of basic facts, given the limited forms of local communication.

Lacking enough knowledge to even mention the Persian roots of 'Baghdad' as a 'God-given' city, or Arab forms of 'Isfahan', as a city of 'armies',[67] Kamal went straight from the customary praises and flowery phrases of his introduction to the bare facts that were the only ways he could compare the two cities: that Baghdad was the resting place of many famous people; that it was closer to the House of God, Mecca; and that its native language was Arabic, the language of Islam's Holy Book. Nothing at the time about Baghdad and Isfahan as the sites of Sunni and Shiʿi sects of Islam; as the ruling grounds of caliphs and kings; or as the rising and setting sites of science. Kamal's lines and arguments were thus limited to heritage, faith, and language. Missing the deeper touches that came with finer forms of transportation, information, and transmission, he proceeded without direct reference to science, and by extension, the trio of institutions, commissions, and communications driving even the earliest phases of scientific development.

The limited flow of information and exchange at the time was not the only curtain falling between the author and his subjects, and ultimately his readers. Caution played its own role. From the very opening of the *Dialogue of Baghdad and Isfahan*, Kamal, describing himself as a traveller with the hard task of choosing between two top candidates for the best residence of the time, brought in a 'companion' as the communicator

64 Menocal, Ornament of the World.

65 Bosworth, Islamic Dynasties, pp. 7–10: ʿAbbāsids; pp. 115–18: Seljūqs; pp. 136–40: Ottomans; pp. 174–5: Afghan rule.

66 Abbott, Nabia, Two Queens of Baghdad: Mother and Wife of Hārūn al Rashīd (Chicago, London, 1986), p. 1.

67 Duri, 'Baghdād', p. 563; Levy, Baghdad Chronicle; Huart, 'Iṣfahān', p. 528: Iṣbahān (Arabic), Sipāhān (Persian); Lambton, 'Iṣfahān', p. 97: Iṣbahān; Lockhart, Laurence, Famous Cities of Iran (Brentford, 1939); Persian Cities (London, 1960).

of a contest between the two cities, in his caution not to offend any local rulers or officials over a sensitive subject. The terms and arguments he used were similarly selected with care, from an introduction to be read most readily, to the boasts and blames that followed and faded successively. If he was not bringing much from the science of his own time into a dialogue between two cities so rich on the subject, there was also a reason. He had to downplay Baghdad as the cradle of science in a work that was to be dedicated to a patron favouring Isfahan; and he had to resist glorifying Isfahan in a place as competitive as Baghdad, with no less of a call for various forms of self-censorship.

Baghdad and Isfahan, he thus started, were two cities that in his exact words, 'rose above others', both in his own experience and the currency of his day. But in addressing an audience he could not completely outguess, he also had to think hard about what he did and did not say. The easiest part was the ruler for whom dialogues of this kind were mostly written, many having, besides the two opposing sides, a third counterpart, a mediator, a judge, often the ruler himself. But the range of courtiers exposed to the contents of a dialogue brought to its author a taint of uneasiness that found its way into many sentences and quotes, thereby cautiously transmitted from mostly dead authors to be on the safe side. Kamal was writing his *Dialogue* with all these in mind. So when he opened his introduction with talk about his travels, he was sure to mention a 'Prophetic saying', quoting 'Those who travel are enriched', instead of the famous 'Seek Knowledge as Far as China',[68] the Hadith whose long chains of transmission from the early days of Islam had accumulated some controversy along the way.

Kamal thus put the body of the *Dialogue* itself in the voice of his 'companion' in a similarly self-conscious tone. Just before setting Baghdad and Isfahan in verbal competition he likened the difficulty of distinguishing between them to that between one's own 'life and heart'.

This one is life, the other, heart,
To distinguish life and heart, is not wise.[69]

With the first words in the mouth of the side that was often privileged to have the last word, Isfahan began through messengers sent to Baghdad:

O' Baghdad, are you making your claims and boasts,
in ignorance of my admired qualities and privileges.[70]

Next came the ancient 'qualities' of water, air, earth and fire, to remind the opponent, in turn, of Isfahan's water and its 'extreme transparency', air and its 'outmost purity', earth and its 'growing supremacy', and fire and its 'innate spirituality'. Isfahan's outstanding

68 Kamāl-i Iṣfahānī, Munāẓirāt-i Baghdād va Iṣfahān, fol. 166v: 'Sāfarū Taghnamū'. Robson, J., 'Hadith', Encyclopedia of Islam (EI^2), 3, 41–2 (1971), pp. 23–8.

69 Kamāl-i Iṣfahānī, Munāẓirāt-i Baghdād va Iṣfahān, fol. 166b, right margin:
'Kih īn jān ast u ān dil, jān u dil rā,
Zi yik dīgar judā kardan nah nikū-st'.

70 Kamāl-i Iṣfahānī, Munāẓirāt-i Baghdād va Iṣfahān, fol. 167a:
'Ay Baghdād, magar tu az man ki Iṣfahān-am ghāfil būd-ī,
Va dhikr-i maḥāmid va khavāṣṣ-i man nashinūd-ī,
Va gar nah īn daʿvī khud-namāʾī nakard-ī'.

features and privileges were then stretched to pre-Islamic times when the city was claimed as the primary seat of famous rulers and battles, and principal site of superb buildings and monuments:

Kings and beggars, dervishes and emirs . . .
None hold another city over my land
Not the whole of Baghdad, in all fairness,
Is a fist of my soil in the palm of one's hand.[71]

'*O' Isfahan*', followed Baghdad messengers, reciting in the philosophical language of body and soul:

How can now live in a world where one,
Is talked down by a city like Isfahan . . .
Clear as a day, if cities were all bodies,
I'd be the soul running through each one.[72]

The lines of prose interspersed along those of poetry throughout the text similarly fell short of the literature of the time. When Baghdad boasted of being the resting place of great minds, having a distance closer to the House of God, and language of Islam's Holy Book, Isfahan returned with matching couplets: a place with high profiles does not lift it any higher, a distance closer to Mecca does not make it any closer to God, and the 'Arab tribe' not well-disposed to learning other languages does not turn their's into a voice of faith.[73] As the *Dialogue* fiercely consuming Kamal's pen came closer and closer to its final sections, it carried more and more tilts towards his native land; and as he raised one city over the other in anticipation for a grand finale, Isfahan came to win over Baghdad on account of something not unveiled until the very end for optimal effect: the presence of a patron in Isfahan named Shahab, meaning Shooting Star, one later titled by Kamal an 'Illuminating Sun'[74] whose radiance shone beyond his own lands, was enough to act as a lifting lever for the city of Isfahan, the first voice in that dialogue.

71 Kamāl-i Iṣfahānī, Munāẓirāt-i Baghdād va Iṣfahān, fol. 167a, left margin:
'Zi shāh u gidā u zi darvīsh u mīr,
Na shahr-ī digar bar man afzūn dah-and
Kih az rū-yi inṣāf u az dād u dih,
Kaf-ī khāk-am az jumlih Baghdād bih'.

72 Kamāl-i Iṣfahānī, Munāẓirāt-i Baghdād va Iṣfahān, fol. 167b:
'Z-īn pas chi-gūnih zindih tavān būd dar jahān,
Kam zīn namṭ khaṭāb kun-ad shahr-i Iṣfahān . . .
Chun rūz ruwshan ast kih īn shahr-hā hamih,
Ham chūn tan-and u man zi miyān-i hamih ravān'.

73 Kamāl-i Iṣfahānī, Munāẓirāt-i Baghdād va Iṣfahān, fol. 175b right margin, 176r left margin:
'Ān-chih guft-ī man bi-vāsiṭih-i mujāvirat-i zamīn-i Ḥijāz az tu mumtāz-am,
Īn maʿnī sabab-i imtīyāz va faḍīlat nashav-ad . . .
[Va na] muṣāḥibat va mujāvirat bā karīmān va nikū-kārān . . .
Va [ham] Ān-chih guftī kih man ʿArab-am va az Tāzī-gūyān
Va tu ʿAjam-i va az jumlih-i Fārsī-zabānān . . .
Chun ṭāyifih-i Aʿrāb rā istiʿdād-i dīgar-i zabān-hā nabuv-ad . . .'.

74 Kamāl-i Iṣfahānī, Munāẓirāt-i Baghdād va Iṣfahān, fol. 177a left margin:
'Shahāb al-Ḥaq . . . Makhdūm Mubārak-Shāh'
fol. 177b, right margin-178r central text:
'Baghdād guft: Iṭālat-i madḥ-i mādiḥān-i Khurshīd-i tābān rā, ruwshanī ziādat nakun-ad,
va ḥamd u sitāyish-i vāṣifān sabab-i izdiyād-i Āftāb-i munīr nashav-ad. . .'

Not long before that time, the physical settings had been different; but now the earlier rulers in Baghdad had been replaced with those much too weak for Kamal to chance longer residence in a city in whose bosom he had resided with open arms till then. The time had come to end the *Dialogue* that Kamal was composing with random characters and dead authors, and to take it to a patron in Isfahan. This came at a time as 'perfect' as the meaning of Kamal's own name, a time when Baghdad, the Arab city with a lunar calendar, was being partially eclipsed; and Isfahan, the Persian city with a solar calendar, was to outshine it with brighter glories for some time to come. More perfect still, as Baghdad, the 'Navel of the World' was to hide in a shadow falling upon its edges, Isfahan, 'Half of the World', was emerging with the 'Plan of the World' cast in the very name of its central square, 'Naqsh-i Jahan'.[75] But more was in store: not before long, Isfahan was to turn into less than 'half' of itself.

1.4 *A Persian City with Western Links*

It was the month of March in a solar year corresponding to sometime before the year 1750, a time when Isfahan was not far from the depths of its lowest downfall. On this first day of a new year in a Persian city with a solar calendar,[76] a man named Jamal, meaning beauty, was copying, in a beautiful hand, the manuscript of a 'dialogue' between the two cities of Baghdad and Isfahan. The volume in which the text was to rest as its single known copy for a long time to come was a fine production (Plate 1): its scripts, borders, colours and illuminations carried the marks of a city as refined in crafts as Isfahan, even if the 'residence' of the volume's copyist at the time of signing was given as a site as remote to both Baghdad and Isfahan as Kanauj in India.[77] It had taken Jamal forever to transcribe the volume's manuscript, and it had been close to the end of that meticulous job when he realised that the piles of prose and poetry next to him were mixed up with the genre of contesting 'dialogues'; and while sorting these out, he could not help being distracted by a few titles as he slaved through that tedious process. Next to major collections like the *Flower Garden* and *Orchard*, by the prose and poetry master Sa῾di of centuries before, a few 'dialogue' poems by a closely named Asadi[78] of even older times had jumped out to

[75] 'Naqsh-i Jahān' is Isfahan's central square: Sourdel-Thomine, 'Iṣfahān' and Blunt, Wilfrid, Isfahan Pearl of Persia (New York, London, 1966; repr. 2009), p. 60, have 'image of the world' and 'picture of the world' respectively. Melville, 'New light on Shah ῾Abbas', and Emami, Farshid, 'Coffee houses, urban spaces, and the formation of a public sphere in Safavid Isfahan', in Necipoğlu, Gülru (ed), Muqarnas: An Annual of the Visual Culture of the Islamic World (Leiden, 2016), pp. 155–76, p. 155 and pp. 177–220, p. 179: 'plan of the world'.

[76] The solar calendar Jalālī is associated with ῾Umar Khayyām in the court of Seljūq King, Malik-Shāh I (465–85/1072–92): Bosworth, Islamic Dynasties, p. 115–18; Browne, Literary History, Vol. 2, p. 181: 1079.

[77] Kamal-i Iṣfahānī, Munāẓirāt-i Baghdād va Iṣfahān, fol. 197a: codex copyist '… Shaykh Jamāl … resident of Qunūj': full text below.

[78] Sa῾dī, Gulistān (prose) and Būstān (poetry): Browne, Literary History, Vol. 2, pp. 525–39. Losensky, Paul, 'Sa῾dī', Encyclopedia Iranica (EIr), 2000. www.iranicaonline.org/articles/sadi-sirazi. Khaleghi-Motlagh, Djalal, 'Asadī Ṭūsī', Encyclopedia Iranica (EIr), 2, 7 (1987), pp. 699–700. www.iranicaonline.org/articles/asadi-tusi. Massé, H., 'Asadi', Encyclopedia of Islam (EI^2) 1, 11 (1958), pp. 685–6; Browne, Literary History, Vol. 2, p. 116, p. 149.

capture his attention: 'dialogues' like those between arrow and bow, earth and sky, night and day: but one in particular, a 'dialogue' between two cities Jamal knew well, bearing on its opening page the name of a certain Kamal-i Isfahani he could neither place nor date, seemed to have enough of an overlay with the volume at hand to be included in it, even if the subject or author did not fit all aspects of that volume perfectly.

The inclusion of a 'dialogue' with a mix of Arabic and Persian, prose and poetry, and text and margin, in the final folios of a volume 'in the hands of' Jamal would have been enough of a fit, if only for filling the number of blank folios left to close the volume. But the two cities in dialogue being Baghdad and Isfahan, both directly related to the Persian literary master Saʿdi, the main figure associated with that volume, made it an even more perfect fit. The first city, Baghdad, was the city giving Saʿdi an education and fame fitting for the links of his name to 'fortune': this was in a past distant from Jamal's time reflected through odes like the *Lament on the Fall of Baghdad*,[79] when conquered by the Mongols over five centuries before; but the fame of Saʿdi was to spread in a future even more distant from Jamal through verses like '*Children of Adam . . . members of a whole, in essence and soul*',[80] verses with verbal gems far-reaching enough to crown the words of a modern Western thinker, entrance of a United Nations building, and speech of a world leader,[81] all in different times and places. The second city of the *Dialogue* in Jamal's hand, Isfahan, had its own fit for a Saʿdi-rich volume: this was beyond bordering Shiraz, the city of poetry, and of Saʿdi himself, to which he later returned, despite reports of his mention of 'homes to die in' away from his beloved homeland of Persia, from Syria and Byzantium to Basra and Baghdad.[82] Isfahan was a city to which Saʿdi devoted poems directly, from a time after the Mongol sack of Isfahan, itself shortly before that of Baghdad. Given Saʿdi's poems on both cities were part of collections central to the volume under transcription, a dialogue between them through the mouthpiece of a wandering resident of both seemed more than fitting.

Among Saʿdi's collection of poems titled *Bustan*, meaning *Orchard*, the masterful poet had captured Isfahan under the sharp blades of the Mongol invasion, far enough to the east of Baghdad to fall to the invaders shortly before the ʿAbbasid capital. The capture of that Persian city was versified through a 'Soldier in Isfahan',[83] whom Saʿdi depicted with the comparable imagery of a youth first 'robust as an arrow', then 'aged as a bow'. From a matchless fighter from Isfahan taking a ring with a spear from his palm, to an archer encircled by the ring of a deadly war, Saʿdi brought to life images of a fast-falling city with strong visual graphics. The days of the 'battle of Tartary' were drawn as:

79 Browne, Literary History, Vol. 2, pp. 29–30; Saʿdī, Ghazaliyāt-i Saʿdī, Arjang, Gh. (ed) (Tehran, 1383 [2002]).

80 Saʿdī's poem '*Banī Ādam . . .*': inscribed on United Nations Entrance: www.zaufishan.co.uk/2011/09/iranian-poetry-bani-adam-inscribed-on.html

81 Horton, Scott, 'Emerson's Saadi', Harper's Magazine, 21 June 2009: http://harpers.org/blog/2009/06/emersons-saadi/. The United Nations Visitors Entrance: 46th Street and 1st Avenue, New York. Mackey, Robert, 'Obama, Peres and Colbert on the Persian New Year', 20 March 2009. https://thelede.blogs.nytimes.com/2009/03/20/obama-and-colbert-on-the-persian-new-year/

82 Browne, 'Account of a rare manuscript', pp. 411–46, p. 413, p. 415; Āvī, Mahāsin Iṣfahān, p. 2: '*Saʿdī-yā ḥubb-i vaṭan gar-chih ḥadīth-īst ṣaḥīḥ, Natavān murd bih sakhtī kih man īnjā zād-am . . . Nah-kih birūn-i Pārs manzil nīst, Shām u Rūm-ast u Baṣrih u Baghdād*'.

83 Saʿdī, Būstān, Hart, Edward, A. (tr) (Būstān of Saʿdī) (London, 1911), p. 91. www.sacred-texts.com/isl/bus/bus09.htm

The raining of arrows that descended like hail,
The storm of death arose in every corner
Not one of our troops came out of the battle,
But his cuirass was soaked with blood . . .[84]

Images of blood filled Saʿdi's *Lament on the fall of Baghdad*, and the ʿAbbasid Caliphate itself, bloodshed mixing with words as strong as 'revolution' (*inqilab*):

Well it were if from the heavens tears of blood on earth should flow,
For the ruler of the Faithful, al-Mustaʿsim brought so low . . .
Fear vicissitudes of fortune; fear the Sphere's revolving change
Who could dream such a splendor such a fate should overthrow . . .?[85]

The fall of Isfahan was itself painted with fateful imagery:

Not that our swords were blunt,
It was the vengeance of stars of ill fortune . . .
Since fortune averted her face,
Useless was our shield against the arrows of fate.[86]

But the city of Isfahan was to rise to the powerful imagery of its higher peaks, not long before falling again under the harshest blows of an Afghan attack to a point of no return. Over a century before that fall in 1722 had come the powerful words of a poet-physician with the fitting name, Shifaʾi, the very meaning of which captured the message of 'healing':

The revolving sphere is the father, and its pillars, the mother,
But Isphahan, the child, is better than the parent . . .
A hundred hours strike in it, at one and the same instant . . .
Both East and West have places within it . . .

Past glories of Isfahan rose in verses that sank hearts beyond those of natives:

At the gate of this world of wisdom, Greece is a beggar for a trait,
In every street, is an Aristotle standing up, At every step, a Plato on the ground . . .
The lowest populace are inventors of such Mejistis [as Ptolemy's],
The very children carry [The Book of] Healing [by Ibn Sina] in their sleeves. . .[87]

[84] Saʿdī, Būstān, Hart (tr), p. 93.
[85] Saʿdī, Būstān; Browne, Literary History, Vol. 2, pp. 29–30.
[86] Saʿdī, Būstān, Hart (tr), p. 97.
[87] Ḥakīm Shifāʾī, quoted by Ḥazīn-i Lāhījī (d. 1766), The Life of Sheikh Mohammed Ali Hazin, Belfour, F. C. (ed, tr) (London, 1830–1831), pp. 43–9; p. 306: memoirs: 1742; Kheirandish, Elaheh (tr, adaptation).
'*Gardūn pidar ast u mādar arkān, Farzand bih az pidar Sipāhān . . .*
Ṣad vaqt dar ū shav-ad bih yik gām . . . Chih sharq u chih gharb rā dar ū jāy . . .
Bar dar-gah-i īn jahān-i ḥikmat, Yunān bāsh-ad gidāy-i fiṭrat . . .
Har kūchih muʿallim-ī sitādih, Har gām Filāṭun-ī fitādih . . .
Awbāsh Majisṭī afārin-and, Aṭfāl Shifā dar āstin-and'.

The transmitter of those verses was a scholar of over a hundred years later than that 17th-century poet, one on the run from the afflicted Persia of his own time, who writing under the pen name *Hazin*, meaning 'sad', was to say nostalgically of 'Isphahan' that 'nowhere in the world [is] to be found a city, however large, that contains the universality to be met with here'. More than a century later, an English translator of Hazin's history-travelogue would have the hindsight of a very different Isfahan, adding a note under those very same verses that they 'have very little merit, but as a magnificent sample of Eastern "Hyperbole"'.[88]

Jamal, the transcriber of a 'dialogue' between Baghdad and Isfahan during the fast-changing pace of his own time, who signed that text with a name ending with 'Shaykh Jamal',[89] was well suited to carry a name meaning 'beauty' on account of the admirable quality of his calligraphic craft. While writing diagonally from right to left, he was circling his text on each page and margin to save paper (Plate 1). Several centuries before, when next-door Europeans wrote on tree trunk layers, paper from the East had brought his native land unimaginable riches; now, at a point where Europe had been multiplying hundreds of text copies per hour,[90] it was taking Jamal hundreds of hours to produce a single text. Too far and too cut off from both the Far East and West to know what was happening in each, he firmly pressed the dark letters and dots of each text line before him on the pale paper. The job was made slower by the frames where the text was supposed to fit; and the ruler occasionally slipped from his tired hands. Measuring, tracing and drawing the double outer lines for central texts, inner lines for interspersed verses, and slanted lines for side margins, amounted to hours and hours of labour. Framing, polishing and colouring with alternate colours of blue, red and black for the outer lines, gold and black for the inner lines, and red for titles and highlights, took their own time. But the *Dialogue* text being inserted towards the end of that labour-intensive volume, it was well on its way of reaching its very last lines.

When Jamal completed his transcribed volume with the closing lines 'ended' in mixed Arabic and Persian, starting with the day, Friday the 22nd, time, before morning prayer, and month, the sixth lunar Hijri month, he did not take the same care with his own name, place, and dates. His name, Jamal, was preceded with a stroke that looked like the term 'bin', as if it followed a paternal line through his father's title as 'Shaykh Jamal'; and 'Qunuj' as a 'residence'[91] was a reference unclear enough to be noted in later annotations as 'inaccurate'; but somehow neither the year of transcription nor that of the original composition, typically from centuries before, were given. There were only

[88] Belfour, Life of Sheikh Mohammed Ali Hazin, p. 44: 'Eastern 'Hyperbole'; also applicable to p. 41: 'nowhere in the world'; p. 49: '. . . the best of all the countries in the world'.

[89] Kamāl-i Iṣfahānī, Munāẓirāt-i Baghdād va Iṣfahān, colophon, fol. 197a: ''Ala yadd ʿAbd al-ḍaʿīf piārah Ibn[?] Shaykh Jamāl, Sākin-i Qunūj, bih tārīkh-i bīst u duvvum-i māh, shahr-i jamādī al-ākhir, bi rūz-i jumʿih baʿd az namāz-i pīshīn' [In the hands of. . .].

[90] Bloom, Jonathan, Paper before Print: The History and Impact of Paper in the Islamic World (New Haven, 2001); Eisenstein, Elizabeth L., The Printing Press as an Agent of Change: Communications and Cultural Transformations in Early Modern Europe (Cambridge, MA, New York, 1979); Blair, Ann, Too Much to Know: Managing Scholarly Information before the Modern Age (New Haven, 2010).

[91] Kamāl-i Iṣfahānī, Munāẓirāt-i Baghdād va Iṣfahān, colophon fol. 197a, copyist; '. . . Ibn[?] Shaykh Jamāl . . . Sākin-i Qunūj'

clues if one looked closely: names within the text, like those buried in Baghdad, including one 'Awhad al-Din Kirmani', to hint at the earliest composition date as falling within decades of Baghdad's surrender to the Mongols after 1250; or seals on the volume's cover naming 'Padshah Ghazi',[92] the Indian Mughal ruler, Awrangzib, to point through him to the latest transcription date, this time within decades of Isfahan's fall to the Afghans before 1750.

By 1750, Isfahan had much to recover from the devastating Afghan attack; and the surviving natives, sometimes too young to remember anything beyond vague images, often without immediate family to report the horrific stories, would have had to learn about the details of the nightmares from the works of a few non-natives: one being the author of the chronicle the *Fall of Isfahan*, a Christian missionary whose personal reports of the critical period from March 1722 to August 1723 of the Afghan siege of Isfahan in a book bearing that title would be written in Armenian and not in the native language of Persian; another, an eyewitness Polish father, whose account in Latin was to be translated into English as a *Traveller's Chronicle*, with a view of putting European accounts of that 'Dark History' in different lights; and yet another *Historical Account*[93] by a British visitor to the court of the rising power, Nadir, as King of Persia, who in talking about the 'genius of Eastern nations giving their history an air of romance', had prophetically said 'perhaps future generations may have occasion to refer to what has passed in our time'.

This was, of course, not the only time when names of Westerners were associated with various encounters with 'Persia', the land of 'flower and nightingale'. Besides the *Historical Account* of the visitor, Jonas Hanway, whose journal of travels from London to Russia and Persia in the early 1750s, included voyages to the Caspian Sea, or the 'Mediterranean Lake' as he called it, there were accounts by travellers to Isfahan in particular, who poured in from all over Europe both before and after that period. European visitors to the Safavid Court[94] of the previous century alone ranged widely in nationality, from British, French and Germans, to Dutch, Belgian and Italian; in age, from teens and twenties to thirties and fifties; in motive, from personal and intellectual to economic and political; and in port of entry, from Iraq and Russia to Azarbaijan and Armenia. The case of Poles and Portuguese as well as non-European residents from Arabs and Turks to Indians and Muscovites were noted by the young Venetian nobleman, Ambrosio Bembo, whose detailed travel accounts on both Baghdad and Isfahan included elaborate drawings by the French Joseph Grélot.[95] Impressed by both

92 Rieu, Catalogue of Persian Manuscripts, Vol. 2, p. 601: Awḥad al-Dīn Kirmānī buried in Baghdad; p. 601: 'Ālamgīr stamps: 1069, 1113 [1658, 1701]; Bosworth, Islamic Dynasties, p. 210–11: 'Awrangzīb'.

93 Gilanentz, Suqūt-i Iṣfahān [Fall of Isfahan]: March 1722 to August 1723; Krusinski, Tadeusz Jan, The Chronicles of a Traveller: or, A History of the Afghan Wars with Persia . . . 'Ta-reekh-i-Seeah', from the Latin of J. C. Clodius, by George Newnham Mitford esq (tr) (London, 1840); Hanway, Jonas, An Historical Account of the British Trade Over the Caspian Sea: With a Journal of Travels from London through Russia into Persia (London, 1753), Vol. 1, p. 156: 'Mediterranean Lake'.

94 Stevens, 'European visitors'; Welch, 'Safavi Iran as seen through Venetian eyes'; Brentjes, Sonja, 'Early modern European travellers in the Middle East and their reports about the sciences', in Pourjavady, N. and Vesel, Ž. (eds), Sciences, techniques et instruments dans le monde iranien (Xe–XIXe siècle) (Tehran, 2004), pp. 379–430.

95 Welch, 'Safavi Iran as seen through Venetian eyes', pp. 97–119, p. 100, and p. 106; Welch, Travels and Journal of Ambrosio Bembo, p. 119 and p. 322: Grélot's Panoramas of Baghdad and Isfahan, respectively.

cities, he had described the most beautiful mosque in Baghdad as being 'made by the Persians' and the main square of Isfahan as surpassing 'many of the most beautiful in Europe'. Other European attractions included a 'clock tower'[96] above the entrance of Isfahan's bazaar, with reports on its successive states, from a striking clock 'made by an Englishman', being 'of no use' or 'ever likely to be', 'disconnected', and 'beyond repair', to its sound being 'hated by Persians' or 'forbidden in religion', and most notably, being 'the only one in all of Persia'. After all, there was a clock in that 'greatest of cities', said the poet of a very close time and place, in which 'a hundred hours strike, at one and the same instant'.

There were to be very different stories of Isfahan's life and times both before and after that time; the fluctuations were shown by a modern author who would cleverly write a chronicle of the city's 'rise and decline' as traceable in the chronological order of its reports by various visitors over time. Multiple quotes would come from Anthony Sherley's steward in the 1590s, that 'Spahan is very large but has no fort or beautiful palace', from Thomas Herbert in the 1620s, that it has 'several good buildings but more large gardens', and from Belgian Tavernier in the 1630s, that it still 'seemed rather a forest than a city'. Chardin in the 1660s could write that 'the beauty of Isfahan consists particularly of a great number of magnificent palaces, gay and smiling houses, spacious caravanserais, very fine bazaars, and canals and streets lined with plane trees'; and Cornelius le Bruyn in the early 1700s could add 'mosques, towers, or large buildings' as 'shaded with trees'.

But things changed so fast and dramatically that the modern narrator of those reports could now add more to le Bruyn's account of shaded buildings that 'he was not to know a few years later, they would be ashen with corpses', referring to when 'following the Afghan siege of 1722, with its attendant horrors of starvation, cannibalism, and mass murders, the dynasty went into pawn and the glories of Isfahan into eclipse'. The modern author would quote from among 'the few remaining foreigners', a monk describing Persia in 1754 as a country of 'danger' both for the soul and the body; and a much later Morier in 1811, writing of 'houses, bazaars, palaces, whole streets, seen in total abandonment' and of 'riding for miles among its ruins without meeting any living creatures'.[97]

Post-1750s Isfahan was a time and place where, with the recent fall of the city to Afghan invaders, fond images and memories of the city before its fatal blow clung hard to the hearts of natives, while rhymed verses about the sites and streets of an Isfahan long hosting visitors including Europeans hardly left their tongues: 'Both East and West have places within it', had said the poet from a time long gone, an Aristotle in every street, a Plato on every step', Ptolemy's *Almagest* in the bags of rogues, Ibn Sina's *Shifa* in the sleeves of children.[98] But most natives had no idea who these people or books were, and such names as 'Aristu' for Aristotle and 'Aflatun' for Plato rolled on their tongue by the force of harmony and rhyme, not any formal education. In a place where even scribes were trained in their trade mostly in madrassas, there was little secular

96 Stevens, 'European visitors', p. 435.
97 Stevens, 'European visitors', p. 429 and p. 449: quotes.
98 Ḥakīm Shifā'ī: Belfour, Life of Sheikh Mohammed Ali Hazin, pp. 43–9: quotes.

education. As popular as science and philosophy were in those days, the place for everything called theoretical knowledge was private homes or circles, not formal schools. These were places, often within or next to a mosque compound, for learning to read or write or study disciplines like grammar, rhetoric and logic. Theoretical sciences from mathematical, physical, and medical branches, to any crossovers between them, could still be studied at religious schools; but mostly through a teacher or mentor learned in secular subjects informally. Practical sciences had more room to maneuver, sometimes exposing sciences through their back doors.

Post-1750s Europe, on the other hand, was an entirely different place where people far from both Baghdad and Isfahan now carried the ball of sciences and crafts in both hands, a time and place producing many larger than life figures. It was a time with the heritage of a Copernicus from Poland, a Galileo from Italy, a Kepler from Germany, a Descartes from France, and a Newton from England, the latter directly associated with the phrase 'standing on the shoulders of giants';[99] Europe was also a place further enriched by universities like those in Bologna, Padua, Paris, Oxford, and Cambridge, and institutions like the British 'Royal Society' and French 'Academy of Sciences'.[100]

One day, the names of outstanding figures from the East acting as 'giants' lending shoulders to later generations were to find their way into the forming chapters of a 'world science'. This would occur through specialised fields within history increasingly integrating contexts relevant to scientific development, from their 'roots' in ancient Greece, Persia, India, and China, to their 'routes' through the Islamic Middle Ages, and Medieval and Early Modern Europe.

[99] Dictionary of Scientific Biography (DSB): Rosen, Edward, 'Copernicus, Nicolas', 3 (1971), pp. 401–11; Drake, Stillman, 'Galilei, Galileo', 5 (1972), pp. 237–50; Gingerich, Owen, 'Kepler, Johannes', 7 (1973), pp. 289–312; Crombie, A. C., 'Descartes, René', 3 (1971), pp. 51–5; Cohen, I. Bernard, 'Newton, Isaac', 10 (1974), pp. 42–101. Merton, Robert K., On the Shoulders of Giants: A Shandean Postscript (New York, 1965; San Diego, 1985; Chicago, 1993), pp. 9–10: Newton's 'paraphrase of the Aphorism': 'If I have seen further it is by standing on the shoulders of giants'.

[100] Baldwin, John W., The Scholastic Culture of the Middle Ages (Lexington MA, 1971), pp. 41–2: Bologna; p. 41, 44, 54: Padua; pp. 42–4: Paris; p. 44, p. 52: Oxford and Cambridge. Dolnick, Edward, The Clockwork Universe: Isaac Newton, the Royal Society, and the Birth of the Modern World (New York, 1952). www.britannica.com/EBchecked/topic/511584/Royal-Society. Hahn, Roger, The Anatomy of a Scientific Institution: The Paris Academy of Sciences, 1666–1803 (Berkeley, 1971). www.britannica.com/EBchecked/topic/528892/Academy-of-Sciences

2

Moon and Sun

500 Hundred Years (ca. 750–1250; 1250–1750)

It was the best of times, it was the worst of times . . .
It was the season of light, it was the season of darkness . . .
Charles Dickens, *A Tale of Two Cities*, 1859, opening[1]

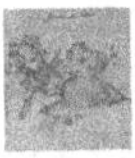

2.1 An Old Manuscript with Gold Illuminations

It was April 2006, and the old manuscript of the *Dialogue of Baghdad and Isfahan* had not been touched since March of the year before when it was returned to the library guard by a young reader requesting it day after day. The manuscript, bound in a dark leather cover, had been treasured at London's British Museum for the longest time before being transferred to the nearby British Library. The old, gold-illuminated manuscript, beautifully transcribed and hand-crafted in a rare mix of Arabic and Persian, prose and poetry, text and margin, all tastefully framed, coloured, calligraphed and bound, was kept at a place where time seemed to have stood still. For a manuscript whose transcription went back a few hundred years, the course of a few hundred days during which its covers had stayed unopened was still too long compared to the constant calling and recalling of comparable manuscripts there, in a continuous, clockwork, pace. The rich hosting library would soon give its 'facts and figures'[2] as a diverse collection of 'over 150 million in almost every language and faith group', one so vast that 'if you see five items each day, it would take you over 80,000 years to see the whole collection'.

The old *Dialogue* manuscript was, along with various other treasures, kept in a new building with a rust-coloured structure shaped as a long ship overlooking a 'forecourt'.[3] To get to the treasury of manuscripts such as the one covered with gold illumination and exquisite transcription on successive folios, one had to navigate the maze of the

1 Dickens, Tale of Two Cities, opening lines. www.sparknotes.com/lit/a-tale-of-two-cities/quotes/
2 Numbers: Library website, 2006: 150 million; 2020: 170 million. www.bl.uk/aboutus/quickinfo/facts/index.html
3 British Library: building and shape. www.bl.uk/about-us/our-story/explore-the-building/ Background: St Pancras compound.

library ground itself: outside, from a set of wide curving steps to a mega size open space; and inside, from a lobby with a fountain, music room, iron sculptures, and electronic flip-through books through a set of stairs and lifts next to rows and rows of see-through stacks visible from a far distance. Between the locked manuscript stacks and the gated library entrance there were many treasures acting as various forms of textual and material source. Indoors, there were walls of invaluable paintings hung in reading rooms alone, among which an attractive portrait stood out in the reading room of the Asian and African Studies from a period not long after the transcription of the *Dialogue* manuscript. The portrait was that of Nadir Shah,[4] literally the 'Rare-King' of Persia from three centuries before, featured in agate-coloured and gem-covered royal garb. The once-called 'Napoleon of Persia',[5] best known for land conquests far and wide, stood at the centre of a thick gold frame, his upper torso covered with jewels, and his head topped with a feathered crown. The portrait had a detailed caption about its owner, a former governor and president of the East India Company buying the painting in India. This was the place where treasures captured by the world-conqueror himself included the world's largest uncut diamonds, 'Mountain of Light' and 'Sea of Light',[6] now living separate lives in England's Tower of London and Iran's National Treasury. But neither the painting nor its caption revealed much about the subject behind that treasure: the painting portraying the warrior turned ruler with a sword in belt still fell short of capturing the fearless man; and its caption did away with all the rarities associated with him, from his rare acts of driving out invading Afghans from Persia and protecting Islamic lands from growing threats of sectarian divide, to the not-so-rare royal habit of blinding one of his offsprings for the mere protection of power itself.

The realm of power captured through a classic painting hanging among the library's indoor treasures, with the acquisition date not far from the death date of the Persian King, sharply contrasted with the realm of knowledge captured through the statue of a famed early modern British scientist not physically far from it among the walled-in outdoor treasures. This was a giant bronze statue[7] of Isaac Newton from the same century as the portrayed king, which, seated nude in a bowed posture holding a compass, sharply contrasted with the image of a standing king holding worry beads. The Newton sculpture, soon turned into a 'talking statue',[8] dwarfed most things around it, starting with a small round courtyard with eight planets sculptured from age-old stones reminiscent of an old Earth-centred cosmos, with the Moon, Mercury Venus,

[4] Nādir Shāh (ca. 1688–1747), founder of the Afshār dynasty (r. 1148–60/1736–95): Bosworth, Islamic Dynasties, p. 175; Painting acquired in India (1760–1767); presented by Nicholas Vansittart, 1822. https://www.artuk.org/discover/artworks/nadir-shah-shah-of-persia-17321747-191186

[5] Axworthy, Michael, Sword of Persia: Nader Shah, from Tribal Warrior to Conquering Tyrant (London, New York, 2006), p. xvii.

[6] Kūh-i Nūr (Mountain of Light): diamond on crown worn by Queen Elizabeth. www.britannica.com/topic/Koh-i-noor. Daryā-yi Nūr (Sea of Light): diamond on crown in jewels of Iran. www.britannica.com/topic/Darya-e-Nur

[7] Paolozzi, Eduardo (1924–2005), statue of Isaac Newton (1643–1727): Four meter tall bronze statue, commissioned for the new British Library in 1995, based on a 1795 engraving by Willian Blake. http://blogs.nature.com/london/2007/03/28/profile-isaac-newton-statue

[8] The statue was given a voice as part of the project, 'Talking Statues' in 2004. www.bl.uk/press-releases/2014/august/isaac-newton-joins-talking-statues

Sun, Mars, Jupiter, Saturn, and the Fixed Stars surrounding it in that order; the giant Newton, on the other hand, was the symbol of a Sun-centred universe,[9] a superceding model given critical weight by an extraordinary man whose decisive astronomical observations were to be repeated on the deck of the nearby Westminster House in a few centuries. The eyes of the Newton statue fit the gaze of a great man whose 'three laws'[10] in physics were to be long taught worldwide, without three laws about life itself: that the lesson about Newton the man is not only about his genius or theories, but his mere survival as a weak infant;[11] that if one dared to think of miracles, the life of Newton was enough to define the word; and that one not only could, but should, imagine what a world this would be without a life such as Newton's in it.

Contrary to the lives of the likes of Newton, preserved against all odds to touch those of so many others, the lives of manuscripts, and of classic works, survived in proportion to how many lives they touched before they could be preserved. For masterpieces like the *De Revolutionibus* of the fifteenth-century Polish scholar Nicolas Copernicus, a work whose many annonations spoke against it as 'The Book Nobody Read',[12] it was enough for it to touch a single life, that of the 'father of science', Galileo, whose own *Dialogue of Two World Systems*[13] was to predate the *Principles of Mathematics* of Newton,[14] the 'scientist who changed everything'. The larger-than-life lives of these scientific authors were what helped their works be preserved in whatever form they were: with Copernicus, collecting so many owner marks on the copies of one book alone; with Galileo, multiplying so many copies of his hypothetical dialogue between Sun- and Earth-centred universes; and with Newton, beating so many odds for the gift of life itself so that he could offer posterity proofs for the unthinkable vision of a new world that would impact so many, in so many ways.

That was how these and other outstanding works of science often overpowered any physical or political obstacles in their way. But with a *Dialogue* in which the term 'science' was curiously not mentioned once by two talking cities of incomparable status at the time, odds were mostly against it for surviving even as a single manuscript. But somehow it would; a transcription signed by a certain *Jamal* without a year would even come to overlap with the dates of Newton whose statue lived on the same grounds; the

9 Crowe, Michael, Theories of the World from Antiquity to the Copernican Revolution (New York, 1990). Gormley, Anthony, *Planets*: rocks of different material, at equal distances around a circle. www.artfund.org/whats-on/more-to-see-and-do/features/top-six-antony-gormley-sculptures. Our observation at the deck of Westminister Arts Library, old home of Newton: 18 September 2018. www.londonremembers.com/memorials/sir-isaac-newton-s-house-simple

10 Cohen, I. Bernard, The Birth of a New Physics (Garden City, NY, 1960; repr., Ontario, 1985).

11 Cohen, 'Newton, Isaac', p. 42. Westfall, Richard S., The Life of Isaac Newton (Cambridge, 1993).

12 Gingerich, Owen, The Book Nobody Read: Chasing the Revolutions of Nicolaus Copernicus (New York, 2004), p. vii, disqualifies the depiction of Copernicus's De Revolutionibus in Arthur Koestler's 1959, The Sleepwalkers as 'The Book Nobody Read' through the evidence of its various annotations, p. 255: 'Koestler had been wrong, dead wrong'.

13 Galilei, Galileo, Dialogue Concerning the Two Chief World Systems, Ptolemaic & Copernican, Drake, Stillman (tr) (Berkeley, 1953).

14 Newton, Isaac, The Principia: Mathematical Principles of Natural Philosophy; Cohen, I. Bernard and Whitman, Anne (tr), assisted by Julia Budenz (Berkeley, 1999); Buchwald, Jed Z., Cohen, I. Bernard and Smith, George E. (eds), Isaac Newton's Natural Philosophy (Cambridge, MA, 2001); Steele, Philip, Isaac Newton: The Scientist Who Changed Everything, (Washington DC, 2007).

date March 20th, reported as the Month and day of Newton's death,[15] would itself coincide with that old manuscript's first visit by a young viewer, centuries later.

2.2 A Young Viewer with Rich Inspirations

It was May 2006, and Leo was getting ready for his second visit to the site of the *Dialogue* manuscript as part of his time away that year. But even at the closing of his gap year, he could not imagine a gap wider than his knowledge of the subjects he had embarked upon. Spending time on a 'dialogue' between two cities as far distant to him as Baghdad and Isfahan had only reinforced the need to learn more about them and their settings; and having been on the lookout for any leads along the way, he had made some headway during the two gap terms that defined that exceptional year. The fall of the year before had brought unexpected advances through participation in a course at the university's liberal arts program known as Harvard College:[16] the course, titled, 'From Alexandria to Baghdad', offered by Leo's old advisor, had occasioned closer looks at subjects like science, books, experiments, and instruments in the respective course events of September, October, November and December. For Leo, the course had been a good icebreaker, as well as the first leverage for nailing an application by the following January to a 'college' he had always considered out of reach. The spring term had poured in its own resources, including another year of prep work for acceptance to a university long associated with 'open books', as repeated in a poem composed for the university's 350th anniversary, and recited by the poet himself in its 375th celebration.[17] Leo's strategy to delay his college application for another year to expand his knowledge through a course taught by that same instructor in the following fall was to be another path-changer. The Harvard Extension[18] where the course was offered was a wing of that institution literally 'extending to the public' to give new meanings to not only a place where 'books stood open', but also the expression 'gates unbarred',[19] one forming the title of the centennial history of that unique institution for characterising its 'distinctive feature of the open enrollment and ready access'. The Extension course, 'Science in the Islamic Middle Ages', was where Leo would navigate through many uncharted territories as revealed by the very titles of course events and lectures: documentary films, 'From Baghdad to Cordoba' and 'From Arabic into Latin'; guest lectures, from

[15] Cohen, 'Newton, Isaac', p. 42: 'd. London, England, 20 March, 1727'.

[16] Harvard College 'founded in 1636 as the oldest institution of higher education in the United States'. https://college.harvard.edu/. Kheirandish, 'From Alexandria to Baghdad': See Introduction. https://www.scholar.harvard.edu/ekheirandish/teaching

[17] Ireland, Corydon. 'A poem for Harvard: Seamus Heaney will reprise a favorite villanelle, written for 350th', Harvard Gazette, 24 May 2012: refers to the 19-line poem and the lines: 'a spirit moved. John Harvard walked the yard . . . the books stood open and the gates unbarred'. http://news.harvard.edu/gazette/story/2012/05/a-poem-for-harvard

[18] Harvard Extension: short for Harvard University's 'Extension School'. www.extension.harvard.edu/ The Division of Continuing Education: www.dce.harvard.edu/

[19] Shinagel, Michael, The Gates Unbarred: A History of University Extension at Harvard, 1910–2009 (Cambridge, MA, 2009), p. xvi: includes text of 'Villanelle for an Anniversary' and quotes on open access.

'Understanding geometry' to 'Patterning knowledge';[20] and 'Personal enrichments', from 'Need for collaboration', 'Personal vocation', 'Lessons in communication', and 'Public service' to 'Unweaving the Web', 'Two-culture problem, Three-culture solutions', 'Philosopy in everyday life', and life in 'Tokyo, Beijing, Cairo, Isfahan'.[21]

As Leo turned the pages of the two academic years behind him, he was labeling images as requested by his mentor of various course events and lectures; and as he sorted these, he was drawn closer to not only lands where cities such as Baghdad and Isfahan stood taller than many others in more distant times, but also places where the Moon and Sun of the lunar and solar calendars of their respective Arab and Persian lands shone brighter than other stars. The two 'brightest stars', as the Sun and Moon were historically called, reminded Leo of an ornamental sun and moon shaping the hands of a round golden clock at the entrance of a rare book library[22]where both classes first met, a place becoming more and more special to him over time: the 'time' seized by the turning sun and moon hands of that unique clock recalled the hundreds of hours and minutes that took the events and lectures of the two courses to bind together a handful of students, often through a lifetime.

Introductory meetings for setting the tone of courses had been often followed by events capturing their main themes. The 'Alexandria to Baghdad' course had directed its first event towards 'science', and the workings of scientific concepts and shifts, starting with a chance for students to perform in a historical play to learn about changing scientific concepts, and subtle linguist shifts. The play had been occasioned by an invitation of 'a different kind' received by Leo's mentor in a calligraphed envelope for a venue created as the brainchild of a scientist-poet for a public education series called 'Entertaining Science' to attract audiences both open to, and amused by, science. The course's historical play had then followed after a rehersal in the venue's 'Science Cabaret' in New York City's Greenwich Village, and a campus performance just before the September event of the 'Alexandria to Baghdad' course.[23] Leo appreciated learning about science and its early shifts from culture to culture, and language to language, not just through a historical play captured through his camera as part of the first 'course event', but especially through its featuring of Baghdad as one of the two cities in his

20 Kheirandish, 'Science in the Islamic Middle Ages', 2006. https://www.scholar.harvard.edu/ekheirandish/teaching. Film: 'From Baghdad to Cordoba' (excerpt): 'Islam: Faith and Power' (PBS, 2000); companion piece: 'The Golden Age: 1250–1750', in Bloom, Jonathan and Blair, Sheila (eds), Islam: A Thousand Years of Faith and Power (New Haven, 2002); Film: 'From Arabic to Latin: The Assimilation of Arab Knowledge', in 'When the World Spoke Arabic' (Films for the Humanities and Sciences, 1999); Guest lectures: 'Understanding geometry' by John Bremmer and 'Patterning knowledge' by Carol Bier.

21 Kheirandish, 'Science in the Islamic Middle Ages', 'Personal enrichments', Year Up, Cambridge MA. 2005 lectures: 'Need for collaboration': Leon Golub; 'Personal vocation': Anne Davenport; 'Lessons in communication': Christina Kasica; 'Public service': Timothy McCarthy; 'Unweaving the web': Hormoz Goodarzy; 'Two-culture problems, Three-culture solutions': Elaheh Kheirandish. Proposed: 'Philosophy in everyday life': Marina van Zuylen; 'Tokyo, Beijing, Cairo, Isfahan': Timothy Brown.

22 Sun and Moon were referred to as 'the brightest stars' (nayyirayn aʿẓamayn) in Arabic and Persian. Houghton is a rare book library at Harvard University, Cambridge, MA. http://library.harvard.edu/libraries/houghton/

23 Kheirandish, 'From Alexandria to Baghdad', Performances: 'Entertaining Science: Science Cabaret': www.roaldhoffmann.com/entertaining-science. Venue: Cornelia Street Café, New York City, August 2005. www.corneliastreetcafe.com. Campus: Harvard University, Quincy House, September 2005. https://quincy.harvard.edu/

own ‘Dialogue’ project. The play was an adaptation of a short story set during the Islamic Middle Ages by the modern literary master, Borges, known to Leo through a poem about his native city of Cambridge: in that clever story, titled ‘Averroes's search’, Averroes, the Latinised ‘Ibn Rushd’[24] of medieval Cordoba in Andalusian Spain, and the prominent Arabic commentator of Aristotle, was creatively brought to life to recreate, then highlight, barriers of language and culture lasting beyond his own age. The leading role of that philosopher, physician and judge skillfully played by a female Averroes in a long cloak, coloured a scene authenticated by the genuine poise of a volunteer cast, including a young writer-director appearing as Borges in his slightly adjusted Play in One Act:[25] the lines jumping out from the page onto the stage through the voice of a narrator made the opening lines all the more powerful, with Averroes writing ‘with sureness from right to left’: ‘Few things more beautiful and more pathetic are recorded in history’, had recited the narrator, ‘than this Arab physician's dedication to the thoughts of a man separated from him by fourteen centuries; to the intrinsic difficulty we should add that Averroes, ignorant of Syriac and of Greek, was working with the translation of a translation. The night before two doubtful words had halted him . . . “tragedy and comedy” . . . no one in the whole world of Islam could conjecture what they meant . . . Averroes put down his pen’.

What pressed most on Leo's mind was more than any cast member on stage dressed as a philosopher in Athens, translator in Baghdad, or commentator in Cordoba, or concepts meaningless or transformed across cultures. It was rather a post-play class exercise to ‘evaluate’ the contrasting words of a modern scholar with reference to the same exact passage: ‘The Greek scientific tradition’, had written a distinguished scholar in an unpublished lecture,[26] ‘came to life in a different language and civilization, which . . . came more and more to adopt Greek ways of thinking as its own’; adding that ‘if I were to choose, more or less at random, a section from a mathematical work by one of the best Arabic mathematicians, Ibn Haytham (fl. 1000), who himself knew no Greek, I could with little difficulty translate it into ancient Greek, and . . . produce something which would be indistinguishable in form, style and terminology from the kind of work which was read in Alexandria in the 4th century’. The puzzle of the assigned class exercise was to evaluate the two contradictory views ‘in the light of sources closer to the time’; and the ‘clue’ had been a manuscript illustration[27] (Plate 2) featuring the ‘Alexandria to Baghdad’ course poster where Greek scholars like Euclid and Galen sat

[24] Arnaldez, Roger, ‘Ibn Rushd’, Encyclopedia of Islam (EI^2), 3, 55–6 (1969), pp. 909–20; Arnaldez Roger, and Iskandar, Albert Z., ‘Ibn Rushd, Abū al-Walīd Muḥammad ibn Aḥmad ibn Muḥammad, also known as Averroës’, Dictionary of Scientific Biography (DSB), 12 (1975), pp. 1–9. Forcada, Miquel. ‘Ibn Rushd: Abū al-Walīd Muḥammad ibn Aḥmad ibn Muḥammad ibn Rushd al-Ḥafīd’, The Biographical Encyclopedia of Astronomers (BEA) (New York, 2007), pp. 564–5. http://islamsci.mcgill.ca/RASI/BEA/Ibn_Rushd_BEA.htm

[25] Borges, ‘Averroes’ search’, pp. 148–9: ‘Abulgualid Muhammad Ibn-Ahmad ibn-Muhammad ibn-Rushd (a century this long name would take to become Averroes . . .) was writing . . .’. Daniela Helbig: Averroes; John Mathew: director and Borges.

[26] Toomer, Gerald J., ‘The mathematical sciences: The role of the Islamic world in the development and transmission of the ancient heritage’ (unpublished lecture, Marlboro College, 1984), p. 7.

[27] Hayes, John R. (ed), The Genius of Arab Civilization: Source of Renaissance (New York, 1975; Cambridge, 1978), p. 147.

cross-legged in Islamic garb with Arabised names, Uqlidis for Euclid and Jalinus for Galen, to point to the inevitable cross-cultural shifts, however discrete.

The second event of the 'Alexandria to Baghdad' course had centred on 'Books', and before the effect of the 'Science event' had worn off, the class had been taken on a fine October day to a memorable visit to see scientific books and prints in an institute in its last months of existence. The institute and its library, named the Dibner Institute and Burndy Library to preserve the memory of their entrepreneur founder Bern Dibner, were fittingly located at 'Memorial' drive along the Charles River on MIT campus, one of four prominent consortium members housing that Institute.[28] The compound's garden, shaped symbolically as the solar system with a central sundial and circular designs of a landscape architect, would also become a memory; as would its bronze head of Copernicus, the celebrated founder of a heliocentric or Sun-centred universe.[29] Leo's Dibner Institute visit had become most memorable through his encounter in the lobby with a life-size image of Leonardo da Vinci's drawing 'Man', a wide-armed figure later living as a framed print in his mentor's office: the humanist-scientist and 'Renaissance man' had been introduced as a favourite of the industrialist turned Institute founder with the vision of historical studies for the good of humankind.[30] On that October visit, Leo's records in one and the same day amounted to numerous shorthands on multiple subjects:[31] on the holdings, *numbers*: 50,000 rare books, 1,600 manuscripts, 400 instruments, 400 artworks; on paper, *timelines*: China in the 2nd century, the Middle East in the 7th century, and the Mediterranean coast by the 12th century; on printing, *dates*: Gutenberg ca. 1450–1455, Koreans, movable type, ca. 1375; on economics, *maths*: a year for one scribe to write a volume, and a team of two to print 500 copies; on production, *stats*: from one or two to 300–400 scribes in monasteries; on transcription, *norms*: in Muslim tradition, handwriting as a pious act; in Christian tradition, written mistakes as a sin; on tools, *records*: lenses on nose in 1265, in frames, 1497; on copyright, *stakes*: as many and as fast as possible; on annotations, *styles*: earliest forms citing sources or adding notes; on circulation, *drives*: benefits from producing books at high speed, 100s of copies more in print.

The rest of Leo's notes were about some 'rare treasures' as they continued to be labeled in their new home some years later,[32] treasures like Euclid's *Elements of*

28 Dibner Institute and Burndy Library: MIT, 38 Memorial Drive, Cambridge MA, until 2005. http://web.mit.edu/dibner/. Founder: Bern Dibner (1897–1988). www.nytimes.com/1988/01/08/obituaries/bern-dibner-dies-at-90-historian-and-engineer.html. Consortium member organisations: MIT, Boston, Brandeis, and Harvard Universities. http://news.mit.edu/1992/dibner-1021

29 Fabricius, Talitha, landscape architect of the garden that 'symbolized the shape of the solar system', housing Copernicus's sculptured head on a pedestal, a central sundial and other circular shapes. http://news.mit.edu/1992/dibner-1021

30 da Vinci, Leonardo, 'Vitruvian Man' (L'Uomo Vitruviano) circa 1490, based on Vitruvius's, De Architectura: life-size print gifted to me when the collection moved to the Huntington Library, California. www.huntington.org/uploadedFiles/Files/PDFs/pr_dibner_collections.pdf. Sarton, 'An Institute for the history of science and civilization'.

31 Kheirandish, 'From Alexandria to Baghdad', Fall 2005, Burndy Library visit at the Dibner Institute on 25 October. Details: Director Philip Cronenwett, and Institute Fellow at the time, Dr Elizabeth Cavicchi.

32 Huntington Library: Burndy Library added to holdings in 2006: '47,000 rare monographic and serial volumes and 50 archival collections … largest assemblage of Isaac Newton materials outside England … '. www.huntington.org/collections/science-medicine

Geometry, in the first of over 1,000 printed editions in 1482, the *Optics* of Ibn al-Haytham, or Alhazen, in one of its few printed editions in 1572, Copernicus's *De Revolutionibus* in 1543, and Newton's *Principia* in 1789, and busts of Pasteur and da Vinci, some with an inside story, like that of the latter related by the touring librarian: that Dibner, the collection founder had 'read a book on da Vinci, did not believe he could have invented those things, and spent the rest of his life building 'one of the world's premier private collections of the history of science and technology'[33] where, the librarian could still say that day, 'you are right now'. Among the collection was an item of a different kind, a birth horoscope from close to the time of da Vinci captioned with a verse about a place, not so close, on the folios of an art-rich, quality-poor manuscript: '*When Isfahan is called half the world, only half of its world is that described*'; this play in words with the 'half-world' image of Isfahan was simpler than the 'half-Isfahan' image of Baghdad in the verse: '*If we gain all of Baghdad in exchange for Isfahan, we would be a half loser*'.[34] Without knowing much about either city at the time, Leo could still calculate that in the first verse, Isfahan's status doubled from a half to a whole world, while in the second verse, an exchange of Isfahan with Baghdad would be 'half a loss' only if Baghdad's status was half of Isfahan's.

If Baghdad and Isfahan of the historical play and historic visit in September and October of Leo's gap year filled gaps in his education, their less direct presence in the historical experiment and instument tour that followed in November and December opened windows of inspiration by demystifying scholarship itself.

November had been the month of historical experiments, with Leo's class meeting around noon on their balcony on the curved 'Bow Street' to catch the strongest sunlight for an experiment related to the age-old and newly recreated 'death ray' of Archimedes,[35] named after the ancient Greek scientist best known for two phrases he either never uttered, or not in those terms: one being the well known 'Eureka' after the Greek expression 'I have found [it]', famously giving rise to 'Eureka moments' of brainstorming; the other, 'Give me a place to stand, and I will move the Earth', being a less known 'boastful claim about the marvelous properties of the lever', bestowing powers on Archimedes 'to perform previously unimaginable tasks', and through it a team of 'scholars leveraging 21st century technology for wonders of its own in an aptly named Archimedes Project'.[36] The Archimedes of the November historical experiment was neither the Archimedes of reported fragments discovering new laws, nor the translated

33 Huntington Libray: quote. https://hdl.huntington.org/digital/collection/p15150coll1/id/9096/rec/2

34 Anonymous, The Birth Horoscope (Tāliʿ-i Muwlūd) of Rustam Bahādur [brother of Iskandar Sulṭān, Tamerlane's grandson]: Burndy Library MS Codex 65 (Persian), 822 [=1419], gift of I. Bernard Cohen:
'Iṣfāhān nīmih-i jahān guft-and, nīmī az vaṣf-i Iṣfāhān guft-and', anonymous.
Nīm ḍarar mikun-īm gar bisitān-īm, khiṭṭih-i Baghdād dar izā-yi Ṣifāhān'
Attribution: Khāqānī; Beelaert, Anna Livia, 'Khāqānī Shīrvānī', Encyclopedia Iranica (EIr), 15, 5 (2010), pp. 522–3. www.iranicaonline.org/articles/kaqani-servani-poet

35 Kheirandish, 'From Alexandria to Baghdad', Fall 2005, 17 November: experiment recreated at MIT: 'Ancient historians recorded that … Archimedes … constructed a burning glass to set the Roman warships … afire'. http://web.mit.edu/2.009/www/experiments/deathray/10_ArchimedesResult.html

36 Archimedes Project. http://archimedes.fas.harvard.edu/. Attiyeh, Jenny, 'Scholars resuscitate dead languages: Tech advances help illustrate how Arabs preserved ancient wisdom', Harvard Gazette, 13 November 2003. http://news.harvard.edu/gazette/story/2003/11/scholars-resuscitate-dead-languages/

Archimedes of dead languages preserving old texts, but the name behind a death ray, ironically giving life to a few others: the myth-testers of modern times setting up experiments to check Archimedes 'burning glass to destroy the Roman fleet in 212 BC'; the myth-busters of modern television, who dismissed the whole thing as 'myth'; and the feasibility-testers of an MIT class, who confirmed that it 'could be possible'.

The noon classroom balcony activity had been much simpler: to show that in the direct path of a concave mirror, it takes only a moment to ignite paper. Leo had jotted down that the Sun was high and bright, the mirror, small and concave, and the paper, the university's newspaper from that day held with tweezers, started to smoke, stopped burning, and then reignited again; and more notably, that with two mirrors casting the sunlight together, the effect intensified. Then something underlined: that the paper's burnt part shaped into a big brown round spot, and to the surprise of all, happened to fall on a part of that day's paper with a photo of a moonlit tower in sunset, one titled above as 'Heavenly Bodies', and captioned below as 'Burnished by a setting sun and keeping company with a rising moon'.[37]

December had followed with the experience of a newly launched gallery that captured the Sun and Moon in a different light: a 'Collection of Historical Scientific Instruments'[38] in a building called the 'Science Center' where, while every object in it was scientific from 'across all major fields of science', some were more historical than others. The Collection having lived in Cambridge, Massachusetts, since the 1600s, and in its famous Harvard College shortly after, was full of instruments and devices where the Sun and Moon slept as two timeless objects through time measuring instruments and timekeeping devices. Behind the double doors that would soon have some 'interactive' touches to match the modern appearance of a camera-looking building and its computer-filled lobby,[39] some sun and moon items first greeting visitors were still historical in comparison: an astronomical instrument called an astrolabe, 'Usturlab' in Arabic and Persian, a hand-held device for measuring, among other things, the height of the Sun or a star or Moon above the horizon, not a typical 'Eastern Astrolabe'[40] as termed in a book with that title; then, another 'astrolabe' displayed there as 'Paris, ca. 1400s'. But the astronomical object overshadowing all else upon entrance was a so-called orrery[41] from Boston, ca. 1700s: a sizeable mechanical model of the solar system under a see-through dome with sun and moon balls, planets near and far, and cast-iron

37 Ide, Justin, Harvard Gazette, 17 November 2005 (base photo), https://www.news.harvard.edu/gazette/story/2005/11/heavenly-bodies

38 Harvard University, Collection of Historical Scientific Instruments (CHSI), Department of History of Science, Science, Center. Director: Peter Galison; Curator: Sara Schechner. https://scictr.fas.harvard.edu/

39 Harvard University, Science Center lobby: History of computers display. https://scictr.fas.harvard.edu/

40 Pingree, David, Eastern Astrolabes, Vol. 2, Kheirandish, Elaheh (ed), in Chandler, Bruce (ed), Historic Scientific Instruments of the Adler Planetarium (Chicago, 2009); Astrolabe: Arabic/Persian usṭurlāb.

41 The Pope Orrery, ca. 1700 once housed in the basement of Harvard's Houghton Library, resides at the Collection of Historical Scientific Instruments (CHSI); displayed in 'The Philosopher's Chamber: Art and Science in Harvard's Teaching Cabinet, 1766–1820', 19 May–13 Dec, 2017. https://chsi.harvard.edu/

figures from scientists Isaac Newton and Benjamin Franklin to politicians James Bowdoin and Paul Revere, supporting the variously sized balls kicking the Earth out of its central place, in that visual signature of a Sun-centred universe.

Some companion 'readers' assigned for the December visit were reminders of the special place of not just the Earth, but also the Sun, the Moon, and the stars: first, a recently published book titled *Planets* by an author drawing readers to her magnetic pen through award winning books; among them wordings like the oddity of the Sun and Moon appearing as the same size due to a 'coincidence of size and distance', the Sun's diameter being 400 times more, the Moon's distance from Earth 400 times less;[42] next, the book *Nearest Star*, bringing the Sun closer by another memorable line from its co-authors about the Earth being at 'just the right distance' from just the 'right star' for life to be possible; then, the lecture notes of one of those co-authors about 'how the Sun teaches us patience', far ahead of their forthcoming *Sun*, 'the most fascinating object humans have ever adored'.[43]

In the older of the two cities called Cambridge, where Leo was to spend time as part of the spring term of his gap year under distant supervision, a series of events came to fill more gaps in his knowledge. On a typically rainy English day when Leo arrived, he first had a few atypical experiences: as he walked the stone steps toward the historic edifice of the Cambridge University Library, a rare sunshower was followed by a rainbow peaking above the path long crossed by many brilliant minds, including Isaac Newton, the master of coloured spectrums;[44] and once Leo reached the long walls and tall ceilings filled with countless years of labour and wisdom from both Eastern and Western hemispheres, a different kind of light emerged from the one coming through the colours of aged stained-glass windows. The experiences inspired Leo to think of science itself as a light passing through the prism of time, and of its ups, downs and middle ranges, as a spectrum of colours that may be measured, much like modern wavelengths: historical factors affecting science at different times and places could then extend the 'identifiers' Leo had studied and put into rhymes in similar quantifiable terms: identifiers like roots for foundations, routes for transmissions, rules for directions, books for conceptions, schools for instructions, tools for manipulations, and loops for communications, initially excluding outlooks as a less measurable identifier.

For his Cambridge University campus housing, Leo was placed on Herschel Road, a street named after a family of scientists in England of about two centuries before whose

42 Sobel, Dava, The Planets (New York, 2005), p. 25: 'This uncanny coincidence of size and distance enables the puny Moon to block out the Sun whenever the two bodies converge on their shared path across Earth's sky'; award winning: Longitude: The True Story of a Lone Genius Who Solved the Greatest Scientific Problem of his Time (New York, 1995, 2005).

43 Golub, Leon and Pasachoff, Jay M., Nearest Star: The Surprising Science of Our Sun (Cambridge, MA, 2001), p. ix: 'We are in the position of Goldilocks, living at just the right distance from a just-right star'. Golub, 'How the Sun teaches us patience and the need for collaboration:' talk: Year Up, 2005. Golub, Leon, and Pasachoff, Jay M., The Sun (Kosmos) (London, 2017).

44 Cambridge University Library, UK. www.lib.cam.ac.uk/. Newton's 1661 notebook: www.bbc.com/news/uk-england-cambridgeshire-53948693. Newton, Isaac, Opticks, or, A Treatise of the Reflections, Refractions, Inflections & Colours of Light (London, 1730; New York, 1952). Descriptions of the day's sunshower and rainbow are accurate.

names rang stars and planets in one's ears: the father, William, well known for discovering the planet Uranus, his son, John, for naming moons for both Saturn and Uranus, and 'assistant' Caroline, for being a sister and aunt to them more than a discoverer of comets and nebulae herself, as occasionally noted in books like *The Sun and the Moon*.[45] The father and son Herschels were linked to a later British father and son named King, with comparable astronomical fame: the father, Henry, passing away at ninety the previous year,[46] had resided in Slough, the site of William Herschel's 'Observatory House' accessing his library through William's granddaughter; while Henry's son, David, aged to see that observatory demolished around 1960, would carry a high profile well into the next century.[47] Two sketches drawn by father Henry, the 'first and last scientific director of the new London Planetarium', were recently published in his son's *Synchrony with the Heavens*, next to his own provocative titles from 'Instruments of mass calculation' to 'When the night-sky over Qandahar was lit only by stars'.[48] Leo, who had synchronised scans of those images, had an astronomical bend that resonated well with the father and son 'Kings': with the father, for attractive titles like *Exploration of the Universe*; and with the son, spending his teenage years under the wings of someone literally *Geared to the Stars*,[49] for inspiring Leo and other youth to become 'watchers', not just of sky and heavens, but also of 'doubts and errors',[50] the expression used by the younger King's students and colleagues in a venue in honour of his scholarly career. Leo could hardly erase the image relayed to him by his mentor of how back in the days of coloured markers and transparency projections, the younger King had crossed out long lingering errors, word after word, in synchrony with the sound 'wrong', for each and every faulty case; nor his mentor's own dedicatory words on that 'honouring' occasion in the form of a few-line translation of a 100-verse astronomical poem, posted in Persian and English as a timeless gift on a 'webpage', before the days of websites:

O' King, we're at war with the times, how it keeps us sad [and in pain],
May your palm be a hand to lift up, from between us the dusts [of disdain]
For as long as the Sun's out shining, and the secrets of skies are in veil,

45 Hoskin, M. A. 'Herschel, William', Dictionary of Scientific Biography (DSB), 6 (1972), pp. 322–3; Goodman, Matthew, The Sun and the Moon (New York, 2008), p. 141.

46 King, David A., 'Henry C. King (1915–2005)', Journal for the History of Astronomy, 38, 4 (2007), pp. 526–7; 'Observatory House', Encyclopedia Britannica, 27 November 2008. www.britannica.com/place/Observatory-House

47 King, David A, publications: https://uni-frankfurt.academia.edu/DavidAKing. The 'Observatory House' was demolished around 1960: Science Photo Library. www.sciencephoto.com/media/321096/view/observatory-house-slough-1924

48 King, David A., In Synchrony with the Heavens: Studies in Astronomical Timekeeping and Instrumentation in Medieval Islamic Civilization, 2 vols. (Leiden, Boston, 2004–2005): Studies I-XVIII; quoted titles: Vol. 2, title, and Vol. 1, pp. 887–96, respectively.

49 King, 'Henry C. King', p. 526: Exploration of the Universe: From the Astrolabe to the Radio Telescope (1964); Geared to the Stars: The Evolution of Planetariums, Orreries, and Astronomical Clocks (1978).

50 Brentjes, Sonja, van Dalen, Benno and Charette, François (eds). Early Science and Medicine (ed: Christoph Lüthy), 7, 3, (2002). Special Issue: Certainty, Doubt, Error: Aspects of the Practice of Pre- and Early Modern Science: In Honor of David A. King, pp. 173–8.

May your night and day's works, be giving, and your month and year,
Nothing but cheer.[51]

Leo's favourite astronomical subjects included titles like the *Starry Messenger*,[52] addressed to an Italian prince his own age by his all-time hero, Galileo, the genius of about four hundred years before with whom he was especially excited to share the sign of Pisces with a rising of Leo. He had read over and over how Galileo, the 'father' of modern science, and of his now-famous daughter,[53] had first turned his self-made telescope, then called 'spy-glass', towards the skies; how his belief in the Sun-centred model of his time had affected what he 'saw in the heavens',[54] and above all, how his trial and eventual raising of the authority of science above that of religion and politics marked a new age. One of the Galileo websites Leo had recently come across was hosted by a museum in Florence[55] Leo remembered from childhood visits: the website 'Galileo//Thek' set up by a scholar-director and his team had instantly caught him as a clever website design with multi-coloured spheres mounted on planetary orbits as links around a central 'index' in a way that matched the pre- and post-Galileo universes with respective Earth-centred and Sun-centred models: the long known seven 'wanderers' around the Earth, as the Moon, Mercury Venus, Sun, Mars, Jupiter, and Saturn; and the nine 'planets' around the Sun, as Mercury, Venus, Earth, Mars, Jupiter, Saturn, Uranus, Neptune, and Pluto, with the Moon as an Earth Satellite reflecting new discoveries. In a later visit to the new 'Museo Galileo',[56] a jewel of a mini museum with physical and digital astronomical items and images, and the excavated finger and tooth of Galileo, Leo would encounter the twelve zodiac constellations on the front pavements of the entrance, followed by a 500-year anniversary exhibit on Leonardo da Vinci, a figure whose rotating digital drawings Leo had gone to visit in Milan's Ambrosian Library[57] every time he had stepped into Italian territory.

But that day Leo was in British territory, walking from Herschel Road to Free School Lane in the centre of Cambridge to visit the university's museum of the history of science, named the Whipple Museum.[58] Described as 'a fabulous chocolate box …

[51] Kheirandish, Elaheh, 'O' King' …: translation and adaptation for the occasion, 11 November 2001: Qavāmī Ganjavī, brother of Niẓāmī Ganjavī (ca. 1140–1209), Qaṣīdih-i muṣanna' (selection):
'*Khusru-vā bā zamānih dar jang-am; kih bih gham miguzār-ad-am ham-vār,*
Chih buv-ad gar kaf-i tu bar-gīr-ad; az miyān-i man u zamānih ghubār
Tā miyān ast Mihr rā tābish; tā nahān ast charkh rā asrār,
Rūz u shab juz sakhā' mabād-at shughl; sāl u mah juz ṭarab mabād-at kār …'

[52] Galilei, Galileo, Starry Messenger, in Drake, Stillman (tr), Discoveries and Opinions of Galileo (Garden City, 1957); Sobel, The Planets, p. 139: Galileo's birth sign.

[53] Sobel, Dava, Galileo's Daughter: A Historical Memoir of Science, Faith, and Love (New York, 1999).

[54] Cohen, I. Bernard, 'What Galileo "Saw" in the Heavens', in Birth of a New Physics, pp. 189–93.

[55] The 'Museum of the History of Science' directed by Paolo Galluzzi, became 'Museo Galileo' in 2010. www.museogalileo.it/en. 'Galileo//Thek' once included images of the planets in orbit and Galileo's signature. www.museogalileo.it/en/explore/egalileoteca.html

[56] www.museogalileo.it/en. In 2019, the 'Year of Leonardo', Museo Galileo celebrated the fifth centennial of his death by hosting the special exhibit, 'Leonardo and His Books: The Library of the Universal Genius'.

[57] Biblioteca Ambrosiana, a historic library in Milan, Italy, has long hosted Leonardo's Codex Atlanticus. www.ambrosiana.it/en/

[58] Whipple Museum of the History of Science, Cambridge, UK. www.sites.hps.cam.ac.uk/whipple/visitorinformation/. Description: Varsity Magazine, 24 October 2008. www.information-britain.co.uk/showPlace.cfm?Place_ID=12561

crammed with fascinating instruments, bizarre models, and wonderful ideas', the museum's website had long hosted a section called *Starry Messenger* as a teaching resource. In the physical Gallery covered by midnight blue starry night motifs and constellation patterns in its upper galleries, Leo met with the Faculty member curating the museum to learn more about the website's *Gallery Challenge*,[59] a curating resource, this time choosing objects, designing cases, writing labels and displaying items. As Leo's interest areas and periods were not immediately visible among the museum's collection of mostly Western astronomy and modern instruments, he was thinking creatively about that inviting 'challenge'; and as his eyes were drawn to attractive manuscript illustrations centrally displayed in the entrance Gallery, his interests took the colour of excitement with the sight of something that gave him an idea. Twelve beautiful zodiac constellations stood out all around the sides of an 'Orrery'[60] from ca. 1750, replicating celestial motions under a glass dome. This and another version in the other Cambridge with constellation drawings dwarfed by cast-iron figures, induced images of constellation illustrations in some Arabic and Persian manuscripts, inspiring Leo to take that Gallery Challenge outside that Gallery: these were illustrations like those in a *Book of Constellations*[61] by an author named ʿAbd al-Rahman Sufi, a work with links to both Baghdad and Isfahan; or a *Book of Instruction*,[62] by a certain Abu Rayhan Biruni, known to Leo in an illustrated version in the British Library for being uniquely composed in both Arabic and Persian, and dedicated to a female patron. Of the worldwide manuscripts of that work, an illustrated one dated just before '1200' had caught Leo's eyes on an auctioneer's handlist given to his mentor on an outdated type-written sheet[63] for the puzzle of its post-auction location: marked on that sheet as authored by 'one of the greatest figures' of his time, and with an early illustrated manuscript in nearby London, the work was too appealing for a Gallery Challenge, starting with whether the 'earliest' one reported was circling in the hands of more dealers or auctioneers, or awaiting identification in a public or private library: spotting that copy alone was a challenge not easily met, even through a twenty-first century[64]

59 'Starry Messenger' as a teaching resource. www.sites.hps.cam.ac.uk/starry/. 'Gallery Challenge' as a curating reseource. www.sites.hps.cam.ac.uk/whipple/explorecollections/gallerychallenge/. The Director and Curator of the Museum featured here is Professor Liba Taub, Cambridge University. www.people.hps.cam.ac.uk/index/teaching-officers/taub

60 Taub, Liba, 'The "grand" orrery: Explore Whipple collections', Whipple Museum of the History of Science (Cambridge, 2006). The grand orrery, ca. 1750, Whipple Museum. http://www.sites.hps.cam.ac.uk/whipple/explore/astronomy/thegrandorrery/

61 Ṣūfī, ʿAbd al-Raḥmān, Ṣuwar al-kawākib [An Islamic book of Constellations] (Bodleian Library MS. Marsh 144) (Bodleian Picture Books, No. 13) (Oxford, 1965); link to Isfahan: author; to Baghdad: copy. Savage-Smith, Emily, 'The most authoritative copy of ʿAbd al-Rahman al-Sufi's tenth-century Guide to the Constellations', in Bloom, Jonathan and Blair, Sheila (eds), God Is Beautiful and Loves Beauty: The Object in Islamic Art and Culture (New Haven, 2013), pp. 123–55, p. 125: 'made in Baghdad in 1125'.

62 Bīrūnī, Kitāb al-Tafhīm [Book of Instruction]; Wright and Humāʾī editions: no constellation figures. Illustrated manuscript, 1286: Titley, Norah, Persian Miniature Painting (London, 1983; Austin, 2009), pp. 18–19, fig 4.

63 A typewritten list of manuscripts including Abū Rayḥān Bīrūnī's Kitāb al-Tafhīm and its 'earliest' known manuscript (current location unknown) came for evaluation from Ars Libri Ltd, Boston, MA.

64 Hogendijk, Jan P., 'Abū Rayḥān Bīrūnī in the 15th/21st Century', Third International Summer School, Istanbul, 26 August 2014. www.jphogendijk.nl/biruni.html

treatment of the author and his works. What was not similarly known at the time was the exercise of a Gallery Challenge itself being of use one day, in real time.

Leo started learning about Biruni, a name sticking to his mind for its connotation as an 'outsider', first through a scientific biography colourfully painting his times as 'kaleidoscopic', and his vast output under six patrons.[65] Working on both sides of the year 1000, from Central Asia all the way to India, the life and times of this so-called outsider seemed like a perfect kaleidoscope itself for a 1000-year project, and the spectrum of seven colours within the prism of science from its earliest 'roots' to its latest 'loops'. Focusing on Biruni's *Book of Instruction*, Leo read in its dedication not only about a female patron named 'Rayhana daughter of Hasan',[66] with a first name comparable to 'Rayhana daughter of Zayd', the Jewish wife' of Prophet Muhammad, and Biruni's own first name as 'Abu Rahyan'; but one who had 'requested' over five hundred questions from the master, from geometry and arithmetic to astronomy and astrology. The book dedication of Biruni's contemporary, Ibn Sina with whom he corresponded, to a Persian princess named 'Zarrin Gis' as reported in one of Biruni's own books,[67] did not make the case of Rayhana unique. But Biruni's name long remaining little known or mistransmitted in the West, in contrast to the Latinised 'Avicenna', did make his own case rather unique: Biruni's name occasionally popped up as being far ahead of his time: a modern preface to his *Book of Chronology*[68] referred to him as a 'modern spirit' and 'historic phenomenon', and to his role in bringing to light Zoroastrian, Jewish and Christian traditions from far back and far away. The same modern author prefacing his *Book of India*[69] praised him for pulling down 'walls between different nations' and 'learning from opponents'; others wrote on 'Biruni between Greece and India' or research on him from Germany to the Netherlands,[70] on manuscripts of his works worldwide, and surviving copies in his own hands. But it was

65 Kennedy, E. S., 'Bīrūnī (or Berūnī), Abū Rayḥān (or Abu'l Rayḥān)', Dictionary of Scientific Biography (DSB), 2 (1970), pp. 147–58, p. 148: quotes.

66 Bīrūnī, Kitāb al-Tafhīm: preface names Rayḥāna bint al-Ḥasan/Bint-i Ḥasan. Esposito, John L. (ed), 'Rayhana bint Zayd ibn Amr (d. 632)', Oxford Dictionary of Islam (New York, 1990). www.oxfordislamicstudies.com/article/opr/t125/e1990

67 Ragep, Sally P., 'Ibn Sīnā: Abū ʿAlī al-Ḥusayn ibn ʿAbdallāh ibn Sīnā', The Biographical Encyclopedia of Astronomers (BEA), pp. 570–2, p. 570: Ibn Sīnā's Fī tūl Jurjān (Longitude of Jurjān) 'was written in Jurjān (1012–1014) and dedicated to Zarrayn Kīs [sic], daughter of Amīr Qābūs (= Shams al-Maʿālī). It is not extant but is discussed by Bīrūnī in his Tahdīd al-amākin. https://islamsci.mcgill.ca/RASI/BEA/Ibn_Sina_BEA.htm. Nasr, S. H., 'Bīrūnī versus Ibn Sīnā on the nature of the universe', in Nasr, S. H. and Amin Razavi, Mehdi (eds), The Islamic Intellectual Tradition in Persia, Vol. 9 (Richmond, 1996), pp. 100–2. Yano, Michio, 'Bīrūnī: Abū al-Rayḥān Muḥammad ibn Aḥmad al-Bīrūnī', The Biographical Encyclopedia of Astronomers (BEA), pp. 131–3, p. 133: 'Aliboron' [ignorant] in a French dictionary. https://islamsci.mcgill.ca/RASI/BEA/Biruni_BEA.htm

68 Bīrūnī, Abū Rayḥān, Āthār al-bāqiyah, Sachau, C. Edward (ed, tr, notes) (The Chronology of Ancient Nations or Vestiges of the Past) (London, 1879), preface.

69 Bīrūnī, Abū Rayḥān, Fī Tahqīq mā lil-Hind: India, Sachau, Edward (ed, tr) (An Account of the Religion, Philosophy, Literature, Chronology, Astronomy, Customs, Laws and Astrology of India about A.D. 1030) (Leipzig, 1925), preface.

70 Rosenthal, Franz, 'Al-Biruni between Greece and India', in Yarshatir, E. (ed), Biruni Symposium (Persian Studies Series, No. 7) (New York, 1976), pp. 1–12; Roemer, Hans Robert, 'Research on al-Biruni in Germany' in Chelkowski, Peter J. (ed), Scholar and the Saint: Studies in Commemoration of Abu'l-Rayhan al-Biruni and Jalal al-Din al-Rumi (New York, 1975), pp. 95–102; Hogendijk, Jan P.: works dedicated to the memory of scholars from East and West. www.jphogendijk.nl/biruni.html

in the kaleidoscopic entry on Biruni that its young reader found a clue as to why Biruni long remained out of the radar of Western scholars, with no Latin translations of his works: the glittering expression of Biruni's 'tongue of silver and gold',[71] used in that entry in the context of worldly affairs, which in his own words 'excited the envy of fools' but the 'pity of the wise', could be extended to how his being dragged from court to court during the peak of his creativity and productivity could have made him fall out of the 'loop'; and how distance from places beyond Baghdad and Isfahan at the time could be decisive in analysing the 'why's and 'why-not' questions of early science.

Biruni did not fall out of the loop of his own native lands, however. The young reader could follow the footsteps of Biruni in a Persian poem closely depicting his signature constellations of the sky in a period *Description of the Night*, and through it, those of the modern commentator placing the Persian poet, named 'Gurgani', in the 'Isfahan of around 1050', the estimated year of Biruni's death.[72] The description of a 'fateful' night painted by a 'poetical genius' with effects as dramatic as the Moon and Sun 'hiding their faces', and the constellations of the never-changing 'fixed stars' changing forms, included rare representations of all forty-eight stellar constellations by the so-called poet of Isfahan: these linked to not only the tradition of the ancient Greek mathematician Ptolemy in the *Star Catalogue* of his famous *Almagest*,[73] but dependent works of a thousand years later, from Sufi's *Book of Constellations* to Biruni's *Book of Instruction*. But it was to Biruni's *Book of Instruction* that the museum's zodiac constellations and Gallery Challenge would lead to, followed by chases of manuscripts of Biruni's bilingual *Book of Instruction*, through which a detective touch would be added to Leo's project.

In the dark hours of the night, Leo was madly searching for four volumes penciled on his course list as *A Literary History*, a search which in that fateful night in his own time led to his consultation of a rich digital archive, coordinated by Leo's mentor with overlaps with the 'Dialogue' project: the archive, 'The Classical Library of Islam',[74] being the product of synergy between a classics-educated entrepreneur and medieval Islamic historians, made accessible four volumes that while titled 'literary' were much more than that in their coverage of over a thousand years after the year 1000; a browse through those never-outdated volumes turned up the names and dates of some of the 'stars' that were to fill Leo's pages. In rising above Baghdad and Isfahan themselves as twin stars of a blinking universe during their phases of radiance and eclipse, he found

71 Kennedy, 'Bīrūnī (or Berūnī)', p. 149.

72 Kunitzsch, Paul, 'Description of the night in Gurgānī's Vīs u Rāmīn', Der Islam, 59 (1982), pp. 93–110. As'ad Gurgānī, Fakhr al-Dīn, Vīs va Rāmīn, Davis, Dick (tr, intro) (Fakhraddīn Gorganī Vīs va Rāmīn) (Washington, DC, 2008), pp. 51–2. Kheirandish, Elaheh, 'Astronomical poems from the "four corners" of Persia (c. 1000–1500 CE)' in Korangy, Alireza, Thackston, Wheeler, Mottahedeh, Roy and Granara, William (eds), Essays in Islamic Philology, History, and Philosophy, Vol. 31 (Berlin/Boston, 2016), pp. 51–90. Bīrūnī's death date is debated.

73 Ptolemy, The Almagest, Toomer, Gerald J. (tr., annot.) (Ptolemy's Almagest) (New York, 1984); Grasshoff, Gerd, The History of Ptolemy's Star Catalogue (New York, 1990). Nasr, S. H., Islamic Science: An Illustrated Study (London, 1976), pp. 102–3.

74 Kheirandish, Elaheh, 'Classical Library of Islam' (Coordinator), Packard Humanities Institute (PHI), Cambridge MA (2000–2004); Founder: David W. Packard; Director: Roy Mottahedeh; Assistants: Stephanie Bass, Kevin Schwarz. https://persian.packhum.org

rich inspirations from other directions. A goldmine of a source titled *Mathematicians, Astronomers, and Other Scholars of Islamic Civilization and their Works*[75] supplied his casting repertoire: for figures, not just names and dates, but also their works and manuscripts; and for settings, not just cities and libraries, but also courts and observatories. For the earlier periods, he picked figures named Musa Khwarizmi and ʿUmar Khayyam representing Baghdad and Isfahan of better times; and for the later periods, Yahya Maghribi and ʿAli Qushji, as suitable contrasts. Thus began the best years of Baghdad and Isfahan: Baghdad of the year 850 and Isfahan of the year 1050 as crescent and quarter moons; and their worse years through nearby Damascus and Constantinople of years 1250 and 1450, as half-moons and partial eclipses. Under their respective skies of Mesopotamia, Persia, Andalusia and Central Asia, then passed, in sequence, other times, places, names and dates (Chart: Names and Dates), covering between them a chapter on cosmology, from chronology and astrology to astronomy and cosmography. All that set Leo on a course leading to new terms, frames, traces, and chases, refining 'the best and worst times' of his thousand years to their 'best and worse halves': searching for curves, rather than breaks, of a supposed 'turning point', and mindful of both brighter and darker sides and their inevitable overlaps, he found a *Dialogue of Night and Day* from around the year 1000, to act as a fitting opening preface for his chapter sections, focusing on the role of routes, and not just roots, of key developments in science, in both their progressive and regressive senses.

Chapter 2: 'Dialogue' of Night and Day

Best Half, Worse Half (ca. 750–1250; 1250–1750) – Routes

By Charles Leo Scribner, May 2006

Best Half (ca. 750–1250): From A Crescent to Quarter Moon

[*Night: O' Day*]
I am a King whose throne is the Earth, and whose palace, the heaven,
Guarded by the Moon, all wandering stars, serve at my command . . .
[*Day: O'Night*]
From my Sun your Moon derives the light that increases its glow,
In allegiance to the Sun it bends its back in homage low . . .

Asadi Tusi, '*Dialogue' of Night and Day*', ca. 1000, English translation: Elaheh Kheirandish; variation: Browne, Edward, G., *Literary History*, Vol. 2, 1906, pp. 150–2[76]

[75] Rosenfeld, Boris. A. and Ihsanoğlu, Ekmeleddin, Mathematicians, Astronomers, and Other Scholars of Islamic Civilization and their Works (7th–19th c.) (Istanbul, 2003), pp. 21–3, No. 41: Khwārizmī; pp. 168–70, No. 420: Khayyām; pp. 226–7, No. 635: Maghribī; pp. 285–7, No. 845: Qūshjī.

[76] Asadī Ṭūsī (attribution), ca. 1000, Munāẓirih-i Shab va Rūz, Khaleghi-Motlagh (ed), 'Asadī Ṭūsī', pp. 91–95, p. 92, line 12; p. 95, line 36, Kheirandish, Elaheh (tr, excerpts); variation: Browne, Literary History, Vol. 2, pp. 150–2:
'[*Night:*] *Man-am ān Shāh kih takht-am zamī ast, īvan, charkh*
Mah sipar-dār u hamih anjum-i sayyārih, khidam
[*Day:*] *Māh-i tu az ḍūʾ-i Khurshīd-i man afzāy-ad nūr*
va-z pay-i khidmat-i Khurshīd kun-ad pusht bih kham . . .'

2.3 *An Arab City with a Growing Moon*

It was April circa 850, and Baghdad, the city with a round plan, was still growing to complete the circle of its most notable days in science when one of the biggest names on the subject was writing his very last book. This was a man whose name, Al-Khwarizmi, and book title, Al-Jabr,[77] named respectively after his native Central Asian town and novel mathematical subject, were to live immortally through the Latinised terms 'algorithm' and 'algebra'.[78] But that day Khwarizmi was working on a book on chronology, titled *Ta'rikh*,[79] as it was called in its original Arabic for its links to history, a book that was itself not to survive to posterity. Immersed in interpreting history with an eye on chronology, the aged author was especially mindful of his own mortality, and that mindset made him painfully aware that he would soon be closing his eyes to a glorious world at a glorious time and place: the glorious world was the fast growing Islamic Empire surrounding him, the glorious time, the second century of ʿAbbasid rule[80] patronising him, and the glorious place, the high court of Baghdad housing him. What was distressing to that associate of a 'House of Wisdom',[81] long celebrated before shadows of doubt would surround its very name, was the thought of the time it would take him to finish his final work. His other works, often the first to be composed in Arabic on subjects like geometry, astronomy, geography and cartography, were what his patrons had wanted; he now wished to write on a subject that he wanted; and the time needed for fulfilling that wish was neither measurable nor predictable, even to a master calculator such as himself.

To Muhammad son of Musa, who was named after the Prophet of the Muslims, by a father named after the Prophet of the Jews, the only comforting thought was that he could pray, in the tradition of both faiths, for the number of months, weeks, and days that he assumed he needed to finish what would be his last book. This was based on the time it had taken him to finish his 'Algebra of Inheritance', a work he had invented for the Muslim community based on a tradition in the Jewish community, much in the order of his own given name. The name itself was not at all uncommon in form, content, or sequence, as in the case of the contemporary Muhammad son of Musa, son of Shakir, the eldest of three influential Persian brothers known as the 'Banu Musa',[82] and a rival, not of al-Khwarizmi, but of others in the court of the Caliph at the time.

77 Toomer, Gerald J., 'Al-Khwārizmī, Abū Jaʿfar Muḥammad ibn Mūsā', Dictionary of Scientific Biography (DSB), 7 (1973), pp. 358–65. Brentjes, Sonja, 'Khwārizmī: Muḥammad ibn Mūsā al-Khwārizmī', Biographical Encyclopedia of Astronomers (BEA), pp. 631–3. https://islamsci.mcgill.ca/RASI/BEA/Khwarizmi_BEA.htm. Saliba, George, 'The meaning of al-Jabr wa al-Muqabalah', Centaurus, 17 (1972–1973), pp. 189–204.

78 Berggren, J. Len, Episodes in the Mathematics of Medieval Islam (New York, 1986), pp. 6–9.

79 Toomer, 'Al-Khwārizmī', p. 362.

80 Bosworth, Islamic Dynasties, pp. 7–10.

81 *Bayt al-ḥikma*: Berggren, Episodes, pp. 3–6; Rosenthal, Franz, The Classical Heritage in Islam, Marmorstein, Emile and Marmorstein, Jenny (tr) (London and New York, 1975), pp. 5–12; pp. 45–51; Gutas, Greek Thought, Arabic Culture, pp. 53–60: reexaminations.

82 Berggren, Episodes, pp. 63–65: 'Algebra of Inheritance'. Al-Dabbagh, J., 'Banū Mūsā: Three brothers – Muḥammad, Aḥmad and Al-Ḥasan … "sons of Mūsā"', Dictionary of Scientific Biography (DSB), 1 (1970), pp. 443–6.

Baghdad of the 850s shone brightly when it came to science, even if the ruling Caliph of the time was nothing like the ʿAbbasid rulers before or after him. The rule of the ʿAbbasids, the Caliphate named after ʿAbbas, the uncle of Islam's Prophet Muhammad,[83] had many patrons for science: not the first Caliph, ruling from the year 750 under the name of Al-Saffah, the 'Shedder', that of Blood and the reign of the previous Caliphate, the Umayyads based in Damascus; but starting with his half-brother, Mansur, the 'Victor', and his son, Mahdi, the 'Well-Guided', as well as the next set of fathers and sons, Harun al-Rashid, 'Aaron the Rightly Guided', and his son, Maʾmun, the 'Trusted', both made especially famous by the stories of the *Thousand and One Nights*. Then there was Muʿtasim, the 'Guarded', and later, Mustaʿin, the 'Assisted', both with a much lesser fame without much less of a role in science. But the reign of the ʿAbbasid Mutawakkil, the 'Designated', was clearly different: in 850, three years into the reign of that Caliph of many unfit associations, from the intolerance of Christians, Jews, and Shiʿite Muslims, to the slaying of his own minister, scholarship miraculously stayed on course. This was a Caliph whose dark sides were captured as remotely in time as a century after his death in a poem addressing him directly:

The heart was like to leave me for distress,
When it was said, "The Wazir is slain!"
O Commander of the Faithful, thou hast slain one,
Who was the axle on which your mill revolved![84]

It was no accident that the poets could capture the lasting strength of scholarship by placing 'pen' above 'sword' in other lines of verse from those notable times:

'Pleasant to the people of the sword be that idleness,
Whereby their days are passed in self-indulgence! . . .
But as for the people of the pen, at no moment,
Are their swords dry of blood.[85]

So rich and high were the states of scholarship and science, both during and after mid-ninth-century Baghdad, that the book commissions extended as far as Caliph Mutawakkil's own concubine slave and active mother. Such cases, however, were much more discrete than the 'two queens of Baghdad'[86] of earlier times whose names were to fill the pages of a modern book so titled by a historian of the same gender. Caliphs and queens, viziers and courtiers, sometimes translators and scholars themselves, were still engaged in an unexplainable scientific surge in this slightly later time. The momentum,

[83] Bosworth, Islamic Dynasties, p. 8: ʿAbbās: uncle of Prophet Muḥammad. Abbott, Two Queens of Baghdad: Caliph name translations.
[84] Browne, Literary History, Vol. 1. p. 253: quoting Ibn Kushājim; n. 1: 'd. 961 or 971'.
[85] Browne, Literary History, Vol. 1. p. 253. Pen and sword 'dialogues': Introduction and Chapter Six.
[86] Abbott, Two Queens of Baghdad.

no doubt, could be explained by the vigor of early Baghdad itself. The city was new, vibrant and, most importantly to science, diverse. It was new, as the capital of an expanding empire founded hardly a century before; it was vibrant, as the seat of a powerful Caliphate strengthening exponentially in one century alone; and it was diverse as an embracing society integrating Greek, Syriac, and Persian scholars into its Arab community, and Christians, Zoroastrians, and Jewish ones into its Muslim community.

For a scholar such as Musa Khwarizmi, whose name would be associated by historians with the epithet 'Majusi' for possible Zoroastrian' origins,[87] and his work with Greek and Hindu traditions, Baghdad was an important 'route' for the assimilation and transmission of the sciences; and for entities such as the sciences taking 'root' in a city with such a rich past and fast pulse, this was a time not only for massive translations and compositions[88] involving a diverse group of scholars, but of perceptions and predictions regarding the development of science at large.

It was not long before the year 850 that predictions about an end to the golden days of Islam already found their way into written records. A forecast about an end to the reign of one of the Caliphs by Khwarizmi himself was more of a self-preservation than prediction when he reportedly gave a very sick Caliph[89] fifty years to live, though the Caliph would die in ten days according to the historian Tabari. Among other predictions, one recorded by Ibn Khaldun, a later figure considered to be among the founders of history as a field, was that Theophile son of Thomas, the chief astrologer of the ʿAbbasid Caliph, Mahdi, had predicted not just the fall of the Caliphate at the peak of power, but the fall of science at the peak of productivity, basing his forecast on the astrological theory of conjunctions, marking the big year as 1530 of the 'common era', 960 years after the great conjunction of the year 571: decades later, a famous Arab scientific author called Yaʿqub al-Kindi would make his conjectured turning point closer to the year 1315, '693 years after the equinox preceding the Hijra . . . or about twenty years earlier if it refers to Muslim years'.[90] But no one had put a finger on the 'when' and 'how' of a scientific phase out, and no dimming of the lights of science was in sight when a man of a different time and place was to make conjectured predictions of a different kind.

87 Toomer, 'Al-Khwārizmī', p. 358, cites historian al-Ṭabarī for that epithet; p. 362: quotes.
88 Gutas, Greek Thought, Arabic Culture, pp. 182–3: list.
89 Berggren, Episodes, pp. 6–7. ʿAbbasid Caliphs: Bosworth, Islamic Dynasties, p. 8.
90 Hartner, 'When and how', p. 99: Theophile, astrologer of Caliph al-Mahdī; p. 100: Al-Kindī. Jolivet, Jean and Rashed, Roshdi, 'Al-Kindī, Abū Yūsuf Yaʿqūb ibn Isḥāq', Dictionary of Scientific Biography (DSB), 15 (Supp. I, 1978), pp. 261–7. Atiyeh, George N., Al-Kindi: The Philosopher of the Arabs (Rawalpandi, 1966): works.

2.4 *A Persian City with a Glowing Sun*

It was May circa 1050, and Isfahan, the city whose square-shaped 'square' would one day be world famous, was to soon host a young man who was to become world famous himself. Carrying the name Khayyam[91] for couplets as creatively turned into English as they rhymed in Persian, the would-be poet-scientist could not be moved further from his family trade name of 'Tent-maker'. Nor could he be moved further from his birthplace of Nayshabur in northern Persia, as the celebrated scholar of Samarqand, later known as part of Uzbekistan. Khayyam's first name, ʿUmar, being the same as the second successor after Prophet Muhammad four centuries before, was not so well matched either; his disposition was far from the reputation of the ill-temper of 'Caliph ʿUmar', whose fearful rule had pushed the conquering Empire of Islam into Persia within the first decade of his rule. ʿUmar Khayyam's contrasting 'gentle nature', was itself only one of many traits later thrown at him under a long chain of labels that ranged from a 'free thinker, atheist, and materialist' to a 'hypocrite, blasphemer, and skeptic', and from 'Persian Abu'l-ʿAla', the first name of the blind Arab poet Maʿarri, to 'Voltaire' of the French Enlightenment.[92] The chain of labels thrown at Khayyam's well known 'Quatrains' were to be no less long: 'scarcely any book in the world', would write a modern literary figure, 'has been admired, rejected, hated, altered, calumniated, condemned, carded, renown the world over, and finally remained unknown':[93] the mix of 'conflicting ideas' in the quatrains estimated by the same literary figure 'from eighty to one thousand two hundred' would raise by him questions of part authorship, not as the involvement of a 'twin of the famous Khayyam' from the same time and place, but 'his very clever followers' from a different age. Khayyam, whose skills in mathematics and poetry overshadowed everything else, came to have other profiles through the literary genre that made him famous by his modern interpreter, Edward Fitzgerald, in his popular *Rubaiyat*. Though the Persian poet and his English translator-interpreter would become so inseparable that their names sometimes merged as 'Omar-Fitzgerald',[94] it was through a combination of his first and last names, from Omar and ʿUmar to Khayyam and Khayyami, that poetry and mathematics combined to strike a harmonic chord captured and identified through his verses.

An instance of the fusion of mathematics and poetry would involve the city of Isfahan, where Khayyam spent close to twenty years towards the end of his life. One day, a man far distanced from his age and land would publish a piece titled 'A

[91] Youschkevitch, A. P. and Rosenfeld, B. A., 'Khayyāmī (or Khayyām), Ghiyāth al-Dīn . . . al-Nisābūrī (or Al-Naysāburī) . . . also known as "Omar Khayyām"', Dictionary of Scientific Biography (DSB), 7 (1973), pp. 323–34. Hashemipour, Behnaz, 'Khayyām: Ghiyāth al-Dīn Abū al-Fatḥ ʿUmar ibn Ibrāhīm al-Khayyāmī al-Nīshāpūrī', Biographical Encyclopedia of Astronomers (BEA) (2007), pp. 627–8. https://islamsci.mcgill.ca/RASI/BEA/Khayyam_BEA.htm

[92] Youschkevitch and Rosenfeld, 'Khayyāmī (or Khayyām)', p. 331: 'gentle nature . . . Abū'l-ʿAlā [Maʿarrī], Voltaire'.

[93] Rubaiyat Hakim Omar Khayyam, 2nd Edition, 1868. Includes Fitzgerald, Edward, Quatrains (Tehran, 1934/1964); Hedayat, Sadegh, Tarānih-hā-yi Khayyām (intro), Ostovar, Mohammad Karim (tr), pp. 23–53, p. 23, pp. 52–3: quotes.

[94] Khayyām, ʿUmar, Rubaiyat of Omar Khayyam, Fitzgerald, Edward (tr), Louis Untermeyer (ed, intro) (New York, 1947), p. xviii.

mathematical sonata for architecture',[95] where Khayyam would take centre stage through several stretches to be associated with the mathematics behind one of Isfahan's 'architectural masterpieces'. The author of the 'sonata', referring to the North Dome chamber of Isfahan's Masjid-i Jami' or 'Atiq, built in 1088–1089, noting a reflection of the ratio known as the 'golden section', would argue for the hand of Khayyam in it; but the evidence for the loose argument that 'the elegance of the procedure suggests its possible creation by Omar Khayyam', coupled with a mistranslation of a key Khayyam verse,[96] would be the first of a series of insensitive historical treatments of that mathematician-poet.

Khayyam's life with which such association went beyond figures as high-profiled as the Seljuq Sultan Malik-Shah and his vizier Nizam al-Mulk, and events as prestigious as their commission of a new solar calendar from him, was quite long; but Khayyam's afterlife was even longer, generating discussions beyond those about his symbolic quatrains or cubic equations. It would only take a few years after Khayyam's death before his alleged companion, the literary figure, Nizami 'Arudi, would write in his highly amusing *Four Discourses* about the man he called 'Proof of Truth' on matters that begged their own test for 'proof':[97] relating from his companion Khayyam that his 'grave will be in a spot where the trees will shed their blossoms twice a year' and arriving in 'Nishapur', finding 'many flower-leaves' hiding his dust, his account misleadingly placed Khayyam outside his own age through dates and places not matching standard historical records.

Still, if Khayyam or any of his contemporaries, including the imaginative visitor to his grave, had any predictive powers, they could not have imagined the fate of a long-dead mathematician-poet much later in time. First, that he would be the subject of books and films, words without meanings for some time; and second, that he would be half-portrayed, if not misportrayed, through both those mediums. In most of what became modern books, including one by the same Fitzgerald that made him famous in a language and land far from his own, he was first and foremost a poet, even if not the composer of all the poetry of the *Quatrains*; and in one of those books, self-described as a novel, and circulated in modern languages and editions, Khayyam would be featured, as both hesitant about the truth of 'truth', and subject of halfway truths:[98] the words uttered from a popularised Khayyam would extend from 'do not speak to me of truth' to conceptions placed outside of his own time, from cubic equations to symbolic

95 Özdural, Alpay. 'A mathematical sonata for architecture: Omar Khayyam and the Friday Mosque of Isfahan', Technology and Culture, 39, 4 (1998), pp. 699–715; p. 699 and n. 2: definition of the 'golden section' citing Oleg Grabar and other sources.

96 Özdural, 'Sonata', p. 703: 'elegance of the procedure . . .'; p. 714: 'pleasure-dome of Earth . . . the delightful package in which is wrapped the evidence we seek': English verse: Elwell-Sutton, L. P., In Search of Omar Khayyam (London; New York, 1971) mistranslates the original Persian: Dashti, Ali, Damī bā Khayyām (Tehran, 1344 [1965]), p. 204: '*ṭarab-khāna-i khāk*', translates as pleasure *house*, not *dome*, of Earth; and '*gunbad-i khākī*', even if in the original Persian, more literally as 'clay dome'.

97 Niẓāmī 'Arūḍī Samarqandī, Chahār maqāla, Browne, Edward G. (tr) (Four Discourses) (Hertford, 1899; repr., Journal of the Royal Asiatic Society, July and October 1899; London, 1900), Anectode XXVIII: pp. 71–2: Khayyām's title, 'Ḥujjat al-Ḥaq' is given as 'Argument of Truth', his arrival in Nīshāpūr as year 530 H [1135–36], and the prediction as reported from 'the city of Balkh'.

98 Maalouf, Amin, Samarkand, Russell, Harris (tr) (Northampton, 2004), p. 28: quotes.

designations: that 'Khayyam used the Arabic term "shay", which means thing . . . spelled xay in Spanish scientific works, and gradually replaced by its first letter, x' to become 'the universal symbol of the unknown'. Part of the truth left out of such incomplete narratives would be that the Arabic term 'shay'', a non-symbolic concept for an unknown entity in early algebra, went as far back as early Arabic translations of corresponding Babylonian, Greek, and Indian works, and to early Arabic authors like Khwarizmi long before Khayyam.[99]

The zoom on only one or two sides of the many-sided Khayyam, sometimes at the expense of inverting his profile altogether, would get further and further from him through the lens of a camera that was to feature the *Legend of Omar Khayyam*:[100] there, he would be in another historical depiction, this time inverting, besides Khayyam's name from 'Tent-maker' to a more marketable 'Keeper' in the film title, the astronomy of his time, from an Earth-centred to a Sun-centred universe long before 16th-century Europe when this would actually happen. It was as if the director were to miss the notes of the film's science consultants in having Khayyam the film-star[101] draw the model of the sky for his fellow cast members according to the much later heliocentric model of Copernicus and Galileo, and not that of the geocentric model actually known to Khayyam and his near contemporaries.

Isfahan of the 1050s was slightly before the time when Arab and Persian scholars of the highest caliber would work in great luxury in the court of the Turkish-origined 'Seljuq'[102] rulers, among them Khayyam regulating the solar calendar among other things. What 'celestial' work there was at the time, whether a 'star catalogue' or 'birth horoscope', relied much more on astronomical tables and celestial globes than sky watchers and star finders; and onlookers on the constellations of northern and southern hemispheres, or zodiac signs, mostly drew from ancient traditions such Ptolemy's *Great Syntaxis*, becoming *The Almagest* from the Al of its Arabic title. One such onlooker in the 'Isfahan of about 1050' was neither a strict astronomer nor Ptolemaic follower, nor a recorder or reader of observational data or tables; but it was he who noted most, and described best, the sinister aspects of the moments defining the coordinates of his particular time and place: as a poet, not astronomer or astrologer, creating a critical moment when an ancient king were to face a fatalistic night, he left his readers in awe by recreating a sky with all the stars and constellations known to him from the *Book of Instruction* of his near contemporary, Biruni, in a form dramatising their effects in his *Description of the Night*: [103] the Sun becoming '*black by the dark drape of slipping hope and grave upset*', the Moon '*fallen from its wheel into a well, as if dug by the night's westward Sunset*'; the Zodiacs, the ring of twelve constellations lining the yearly visible path of the Sun, being neither less dramatic, nor graphic; even

99 Kheirandish, Elaheh, Problems Corresponding to Quadratic Equations in Early Mathematical Texts: A Chapter in the History of Algebra, (unpublished MS Thesis, University of Rhode Island, 1987).

100 Mashayekh, Kayvan (writer/director), The Keeper: Legend of Omar Khayyam, released 10 June, 2005. www.imdb.com/title/tt0294806/plotsummary?ref_=tt_ov_pl

101 Mashayekh, Keeper: 'for future generations'; scene: Khayyam wrongly draws a Sun-centred model. www.imdb.com/title/tt0294806/plotsummary?ref_=tt_ov_pl

102 Bosworth, Islamic Dynasties, p. 129–31.

103 Kunitzsch, 'Description of the Night': 'poetic devices'. Gurgānī, Vīs va Rāmīn, Davis (tr), pp. 51–2.

constellations named 'fixed stars' for never changing positions or shapes turning to 'poetic devices' for having the signs of the coming dark overblown: the lines of a poem on the maleficent signs of the Sun, the Moon, and the stars were to be one day not just translated, but contextualised and reconstructed in modern times.[104]

The little-known words of that little-known poet of Isfahan from a millennium before were to turn frightfully prophetic when it came to the years immediately following the year 1050 when the *Description of the Night* was composed, and dated, based on period data.[105] A major disaster on the rise was 'about the time of the appearance of the comet in Gemini' in a year corresponding to 1054–1055; this was one of the 'widely known plagues' recorded by a well known physician from Baghdad, as restored by a historian of the time; a plague devastating lands far beyond Baghdad and Isfahan, confirming a Ptolemaic prediction especially for Egypt, and counting among many victims from the 'ancient sciences' one 'Ibn al-Haytham', spelling out that after his demise 'the lamps of knowledge were put out, leaving the surviving minds in darkness'.[106]

A scholar of a much later time reporting all such details would add that such destructive events happening 'at the end of the most creative period of scientific activity in the Middle East . . . have yet to be seriously considered . . . in connection with the important "Problem of Decline"':[107] as the foremost scholar of one of the brightest stars of science, Ibn al-Haytham, the words he would quote from one whose works he knew, almost by heart, translated as 'the duty of the man who investigates the writings of scientists . . . is to make himself an enemy of all that he reads, and, applying his mind to the core and margins of its content, attack it from every side'.[108] But attacks from every side, political as well as natural, on the cores and margins of his native lands, were to turn things around a few times.

In slightly over a couple of centuries, the army of the Mongols would advance upon Baghdad from both East and West: a 'personal account' of no more than a few decades later would chronicle the critical moments of political turnover in disbelief, reporting on Baghdad and its sack, the last ʿAbbasid Caliph's love of books and ignorance in statecraft', as well as his wazir's library of ten thousand volumes of rare and precious works.[109] All that changed in the course of a shift, not from the direct blows of the armies of invaders such as the Mongols, but the indirect breaks in the 'routes' of transmission, through both man and nature.

104 Kheirandish, 'Astronomical poems', includes commentaries; 'Early science and craft: When astrology was part of astronomy', Harvard University, 17 Jan 2014: reconstruction of Gurgānī's Poem: painting commissioned from Artemis Akchoti-Shahbazi.
105 Neugebauer, Otto, 'The date of the "horoscope" in Gurgānī's poem', Islam, 59 (1982), pp. 297–301, p. 297: problems of dating raised in Kunitzsch, 'Description of the Night'.
106 Sabra, A. I., 'The "commentary" that saved the text: The hazardous journey of Ibn al-Haytham's Arabic optics', Early Science and Medicine, 12 (2007), pp. 117–33; Ibn Buṭlān translation: pp. 129–31.
107 Sabra, 'Appropriation and subsequent naturalization', pp. 238–42: decline.
108 Sabra, A. I., 'Ibn al-Haytham', Abū ʿAlī al-Ḥasan Ibn al-Ḥasan . . . also known as Alhazen', Dictionary of Scientific Biography (DSB), 6 (1972), pp. 189–210; 'Vita: Ibn al-Haytham: Brief life of an Arab mathematician, died circa 1040', Harvard Magazine, October 2003, pp. 54–5, p. 55: quote. www.harvardmagazine.com/2003/09/ibn-al-haytham-html. Kheirandish, 'Eloge: A. I. Sabra', pp. 281–6.
109 Browne, Literary History, Vol. 2, pp. 462–3: Mongol war costumes; pp. 465–6: the last ʿAbbasid Caliph and his wazir on books.

Worse Half (ca. 1250–1750): From A Half Moon to Partial Eclipse

[Night: O' Day]
While your erect Sun takes a year to take its course
My Moon [only] takes less than a month [to get full], in quality or quantity
[Day: O' Night]
If by your Moon the Arab months and years are recognized
It is by my Sun that all know the Persian months and years

Asadi Tusi, *'Dialogue' of Night and Day'*, ca. 1000, English translation: Elaheh Kheirandish; variation: Browne, Edward, G., *Literary History*, Vol. 2, 1906, pp. 150–2[110]

2.5 *An Arab City with a 'Westerner'*

It was April circa 1250, and scholars who considered themselves high up in astronomy and astrology, at a time when the two subjects were still close enough to share the root of the word 'star' in Arabic and Persian,[111] were no longer observing the heavens mostly under the skies of Baghdad. One night, in a historic city to the west of Baghdad, a man whose name in Arabic, Maghribi, translated into 'Westerner' for being from the western parts of Islamic lands,[112] was observing the sky with naked eyes. But even as an avid sky watcher whose 'obserational notebook', would be discovered and published in modern times, he would still not register 'the brightest star in the sky around the year 1250', one perplexing future astronomers, by then called astrophysicists, for why it 'is missing from ancient records': reported in a modern news release,[113] as a 'newly detected supernova' that 'presumably the great astronomers of the Orient would have seen above their horizon' around the year 1250, the piece added that the 'blast actually occurred around the year 600, but its light took about 650 years to reach Earth'; that it 'should have beamed for months, and brighter than anything but the moon at night'; and that

[110] Asadī Ṭūsī (attribution), Munāẓirih-i Shab u Rūz, Khaleghi-Motlagh (ed), 'Asadī Ṭūsī', p. 92, line 16; p. 94, line 33; Kheirandish, Elaheh (tr, excerpt); variation: Browne, Literary History, Vol. 2, pp. 150–2:
[Night:] Rāst Khurshīd-i tu chandān kih bih sāl-ī birav-ad
Kam bih yik mah birav-ad Māh-i man az kayf u zi kam
[Day:] Gar zi-Māh-i tu shinās-and mah u sāl-i ʿArab
Z-aftāb-am hamih dān-and mah u sāl-i ʿAjam [based on critical apparatus]

[111] Kunitzsch, Paul, 'Al-Nudjūm, the stars', Encyclopedia of Islam (EI2), 8, 131–2 (1992), pp. 97–105; Pingree, David. ''Ilm al-hay'a, the science of the figure of the heavens or astronomy', Encyclopedia of Islam (EI^2), 3, 57–8 (1970), pp. 1135–8; Forcada, Miquel, 'Astronomy and astrology and the sciences of the ancients in early al-Andalus (2nd/8th–3rd/9th centuries)', Zeitschrift für Geschichte der arabisch-islamischen Wissenschaften, 16 (2004–2005), pp. 1–73.

[112] Tekeli, S., 'Muḥyi 'l-Dīn al-Maghribī … Yaḥyā … al-Maghribī al-Andalūsī', Dictionary of Scientific Biography (DSB), 9 (1974), pp. 555–7. Comes, Mercè, 'Ibn Abī al-Shukr: Muḥyī al-Milla wa-'l-Dīn Yaḥyā … al-Maghribī al-Andalūsī …', Biographical Encyclopedia of Astronomers (BEA), pp. 548–9. http://islamsci.mcgill.ca/RASI/BEA/Ibn_Abi_al-Shukr_BEA.htm. Saliba, George, 'An observational notebook of a thirteenth-century astronomer', in A History of Arabic Astronomy: Planetary Theories During the Golden Age of Islam (New York, 1994), pp. 163–76.

[113] Associated Press, 'Was supernova invisible in 1250?', Deseret News, 12 November, 1998. www.deseret.com/1998/11/12/19411899/was-supernova-invisible-in-1250

the 'puzzle' of the absence of any historical reference to it, even in China, was whether 'Mongol rule disrupted the work of astronomers'.

Even if Yahya Maghribi, whose name translated into 'John, the Westerner', and whose life was reportedly saved because he knew astrology when Mongols invaded Damascus,[114] had seen such an odd object in the sky before moving to the Mongol founded observartory in Maragha in north west Peria, he could not have marked it in his 'observational notes': this would have been not a symmetrical object like the planets and the stars he was so used to, or a 'meteor' of a falling or shooting kind, a 'tailed star', as comets were called; 'stars having tails', as spear, stick, bearded, hunched back, even the kind 'kaid' or deceit he had recorded.[115]

That 'Westerner' from Southern Spain, according to his name's ending, 'Andalusi', though not half as famous as many of his contemporaries, despite the diligence with which he treated any subject he touched, was still intimately connected to the sky. In the years following the 'exploding star' of 1250, detected centuries later, he moved from Damascus to the west of Baghdad, where he was at the service of an Ayyubid ruler[116] for some years, then to Maragha, north west of Isfahan, where he was to live for the rest of his life at one of the first observatories of its kind. Working in Damascus as a court astrologer, something Maghribi knew particularly well, had not stopped his patron from giving him the title of the 'Revival of Faith' after his earlier studies in Islamic Law; and it was under the expression 'Muhyi al-Din' of that given title that John became known to his later contemporaries. Among these was a figure named Nasir al-Din Tusi with the honourific title of 'Ustad al-Bashar', meaning 'Teacher of Mankind',[117] one who would stand above many others as the director of the celebrated observatory recently established in Maragha.[118] This was an observatory that Khwaja Nasir al-Din Tusi, named as such after his origin of 'Tus', would found and direct through the patronage of the recently invading Mongols, that paradoxically savage and supportive tribe from the Far East, who first ripped, then enriched the lands of Islam from the 1250s onwards. At Maragha, a dwarfed Maghribi was to be known for things beyond his carefully handled astronomical records, still known with the ancient term 'zij'.[119] He would

[114] Saliba, 'Observational notebook', p. 167; Comes, 'Ibn Abī al-Shukr … al-Maghribī', p. 548. http://islamsci.mcgill.ca/RASI/BEA/Ibn_Abi_al-Shukr_BEA.htm

[115] Kennedy, E. S., 'Comets in Islamic astronomy and astrology', Journal of Near Eastern Studies, 16, 1 (1957), pp. 44–51, p. 44: tailed stars (kawākib mudhanniba, kawākib dhawāt al-adhnāb); spear (naizak), stick (al-ʿaṣā), bearded (dhū al-laḥya), hunchback (dhū al-qaṣaʿa); p. 48: kaid, from Maghribī's Zīj.

[116] Saliba, 'Observational notebook', p. 167: Ayyubid 'Malik al-Nāṣir of Damascus (AD 1250–1260); Bosworth, Islamic Dynasties, p. 59.

[117] Nasr, S. H., 'Al-Ṭūsī, Muḥammad ibn Muḥammad ibn al-Ḥasan … Naṣīr al-Dīn, Dictionary of Scientific Biography (DSB), 13 (1976), pp. 508–14. Daiber, H. and Ragep, F. Jamil, 'Al-Ṭūsī, Naṣīr al-Dīn, Abū Djaʿfar Muḥammad … or Khwāja Naṣīr al-Dīn', Encyclopedia of Islam (EI²), 10, 175–6 (2000), pp. 746–52. Masoumi Hamadani, Hossein, 'Ustād-i Bashar' [Teacher of Mankind], in Pourjavady, N. and Vesel, Živa (eds), Naṣīr al-Dīn al-Ṭūsī: philosophe et savant de XIIIe siécle (Tehran, 2000), pp. 1–38. Ragep, F. Jamil, 'Ṭūsī: Abū Jaʿfar Muḥammad … Naṣīr al-Dīn', Biographical Encyclopedia of Astronomers (BEA) (2007), pp. 1153–5. http://islamsci.mcgill.ca/RASI/BEA/Tusi_BEA.htm

[118] Sayılı, Observatory in Islam; Varjavand, Kāvush-i raṣad-khānah-i Marāgha.

[119] King, David A. and Samso, Julio, 'Zīdj, in Islamic science an astronomical handbook with tables', Encyclopedia of Islam (EI²), 11 (2002), pp. 496–508.

skillfully construct mechanical clocks, known with the Persian term 'binkam',[120] after their assumed place of origin. The librarian of the Maragha Observatory knew him well enough to report on his learnings and leanings; but it was from a better known resident of the Maragha complex, Bar Hebraeus, that reports would come from Maghribi himself that his life had been spared by the Mongols 'because he was an astrologer'.[121]

Baghdad of the 1250s was still years before Maghribi would visit the city with one of Tusi's own sons. Before that trip, sometime after 1274, the year of Tusi's death, Maghribi was at the service of that observatory director in Maragha, a period consuming the pen of many modern historians: one would discover some of his astronomical records and publish his 'observational notebook' from a single surviving copy with his own new findings and datings;[122] another writing on 'comets in astronomy and astrology' would place Maghribi's astronomical tables next to several others in claiming 'none of it is based on observations', but 'passed along as a matter of tradition'.[123] Others would say that most astronomical theories within the Islamic 'scientific enterprise' had little to do with actual observations.[124] But at the time Maghribi was looking at the sky night after night, he could never have guessed that his records, let alone script and style, could once be such subjects of scrutiny. Neither could he imagine that the very separation of astronomy from astrology would one day be considered the mark of a new age. There had been attacks on astrology earlier from an author named Ibn Sina or Abu ʿAli Sina in the East, and Avicenna in the West,[125] and on the ranking of astrologers as 'complete', 'competent', 'dependent', and 'incomplete', from a much less known Al-Qabisi.[126] But being in the company of Nasir al-Din Tusi, who was no different in practicing astronomy through the appeals of astrology in royal courts, meant that astronomy and astrology were still hand in hand, and that masters of such subjects worked in both the astronomical tradition of Ptolemy's *Almagest* and astrological tradition of Ptomely's *Tetrabiblos*.[127] But more came with Tusi, the man at the head of not just the Maragha Observatory, but school of non-Ptolemaic astronomy all the way to the early modern Copernicus in Europe: besides correspondences of his

120 Archimedes, Kitāb Arishmīdis fī ʿamal al-binkāmāt, Hill, Donald R. (ed, tr) (On the Construction of Water-Clocks) (London, 1976).

121 Saliba, 'Observational notebook', p. 167; Comes, 'Ibn Abī al-Shukr' [Maghribi], pp. 548–9, p. 548. https://islamsci.mcgill.ca/RASI/BEA/Ibn_Abi_al-Shukr_BEA.htm. Librarian: Melville, Charles, 'Ebn al-Fowaṭī, Kamāl al-Dīn ʿAbd al-Razzāq' Encyclopedia Iranica (EIr), 8, 1 (1997), pp. 25–6, p. 25: www.iranicaonline.org/articles/ebn-al-fowati

122 Saliba, 'Observational notebook', p. 167.

123 Kennedy, 'Comets in Islamic astronomy and astrology'.

124 Sabra, A. I., 'The scientific enterprise: Islamic contributions to the development of science', in Bernard Lewis (ed), The World of Islam: Faith, People, Culture (London, 1976), pp. 181–99.

125 Goitchon, A. M., 'Ibn Sīnā', Encyclopedia of Islam (EI^2), 3, 55–6 (1969), pp. 941–7; Anawati, G. C., 'Ibn Sīnā, Abū ʿAlī al-Ḥusayn Ibn ʿAbdallāh, also known as Avicenna', Dictionary of Scientific Biography (DSB), 15 (Supp. I) (1978), pp. 494–8. Gutas, Dimitri, 'Avicenna ii. Biography', Encyclopedia Iranica (EIr), 3, 1 (1987), pp. 67–70. www.iranicaonline.org/articles/avicenna-ii. Ragep, 'Ibn Sīnā'. http://islamsci.mcgill.ca/RASI/BEA/Ibn_Sina_BEA.htm

126 Burnett, Charles, 'The certitude of astrology: The scientific methodology of Al-Qābisī and Abū Maʿshar', Early Science and Medicine, 7, 3 (2002), pp. 198–213.

127 Burnett, 'Certitude of astrology', pp. 198–200: Astrology according to Ptolemy's Tetrabiblos.

models – figures, especially letters – to their much later Latin counterparts,[128] and comparable arguments and references to comets, Tusi's physically oriented mathematical models and a novel rolling device later known as the 'Tusi Couple'[129] were known enough to the Polish astronomer for the names 'Tusi' and 'Copernicus' to be joined in more than one modern title.[130] Tusi's differently worded 'mathematical' and 'physical' methods of proof, the 'That' and 'Why' proofs,[131] proving that something is, and why it is, were no less important.

The cosmological problems themselves went as far back as when watchful eyes on both the sky and Earth were first misled by appearances. Eyes turned to the sky told such 'watchers' that everything including the rising and setting of the Moon, Sun and the stars revolved around them; and eyes fixed on the Earth told them that it was around a 'standing' Earth that all these circled. Eyes on the sky also told them that what they 'saw' as motion in the sky periodically involved looped and reversed patterns; and eyes on the Earth showed that if something was thrown upwards it would not come to the right or left, but only the centre. But long before up and down looks would yield misleading appearances, there was talk of 'accounting for' those appearances. Such phrases went as far back as the time of Plato from ancient Greece, through other testimonies of Greek antiquity:[132] Plato is reported as formulating 'what circular motions, uniform and perfectly regular, are to be admitted to save the appearances presented by the planets'; his disciple, Aristotle, responding with an Earth-centred model to conform to visible phenomena with reference to a stationary Earth; and later Ptolemy,[133] elaborating that model to account for visible paths and irregularities through multiple components with technical expressions like 'epicycle's, 'deferent's, 'eccentric's, and 'equant's: an epicycle being the circular path of a planet's motion; a deferent, the carrier of the centre of epicyclic paths; an eccentric the point about which circular motion is uniform; and an equant, a point with reference to which 'retrograde' motion is also uniform. Successive responses to the challenge of 'saving appearances' throughout Greek, Islamic and European lands would then yield model after model, for both the 'lower' planets, Moon, Mercury, Venus and Sun, and 'upper' planets, Mars, Jupiter, and Saturn. In the case of Islamic lands, the models had so many components comparable to those later proposed by Copernicus, the Polish scholar of early Modern

128 Hartner, Willy, 'Naṣīr al-Dīn al-Ṭūsī's lunar theory, Physis, 11 (1969), pp. 287–304.

129 Ragep, Ṭūsī's Memoir on Astronomy; Ragep, F. Jamil, 'The Persian context of the Ṭūsī Couple', in Pourjavady, N. and Vesel, Ž. (eds), Naṣīr al-Dīn al-Ṭūsī: Philosophe et savant du XIIIe siècle, (Tehran, 2000), pp. 113–30.

130 Ragep, F. Jamil, 'Ṭūsī and Copernicus: The Earth's motion in context', Science in Context, 14, 1/2 (2001), pp. 145–63; Barker, Peter and Heidarzadeh, Tofigh, 'Copernicus, the Ṭūsī Couple and East-West exchange in the fifteenth century' in Granada, Miguel Á, Boner, Patrick J. and Tessicini, Dario (eds), Unifying Heaven and Earth: Essays in the History of Early Modern Cosmology (Barcelona, 2016), pp. 19–57.

131 Ragep, Ṭūsī's Memoir on Astronomy, Vol. 1, p. 39; Vol. 2, pp. 386–7.

132 Duhem, Pierre, To Save the Phenomena: An Essay on the Idea of Physical Theory from Plato to Galileo, Edmund Dolan and Chaninah Maschler (tr) (Chicago, 1969, 1985).

133 Owen, G. E. L., 'Aristotle', Dictionary of Scientific Biography (DSB), 1 (1970), pp. 250–8. Aristotle, On the Heavens, W. K. C. Guthrie (tr) (Loeb Classical Library, No. 6) (Cambridge, MA, 1971). Toomer, Gerald J., 'Ptolemy (Claudius Ptolemaeus)', Dictionary of Scientific Biography (DSB), 11 (1970), pp. 186–206; Ptolemy's Almagest (New York, 1984).

Europe, that they would sometimes be described by modern expressions as clever as 'pre-Copernican Copernican models'.[134] Many such models in Arabic and Persian were directed against violations of the Aristotelian principle of uniform and circular celestial motions, and towards Ptolemaic reforms. They were 'non-Ptolemaic' in the sense of challenging Ptolemaic models that produced irregular motions: these would begin with Ibn al-Haytham in an Arabic work titled *Doubts on Ptolemy*,[135] with alternative models presented by Nasir al-Din Tusi from the 13th century, first in Persian, then Arabic,[136] followed by scholars in and beyond the 'Maragha School'. Treatments from Western Islamic lands came mostly from 11th- to 12th-century Andalusia[137] through authors ranging from Ibn Rushd, Latinised as Averroes, to Bitruji, Latinised as Alpetragius. From all these the name of Yahya Maqribi would often be left out as a Western resident in Eastern Maragha, even if he had produced major alternative models. The story of 'late medieval planetary theory'[138] would itself be retold by a new generation of modern scholars as Copernicus being 'influenced by this late tradition of non-Ptolemaic astronomy' ouside of heliocentrism, and 'the balance of evidence' being 'decisively on the side of transmission'.[139] Soon enough, more missing links in transmission were to emerge to connect more dots, some by the very same scholars placing the first few on the open-ended skies of evolving knowledge.

2.6 *A Persian City with a 'Falconer'*

It was May circa 1450, and a new generation of scholars from both the Eastern and Western parts of Islamic lands were assuming their own roles in transmission, this time not from the north east of Baghdad, as in the Maragha of post-1250s, but from the north east of Isfahan, in the much later scholarly sanctuary of pre-1450s Samarqand.

Around the year 1450, a man named Qushji,[140] meaning 'Falconer' after the profession of his father in the high-profiled court of Samarqand, could no longer stay

[134] Roberts, Victor, 'The solar and lunar theory of Ibn al-Shāṭir: A pre-Copernican Copernican model', Isis, 48 (1957), pp. 428–32.

[135] Sabra, 'Ibn al-Haytham'; Ibn al-Haytham, al-Ḥasan, Ibn Al-Haytham: Al-Shukūk ʿala Baṭlamyūs (Dubitationes in Ptolemaeum), Sabra, A. I. and Shehaby, N. (eds) (Aporias Against Ptolemy) (Cairo, 1971); Langermann, Y. Tzvi , 'Ibn al-Haytham: Abū ʿAlī al-Ḥasan ibn al-Ḥasan', Biographical Encyclopedia of Astronomers (BEA), pp. 556–7. http://islamsci.mcgill.ca/RASI/BEA/Ibn_al-Haytham_BEA.htm

[136] Ṭūsī, Naṣīr al-Dīn, Risālah-i Muʿīnīyah, Danish-Pazhuh, Muhammad-Taqi (ed) (Tehran, 1956); Al-Tadhkira, Ragep (ed, tr), Ṭūsī's Memoir on Astronomy.

[137] Sabra, A. I., 'The Andalusian revolt against Ptolemaic astronomy: Averroes and al-Bitrūjī', in Mendelsohn, Everett (ed), Transformation and Tradition in the Sciences: Essays in Honor of I. Bernard Cohen (Cambridge, 1984; Aldershot, 1994), pp. 133–53.

[138] Kennedy, E. S., 'Late medieval planetary theory', Isis, 57, 3 (1966), pp. 365–78.

[139] Ragep, 'Ṭūsī and Copernicus', pp. 145–6; and Barker and Heidarzadeh, 'East-West exchange', pp. 54–7, respectively.

[140] Adivar, A. Adnan, 'ʿAlī ibn Muḥammad al-Kūshdjī', Encyclopedia of Islam (EI^2), 1 (1960), p. 393; Heidarzadeh, Tofigh, The Astronomical Works of ʿAlī Qūshjī (unpublished MA Thesis, Istanbul University, 1997); Fazlıoğlu, İhsan, 'Qūshjī: Abū al-Qāsim ʿAlāʾ al-Dīn ʿAlī ibn Muḥammad Qushči-zāde', Biographical Encyclopedia of Astronomers (BEA) (2007), pp. 946–8. http://islamsci.mcgill.ca/RASI/BEA/Qushji_BEA.htm

there, much less serve as the director of the grand complex housing its school and observatory. This was the first year of the assassination of the illustrious founder of the Samarqand School, Prince Ulug Beg,[141] the learned grandson of the Timurid ruler Tamerlane to whom Qushji was particularly close. A mathematician and astronomer, and a forerunner to Copernicus, increasingly more studied by modern historians,[142] young Qushji was raised with much more privilege than that granted to a servant's son at a royal institution; and he was especially 'envied' as one of the favourite protégés of Ulug Beg, that student-prince of Samarqand turned 'world-conqueror',[143] in the short course of his reign. During the two years when Ulugh Beg had ruled Samarqand as a Timurid Sultan before being killed reportedly on the order of his son, that 'Great Prince' – as 'Ulugh Beg' meant in Turkish – had come to refer to Qushji as his own son.[144]

Qushji's given name was ʿAli, like Prophet Muhammad's son in law, cousin, foster-brother, and fourth succeeding Caliph,[145] a first name already charged as the first perceived successor to the Prophet of Islam by his growing followers. ʿAli Qushji's life was, by contrast, not on the 'path' of politics, one literally called 'Shiʿa' as a sectarian 'path' naming followers of ʿAli ibn Abi Talib, holding him as the first 'Shiʿi Imam', not the fourth Caliph after three others. The life of the much later ʿAli, a leader with a far different form and number of followers, was on quite a different path: this was not only the path of science, but one 'freeing' itself from established traditions to the point of entertaining the 'possibility' of Earth in motion,[146] in a crucial step both within and beyond Islamic lands. So outstanding would ʿAli Qushji's profile be in his own time and place that a local historian, born about twenty years after his death, would devote more pages to him than most of the other five hundred odd names in his *Scholars of the Ottoman Empire*.[147] Through these and other historical sources, Qushji's footsteps could be followed much later in time, starting from Samarqand, and a trip to Kerman

141 Kary-Niiazov, T. N., 'Ulugh Beg', Dictionary of Scientific Biography (DSB), 13 (1976), pp. 535–7; Manz, Beatrice F., 'Ulugh Beg', Encyclopedia of Islam (EI^2), 10 (2000), pp. 812–14; van Dalen, Benno, 'Ulugh Beg: Muḥammad Ṭaraghāy ibn Shāhrukh ibn Tīmūr', Biographical Encyclopedia of Astronomers (BEA), pp. 1157–9. http://islamsci.mcgill.ca/RASI/BEA/Ulugh_Beg_BEA.htm

142 Saliba, George, 'Qushjī's [sic] reform of the Ptolemaic Model for Mercury', Arabic Sciences and Philosophy, 3 (1993), pp. 161–203. Ragep, F. Jamil, 'Freeing astronomy from philosophy: An aspect of Islamic influence on science', Osiris, Science in Theistic Contexts: Cognitive Dimensions, 16 (2001), pp. 49–71; 'ʿAlī Qushjī [sic] and Regiomontanus: Eccentric transformations and Copernican revolutions', Journal for the History of Astronomy, 36 (2005), pp. 359–71; 'Copernicus and his Islamic predecessors: Some historical remarks', History of Science, 45 (2007), pp. 65–81. Barker and Heidarzadeh, 'East-West exchange'.

143 'World-Conqueror' (kishvar-gushā, as land conquerer), is used by Kāshī for Ulugh Beg: Bagheri, Az Samarqand bih Kāshān, p. 38; 'Newly found letter', pp. 241–56, 243–4; 'envy' (ḥasad) is used by Qūshjī: Saliba, 'Qushjī's reform', pp. 164–5.

144 van Dalen, 'Ulugh Beg', pp. 1157–9: Great Prince (Ulugh Beg); names his accused son. Fazlıoğlu, 'Qūshjī', p. 946: son/offspring (ferzend).

145 Bosworth, Islamic Dynasties, pp. 3–4.

146 Ragep, 'Freeing astronomy', pp. 49–71.

147 Ṭāshkubrī-zādah, Aḥmad ibn Muṣṭafa, Al-Shaqāʾiq al-nuʿmānīyah fī ʿulamāʾ al-Dawlat al-ʿUthmānīyah, Furat, Ahmet Suphi (ed) (Istanbūl, 1985); Rosenfeld and Ihsanoğlu, Mathematicians, Astronomers, and Other Scholars, p. 324: 'Flowers of Anemones for the Scientists of the Ottoman Empire'.

where he reportedly drafted his important *Commentary on the Epitome of Belief* of Nasir al-Din Tusi;[148] next a pilgrimage to Mecca after the loss of his beloved patron while still mourning;[149] a residence in Herat, where he may have completed that *Epitome*; then a stay in Tabriz, where after the defeat of his patron in Herat, the Timurid Sultan Abu Saʿid, he would be welcomed by a ruler called Uzun Hasan; and finally, after a mediation between the latter and the Ottoman Sultan Mehmet, titled the 'Fatih', meaning 'Conqueror', a brief but fateful residency in Istanbul, where he would move with an entourage of relatives and students, become director of the Ayasofya Madrasa, and be buried in that city with a long legacy.[150] Some historical puzzles about Qushji's works and contributions were to be later teased out of what could be considered period clues, like the puzzle of the actual content versus reported title of a notable work dedicated to Ulugh Beg;[151] or his actual versus assumed inputs in a *Zij* named after that patron, since he critiqued and corrected aspects of it in his own later *Commentary* on that work.[152]

Constantinople of post-1453, when the city had fallen to the conquering Ottoman Empire, would be the place where these and other works by Qushji were to crown several libraries of the newly renamed Istanbul, all at a time when science was just starting to thrive in Western Europe. A single work by Qushji, a treatise on the science of 'hayʾa', meaning astronomical configurations, was not only to circulate in Qushji's own original versions in Persian and Arabic, but in later translations into Turkish and Sanskrit.[153] The worldwide manuscripts of the later works of that junior student in Samarqand, rising to the status of a senior observation director in Istanbul, would still not reach Europe in the way the *Star Catalogue* of Ulugh Beg would in European records as major as London's Royal Astronomical Society.[154] But the name of Qushji himself would increasingly turn up in one modern study after another for scientific breakthroughs, even if not with reference to 'The Copernican Revolution':[155] one study would highlight Qushji's 'reform of astronomy' as an example of breaks with the past; another of breaks with Aristotelian Physics and observational deceptions like a

[148] Ṭāshkubrī-zādah, Al-Shaqāʾiq, p. 159–60: drafted 'sawwada': made black; Adivar, 'al-Kūshdjī', p. 393; Saliba, 'Qushjī's Reform', 164–5; Fazlıoğlu, 'Qūshjī', p. 946, cite the work, and the city of Kerman.

[149] Ṭāshkubrī-zādah, Al-Shaqāʾiq, p. 160. Browne, Literary History, Vol. 3, p. 407.

[150] Ṭāshkubrī-zādah, Al-Shaqāʾiq, p. 161; Fazlıoğlu, 'Qūshjī', p. 946: entourage, positions, burried in Istanbul. Barker and Heidarzadeh, 'East-West exchange', p. 51: Tabriz.

[151] Adivar, 'al-Kūshdjī', p. 393: cites it as a Moon treatise, 'Ḥall Ashkāl-Qamar'; Saliba, 'Qushjī's reform', p. 163: a Mercury treatise (Moon title: 'possibly false' or not 'located').

[152] Fazlıoğlu, 'Qūshjī', p. 946 treats Zīj Ulugh Beg as a Qūshjī work, but cites his criticisms of mistakes in it in his own Sharḥ-i Zīj Ulug Beg. Rosenfeld and Ihsanoğlu, Mathematicians, Astronomers, and Other Scholars, p. 287.

[153] Qūshjī, ʿAlī, Risāla dar ʿilm al-hayʾa (Persian): Rapep, 'Freeing astronomy', p. 62; Fazlıoğlu, 'Qūshjī', p. 948: Arabic and Turkish versions, Arabic made by Qūshjī from Persian; Sanskrit: Pingree, David, 'Indian reception of Muslim versions of Ptolemaic astronomy', in Ragep, F. Jamil and Ragep, Sally P., with Livesey, S. (eds), Tradition, Transmission, Transformation (Leiden, 2000), pp. 471–85, p. 474.

[154] Baily, Francis, The Catalogues of Ptolemy, Ulugh Beg, Tycho Brahe, Halley, Hevelius: Memoirs of the Royal Astronomical Society, Vol. 3 (London, 1843), pp. 19–28: Preface to Ulugh Beg's Catalogue; Knobel, Edward Ball, Ulugh Beg's Catalogue of Stars: Revised from all Persian Manuscripts Existing in Great Britain, with a Vocabulary of Persian and Arabic Words (Washington, 1917).

[155] Kuhn, Thomas S., The Copernican Revolution: Planetary Astronomy in the Development of Western Thought (Cambridge, MA, 1957).

stationary Earth; another breaks from Ptolemaic astronomy and its coincidence with pre-Copernican models; and yet another with 'East-West exchanges' to dispense with 'outmoded Eurocentric viewpoints' and 'lone genius models'.[156] Among modern period reevaluations,[157] were other studies, some involving Qushji with critical texts and figures and comparative Arabic-Latin models to establish knowledge transfers; others, new clues for exact times, places and routes of such East-West transmissions, rather than independent developments.[158]

In the opening years of the 1450s, during the first phase of his unfamiliar life moving from patron to patron following the death of the 'Great' Ulugh Beg, ʿAli, the falconer, was working in Herat not far away from Samarqand in what was by then a 'Greater Persia'. He was struggling with a commentary he had long been drafting on Tusi's *Epitome of Belief* from two centuries before, and mindful of the religious context of the work, and the needs of his own time, he was trying to give that work enough of a twist to make it more than yet another commentary. He was cleverly including examples of heavenly phenomena 'in the manner in which they are observed' to win the attention of his audience, such as the 'sighting of the full and crescent shapes' of the Moon to state that 'the light of the Moon is derived from the Sun', or that 'a lunar eclipse occurs because of the interposition of the Earth between the Sun and Moon, and that a solar eclipse occurs because of the interposition of the Moon between the Sun and the eye'. While leaving room for the Almighty to have the power to intervene in these and other matters, giving the vivid example of 'God darkening the Moon without the Earth's shadow causing an Eclipse', he was arguing for human experiences to the contrary, and of the likelihood of the rule of 'ordinary' and 'regular' patterns, over extraordinary and forced matters: above all, he was crafting his most critical point in a way that the resulting argument would go down much later in time as a breakthrough that was not only 'freeing' astronomy as a discipline, but relieving any 'provisional' astronomical premise from being the only possible one.[159] Qushji was aware of breaking ground against Aristotelian physics, and its reliance on the observational premise of a stationary Earth. But the critical parts of his arguments amounted to exploring reasonable possibilities, including those like a moving Earth, however unfamiliar to sense. He was especially aware that he needed a much fuller bag of tricks than all those he had pulled before in purely astronomical works. In that subject, he felt such ease with the technical details that he had even opened praises of his Lord and Patron in astronomical language: in his novel treatise dedicated to Ulugh Beg, the 'Lord' was a

156 Respectively: Saliba, 'Qushjī's reform'; Ragep, 'Freeing astronomy'; Ragep, 'ʿAlī Qushjī and Regiomontanus'; Barker and Heidarzadeh, 'East-West exchange'.

157 Period reevaluations include: Ragep, 'Copernicus and his Islamic predecessors'; Saliba, George, Islamic Science and the Making of the European Renaissance (Cambridge, MA, 2007); Morrison, Robert, 'A scholarly intermediary between the Ottoman Empire and Renaissance Europe', Isis, 105 (2014), pp. 32–57; and Ragep, F. Jamil, 'From Tūn to Torun: The twists and turns of the Ṭūsī Couple', in Feldhay, Rivka and Ragep, F. Jamil (eds), Before Copernicus: The Cultures and Contexts of Scientific Learning in the Fifteenth Century (Montreal, 2017), pp. 161–97.

158 Saliba, 'Qushjī's Reform', text: pp. 187–203, translation, pp. 168–77; Ragep, 'Freeing Astronomy', text and translation: pp. 66–71; 'ʿAlī Qushjī and Regiomontanus', text, pp. 366–8; Arabic and Latin figures, p. 362; Barker and Heidarzadeh, 'East-West exchange', p. 54: possible 'Persia-Venice' route.

159 Ragep, 'Freeing astronomy, p. 65: 'God darkening the Moon', includes text.

'director' in the movement of the planets, as well as the 'adjuster of their motion', both technical expressions for important spheres within ancient heavenly models; the Patron's throne had then been placed 'above the northern stars', and he himself, at the centre of the circle of the learned men; and at least one poem in his dedication had placed 'the learned swarm around his majestic heights, just as the pilgrims do around the House of God'.[160] The clever use of such language would project a more balanced position within both scientific and religious circles of Qushji's specific setting. Echoes of his life and times, ups and downs, friends and foes, thoughts and words, and lines of verse, would also bounce loudly into the future.

The 'most learned of recent scholars',[161] as Qushji was known to people of his own age, had done his most important work by the 1450s, something which went far beyond his own time and place: He had shown not only that Ptolemy, the Greek master of the Earth-centred universe more than a thousand years before him, was wrong; he was walking in the same direction as 'Copernicus', the Polish father of the Sun-centred universe about a hundred years later, who could hardly be seen as making his other dramatic switches without clues from predecessors from further East. Still, with the much later question of why the 'Scientific Revolution' that was agreed Copernicus fathered in the West did not happen in the East, Qushji would be perceived not so much as a 'precursor of Copernicus', but 'predecessor of Osiander',[162] whose preface to Copernicus's book would use the language of 'hypothesis': explicit about 'Ptolemy being wrong', Qushji had proposed the Earth's motion as a 'possibility', arguing just as Osianders's Preface to Copernicus's *De Revolutionibus* that assumptions can freely be made to 'save the phenomena', without these being the only possible ones. The name of Qushji would still not be raised to the level of Copernicus because the revolutionary model of a Sun-centred universe would remain unexpressed by him: by raising questions of 'possibility' at all, Qushji's provisional premises could be compared to Osiander's 'hypotheses'; but in not making the further leap of placing the Sun at the centre of the universe, he could hardly reach the status of a Copernicus.

The case of Qushji, much more than his name, were still to be central to a later-posed 'why not' question, regarding why the European Scientific Revolution did not take place in a different time and place, one like Qushji's time in a pre-modern age, and his place, in pre-modern Islamic lands. Later studies would adjust misguided expressions of 'decline' in pre-modern times, and non-western places, from a refutation of a 'universal scientific decline' through texts such as Qushji's Mercury model, to a position with reference to his other works, and of 'science in Islam', being far from 'steep decline'.[163] But not only did Qushji remain unaware of the importance of his own legacy, and its soon recognisable links to Europe; his name and that of his predecessors

[160] Saliba, 'Qushjī's reform', p. 171: poem.

[161] Kheirandish, Elaheh (ed, tr, comm), The Arabic Version of Euclid's Optics: Kitāb Uqlīdis fī Ikhtilāf al-manāẓir, 2 vols., in Toomer, Gerald J. (ed), Sources in the History of Mathematics and Physical Sciences Vol. 16 (New York, 1999), Vol. 1, p. l; Vol. 2, p. lviii, n. 37: 'afḍal al-muta᾽akhirīn' used for Qūshjī.

[162] Ragep, 'Freeing astronomy', 63: 'Instead of being the precursor of Copernicus, is he [Qūshjī], rather the predecessor of Osiander . . .?'

[163] Saliba, 'Qushjī's reform', p. 164; Ragep, 'Freeing astronomy', p. 64.

like Tusi would remain unfamiliar, if not to their immediate successors, to those working centuries later, when Western names would typically pop up without their Eastern counterparts.

A good 500 years after Qushji, and 700 years after Tusi, an essay would be written with the words 'Something old, something new, and something borrowed . . .'[164] in its title, next to 'Copernicus, Galileo, and Newton', with statements like it was 'lucky for Copernicus (and lucky for us) that Ptolemy followed the solar and not the lunar calendar year'; how 'lucky it was for Galileo (and for us) to hear about the existence of the spyglass', namely telescope, and with Newton there was 'a new sound, never before produced upon this planet'. But it was as if the words 'Something missing' were themselves missing from the title and body of an essay where names as largely printed and as loudly echoed as Copernicus, Galileo and Newton stood next to Plato, Aristotle and Ptolemy, while 'missing' many 'giants' of Islamic and European lands in between. 'Giant' was the very word used by Newton in the context of an expression that was itself 'something borrowed': when Isaac Newton would write that 'if I have seen farther, it is by standing on the shoulders of giants',[165] he was himself using a repeated expression whose earlier form 'A dwarf standing on the shoulders of a giant may see farther than the giant himself' would reach the twentieth and twenty first century with addendums: a book titled *On the Shoulders of Giants*[166] by historians and scientists would follow the history and associations of that 'aphorism' beyond Newton and astronomy; a historian reporting Newton's biographer about Newton's small beginning and grand conclusion, with reference to that aphorism; and a scientist covering other celebrated names from Copernicus to Einstein, citing Newton's use of that aphorism in optics, rather than mechanics.[167]

The case of the earliest of the scientific 'giants' covered there, Copernicus, whose shoulder Newton would be said to not only stand on, but 'leap' from, was different. From Copernicus's *Commentariolus*, to his later *De Revolutionibus*, the progression was slow: the first, a *Commentary on Motion of the Heavens* with components of his 'revolutionary' models not officially published during his lifetime; and the second, on the *Revolution of the Heavenly Spheres*, withheld from publishing for even longer:[168] but the three most revolutionary components of their model, namely placing the centre of

164 Clark, Joseph T., 'Something old, something new, something borrowed, something blue: Copernicus, Galileo, and Newton', in Mendehlsohn, E. (ed), Transformation and Tradition in the Sciences (Cambridge, New York, 1984).

165 Newton, Isaac, 'Letter to Robert Hooke, 5 February 1675-6: The Newton Project, Oxford University: Brewster, David, Memoirs of the life, writings, and discoveries of Sir Isaac Newton, Vol. 1 (Edinburgh, 1855). www.newtonproject.ox.ac.uk/view/texts/normalized/OTHE00101. Merton, On the Shoulders of Giants: expression's origin.

166 Merton, On the Shoulders of Giants; Hawking, Stephen, On the Shoulders of Giants: The Great Works of Physics and Astronomy (Philadelphia, 2002).

167 Merton, On the Shoulders of Giants, pp. 9–10, cites Newton's biographer, David Brewster on Newton's 'diminutive size' as an infant; Hawking, On the Shoulders of Giants, p. ix: in using that aphorism 'Newton was referring to his discoveries in optics . . . rather than gravity or laws of motion'.

168 Hawking, On the Shoulders of Giants, p. xiii: 'Sometimes as with Copernicus and Einstein, we have to make a leap to a new world picture'; pp. 3–5: composition years of the two Copernican works in 1514 and 1530, the latter's publication in 154; also quotes.

the Earth not at the centre of the universe but 'at the centre of the Moon's orbit', placing the Sun, not at, but near, the centre of the universe, and getting the Earth 'revolving around the Sun . . . like any other planet', would all be giant 'leap's from Aristotelian and Ptolemaic models. Some of Copernicus's non-Ptolemaic models were to have identifiable overlaps with his 'Islamic predecessors',[169] some of whom he would name himself. But the name of 'Ali Qushji, would not always be among them for any comparable cases, in spite of their common admission of 'possibilities' like the Earth's motion. A puzzle for future analysts would be why someone like Qushji would not make any 'leap's to one of the three major components of Copernicus's 'revolutionary' model. Such puzzles could generate partial explanations, from the absence of Copernicus's astronomical instruments and observation tower and Galileo's self-made 'telescope',[170] to the times of Qushji and the disruptions and dispersions of scientific communities as compared to the much tighter European cases. Over time, studies on sciences in Islamic and European lands would increasingly change the traditional image of a century or millennium as having linear highs and lows, or ups and downs. The binary black and white images of these and other historical matters would, in turn, assume first grey borders, then colours, and eventually, a spectrum of shades.

[169] Ragep, 'Copernicus and his Islamic predecessors', p. 77, n. 1; names cited: 'al-Battānī, al-Biṭrūjī, al-Zarqāllu, Ibn Rushd, and Thābit ibn Qurrā'.

[170] Hawking, On the Shoulders of Giants, p. 3: 'observation tower' built by Copernicus and 'astronomical instruments' other than telescope, to observe, the sun, moon, and stars'; Cohen, 'What Galileo "Saw"', p. 188: Newton on 'large' and 'ancient' spots 'not been seen by anyone before'.

3

Round and Square

100 Years: A Crescent Phase (ca. 750–850)

Cast your eyes from all sides like a sun towards Baghdad,
Then rise like heaven around it until you see it.

Hamdallah Mustuwfi, *Nuzhat al-qulub* (ca. 1340),
English translation: Elaheh Kheirandish[1]

'The revolving sphere is the father, and the pillars of heaven the mother,
But Isphahan, the child, is better than the parent . . .'

Hakim Shifa'i (d. ca. 1627), *Divan*, English adaptation: Elaheh Kheirandish[2]

3.1 An Old Manuscript with a Microfilm

It was June 2007, and a microfilm of the manuscript of the *Dialogue* of Baghdad and Isfahan, ordered by a reader at London's British Library as a black and white copy of a coloured, gold-illuminated manuscript, had been sitting in an envelope mailed by post to Cambridge University Library according to the instructions on the order slip. The microfilm, which was the top reproduction technology of the time, was to be kept there for pick up by a young visiting student to look up sources related to his 'Dialogue' project in that library's own collection of rich oriental manuscripts. Cambridge was a natural place for oriental manuscripts related to that assigned project, not least for those like the *Dialogue* manuscript itself filled with a heavy dose of Persian intervowen with Arabic. It was to Cambridge that the cataloguer of the assigned *Dialogue*, the Swiss born Charles Rieu, had moved after the late 1800s upon leaving his position as the 'keeper of oriental manuscripts' at London's British Library; and it was in Cambridge

1 *'Hamih sar dīdih chu khurshīd shu an-dar Baghdād,*
Va-ān gah-ash ham-chu falak gird bar-ā tā bīnī . . .'
Mustuwfī, Nuzhat al-qulūb, quoting Athīr al-Dīn al-Umānī (ed), pp. 37–8; Le Strange, G. (ed), The Geographical Part of the Nuzhat-al-qulub (Gibb Memorial Series) (Leyden, 1915–1919): '*tharāyā* [*thurayyā? = Pleaides*] *bīnī*', quoted in Bayani, Tisfūn va Baghdād, p. 279; Kheirandish, Elaheh (tr, excerpt); Browne, Literary History, vol. 3, pp. 87–8: author.

2 *Gardūn pidar ast u mādar arkān, Farzand bih az pidar Siphāhān . . .:*
Ḥakīm Shifā'ī: Browne, Literary History, vol. 4, p. 256: 'd. 1627'; Dīvān, quoted in Belfour, Life of Hazin, pp. 43–5; Kheirandish, Elaheh (tr, excerpt).

that had long resided the successor of Rieu's chair as Professor, the distinguished Edward Browne, a British medical student turned orientalist, and author of Rieu's obituary,[3] one whose tilt towards all things Persian was to live long after his own life. This was not merely reflected by titles of masterpiece volumes modestly reduced to *A Literary History of Persia* or *A Year Amongst the Persians*,[4] but through local landmarks of a country called 'Iran' in modern times awarding their author the Persian order of the Lion and the Sun, and honouring him through statues and street names.[5]

Cambridge University was itself an old host of many things Persian in particular. Besides Browne's *Catalogue of Persian Manuscripts*[6] next to many others, whoever else who was anyone in Persian studies either came from or went to Cambridge, one way or another. The vibrant network of the subject in that university from a century before included many famous names: Charles Storey, the British scholar, whose classic volumes of *Persian Literature*[7] went beyond 'literature'; Vladimir Minorsky, the Russian Persianist and Professor in London retiring in Cambridge; A. J. Arberry, the Professor of Persian literature and poetry as well as Arabic; Laurence Lockhart, the author of *Persian Cities* and an educational liaison; and Peter Avery, the scholar with his own multiple Persian associations: all such names were to be covered in a thorough piece on 'Iranian Studies in Britain', qualified as research 'built on, and in response to' work including that by 'foreign scholars' residing in Britain.[8] Experts of a slightly later time included the author of that piece, sharing the first name, Charles, with Rieu and Storey, standing tall as a scholar resurrecting Persian studies through a monumental 'Shahnama Project' and emerging 'Center';[9] then, a literary specialist acting as the research director of the 'Shahnama Center', authoring pieces from a 'poetic debate' between an 'Arab and a Persian' to the 'origins' of the literary genre,[10] with manuscripts in Cambridge itself; and still later in time, another scholar with contributions to directing and redirecting paths to a wider 'Persianate World'.[11]

3 Browne, 'Obituary notices'; Wickens, G. Michael. 'Browne, Edward Granville', Encyclopedia Iranica (EIr), 4, 5 (1989), pp. 483–8. www.iranicaonline.org/articles/browne-edward-granville

4 Browne, Literary History, 4 vols.; Browne, Edward G., A Year Amongst the Persians: Impressions as to the Life, Character, and Thought of the People of Persia, Received During Twelve Months' Residence in that Country in the Years 1887–1888 (London, 1893).

5 Wickens, 'Browne, Edward Granville'; Bosworth, C. Edmund, 'E. G. Browne and his "A Year Amongst the Persians"', Iran, 33 (1995), pp. 115–22, p. 121: Browne's statue in Tehran 'spared'.

6 Browne, Edward G., A Catalogue of the Persian Manuscripts in the Library of the University of Cambridge (Cambridge, 1896).

7 Storey, Charles Ambrose. Persian Literature: A Bio-Bibliographical Survey, Vol. 2, Part 1: A. Mathematics, B. Weights and Measures, C. Astronomy and Astrology, D. Geography (London, 1927).

8 Melville, Charles, 'Great Britain x. Iranian Studies in Britain, the Islamic period', Encyclopedia Iranica (EIr), 11, 3, (2002), pp. 260–7. www.iranicaonline.org/articles/great-britain-x

9 Melville, Charles, Director: Project Shahnama: first phase: 1999 to 2004. http://shahnama.lib.cam.ac.uk/. Shahnama Centre for Persian Studies' launched at Pembroke College, Cambridge University, 26 May 2014: Iranian studies beyond the *Shahnama*. http://persian.pem.cam.ac.uk/projects/

10 [Abdullaeva-] Melville, Firuza, Research Director: Shahnameh Centre for Persian Studies, Cambridge University. Author of 'The Bodleian manuscript of Asadī Ṭūsī's Munāẓara between an Arab and a Persian: Its place in the transition from ancient debate to classical panegyric', Iran, 47 (2009), pp. 69–95; and 'The origins of the Munāẓara genre in new Persian literature', in Seyed Gohrab, A. A. (ed), Metaphor and Imagery in Persian Poetry (Leiden, Boston, 2012), pp. 249–73.

11 Ashraf, Assef, 'Pathways to the Persianate', in Abbas Amanat and Assef Ashraf (eds), The Persianate World: Rethinking a Shared Sphere (Leiden, 2019).

An upcoming obituary for the distinguished 'orientalist' Avery,[12] in the engaging pen of his once-student and later director of Shahnama Center for Persian Studies, was a good indicator of what Cambridge University meant to anything Persian. This was a place well fit for a 'dialogue' between a Persian and Arab city, a text whose microfilm was sitting in Cambridge University Library that day with its own uneven weight of Persian over Arabic. The Avery obituary would read that Cambridge 'received a stream of visitors' in the elegant rooms referred to by that deceased Persianist as 'a corner of Iran'; that 'he was often moved to tears in discussing Iran's history and the beauties of her poetry'. Before the occasional notes of that obituary and its author's earlier 'Iranian Studies in Britain', such 'source' studies had come from the other Cambridge with similar switches between 'Iranian' and 'Persian' for their subject: a rich article titled 'Sources for the Study of Iran', had published major sources from 'old Iranian subjects' to 'Iranian area studies'; in the same year, a book titled *Persia* by a senior specialist, had covered sources with 'categories not usually found in bibliographies';[13] and by the turn of the century, there would be not only more publications and departments, but also organizations and foundations, as well as centres and programs,[14] all emerging to the left and right of both 'Cambridge's, covering between them subjects anywhere from wider Islamic studies to narrower pre-Islamic ones.

Today, seven years into the dawn of a new century, and a new age in studies from Arabic, Islamic and 'Arabic-Islamic' to Persian, Iranian and 'Persiranian',[15] was to be not like any other: as the manuscript of a *Dialogue of Baghdad and Isfahan* lay in London's British Library not far from other unique and colourful items, from the portrait of a rare oriental king to the statue of a giant occidental scientist, a black and white microfilm of that *Dialogue* sat in a padded envelope waiting for a reader in Cambridge University Library to start the next phase of its many lives.

3.2 A Young Reader with a 'Micromap'

It was July of 2007, and Cambridge was a city in England Leo had long wanted to spend more time in for reasons beyond its fame for oriental studies. Besides sharing a name with his own native city across the Atlantic Ocean, the university called Cambridge was known to Leo as a major centre for studies related to his passion-driven high-school thesis work. For him, it was enough that 'the other Cambridge', was the birthplace of a 'Shahnama Project', named after the *Book of Kings*, not knowing a so-called 'Cambridge

12 Melville, Charles. 'Obituary: Persian scholar Peter Avery', The Times, 16 October 2008. Mellville, 'Iranian Studied in Britain'.

13 Mottahedeh, Roy P., 'Sources for the study of Iran', Iranian Studies, 1, 1 (1967), pp. 4–7; Frye, Richard N., Persia (London, 1967), pp. 124–5.

14 Examples: ecademics.org Inc.: non-profit organization founded, 2000, Cambridge US; Soudavar Memorial Foundation: est. 2001 in London. http://soudavar.org/. The Samuel Jordan Center for Persian Studies and Culture est, 2009. https://www.humanities.uci.edu/persianstudies/about/. Pourdavoud Center for the Study of the Iranian World, est, 2017. http://pourdavoud.ucla.edu/

15 Examples of combined expressions: Institut für Geschichte der Arabisch-Islamischen Wissenschaften. https://web.archive.org/web/20100201182256/http://web.uni-frankfurt.de/fb13/igaiw/. Gharagozlou, Yahya, 1001: Persiranian Stories of Love and Revenge (Boston, 2016).

Shahnama Center for Persian Studies' would follow in a few short years.[16] The powerful epic poem of the *Book of Kings* from about a thousand years before had formed one of the main subjects of Leo's high-school 'honours thesis':[17] there the book's attractive messages of personal integrity and national identity had been communicated firsthand with the timely publication of a new Persian edition and English translation of that work of some thirty thousand verses.[18] The power that the magical poems of the *Book of Kings* and its miniature scene paintings had cast upon Leo from childhood had made him go as far as choosing the opening title of 'Heroes' for his thesis after the book's main character, and titles of 'must reads' on his advisor's list.[19] But that day, Leo was looking not at a warrior Hero, but at an obscure figure for his authorship of some early 'dialogues' as part of his post-thesis work: this was a teacher of the celebrated poet of the *Book of Kings*, Firduwsi Tusi,[20] one called Asadi Tusi[21] also from Tus; a figure who carried the surname 'Asadi' related to both 'Leo' and 'Lion' in Arabic and Persian, as well as a debated role in the completion of Firduwsi's literary masterpiece. Having been read to night after night from a book he thought of as a 'Great' Book more than Book of 'King's – knowing the word 'Shah' in the Persian title meant 'Great' as well as 'King' – Leo had long been curious about the figure named Asadi; but this was mostly about the identity of a poet credited with possibly composing the closing lines of a great book; never as a figure to 'look up' in connection with a historical dialogue. At least not until he would take a course titled 'Historical Dialogues from the Near East'[22] in his first year of university enrollment.

Leo would be choosing the course from among many other 'freshman seminars',[23] first because it was a course tailor-made to his post-thesis work by his mentor who was offering it that one time; and second, because he would have inside information that the course would go beyond the stated focus of its description in the university catalogue: this was to be more than a course on early science focused on the Near East during one thousand and one years, through selective primary and secondary sources; it was to involve premodern case studies introduced through historical dialogues between such counterparts as cities (Baghdad, Isfahan), faiths (Muslim, Zoroastrian), cultures (Arab, Persian), cosmologies (Heaven, Earth), objects (pen and sword), and

16 'Cambridge Shahnama Centre for Persian Studies', Cambridge University, launched 2014. http://persian.pem.cam.ac.uk/projects/shahnama-project

17 Goodarzy, Asad, Heroes in Fiction, Heroes in Action (unpublished 'honours thesis', Boston University Academy, 2005).

18 Firduwsī Ṭūsī, Abu al-Qāsim. Stories from the Shahnameh of Ferdowsi, Selections in English, Davis, Dick (tr) (Washington, DC, 2005); Afshar, Iraj and Omidsalar, Mahmoud, Firdawsī, Shāhnāmah (facs) (Tehran, 2005).

19 Davidson, Olga M., Poet and Hero in the Persian Book of Kings (Ithaca, 1994); Nagy, Gregory, 'The epic hero', in Foley, J. M. (ed), A Companion to Ancient Epic (Oxford, 2005), pp. 71–89.

20 Browne, Literary History, Vol. 2, pp. 129–49; Ménage, V. L., 'Firdawsi' (Ferdosi)', Encyclopedia of Islam (EI2), 2, 37 (1964), pp. 918–21.

21 Browne, Literary History, Vol. 2, pp. 148–52; Khaleghi-Motlagh, 'Asadī Ṭūsī'. www.iranicaonline.org/articles/asadi-tusi

22 Kheirandish, 'Historical Dialogues from the Near East', Freshman Seminar, 2007–2008. https://www.scholar.harvard.edu/ekheirandish/teaching

23 Freshman Seminar Program: Harvard University, est., 1959. https://freshmanseminars.college.harvard.edu/

worldviews (chess, backgammon) according to the course poster featuring facing human counterparts from a scientific manuscript illustration[24] (Plate 3). In addition to the creative exercises and events that would make a course subtitled 'case studies in early science' more than a mere requirement, the participation of students cross-registering in it from a neighbouring university with a technical reputation[25] would give it a balanced theoretical and practical touch. Especially inviting for Leo in that Freshman seminar were to be its extra-curricular activities and hands-on events; this would include a guest-lecturer[26] they were assigned to read about in advance in a piece by one of Leo's favourite science writers soon known to him beyond her book, the *Planets*, through titles from *A More Perfect Heaven* and *The Glass Universe* to *And the Sun Stood Still*.[27] The piece assigned in the course carried the equally intriguing title of 'The shadow knows',[28] followed by 'Why a leading expert on the history of timekeeping set out to create a sundial unlike anything the world has ever seen'. The 'leading expert' of the subtitle, once acting as the curator of a 'Collection of Historical Scientific Instruments', lecturer on 'Instruments of Time and Space' and designer of a bluestone sundial hosted on the campus of the same university,[29] would then bring to life in a live lecture the words of the assigned piece, published just that year. Holding a gold-cardboard model of an astronomical instrument without a need for his famously protective white gloves, the guest-lecturer would capture student attention by some unforgettable food for thought through the assigned piece: what instantly stood out about sundials measuring time through shadows since ancient times was that regardless of the old belief that the Sun circles around a fixed Earth, or vice versa centuries later, 'the Sun shines on the dial, protruding a "gnomon", from the Greek for "one who knows" – presumably, who knows what time it is',[30] hence the title of the piece assigned for that lecture, 'The shadow knows'.

But what would stay with Leo most would be not any one early science subject or instrument he had the privilege of experiencing so close; it was rather a single sentence

24 Jazarī, Badīʿ al-Zamān. Al-Jāmiʿ bayn al-ʿilm wa al-ʿamal al-nāfiʿ fī ṣināʿat al-hiyal, Hill, Donald K. (tr) (The Book of Knowledge of Ingenious Mechanical Devices) (Dordrecht, Boston, 1974); Compendium of Theory and Useful Practice in the Mechanical Arts, al-Ḥassan, A. Y. (ed) (Aleppo, 1979).

25 Cavicchi, Elizabth, 'Recreate Historic Experiments', MIT, 2008: cross-registered students in my Freshman Seminar.

26 Andrewes, William: former director of Harvard University's Collection of Historical Scientific Instruments and author of many works. https://www.scientificamerican.com/author/william-j-h-andrewes/. www.longitudedial.com/about_will.html

27 Sobel, Dava, A More Perfect Heaven: How Copernicus Revolutionized the Cosmos (New York, 2011); The Glass Universe: How the Ladies of the Harvard Observatory Took the Measure of the Stars (New York, 2016); And the Sun Stood Still (New York, 2016).

28 Sobel, Dava, 'The shadow knows: Why a leading expert on the history of timekeeping set out to create a sundial unlike anything the world has ever seen', Smithsonian Magazine, January 2007. www.smithsonianmag.com/science-nature/the-shadow-knows-142866936/

29 Lincoln, Rose, 'Hidden spaces: Secret garden', Harvard Gazette, 2 September 2014: William Andrewes spoke at the unveiling in 1999 of the garden, where time is measured in shadows. https://news.harvard.edu/gazette/story/2014/09/secret-garden/

30 Sobel, 'The shadow knows': 'a sundial is one of the oldest – it may be the oldest – of all scientific instruments . . . where the Sun shines on the dial, protruding "gnomon". . .'. www.smithsonianmag.com/science-nature/the-shadow-knows-142866936/

by an eloquent guest-lecturer with examples that long stuck in his mind: that technology could mean different things at different times and to different people, such that even a pencil could count as an early form of technology.[31] Described in the 'Shadow' piece as being himself the 'first to build a sundial showing the time in multiple places', Leo became instantly drawn to subjects like shadows and timekeeping by someone creating life size timekeeping devices including a sundial in the maker's home country of England, 'etched into a black gabbro stone' with a world map,[32] among other constructions by him worldwide.

Before Leo's cross-Atlantic trip to England's Cambridge the summer before, and a special visit to the historic garden housing that sundial with a world map, he had been working with what in his course was called a 'micromap' for conducting microscopic studies in both the physical and digital sense of the term. The physical micromap had a colour-coded base-map adopted from a publication edited by another Cambridge-based scholar, representing land expansions in what it called the 'Islamic World',[33] as if that was a different *world*; the published base-map was colour-coded in the sense that different colours represented successive regional expansions, which in the case of 'Islamic lands' – the form used throughout Leo's courses – had grown exponentially over time: the colour purple represented expansions up to the year 750, about a century after the start of the Islamic calendar corresponding to the year 632: the colour yellow, up to the year 1250, shortly before the fall of Baghdad to the Mongols; the colour orange, up to the year 1500, with two small red and pink regions to represent European retakes up to 1250 and 1500 respectively. The reconstructed digital micromap,[34] on the other hand, was designed for representing diverse regions within the expanding lands themselves, and was colour-coded differently: here, colour-codes were assigned to specific cities as 'hotspots' to highlight the distinction of areas within both Islamic and European lands: red and green highlighted Arab and Persian lands, blue and purple, those of ancient Greek and medieval European lands, and so on; historical maps, supplied with colour-coded hotspots for the years 750, 1000, 1250, 1500 and 1750, could then be used to zoom in and out of select cities for various exercises. The 'case studies in early science' – the subtitle of Leo's upcoming course 'Historical dialogues from the Near East' – included exercises involving items, from historical episodes and literary genres to focused themes and contexts, all further narrowed through select figures whose time and space coordinates were identifiable on such maps. Figures could, in turn, range from translators and authors to patrons and scribes, and from Persian Zoroastrians and Greek Christians, to later Muslim, Jewish, Arabs, Persians, and Turks; many were obscure figures, and some were to become characters in Leo's 'Dialogue' project.

31 Andrewes, William, Guest lecturer: Freshman Seminar: 'Historical Dialogues from the Near East'.

32 A longitude sundial with a world map designed by William Andrewes is at Burghley House. www.burghley.co.uk/?s=sun+dial+

33 Robinson, Francis (ed), The Cambridge Illustrated History of the Islamic World (Cambridge, 1996). The courses featuring the physical and electronic maps used the expression 'Islamic Lands'.

34 Tübinger Atlas, Harvard University, Pusey Collection (Middle East, ca. 750 to 1750) (Plate 11): Micromapping Early Science: http://www.scholar.harvard.edu/ekheirandish/multimedia

Cambridge University Library was a promising place for finding things on obscure figures; and Asadi, the author of some of the earliest 'dialogues' introduced for the first time to a handful of first-year students, was no exception. Browne, the renowned name in Persian studies, had written a few pages on a certain Asadi, often mixed up by ancient bibliographers with someone else with that name as a 'father and son',[35] speaking of 'Asadi the father' as the author of Persian 'munazara's between counterparts beyond night and day translated by Browne himself, and of 'Asadi the son' as the author of the oldest Persian Lexicon in whose handwriting the earliest Persian manuscript transcribed had been cited. Leo was taking detailed notes on everything about the authorship questions regarding the 'Great Book of Kings' through Browne's warnings of different scenarios about the composition: that 'Asadi was pressed to undertake the composition of the *Shahnama*, but excused himself on the ground of his age, and passed on the task to his pupil Firdawsi [sic]', or 'when the latter lay dying at Tus, with the last four thousand couplets of the Epic still unwritten, Asadi finished it for him in a day and a night'.[36] As for the authorship of verses which 'extend from the first invasion of Persia by the Arabs to the end of the book', a literary historian named Dawlatshah-i Samarqandi was cited for writing much closer to the time that 'men of letters are of opinion that it is possible to detect by close attention where the verse of Firdawsi ends and that of Asadi begins'. Careful not to leave anything out, including quotes within quotes, Leo followed every detail, like a marginal comment on one of the manuscripts of Dawlatshah's *Memoir of the Poets* in Cambridge University Library, where Leo could check the original, that Firduwsi 'himself completed the *Shahnama*', that 'it is evident that no other person collaborated with him in its versification', and even a note in a different hand adding the words, 'Niku gufti' meaning well said.[37]

The marginal note on the original manuscript was simple enough in Persian for Leo to understand, and convincing enough for him to consider the case closed.

Still, he would not have been surprised if Asadi, being a 'father' regardless of the authorship of a 'son' he reportedly had, were to have a role in the composition of a book most remembered for its famous story of a father and son, that tragic episode of the Hero, Rustam in the *Book of Kings*, finding out to his great horror that he has killed in battle someone whom he recognizes as his own son, Suhrab, on the sight of his identifiable wristband.[38] Disregarding the coincidence of the 'fathers and sons' of the *Shahnama* with the 'elder and younger' Asadi of Browne, Leo finally turned to leads on the literary works of the supposed father that were closer to the mysteries of his own work: 'Asadi's chief claim to distinction', had written Browne, 'rests on the fact that he developed and perfected, if he did not invent, the species of . . . *munadhara*', or "strife-poem"', acknowledging 'an admirable monograph published' in 1882 by a 'Dr. Ethé'[39] on

35 Browne, Literary History, Vol. 2, p. 148: father, Abū Naṣr Aḥmad ibn Manṣūr of Ṭūs; son: 'Alī ibn Aḥmad al-Asadi, and the Vienna manuscript dated as A.D. 1055–56.

36 Browne, Literary History, Vol. 2, pp. 148–9.

37 Dawlatshāh-i Samarqandī, Tadhkiratu al-shuʿará, Browne, Edward G. (ed, tr) (Memoirs of the Poets) (London, 1901), p. 9: identifies three manuscripts of the text at the Cambridge University Library, and 12 at Oxford's Bodleian Library; Browne, Literary History, Vol. 2, p. 149: 'Nīkū guftī'.

38 Browne, Literary History, Vol. 1, pp. 110–24; Vol. 2, pp. 144–5.

39 Browne, Literary History, Vol. 2, p. 149.

five such '*munadharat*', the titles of which were translated by Browne as a 'strife' between 'Arab and Persian', 'Heaven and Earth', 'Spear and Bow', 'Night and Day', and 'Muslim and Gabr (Zoroastrian)'; included was a bilingual text of the fourth 'strife poem' of Night and Day, the one poem reproduced by Dawlatshah in his *Memoirs of the Poets*, about four centuries distant from both Asadi and Browne.

Leo could not help noticing the parallels between the 'Night and Day' of that poem and 'Baghdad and Isfahan' of his own project as he was copying down the verses of Browne in his English translation of the original Persian. As a 'munazara' meant nothing more to him than a 'dialogue' between two or more counterparts, he was puzzled about the words 'strife' and 'dispute' in Browne's translation of what he had titled a 'strife-poem between Night and Day'. To Leo the dance of verses taking turns between two facing counterparts made a 'munazara' more of a 'dialogue', or 'debate', as it was sometimes translated as.

> '*Hear the fierce dispute and strife*', read Browne's translation of the opening lines, about a munazara '*which passed between the Night and Day . . .*'
>
> '*Surely Night should take precedence over Day*', began Night, '*since at first the Lord Eternal out of darkness called the Light . . .*'

To which Day returned with its own verses, through the lines:

> '*I am born of Heaven's sunshine*' and '*from the Sun the Moon derives the light*'.[40]

The verse in Asadi's Night and Day 'dialogue', where the Moon stood for the Night, and the Sun for the Day, reminded Leo of the lunar and solar calendars of Arab and Persian cities like Baghdad and Isfahan, cities he had long linked to the silver Moon and golden Sun; and the part 'the Moon derives its glowing light from the Sun' pointed to something he had come across from a time both before and after Asadi: before him, the Aristotelian concept of the Moon illuminated by the Sun;[41] and after him, that of the Sun and Moon being self-luminous bodies with primary and secondary or essential and accidental lights.[42] It was puzzling to Leo when and how a literary figure like Asadi could have had such 'scientific' knowledge to bring into a 'literary' production such as a poem. But as interested as Leo was in literature, science, and especially puzzles, he knew it would take him months of work and miles of travel to pursue any such questions. Having

40 Browne, Literary History, Vol. 2, pp. 150–2; Khaleghi-Motlagh (ed), 'Asadī Ṭūsī', p. 91, lines 1 and 3; p. 93, line 24, and p. 95, line 36.
[*Narrator:*] *Bishnu az ḥujjat-i guftār-i Shab u Rūz bi-ham . . .*
[*Night:*] *Gutf Shab faḍl-i Shab az Rūz fuzūn ām-ad az-ānk,*
Rūz rā bāz zih Shab kard Khudā-vand qalam . . .
[*Day:*] *Man bih aṣl az Khur-i charkh-am . . . Māh-i tu az ḍū'-i Khurshīd-i man afzāy-ad nūr . . .*

41 Reeves, Eileen, Painting the Heavens: Art and Science in the Age of Galileo (Princeton, 1999), p. 40: 'Averroes proved by the authority of Aristotle that . . . just as the earth is illuminated by fire, so the moon is by the sun'.

42 Ibn al-Haytham, Sabra, Optics of Ibn al-Haytham, Vol. 2. p. 29: 'In I. H.'s treatise *On the Light of the Moon* . . . the "accidental light" of the moon radiates in the same way as the "essential light" of the sun or fire . . .'; in his post-*Optics On the Quality of Shadows*, the moon is mentioned among self-luminous bodies.

more immediate tasks to attend to in the little time he had in Cambridge, and England for that matter, he directed his attention back to the 'dialogues'.

The original Persian verses of *A Dialogue of Night and Day*, readily accessible to Leo that summer through reproductions of historical manuscripts at Cambridge University Library, were literally at his fingertips for other on-spot inspections. Through day trips to Oxford's resourceful Bodleian Library he also went after the original manuscripts of this and the other four such '*Munadhara*' listed by Browne: according to his Project list, these were all published in a Journal from a university in Mashhad,[43] one coincidentally called 'Firduwsi', honouring the epic poet developing enough worldwide fame for a modern statue of him to be placed in places as unexpected as a garden in Rome.[44] A university journal from an 'eastern' city such as Mashhad, Iran, reaching the shelves of a library as far west as Cambridge, England, contained the critical edition and generous annotations of the five '*Munazara*'s in Persian, all of whose titles Leo replaced with his own translations on his hand-held device as dialogues between an *Arab and Non-Arab* for '*Arab va Ajam*', *Muslim and Zoroastrian* for '*Musalman va Gabr*', *Heaven and Earth* for '*Asman va Zamin*', *Arrow and Bow* for '*Ramh va Qaws*', and *Night and Day* for '*Shab va Ruz*'. The first of these '*Munazara*'s, that 'between an Arab and a Persian', as 'Ajam' could rightly mean there, would undergo a thorough study by someone who would place it and the 'literary genre' itself under a magnifying glass,[45] one simultaneously merging the 'father and son Asadi's back into one, and split the genre of 'debates' into two.

But while both those modern works were literary 'in the works', the common threads between the five historical dialogues and the polarity that manifested itself to Leo in the seemingly Zoroastrian contrast of opposites were slowly starting to emerge. It did not take much imagination to correlate a '*Dialogue between Baghdad and Isfahan*' with one between an Arab and Persian city or Muslim and Zoroastrian faith; and it was just as easy to relate the black and white contrast of Night and Day to a contest between Heaven and Earth or an Arrow and Bow. The most challenging opposites Leo was faced with at this stage of his project was the case of Baghdad and Isfahan as the perceived rising and setting points of science with many ups and downs in between. He had already gone through great effort and much research to touch the ups and downs of science through a 'Khwarizmi' and 'Khayyam' on the upward curve, and a 'Maghribi' and 'Qushji' on a downward one; he had also balanced the opposite extremes of rise and fall by thinking in non-linear terms in historical matters. In a leap of imagination, he visualized the circular path of the rising and setting of the seven planets of the time as the parallel orbs of the seven indicators of the rise and fall of science in his two cities,

43 Asadī Ṭūsī, Munāẓirāt, Khaleghi-Motlagh, Djalal (ed), 'Asadī Ṭūsī'.

44 A statue of Firduwsī by Abu al-Ḥasan Ṣadīqī is in Rome's Villa Borghese. https://theotheriran.com/2014/04/11/statue-of-persias-homer-in-rome-italy/

45 Abdullaeva, 'Bodleian manuscript of Asadī Ṭūsī's Munāẓara', p. 70: 'the author of the Munāẓaras, and that of the other works sometimes ascribed to an earlier figure of the same name, are one and the same person'; 'The origins of the Munāẓara genre', p. 259: the mixed heritage of 'an old tenzone and young Arabic qaṣīda'.

and how geometry alone could not be carried by any one of them in isolation of the others. His sample cases for the Baghdad and Isfahan of the 850s, 1050s, 1250s and 1450s had made it clear that roots and routes, the prerequisite of any cultivations and transmission of science, leave the why and why-not questions of his assignment open-ended without other sample cases and indicators. As cautious as he was of embarking on an overly ambitious project, that of a thousand years by examining such indicators one by one, he began the monumental task of including sample cases for each, starting with the first hundred years and the case of 'rules'.

Rules were Leo's way of thinking about 'science and authority', the first theme on his earlier course syllabus. Just as authorities, rules could be both intellectual and political. But rules were also astrological. As Leo soon learned, this was a science devoted to the rules of the heaven on earth, and the first to charm the many rulers of that earth. He first learned that the historical meaning of astrology was distinct from the occult or pseudo-sciences that it would become much later; that like all scientific subjects it came to Islamic lands from the ancient world; and that the twin disciplines of astronomy and astrology went far ahead of the other sciences due to the interest of so many rulers in them. But what Leo also learned was that even as the 'queen of sciences', the two subjects were not that different from other disciplines when it came to scarcity of published sources on them. He could soon see that the 'sciences of the stars' did not turn up too many primary sources in original languages; and that early histories of such disciplines in the form of secondary sources were written by a few modern scholars at best.

In the case of early astronomy and astrology, one of those scholars had earned the deserving title of 'Hakim extraordinaire'[46] for his vast knowledge and combination of classical subjects and languages ranging from Greek, Arabic and Latin to Pahlavi, Syriac, and Sanskrit. The name of that 'extraordinary' scholar had stuck in Leo's mind in a number of ways: besides volumes published by him, even posthumously,[47] there were those in his honour whose dedications included titles as extraordinary as texts 'worthy of being penned in gold ink'.[48] Most outstanding for Leo, however, was the reputation of that honour-deserving scholar for not only producing meticulous and exhaustive works submitted for publication in his own minuscule hand, but for 'refusing to touch' computers or modern tools for their 'false senses of precision': who could forget the name of such a truly extraordinary figure after whom, in the words one of his students quoted in his obituary, the field would be 'regressing about ten years because of his passing'.[49] The volumes that were yet to be published, whether continuing

[46] Ragep, Tūsī's Memoir on Astronomy, Preface, Vol. 1, p. viii.
[47] Pingree, Eastern Astrolabes.
[48] King, David A., 'A Hellenistic astrological table deemed worthy of being penned in gold ink: The Arabic tradition of Vettius Valens' auxiliary function for finding the length of life', in Burnett, Charles, Hogendijk, Jan P., Plofker, Kim and Yano, Michio (eds), Studies in the History of the Exact Sciences in Honour of David Pingree (Leiden, Boston, 2004).
[49] Sripada, Kam, 'David Pingree obituray', The Brown Daily Herald; Campus News: 18 November 2005: quote from Kim Plofker.

the 'pathways'[50] of that great scholar's unfinished work through the efforts of his knowledgeable wife and close students, or being produced 'in his memory'[51] by his colleagues in more distant lands, would all bear witness to the everlasting presence of his mind.

Leo was far from all that at first, beginning his century by century project with an electronic 'search' on the earliest Islamic centuries, and coming across works that were mostly about things other than science. Some of these included chronologies and genealogies of the two cities and their rulers with details of dates, and events under self-explanatory titles like a *Chronicle* and *Topography of Baghdad*, or *Studies on Isfahan*.[52] Other genres of work contained reports and stories about the period, with titles on both Baghdad and its Caliphs, from *Two Queens of Baghdad* with a chart of female courtiers,[53] to the *Courts of the Caliphs* and *When Baghdad Ruled the Muslim World*.[54] The little coverage there was of 'early science' was further limited by a searchable term like 'science' missing in most titles, of which only a few were relevant to Leo's first centuries of focus: a book titled *The Classical Heritage in Islam*[55] was rich with firsthand reports of 'primary sources', edited by an author who never stopped impressing readers for his knowledge and coverage of subjects; those not simply on 'intellectual and social history', 'art and literature', or the 'concept of knowledge', but themes as rarely touched upon as 'humor', 'hope', 'gambling' and 'suicide', many in titles soon to be republished in a single volume by his distinguished successor and editor.[56] The latter's own major publication, *Greek Thought, Arabic Culture*,[57] also drew heavily from classical sources for subjects with wide appeal, here with a high dose of modern expressions[58] spilled over, from the 'architect' of a 'policy' behind a translation movement in Baghdad of early Islamic centuries, to 'factions', 'coalitions', 'contingents' and 'constituencies' of an early ʿAbbasid society; and from conjoined buzzwords like 'lawsuits', 'public relations', and 'social promotion' to those like 'international community' and 'imperial ideology', with modern appeals beyond the 8–10th centuries of the book's subtitle.

In the *Classical Heritage*, Leo read through historical sources like an early Arabic Catalogue by a book-collector and seller called Ibn al-Nadim, about questions formulated as 'how the Arabs became acquainted with the Greek heritage', 'why there are so many books to be found in these parts on philosophy and the other ancient

50 Pingree, Isabelle and Steele, John M. (eds), Pathways into the Study of Ancient Sciences: Selected Essays by David Pingree (Philadelphia, 2014).
51 Gnoli, Gherardo and Panaino, Antonio (eds), Kayd: Studies in History of Mathematics, Astronomy and Astrology in Memory of David Pingree (Roma, 2009).
52 Reuben, A Baghdad Chronicle; Lassner, The Topography of Baghdad; Holod (ed), Studies on Isfahan.
53 Abbott, Two Queens of Baghdad.
54 Abbott, Two Queens of Baghdad. Kennedy, Hugh N., The Court of the Caliphs: The Rise and Fall of Islam's Greatest Dynasty (London, 2004); When Baghdad Ruled the Muslim World: The Rise and Fall of Islam's Greatest Dynasty (Cambridge, 2005).
55 Rosenthal, Classical Heritage.
56 Rosenthal, Franz, Man versus Society in Medieval Islam, Gutas, Dimitri (ed) (Leiden, 2014).
57 Gutas, Greek Thought, Arabic Culture.
58 Gutas, Greek Thought, Arabic Culture, p. 29: 'architect' of a 'policy': 'factions', 'coalitions', 'contingents', p. 41: 'constituencies'; p. 107: 'public relations', p. 113: 'law-suits', 'social promotion and consumption'; p. 15, 116, 192: 'international community'; p. 28, 108, 191: 'imperial ideology'.

sciences', and how a Caliph called Ma'mun, and his dream of Aristotle[59] was an early spark for the 'translation activity'; in *Greek Thought, Arabic Culture*, he read about an earlier Caliph Mansur, being behind major translations into Arabic, and the translation movement itself tied to 'a recovery of ancient Persian knowledge': among the historical reports reproduced there, a 'version' by Abu Sahl son of Nawbakht, the Persian court astrologer, presented a so-called 'astrological' history of the transmission of the sciences in reporting that:[60] when 'Alexander, king of the Greeks' – who would rightly not be called Great in Persia – invaded that country, before burning 'archives and treasuries', had them copied and translated into Byzantine; that ancient Persian knowledge was also preserved through copies made by ancient 'kings of Persia' in places like India and China, and collected by Sasanid kings from those regions and Byzantium. That the recovery of all this was behind a translation movement in early Islamic centuries when scientific translations into Arabic included ancient Greek, Persian Indian and Chinese was one explanation for motivations behind the translations: Ibn Nawbakht's closing lines that 'people of every age . . . have knowledge renewed for them in accordance with the decree of the stars', then provided documentation for how such a 'message' to the 'Abbasids Caliphs about their 'turn to renew the sciences' could have placed them at the forefront of secular as well as religious sciences of the time, all collectively termed ''ilm', for knowledge.

It was now only natural for Leo to turn to the writings of a frequently quoted modern author in that work, in observance of their chronological order: this was the 'extraordinary scholar' with expertise in multiple languages and cultures and an astronomical number of publications devoted to the transmission of the early sciences, which according to his recent obituary, was about one tenth of what was 'taken away with him'.[61] This was in preparation for Leo's mounting work not just on the early days of Baghdad and Isfahan, but especially their roles in the rise of early science: in the works of that late scholar, Leo read with great interest, about early Baghdad and the details of a horoscope drawn for its foundation in 762, about Fazari, the Muslim, and Nawbakht, the Zoroastrian, the two astrologers involved in drawing that horoscope with their Jewish contemporary Masha'llah, and accounts of early Isfahan, in preserving early sciences;[62] about the reports of Abu Ma'shar, better known in the West as

59 Ibn al-Nadīm (d. ca. 995), Fihrist, Flügel, G. (ed) (Leipzig, 1871–1872), pp. 241–3; Fihrist, Dodge, B. (tr) (New York, London, 1970), pp. 336–40: 'How the Arabs became acquainted with the Greek heritage'; Rosenthal, Classical Heritage, pp. 45–50.

60 Gutas, Greek Thought, Arabic Culture, pp. 28–46, p. 39: 'Alexander, king of the Greeks, set out from a city of the Byzantines called Macedonia to invade Persia . . .'; p. 46: 'The people of every age and era acquire fresh experiences and have knowledge renewed for them in accordance to the decree of the stars'.

61 Sripada, 'David Pingree, obituary': quote from Kim Plofker.

62 Pingree, David, 'Fazārī: Muḥammad ibn Ibrāhīm', Dictionary of Scientific Biography (DSB), 4 (1971), pp. 555–6; 'Abū Sahl B. Nawbakt', Encyclopedia Iranica (EIr), 1, 4 (1983), p. 369. www.iranicaonline.org/articles/abu-sahl-b. Rosenfeld and Ihsanoğlu, Mathematicians, Astronomers, and Other Scholars, nos. 6–7, pp. 14–15. Plofker, Kim, 'Fazārī: Muḥammad ibn Ibrāhīm al-Fazārī', Biographical Encyclopedia of Astronomers (BEA) (2007), pp. 362–3. https://islamsci.mcgill.ca/RASI/BEA/Fazari_BEA.htm

Albumasar, his little known student Shadhan, and an 'unknown' scholar reported by the much later and better-known Biruni.[63] What the single pen of that all too well known scholar brought Leo came magically at a time when it was possible to check a manuscript in Cambridge University Library where he was working; and what the recently dried pen of that extraordinary teacher underscored was the broader lesson of the transmission of knowledge itself: a lesson not simply that sciences like astronomy and astrology had long been transmitted from culture to culture, but that their transmission, while non-linear and complex, could still be expressed in simple terms. The title 'From Alexandria to Baghdad and Byzantium',[64] from the latest pen of that expert scholar on classical cultures, had two simply expressed messages about scientific transmission: one for the recipient cultures, and the other within a single culture.

When it came to the first century of his project, however, Leo did not choose his main characters from an Arabic manuscript of a *Mudhakarat* that sounded like discussions on Astronomy and Astrology between a teacher and student – in this case, Abu Maʿshar, and his pupil, Shadhan. Mindful of the living remnants of the work of that extraordinary scholar, writing with great skill on all such subjects and figures, and specialties in several ancient and medieval cultures at once, Leo extended the Indian and Greek expertise of that scholar to the Arabic and Persian focus of his own project as representatives of Baghdad and Isfahan. He now had to find characters that well represented those cities and cultures of the time, using besides sources like the *Dictionary of Scientific Biography* and *Mathematicians, Astronomers, and Other Scholars*, those with 'online' supplements, like the *Encyclopedia Iranica*, and a newly published *Biographical Encyclopedia of Astronomers*.[65] To represent Baghdad and Isfahan of the earliest centuries, he picked the years 750 through 850, and figures like 'Fazari' and 'Ibn Nawbakht', for not merely corresponding to the Muslim and Zoroastrian of one of the five Asadi dialogues, but acting as representatives of the transmission of ancient Indian and Greek sciences into Arab and Persian lands. Through them Leo could transmit early scientific concepts both across and within cultures; and he could do so by choosing the language of geometry to pass his two selected historical characters through the many rounds and squares of his assigned two cities. Now he could test the role of the third of his seven indicators, namely rules, in and beyond its geometrical sense to underline key moments in the story of science.

Leo's historical narrative would next turn to the role of rules in scientific development, focusing on geometry in both its theoretical and practical aspects, and on rules in both geometrical and non-geometrical senses: here, the selected historical cases would show that rules, when coming from political rulers as patrons of science, advanced developments in and beyond geometry; and those applied to scientific authority or conventions held it back, if strict and inflexible.

63 Pingree, David, The Thousands of Abū Maʿshar , pp. 5–6; 20: 'Mudhākarāt of Shādhān'.
64 Pingree, David, 'From Alexandria to Baghdad and Byzantium: The transmission of astrology', International Journal of Classical Traditions, 8, 1 (2001), pp. 3–37, p. 3.
65 Yarshater, Ehsan (ed), Encyclopedia Iranica (EIr): www.iranicaonline.org. Hockey, Thomas et al. (eds), The Biographical Encyclopedia of Astronomers (BEA) (New York, 2007; 2nd edn 2014): https://islamsci.mcgill.ca/RASI/BEA/

Chapter 3: 'Dialogue' of Muslim and Zoroastrian
Round City, Square Pillars – Rules
By Charles Leo Scribner, July 2007

[*Zoroastrian:*] *From the sky, night and day, to the Moon, Sun and stars*
It is through the [fire]'s ignite, that all come to light
[*Muslim:*][*Earth is*] *like a book, [and] trees, like letters of speech*
[*Earth is*] *like a point, [and] heavens, like the [encircling] line of compass . . .*

Asadi Tusi, *'Dialogue' of Muslim and Zoroastrian*, ca. 1000, English translation: Elaheh Kheirandish[66]

3.3 *An Arab City with a 'House of Wisdom'*

It was June circa 750, and one of the earliest scientific figures from Islamic lands named 'Muhammad Al-Fazari'[67] from an old Arab family in Kufa near Najaf in historic Iraq – one to be soon attached to the 'astrological moment for laying the foundations of Baghdad'[68] on 30 July 762 – was finishing his multiple tasks at the end of a full day's work. Baghdad of post-750s was a city associated with a 'house of wisdom' involving a palace 'treasury' of books,[69] and a royal court filled with Arabs and non-Arabs, translators and scholars, theoreticians and practitioners, individuals and circles: all were reportedly housed in a city with a 'circular' plan meant to measure equal distances from all points around the Caliphs' 'rule'. That day, about twelve years before the foundation of Baghdad as a capital city, Fazari had to be a multi-tasker embodying various trades and activities at once. As he was putting away the paper sheets recently received from far away China, and metal tools brought from nearby Persia, he could not have imagined that the benefits of mediums to be someday known as early 'technologies' could actually be outweighed by their harm; that when it came to transcriptions or inscriptions involving these and other crude mediums, the long chain of transmission around authors, copyists, biographers, and bio-bibliographers could make their names interchangeable with others like them; that his own full name, Muhammad ibn Ibrahim ibn Habib al-Fazari, would soon give his very identity 'some ambiguity' next to Ibrahim ibn Habib al-Fazari, as references to 'two different people,

66 Asadī Ṭūsī (attribution), Munāẓirih-i Musalmān va Gabr (ca. 1000), Khaleghi-Motlagh, 'Asadī Ṭūsī', pp. 79–90: p. 82, line 22; p. 86, line 57, Kheirandish, Elaheh (tr, excerpts).
'[*Zoroastrian:*] *Zih charkh u layl u nahār u zih māh u anjum u khur*
Chu bar-furūz-ad [u] dar vay buv-ad padīd athhār . . .
[*Muslim:*] *Chu nāmih shud-dī u ashjār chun hurūf-i sukhan*
Chu nuqṭih shud-dī u aflāk chun khaṭ-i pargār . . .'

67 Pingree, 'Fazārī'; Pingree, David, 'The fragments of the works of Al-Fazārī', Journal of Near Eastern Studies (JNES), 29, 2 (1970), pp. 103–23; Plofker, 'Fazārī'.

68 Pingree, 'Fazārī', p. 555; Pingree, 'Nawbakt', p. 369.

69 Pingree, Thousands, p. 6, n. 3, cites Ibn al-Nadīm's, Fihrist, pp. 396–7: 'Treasure-house of Wisdom'; p. 11: 'Khizānat al-ḥikma'; Gutas, Greek Thought, Arabic Culture, pp. 53–60: reexamines 'the question of the bayt al-ḥikma', pp. 54–6 includes expressions and translations: 'bayt/buyūt al-ḥikma (house/houses of wisdom)', 'khizānat al-ḥikma (storehouse of wisdom)'; 'khizānat kutub al-ḥikma' (storehouses of books on wisdom)'.

namely father and son',[70] splitting up with it all the scientific credit that he alone deserved. Neither could he have foreseen something else, as expert as he was in foretelling, in his case through the 'science of the stars' and associations with the horoscope of Baghdad: this was foreseeing that the name of this and other cities in his native Iraq would one day be far more familiar around the world than the epithet Fazari that represented him and his ancestors of 'twenty seven generations'.[71] Here was a man recorded as 'first' in many things: first to construct a plane astrolabe, first to translate a Sanskrit text into Arabic, and first to compose an astronomical poem with technical content; a man whose other 'first's would be known through titles like *On the Measurement of Noon* or *Use of Armillary Spheres and Astrolabes*.[72] But ironically, the transmission of his very name would be far from firsthand: through various channels of transmission, from one text and medium to another, even his first name, Muhammad, while named after the Prophet of Islam, would go down in history either as dropped altogether[73] or as second to the name Ibrahim, this time the name of the Prophet well known for sacrificing his son.

That day, Muhammad son of Ibrahim son of Habib, who was about to leave a work space with an unfinished astrolabe construction, scientific translation, and poem composition for his next days' labours, was far from the thought of how the rule of Arabic names, the sequence of 'such and such', son of 'such and such', could make him indistinguishable from the name of any of his ancestors with the mere drop of a prefix or two in later treatments. But young Fazari could hardly be oblivious to other rules affecting him and his work, which were many at the time: in his case, the political rule that commissioned his astrolabe, the scientific rule that guided his translation, and the astrological rule that inspired his poem. It was at the court of the ʿAbbasid Caliph Mansur, a literal Victor on many fronts, that Fazari excelled as one of the masters of the sciences; it was by the Barmakid Viziers, the powerful Persian ministers at this and other ʿAbbasid courts that he was ranked as one of the best of four within their own specialties; and it was under an overall political rule, whose frequent disfavours did not typically extend to scientists, that Fazari's work could evolve into volumes of astronomical handbooks with tables, and astrological verses with calculations.

The rule of science itself in the life of a dedicated scholar such as Fazari was no less dominating than the rule of patrons supporting that science. As a transmitter of science from regions in the ancient world besides India, Fazari was no different from older contemporaries such as Mashaʾllah and Nawbakht, the Jewish and Zoroastrian court scientists who were similarly credited for the casting of the Baghdad horoscope:[74] he had to know the Greek astronomical authorities starting with Ptolemy, the author of the masterpiece *The Almagest*, named after its Arabic title, 'Al-Majisti', meaning 'The Great' work. But when it came to ancient Persia, an Arab scientist such as Fazari was different from someone like Nawbakht, the head of the family of ancient Persian

70 Pingree, 'Fragments', 103–4; Plofker, 'Fazārī', p. 362 include identity discussions.

71 Pingree, 'Fazārī', p. 555; Pingree, 'Fragments', p. 104.

72 Plofker, 'Fazārī', p. 363.

73 Pingree, 'Fragments', 103–4: considers 'only one person is referred to in the passage but that ... Ibn al-Nadīm or his manuscript tradition has omitted the "Muḥammad ibn"'.

74 Gutas, Greek Thought, Arabic Culture, p. 33, p. 34: Barmakid family.

Zoroastrians:[75] Nawbakht, whose name meant 'new fortune', lived up more than any other to the meaning of his name when he was released from prison by Caliph Mansur to become a resident of that Caliph's court and author of an *Epistle on the Secrets of Astrology*: young Fazari was to be especially different from the son and successor of the newly converted Nawbakht, someone with a long name opening with 'Kharshad-Mah' to mean Sun-Moon:[76] to start with, Fazari was a mere transmitter, and not active promoter, of the Persian astronomical tradition.

By contrast, Abu Sahl Ibn Nawbakht, as he was known after the supposed conversion of his father from Zoroastrian to the Muslim faith, would become known as a pioneer in promoting the Persian roots of an Islamic scientific tradition that started as a massive translation and scientific movement in Baghdad.[77] The more Ibn Nawbakht would penetrate into the ʿAbbasid court, as one accompanying Caliph Mansur on his last Pilgrimage to Mecca in 775, and serving under the next few Caliphs, the brothers Mahdi and Hadi,[78] the more weighty his position were to become. Under those Caliphs' direct descendant, Harun al-Rashid, the ʿAbbasid Caliph of twenty-four years, Ibn Nawbakht was to be linked to a so-called 'House of Wisdom' translating books from his native Middle-Persian tongue of 'Pahlavi' into the state language of Arabic. No such royal honours were to be carried by the name Al-Fazari. Besides being 'split into two' personalities[79] in some early sources for similar reasons, Al-Fazari had little in common with Ibn Nawbakht. For one thing, their works, which were both passed on through extracts in later transmissions, had a sharply different fate in both the quantity and quality of that transmission. Fazari would have his works preserved through a channel as great as that of the slightly later Biruni. But while Fazari would get some unfavourable reviews from that great historical figure despite his multiple efforts, a single extract from Ibn Nawbakht's *Book of Nativities* would bring its author literal 'new fortune' in becoming part of the story of the transmission of the sciences as uncovered by modern scholars centuries later.[80]

Nothing associated with Fazari had any such fortunes when it came to later transmission, whether of his works or his name. About a quarter of a millennium before the time when Biruni lived and worked with great authority, a young Fazari had written works whose problematic transmission, from one hand to another, would bring Biruni cause for alarm. Being a resident in and expert on India, an alert Biruni would later write in his famous book titled after that ancient region, that in the case of al-Fazari 'if we compare his secondary statements to the primary statements of the Indian' who came to Baghdad as a member of a political mission,[81] 'we discover discrepancies,

[75] Pingree, 'Nawbaḵt'; Massignon, Louis 'Nawbakht', Encyclopedia of Islam (EI^2), 1913–16, 1987, p. 887; Iqbal, Abbas, Khāndan Nawbakhtī (Tehran, 1345 [1966]); Anthony, Sean W., 'Nawbakhtī Family', Encyclopedia Iranica (EIr), 2000: www.iranicaonline.org/articles/nawbakti-family
[76] Pingree, 'Nawbaḵt', p. 369: 'Risāla fī sarāʾir aḥkām al-nujūm'; 'Kharshād Māh . . .'
[77] Gutas, Greek Thought, Arabic Culture, p. 7.
[78] Bosworth, Islamic Dynasties, p. 7: The two ʿAbbasid brothers reigned for ten and two years respectively.
[79] Pingree, 'Nawbaḵt', p. 369: refers to medieval sources 'that split [Abu Sahl] into two astrologers'.
[80] Gutas, Greek Thought, Arabic Culture, pp. 38–40: Book of Nahmuṭān on the Nativities.
[81] Pingree, 'Fragments', 108: sent to Caliph, al-Manṣūr in AH 154 (24 Dec. 770–12 Dec. 771).

the cause of which is not known', this being either 'due to the translation of al-Fazari . . . or to the dictation of that Indian'. Fazari would even be written out of Biruni's dating of the horoscope for the foundation of Baghdad as one 'drawn by Nawbakht' without mentioning Fazari's name. It would be an early historian, named Yaʿqubi, who would mention the name Fazari next to Nawbakht, even if it came in a sequence that reversed 'Ibrahim ibn Muhmmad' for 'Muhammad ibn Ibrahim'.[82]

Muhammad al-Fazari may never have thought of himself as careless as an Indian missionary dictating to him or the Arabic scribes naming him. He always tried to be systematic; he had to, if he were to write a work as long as his 'ten volumes'. Being not only an Arab, but also a Muslim, instead of a Persian and Zoroastrian like Ibn Nawbakht, he would start even the celestial poems surviving from those volumes with the names and praises according to his native rules: his 'qasidah', the genre of verse from pre-Islamic times before it became a form of praise of kings in Persia, would have an astronomical bend with specific reference to higher forms in its first lines as quoted by a biographer-geographer named Yaqut: the poem began with 'the high and mighty . . . creator of the highest seven' before it would turn to the Sun and Moon, where 'the Sun's light brightens the darkness' and 'full Moon's light spreads to the horizon'; the poem would follow by turning to 'the sphere, revolving in its course'; and to the stars, noting all of them as agents, some permanent, some transitory, some rising, others setting.[83]

Fazari's systematic approach was also to be captured in a creative calculation expressed in that same astronomical poem, as transmitted in Biruni's *Treatise on Shadows*; but this too was in a form that threw more shadows than light on its meaning. Here problems of transmission did not involve Fazari's full name: Biruni had no problem getting the sequence right; it was the calculation of 'the remainder of daylight' that required first interpretation, then simplification: the interpretation required would make an 'extraordinary' scholar turn editor to add parenthetical marks to rephrase the Fazari shadow problem and offer a formula.[84]

As creative as the calculation of the remainder of light of a given day was in the formulaic verse of Fazari, the fragmentary nature of its transmission would give it little chance of being properly preserved even by Biruni, whose mere naming of Fazari next to any defects would have been enough of a blow to his reputation, and so historical 'place'. By contrast, the single extract of Fazari's younger contemporary, Ibn Nawbakht, preserved in more than one source, and through more than one reputable scholar,[85] was enough to create – both through the form of the medium presenting it, and the force of arguments supporting it – something unprecedented: this was a real chance for further transmission of its content, namely a new explanation for the transmission of early sciences at the time, and by extension new lights on cultures as old as the ancient Persian kingdom.

82 Pingree, 'Fragments', p. 104.
83 Pingree, 'Fragments', p. 104.
84 Pingree, 'Fragments', pp. 121–2: 'the full meaning of this passage alludes us' but 'the general procedure which is described remains clear' as '12/(S + 12 – Sn) = X/6', if 'the shadow at any given time [is] S . . . at noon Sn, and the hours since sunrise or before sunset X', then the latter, unknown quantity, could be calculated for the seasonal hours passed, since sunrise is 'as in a geometric progression'.
85 Pingree, Thousands; Gutas, Greek Thought, Arabic Culture: historical sources for Abu Sahl's fragments.

3.4 *A Persian City with an Ancient Kingdom*

It was July circa 850, and a man with the longest string of words forming his full name could make that name one of further distinction through very different circumstances: his first name, starting with the word 'Sun', the focal point of his Zoroastrian origin, was 'Kharshad', followed by 'Mah' for 'Moon' and a few other Middle-Persian terms;[86] and his last name, 'Nawbakht, or naybakht' in pre-Islamic Persian dialect,[87] had its own long sequence, descending from the ancient Persian Giv son of Gudarz of the Kiyanid Dynasty, living on through the much later *Book of Kings*. Upon his father's move to Baghdad and conversion to Islam on the testimony of Nawbakht, the elder, the young Sun-Moon's name would become Arabised as Ibn Nawbakht, meaning Son of Nawbakht according to the rule of Arabic names. But his first name, Abu Sahl, meaning father of Sahl, had a more interesting story than a simple reference to a son rather than father. This was reportedly chosen by the ruling Caliph to simplify his long Middle-Persian name: early biographers would report from his own mouth the charming story of when Caliph Mansur, in whose service he had followed his aging father, heard him introducing himself with that long string of names, said while laughing, either be only one of those names, or accept from me Abu Sahl,[88] a name that ending with a word meaning 'ease', could easily void all the others.

But as the reported 'only child' of the famed Nawbakht, Abu Sahl would long be known not only as the father or 'Abu' of his son, Sahl, but as the son or 'Ibn' of his distinguished father, Nawbakht; and as the only Ibn Nawbakht there was, he would have, besides little trouble climbing up that high ladder, a lesser chance of having that shorthand name split into more parts or be mixed up or misreported. Such was the case with many of the sons he would reportedly have himself, ten including one called Sahl, at least seven of whom were said to have been from his wife Zarrin; and while the descending line of the Nawbakht family would go down in history with some distinction in many areas, as in the case of Ibn Nawbakht's first son, Isma'il,[89] his own case was to be quite exceptional.

The great distinction that would come with the name Abu Sahl Ibn Nawbakht involved elements of fortune beyond those simply inherited. He would be credited with seven books on various branches of astrology by the book dealer Ibn al-Nadim,[90] not long after his own time. But it was through a single book called *Book of Nativities* that a long extract would not just survive, but was noted for an important history of the transmission of the ancient sciences, a history preserved through multiple channels all the way to modern times.[91] Neither a name as lofty as Nawbakht nor a subject as

[86] Pingree, 'Nawbaḵt', p. 369: gives the full name as Kharshād Māh Taymāḏā Mābāḏār Kusirvā Bihshād. Anthony, 'Nawbakhtī Family', follows 'Mābāḏār' by '(Māh-bādān? . . .)'.

[87] Pingree, 'Nawbaḵt', p. 369; Iqbal, Khāndān Nawbakhtī, pp. 5–6.

[88] Iqbal, Khāndān Nawbakhtī, pp. 8–11.

[89] Iqbal, Khāndān Nawbakhtī, pp. 15–20, p. 20: Sahl; Massignon, 'Nawbakht', p. 1043.

[90] Pingree, 'Nawbaḵt', p. 369.

[91] Pingree, Thousands; Gutas, Greek Thought, Arabic Culture.

popular as astrology could add up to the 'fortune' that made him and his work stand above many others in and beyond his own time. He would have, not unlike his many colleagues, the good fortune of close links to Baghdad, a city founded with astrological help credited to his father and his own colleagues; history would even record him as being brought to Baghdad as a young boy following the fateful meeting of his father in an Ahwaz prison with a 'tall and handsome' Caliph Mansur to be.[92] Links to the city of Isfahan, then made up of two ancient districts of Jay and Yahudiya, also came from reports not directly involving Ibn Nawbakht: like manuscripts discovered in ʿAbbasid times in an Isfahan wall in Greek script, or in the citadel of Jay copied on the bark of trees used by Indians and Chinese, and deposited in vaults in places as high as Jay in old Isfahan for protection from natural disasters like earthquakes or storms.[93]

But the report of Sun-Moon, later Abu Sahl, son of Nawbakht, on the transmission of early sciences was at the right time and place for a credit given to him in modern times beyond translations from Pahlavi into Arabic, which he was himself linked to as part of that transmission movement.[94] He would write in his *Book of Nativities*, as reported by later sources like the *Catalogue* of Ibn Nadim the book-collector, and reproduced by modern scholars, that 'a knowledge of astronomy and astrology is especially associated with' ancient Persian kings; and that one of these built, in the 'period of Jupiter', a city named after that planet, and 'constructed twelve palaces named after the twelve signs of the zodiac, and installed in each a library and a group of scholars';[95] and most notably, that in invading Persia, Alexander 'took whatever he needed of the sciences of astronomy and medicine . . . along with learned men he came upon.'[96] The historical reports on the 'pillage of Alexander and the translation of the Persian books into Greek' would continue to be given in other versions, and in at least one case with reasons for Alexander's burning of Persian books after their translation into Greek: this would be by a Persian writer named Hamza Isfahani, writing about two centuries after Ibn Nawbakht, that Alexander 'envied the fact that' they, meaning the Persians, 'had gathered together sciences the likes of which no other nation had ever gathered.'[97] These and other accounts reported would then be read and understood much later in time as signaling not just the pivotal role of Persian elements, including rules in the early transmission of the sciences even during pre-Islamic times, but also the mention of Isfahan in such connections. People would continue to read about Baghdad as a 'round' city at the centre of rules with four gates modeled after Persian palaces; but only those with access, and patience, of reading through layers of text, would know about the case of Isfahan, a city with an ancient citadel before a square-shaped square of a much later age.[98] This was a notable city itself hosting various

92 Iqbal, Khāndān Nawbakhtī, pp. 7–8.
93 Pingree, Thousands: pp. 1–3.
94 Pingree, 'Fazārī', p. 555; Pingree, 'Nawbakt', p. 369.
95 Pingree, Thousands, p. 9: report from Ibn al-Nadīm, quoting Ibn Nawbakht's 'Kitāb al-Nahmaṭān'.
96 Gutas, Greek Thought, Arabic Culture, pp. 38–40: report from Ibn Nawbakht's 'Kitab an-Nahmuṭān'.
97 Gutas, Greek Thought, Arabic Culture, p. 40.
98 Pingree, Thousands, p. 3: The citadel of Isfahan is where Persian manuscripts were found during ʿAbassid times. Maydān-i 'Naqsh-i Jahān' (Plan of the World).

visitors including Europeans, who by the time they visited or resided in it would be far ahead of the sciences to their east. Isfahan of post-850s was a central city within an ancient kingdom despite the gravitation of many to Baghdad of the time. Long documented for its own role in the early transmission of the sciences, Isfahan was a city reported to have preserved early sources from natural as well as political harm, a city about whose transmissional role historical evidence would keep piling up into modern times.

As early as a generation after Ibn Nawbakht, his own family line would go down in history with different associations with science. Even before the time of those working directly on scientific subjects – namely, a son called Sahl and his own son, Hasan – Ibn Nawbakht's first son Isma'il, and his own nephew, Abu Muhammad, were two figures[99] who, while not directly involved with science, were both closely associated with someone who was; someone from Harran, an ancient 'city of stars and star-worshippers':[100] this was a polymath named Thabit ibn Qurra[101] who, through an 'inherited fortune', would turn from a young money changer in Harran to a man of all trades in Baghdad, credited with subjects from science and philosophy[102] to many others including a 'chess problem';[103] it was through him in the 'circular city' of Baghdad, not his ancestors' city of Harran, that science would have major leaps forward; and it was through a house in the province of Isfahan, named after him in modern times, that a 'House of stars' would restore the planet and zodiac houses of his ancestors.[104] So wide was the radius of subjects and languages mastered by Thabit son of Qurra, surnamed Harrani, that it would take more than one modern scholar to write his intellectual biography;[105] and so far went the range of his scientific activities that of the two meanings of his first name in Arabic, the language adopted after his native Syriac, only one would fit his scientific profile: Thabit meaning 'fixed', as in the 'fixed' stars, did not quite do justice to his active, indeed dynamic, scientific input; but Thabit having a meaning like 'proven', from the root, 'proof', could not have been a better fit for a novel concept of 'proof' that he would help push forward.

Up until his own time, Thabit and his colleagues, some associated with an increasingly active 'Abbasid Baghdad, had mostly dealt with a concept of proof that was rhetorical and visual much more than logical or geometrical. Ancient authors like Euclid of Alexandria, writing as far back as three hundred years before the common era, with volumes and volumes devoted to the *Elements of Geometry*, had dealt with

99 Iqbal, Khāndān Nawbakhtī, pp. 2, 15, 20, 120.

100 Weir, T. H. 'Ḥarrān', First Encyclopedia of Islam (EI¹), 3, 19 (1987), p. 270.

101 Ruska, J., 'Thābit ibn Kurra', First Encyclopedia of Islam (EI¹), 8 (1987), p. 733; Rosenfeld, B. A. and Grigorian, A. T., 'Thābit ibn Qurra, Al-Ṣābi Al-Ḥarrānī, Dictionary of Scientific Biography (DSB), 13 (1976), pp. 288–95; and Palmeri, JoAnn, 'Thābit ibn Qurra', Biographical Encyclopedia of Astronomers (BEA) (2007), pp. 1129–30. http://islamsci.mcgill.ca/RASI/BEA/Thabit_ibn_Qurra_BEA.htm

102 Rashed, Roshdi, Thābit ibn Qurra: Science and Philosophy in Ninth-Century Baghdad (Berlin, 2009).

103 Masood, Ehsan, Science and Islam: A History (London, 2009), pp. 48–9: chess problem.

104 Pingree, Thousands, p. 9: quoting Ibn al-Nadīm; 'Thābit house', Kashan: Chapter Seven, 7.4.

105 Ruska, 'Thābit ibn Kurra'; Rosenfeld and Grigorian, 'Thābit ibn Qurra'; Palmeri, 'Thābit ibn Qurra'.

'proofs', of which many were geometrical 'identities' rather than proofs. The simplest of these, long associated with a legendary sage named Pythagoras, could not have even been properly called the Pythagorean 'theorem' for the same reason. The forty seventh proposition of the first Book of Euclid's *Elements* had simply shown that in a right angled triangle, the square area constructed on its hypotenuse, the longest side opposite to the triangle's right angle, is equal to the sum of the two square areas constructed on the other two sides of the same triangle. There was no formal 'proof' for that geometrical problem other than a check mark on equality of those areas based on given numbers: in the simple case of a right-angled triangle with sides 5, 4, and 3, the square of 5, the area of a square figure with side 5 as 25, being equal to the area of the square on 4, namely 16, plus that of 3, namely 9: the proof of that identity would then be based on the equality of the areas of the larger square, to the sum of the two smaller squares, each being 25. The second book of Euclid's *Elements* would continue to be known for such 'geometric identities' like the fourth, fifth, and sixth proposition, those that would one day be called 'application of areas' for the very reason that an equality could be drawn between areas of the figures involved in them, in this case mostly squares and rectangles. There were also other kinds of Euclidean proof, which were at once geometrical and logical: those that followed the Aristotelian method of finding the causal premise of a three-part identity. A recurring example of these, which carried the complex name of 'syllogism', would be the trio: 'All men are mortal, Socrates is a Man, therefore Socrates is Mortal': here the middle term, Socrates is a Man, would provide the 'causal premise' to explain why something is the way it is, a method long applied in a range of 'geometrical' proofs.

Thabit, like many of the colleagues of his time, from his sponsors, the Banu Musa Brothers best known for their work on mechanics, to Musa Khwarizmi, most closely associated with the 'science of algebra', were all familiar with the *Elements* of Euclid and its thirteen books with numerous propositions: this was one of the first books transmitted into Arabic[106] as part of the ʿAbbasid translation movement. Thabit himself had also revised many mathematical translations from Greek, including Euclid's, some with another Syriac speaking scholar, Ishaq ibn Hunayn, the son of the Nestorian Christian, Hunayn ibn Ishaq,[107] the founder of an early school of translation in Baghdad with other members of his family. But Thabit did not have his 'translating hat' when he was composing a brief treatise which was to change the face of geometrical proofs by its very title: 'On the verification of algebraic problems with geometrical demonstrations'.[108] Here, Thabit would be explicit about establishing 'justifications' of the equality of areas for those geometrical propositions of the second book of Euclid's *Elements*: loyal to one of the senses of Thabit's own name as 'proven', these were 'proof's of geometry applied to arithmetic and algebra. No one had done that before him, at least explicitly – not even Khwarizmi, whose name would be long wedded to both

106 Murdoch, John E., 'Euclid: Transmission of the Elements', Dictionary of Scientific Biography (DSB), 4 (1971), pp. 437–59; Gutas, Greek Thought, Arabic Culture, pp. 182–3.

107 Gutas, Greek Thought, Arabic Culture, p. 136. Anawati, G. C., 'Ḥunayn ibn Isḥāq al-ʿIbādī, Abū Zayd, known . . . as Johannitius', Dictionary of Scientific Biography (DSB) 15 (Supp. I) (1978), pp. 230–4.

108 Berggren, Episodes, pp. 104–8; Rashed, Thābit ibn Qurra, p. 8.

algebra and geometry. A more forceful move in the direction of advanced concepts of proof was an ingenious turn of an individual 'algebraic' identity to a generalized 'rule',[109] a concept far ahead of its time, even without the use of algebraic symbols which were to appear much later in time. More advanced concepts of proof, however, including physical set ups leading to generalizations based on cases 'with no variation or change',[110] would follow not long after.

[109] Sayılı, Aydin. 'Thâbit ibn Qurra's generalization of the Pythagorean Theorem', Isis, 51, 1 (1960), pp. 35–7. Al-Daffa, Ali, 'Thābit ibn Qurra's extension of the Pythagorean Theorem', Proceedings of the First International Symposium for the History of Arabic Science (Aleppo, 1976), pp. 33–4.

[110] Sabra, Optics of Ibn al-Haytham, Vol. 1. pp. 7–8, includes a passage by Ibn al-Haytham regarding observations 'always found to be so, with no variation or change'; Kheirandish, Elaheh, 'The footprints of "experiment" in early Arabic optics', Early Science and Medicine, 14, 1–3, Special Issue: Newman, William R. and Sylla, Edith Dudley (eds), Evidence and interpretation: Studies on early science and medicine in honor of John E. Murdoch, (2009), pp. 79–104, pp. 99–100.

4

Word and Line

200 Years: A Quarter Phase (ca. 850–1050)

The duty of the man who investigates the writings of scientists . . . is to make himself an enemy of all that he reads, and . . . attack it from every side.
Ibn al-Haytham (d. aft. ca. 1040), *Aporias Against Ptolemy*, English translation: A. I. Sabra[1]

When I became great, no city was big enough for me;
When my price went up, no one would buy me . . .
Ibn Sina (d. ca. 1037), 'Autobiography', English translation: Dimitri Gutas[2]

4.1 An Old Manuscript with Colour Scans

It was August 2008, and the *Dialogue of Baghdad and Isfahan* had started the next phase of its life through colour scans of its manuscript, where its opening gold-illuminated folio was printed and framed in a matching border for display in a recent exhibit.[3] The *Dialogue*'s colour scans were also saved on compact discs and DVDs along with a few other manuscript copies and prints as part of the exhibit's 'gallery tour'. The light, bone-coloured background of the *Dialogue* folios framed within a midnight blue gold-illuminated border to match its manuscript's opening page stood out sharply like a star shining through a dark night sky. Much had gone into decorating the

1 Ibn al-Haytham, Aporias Against Ptolemy, Sabra, A. I. and Shehaby, N. (eds); Sabra, 'Vita: Ibn al-Haytham', p. 55.

2 Ibn Sīnā, Autobiography, Sar-gudhasht-i Ibn Sīnā, Nafīsī, Saʿīd (ed, tr) (Tehran, 1332 [1953]); Autobiography, The Life of Ibn Sīnā: A Critical Edition and Annotated Translation, Gohlman, William, E. (ed, tr) (Albany, 1974); Autobiography, Avicenna and the Aristotelian Tradition: Introduction to Reading Avicenna's Philosophical Works, Gutas, Dimitri (tr), in Hans Daiber (ed), Islamic Philosophy and Theology: Texts and Studies, Vol. 4 (Leiden, 1988), pp. 22–30, p. 30: poem above.

3 Kheirandish, 'Windows into early science': Harvard University, Houghton Library. https://www.scholar.harvard.edu/ekheirandish/exhibits. Ireland, 'Houghton exhibit features Islamic sciences'. http://news.harvard.edu/gazette/story/2008/04/houghton-exhibit-features-islamic-sciences/

bordered frame alone, including gold-illumination in a specialised craft school, with the help of a historian-artist.[4]

The write-up on the 'Windows' exhibit, held in a rare book library later described as a 'mother ship' of the university's literary collection,[5] captured other forms and colours through the dynamic and graphic nature of the words and images imaginatively selected in that piece: that the exhibit's three display cases offered the 'latest time machine', [6] that walking up the curving stairs to the second-floor, 'between shelves of rare books – Melville, Longfellow, Whitman, and others –' eyes would be set on three glass cases that 'bottle up time . . . from an era when scholars from the Middle East were translating the works of ancient Greek scientists, making science of their own, and preserving a legacy of knowledge that would one day help power the Renaissance in Europe'. The exhibit was held at an architecturally rich classic building[7] that was much more than a treasury housing the variously dated manuscripts and editions on display among its rare items; other forms of periodic progression were captured by introductory labels showcased next to a visitor's book: that the three display cases were prepared in conjunction with three successive courses taught by an instructor acting as a guest curator; that the courses were offered at different departments, terms, and levels; and that students were invited to contribute captions on manuscripts and primary sources assigned in courses with titles reflecting their distant times and places.[8]

The exhibit's three course-inspired display cases were placed on the second floor of that rare book library adjacent to an elegant event room and presentation area with a newly installed LCD projector, the 'liquid crystal display' beaming images of manuscripts and rare books as part of newly designed class sessions held in preparation for the Windows exhibit. For each display case, there were themes and objects: at the centre, the theme of 'science and locality' with the two-city dialogue manuscript representing regional and cultural diversity; and on its sides, the themes of 'science and authority', and 'science and universality', with a reed pen and brass sword representing scientific and political authority, and facing chess and backgammon sets representing strategy and chance through cosmology. Together, the texts and objects, some coming from private collections, captured three course themes through twelve items and seven languages in line with the cosmological matches of such numbers, from three months in a season, to seven days in a week and twelve months in a year.

Most striking among the displays was the colour image of the *Dialogue* manuscript printed inside a matching gold-illuminated frame in the central glass case of the Windows exhibit capturing subjects well beyond Baghdad and Isfahan of a specific

[4] North Bennet Street School, Boston, MA: workshop for gold illumination. www.nbss.edu/. Elizabeth Cavicchi, science historian, MIT instructor, and artist contributed to the 'Windows' exhibit.

[5] Ireland, Corydon, 'Treasure island', Harvard Gazette, 9 November 2011: 'Houghton is the mother ship for Harvard's literary collections'. https://news.harvard.edu/gazette/story/2011/11/treasure-island/

[6] Ireland, 'Houghton exhibit': 'If scholarship is the only reliable means of time travel, the Houghton Library offers up Harvard's latest time machine: "Windows into Early Science"'.

[7] Houghton Library, opened in 1942: https://library.harvard.edu/libraries/houghton

[8] Kheirandish, 'From Alexandria to Baghdad'; 'From Baghdad to Isfahan', and 'Historical Dialogues from the Near East' formed the opening titles respectively. https://www.scholar.harvard.edu/ekheirandish/teaching

time and place; as did the other cities featured in cases on either side of it, from Alexandria and Cairo to Maragha and Samarqand: micromaps placed in all three display cases, coming from archives next to the hosting library, featured Baghdad and Isfahan of a range of periods, those as early as the Umayyad Caliphate up to ca. 750, and ʿAbbasids of the Local Dynasties', ca. 1000, and as late as the 'Middle East' of years 1500 to 1750,[9] stretching to a thousand years.

All such features of the Windows exhibit were to stand out still further by its coincidence with an 'exhibition' in that same building with a close enough time and place: it so happened that the exhibition 'European travelers to Safavid Iran', was launched on the level below the Windows exhibit with enough date and subject overlaps to occasion combined gallery tours and summer visitors, and joint publications in academic journals:[10] the displays of the exhibition 'From rhubarbs to rubies' similarly featured seven languages, those of Latin, French, English, Dutch, Italian, German, and Persian, instead of Greek, Arabic, Middle Persian, Persian, Latin, Hebrew, and Turkish; their opening lines also quoted a European visitor to both Baghdad and Isfahan where images through the eyes of a young seventeenth-century Italian and his French sketcher included a line partly inspiring the Windows exhibit about the world itself as a 'great book':[11] this was a line with not only old resonances, but renewed inspirations for a young viewer of a much later age, one with open-book visits away from home as part of a related project.

The young viewer's open-book visits were first occasioned by the puzzles of a 'Dialogue' project related to the centrepiece of the 'Windows' exhibit: there, the opening manuscript folios of the *Dialogue of Baghdad and Isfahan* occupying a prominent place in its colourful indigo frame posed immediate problems of dating next to three other items representing the two cities featured: one case next to the *Dialogue* was a *Calendar of Timekeeping* attributed to an author working in Baghdad with a questionable authorship marking his name in the library handlist: a pressing puzzle here was that the attribution of that text to an early author like 'Abu al-Wafaʾ Buzjani' followed by a question mark seemed off, because the name of a later figure 'Muhyi al-Din Maghribi', identified on the displayed manuscript in a gallery tour,[12] did not allow it. Another case was a fully annotated *Canon* of medicine by the well-known scholar Ibn Sina, Latinised as Avicenna, an author closely associated with Isfahan, this time with a questionable

9 Base historical maps: ca. 750, 1000, 1250, 1500, 1750, Tubingen Atlas, Harvard University Archives. http://library.harvard.edu/university-archives. Colour-coded digital maps: Internal access. https://www.scholar.harvard.edu/ekheirandish/multimedia

10 Kheirandish, 'Windows into early science', pp. 581–91; and Brancaforte, Elio and Brentjes, Sonja. (2008). 'From rhubarb to rubies', Iranian Studies, 41, 4, Special Issue: Bier, Carol, Kheirandish, Elaheh and Yousefi, Najm al-Din (eds), Sciences, Crafts, and the Production of Knowledge: Iran and Eastern Islamic Lands (ca. 184–1153 AH/800–1740 CE), and 595–600 respectively (overlap: May 23 to July 23, 2008).

11 Brancaforte and Brentjes, 'From rhubarb to rubies', p. 595: 'Ambrosio Bembo (1652–1705), Venetian traveler to Safavid Iran (1671–1675)'.

12 The manuscript of the Calendar of Timekeeping naming 'Shaykh Wafāʾ' had a question mark after Abu al-Wafāʾ al-Būzjānī on the description of Widener Library's Middle-Eastern Division. The manuscript, now at Houghton Library, was first identified by Michael Hopper, and the name Muḥyī al-Dīn Maghribī by Nasser Rabbat.

authorship of another text with Isfahan connections;[13] and yet another case was an arithmetical *Summary*,[14] with a gold-illuminated crown posing questions about a much later period, and beyond associations with Isfahan among other cities. The side display cases posed different puzzles, like the one with two items involving Baghdad through authors as prominent as Hasan Ibn al-Haytham and Nasir al-Din Tusi, spending the start and end of their active lives in that city, both producing works later printed in Europe.[15] Combined with standing questions around the very text of the *Dialogue* of Baghdad and Isfahan, from author and patron identities to composition and transcription dates, such open-ended questions would soon occasion visits by a young student to Europe and beyond.

4.2 A Young Visitor with Secret Plans

It was September 2008, and Leo had just arrived on a speed train from London to Paris on a day that completed the British cycle of his manuscript adventures. Earlier that summer he had started his overseas visits to cities in and beyond Europe as part of the exhibit 'Windows into early science': his later summer visits were occasioned by the extension of that exhibit into related projects, like one titled 'Windows into early science and craft', scheduled for another rare book library in another Ivy League university.[16] Acting as a helper in both 'Windows' exhibits, Leo had been assigned to overseeing caption contributions for the selected text and objects on display: for the 'Early science' exhibit, from fact-checking to choosing micro-maps for each display case;[17] and for its 'Early craft' sequel, inviting contributors anywhere from high-school students and course instructors to independent scholars and lecturers for its own twelve-item selections.[18]

The showcasing of the selected manuscripts of the 'Early science' exhibit and its various extensions had already taken that exhibit beyond its launching city and site; the

[13] Ibn Sīnā, Shaykh al-Raʾīs, ʿAbū Alī al-Ḥusayn ibn ʿAbdallāh, Al-Qānūn fī al-ṭibb, Manuscript: Harvard University, Houghton Library. Persian mechanical text attribution: Miʿyār al-ʿuqūl [Rational Measures], Humāʾī, Jalāl al-Dīn (ed) (Tehran, 1331 [1952]); questioned: Shah, Mir Hussein, 'Athār-ī mansūb bih Shaykh al-Raʾīs' ('A work attributed to Shaykh al-Raʾīs [Ibn Sinā]'), Indo-Iranica, 8, 3 (1955), pp. 1–14.

[14] ʿĀmilī, Bahāʾ al-Dīn, Muḥammad ibn Ḥusayn (Shaykh Bahāʾī), Khulāṣat al-ḥisāb: Harvard University, Houghton Library Manuscript Arab SM4284. Edition based on other manuscripts: Khulāṣat al-ḥisāb (Tehran, s.n. [1311]).

[15] Alhazen, Opticae Thesaurus [Latin] Risner, Friedrich (ed) (Basel, 1572, repr. New York 1972); Ṭūsī, Naṣīr al-Dīn, Recension of Euclid's Elements. [Arabic], Rome, 1594, Harvard University, Houghton Library Typ 525.94.373F.

[16] Kheirandish, Elaheh, 'Windows into early science and craft', Spring 2010: John Hay Rare Book Library, Brown University: Exhibit dedicated to the memory of David Pingree. Elizabeth Cavicchi (image illumination). https://blogs.brown.edu/libnews/27/. https://www.scholar.harvard.edu/ekheirandish/exhibits

[17] 'Early science' caption contributions: Elaheh Kheirandish (1, 5, 9); Daniela Helbig (2); Sonam Velani: (3); Cecily Lopes and Julia Kinsgdale (4); Patrick Brennan (6); Abigail Darby and Mary Brazelton (7); Maham Siddiqi (8); Colin Donovan (10); Ayodeji Ogunnaike (11); Avigail Noy (12).

[18] 'Early science and craft' caption contributions: Elaheh Kheirandish (1–5, 12); Farzan Vafa (6); Asad Goodarzy (7); Asadollah Kheirandish (8); Arash Afraz (9–11).

evolving puzzles involving more authors, texts, cities and sites were now generating not just newly assigned tasks, but a series of unfolding secret plans.

It had all started with the display case labeled 'From Alexandria to Baghdad' and authors and texts associated with its theme of 'science and authority'. In the spring of that year, Leo had been given a grant to extend his intellectual horizons beyond academic courses to participate in field work, including an international conference in a city none other than Alexandria, Egypt, once part of Greece. That occasion had landed him in the new 'Bibliotheca Alexandrina',[19] an impressive site reminiscent of the ancient Library of Alexandria. This was long before 'Alexandria' and 'Baghdad' would appear side by side, not just in the title of articles long published,[20] but those of forthcoming works, from book titles to projects and lectures, some sponsored by the library itself.[21] But the event that had taken Leo to historic Alexandria and its great modern library was different from all of these. Attending session after session of a specialised conference titled 'Lost and embedded manuscripts', and hearing 'paper' after 'paper' from across the world firsthand, was not an everyday occasion; and Leo had been instantly drawn to the themes of that conference through its website,[22] without knowing the first thing about what the word 'embedded' in its title exactly meant: this was a word he had only heard of in the context of journalists 'embedded' with troops in the expanding war zones of his own time; and learning from the conference website that the original Arabic word could mean 'disappearance, concealment, fading into oblivion' had made him especially curious. So had other descriptions on the conference 'home page', such as 'building and raising awareness of Arabic manuscript heritage', and conferences, with the word 'manuscript' all over them, from 'millenary, signed, commentary and translated' manuscripts of the years before to the 'lost and embedded' manuscripts of that year. This one had a broad coverage: the part 'lost' applied to cases from arbitrary disappearance to intended concealment, and 'embedded', to both partial and complete cases, all in the course of four days.

The theme of that year's Alexandria conference fit well into Leo's project of a 'dialogue of two cities', one whose only known manuscript was inserted into a volume of literary genres containing subjects far from contests between objects or people; the conference being focused on manuscripts had exposed Leo to related handwritten volumes, or 'codices', the word used by specialists there as a plural for a manuscript volume called a 'codex'. It was these strange sounding sources and collections which

19 The Library of Alexandria, Bibliotheca Alexandrina, opened in 2002. www.bibalex.org/en/default

20 Meyerhof, Max, From Alexandria to Baghdad, Heinen, A. (tr), in Introduction to the History of Science: Course Source Book compiled by A. I. Sabra (Cambridge, MA, 1978); Gutas, Dimitri, 'The "Alexandria to Baghdad" complex of narratives: A contribution to the study of philosophical and medical historiography among the Arabs', Documenti e Studi Sulla Tradizione Filosofica Medievale, 10 (1999), pp. 155–93; Pingree, 'From Alexandria to Baghdad to Byzantium'.

21 Sidoli, Nathan and van Brummelen, Glen (eds), From Alexandria, Through Baghdad: Surveys and Studies in the Ancient Greek and Medieval Islamic Mathematical Sciences in Honor of J. L. Berggren (Berlin, Heidelberg, 2014). Bibliotheca Alexandrina: Alexandria Project. www.bibalex.org/en/Project/Details?DocumentID=189&Keywords. Lecture: From Alexandria to Baghdad. www.bibalex.org/en/News/Details?DocumentID=3736&Keywords.

22 Bibliotheca Alexandrina: 6–8 May 2008, 5th International Conference: Lost and embedded manuscripts. www.bibalex.org/en/events/eventdetails?id=5269

advanced some of the puzzles of both his project and its companion exhibit through various leads and inspirations. Most inspiring among the sources were manuscripts and volumes related to the works of outstanding historical figures challenging the words of authorities from ancient Alexandria, those like Euclid and Ptolemy, associated with the Alexandria of a few hundred years before and after the 'common era'; and most challenging among the subjects were the visual theories[23] of such age-old authorities assuming rays issue from the eye to objects to perceive them, assumptions which were literally 'turned around' with the ingenious reversal of the direction of radiation from the object to the eye by ground-breaking historical figures of hundreds of years later. The most critical breakthrough carried the name of someone called 'Ibn al-Haytham' working not far from Baghdad in a multi-volume work on optics, still mainly devoted to the subject of vision. The name of that 'revolutionary' figure, his 'masterpiece' in optics, and the relevant Greek, Arabic and Latin manuscripts in both Islamic and European lands had come up again and again in the Alexandria conference, not only more than once, but from quite different angles. Two world-famous scholars who held quite different views on the subject, including whether there was one or two 'Ibn al-Haytham's in the first place, had opened and closed the conference: the scholar holding that the name 'Ibn al-Haytham' represented two different people from around the same period and area had started with a paper under the broad title of 'Mathematics and science';[24] and the scholar with not one but two published works with the title of 'One Ibn al-Haytham or two' had presented different conclusions, not only in hundred-page long publications, but in a 'keynote address' towards the end of the conference:[25] in a spacious auditorium full of eager participants in his native Alexandria – and in the last public lecture of that scholar on a flower-filled podium – he had made a distinction between not two but three 'Ibn al-Haytham's, this time representing one and the same man passing through the records of time: the Arabic author of a *Book of Optics* titled *Kitab al-Manazir*, and the 'Alhacen' and 'Alhazen' of Latin translations and printed editions of it after his first name, Al-Hasan. Such key distinctions made in a presentation titled the 'European journey' of the work's manuscripts, called to life the words of that modern scholar's own lifelong, multi-volume work on the *Optics* of Ibn al-Haytham where the sharp contrast of the fate of that book in Islamic and European lands coined the terms 'checkered history'.[26]

That was where Leo's inspiration to follow the footpaths of that fateful book and its author had started to take shape. The idea was similar to what he had seen in the published footpaths of another scholar of the same period called Ibn Sina,[27] a scholar of Persian, not Arab origin, associated with Isfahan not Baghdad, and well known in

[23] Lindberg, David C., Theories of Vision from Al-Kindi to Kepler (Chicago, 1976); Lindberg, David C. 'The intromission-extramission controversy in Islamic visual theory: Alkindi versus Avicenna', in Machamer, Peter K. and Turnbull, Robert C. (eds), Studies in Perception: Interrelations in the History and Philosophy of Science (Columbus, 1978).

[24] Rashed, Roshdi, 'Mathematics and Science', 6 May 2008.

[25] Sabra, A. I., 'One Ibn al-Haytham or two: An exercise in reading bio-bibliographical sources', Zeitschrift für Geschichte der arabisch-islamischen Wissenschaften, 12 (1998), pp. 1–50; 15 (2002/3), pp. 95–108; 'The European Journey of Ibn al-Haytham's MSS of his *Optics*', 8 May 2008.

[26] Sabra, Optics of Ibn al-Haytham, Preface, vol. 2, p. xi.

[27] Nafīsī (ed, Persian tr), Autobiography, Sar-gudhasht-i Ibn Sīnā: map with footpaths on final page.

Europe through the Latinised name of 'Avicenna'. Helping to design digital, searchable, versions of such maps with the aim of following the footpaths of these and other historical figures who were important enough to be showcased in his ongoing project was to be a critical part of Leo's own onward 'journeys'.

That day in September, Leo had just arrived in Paris from London as part of a related journey. The visit before that had been to nearby Oxford, where he had found much more than he expected. At Oxford's Bodleian Library, he had seen not only many of the manuscripts of Asadi's *Dialogue of Night and Day* in one place, before chasing another dozen in Paris;[28] he had looked at multiple other manuscripts with texts and figures associated with names involving both Baghdad and Isfahan: among them a manuscript volume involving Abu al-Wafa' Buzjani,[29] the scholar in Baghdad to whom the Window exhibit's displayed *Calendar of Timekeeping* was misattributed, as well as a scholar whose name as 'Abu al-Fath Isfahani'[30] went far beyond Isfahan through a Latin translation of his work. Leo had read with interest the type-written introduction to that codex[31] about how 'a letter . . . found between the leaves of a seventeenth-century Atlas in the Bodleian throws some light on the circumstances under which the manuscript had reached' it; how 'it had fallen into the hands of a bookseller' when it did; and how 'in the light of the facts . . . the story can be reconstructed'. That unexpected experience had set Leo's mind on treating the puzzles of his own project like a detective story. But through other one-of-a-kind manuscript codices, this time in Paris, he could figure out, not just who to pick for the reconstruction of his next 'Dialogue' sections, but how to piece together other puzzles through manuscript codices to be viewed and deciphered in Paris and elsewhere.

The first of those manuscript codices was one so remarkable for the unique items contained between its covers that it would come to be known as the 'Paris Codex', after the city of its location in the Bibliothèque Nationale de France.[32] The written words and drawn lines in that volume, transcribed in a seemingly single hand, and in a combination of black and red script for the lines and letters, presented many atypical features and questions: why the volume was directed to the crafts more than the sciences, and to the practical more than the theoretical aspects of geometry; why most of the items in it were written in Persian rather than the standard language of Arabic for the sciences of the time; and when, where, by whom, and for whom were some of these items composed, transcribed, illustrated and coloured, and why. There were some rare items in that manuscript volume that caught Leo's attention: the first item was an Arabic version of an *Elements of Geometry* by the ancient Greek author Euclid, with propositions and figures just like the one Leo had written about in his 'Dialogue'

28 Browne, Tadhkiratu al-shu'ará (Memoirs of the poets), p. 11.

29 Pingree, David, 'Abu'l-Wafā Būzjānī', Encyclopedia Iranica (EIr), 1, 4, pp. 392–4. www.iranicaonline.org/articles/abul-wafa-buzjani. Hashemipour, Behnaz, 'Būzjānī: Abū al-Wafā' Muḥammad ibn Muḥammad ibn Yaḥyā al-Būzjānī', The Biographical Encyclopedia of Astronomers (BEA) (2007), pp. 188–9. https://islamsci.mcgill.ca/RASI/BEA/Buzjani_BEA.htm

30 Pingree, David, 'Abu'l-Fatḥ Esfahanī', Encyclopedia Iranica (EIr), 1, 3 (1983), pp. 284–5. www.iranicaonline.org/articles/abul-fath-b

31 Oxford University, Bodleian Library, Thurston 3: Introduction: pp. 152–3.

32 Necipoğlu (ed), Arts of Ornamental Geometry. https://brill.com/view/title/32181

chapters with reference to mathematicians named Khwarizmi and Thabit ibn Qurra; but this item atypically mentioned craft-related pieces like gems; the second item was a Persian version of an Arabic text on practical geometry, naming its author Abu al-Wafa' Buzjani in its Persian form 'Abu al-Vafa'', the only work of its kind citing geometers and craftsmen in the same 'gathering' with different methods for the same problems; the third item was an anonymous text in Persian with multiple repeat geometrical patterns and constructions, as well as a mention of the name Ibn al-Haytham Persianised as 'Ibn-i Heytham'; and the fourth item was a flat 'map' in a square frame featuring cities that included Baghdad and Isfahan, the latter, magnified (Plate 12).[33]

Each item introduced its own puzzles, while offering clues or leads along the way. The first item introduced the puzzle of what an Arabic Euclidean text was doing in a mostly Persian practical geometry volume; the clue it offered was that crafts too required forms of proof, in this case applying equality of areas[34] from Arabic Euclidean geometry to Persian 'ornamental geometry'. The second item introduced the puzzle of why a text by Buzjani, from Buzjan in north west Iran, who lived most of his life in Baghdad in south east Iraq, was translated into Persian more than once; the clue it offered was that the text had wide reception and application in Persian lands including a late Persian translation involving a figure with a possible Isfahan connection.[35] The third item introduced the puzzle of what the name of 'Ibn al-Haytham', mostly associated with theories of light and vision, was doing in a text containing repeat geometrical patterns;[36] the clue it offered was about the role of surveying in practical geometry, and the relevance of an early work by Ibn al-Haytham on measurement;[37] and the fourth item introduced the puzzle of why a map featuring Isfahan so prominently was included in that volume in the first place; the clue it offered was that the map itself may have been drawn by the same figure drawing and illustrating the entire volume.[38] Other manuscript codices offered other leads or pieces of information. A manuscript volume in Paris containing a copy of the *Calendar of Timekeeping*[39] displayed in the first Windows exhibit seconded the unlikely nature of a 'Shaykh Vafa'' named there as author, intended as 'Abu al-Wafa' Buzjani', the author of a manual on

[33] Kheirandish, Elaheh, 'An early tradition in practical geometry: The telling lines of unique Arabic and Persian sources', in Necipoğlu (ed), Arts of Ornamental Geometry, pp. 79-144: pp. 92, 96, 106, and 118. https://brill.com/view/title/32181

[34] Kheirandish, 'Early tradition in practical geometry', p. 116.

[35] Abū Isḥāq Kūbanānī: Kheirandish, 'Early tradition in practical geometry'. The Isfahan connection: Ghanbari, Vahid, 'The literary works and letters of Abū Isḥāq Kūbanānī' (unpublished lecture: Nashr-i Tārikh-i Iran, founder: Mansoureh Ettehadieh, Tehran, May 2016); suggestion: 'Kujān' near Isfahan (inconclusive). Karamati, Younes, 'Abū Isḥāq al-Kūbunānī', Negahban, Farzin (tr), in Madelung, Wilfred and Daftary, Farhad (eds), Encyclopedia Islamica (London, 2008–09).

[36] Necipoğlu, Arts of Ornamental Geometry (facs).

[37] Rashed, Roshdi, Ibn al-Haytham's Theory of Conics, Geometrical Constructions and Practical Geometry, Field, J. V. (tr), Vol. 3, in Nader El-Bizri (ed), A History of Arabic Sciences and Mathematics, 4 vols. (London, New York, 2013), p. 573.

[38] Kheirandish, 'Early tradition in practical geometry', pp. 117–19.

[39] Rosenfeld and Ihsanoğlu, Mathematicians, Astronomers, and Other Scholars, No. 872, p. 293.

geometrical constructions,[40] despite the latter's title as 'Shaykh' in his old age; another manuscript codex containing a mechanical text in Persian presented features that partially explained why that text, later published under the name of Ibn Sina, could be a misattribution,[41] even if Ibn Sina partly carried the title of 'Shaykh' as 'Shaykh al-Ra'is', meaning Chief Master, far in advance of old age.

Leo would continue to engage with matters related to Baghdad and Isfahan through pairs like science and craft, Arabic and Persian, texts and figures, as well as words and lines. But his selection of themes and characters representing such pairs in his next section would come through other unique volumes both in and beyond that library and city. The last leg of Leo's visits in that year would take him to an outstanding city with a known record of the most illustrious oriental manuscripts and codices for rewarding inspirations from even the smallest pool of items scattered between the city's various resourceful and renowned libraries. The city was Istanbul, a historic site sitting on coastal waters at a point where East and West physically met through the city's own European and Asian sides. This was a city filled with other corresponding pairs: two magnificent architectural structures facing each other as a stunning 'blue mosque' and a rust-coloured church-turned-mosque called Ayasofya, crossing ages and cultures through daily laser shows in several languages;[42] and at a short distance, arose two outstanding libraries, one called Süleymaniye after the name of the Ottoman Sultan Suleyman the Magnificent, and built as part of a school complex;[43] the other called Topkapi, spread out above a vast water view with a name capturing the form of the dome structure beautifying one of many parts of its once palace complex.[44] The two libraries housed between them textual and visual masterpieces of various kinds. Among the former's notable textual productions were all the known transcriptions of the important and influential *Book of Optics* by Ibn al-Haytham, including those transcribed in his native city of Basra by his own son in law;[45] so were various manuscripts of the surviving works of Ibn Sina,[46] to the exclusion of a *Book of Mechanics*,[47] weakening its attribution to him. As for beautiful visual productions, there was a *Book of Constructions*[48] by Abu al-Wafa' Buzjani in its original Arabic, shining

40 Kheirandish, 'Early tradition in practical geometry' includes reference to the works of the author relevant to practical geometry and astronomy, including: Būzjānī, Abu al-wafā', Fī Mā yahtāju ilayhi al-ṣāni' min a'māl al-handasa [On What is Needed by the Craftsman from Geometrical Constructions], Ghorbanī, Abu al-Qāsim and Sheykhan, M. A. (facs), Būzjānī-nāma (Tehran, 1371 [1992]).

41 Blochet, E., Catalogue des Manuscrits Persans de la Bibliothèque Nationale, No. 803, pp. 73–4: 'François Pétis de la Croix, the teacher to the son of Mir Morteza, the son in law of Shah 'Abbās II, from 1674 to 1676'. Text comparable to Mi'yār al-'uqūl, Humā'ī, J. (ed).

42 Arabic, English and French.

43 Süleymaniye school complex: library and mosque named after Sultan Suleyman the Magnificent. http://hazine.info/suleymaniye-library/

44 Topkapi palace complex: library and mosque, takes its name from a dome shape. https://hazine.info/topkapiarchiveandlibrary/

45 Sabra, Optics of Ibn al-Haytham, Vol. 2, p. lxxx; Sabra, '"Commentary" that saved the text', p. 123.

46 The Süleymaniye Manuscript Library in Istanbul houses many manuscripts of works by Ibn Sina ... https://en.unesco.org/silkroad/silk-road-themes/documentary-heritage/works-ibn-sina-suleymaniye-manuscript-library

47 Humā'ī (ed), Mi'yār al-'uqūl.

48 Būzjānī, Kitāb A'māl al-handasa (Geometrical Constructions); Kheirandish, 'An early tradition in practical geometry', p. 87. Qurbanī and Shaykhan, Būzjānī-nāma (facs), Ulugh Beg MS, Istanbul.

through an illuminated seal from the court of that student-prince in Samarqand named Ulugh Beg; a heavily illustrated *Book of Instruction*[49] by Abu Rayhan Biruni, dedicated to a mysterious female figure with the first name of Rayhana in both Arabic and Persian; and a *Book of Constellations*[50] in Arabic in the tradition of the celebrated *Star Catalogue* of Ptolemy by ʿAbd al-Rahman Sufi, himself a near contemporary of Ibn al-Haytham, Ibn Sina, Buzjani, and Biruni. In the case of the latter text, there also stood out the same Arabic work, this time in its later Persian translation by Nasir al-Din Tusi,[51] a text claimed to be in the hand of its author, one credited with a constellation poem: the assumed 'autographed' Persian translation in the bound volume living in Istanbul had the additionally rare feature of combining an attractive script, name of translator, and assumed transcriber, with the date, year and place of the text's completion.[52]

Such was the state of these and other unique manuscripts in modern day Istanbul: they were unique not always as a single surviving manuscript of the texts they represented; but as precious compositions, transcriptions, illumination, or illustrations, that were explicitly stated as being 'preserved for present and future generations'. And yet, in September of the year 2008 when Leo was completing his European visit in that city to return to his second year of university half way around the world, the physical manuscript holdings in the treasure houses of such libraries were already replaced by scans of their successive folios, and were only to be viewed through manuscript readers in the library's reading room.[53]

For Leo, who still enjoyed the quiet moments and charming spaces of those reading rooms overlooking inviting courtyards, even if it meant flipping manuscript scans on a static screen, the nature of the puzzle behind the secret plans of his visits were fast expanding. The puzzle of why any such manuscripts or codices were housed in such cities or libraries in the first place, as opposed to places of their original productions or acquisitions, was becoming the puzzle of all puzzles; and the highest collections in both quality and quantity, being in a city like Istanbul, was at the time still an uncovered mystery.

In the quiet moments of reading rooms far away from what was becoming Leo's most favourite city and library, he would find partial answers to such questions. And in a reading room back in his home university, one looking up at a turquoise dome and over a green campus,[54] he would soon be flipping physically through multiple pages of two old sources devoted to oriental manuscripts in Istanbul. A long monograph from the 1930s in German[55] quickly gave him title after title of manuscripts in Arabic, Persian and Turkish, and name after name of multiple libraries and collections in Istanbul alone. But a slightly shorter publication from the 1950s, under the inviting title

[49] Bīrūnī, Kitāb al-Tafhīm; Rosenfeld and Ihsanoğlu, Mathematicians, Astronomers, and Other Scholars, No. 348, pp. 148–9: list includes MSS in Istanbul.

[50] Ṣūfī, Kitāb Ṣuwar al-kawākib, Istanbul, Süleymaniye Library, MS Fatih 3422.

[51] Tūsī, Tarjamah-i Kitāb Ṣuwar al-kawākib, Istanbul, Süleymaniye Library MS. Ayasofya 2595.

[52] Ṭūsī, Naṣīr al-Dīn, Tarjamah-i Suwar al-kawākib (facs), p. 196.

[53] Süleymaniye Library reading room is where manuscript scans have long been viewed on screens.

[54] Harvard's Widener Library, Locker Reading Room, has a high ceiling with a turquoise-coloured dome.

[55] Krause, Max, 'Stambuler handschriften islamischer mathematiker', Quellen und Studien zur Geschichte der Mathematik, Astronomie und Physik, 3 (Abt. B) (1936), pp. 437–532.

of 'Autographs in Turkish libraries'[56] took much longer to go through, with pages of readings he could not put down about Istanbul libraries and their colourful stories. The opening drew him right in, with the author writing he had 'walked from library to library' for 'the exact official numbers of the manuscripts entrusted to their care'; more capturing than numbers were the lively descriptions, starting with a 'highly learned collector of manuscripts in modern Turkey', how his collection came from 'everybody, who had inherited Arabic or Persian books from his fathers and did not know what to do with them'; how 'most of his books were stored in an unused old oven', and after his death when the government purchased his library, books were 'taken out of the oven, registered and counted'; how the records of the time showed 'Istanbul libraries alone as composed of about 150 different bequeathed funds distributed among 16 libraries with works from 'the latest period of the Caliphate of Baghdad', and some like one by Biruni 'written by the famous scholar himself', to become an 'autograph'; and most notable of all, how had 'these treasures come together' through swords, purchases or gifts. Still, not a word in this half-a-century-old record, of an Ottoman Palace Library Inventory discovered and published,[57] with previously unknown manuscripts in Istanbul, a city with forthcoming 'tales' of its own.[58]

Meanwhile, sitting day in and day out under a tall turquoise dome overlooking a green campus far from Istanbul, each day led Leo to more sources, and with it, new ideas. It was under that tall turquoise dome looking over the green campus of his university that Leo had recently heard a graduation address by the worldwide famous author of a 'seven-book' series; and it was the powerful message of that address on the 'Importance of imagination'[59] that would colour his seven-chapter narrative through closer identifications with historical characters. The collective effect of all such experiences then brought to life the next two characters of Leo's 'Dialogue' from among many stars shining above and beyond a city now treasuring most their works: thus emerged an 'Arab and Persian' representing Baghdad and Isfahan, and through them, other pairs, from science and craft, to words and lines. Leo would next turn to the fourth of his seven indicators, 'books', to test their role in the case of other key moments and developments. Little did he know at the time that his first selected character, the 'Ibn al-Haytham' and 'Ibn-i Heytham' of Arabic and Persian, and the 'Alhacen' and 'Alhazen' of his Latinised first name Al-Hasan, would return to the site of an architecturally rich 'rare' book library once called a 'mother ship', and soon, a rare 'enchanted palace';[60] and that signicantly, his ever-lasting book on optics, the *Optika*

56 Ritter, Hellmut, 'Autographs in Turkish libraries', Oriens, 6, 1 (1953), pp. 63–90.

57 Necipoğlu, Kafadar, and Fleischer, (eds), Treasures of Knowledge: An Inventory of the Ottoman Palace Library (1502/3–1503/4), 2 vols. (Leiden, Boston, 2019); Maróth, Miklós, 'The library of Sultan Bayazit II', in Jeremiás, Éva M. (ed), Irano-Turkic Cultural Contact in the 11th-17th Centuries (Piliscsaba, 2003).

58 Hughes, Tale of Three Cities.

59 Ireland, Corydon, 'Yes, it was a magical talk: Rowling casts spell at afternoon exercises', Harvard Gazette, 5 June 2008: themes: "The Fringe Benefits of Failure, and the Importance of Imagination". https://news.harvard.edu/gazette/story/2008/06/haa-annual-meeting/

60 Carling, Jennifer and Rosenberg, John S., 'An "enchanted palace": A humanistic "masterclass" for Houghton Library's seventy-fifth anniversary', Harvard Magazine, March–April, 2017, pp. 36–41, p. 36: In a 1924 letter, Coolidge, director of the Harvard University Library, imagined an 'enchanted palace on the raised ground close to Widener'. https://harvardmagazine.com/2017/03/an-enchanted-palace

and *Manazir* of Greek and Arabic, and *Aspectibus* and *Perspectiva* of Latinised Europe, would turn full circle to act as a strong case for the historical significance of 'books', and the consequence of their transmission.

Chapter 4: 'Dialogue' of Arab and Persian
Science of Words, Craft of Lines – Books
By Charles Leo Scribner, September 2008

> [*Arab:*] *Of all the creatures, humans are the greatest in speech,*
> *and of all humans, none are better in speech than us . . .*
> [*Persian:*] *We know all your crafts, all the way, while you are,*
> *helpless and perplexed from every one of ours . . .*
>
> Asadi Tusi, *'Dialogue' of Arab and Persian*, ca. 1000,
> English translation: Elaheh Kheirandish[61]

4.3 *An Arab City with a 'Critical' Mind*

It was August circa 950, more than a decade before one of the brightest stars of early science was to be born not far from Baghdad.[62] No one would have cared about the exact details of his birth, death, life and works, had he not gained such increasing fame, with so many credits to his name. About a thousand years after he lived, at the turn of the year 2000, he was to be credited by globally well-known journals for 'setting in motion the most important idea of the millennium – the rise of the scientific method',[63] and with even more exaggeration, for 'work on refraction and lenses . . . led to the invention of the telescope and microscope'.[64] This was a year when lenses were to be 'nominated' in the form of 'eyeglasses', as 'the most important inventions of the last thousand years', as part of 'The Power of Big Ideas';[65] and such credits were to multiply exponentially through time. In the year 2005, one that happened to add the years 965 and 1040 of the approximate birth and death dates of that shining star, would come

[61] Asadī Ṭūsī, Munāẓirih-i ʿArab va ʿAjam, Khaleghi-Motlagh (ed), 'Asadī Ṭūsī', pp. 69–79: p. 70, line 23; p. 73, line 49, Kheirandish, Elaheh (tr, excerpt)
'[*Arab:*] *Insān mah-i har jānivar az lafẓ-i lisān-ast, V-az mā bih lisān nīst kasī bihtar az insān . . .*
[*Persian:*] *Mā ṣunʿ-i shumā yik-sarih dān-īm u shumā pāk*
Hast-īd zih har ṣunʿ zi-mā ʿājiz u ḥayrān . . .'

[62] Sabra, 'Ibn al-Haytham', p. 189: 'al-Baṣrī', Optics of Ibn al-Haytham, pp. xxi–xxiii; '"Commentary" that saved the text', p. 121; Langermann, 'Ibn al-Haytham', p. 556; Rosenfeld and Ihsanoğlu, Mathematicians, Astronomers, and Other Scholars, No. 328, pp. 131–8; Kheirandish, Elaheh, 'Light and dark: The "checkered history" of early optics', in Bloom, Jonathan and Blair, Sheila (eds), God Is the Light of the Heavens and the Earth: Light in Islamic Art and Culture (New Haven, 2015), pp. 61–85.

[63] Powers, Richard, 'Eyes wide open: When an obscure Arab scientist solved the riddle of light, the universe no longer belonged to God', The New York Times Magazine: The Best Stories and Inventions of the Last Thousand Years, 18 April 1999. www.nytimes.com/library/magazine/millennium/m1/powers.html

[64] Powers, 'Eyes wide open'.

[65] Begley, S., 'The power of big ideas', Newsweek, 11 Jan. 1999, pp. 58–9.

another notable honour. The celebration of the 'International Year of Physics', marking the centenary of the 1905 'special relativity' of the bright luminary, Albert Einstein, was to not only bombard the scientific star of the millennium before with numerous credits, from breakthroughs in the study of light and vision, to experiments and instruments guiding future generations; a crater on the Moon was to be named after him as 'Alhazen' in what was to be described as a 'fitting coincidence' that made his crater lie 'in the east whereas Einstein crater lies in the west beautifully reflecting their birth places back on Earth – Basra in Iraq and Ulm in Germany'.[66] Another high honour would come in 2015, the year named as 'The Year of Light':[67] events and publications featuring him with a high profile were to sweep across 'Western' cities, events from Palermo and Paris to Istanbul,[68] and publications from New Haven and New York to Washington. Yet another high honour would come in 2017 through the selection of a European print of his most celebrated book for prominent display in a prestigious rare book library named an 'enchanted palace'.[69] And more and more occasions were to follow to move him not just higher and higher on the ladder of distinction, but further and further from his increasingly far native lands and languages.

The credits of that scientific star, shining upon a boundless sky above many lands and languages, were not the only things that raised him so high up in comparative scale. Everything about him made him stand out. Even his name was not to go down in history as a single identity, as everyone else's did before and after him. Not only was there a dispute about his first name, as late as a thousand years after his own time, with over a hundred pages devoted to whether there were 'one or two' historical figures corresponding to the immortalised form of his name as 'Ibn al-Haytham'.[70] The more he became known beyond the borders of his own land, the more names his fame brought him, first through the foreign forms of his first name, Al-Hasan, as Alhacen and Alhazen, and later through the acronym form of his name, Ibn al-Haytham, as 'IH'.[71] His titles got more and more varied with time as well, from a 'Second Ptolemy', after the name of that scientific icon of ancient Greece living several centuries before him, to the 'First True Scientist'[72] that he was broadcast as by a scientist succeeding him by about a thousand years. Imaginary portrayals of him were to similarly abound in various forms in and beyond Arab and Persian lands, a 'face' printed on paper money, another sketched above a 'Visual Arts' gallery, another sculptured for a film academy,

66 Salih, H., Al-Amri, M. and El Gomati, M., 'The miracle of light', UNESCO, October, 2005. www.unesco.org/science/infocus_full_oct_05.shtml#1

67 United Nations Educational and Cultural Organization (UNESCO) named 2015 the year of light. www.light2015.org/Home.html

68 'Year of Light' events: Palermo, Italy, 2013, Paris, France, and Istanbul, Turkey, 2015.

69 Kheirandish, Elaheh, 'The spread of science: Alhazen, Opticae Thesaurus, 1572' in Carling and Rosenberg, 'An "enchanted palace"'. https://harvardmagazine.com/2017/03/an-enchanted-palace

70 Sabra, 'One Ibn al-Haytham or two'.

71 Sabra, 'Vita: Ibn al-Haytham'.

72 Meyerhof, Max, ''Alī Bayhaqī's Tatimmat Ṣiwān al-ḥikma. A biographical work on the learned men of Islam', Osiris, 8 (1948), pp. 122–216: pp. 155–6; Sabra, Optics of Ibn al-Haytham, vol. 2, p. lxv. Al-Khalili, Jim, 'First true scientist', BBC News, 4 January 2009. http://news.bbc.co.uk/2/hi/science/nature/7810846.stm

another faceless behind an exhibit of calligraphy,[73] and yet another in full view in a frontispiece standing not only tall, but next to Galileo[74] (Plate 4).

Things about 'Hasan, son of Haytham' that were to make him stand out much closer to his own time were themselves too many and unordinary for anyone, in any age, to wrap their heads around. Not long after his death, reports of his extra-ordinary life were to come in several shapes and colours by his immediate successors. Even the most common and commonly reported aspects of his life were far from ordinary. Not so much his name, given in the customs of the time with reference to a son or a father, in this case, 'father of ʿAli' as Abu ʿAli, and 'son of Haytham' as Ibn al-Haytham; and not so much his place, given as his native Basra, near Baghdad, later displaced to Cairo, as many were before and after him traveling both near and far to find a patron, a commission, or a teacher, here and there; not even his work, under a patron as odd as Caliph Al-Hakim of the ruling Fatimid Dynasty,[75] the founder of the 'House of Knowledge', the Dar al-ʿilm of Cairo, modelled after the 'House of Wisdom', the 'Bayt al-hikma' of Baghdad,[76] associated with ʿAbbasid Caliphs a century before. More uncommon was the nature and sequence of the reported circumstances surrounding his work: that he had first tried not only to get out of a patronised life which was so much sought after, but to pretend to be insane under a ruler considered to have been actually 'imbalanced'; that he had managed not only to earn his living from copying scientific manuscripts under the dome of the famous Azhar mosque in Cairo, but to lead a productive and effective scientific life free of distractions; and most critically, that his clever engineering of freedom had succeeded not just to free him from the demanding, and often degrading, shadow of patrons altogether, but take him far beyond the riches of any 'engineering project' to produce works whose multiple lists were reproduced by those same biographers. But what stood above all when it came to the man whose name was included in the list of those perished in a devastating plague in the same breathe as the extinction of the 'lamps of knowledge . . . leaving the surviving minds in darkness',[77] was something else: it was to be found, not in any later 'reports' involving him, but in the words of his very own writings. This time, what outshone everything else was a sign of not just a sharp critical mind behind truly superior work, but one with a strong and decisively 'critical' voice: to make oneself an enemy of all one reads, applying one's mind to the core and margins of its content, and attacking it from every side,[78] was a call set in words found nowhere as explicit or effective, much less expressed in such terms, by any one early author of a comparable setting.

[73] Belting, Hans, Florence and Baghdad: Renaissance Art and Arab Science, Lucas Schneider, Deborah (tr) (Cambridge, 2011). 'Dar Ibn al-Haytham for Visual Arts', Dubai, United Arab Emirates, December, 2012. 'Farabi Film Academy', Bāgh Firduws, Tehran, Iran, first visited in March 2012. Boullata, Kamal, 'Homage to al-Hasan Ibn al-Haytham', Artspace Gallery, Dubai, United Arab Emirates, December 2009.

[74] Frontispiece: Alhazen and Galileo, Selenographia, Johannes Hevelius, 1647, Harvard University, Houghton Library.

[75] Bosworth, Islamic Dynasties, pp. 46–8: Caliph al-Ḥākim (r. 996–1021); p. 48: 'unbalanced'; Sabra, 'Ibn al-Haytham', p. 189: 'capricious and murderous al-Ḥākim'.

[76] Gutas, Greek Thought, Arabic Culture, pp. 53–60: reexaminations.

[77] Sabra, "Commentary" that saved the text', p. 131.

[78] Sabra, 'Vita: Ibn al-Haytham', p. 55.

When Ibn al-Haytham was writing his timeless scientific works sometime after the year 1000, he could hardly have imagined the colourful stories that were to be attached to his name not so far from his own time and place: one story came from someone named Ibn al-Qifti[79] living over two hundred years later in both Egypt and Syria, in his valuable *History of Philosophers*, where philosophy embraced most of the sciences of the time: under the entry 'Hasan Ibn al-Haytham', among many other select figures, came from Ibn al-Qifti the story about the harsh Caliph al-Hakim first meeting Ibn al-Haytham in person outside of Cairo, then relieving the pretending 'mad' scientist from the unpromising project of regulating the flow of the Nile, before placing him under house arrest until the Caliph died himself; another story came from an author who revealed his source as his well-travelled friend Ibn Fas, one whose own name would be mostly remembered as an associate of Ibn Maymun, the Jewish scholar writing in Arabic and increasingly more celebrated through his Latinised name Maimonides;[80] another story came from a biographer called Bayhaqi,[81] living only about hundred years after Ibn al-Haytham in more distant Persian lands, still writing in Arabic, one who placed him first outside an Inn near Cairo, with the Caliph on a donkey and Ibn al-Haytham on a 'bench' under his feet to rise to the occasion with a height depicted as short;[82] and then, in a position where a disappointed Caliph looking over his plan, ordered the bench to be demolished right then and there, rather than having his shadow over his subject for the rest of his life, in that particular story. Through yet another story, in a *History of Physicians* compiled by someone named Ibn Abi Usaybiʿa,[83] the latest of the three authors who, being from Egypt and Syria, was to repeat some of the stories of the first author to the exclusion of the second, a very tall Ibn al-Haytham in status was to be given a very long list of scientific writings, more than a hundred surviving by then, some in his own hands, one providing a clue to his death date as after the year 432 AH corresponding to 1040–1041 of the 'common era', this time with a first name cited as 'Muhammad', not Hasan, striking a dispute centuries later.

Of all the authors on Ibn al-Haytham, it was he himself who portrayed the clearest image of his own exceptional case, of who he was, and what he should or should not be credited with. From the time he was writing scientific works in his youngest years, to the time he was completing his key works in later life, he also wrote with words that clearly reflected his mindfulness of the fact that he was different. From his autobiography, in which he expressed his 'good fortune, or a divine inspiration, or a kind of madness' reminiscent of Galen,[84] to his 'Doubts' on Ptolemy,[85] the Greek contemporary of Galen,

79 Ibn al-Qifṭī, Tāʾrīkh al-ḥukamāʾ Lippert, Julius (ed) (Leipzig, 1903).

80 Pines, Shlomo, 'Maimonides, Rabbi Moses Ben Maimon…', Dictionary of Scientific Biography (DSB), 9 (1974), pp. 27–32.

81 Meyerhof, 'ʿAlī Bayhaqī's Tatimmat Ṣiwān al-hikma, pp. 155–6.

82 Sabra, Optics of Ibn al-Haytham, Vol. 2, p. xxxi and n. 30 refer to Bayhaqī's Tatimmat, pp. 77–80.

83 Ibn Abī Uṣaybīʿa (d. ca. 1270), ʿUyūn al-anbāʾ fī Ṭabaqāt al-aṭibbāʾ [Classes of Physicians], Müller, August (ed.), 2 vols. (Köninsberg, 1884).

84 Sabra, 'Ibn al-Haytham', p. 190; Sabra, A. I., 'Sarton Medal Award Acceptance Speech at the History of Medicine Society Meeting, 5 November, 2005, Minneapolis, Minnesota', mentioned in Russel, Gül A., 'In Memoriam: A. I. Sabra (June 8, 1924–December 18, 2013)', Journal of the History of the Neurosciences, 24, 2 (2015), pp. 193–8. http://dx.doi.org/10.1080/0964704X.2014.998521

85 Sabra, A. I., Ibn al-Haytham: Aporias Against Ptolemy; Kennedy, 'Late Medieval Astronomical Theory'.

himself associated with 'doubts' by a slightly earlier independent thinker Razi, turned Rhazes,[86] Ibn al-Haytham knew he was breaking ground; and from his most mature works, following those in the third 'list' preserved by the latest of those historical reports, to visual theories introduced in his *Optics* as a continued central subject, his breakthroughs were solid and explicit. In the centuries immediately following Ibn al-Haytham, from when his European successors came to be called 'Alhacen's Ape',[87] to a much later time when his scientific gems won him chapters and books written by modern historians in languages from Arabic to German, English, and French,[88] his intellect was to be celebrated beyond his own imagination; and in a much later age, one of increasing information and documentation where matters beyond dates or states of a life or a work were to be preserved through more effective mediums, other aspects of his life would have chances to shine through: above them all shone the critical thinking of a clear and self-conscious mind, that of a man behind some outstanding and groundbreaking works. It would become clearer through time that he applied the clarity of his mind to every subject he touched, from eclipses to the camera obscura.[89]

When Ibn al-Haytham started to write his voluminous *Optics* in seven books, naming it Kitab 'al-manazir' in the manner of books devoted to 'optics' by his ancient Greek predecessors, he had already written a *Summary* of the works of the two main authorities on the subject of vision, which long formed the main subject of optics: Euclid and Ptolemy.[90] Quick to ask his readers to disregard his earlier *Summary* of those works in favour of his superseding *Optics*, a mature Ibn al-Haytham, was to begin by dispelling all earlier visual theories that amounted to centuries and centuries of writings preserved through volumes and volumes of manuscripts, all of which he explicitly refuted in favour of his own 'combined' and lasting alternative: his solution first made 'futile and superfluous' the long-held assumption of 'visual-rays' reaching objects to make them be seen, one later called 'extramission theory' and linked to mathematicians like Euclid and Ptolemy and physicians like Galen. Ibn al-Haytham also adopted an upgraded version of the reception of form without matter in the eye, later called 'intromission theory' and linked to natural philosophers from Presocratics to Aristotle.[91] His was a creative 'combination', one that not only mixed the imaginary visual cone of the mathematicians with the layered anatomy of physicians and perceptive psychology of natural philosophers; it also introduced a concept such as

[86] Shoja, Mohammadali M., Agutter, Paul S. and Tubbs, R. Shane, 'Rhazes doubting Galen: Ancient and medieval theories of vision', International Journal of History and Philosophy of Medicine, 5 (2015), pp. 1–6, p. 1, 'Zakariyā Rāzī, Latinized Rhazes: I never wrote about things unless I first examined them myself'.

[87] Lindberg, Theories of Vision, p. 118.

[88] Naẓīf, Muṣṭafā, Al-Ḥasan ibn al-Haytham: buḥūthuhu wa-kushūfuhu al-Baṣariyya [al-Hasan ibn al-Haytham, His Researches and Discoveries in Optics], 2 vols. (Cairo, 1942–1943); Schramm, Matthias, Ibn al-Haytham Weg zur Physik (Weisbaden, 1963); Sabra, Optics of Ibn al-Haytham; Rashed, Roshdi, Géométrie et dioptrique au Xe siècle: Ibn Sahl, al-Quhi, et Ibn al-Haytham (Paris, 1993).

[89] Ibn al-Haytham, al-Ḥasan, Maqāla fī surat al-kusūf, Raynaud, Dominique (ed, tr), A Critical Edition of Ibn al-Haytham's On the Shape of the Eclipse: The First Experimental Study of the Camera Obscura (Cham, 2016).

[90] Sabra, Optics of Ibn al-Haytham, Vol. 2, p. xxxii.

[91] Lindberg, Theories of Vision; Kheirandish, Elaheh, 'Optics, History of', Encyclopedia Iranica (EIr), 2010. www.iranicaonline.org/articles/optics

'experimentation' into optics, not to merely test something as simple as the linear propagation of light through artificially produced tools from flat screens to manipulated tubes,[92] but especially to show that the results occurred 'without variation or change' in every single trial. But there came something even more critical than an advanced concept of experimentation, adopted from astronomy along with Arabic terms such as 'iʿtibar' to become 'experiment' in Latin, as distinct from Arabic 'tajriba' for Greek emperia, meaning experience:[93] these were the terms through which Greek optical theories had reached Ibn al-Haytham in his native language of Arabic. Despite all his gifts, he was no different than others in his time in not reading ancient languages such as Greek, and having to rely on Arabic translations of the Greek optical corpus, made two centuries before him.

Of the Greek optical corpus, the most influential for Ibn al-Haytham was the *Optika* of Ptolemy, a work in five books which had reached him missing its critical first book on light and colour in Arabic, one which he had reconstructed in his *Summary* according to the title of that work, later lost itself. From the text of Ptolemy, Batlamyus in Arabic, it was the concepts rather than the language that had affected Ibn al-Haytham's own great work on optics, some occasioning criticisms.[94] But the case of Euclid, Uqlidis in Arabic, was quite the opposite. Not only was that work much more widely circulated in Islamic lands; the book's Arabic translation, having been among the earliest translations made from Greek, was carried out by an early translator who had picked nonstandard terms for critical optical concepts in Greek, thereby transforming the original concepts and models through language alone. One of these was the term for the most central concept of ancient geometric optics: the Euclidean, 'visual-ray', opseis in Greek, shifting to ray, shuʿaʿ in Arabic, a term significantly without an inherent link to the eye; another case was the concept of the 'indefinite magnitude' of rays, 'megathon megalon' in the original Greek, shifting to the very different 'indefinite multitude' in its Arabic translation, one turning with it the single visual cone of Euclid and Ptolemy into a consequential multiple-point conic radiation; yet another term was the origination point of such cones, shifting from 'inside' the eyes to their surface, through an orthography similarly turning the word for 'magnitude' itself into one for 'multitude' through a transmission missing the dots alone. Ibn al-Haytham's dependent visual model was thus based on point by point radiation of rays, not visual-rays, extending in multitude, not magnitude, and originating on the surface, not inside, of a luminous object, not the eye. Formulated without any knowledge of the striking, and *unintended*, shift from the original Greek model to its Arabic 'version', his was an extension of what 'Euclid had said to his Arabic readers'[95] at first.

92 Kheirandish, 'Footprints of "Experiment" in Early Arabic Optics'.

93 Sabra, A. I., 'The astronomical origin of Ibn al-Haytham's concept of experiment', In Actes XIIe Congrès International d'Histoire des Science (Paris, 1971), pp. 133–6.

94 Sabra, A. I., 'Ibn al-Haytham's criticisms of Ptolemy's *Optics*', Journal of the History of Philosophy, 4, 2 (1966), pp. 145–9. http://muse.jhu.edu/journals/journal_of_the_history_of_philosophy/summary/v004/4.2sabra.html. A.I. Sabra, 'Vita: Ibn al-Haytham', p. 55.

95 Kheirandish, Elaheh, 'What "Euclid said" to his Arabic readers: The case of the optics', in De Diversis Artibus (Collection of Studies from the International Academy of the History of Science), Tome 55 (N.S. 18), Vol. 12, in Simon, Gérard and Débarbat, Suzanne (eds), Proceedings of the XXth International Congress of History of Science (Turnhout, 2001), 55, 18, pp. 17–28.

The day Ibn al-Haytham was writing the opening pages of his great *Optics*, this time with *intended* transformations on the subject, was like any other day, until it wasn't. Looking at the manuscripts of earlier optical authors – Greek authorities, like Euclid, Ptolemy, Aristotle and Galen, whose works in Arabic translations were followed by original Arabic compositions up to his own time[96] – he knew how confusing these would be to anyone not familiar with the subject. That day was when he decided on how to correct and transform the subject once and for all, starting with a long preface. He was writing with clarity and confidence some key premises whose meaning and elegance were far from lost in their modern translation:[97] first that 'views on the nature of vision are divergent and their doctrines regarding the manner of sensation not concordant. Thus perplexity prevails, certainty is hard to come by, and there is no assurance of attaining the object of inquiry'; next, that 'in addition to all this, how strong is the excuse for the truth to be confused, and how manifest is the proof that certainty is difficult to achieve'; adding that 'the truths are obscure, the end hidden, the doubts manifold, the minds turbid, the reasonings various: the premises are gleaned from the senses, and the senses (which are our tools) are not immune from error'; and finally that 'the path of investigation is therefore obliterated and the inquirer, however diligent, is not infallible. Consequently, when inquiry concerns subtle matters, perplexity grows, views diverge, opinions vary, conclusions differ and certainty becomes difficult to obtain'. Other key premises would then follow in a similarly logical order, starting with 'the nature of our subject being confused, in addition to the continued disagreement through the ages among investigators who have undertaken to examine it'; next explaining that 'because the manner of vision has not been ascertained, we have thought it appropriate that we direct our attention to this subject as much as we can, and seriously apply ourselves to it, to examine it, and diligently inquire into its nature'; then stating that 'we should, that is, recommence the inquiry into its principles and premises, beginning our investigation with an inspection of the things that exist and the survey of conditions of visible objects' and to 'distinguish the properties of particulars, and gather by induction what pertains to the eye when vision takes place and what is found in the manner of sensation to be uniform, unchanging, manifest and not subject to doubt'; only 'after which we should ascend in our inquiry and reasoning, gradually and orderly, criticizing premises and exercising caution in regard to conclusions'; the final 'aim' being to 'make subject to inspection and review' all that, and 'to employ justice, not to follow prejudice, and to take care in all that we judge and criticize that we seek the truth and not to be swayed by opinion'.

The multiple sections and subsections of Ibn al-Haytham's *Optics* volumes followed with the same striking consistency, including the structure of arguments as either a mathematical demonstration, experimental proof, or inductive generalisation.[98] But not surprisingly, the volumes, did not have the fate their author had intended. A couple of centuries after the work's composition, its paths in the East and West were to part in what was to be described by its modern editor and translator as a 'checkered history',

[96] Lindberg, Theories of Vision.
[97] Sabra, Optics of Ibn al-Haytham, Vol. 1, pp. 3–6.
[98] Sabra, 'Astronomical origin', p, 133.

one with an 'overlap' of fortune and misfortune.[99] In this case, the misfortune was that the natives of his own land were deprived of it for over two centuries due to the poor internal circulation of that masterpiece, while a scholarly King in Spain was benefiting from the brain power of that author much earlier. The fortune, on the other hand, was that the Europeans came to recognise Ibn al-Haytham's *Optics* as important enough for it to occasion two Latin translations by the thirteenth century, an Italian version within the next century, and a printed edition within the next two centuries.[100] In another several centuries, the printed version would be written up by a modern reporter as part of an 'Early science' exhibit, there described as the 'latest time machine': the reporting author would write in detail that 'among the other ornate manuscripts and drawings . . . there is a facsimile reproduction of the frontispiece of a 1572 Latin edition of *Optics*, the magnum opus of al-Hasan ibn al-Haytham (also known by his Latinised name, Alhazen or Alhacen). The 11th century empiricist, polymath, and skeptic – born in what is now Basra, Iraq – was known as the 'father of optics. He copied Arabic translations of Euclid and Ptolemy, reveled in geometry, and went on to revolutionise the science of optics with his mathematical theory of vision'.[101] Less than a decade later, another exhibit write-up[102] on that same volume among other select pieces would zoom in on other aspects of the featured book: that 'although this book is on optics and from Europe of the early modern period, it represents subjects, figures, mediums, languages, places, and times much beyond what is embodied between the covers of its single volume'; adding that besides 'subjects from early perception and natural philosophy to pre-perspective geometry and epistemology, the work is of interest for representing mediums beyond print, and languages beyond Latin'.

In the years preceding the dimming of the life of that shining star of science, he had not been able to produce more of the extraordinary pieces of works he had so insightfully conceived and examined: this was due to the light of his own eyes dimming in an age that had not fully begun the study of lenses in which he himself had no small part for the benefit of humankind. He, like many others living both before and after him, had the disadvantage of working not only in the dim light of a candle, night after night, but with the weak force of his aging eyes day after day, without any hopes of simply seeing better by means of a visual aid, one to be called a 'spectacle' by Europeans of a slightly later age.[103] In that sense, in addition to 'books', the 'tools' involved affected key developments in dependent fields of knowledge for years to come.

Ibn al-Haytham's was a very different place than the Europe of the Middle Ages: it was where not just the lights of the eye, but the candles of life were dimming due to various physical causes including diseases then without cure. While some reports

[99] Sabra, Optics of Ibn al-Haytham, Vol. 2, Preface.

[100] Hogendijk, Jan P., 'Discovery of an 11th-century geometrical compilation: the Istikmāl of Yūsuf ibn Hūd, King of Saragossa', Historia Mathematica, 13 (1986), pp. 43–52; Sabra, Optics of Ibn al-Haytham, Vol.. 2, p. lxiv, n. 94: 'al-Mu'taman ibn Hūd, King of Saragossa from 1081 to 1085'; Lindberg, David C., A Catalogue of Medieval and Renaissance Optical Manuscripts (Toronto, 1975), pp. 17–21.

[101] Kheirandish, Exhibit 'Windows into Early Science'; Ireland, 'Houghton Exhibit'. http://news.harvard.edu/gazette/story/2008/04/houghton-exhibit-features-islamic-sciences/

[102] Kheirandish, 'The spread of science'. https://harvardmagazine.com/2017/03/an-enchanted-palace

[103] Lindberg, Theories of Vision, pp. 180–2.

[104] Sabra, '"Commentary" that saved the text', p. 131.

would come to associate a certain Abu ʿAli Ibn al-Haytham with a 'devastating plague',[104] others would link the demise of a contemporary figure who devoted his whole life to medicine among other scientific fields he mastered quite early in life, with a much simpler illness. The latter was a figure whose life's work would be exhibited in a display case adjacent to that of the former in an 'Early science' exhibit more than a thousand years after their lifetimes, and thousands of miles from their neighbouring lands: they would display between them various differences not merely in vision, including distinct 'theories of vision',[105] but also parallel paths: books composed and transmitted through those paths would in turn reflect, besides 'roots', 'routes', and 'rules' involved in book production, 'tools', 'schools', and 'loops' in their circulation.

4.4 *A Persian City Left Behind*

It was September circa 1050, and another bright star in the sky of early science had stopped shining for over a decade in a place not far from Isfahan.[106] Just like his near contemporary Arab counterpart, Al-Hasan, whose first name had become so well known in Europe to produce the Latinised forms Alhacen and Alhazen, the Persian, Abu ʿAli, father of ʿAli, in this case also known as the son of 'Sina' rather than 'Haytham', was to similarly develop widespread fame in Europe under his Latinised name Avicenna, this time with corresponding Arab and Persian prototypes as Ibn Sina and Pur Sina respectively.[107] But in contrast to Ibn al-Haytham, whose first name as Al-Hasan was the same as that of the first grandson of Prophet Mohammad, the given name of Ibn Sina, Husayn after Prophet Muhammad's second grandson, was highly noted due to the decisively more important role of the younger grandson in Shiʿite history after his fateful martyrdom along with his followers in the hands of rival Sunni factions. Husayn was also a more popular name in post-Islamic Iran, due to the marriage of Husayn, the third Imam of Shiʿite Muslims, to Shahr Banu, the daughter of the last Persian Sasanid King at the time of the Islamic Invasion of Persia.[108] Still, the omission of a first name like Husayn in favour of a second name like Ibn Sina would not have been as unexpected at a time when post-Islamic Iran was still not an official Shiʿite state, and the Shiʿi-Sunni division not so sharp. The problem of the succession of Prophet Muhammad as the leader of the Islamic community went as far back as few hundred years to the split between the followers of his first three successors, Caliphs Abu Bakr, ʿUmar, and ʿUthman, known as 'Sunni' after the 'community' of Arab Muslims, and his fourth successor, ʿAli, triply related to the Prophet, and the father of his grandsons Hasan and Husayn; and it would not be for another few hundred years

[105] Lindberg, Theories of Vision; Lindberg, 'Intromission-Extramission Controversy'.
[106] Nafīsī (ed) Sar-gudhasht-i Ibn Sīnā; Goitchon, 'Ibn Sīnā'; Ibn Sīnā, Life of Ibn Sīnā, Gohlman (ed, tr); Anawati, 'Ibn Sīnā'; Gutas, 'Avicenna: Biography'; Rosenfeld and Ihsanoğlu, Mathematicians, Astronomers, and Other Scholars, No. 317, pp. 122–8; Ragep, Sally, 'Ibn Sīnā'. https://islamsci.mcgill.ca/RASI/BEA/Ibn_Sina_BEA.htm
[107] Nafīsī, Saʿīd, Zindigī va kār va andīshah va rūzgār-i Pūr Sīnā (Tehran, 1333 [1954]).
[108] Browne, Literary History, Vol. 1, pp. 130–1; Bosworth, Islamic Dynasties, pp. 3–4.
[109] Browne, Literary History, Vol. 4, pp. 16–24; Bosworth, Islamic Dynasties, p. 3 and p. 172.

that post-Islamic Iran would become a Shiʿi state[109] under a dynasty called the Safavids, with Isfahan as its momentous capital.

Ibn Sina's own life had coincided with a period of upheavals severe enough for some of his books to be reported as written on horseback or in prison,[110] and referred to as illegible or incomplete accordingly. His profile was so diverse that he would one day be called 'not a philosopher who lived in his books', but 'occupied all days by affairs of the state' and 'laboured by night on his great works'.[111] He would still leave behind an exceptionally large corpus and fine legacy through many works including famous philosophical and medical books respectively titled *Shifa'*,[112] meaning healing, and *Qanun*,[113] meaning canon, as well as astronomical and cosmological works of various kinds and lengths.[114]

Abu ʿAli Sina, a man who was to become better known in his own native land as father of ʿAli rather than the 'son of' a father, mother, or any other given name, was a self-proclaimed protégé, with a so-called 'autobiography'[115] in the tradition of Aristotle. This was different from the autobiographical work of his Arab contemporary, Ibn al-Haytham in the Galenic tradition, one whose works would remain largely unknown to Ibn Sina and all but a few of their Arab and Persian successors.[116] In his 'autobiography' completed by a student of his named Juzjani, Ibn Sina would say things that were to illuminate the little known context of science during his time. He would record, not only where, when, and with whom he studied, on what subjects, and in what order, or at exactly what age he read this or that book, and mastered this or that subject between memorising the Quran at the age of 6, and mastering all major subjects by the age of 18;[117] he would also shed light on scientific education, institutions, and classifications of the time: on scientific education revealing that even students as privileged as he, had to learn subjects such as arithmetic informally from 'greengrocers'; on scientific institutions, that royal courts had books in their libraries the likes of which he had not 'seen either before or after that';[118] and on scientific classification, that there was more to it than the trio of natural, mathematical, and metaphysical sciences. In the case of scientific subjects with which Ibn Sina would be associated at a much later time, his readers had to turn to his encyclopedic work, the multi-volume *Shifa'*, where cases

110 Browne, Literary History, Vol. 2, pp. 106–11; Goitchon, 'Ibn Sīnā'; Anawati, 'Ibn Sīnā'.
111 Goitchon, 'Ibn Sīnā', p. 941.
112 Ibn Sīnā, Al-Shifāʾ al-ṭabiʿīyāt, Ibrāhīm Madkūr (ed) (Cairo, 1983–); Gutas, Avicenna and the Aristotelian Tradition.
113 Ibn Sīnā, Al-Qānūn fī al-ṭibb, 3 vols. (Būlāq, 1294 [1878]).
114 Ragep, F. Jamil and Ragep, Sally P., 'The astronomical and cosmological works of Ibn Sīnā: Some preliminary remarks', in Pourjavady, N. and Vesel, Ž. (eds.), Sciences, techniques et instruments dans le monde iranien (Xe-XIXe siècle) (Tehran, 2004), pp. 3–15.
115 'Autobiography' in Gutas, Avicenna and the Aristotelian Tradition.
116 Sabra, Optics of Ibn al-Haytham, Vol. 2, pp. lxiv–lxviii: the generally 'unknown or unused' *Optics* of Ibn al-Haytham in Islamic lands is established by a review of Arabic sources (Persian sources not included).
117 'Autobiography': Gutas, Avicenna and the Aristotelian Tradition; Browne, Literary History, Vol. 2, p. 106.
118 'Autobiography': Gutas, Avicenna and the Aristotelian Tradition; Browne, Literary History, Vol. 2, p. 107.

such as optics and mechanics were both atypically classified under sciences with 'moving devices',[119] the rare expression used being 'hiyal al-mutaharrika'.

By the time Ibn Sina was to be associated with optics, called 'manazir' to mean both 'visual rays' and 'aspects',[120] or mechanics, called 'hiyal', to mean both tricks and devices, the two fields were noted for many overlaps as ancient subjects that were both primarily mathematical with a predominately Greek legacy.[121] Besides subdivisions of geometry, classified by Ibn Sina's inspirer, Aristotle, under plane and solid geometry respectively, the two fields belonged to the Greek tradition of 'Intermediate' or 'Middle' Books,[122] those instructed after Euclid's *Elements* and before Ptolemy's *Almagest*, both well known to Ibn Sina. The two fields further shared the Aristotelian distinction of a 'mixed' science as the more physical of the mathematical sciences.[123] There were other historical parallels: the science of optics was initially a study of vision, its disciplinary status, a subdivision of plane geometry, its subject, primarily sight, rather than light, its method, initially geometrical, rather than experimental, and its branches, the sciences of direct and indirect vision; the science of mechanics was initially a science of devices rather than weights, its disciplinary status, a subdivision of solid geometry, its main subject, machines and powers, not just motion, its method, operative and productive more than demonstrative, and its branches, the science of devices and weights. But optics and mechanics had distinctions besides parallels,[124] those that were not always expressed including distinct treatments by people like Ibn al-Haytham or Ibn Sina associated with both subjects.

Ibn Sina's treatments were not only different from that of his Arab contemporary Ibn al-Haytham in optics, in the case of both vision and rainbows;[125] they were also different in the case of mechanics, in both the content of a text passed on under Ibn Sina's name on the subject, and in the language of that text being atypically Persian.[126] Mechanics itself was a field that had become popular enough in Persian lands to be among the first fields to have Persian compositions devoted to them as early as the time of Ibn Sina. The first set of works in mechanics proper had been composed in Greek in the early centuries of the common era, in this case in the second and fourth centuries by Heron and Pappus of Alexandria, both from a city belonging to Greek lands at the time. Like many other ancient scientific works, the *Mechanics* of Heron and Pappus, pronounced in Arabic as 'Irun' and 'Babus', had also been translated into Arabic in the

[119] Kheirandish, Elaheh, 'The mixed mathematical sciences: Optics and mechanics in the Islamic Middle Ages', in Lindberg, David C. and Shank, Michael H. (eds), The Cambridge History of Science, Vol. 2, Medieval Science (Cambridge, 2013), pp. 84–108.
[120] Sabra, A. I. 'Manāẓir, or ʿIlm al-Manāẓir', Encyclopedia of Islam (EI²), 6 (1987), pp. 376–7. Kheirandish, Elaheh 'The many aspects of appearances: Arabic optics to 950 AD', in Hogendijk, Jan P. and Sabra, Abdelhamid I. (eds), The Enterprise of Science in Islam: New Perspectives (Cambridge, 2003), pp. 55–83.
[121] Kheirandish, 'Mixed mathematical sciences', pp. 90–1.
[122] Kheirandish, Elaheh, 'Organizing scientific knowledge: The "mixed" sciences in early classifications', in Endress, Gerhard (ed), Organizing Knowledge: Encyclopaedic Activities in the Pre-Eighteenth Century Muslim World (Leiden, 2006), pp. 135–54, pp. 138–9.
[123] Kheirandish, 'Organizing scientific knowledge', p. 137.
[124] Kheirandish, 'Mixed mathematical sciences', pp. 107–8.
[125] Sabra, 'Scientific enterprise', p. 188–90.
[126] Kheirandish, 'Mixed mathematical sciences', p. 106, and n. 72.

eighth and ninth centuries, the first, by a Greek Christian scholar long living in Baghdad under the ʿAbbasid Caliphs, and the second by a translator whose identity would remain unknown for centuries to come.[127] But the case of the Persian mechanical text attributed to Ibn Sina, who lived as early as a century after the period of translations in Baghdad, was different from that of most other sciences in other ways. Not only was the Persian text titled *Rational Measures*, a vague yet close equivalent of *Miʿyar al-ʿuqul*, as opposed to the more standard form of a book of 'mechanics' in Greek, and of 'devices' in Arabic. The title of the text was only one of many things that set the text apart from others. The preface had an unusual reference to the 'most illuminating mechanician', Anvar-i mikhaniqi; it also had the famous dictum 'Give me a place to stand and I will move the earth', without direct mention of 'Archimedes',[128] the great Greek mathematician behind both expressions besides the eternal words 'Eureka', 'I found it'. When it came to the body of the text, the description of the five so-called simple machines, 'axle, pulley, lever, screw and wedge' from the second book of Heron's *Mechanics*, the part transmitted most widely in Islamic lands,[129] also appeared in a different order than all other versions of the same book. Not only that. The words for the five 'devices' departed from their standard Arabised form, as in the case of the lever, termed in Persian as 'barim', rather than in Arabic, as 'mukhl'.[130] The description itself, showing how small forces could lift large weights, followed in a way that was not so much in terms of a 'trick' or 'contrivance' as could be read into the Greek or Arabic titles *Mechane* and *Hiyal*, but as a 'rational measure' turning phenomena considered 'against' or 'beyond' nature, from supernatural to natural manipulation.[131] This was simply the case with the lever where a beam on a fulcrum is manipulated to reach a balance through a 'rational' proportion between a force or 'quwwa' applied to one side, and a weight or 'thiql' lifted on the other, in the reverse order of their distances from the fulcrum. This also applied to the science of weights itself, where a rod on a suspension point is manipulated to reach a proportional balance between a scale added to one side and weights measured on the other, in the reverse order of their distances from the suspension point: all it took for the explanation of why, in the case of the lever, a force as small as 1/3 units could lift a weight as large as 3 units, was the demonstration of a proportional relation, itself measured through calculations and represented through demonstrations, that a weight measuring 3 units x a distance of 1/3 units, equals – namely, needs for lifting – a force of 3/2 units x a distance of 2/3 units.[132]

[127] Kheirandish, Elaheh. 'The "fluctuating fortunes of scholarship": A very late review occasioned by a fallen book', Early Science and Medicine, 11, 2 (2006), pp. 207–22; 'Qusṭā ibn Lūqā al-Baʿlabakkī', The Biographical Encyclopedia of Astronomers (BEA) (2007), pp. 948–9. https://islamsci.mcgill.ca/RASI/BEA/Qusta_ibn_Luqa_al-Balabakki_BEA.htm

[128] Attiyeh, 'Scholars resuscitate dead languages'. http://news.harvard.edu/gazette/story/2003/11/scholars-resuscitate-dead-languages/

[129] Heron of Alexandria. (1900). Mechanics, Nix, L. and Schmidt, W. (ed) (Heron von Alexandria Mechanik und Katoptrik) (Leipzig, 1900).

[130] Humāʾī (ed), Miʿyār al-ʿuqūl.

[131] Schiefsky, Mark J., 'Art and nature in ancient mechanics', in Bensaude-Vincent, Bernadette and Newman, William R. (eds), The Artificial and the Natural: An Evolving Polarity (Cambridge, MA, 2007), pp, 67–108, pp. 67–8.

[132] Kheirandish, 'Mixed mathematical sciences', pp. 103–4.

Nothing about the text *Rational Measure* was, therefore, unusual except the attribution of its very authorship to Ibn Sina. In the absence of such a title found among the known works of that celebrated author,[133] the editor of the text over a thousand years later, one who would have the surviving handwritten scripts published in print form, could still not be sure if the author, named in the text as 'Abu ʿAli', was meant as Abu ʿAli Sina. 'I could not sleep for many nights', would write the celebrated scholar from a much later Isfahan, 'to determine an identity I had to leave at this state'.[134] Other modern scholars could not throw much light on the identity of the author of a mechanical text combining mechanical knowledge and practice, either. The impressive library of two scholarly brothers in Tehran,[135] not far from the city of Ray where Ibn Sina had once worked, would not turn up any sources illuminating that subject despite its wealth of historical manuscripts and maps. Nor would whole volumes devoted to 'Avicenna'[136] authored by specialised experts on the renowned 'scholar from the East', nor feature films[137] portraying him as a practitioner of medicine, not of any other scientific subject including mechanics. Clues would start pointing to the mystery of the mechanical text's authorship only through time. A clue would come from one of the handwritten copies of the text in the form of an honourary title long given to Ibn Sina, as a Chief Master or 'Shaykh al-Raʾis', still challenged on the basis of literary style. Another clue, still indirect, would then follow with promising leads later in time, one becoming the subject of a series of 'rational measures' of its own.

About four hundred years after the time of Ibn Sina, something unexpected was to involve the city of Isfahan, a place which was to become a major crossroad for Europeans and non-Europeans alike. A French interpreter and tutor at the court of a Safavid King, and a resident of Isfahan long after Ibn Sina, was to be closely associated with a Persian mechanical text almost identical to the one attributed to the celebrated scholar. The tutor of the young Safavid prince would have the description of the five simple machines of a much earlier mechanics in a closely comparable form, transcribed and illustrated in French next to Persian, in a volume carrying the Frenchman's name on an anonymous Persian text, since kept at a library in Paris.[138] Puzzles over who could have been the anonymous author of one or both mechanical texts, whether the two versions were by the same author in the first place, or whether Ibn Sina could have been the author of one or both of them, would have some clues along the way: among them that an author as highly esteemed as the 'Chief Master' Ibn Sina, residing years of his own life in Isfahan, could be a great candidate to be associated with a mechanical

[133] Mahdavi, Yahya, Catalogue of Manuscripts of the Compositions of Ibn Sīnā (Persian) (Tehran, 1333 [1954]), pp. 1–255, 259–304: definite and doubtful works; Rosenfeld and Ihsanoğlu, Mathematicians, Astronomers, and Other Scholars, No. 317, pp. 122–8.

[134] Humāʾī (ed.), Miʿyār al-ʿuqūl.

[135] Mahdavi, Yahya, Ibn Sīnā library; Mahdavi, Asqar, manuscript and map collections, visited in 1994.

[136] Wickens, G. M. (ed), Avicenna: Scientist and Philosopher: A Millenary Symposium (London, 1952); Wisnovsky, Robert (ed), Aspects of Avicenna (Princeton, 2001); McGinnis, Jon, Avicenna (Oxford, New York, 2010).

[137] Stölzl, Philip (director), The Physician, 2013: Based on Gordon, Noah, The Physician (1986).

[138] De la Croix, François Pétis (1653–1713), 'French orientalist, author, resided in Isfahan (1674–1676)'. Blochet, Catalogue des Manuscrits Persans, pp. 73–4; entry: Encounters with the Orient. www.kent.ac.uk/ewto/projects/anthology/croix.html

text that could have even been a royal gift to the French tutor, regardless of Ibn Sina's actual authorship of that text. As such, the history of mechanics would be on a course which was to be as diametrically opposed to that of optics as that of the Arab and Persian authors associated with those sciences. This was also a time when the city of Isfahan was being set on a course much different from cities of prominence in both Islamic and European lands. In contrast to an Arab city like Baghdad, which had offered gifts as precious to Europe as masterpieces in content and method produced by one of its most 'critical minds', Isfahan was a Persian city left behind of various major cities and centres of learning to its east and west alike. For residents of Baghdad and Isfahan like Ibn al-Haytham and Ibn Sina, having been from about the same time, it was their distinct places, and circumstances, that were to have a direct impact on their respective productions: while in the case of Ibn al-Haytham, his reported pretense to madness would give him 'freedom' from other duties[139] to produce 'books' which were unparalleled beyond his own time, in the case Ibn Sina, he would be literally left behind in the 'fleeing' mode of escaping from place to place[140] for most of his mature life. In these and other ways, not only were the roots, routes, and rules involved in 'book' production different for scholars with different scientific authorities and forms of patronage; the nature of tools, schools, and loops affecting transmission were increasingly changing, not just within Arab and Persian lands, but especially in European lands.

[139] Sabra, 'Ibn al-Haytham', p. 189.
[140] Goitchon, 'Ibn Sīnā'; Anawati, 'Ibn Sīnā'; footpath of Ibn Sīnā: Nafīsī, Sar-gudhasht-i Ibn Sīnā.

5

East and West

300 Years: A Half Phase (ca. 1050–1350)

Few things more beautiful and more pathetic are recorded in history than this Arab physician's dedication to the thoughts of a man separated from him by fourteen centuries; to the intrinsic difficulty we should add that Averroes, ignorant of Syriac and Greek, was working with the translation of a translation . . .

Ibn Rushd = Averroes (d. ca. 1198): Borges, Jorge Luis, 'Averroes' search', 1962, English translation: Irby and Yates, pp. 148–9[1]

That group of people who, as guides, came and passed,
And informed no one with certitude, as they passed
Into that complex tangle, unraveled by anyone,
Each came to place a knot, and so they passed . . .

Tusi, Nasir al-Din (d. ca. 1274) (attribution): Mudarris-i Radavi, *Ahval va Athar*, p. 61, English translation: Elaheh Kheirandish, *The Arabic Version of Euclid's Optics*, 1999, 2 vols., opening[2]

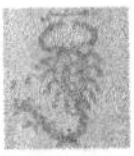

5.1 An Old Manuscript in a Virtual Space

It was October 2009, and the *Dialogue* manuscript was living in a virtual gallery[3] for about a year on a platform called 'Second Life', a virtual 'second' to a physical first, which in the case of the *Dialogue* manuscript had taken it well into its fifth life, after at least four: first as a physical composition and transcription, and then, a digital reproduction

1 Borges, Jorge Luis. 'Averroes' Search', pp. 148–9.
2 Mudarris-i Raḍavī, Muḥammad Taqī, Aḥvāl va athār-i Khwāja Naṣīr al-Dīn Ṭūsī (Tehran, 1355 [1976]; 1356 [1977]), p. 61. Kheirandish (tr, excerpt), Arabic Version of Euclid's Optics: Vols. 1, 2, opening.
Ān quwm kih rāh-bīn fitād-and u shud-and, Kas rā bih yaqīn khabar nadād-and u shud-and
Ān ʿuqdih kih hīch kas natān-ist gush-ād, Har yik girih-ī bar ān fitād-and u shud-and
3 Kheirandish, Elaheh, 'From Baghdad to Isfahan and Beyond', Virtual Gallery based on the exhibit: 'Windows into early science', Houghton Library, 2008, and included in a 'Digital Humanities Fair'. Ireland, Corydon, 'Fair shows progress of humanities in digital world', Harvard Gazette, 18 December 2008: 'Second Life is a virtual world accessible through the Internet . . . where Harvard owns an "island"'. http://news.harvard.edu/gazette/story/2008/12/fair-shows-progress-of-humanities-in-digital-world/

and reconstruction. This next stage of 'virtualisation' was a state that however timeless and endless was not the last life of a manuscript changing form with the technology of the times. The virtual gallery housing the *Dialogue* manuscript was placed on a spacious, attractive, three-dimensional site on an 'Island', with another set of distinct quarters: a front lobby with a fireplace and carpet for walk-throughs around illuminated manuscripts including the virtual *Dialogue*;[4] a back lounge with monitor screens and keyboards for electronically flipping through physically delicate pages; a dividing wall between the two quarters for crossovers of virtual characters called 'avatars',[5] created and monitored by real people, who sometimes 'drove' several characters; and a dividing floor between an upper gallery and a lower library, a virtualised corner of the 'college library'[6] of its hosting university, itself sitting in a much larger scale and open space, real-life landscape. For the virtual Windows exhibit located on the upper gallery, its first avatar had been its creator, one given the name Charles Leo Scribner[7] after Leo's 'pen name', here with the task of 'transcribing' codes not just to create, but dress, style and walk that first avatar. The exhibit's second avatar was different: it was the virtual curator[8] of the college library on the university's 'Island', this time 'driven' by a real librarian, turning first into a shadow visitor, then 'first respondent' to all inquiries of a 'Digital Fair', then in its first year.

The virtual gallery's physical curator was 'among more than 100 real live visitors to a Digital Humanities Fair'[9] on campus, the 'first-ever comprehensive display of digital resources for scholars and students of the humanities', as worded in the December 2008 issue of the university newspaper, where all things came to life in the hands of journalistic writers. The write-up on the Fair and its virtual gallery rose over and above that author's own ingenious imagery of a time machine used earlier for the physical Windows exhibit. In successive lines drawing the reader further and further into a curious world of unfamiliar words and expressions, Second Life appeared as 'a virtual

4 Munāẓirāt-i Baghdād va Iṣfahān was one of three manuscripts transported into the virtual gallery from the display 'From Baghdad to Isfahan' of the Windows exhibit. Ireland, 'Fair shows progress'. http://news.harvard.edu/gazette/story/2008/12/fair-shows-progress-of-humanities-in-digital-world/

5 Ireland, 'Fair shows progress': 'Second Life is peopled with "avatars"—embodied personalities … "they jump, they fly, they go through walls…"'. http://news.harvard.edu/gazette/story/2008/12/fair-shows-progress-of-humanities-in-digital-world/

6 Ireland, 'Fair shows progress': a virtual Harvard College Library was set in an open-air portico. http://news.harvard.edu/gazette/story/2008/12/fair-shows-progress-of-humanities-in-digital-world/

7 An avatar named 'Charles Leo Scribner' was created in 'Second Life' by the curator of the virtual gallery for the 'Windows' exhibit, Caroline M. 'Carrie' Kent, head of research services at Widener Library at the time; the part 'Scribner' was picked from the platform list for its connotations as 'transcriber'.

8 Caroline 'Carrie' Kent, the virtual curator of the Windows exhibit, had her 'redheaded avatar moved around in a stylish black body stocking', Ireland, 'Fair shows progress'. http://news.harvard.edu/gazette/story/2008/12/fair-shows-progress-of-humanities-in-digital-world/

9 Digital Humanities Fair, Harvard University, Humanities Center, Thompson Room, Fall 2008. Ireland, 'Fair shows progress': 'a first-ever comprehensive display of Harvard's digital resources for scholars and students of the humanities … among more than 100 real live visitors … a science historian … and educator'. http://news.harvard.edu/gazette/story/2008/12/fair-shows-progress-of-humanities-in-digital-world/

world accessible through the Internet': the named university as the 'owner of an island'; the virtual gallery as a space with 'reddish stone walls' and a 'bright blazing fireplace . . . peopled by avatars'; and the avatars themselves, as 'embodied personalities – who jump, fly, and go through walls'; the virtual curator, as a 'redheaded avatar' with a 'stylish black body stocking . . . teleporting visitors on an apple computer', and her physical driver, as one telling readers of the university paper, in both physical and digital forms, how in such a virtual gallery 'you could put on display together manuscripts from around the world that you could never, in real life, see together', with 'no limit to the number of pages you can add', as in the twelve exquisite folios on display in that 'exhibit of ornate folios from medieval Islamic science'.[10]

Such was the status of the *Dialogue* manuscript as one of the items displayed next to two others, which in their case came from halfway around the world. The *Dialogue*'s virtual space was far from the 'virtual realities' of phantasy and illusion, or of games 'reconfigured into new high-tech' forms of a much later time.[11] This was, rather, a virtual space with digital, three-dimensional, reproductions of physical objects, one where electronically flipping through manuscript pages were among the most advanced and dynamic modes of the evolving technology of the time.

As a virtual extension of a physical display called 'From Baghdad to Isfahan and Beyond', Baghdad and Isfahan had their own digital representations of such a primitive virtual space: Baghdad was represented by the image of a *Canon of Medicine* by a scholar of Persian origin having lived in Baghdad; and Isfahan, by an arithmetical text composed by a scholar of Arab origin living in Isfahan with a similarly well-known name[12] under a crown of gold illumination. The *Dialogue of Baghdad and Isfahan*, set between virtual representations of those two cities, was then living a timeless life: temporally between an earlier and later text on either side; and spatially, between two manuscripts living their physical lives in Western as well as Eastern cities. The *Calendar of Timekeeping*[13] next to them without an author name identifiable on its eye-catching opening folio was especially notable, since an exact time, let alone place, for such a physical entity could not be determined beyond a composition from the later Middle Ages in the East-West city of Istanbul, even as a 'timekeeping' tool that the *Calendar* was.

The *Calendar* – literally, *Book of Days* (*Ruz-Namih*) – which claimed to 'Keep Time for Day, Night, and other Known Times' according to its full title,[14] had features as exceptional as those of the *Dialogue* itself. For one thing, it was atypically composed in more than one language, in this case, Ottoman Turkish, as well as the Arabic and

[10] Ireland, 'Fair shows progress': quotes from the piece's opening and closing lines. http://news.harvard.edu/gazette/story/2008/12/fair-shows-progress-of-humanities-in-digital-world/

[11] Metz, Rachel. 'Second Life is back for a third life, this time in virtual reality', MIT Technology Review, 27 January 2017. www.technologyreview.com/s/603422/second-life-is-back-for-a-third-life-this-time-in-virtual-reality/

[12] Bahāʾ al-Dīn al-ʿĀmilī also known as 'Shaykh Bahāʾī (ca. 953–1031/1547–1622).

[13] Rosenfeld and Ihsanoğlu, Mathematicians, Astronomers, and Other Scholars, No. 872, p. 293: 'Muṣṭafā al-Qonāwī . . . Sheikh Wafā (d. 1491), from Konya, died in Istanbul', as the author of the 'Rūz-nāma . . . mīqāt.

[14] Rūz-nāma maʿa-hu mīqāt layl wa-nahār wa-sāʾir al-awqāt al-maʿlūma naqla-hu Shaykh Wafāʾ.

Persian of the bilingual *Dialogue*. It also evoked a strong sense of awe by the cosmic dance of script, shape, colour and illumination on successive pages, one that floating in a virtual medium seemed similarly immortal, and not just magical. The opening folio was, by far, the most stunning, with large sun- and moon-like circles filling the page with glaring distinctions. Next to a central gold-filled circular image was a parallel text with the opening title: The *Royal New Day* (*Nowruz- Sultani*), the 'New Year' of the Persians, another item to seize something momentous in that timeless medium. That name was given to a moment known as 'spring equinox', a split second occurring all around the world at the very same time. The adjacent mega-sized wheel contained five concentric circles depicting months, weeks, days, hours, and minutes, all written in Persian on a multi-layered disc inside a rust-coloured square frame; the set of circular layers beautifully transcribed and cosmologically marked with 12 months, 4 weeks, 28 days, 24 hours, and 60 minutes, further glowed above a lower circle,[15] encircling within it a cubic structure illustrating the Ka'ba, the centre of worship in Arabian Mecca (Plate 9).

A *Calendar* with twin circles, capturing a Persian new year and Arab holy site in one and the same timeless, endless virtual medium, was well placed next to a *Dialogue of Baghdad and Isfahan*, two age-old cities of Arab and Persian origin with lunar and solar calendars. Soon, the mega-wheel on the *Calendar*'s opening page was to digitally turn round and round to dial some specific times and places.

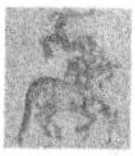

5.2 A Young Traveller with Paths to Trace

It was November 2009, and Leo was turning the dial of time both back and forth in this third year of his undergraduate studies. Into the near future, and the turn of at least another year before him, rested his wishful dreams, from graduation to graduate work. And back in the recent past, the course of the couple of years behind him had been enough to bring him other 'great gifts', from instruction to creativity: instruction had come through classes as general as courses on 'classical sciences', and as specific as 'historical dialogues'. Creativity had, in turn, been nurtured by events developed partly through those same courses, from historical plays and reconstructed experiments, and partly through course-based exhibits as extensions of exhibit-based courses.[16] The next few years would open other 'windows', including new venues adopting that title. A new course with such a title was to be offered that year in his university's summer school, one placed in the 'Windows' series for bringing not just an exhibit titled as such directly into the classroom, but holding classes in the same room where that exhibit was set up and filmed. A new exhibit, adopting the Windows title for displaying Persian traditions in addition to Arabic, and craft traditions in addition to science, would be prompted by

[15] Opening folio: upper image: years, months, weeks, days, minutes and seconds; lower image: Islam's centre of worship, Ka'ba, in Mecca, Saudi Arabia.

[16] Exhibit-based courses: Kheirandish, 'Windows into early science': Harvard Summer School, 2010, 2011; Course-based exhibits: 'Windows into early science' and 'Windows into early science and craft'; https://www.scholar.harvard.edu/ekheirandish/exhibits

the treasury of a rich manuscript collection, donated to a nearby university by an art dealer, occasioning sequels to the Windows exhibit.[17]

The fall of the following year, the last academic year of college for Leo, he was to be consumed by preparation for that sequel exhibit, one to which he would be contributing, not just as an overseer of captions and photographer of the exhibit as before, but to several aspects of it, from its opening and closing to a reception for the Persian New Year, falling on the solar year 1389.[18] The sequel exhibit 'Early science and craft', corresponding to the ancient Greek 'episteme and techne', was to expose related Persian manuscripts from a scattered art collection;[19] and the weaving thread of its displays was to be numbers 'seven' and 'twelve', in accordance with the strong presence of those timeless cosmological numbers in and beyond that exhibit. Fourteen display cases were to be set up in another rare book library, combining two main themes, each with seven cases within a rectangular space: the displays of the 'Science of the stars', set in the gallery's north and east glass cases, and those of the 'Craft of war instruments', in its east and south end, formed a combination of subjects from the seven heavenly bodies to the twelve zodiac signs.

The occasion for setting up the 'Science and craft' exhibit in that particular year was, however, something more than a literal uncovering of material from boxes and boxes of beautiful, valuable manuscript folios. Any part of the collection could have practically been exhibited any time after it was donated to the hosting university, along with various items amounting to 800 plus leaves in Persian alone, nearly four times as many as the Arabic and Turkish manuscripts of the whole collection. The occasion that made the exhibit timely was the millennium anniversary of the Persian *Book of Kings*,[20] a work prominently represented in that collection. The occasion especially called for honouring the memory of an 'extraordinary scholar'[21] behind the documentation of a collection now being leafed through for the exhibit selections. All such details were to be observed for that exhibit, one that was to use numbers as historically illustrious as 'twelve and seven' to promote creative and collaborative work: twelve selections from the Persian manuscript collection and their supplements were to form seven authors, 12 items, and 14 cases.[22]

17 Kheirandish, 'Windows into early science and craft', 2010; 'Science of stars and craft of wars instruments', Brown University, Rockefeller Library 2011: Persian manuscripts: Minassian Collection, donor: Adrienne Minassian, daughter of Kirkor Minassian. https://library.brown.edu/cds/minassian/

18 Persian solar new year of 1389 = 20 March 2010.

19 Kheirandish, Elaheh, 'Catalogue of the Persian manuscripts of the Minassian Collection at Brown University' (unpublished catalogue, 1999): database of over 800 scattered leaves supervised by David Pingree and reported in a 1999 Brown University publication; Exhibits: the first displays of the collection. https://www.scholar.harvard.edu/ekheirandish/exhibits: https://blogs.brown.edu/libnews/27/

20 Abdullaeva, Firuza and Melville, Charles (eds), Iranian Studies, 43, 1, Special Issue: Millennium of the Shahnama of Firdausi (2010).

21 David Pingree is named 'Hakim extraordinaire' in Ragep, Memoir on Astronomy, Preface, Vol. 1, p. viii.

22 In the order of displays: 12 items: (1–2) anonymous and untitled; (3) 'Description of the night': Niẓāmī Ganjavī; (4) Book of Constellation: ʿAbd al-Raḥmān Ṣūfī; (5) Persian Book of Constellation: Naṣīr al-Dīn Ṭūsī; (6) Book of Instruction: Abū Rayḥān al-Bīrūnī); (7–11) Shāh-nāmih: Book of Kings: Abū al-Qāsim Firduwsī; (12) Education of Alexander: Niẓāmī Ganjavī; added displays (13) anonymous: 'Treatise on arrow and bow', 'Dialogue of Arrow and Bow: Asadī Ṭūsī; Dish with war images; (14) 'Science of war instruments': Fakhr al-Dān Rāzī; seven authors: Niẓāmī, Ṣūfī, Ṭūsī, Bīrūnī, Asadī Ṭūsī, Rāzī.

Leo was to wear a different hat in that sequel exhibit, one with more demanding, yet less visible, tasks of chasing supplementary items that were not as openly credited by nature. One of these was finding a suitable item for the opening display case to act as an inviting introduction to the exhibit. For that, Leo was excited to have found an illustration from a book he felt qualified to handle as the subject of his 'manuscript challenge' in the other Cambridge. The illustration, taken from Biruni's *Book of Instructions*, had more than one occasion for its selection: the constellation Sagittarius which Leo had selected from that book on the occasion of the correspondence of the month of November with the making of that selection, had more than one association itself, in line with the combined nature of that constellation as a half-human, half-horse creature known as 'centaur'. Not only did Sagittarius[23] turn out to have close associations with both Baghdad and Isfahan, the twin cities occasioning the first Windows exhibit; as a combined entity it would also embody the two main themes of the sequel Windows exhibit: the Sagittarius archer, coloured as a dark blue sky and covered with gold-illuminated star points all over it embodying the theme 'Science of the stars'; and the archer's 'arrow', painted over in blood-coloured red', the theme 'Craft of war instruments' (Plate 5).

Besides merging two historically rich themes rarely combined, the two wings of that upcoming exhibit would bring Leo closer to the two characters of his next sections. From the wing of the 'Science of the stars' would shine a *Book of Constellations* open on the page of another zodiac sign, now Pisces, with a caption presenting the manuscript as a Persian translation by Nasir al-Din Tusi claimed in the author's hands, next to a date corresponding to 1250, and place Baghdad,[24] to set the first character as that famous scholar and founder-director of the Maragha Observatory. The wing of the 'Crafts of war instruments' offered a candidate for the second character, this time under the striking subtitle of 'The past's improvised explosive devices': here, a Persian classification work with a chapter on 'War Instruments' featuring Tusi's near contemporary Fakhr al-Din Razi, would have anyone's undivided attention reading a caption on the construction of figures[25] on the model of riding and walking warriors, where 'figures split, their centers open and a murky and dark smoke comes out such as no one can tolerate it'. Though the two characters, Tusi, and Razi, with the respective titles of 'teacher of mankind' and 'master of raising doubts',[26] complemented each other there for representing astrology as practical astronomy, and moving devices as practical mechanics, respectively, Leo's finalist for a 'Dialogue' character next to Tusi was not

[23] Sagittarius (Qaws) is associated with Baghdad and Isfahan in geographical works such as Majdī, Majd al-Dīn Muḥammad al-Ḥusaynī, Zīnat al-majālis (Tehran, 1342 [1963]), p. 762 and p. 766 respectively. Sagittarius image: adaptation of British Library manuscript 7697, ca. 1286, possibly from Maragha observatory, which includes zodiac drawings: Titley, Persian Miniature Painting, pp. 18–19, Fig. 4.

[24] Ṭūsī, Tarjamah-i Ṣuwar al-kawākib, p. 196: 'tarjuma va naskh: 647 [1250] bih Dār al-salām, Baghdād'.

[25] Rāzī, Fakhr al-Dīn, Jāmiʿ al-ʿulūm (Kitāb-i Sittīnī), Tasbīḥī, Muḥammad Ḥusayn (ed, intro) (Tehran, 1346 [1967–68]); excerpts: Kheirandish, Elaheh, 'Science and "mithāl": Demonstrations in Arabic and Persian scientific traditions', Iranian Studies, 41, 4, Special Issue: Bier, Carol, Kheirandish, Elaheh and al-Din Yousefi, Najma (eds), Sciences, Crafts, and the Production of Knowledge, pp. 465–89, p. 488–9.

[26] Mudarris-i Raḍavī, Aḥvāl va athār, p. 3; Shoja, Agutter, and Tubbs, 'Rhazes doubting Galen'.

Razi from Eastern Islamic lands, but an earlier contemporary of both from Western Islamic lands.

A suitable second character for Leo's next *Dialogue* section highlighting East and West came from a different direction. This was the direction of recording the paths of selected authors and works to identify parallel or overlapping times and places. The occasion of tracing some of those paths, not just digitally, but physically through travel, was afforded to Leo during his last winter term through an opportunity in January of 2009 to participate in an 'International year of astronomy' honouring the 400th anniversary of 1609, when important discoveries involving Galileo were made. This was a year when a young Galileo had looked into a self-made telescope night after night starting in the same month of January to record observations in the sky that were to not only change the course of astronomy, and through it, science, but shake humankind from the limiting bounds of a self-centred universe.[27] The events that far surpassed the limited boundaries of East and West included the celebration of the breakthroughs of the Italian Galileo in an Iranian city with an 'Institute of Advanced Studies in Basic Sciences' hosting the event 'Astronomy and science before and after Galileo'.[28] The travel path of Leo for attending that event had some stops along the way: from the sites of Galileo's work in Florence and Rome in Italy, to the Persian city of Zanjan hosting that event, there were various key sites in European universities and translation centres like Sicily and Toledo in Italy and Spain – one quite critical: the city of Cordoba in southern Spain, the so-called 'Ornament of the world',[29] housed a statue of Averroes,[30] the philosopher-scientist from the Islamic Middle Ages, one who would act as the Arab counterpart to the Persian Tusi in representing the Baghdad and Isfahan of Leo's next project chapter.

The Galileo event had occasioned exposures which already extended Leo's intellectual horizons far beyond Eastern geographical boundaries starting with a sizeable pool of Western participants from both sides of the Atlantic Ocean. It had also extended his topical horizons from 'Galileo and the Moon' to telescopes, comets, Newtonian natural philosophy, and the historical relationship between astronomy and optics.[31] The first and last of those topics had beamed on a screen, the full size image of Galileo next to Ibn al-Haytham standing on a side by side pedestal:[32] this was a cover-page image called the 'frontispiece' of a work from the year 1647 of the common era, about five years after Galileo's death in 1642: on the right stood Galileo, holding a

27 Galileo, Sidereus nuncius: Starry Messenger, Drake (tr), records Galileo's observations since Jan 1609: Koyré, Alexander, From the Closed World to the Infinite Universe (Baltimore, 1957; New York, 1958).

28 Zanjan, Iran, 29–30 Jan, 2009, on the 400th anniversary of Jan 1609.

29 Menocal, Ornament of the World.

30 A statue of Averroes is in the historic centre of Cordoba, Spain listed as a UNESCO World Heritage Site. https://commons.wikimedia.org/wiki/File:Statue_of_Averroes_in_C%C3%B3rdoba,_Spain.jpg

31 'Galileo and the Moon' and 'Historical relationship between astronomy and optics': presentation titles by Hossein Masoumi Hamedani and Elaheh Kheirandish respectively.

32 Ibn al-Haytham and Galileo: frontispiece of Selenographia, 1647, Johannes Hevelius's description of the moon, projected separately in the above presentations; image: Harvard University. Houghton Library. Typ 620.47.452F; Sabra, 'Vita: Ibn al-Haytham', p. 55. (Plate 4).

telescope, the subject of quite a few presentations from day one; on the left, Ibn al-Haytham, from about five hundred years before that, holding a textual diagram. At the end of those presentations, it had become clear that among adjustments needed to that image were the place of instruments, not just texts, in the hands of Ibn al-Haytham, as was more suitably the case with Averroes's statue holding a book in a historic centre in Cordoba, Spain. In that sense, Ibn al-Haytham, the Alhacen and Alhazen of Europe, had an upper hand over Ibn Rushd, the Latinised Averroes, with whom he shared breaking with Ptolemaic astronomy,[33] in Ibn al-Haytham's case, having advanced experimentation as well as instrumentation. The two-day presentations credited the Eastern counterpart of Galileo on the projected pedestal, with repeated observation records, physical sets-up, and generalised conclusions,[34] all verifiable with the exception of instruments such as the telescope used only by figures as late as Galileo, raising discussions about obstacles critical to breakthroughs earlier or elsewhere.

But the Galileo event had occasioned breakthroughs for one participant when it came to physical visits enhancing related digital projects, those from the footpaths of authors to the footprints of works. The event, having taken place in the mountainous ranges of Alburz Mountains close to the Caspian Sea coast of northern Iran, had occasioned Leo to be close to historic sites both around and beyond that region: to its west, the site of the Maragha Observatory[35] and its director Nasir al-Din Tusi; to its east, the site of Alamut fortress[36] of Tusi, his Isma'ili patrons, and another, possibly older, observatory; to its south, Soltaniyeh and its massive dome on an octagonal building,[37] then, Qazvin, and its little-known colour-glass zodiac;[38] and lastly, historic Ray, the historical name of the much-expanded capital city, Tehran, and the site of important libraries for scientific manuscripts, some holding single copies of works by Tusi and others, and the central core of Leo's travel path.

On that road trip, a visit to a private collection to the south of Tehran had first swept Leo off his feet when the driver assigned to taking him to some libraries in the capital had stopped at the house of an old distinguished teacher with a unique book and instrument collection in the city of Qum.[39] Collectables there ranged from a rare instrument signed at the Maragha Observatory during Tusi's tenure, to a lithograph print of his works composed in the Alamut fortress during the pre-Mongol period when he was in hiding. The few-story house holding that larger than life collection had become doubly memorable, first for having hardly any item in it other than piles of books on the carpeted floors of otherwise unfurnished floors; and then, for the

33 Sabra, 'Andalusian revolt', p. 144; p. 152, n. 44.
34 Sabra, 'Astronomical origin'.
35 Varjavand, Kāvush-i raṣad-khānah-i Marāgha; Ragep, Ṭūsī's Memoir on Astronomy, Vol. 1, p. 23: Chronology of Ṭūsī's Life includes years in Alamut and Maragha.
36 Bier, Carol, 'The decagonal tomb tower at Maragha and its architectural context: Lines of mathematical thought', Nexus Network Journal, 14 (2012), pp. 251–73, p. 269 refers to Alamūt as 'where there was an earlier observatory at which Naṣīr al-Dīn Ṭūsī worked'. Visit during conference on Naṣīr al-Dīn Ṭūsī: Tehran, 1998.
37 The dome of Soltaniyeh constructed in the early 1300s sits as a 50 m tall dome on an octagonal building. http://whc.unesco.org/en/list/1188
38 A stained-glass window consisting of the twelve zodiac signs is in 'Amīnī-hā' house, Qazvin, Iran.
39 The books and instruments included notable items held in a private collection in the city of Qum.

incredible 'memory' system of the collection itself: no catalogues or handlists, merely the memory aid of the collection's owner counting up and down books tied with strings: it was there that the old lithograph of Tusi's work in a distinctly beautiful hand had shown up in a memorised 'count' of the library's inventory on demand. But the moment of thrill, and the highlight of the visit, had been the sight of an astronomical instrument with an inscription dating back to the time of Tusi's Maragha days.[40]

Other rare and single surviving items had emerged during Leo's visits to libraries in the modern capital, Tehran, all of whose names started with the letter M to his great surprise. The first and most impressive had been the precious 'Muttahari' library sitting within a traditional education complex, a library with a great presence first under a different name.[41] Located near a tree-lined square, the tranquil library had a back room with a vault to which Leo felt privileged to be escorted for viewing a few locked up items, including, from the earlier periods, one of the most elegant illustrated and illuminated manuscripts of Biruni's *Book of Instruction*, Leo's 'Gallery Challenge', and the only known manuscript of his work on spherical astronomy.[42] The vault also locked in valuables from later periods, from Tusi's astronomical 'configuration' work in a manuscript read to him with annotations in his own hand, to the earliest manuscripts of Tusi's 'Middle Books'.[43] The second library visited was within the same square named 'Majlis', meaning Parliament, a library known to Leo through beautiful astronomical constellations published in an *Illustrated Study*.[44] The third library, 'Malik', named after its original founder, and once located within the beautiful Bazaar compound of Tehran, and later the 'National Library and Museum', had also rare items in the Malik branch in Mashhad:[45] unique Persian and Arabic versions of Abu al-Wafa' Buzjani's practical geometry endowed by 'Shaykh Baha'i', and the only known Persian text of a work on practical mechanics by a slightly earlier Hafiz Isfahani.[46] The fourth library visited by

40 Ṭūsī, Naṣīr al-Dīn, Taḥrīr al-Mutawassiṭāt, the lithograph edition handwritten by a Persian copyist (Tehran, 1304 [1886]), was tied with strings into a book batch and identified by its owner in a memorized 'count'. Visit to the book and instrument collection: June, 1994.

41 Muṭahharī Library is named after Ayatollah Murtiḍā Muṭahharī (1919–79), replacing 'Sipahsālār Library' named after Mirzā Ḥusayn Khān Sipahsālār (1826–81).

42 Bīrūnī, Abū Rayḥān, 'Maqālīd ʿilm al-hayʾa', in Bīrūnī-nāmah, Qurbānī, Abu al-Qāsim (facs) (Tehran, 1353 [1974]), pp. 461–504.

43 Ṭūsī, Tadhkira fī ʿilm al-hayʾa: Ragep: Ṭūsī's Memoir on Astronomy, Vol. 1, p. 81; Ṭūsī, Taḥrīr al-Mutawassiṭāt: Kheirandish, Arabic Version of Euclid's Optics, Vol. 1, p. xxxvii; and 'A report on Iran's "jewel" codices of Ṭūsī's Kutub al-Mutawassiṭāt' in Pourjavady, N. and Vesel, Ž (eds), Naṣīr al-Dīn al-Ṭūsī: philosophe et savant de x11e siècle (Tehran, 2000), pp. 131–43, p. 131 and p. 140; Danish-Pazhuh, M. T. and Munzavi, A. N, Catalogue of Sipahsālār Library (Persian), Vol. 3 (Tehran, 1341 [1962]). p. 384 and p. 330, respectively.

44 Nasr, Illustrated Study, pp. 102–3: constellations.

45 Malik, Ḥāj Hossein Āghā, founder of Malik Library and Museum, managed and expanded by his daughter, Ezzat-Malek Malek Tehrani/Soudavar. https://www.jadidonline.com/story/03022015/bhr/ezzat_malek_soudavar_profile . 'Malek National Library and Museum, functioning in Malek House until 1996' before its 'larger building in Bagh-e Melli square', is a private, non-profit institution dependent on 'Astan Quds Razavi' in Mashhad. http://malekmuseum.org/en/page/5/History

46 Unique Persian translation of and Arabic commentary on Būzjanī's Geometrical Constructions' [Aʿmāl al-handasa] endowed by Shaykh Bahāʾī; Kheirandish, 'Early tradition in practical geometry'. Ḥāfiẓ-i Iṣfahānī, Muḥammad, Natījat al-dawla, in Binesh, Taqi (ed), Sih risālah dar ikhtirāʿāt-i sanʿatī (Tehran, 1350 [1971]); Kheirandish, 'From Maragha to Samarqand', pp. 162–3; Appendix: IV, pp. 175–6.

Leo had been Tehran University's 'Markazi' library,[47] a library well-named as 'central' in relation to its host university and city: this had been a library with the most impressive of directors for 'photocopies of important Persian manuscripts found in collections abroad',[48] as well as later generation microfilms and discs of any given library in the area. The fifth library visited in Tehran was Iran's National Library called Milli,[49] a library that would report a copy of Ibn al-Haytham's *Optics* that turned out to be a commentary by Farisi. There were also private collections, like that of two distinguished brothers: the 'Mahdavi' private collections,[50] once located in a surprisingly quiet sanctuary in the middle of downtown Tehran, housed besides rare and valuable texts and maps by one brother, a rich assortment of Ibn Sina manuscripts and books by the other.

All these Mega libraries with a capital M, competing in excellence with each other in a capital city, had their own 'back stories'. But the one among them whose memory sank deepest in Leo's mind was the library which reminded him of one he had visited in the city of Istanbul the year before, one which by then felt several decades and thousands of miles away. Tehran's Muttahari library and its setting within a school complex with a mosque's dome looking over it was not far from that of Istanbul's Süleymaniye library: both had the historical settings of traditional institutions regardless of their respective Shiʿi and Sunni leanings.[51] Despite the sharply contrasting settings of their host cities, Tehran with a spectacular mountain range hanging over it, and Istanbul with picturesque blue waters surrounding it,[52] there was something about those two libraries standing out of the few others visited by Leo, without him being able to put his fingers on it – not until he opened the rich manuscript catalogues of the Mutahhari Library, still titled after Sipahsalar,[53] the modern secular figure endowing that school and library. The catalogue's third volume, opened to the 'jewel' codices'[54] of Tusi's 'Intermediate works': these codices were elsewhere called jewels for being the oldest, dating to a year before the author's death; and the works were called 'intermediate' for having been studied intermediately between geometry and astronomy. This had been the same Tusi collection Leo had seen in a modern lithographic print the day before in that private collection of old books rising from carpet to ceiling tied with strings. It had also been the same 'collection' he had seen old copies of the year before in more than one library in Istanbul: one carrying the same old date of 671 H had been in a library to

47 Central Library and Documentation Center of the University of Tehran includes a rich and broad selection. http://ut.ac.ir/en/page/781/central-library-and-documentation-center-of-the-university

48 Yarshater, Ehsan, 'Iraj Afshar (1925–2011)', Encyclopedia Iranica (EIr) (2000): 'Head of the University of Tehran's Central Library and its Center for Documents [1965–79] including 'collections abroad'. www.iranicaonline.org/articles/iraj_afshar_memorial

49 Iran's National, Millī, Library: Manuscript of Kamāl al-Dīn Fārisī, Tanqīḥ al-Manāẓir (Revision of Optics) listed as 'Ibn al-Haytham's Kitāb al-Manāẓir in Dirāyatī, Muṣṭafā, List of Manuscripts in Iran, Vol. 10 (Tehran, 1389 [2010]), p. 36. Fārisī, Kamāl al-Dīn, Tanqīḥ al-Manāẓir li-dhawī al-abṣār wa al-baṣāʾir, 2 vols. (Hyderabad, 1347–48 [1928–30]; Cairo, 1404 [1984]).

50 The manuscript and map collections of the two scholarly Mahdavi brothers are included in section 4.4.

51 Iran and Turkey are historically associated with Shi'ī and Sunnī leanings respectively.

52 Tehran has the view of the Alburz mountain range hanging over it; Istanbul has the picturesque blue waters of the Bosporus surrounding it.

53 Danish-Pazhuh and Munzavi, Sipahsālār Catalogue, Vol. 3.

54 Kheirandish, '"Jewel" Codices'.

which he had taken a ferry; another, with a date reported as 716 H but actually 723, had been in a military museum under a locked glass case, unscrewed and opened only by guards with security weapons.[55] Not so, however, in the case of the one-of-a-kind library known under the names of Muttahari and Sipahsalar: there, Leo had occasion to not only see a massive vault of valuable manuscripts up close, but touch the 'jewel' codices of Tusi's 'Intermediate works' before ordering a CD of those works. He later regretted not ordering other unique items: a little known work on practical geometry by Tusi, the master of theoretical science; an astrological poem attributed to him partly preserved in a 'Paris Codex'; and a much later and more curious 'reply', not just in a letter from 'Shaykh Baha'i', a practical mathematician and statesman in Safavid Isfahan known to Leo through the early science exhibit and its virtual display; but one addressed to 'Shah ʿAbbas',[56] the jewel in the crown of the most glorious days of Isfahan, noting European visitors to that city and their mingles with natives.

The occasion for Leo to travel after Tehran to Isfahan, a 'jewel' of a city itself, coincided with partly uncovering the 'ancient and modern secrets of Isfahan'[57] as worded in an article published the year before under that title. A visit to the 'ancient' mosque of Isfahan, an architectural masterpiece also known as the Jamiʿ or Friday mosque,[58] reopened the links of Isfahan to geometrical patterns of what Leo had seen in a unique Paris Codex.[59] This was an anonymous compendium with repeat patterns of exceptional beauty and complexity drawing attention from historians of science, art, and architecture. A visit to a historic house once owned by a Safavid scholar[60] and teacher in that mosque then uncovered other missing links to an impressive tradition of practical geometry. But these were only partial clues to the puzzles Leo had encountered there and elsewhere. Passing through the great square of Isfahan, an enormous and impressive square called 'plan of the world',[61] inspiring one in Venice, could not spot the whereabouts of a clock tower reported by Europeans in their visit to Safavid Isfahan.[62] Neither could a visit to a long-forgotten part of that city and the 'dome of Ibn Sina' in an old school[63] uncover whether the bearer of that name had actually taught in a school so-named.

55 Kheirandish, Arabic Version of Euclid's Optics, Vol. 1, p. xxxvii: Selīm Agā, Ṭūsī's Taḥrīr al-Mutawassiṭāt, dated 671H, accessible through a short ferry ride to Uskudar; Vol. 1, p. xxxviii, ʿAskeri Museum, Mutawassiṭāt codex turned up in my eventful visit to that library.

56 Danish-Pazhuh and Munzavi, Sipahsālār Catalogue, Vol. 3, p. 347 and p. 78: Ṭūsī, 'Taḥrīr-i Maʿrifat-i Masāḥat' and 'Ikhtiyārāt-i qamar'; Vol. 3, 276: 'Pāsukh-i [Shaykh] Bahāʾī bih Shāh ʿAbbās'.

57 Hogendijk, 'Ancient and modern secrets of Isfahan', Nieuw Archief voor Wis kunde, 5, 9 (2008), p. 121.

58 Seherr-Thoss, Sonia P., Design and Color in Islamic Architecture (Washington DC, 1968), p. 88: original construction and later redecoration: 515 (1121–22) and 1112 (1700–01); p. 186; part of tiling: 1080 (1669).

59 Paris Bibliothèque Nationale MS Pers 169, partly published: Necipoğlu (ed), Arts of Ornamental Geometry.

60 ʿĀmilī, Bahāʾ al-Dīn Shaykh Bahāʾī, 'Isfahan's Hidden House'. www.jadidonline.com/story/26022009/frnk/sheikh_bahai_eng

61 Maydān-i Naqsh-i Jahān has also been translated as 'image of the world': Sourdel-Thomine, 'Iṣfahān'.

62 Stevens, 'European visitors'.

63 Adle, Kamran, Ānān kih khāk rā bi-naẓar kīmiyā kun-and (Tehran, 1371 [1992]).

The peak of Leo's visit to Isfahan was learning about students around his age from European universities in the Netherlands having made not just a study trip to that city under the guidance of their expert mentor, but a groundbreaking discovery: they had discovered 'some extraordinary tiling through their own eyes' at the North Cupola of the Friday Mosque closely corresponding to a complex geometrical pattern in an anonymous compendium in the Paris Codex. Still, the actual superimposition of the mirror patterns could not offer a clue as to which came first, the geometrical pattern or historical tiling, nor to historical relations between science and craft traditions at large.[64] Leo's visit to the scene of the geometrical construction in an Isfahan monument and a textual pattern in Paris was an irreplaceable experience. But pieces to the puzzles of practical geometry, Paris Codex, and links to Isfahan were still far from presenting a clear picture.

So were puzzles related to practical mechanics, despite two other guided visits within the limited time of that Isfahan trip. A visit to the old Bazaar of Isfahan made Leo hear from the locals what he had once read in print about the existence of a clock tower constructed above the entrance of Isfahan's bazaar during the Safavid period: this was reported by a European visitor to Isfahan as a striking clock made by an Englishman claimed to have been 'the only one in all of Persia'. Leo's visit to Isfahan further took him to a city within its province called Kashan where a clock was reported to have been constructed by its maker Hafiz-i Isfahani.[65] The sources and visits offered between them insights into the workings of earthly and heavenly matters, from astronomy and astrology to mechanics and geometry. They also determined the characters selected for representing East and West in Leo's next *Dialogue* section. The characters, in turn, afforded opportunities for adding further threads into the reconstruction of the historical fabrics of Baghdad and Isfahan, and those beyond their central cores.

Leo's historical narrative would next turn not only to the case of other relevant cities from Damascus and Kashan to Samarqand and Istanbul, but to the similarly unexplored case of 'schools' as communities and their role in scientific development, focusing on astronomy and astrology within both their institutional and sectarian aspects: here, the selected historical cases would show that schools, when a forum for patrons and practitioners of science as private or public institutions, advanced developments in and beyond astronomy and astrology, in contrast to cases with sectarian divides within Sunni or Shiʿi settings.

Chapter 5: 'Dialogue' of Sky and Earth
Silver Stick, Golden Ball – Schools
By Charles Leo Scribner, November 2009

[*Sky:*] *I am the home of the polo ball and mallet of that marble field,*
my mallet is from plain silver, and my ball, from pure amber

[64] Hogendijk, 'Ancient and modern secrets of Isfahan', p. 121. Kheirandish, 'Early tradition in practical geometry'.

[65] Kheirandish, 'From Maragha to Samarqand', pp. 167: cites the report from 1004 [1595].

[*Earth:*] *I am a point, you a circle, which, at times, its way,*
Is diverted, without a point, from its circular path...

Asadi Tusi, *'Dialogue' of Sky and Earth*, ca. 1000, English translation: Elaheh Kheirandish[66]

5.3 *An Arab City with a Western Court*

It was October circa 1150, and a man named Ibn Rushd, who would soon be best known through the Latinised form of his name as 'Averroes',[67] was reviewing his notes about the workings of the universe, and the astronomical models developed up to his own time for how well they accorded with appearances versus reality. Though studying mathematical sciences and philosophy with a court physician in Seville, and later serving the court of a dynasty called 'Almohads'[68] in southern Spain long known as al-Andalus, that day Averroes was writing in Cordoba, a city called not only an 'Ornament of the world' as the former seat of a Cordoban Caliphate,[69] but also the 'Baghdad of the West', as a later centre for Arabic into Latin transmissions. This was a time when all major centres of knowledge from Baghdad to cities like Isfahan and Cairo in Islamic lands, or Sicily and Toledo in European lands, had a long way to go to break away from the age-old conception of a stationary earth at the centre of orbs encircling the sky. And the man who would be remembered close to a thousand years after the time he lived for writing commentary after commentary on the works of that long-gone age was taking incremental steps in playing with the idea of a non-Ptolemaic model for a still geocentric universe.

Abu al-Walid, Muhammad ibn Ahmad ibn Muhammad, known as 'Ibn Rushd', had two loops in the long chain of his Arabic name that while not appearing in his own signatures, made it to the many biographies of his long and eventful life up to modern times. One was the identifier 'The Grandson', something to distinguish him from a grandfather with not just a duplicate name, but with a line of work as a religious judge in Cordoba, somewhat similar to Averroes's own father. The other identifier was the honorific, and much more durable, title of 'The Commentator', bestowed upon Averroes with reference to someone as distant in time and place as Aristotle in the Greece of a few centuries before the start of the common era, one with whose works Averroes was as intimately connected as if they had been written next door or the day before.

66 Asadī Ṭūsī, Munāẓirih-i Āsmān va Zamīn (Persian), Khaleghi-Motlagh, 'Asadī Ṭūsī', pp. 96–104: p. 96, line 7; p. 100, line 41, Kheirandish, Elaheh (tr, excerpts).
'[*Sky:*] *Maʾvā-yi gūy u chugān-i maydān-i marmar-am*
Chugān zih sīm-i sādih u gūy-am zih kah-rubā ...
[*Earth:*] *Man nuqṭih-am tu dāʾirih-ī u gah-[ī] ravish*
bī nuqṭih ūft-ad zih khaṭ-i, dāʾirih khaṭāʾ...'

67 Arnaldez, 'Ibn Rushd', p. 909; Arnaldez and Iskandar, 'Ibn Rushd', p. 1; Rosenfeld and Ihsanoğlu, Mathematicians, Astronomers, and Other Scholars, No. 512, pp. 190–1; Forcada, 'Ibn Rushd', p. 564. http://islamsci.mcgill.ca/RASI/BEA/Ibn_Rushd_BEA.htm

68 Bosworth, Islamic Dynasties, pp. 30–1: Almohads (r. 524–667/1130–1269).

69 Menocal, Ornament of the World; Bosworth, Islamic Dynasties, pp. 11–13: Spanish Umayyads (r. 138–422/756–1031).

The year 1150 was a year when correspondences with a Greek nobleman would be recorded with Averroes much later in time, a year when the young 'Ibn Rushd', whose Arabic name literally meant 'Son of Growth', would be reported as having exchanged several letters with a noble Grecian student in Athens named Metrodorus since the year before.[70] Greece had a firm hold upon Ibn Rushd at the time, as firm as it would on a more mature and famed Averroes of a much later period. The thought of a region then known as 'Rum' for Byzantium, the Greater Greece of the time, squeezed his heart more than any other place on earth. He would later write, on more than one occasion, how Greece is higher than other places in both physical and intellectual terms, and how his own homeland of Andalusia similarly 'lies at the beginning of the fifth climate', the 'most temperate' region, as set by none other than Galen, a physician of the 2nd century of the common era from ancient Greek lands himself; and while Averroes would acknowledge capacities beyond Greece, in lands like Iraq and Egypt with Arab speaking inhabitants just like his own, he would be at odds with the more native seven-division geographies of a time and place closer to him. Closest to his own coordinates was a work titled *Category of Nations* by a native countryman even named Andalusi,[71] one who had divided the 'original nations' of ancient times and their branches into those 'cultivating science', as Indians, Persians, Chaldeans, Greeks, Romans, people of Egypt, Arabs, and Hebrews, and those not, naming various nations; even more distant to the western parts of Islamic lands, were the eastern divisions of both Arabic and Persian geographies, where the fourth, not fifth, climate was most privileged, and where, in the case of a bilingual treatment[72] by Abu Rayhan Biruni, himself not so far in either time or place, Persia sat front and centre as 'Iranshahr' (land of Iran) encircled by India, Morocco and Syria on one side, and Greater Greece, Central Asia and China on the other.

Besides giving a privileged position to Andalusia next to Greece, Averroes took a similar stance towards Greek subjects by elevating them to unparalleled heights. The highest place was kept for the singular case of Aristotle to sit above all others, not just as the so-called 'First Teacher', both before and after Averroes, and all over Islamic lands, but as the prime receiver of the most exclusive praises from Averroes, from 'infallible', and 'singled out by God for perfection', to 'always correct regardless of the occasional criticism of his commentators'.[73] The highest points of superiority, however, were still reserved for not just places or people, but regions. The case of 'West' over 'East' in particular seemed to Averroes to gain its strongest leverage when the loftiest names from both Arab and Persian regions of eastern lands were dragged to their lowest possible places. For those as high up in fame as Abu Nasr Farabi, Ibn Sina, and

[70] Averroeana: Transcript of Several Letters from Averroes to Metrodorus, a Young Grecian Nobleman, Student at Athens'...Athens and Cordoba, 1149 and 1150 ... put into English for the benefit of mankind ... (London, 1695), Harvard University, Houghton Library.

[71] Ṣāʿid al-Andalusī Kitāb Ṭabaqāt al-umam, Salem, Semaʿan I. and Kumar, Alok (ed tr), Science in the Medieval World: Book of the Categories of Nations (Austin, 1991).

[72] Bīrūnī, Kitāb al-Tafhīm, Wright (Arabic facs, tr), pp. 142–3: 'Maqrib' translated as Morroco, rather than Andalūs, for the second climate; Humāʾī (Persian ed), p. 196: 'Arab va Ḥabashān' Arab and Ethiopia.

[73] Sabra, 'Andalusian revolt', p. 138, and p. 149, n. 23.

Muhammad Ghazzali, esteemed with the Latinised forms Alpharibus, Avicenna, and Algazel, the mightiest exertion of force was needed. This Averroes would do through a blowing attack on the latest of those figures, Ghazzali, and his landmark book *Incoherence of the Philosophers* directed at secular sciences, in his smartly titled *Incoherence of the Incoherence.*[74] There, he would go after misrepresentations, not just misunderstandings, of the Greek master, much beyond the author, Ghazzali, the highly regarded teacher of the Nizamiyya school in Baghdad. Averroes would pull down the earlier Eastern philosophers, from Farabi, the so-called 'Second Teacher' after Aristotle, to Ibn Sina, the Aristotelian par excellence with a 'poem on medicine'[75] commentated by Averroes himself. All this was before attacking Ghazzali's *Incoherence of the Philosophers*, the book to be one day perceived as exerting one of the deadliest blows to the development of science in both Eastern and Western Islamic lands.

Solidly strong, yet discrete, were the attacks of Averroes on such authorities as al-Kindi and Ibn al-Haytham, the 'Alkindus' and 'Alhazen' of a time and place still not that far from Averroes's own. But in his case, this would be for their departures from Aristotelian teachings on science and its hierarchies, not philosophy.[76] And while Averroes's own brushes with some sciences were to be negatively affected by the limiting hierarchical system of Aristotle,[77] his treatments of other sciences were to benefit from Aristotelian teachings. In the case of astronomy, a science which Averroes became engaged with as early as his astronomical observations, and as late as his old age objections, it was Aristotelian teachings that inspired him to divert from the master of astronomy, Ptolemy, another Greek author from centuries later. But as it happened, the astronomical models of Eastern Islamic authors,[78] those ranging from Ibn al-Haytham and Ibn al-Shatir of 11th-century Cairo and 14th-century Damascus, to Tusi and Qushji of 13th-century Maragha and 15th-century Samarqand respectively, came to have better shots at hitting the right targets than those of Western Islamic authors, from Averroes himself, to the 12th-century Andalusian models of Ibn Tufayl, Al-Birtuji, and Ibn Maymun, the Latinised Abubacer, Alpetragius and Maimonides of Western Europe. Still, when it came to the much later revolutionary model of Copernicus from Eastern Europe, such earlier attempts were 'pre-Copernican Copernican' models[79] at best, even without considering the 'Sun-centred' component missing from them all.

That day in 1150, was a time when Averroes was still taking notes on two ancient Greek schools of thought in astronomy: that of Aristotle and the models of Eudoxus and Callippus, versus the later works of other Greek authors, like Hipparchus, and especially Ptolemy's *Almagest*,[80] those with whose non-uniform models he felt uneasy

[74] Averroes (Ibn Rushd). Tahāfut al-Tahāfut, Bouyges, M. (ed), van den Bergh, Simon (tr) (The Incoherence of the Incoherence) (London, 1954)
[75] Arnaldez and Iskandar, 'Ibn Rushd', p. 8.
[76] Sabra, 'Andalusian Revolt', p. 144, and p. 152, notes 41–3.
[77] Sabra, A. I., 'The physical and the mathematical in Ibn al-Haytham's theory of light and vision', The Commemoration Volume of Biruni International Congress in Tehran (Tehran, 1976), pp. 439–78, pp. 448–50.
[78] Kennedy, 'Late medieval planetary theory'.
[79] Roberts, 'The solar and lunar theory of Ibn al-Shāṭir'.
[80] Arnaldez and Iskandar, 'Ibn Rushd', p. 3; Toomer, Ptolemy's Almagest.

like so many of his predecessors and successors. In his old age, Averroes would write about astronomy that 'in my youth I had hoped to accomplish this investigation. But in my old age, I have despaired of that, having been impeded by obstacles'.[81] But that day, in his early twenties, the young Averroes was still eagerly collecting notes on natural philosophy, a subject with many promises even before becoming established as a discipline called physics. This was a subject to be noted as underlying his correspondence with the Greek student much later in time in a transcript 'long concealed and put into English for the benefit of mankind'. In that recorded correspondence, dated centuries later under the title *Averroeana*, letters were reportedly exchanged over enough distance in time and place as those put in the English of 1695 London,[82] to make everything seem anachronistic to later readers. Metrodorus would open with: 'Most learned and renowned Averroes, having often read over thy Works, I am astonished at the conceivable Activity of thy Wit, which in an imperial and uncontrollable manner extends itself over all the works of Nature, searches into her most Secrets … How much, and upon what accounts Aristotle himself stands Indebted to thee'. Next came other praises: 'Thou art admitted to a particular Intimacy [with nature], and hath been able to trace her through all her windings and turnings and discerned her naked in her bare and simple form … '. 'I in retreat therefore', followed the closing lines, 'thou wouldest send thy Opinion of this Operation of Nature in Writing by this Messenger, whom I have ordered to stay at Corduba till thy leisure shall allow thee opportunity of doing it … Athens, 1149'. The name 'Averroes' would accompany a reply to that nobleman of a seemingly lower intellectual stature, with opening words like 'Worthy Metrodorus', in line with the flattering customs of the time, or 'Noble Metrodorus' in a later letter sent through a friend 'just upon the point of taking his journey into Greece'. In doing so, Averroes would sound more and more modern when words placed into his mouth would come to read: 'There are some things unalterably to be believed upon the sole Credit and Authority of Nature as no humane Inquisition can arrive at any further knowledge of. Such are the Mysteries of our Religion … But in Philosophy we are left to a larger Latitude, like those of our Countrymen, whom they call wild; we are obliged to the Authority of no Person, but at Liberty to pick and choose, change and resettle our Opinion as oft as our Reason directs; as a Ship that has the Port in view, shall not withstanding by reason of a contrary Wind be forced to tack and shift her Sails a great many times before she reach the Haven. Let us, therefore, Metrodorus, launch forth boldly into this part of the Sea of Nature, and try what Discoveries we can make beyond the experience of former Adventures … '.

In some ways, these reported letters, converted into early modern English, were no different from the 'translation of a translation' of Greek into Syriac and Arabic, one that made a fictional Averroes put down his pen in an even more modern 'Search of Averroes' for the meaning of two words: 'tragedy' and 'comedy' in Aristotle.[83] Those were concepts that were inconceivable to even an avid 'Commentator' such as Averroes through cultural gaps far wider than distance of several centuries or regions. But the

81 Arnaldez and Iskandar, 'Ibn Rushd', p. 3; Sabra, 'Andalusian revolt', p. 142, includes key original terms.
82 Averroeana, pp. 1–6.
83 Borges, 'Averroes's search', p. 148.

use of two other Greek words by the later Greek scholar Ptolemy would become so close to the heart and mind of Averroes for violating Aristotelian principles that it would occupy him for a good part of his life. In the early days of such pre-occupations, Averroes's setting was not quite as that imaginatively laid out by one of the most creative literary figures of a much later age. This was the Argentinean author and poet Jorge Luis Borges, who placed him under the limelight of his short story 'Averroes's search' in an unforgettable scene:[84] 'from some unseen patio arose the murmur of the fountain ... down below were the gardens, the orchard; down below the busy Guadalquivir, and then the beloved city of Cordova, no less eminent than Baghdad or Cairo, ... and all around ... stretched out into the limits of the earth, the Spanish lands...'. On that October day, by contrast, Averroes was – far from sitting in broad daylight – bent in the dark shadows of a burning candle over his notes, those on the workings and inconsistencies of nature, especially the appearances and movements of celestial objects, observable at night, still only with bare eyes.

In his large *Commentary* on Aristotle's *Metaphysics* in Arabic, a 'Tafsir', that Averroes would write at an old age after a paraphrase called 'Talkhis' written when he was about fifty, he could still not take his mind off a subject coming up at the Almohad court to which his older contemporary, Ibn Tufayl, had introduced him. He would always recall when the young prince asked about 'the substance of the heavens' and about 'obscurities of Aristotle's texts', asking for commentaries for which a young Averroes would have been more suitable than an old Ibn Tufayl. After about three decades, and a small, middle, and large commentary, Averroes's problems with two floating Ptolemaic words[85] persisted when he wrote: 'the existence of an eccentric sphere or an epicyclic sphere is contrary to nature. As for the epicyclic sphere, this is not at all possible; for a body that moves in a circle must move about the centre of the universe, not aside from it ... It is similarly the case with the eccentric sphere proposed by Ptolemy. For if many centres existed ... the centre would cease to be unique ... It may be possible to replace these two things by the spiral motions assumed by Aristotle in this astronomy in imitation of those who came before him'.

The problem with conceptions like epicycles and eccentrics, as two early models Ptolemy had devised for explaining the apparent motions of the planets – motions assumed to be circular and uniform since ancient times – was discussed long before and after Averroes, in both the eastern and western parts of Islamic lands. From the standpoint of stationary Earth-centred models that were common before the Earth-moving, Sun-centred model not considered by Averroes and his immediate successors, one non-uniform apparent motion in the sky was a retrograde, loop-like motion planets seemed to make. The other non-uniform motion was the case of some planets appearing to speed up and slow down to an observer on Earth in various parts of apparent circular orbits. Ptolemy had followed the attempts of his predecessors to explain the occasional appearance of such non-uniform motions by assuming, in the first case – namely retrograde motion – a conception such as 'epicycles' to explain that the orbit of a planet is around a small circle called an epicycle, which is itself moving

84 Borges, 'Averroes's search', p. 148.
85 Sabra, 'Andalusian revolt', p. 141.

around a bigger circle, called a deferent, centred at the centre of the universe; and that the combined motion creates only the 'appearance' of non-uniform motions. The second, eccentric model was the attempt of the ancients, and later Ptolemy, to assume a position for the Earth, and an observer on it, at some distance from the centre of the universe, and so assuming a unifying centre other than the Earth, and in Averroes's words, a multitude of heavenly bodies outside the place of the Earth.

Averroes knew full well that these conceptions, as well as their problems and solutions, were closely connected with at least two other sets of ancient Greek conceptions: one was rectilinearity and circularity, concepts linked to Aristotelian cosmology, which divided the visible world to one below and one above the Moon, where straight and circular modes of motion respectively operated; another set of concepts were the 'mathematical' and 'physical' conceptions going back to Plato, Aristotle's own teacher, and preserved through successive reports from Greek antiquity: this time, the 'mathematical' explained, or 'saved' the phenomena,[86] like those of apparent retrograde motions, and the 'physical' represented the actual reality of the heavenly bodies. The respective 'hypothetical' and 'real' models were themselves adopted by Ptolemy in two different works:[87] the mathematical-hypothetical *Almagest* of his younger years, and the physical-real *Planetary Hypotheses* of his older age.

Averroes was one of many astronomical authors writing about a thousand years after Ptolemy who had expressed concern about these and other ancient Greek models. In the Arab speaking world, Ibn al-Haytham writing much before Averroes had done so in a work devoted to the subject,[88] including a similarly problematic assumption such as the conception of an 'equant' as a point with the same distance from the centre of the universe as the distance of Earth from it, to offset the non-uniformity problem among others. Closer to Ibn Rushd's time, Ibn Maymun, the Jewish scholar writing in Arabic and Latinised as Maimonides, had a position of compromise in his influential *Guide for the Perplexed*: he had carefully chosen his words in two assumptions of his own:[89] first that 'it is preferable for us to rely on the arrangement postulating the lesser number of motions. For this reason we have chosen, in the case of the Sun, the hypothesis of eccentricity, as Ptolemy mentions, rather than that of an 'epicycle'; and then, the assumption that 'regarding all that is in the heavens, man grasps nothing but a small measure of what is mathematical...the deity alone fully knows the true reality . . . But he has enabled man to have knowledge of what is beneath the heavens, for that is his world. . .', quoting 'The heavens are the heavens of the Lord, but the earth hath He given to the sons of man'.

There would be astronomical writers from the Muslim East who would propose model after model to get closer and closer to what could be the 'real' structure of the heavens. But Averroes, whose position was similarly closer to the 'physical-real' of Ptolemy's later years than the 'mathematical-hypothetical' of his younger age, was also

86 Duhem, To Save the Phenomena.
87 Toomer, Ptolemy's Almagest; Goldstein, Bernard R., 'The Arabic version of Ptolemy's Planetary Hypotheses', Transactions of the American Philosophical Society, 57, 4 (1967), pp. 3–55.
88 Sabra, 'Aporias Against Ptolemy'.
89 Crowe, Theories of the World, p. 75.

one who wrote about his own positions in both young and old age. He would one day write about his hopes in his youth for accomplishments, and his despairs in his old age over obstacles. He would write about astronomy and its discourses at a later time, and about the question of actual realities versus merely workable models, stating that 'let this discourse spur someone else to inquire into this matter ... For nothing of the [true] science of astronomy exists in our time, the astronomy of our time being only in agreement with calculations, and not with what exists'.[90]

5.4 *A Persian City with an Eastern Fort*

It was November circa 1250, and the man known as the 'Third Teacher' after Aristotle and Farabi, as well as 'Teacher of Mankind'[91] closer to his own time – one to soon become a 'cutting edge of 13th-century intellectual life'[92] and 'well-known unknown'[93] of a much later age, was looking at the final page of one of his astronomical works. This was a *Book of Constellations* that he had translated from Arabic into Persian on the request of some friends,[94] something a high-profiled scholar such as he would rarely spend time on instead of an original composition. His target was to finish the book in his favourite month, which was February, not just as the month of his own birth, but the last month of the Persian calendar before Nowruz, the 'New Year' of his native Persian Zoroastrian ancestors. That day, Abu Jaʿfar Muhammad ibn Muhammad ibn al-Hasan, the 'Distinguished Scholar and Teacher',[95] prefixing his better-known first and last name, Nasir al-Din Tusi, was looking at an image above the signature lines of his beautifully illustrated *Book of Constellations*. The image was that of a fish, representing the zodiac sign Pisces, ending the Persian solar year, floating like a large whale over a small legible script.[96] The signature line, lacking the signature itself, posed something never crossing the mind of the book's renowned author: that a different hand placed sideways in the right margins of the closing lines including various Tusi titles next to the phrase 'also in the script of his hand',[97] was something to one day raise questions about the book as a valuable 'autograph copy', needing cross-checks against his various scattered writings.

The post-production life of the Persian *Constellations* was to be even further from the imagination of anyone at the time. The mere move of the uniquely illustrated book

[90] Sabra, 'Andalusian revolt', p. 142.

[91] Mudarris-i Raḍavī, Ahvāl va athār, p. 3; Daiber and Ragep, 'Al-Ṭūsī, Naṣīr al-Dīn', p. 750; Masoumi Hamedani, 'Ustād-i bashar', p. 1; Mudarrisī (Zanjānī), Muḥammad, Sar-gudhasht va ʿaqāʾid-i falsafī-yi Khwāja Naṣīr al-Dīn Ṭūsī (Tehran, 1363 [1984]), p. 29.

[92] Ragep, 'Persian context', p. 119.

[93] Masoumi Hamedani, 'Ṭūsī: nā-shinās-i maʿrūf', in 'Ustād-i bashar', p. 1, section 1: an expression highlighting the imbalance between an unknown (nā-shinās) Ṭūsī, and his well known (maʿrūf) name.

[94] Ṭūsī, Tarjamah-i Ṣuwar al-kawākib, p. 2: 'iltimās-i baʿḍī dūstān'.

[95] Ragep, Ṭūsī's Memoir on Astronomy, Vol. 1, p. 3, n. 4: Ṭūsī's contemporary, Bar Hebraeus, called him 'Khwāja'.

[96] Ṭūsī, Tarjamah-i Ṣuwar al-kawākib, colophon: p. 196.

[97] Sideway marginal note: 'ham bi khaṭṭ-i yad-i ū-st'.

from one time or place to another would be more than dynamic: the original volume was to start from Alamut of the 1250s, the capital of Shiʿi Ismaʿili governors where Tusi had found patrons in the province of Quhistan to work safely midway between his native Khurasan and Isfahan where the Mongol invasion[98] had reached decades before. The volume would then move to the courts and libraries of conquerors and inheritors of lands, gaining through more and more royal routes, more and more distinguished marks along its way: first there would be the post-Mongol Baghdad of the early 1400s, and a Jalayirid ruler, annotating the book; then the Timurid Samarqand of the mid-1400s and their distinguished ruler, Ulugh Beg, signing the book; then the Ottoman Istanbul of 1400 to 1700s, and Sultans from Bayazid, the second, to Mahmud, the first, stamping the book; then back to Persia of the 1600s and 1700s, with a volume in the 1650s duplicating the book; and most unexpected of all, a pre-1750 copy with the conqueror Nadir Shah endowing the book.[99] Inconceivable, not just to the author, but to all readers, owners, and donors of the book up to that time, was that the original and duplicate copies would one day end up split between Sunni Constantinople and Shiʿi Mashhad,[100] of a much later time.

The lively physical life of Tusi's *Book of Constellations* in its kinematic move from city to city, and region to region, would be coupled with an even more dynamic intellectual life. The question of whether this was an 'autograph' work, in the hands of the author himself, would be a living, breathing question, with a life of its own, as the status of the book shifted from a rarity, to a mystery, to a commodity. To its readers, a single translation next to hundreds of original compositions by the same author[101] made it a rarity; to its examiners, the closing lines missing a name next to the dates of a translator-transcriber matching that of Tusi[102] made it a mystery; and to its owners and dealers, the marks of all such names, dates, times and places of distinction, made it a commodity.

But to the author of the Persian *Constellations*, as Tusi was, the book could be none of these: his immediate interest in it was not just a long passion in its subject of astronomy, but also a close association with the author of the book's prototype, Sufi. In subject, the Arabic *Book of Constellations* had been more to him than yet another Arabic composition based on a Greek original, as was its author more than yet another Persian native writing in Arabic or away from home; and if the content of the book had benefitted from an author such as Sufi, a pioneer in observational astronomy, its form followed the book's transcribers and illustrators, possibly

98 Ragep, 'Persian context', p. 121: Khurasan 618/1221; Browne, Literary History, Vol. 2, pp. 4–17: Isfahan.

99 Ṭūsī, Tarjamah-i Ṣuwar al-kawākib, colophon margin: owner 'Ahmad ibn Shaykh Uvays', date (805 H [1402–3]); later copy: 'Madinat al-salām' [Baghdad]; cover page: 'Ulugh Beg' signing; Bāyazīd II stamp; Natil Khanlari, Parviz (Intro): duplicate endowed to Mashhad by Nādir Shāh Afshār; authenticity discussions; periods: Bosworth, Islamic Dynasties, pp. 136–7: Bāyazīd II (r. 1481–1512); Maḥmūd I (r. 1730–54); pp. 172–5: Safavid ʿAbbās II (r. 1642–66); Nādir Shāh (r. 1736–47).

100 Istanbul Ayasofya 2959; Mashhad Astan Quds, 5250.

101 Rosenfeld and Ihsanoğlu, Mathematicians, Astronomers, and Other Scholars, No. 606, pp. 211–19.

102 Colophon page: translation (tarjama) and transcription (naskh), the date in words as 647 H [1249/1250].

Sufi's own son,[103] named in the well-executed *Constellations* dated close to twenty years after Sufi's death. That possibility had the strongest resonance with Tusi, who wished his own sons to become devoted to the cause of astronomy, each in their own way.

Nasir al-Din, whose first name rhymed with that of his three sons, Sadr al-Din, Asil al-Din, and Fakhr al-Din,[104] and whose second name, Tusi, was close enough to that of the father and son, author and debated illustrator, Sufi, had translated that Arabic work from what was one of its earliest illustrated manuscripts.[105] But Tusi's Persian *Constellations* was to do more: it would preserve relics of his native 'Iranian past',[106] some as discrete as an ancient Persian Sasanian headdress for the Constellation Andromeda, 'the woman in the [human] chain in the Constellation of the Northern Fish'. The book would also strengthen the usage of Persian language next to Arabic – the standard language of intellectual discourse at the time. More than a decade before, Tusi had composed two outstanding astronomical works[107] in Persian which, significantly, contained the first version of his non-Ptolemaic astronomical models. This was the first time any major scientific work was to be composed in Persian before Arabic, and not just alongside of it. Tusi would be credited with other works in Persian, including a piece on the body of water called the 'Caspian'[108] in northern Persia, one whose very name as a 'lake' or 'sea' was to change its fate with the changing status of its neighbouring lands. But it would be on the sky above more than the earth below of the much wider landscape of his native lands that the fame of Tusi's Persian works was to lie. Two important Persian works, one on ethics and another on logic, had been dedicated to his Isma'ili patrons, not far in time from his astronomical works. But it was in the 'science of stars', as astronomy was called, that the Persian models of the so-called 'Tusi couple', naming the first Isma'ili patron, would become world famous even before the Arabic. In the same way, Tusi had composed important works in Arabic earlier than his *Memoir on Astronomy*, a spiritual autobiography titled *Journey and Conduct*,[109] and a mathematical collection titled *The Middle Books*, those studied

[103] An Islamic book of Constellations, p. 3: 'a fragment of the colophon . . . written and illustrated in the year 400 A.H. (A.D. 1009/10) by al-Ḥusayn b.ʿAbd al-Rahman b.ʿUmar ibn Muḥammad, alleged to be the son of the author . . . (903–86)'. Savage-Smith, 'Most authoritative copy', p. 152, treats the Oxford manuscript as 'semi-fake', citing Soudavar, Abolala, 'The concepts of "al-aqdamo aṣaḥḥ" and "yaqīn-e sābeq", and the problem of semi-fakes', Studia Iranica, 28 (1999), pp. 255–73.

[104] Mudarrisī (Zanjānī), Sar-gudhasht va ʿaqāʾid, pp. 78–9.

[105] Rice, D. S., 'The oldest illustrated Arabic manuscript', Bulletin of the School of Oriental and African Studies, 2, 1/3 (1959), pp. 207–20, p. 207: 'The oldest scientific illustrations known at present are those of ʿAbd al- Raḥmān al-Ṣūfī's Treatise on the fixed stars' (Kitāb Ṣuwar al-kawākib al-thābita), MSS: Leningrad, dated 396 [1005–6] and 402 [1011], copied from Ṣūfī's holograph completed in 355 [965]; another MS copier long assumed as Ṣūfī's son, dated 400 [1009], now in the Bodleian Library.

[106] Melikian-Chirvani, A. S., 'Khwāje and the Iranian past', in Pourjavady, N. and Vesel, Ž. (eds), Nasīr al-Dīn al-Ṭūsī: Philosophe et savant du XIIIe siècle (Tehran, 2000), pp. 69–104.

[107] Masoumi Hamedani, 'Ustād-i bashar'; Ragep, 'Persian Context'.

[108] Ṭūsī, Naṣīr al-Dīn (attribution), Dhikr-i Daryā-yi Khazar [Commemorating the Caspian Sea], Vienna Manuscript published in Melgunof, Gregory, Kaspischen Meeres oder Die Nordprovinzen Persiens (Leipzig, 1868).

[109] Ṭūsī, Naṣīr al-Dīn, Sayr wa sulūk, Badakhchani, S. J. (ed, tr) (Contemplation and Action: The Spiritual Autobiography of a Muslim Scholar) (London, New York, 1998).

intermediately between Euclid's *Elements* in geometry and Ptolemy's *Almagest* in astronomy. But it was Tusi's Arabic astronomical 'configuration'[110] that would overshadow all the earlier Arabic and Persian astronomical works, itself composed before his Persian *Constellations*.

That day in November, in the cold hidden regions of the Alburz mountains where Tusi worked with a low profile a few years before the much-feared Mongol invasion of Eastern Islamic lands, he was surrounded by many books from the rich library of his outgoing patrons, the Isma'ili's, Shi'ite rulers whose fortress of Alamut would soon be added to the list of Persian regions fallen to the Mongols. Closing his *Book of Constellations*, Tusi reached for his two pioneering astronomical compositions next to that translation, all stacked up in the same batch of Persian works. He felt a mixed sense of pride and regret: pride that he had masterminded such pieces, especially in his native tongue of Persian, even before Arabic, the language of science among other subjects; and regret that he had not yet been able to fulfil his wish of unveiling their clever astronomical models through the *Memoir on Astronomy*[111] that he was putting together in Arabic, a work to broadcast them in a more scientific language. From the day Tusi had composed the first of those Persian astronomical gems more than a decade before, giving it the title of *Mu'iniyya Treatise* after the name of Mu'in al-Din Shams, the son of one of his earliest Isma'ili patrons, Nasir al-Din Muhtasham, to the time he had started working on the *Solutions to the Difficulties of Mu'iniyya*,[112] promised to the same patron, with a first name identical to his as 'Nasir al-Din', he had not stopped thinking about the details of the models he had invented to solve one of the oldest 'doubts' that his Islamic predecessors had raised against important aspects of Greek astronomy. These models, to be one day carrying Tusi's name and credited for direct impacts on later European models, were invented by him through sleepless nights under the starry skies of the dark and vast lands of pre-Mongol Persia to preserve two ancient principles related to uniform motion in the heavens: that of rectilinearity and circularity. His invented device, which would become famous under the expression 'Tusi couple', consisted of two rolling spheres,[113] one inside and tangential to the other twice its radius, and moving twice as fast in the opposite direction. These rolling spheres turning in opposite directions cleverly worked such that a point on the smaller sphere had a uniform *circular* motion around the larger sphere's circumference, and a uniform *rectilinear* motion on its diameter. Adapted to lunar and planetary models, the device kept the accuracy of Ptolemy's model without violating ancient Aristotelian principles, still with a primary aim common in premodern times: that of making the two systems consistent.

The first of Tusi's Persian astronomical treatises was, by itself, a landmark in more than one way: in terms of content, there was the 'serious doubt' Tusi raised with regard

[110] Ragep, Ṭūsī's Memoir on Astronomy: hay'a: configuration.
[111] Ragep, Ṭūsī's Memoir on Astronomy, Vol. 1, p. 23.
[112] Ṭūsī, Naṣīr al-Dīn, Risālah-i Mu'īnīyah, Danish-Pazhuh, Muhammad-Taqi (ed) (Tehran, 1335 [1956]); Hall-i Mushkilāt-i Mu'īnīyah, Danish-Pazhuh, Muhammad-Taqi (ed) (Tehran, 1335 [1956]).
[113] Ashworth, William B., Linda Hall Library, 18 February, 2015: animation of Tusi couple producing rectilinear motion from a rotating circle. www.lindahall.org/nasir-al-din-al-tusi/

to the model of Ptolemy, and the 'elegant way' for which the author claimed originality; and in terms of reference, two other items stood out: mention of 'Prince of Iran', whose will was set as the condition for previous forthcoming treatments; and that of Abu ʿAli ibn al-Haytham,[114] the 'great mathematician' of two centuries before, one whose earlier attempts on that same problem were not acceptable to the author. In the 'Solution' or 'Appendix' to that same treatise in Persian, which just like its prototype was to have two prefaces, one for the outgoing Ismaʿili patron, and one for the incoming Mongol ruler,[115] Tusi's various chapters included additional features, still without alternatives to the models he found unacceptable. The same could not be said of Tusi's later *Memoir on Astronomy*, a work in Arabic with its own two versions, one composed soon after he became the director of an observatory founded by the Mongol ruler, Hulaku in Maragha; and the other, completed the year Tusi died in Baghdad.[116] Tusi's experience in other places were to be similarly remarkable: highlights in Alamut, where he spent his earlier years in hiding, included key moments when he was not only eyewitness, but negotiator during the submission of the Ismaʿili Rukn al-Din Khurshah, to the Mongol conqueror, Hulaku; those in Maragha included experiences with scholars pouring in from various parts of the fast expanding Islamic lands, places as far as China and India, into that early Islamic institution funded by state endowment.[117]

But in the year 1250, Tusi was still in hiding from the invading Mongols, somewhere between Khurasan in the east, where he grew up, and Azarbaijan in the west, where he would soon excel high, while some of his fellow observatory colleagues-to-be, who would join him in Maragha close to a decade later, were also breathing under different skies. One of these, Yahya Maghribi whose name translated into 'John the Westerner',[118] would come to Maragha after his life had been spared by the Mongols invading Damascus in 1258 because he knew astrology, according to another Maragha resident, Bar Hebraeaus; another one was a young man named Ibn Fuwati, enslaved by the Mongols at the siege of Baghdad in the same year, who would be taken to Azarbaijan and become an attendant of the Maragha Library.[119] In the walkway between an observatory and a library, among so many other spaces that Tusi occupied day and night in both Alamut and Maragha, there was a natural place for not only history in the sense of chronology, but also poetry as a form of narrating history. The genre of poetry, to which many Persian speakers would lose their hearts, both before and after Tusi, included astronomical subjects, with reference to various chronologies and constellations, some attributed to Tusi and his own contemporaries. In the case of astronomical chronologies, the poems were simple, many in the form of rhyming quatrains, recording years of some significant event including those involving Tusi: one poem was about the fall of the fortress of Alamut and his Ismaʿili patrons in the year

[114] Ragep, 'Persian context', pp. 124–5.
[115] Ragep, Tūsī's Memoir on Astronomy, Vol. 1, p. 13.
[116] Ragep, Tūsī's Memoir on Astronomy, Vol. 1, p. 23.
[117] Ragep, Tūsī's Memoir on Astronomy, Vol. 1, p. 9.
[118] Reference to Muḥyī al-Dīn [Yaḥyā] al-Maghribī. Ragep, Tūsī's Memoir on Astronomy, Vol. 1, p. 14.
[119] Comes, 'Ibn Abī al-Shukr' [Maghribi], pp. 548–9, p. 548: https://islamsci.mcgill.ca/RASI/BEA/Ibn_Abi_al-Shukr_BEA.htm; and Melville, 'Ebn al-Fowaṭī', pp. 25–6, p. 25: www.iranicaonline.org/articles/ebn-al-fowati

1256;[120] another, about the fall of a city such as Baghdad, and the rule of the ʿAbbasid Caliphate in 1258;[121] and yet another, the death of Tusi's Mongol patron Hulaku in 1261.[122] Chronological poems about important dates included those involving Tusi directly: the year of his death in 1274 generated quatrains which in one case included its day and month;[123] and in another case, its date and the time.[124]

Besides astronomical dating, there were poems with subjects such as stellar constellations including verses attributed to Tusi: these extended from short verses with successive names for the zodiac signs[125] and their relations to the planets,[126] to long poems establishing a legacy that would be followed in poems beyond those of his contemporaries. Astronomical poems[127] written close to or earlier than Tusi's own age were by poets as far back as Firduwsi and Gurgani, and as late as Sanaʾi and Rumi; and those after Tusi included astronomical poems by authors like Khaju-yi Kirmani and Shah Niʿmatullah-i Vali, succeeding him by one and two centuries. Such poems also included those on the 'observatory' as an institution,[128] and the fate of astronomy itself in a period following Tusi by as much as three centuries. Each of these poets had at least one poem describing astronomical objects that would have been visible to them from various parts of Persia, from deserts to mountains, under the same sheltering sky. But being as far apart as they were in both time and place, these poems were to act as mirrors below star-filled skies to reflect their respective ages from the 'four corners of Persia': the *Shah-namih* or *Book of Kings of Firduwsi,*, in whose old preface the expression 'four corners of Persia'

[120] Muʿaẓẓamah Iqbālī (aʿẓam), Shiʿr va Shāʿirī dar āthār-i Khwājah Naṣīr al-Dīn Ṭūsī (Tehran, 1379 [2000]), p. 157, Kheirandish, Elaheh (tr, excerpt).
'When the Arab year reached six hundred and fifty-four years, on a Sunday morning when Dhū qaʿdih was the month, Khur-Shāh, then, the Ismāʿīlī King, from the throne, rose up facing Hulākū in his step down'
Sāl-i ʿArab chu shish-ṣad u panjāh u chār shud, yik-shanbih-ī zi avval-i Dhū qaʿdih, bām-dād
Khur-Shāh pād-shāh-i Ismāʿīliyān zih takht, bar khāst, pīsh-i Hulākū bi-īstād'.

[121] Muʿaẓẓamah Iqbālī, Shiʿr va Shāʿirī, p. 157, Kheirandish, Elaheh (tr, excerpt).
'On the [lunar] year, six hundred and fifty six, on a Sunday, the fourth of ṣafar [in day and month], the Caliph came to Hulākū and from then on, the rule of ʿAbbasids was lost and gone.
Sāl-i hijrat shish-ṣad u panjāh u shīsh, rūz-i yik-shanbih, chāhar-um az ṣafar,
shud khalīfih pīsh-i hullākū va-z-ān, duwlat-i ʿAbbāsiyān ām-ad bi-sar'.

[122] Muʿaẓẓamah Iqbālī, Shiʿr va Shāʿirī, p. 157.

[123] Mustuwfī, Ḥamdallāh, quoted in Mudarrisī (Zanjānī), Sar-gudhasht va ʿaqāʾid, p. 75:
'Naṣīr-i millat u dīn, pād-shāh-i kishvar-i faḍl, yigānih-ī kih chu ū mādar-i zamānih naz-ād
Bih sāl-i shish-ṣad u haftād [u] du bih Dhi hajjih, bih rūz-i hijdah-um dar-guzasht dar Baghdād'.

[124] Musāmarah al-akhbār, quoted in Mudarrisī (Zanjānī), Sar-gudhasht va ʿaqāʾid, p. 75:
'Hijdah-um az māh-i Dhi hajjih, du-shanbih vaqt-i shām, sāl-i hijrat, shish-ṣad u haftād-u du, nāqiṣ nah tām, Khwājih-i ʿālam, Naṣīr al-Dīn-i Ṭūsī az gaḍā, naql kard az khaṭṭih-i Baghdād tā Dār al-salām'.

[125] Muʿaẓẓamah Iqbālī, Shiʿr va Shāʿirī, p. 133; Varjavand, Kāvush-i Raṣad-khānah-i Marāgha, p. 136: '*Aries, Taurus, and then Gemini*' (*Ḥamal u Thawr baʿd az ān Jawzā*), '*Cancer, Leo, then Virgo*' (*Saraṭān u Asad digar Adhrā*), '*Scorpio and Sagittarius, after that Libra*' (*ʿAqrab u Qaws d ān pas az Mīzān*); *and then* '*Capricorn, Aquarius, and Pisces comes right after*' (*Jady u Dalv ast u Ḥūt, az pas-i ān*)'. Kheirandish, 'Astronomical Poems', p. 64, n. 31 and p. 82.

[126] Kheirandish, Elaheh, 'Zodiacs of Paris: Verses, places, faces', in Diana Cormos-Buchwald et al. (eds), Looking Back As We Move Forward: The Past, Present, and Future of the History of Science (New York, 2019), pp. 142–53.

[127] Kheirandish. 'Astronomical poems', Appendix, pp. 69–90; Richard, Alain, 'L'astronomie et l'astrologie dans la poésie persane', Luqmān: Annales des Presses Universitaires d'Iran Revue Semestrielle, 20, 1 (1382 [2003]), pp. 81–101.

[128] Sayılı, Observatory in Islam.

appeared,[129] along with the 'seven quarter' division of its 'land from end to end', was only one of many astronomical poems to be identified from successive historical and geographical settings for reflecting the cosmological views of their ages: from the 11th-century northern Persia, the 'Education of Alexander' in the *Shah-namih* of Firduwsi, ca. 1000, another author from Tus; and the 'Description of the Night' in *Vis u Ramin* of Fakhr al-Din As'adi, from Gurgan, ca. 1050, reflecting the views of an age won by the effect of the upper heavens on sublunary realms; from the 12th-century north east and south west Persia, 'On the Twelve Constellations' in *Hadiqa al-haqiqa* of Sina'i Ghaznavi, and 'Description of the Night and Majnun's Secret Prayer' in *Layli u Majnun* of Nizami Ganjavi, both before ca. 1150, reflecting the views of an age engaged with the creator of both realms; from the 13th-century north west Persia, poems by Muwlana Jalal al-Din Rumi complemented those of Tusi in looking upwards to configurations as well as prognostication, however different the nature and order of their treatments; and from the 14th and 15th centuries southern Persia, the respective 'Birth Horoscope' in *Gul u Nowruz* of Khwaju-yi Kirmani, and 'Zodiac Organs' in *The Degrees of Existence* of Shah Ni'matullah Vali, reflecting the new mystical and spiritual tilts of a later age.

The age of Tusi, just as those before and after him, was an age reflecting bonds with not only astronomy, but astronomical poems; the case of the poet, muwlana Jalal al-Din, known as Rumi,[130] residing in Byzantium after the Mongol takeover of his native Persian lands, stood out: this figure, whose birth and death dates closely coincided with Tusi's, wrote an outstanding piece in the form of an astronomical feast in the sky under a full moon, a feast in a 'night of joining, giving, and outpour, in the heaven' where there is 'a wedding by the Moon of ten and four',[131] the full moon of the fourteenth day of the month. Not only was Rumi's imagery of the sky and earth finer than in his better known verses on being neither from 'the skies or of the lands, nor of the circling heavens';[132] he named the planets and zodiacs known at his time, then seven planets next to twelve zodiacs.[133]

While there were discontinuities between the literary and scientific traditions even among those living as close in time and place as Rumi and Tusi, there were continuities when it came to the dominating force of their age. The age of the scientist and philosopher Tusi, and that of his contemporary poet and mystic Rumi,[134] was an age in

[129] Old Preface of the Book of Kings (Shāh-nāmih Abū Manṣūrī):
'Everywhere there was a resting place for people,
In the four corners of the world, from end to end,
this land they granted, and divided into seven quarters. . .'
'Har kujā kih āram-gāh-i mardumān būd, bih chahār sūy-i jahān,
az karān tā karān īn zamīn rā bibakhshīd-and va haft bakhsh kard-and . . . .
[130] Kheirandish, 'Age of Rūmī'.
[131] Kheirandish, 'Astronomical poems', pp. 81–2; details and excerpt: Postscript.
[132] Blodgett, E. D. and Mannani, Manijeh, Speak Only of the Moon: A New Translation of Rumi (Santa Monica, 2014), reference: Arash Afshar, p. 32 (Persian); p. 38 (English: nonliteral):
'Not Eastern or Western, celestial, or of
The lower world, or objects turning above. . .'.
'Nah sharqī-am, nah gharbī-am, nah 'ulwī-am, nah sulfī-am,
Nah arkān-i ṭabī'ī-am, nah az aflāk-i gardān-am. . .'.
[133] Kheirandish 'Astronomical poems': Appendix, pp. 81–2; order: Moon, Venus, Jupiter, Saturn, Mars, Sun, Mercury; Capricorn, Leo, Pisces, Aquarius, Virgo, Gemini, Libra, Aries, Sagittarius, Scorpio, Taurus, Cancer.
[134] Kheirandish, 'Age of Rūmī', Harvard Summer School, 2012.

which the penetration of Mongol warriors through lands stretching all the way from their birth places in Tus and Balkh of the Persian east, to and beyond their respective death beds in Baghdad and Kunya of Arab and Turkish west, was the single most outstanding event of their fateful times. On the other hand, the Mongol takeover that bore the reputation of killing their youth and burning their books for centuries to come, was within the same age that offered them a chance for learning new skills and building new tools, to literally reach for the stars. The conquerors from the east that the Mongols were made them no different from conquerors from the west, north or south, who were passionately interested in the heavens and predictions, to monitor not only the effects of forces above and beyond those below, but their rates of success and survival, through cosmology.

At the same time, the age in which Tusi lived was one where eyes were only partially directed to the sky. Subjects as earthly as light refraction through dense mediums, and outward and inward appearances on flat surfaces, created both puzzles and complexities. The case of light refraction created 'puzzles' for scholars as late as Kamal al-Din Farisi,[135] a student of Tusi's own student, Qutb al-Din Shirazi,[136] when the ray of light ended up, wrongly, with equal angles of incidence and refraction through problems of transmission. This was a 'puzzle' to which Tusi could be a direct contributor through the interchangeability of orthographic twins such as the words for 'reflection' and 'refraction'[137] in his widely circulated manuscripts. The case of non-flat appearances reflected further complexities when Tusi spoke of pre-perspective, perspective effects in an age when rules of perspective[138] were still far from having developed even in Europe. But nowhere were the puzzles of Tusi's age, one witnessing the birth, death, or both, of various luminaries,[139] better captured than in verses carrying Tusi's name in the telling lines that his predecessors, 'who came as guides', did not merely 'come and pass;' but 'each placed a knot into complex tangles unraveled by anyone, as they passed'.[140]

[135] Sabra, Optics of Ibn al-Haytham; Sabra, '"Commentary" that saved the text'; Kheirandish, Elaheh, 'The puzzle of Ṭūsī's optical works', in in Pourjavady, N. and Vesel, Ž. (eds), Les sciences dans la monde iranien (Xe-XIXe siècle) (Tehran, 2004); also, Kheirandish, 'Light and Dark'.
[136] Sabra, '"Commentary" that saved the text'; Kheirandish, 'Light and dark'.
[137] Kheirandish, 'Puzzle of Ṭūsī's optical works'; Kheirandish, 'Light and dark'.
[138] Kheirandish, Elaheh, 'Optics and perspective in and beyond the Islamic Middle Ages: A study of transmission through multidisciplinary sources in Arabic and Persian', in Dupré, Sven (ed), Renaissance Cultures of Optics and Practices of Perspective (Turnhout, 2019), pp. 205–39.
[139] Ragep, Ṭūsī's Memoir on Astronomy, p. 3.
[140] Kheirandish, Arabic Version of Euclid's Optics: Vols. 1 and 2, opening.

6

Old and New

400 Years (ca. 1350–1750): Three-Quarter Phase

It was the best of times, it was the worst of times. . .
We had nothing before us, we had everything before us. . .
Charles Dickens, A *Tale of Two Cities*, 1859, opening[1]

6.1 An Old Manuscript in a Digital Age

It was December 2010, and the *Dialogue* manuscript was now living in the rapidly changing world of digital technology in a different capacity. Hosted by a project called 'Micromapping Early Science',[2] it had been featured in a campus fair on 'digital technology', one with a higher profile than an earlier one on 'digital humanities' through not one but two university write-ups[3] on the fair, and so the project.

The month before, the *Dialogue* manuscript and its hosting micromaps were showcased in both digital and virtual forms next to other items in the new 'fair': 'What's possible' of the November issue of the university paper covered a fair 'in its third year', highlighting 'digital resources available' far beyond those included in the first year on 'progress of humanities in the digital world';[4] the piece, 'Digital drive' of the December issue showed still higher leaps, from its opening lines on 'scholarship changing' and teachings 'driving the technology' through projects from a 'library of the future', 'virtual 17th-century' university, and 3D 'encyclopedia of life' to 'geographic analysis' and 'internet and society' projects, to its closing lines bringing the present into the future by

1 Dickens, Tale of Two Cities, opening.

2 Kheirandish, Elaheh, 'Micromapping early science', Harvard University: Academic Technology Group (ATG). https://www.scholar.harvard.edu/ekheirandish/multimedia

3 Digital Technology Fair, Harvard University, Barker Center, 29 November, 2010. Walsh, Colleen, 'What's possible: Fair highlights Harvard's digital resources', Harvard Gazette, 30 November 2010. http://news.harvard.edu/gazette/story/2010/11/whats-possible/. 'Digital drive: Technological breakthroughs are changing scholarship all across campus', 16 December 2010. http://news.harvard.edu/gazette/story/2010/12/digital-drive/

4 Walsh, 'What's possible'. Ireland, 'Fair shows progress'. http://news.harvard.edu/gazette/story/2008/12/fair-shows-progress-of-humanities-in-digital-world/

drawing its fine lines from the unexpected direction of 'technology driving research' in a Micromapping project, and 'research questions not thought of without that technology'.[5]

The micromaps embedding the *Dialogue* manuscript among other historical sources shared some features with the many projects displayed and covered in that 'feast of digital technology'. But the Micromapping project itself, exposing a *Dialogue* manuscript among other untapped sources, was as different as these were from each other: not only did it represent a different time and place as the only 'Middle Eastern' or 'Early Science' project that day; it held the place of technology not as a facilitator or time-saver, but an inspirer and creator of a new way of thinking produced by the very technology created to serve it.

The project director, faculty aide, and student assistant named on the Micromapping project, making demos with the 'go to' and 'timeline' features of the maps to zoom in and out of places from ancient to pre-modern times, starting with Baghdad and Isfahan, explained to the visitors the distinct features of the project with reference to its own past, present and future: not just 'dynamic' maps, with reference to past 'static' versions taken from historical and colour-coded maps; or 'interactive' maps with reference to present dynamic versions tagged with links to various media; but 'generative' maps, with reference to future, multimedia environments for evolving inputs like the tracks of the footprints of authors and works, and intersections of times and places, all with new directions for setting out historical work not readily 'conceivable' without such forward-looking technologies.

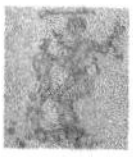

6.2 A Young Curator with a 'Future' Stage

It was January 2011, and Leo was integrating his tech projects into a multimedia platform as part of a new venture in this last year of his university studies. Digitised historical maps from 750 to 1750 were being filled with postings, century by century, and the year 1000, halfway between the first 500 years, was occupying a pivotal point, which included, besides micromaps, covering early science in Baghdad and Isfahan, both before and after that year, two short films, stretched through the year 1500, the mid-point of the second half of that 1000-year period. The medium of film was itself pushed from two recent fronts: a statistical front from the latest coverage of Leo's project as part of a 'digital future' where video appeared as 'one aspect' of it, not just 'risen to the top' in a network of 'millions of open-sources, thousands of servers, tens of thousands of computers, and uncounted mobile devices' at one university alone; but reported as 40% of the traffic there, and predicted to double in a short few years in an

[5] Walsh, 'Digital drive', p. 3: Katie Vale, director of Academic Technology Group: 'what we want to be able to do is make sure the teaching is driving the technology'; p. 5: library of the future; p. 3: virtual 17th-century Harvard Yard; p. 7: database of 3D models; p. 4: Center for Geographic Analysis; p. 8: Internet and Society, animating libraries and museums; p. 13: 'the ways technology can drive the research, said Kheirandish, a science historian' is 'questions we would not have thought of without this technology'.

'explosion of demand for videos'.[6] The other accelerating push for films came from a competitive front through the university's 'Film Archives', a contest where Leo was part-helper in two 'documentary shorts', films with the set duration of three minutes tops as a way of teaching economy of expression on any given subject.[7]

The more general short film titled 'A quartet of early scientific traditions' was to tell the story of four subjects in the film's subtitle: 'Geometry, astronomy, mechanics and optics, ca. 1000';[8] and the more specific film, titled 'When optics was more than physics', had besides the subtitle of 'Forward into the past', a closing title as 'A symphony of word and line, eye and mind, light, art and sight',[9] thereby capturing seven distinct stories in the same blink of maximum viewer attention. The styles of the two documentary shorts were different. The 'Quartet', which was to extend to a longer version for an academic event on 'World culture',[10] showed how some prime players in a quartet of early science, those in the film's subtitle, became key players in the quartet of 'world science', each subject rising, in turn, above the other, against the background of a rhythmic string quartet.[11] The 'Symphony' focused on the last of those subjects to show how optics, once called the 'most perfect' of the early sciences, shifted from a plural multi-disciplinary optics, to a single specialised subject: here the climax was a powerful symphony[12] behind the celebrated light model of a single prism converging the seven-colour spectrum of the film's subtitle.

The ceiling of three-minute film submissions confined their contents to a dozen sentences in between opening and closing lines, all narrated and subtitled over a musical piece which in the case of the 'Quartet', was produced in the form of two voices in continuous dialogue:

'That the world was once defined in terms of its four corners, may be well known', started one voice: 'Much less known is a time and place, as long as a thousand years ago and as far as Mesopotamia and Persia, where a quartet of geometry, astronomy, mechanics and optics, had a rich and long life beyond the Islamic Middle Ages'.[13] But what was the early history of these sciences, it continued, and their impacts beyond Arab and Persian lands?

6 Walsh, 'Digital drive', p. 8; Anne Margulies, Harvard's chief information officer: '... we need to make sure that our infrastructure is able to keep up with that and support it'.

7 Kheirandish, Elaheh, Harvard Film Archives documentary shorts, produced and narrated with Maera Siddiqi. https://www.scholar.harvard.edu/ekheirandish/films. https://harvardfilmarchive.org/cinematheque/history

8 Kheirandish, Elaheh, 'An Early Science Quartet: Geometry, astronomy, mechanics, optics, ca 1000 CE'. http://vimeo.com/51476052

9 Kheirandish, Elaheh, 'When optics was more than physics: Forward into the past, a symphony of word and line, eye and mind, light, art, and sight'. http://vimeo.com/51476183

10 Kheirandish, Elaheh, 'A quartet of Persian scientific traditions: Persian culture as a world culture'. London University, School of Oriental and African Studies (SOAS), November, 2011 (Soudavar Memorial Foundation anniversary, Invitation: Fatema Soudavar).

11 Dang Show, 'Piano, Piano' from the album '40-year-old Shiraz' (Shīrāz-i chihil sālih).

12 Beethoven: Symphony no. 7, 2nd Movement, Allegretto, Op. 92 in A Major.

13 '. . .Geometry and astronomy, two prime players in the quartet of early science were a rich pair in the curriculum, not just keys to the so-called Middle Books studied in between them. Mechanics and Optics, at centre stage as outstanding intermediary subjects and mixed mathematical-physical sciences, were the other twin stars with similar starts, yet different ends. . .'.

Here, a *Calendar of Timekeeping* rotating like a wheel of chance, turned a few times to dial the first selected time and place, before the other voice entered that 'dialogue': 'In Baghdad of around the year 1000, where the early growth of sciences coincided with court patronage, science was in full bloom in the lands of thousand and one nights'. Once the film's periphery of circular Baghdad was filled with scientific marks next to places from nearby Isfahan to faraway Europe, the first voice ended with four 'stars' with 'similar starts, yet different ends', each with their own marks in becoming a 'player in the quartet of world science'.

In contrast to the first film staging four 'players' over a musical quartet with varying overtones, the second film on the last of those sciences featured a single player over a powerful symphony with an escalating climax: the 'Symphony' told the story of 'when optics was more than physics' through the microscopic lens of language, zooming in on key concepts and terms, and their shifts, however slight, with Greek, Arabic and Latin dancing on the screen in the order of the path of early science itself: that 'For Euclid and Ptolemy in ancient Alexandria, then a part of Greece, the *word* "optika", meant a mathematical study of vision, and "opseis", meant "visual-rays" extending as outward *lines*'; that 'In the Islamic Middle Ages, Greek "opseis" became Arabic "shuʿaʿ", to mean "luminous-rays" multiplying indefinitely through translation alone, and with the pioneer Ibn al-Haytham, the *eye* became a receptive organ of the *mind*, combining mathematical and physical models with psychological and experimental dimensions'; that 'With transmissions to Renaissance Europe, came Latin "perspectiva", surveying and the *art* of projecting images on a plane'; with 'Kepler, *sight* turned into a visual instrument to invert inward images forming on the retina, like the camera obscura of his day, and the camera of our's; and with 'Newton, his celebrated *Opticks* brought *light* to the subject with a single prism of colour to converge the seven spectrums of *word, line, eye, mind, light, art*, and *sight*, into the single term "optic"'.[14]

Up until this last scene, Leo had been involved with film production that set in motion clips of what were mostly manuscripts and maps fed into image programs such as iMovie and Keynotes, mixed with sound programs like iTunes and Garage Band. But with the closing scene of the optics film, came the only 'live' scene of the film, a scene where Newton came to life, not through a painted portrait, but the 'walls' that held his portrait. A 'Newton Room', transported with its pine-paneled walls and carved mantel from the 'fore-parlour' of his last house in London, had come to a nearby college named after the school's founder, one whose wife was a 'collector of Newtonia';[15] the founder's own interest was in Newton's laws of motion for applications in economics and business, and in 'predicting and, if possible, controlling shifts' in their

[14] 'In classical Greek, the *word* for optics was optike from the root 'ops', meaning the eye, and 'opseis', meant visual-rays extending as outward *lines*; with the linguistic shift from Greek into Arabic, visual-rays, opseis, became luminous rays, 'shuʿāʿ' multiplying indefinitely; and with the pioneer Ibn al-Haytham, inward rays reversed all extramission models, adding psychological and experimental dimensions . . .'.

[15] Newtonia Collection of Grace Babson, first wife of Roger Babson, founder of Babson College, 'largest in the US', included the fore-parlour of Newton's last London residence. https://centennial.babson.edu/past/grace-k-babson-collection-of-newtonia/

cycles.[16] What that visionary couple could not have foreseen was that, one day, the Newton Room would not only turn from a library and museum to a meeting room in the business-rich college named after them, but where the room's 'fore-parlour' walls would form the only live scene of a digital film.

While the two films and their capturing shots were being posted on a multimedia site where the Newton walls could have their own virtual versions of fly-through Avatars of a time and place as critical to early science as post-1750 Europe, their embedded micromaps focused on pre-1750 Islamic lands as they kept moving 'forward into the past'. The micromaps were moving fast to link to earlier sources; but the earlier the sources, the harder the catch. The first half of the maps from 750 to 1750 were filling up with some postings for the year 1000, from the static profiles of authors and texts, to dynamic links for relevant files and sites; but the second half of those maps, and mid-point years like 1500, lent themselves well to more diverse historical sources by virtue of the mere survival of more sources, those that were exponentially more and more discovered, edited, translated, and simply read. These historical 'logs', as they were called in the Micromapping project, were entries that were used for producing historical 'plots' through codes and programs, those as simple as graphs, to connect historical 'dots'; and the later the sources, the more likely the chances of coming across them to connect those dots, or produce such 'plots'.

Leo was particularly fond of two such 'late' sources from his coursework in the form of detailed letters from a scholar named Kashi, short for Kashani,[17] after the city of Kashan in central Iran from which that protégé had been recruited to the newly founded school and observatory in Samarqand. The letters, addressed by Kashi in Samarqand to his father in Kashan, reflected a period labeled anywhere from a 'century of princes',[18] namely the 1400s that included a 'student prince', to a period of lapses through at least another century, where lines of downfall were often drawn in the early 1500s. The two letters,[19] discovered, published, and translated into a few languages more than half a millennium after their composition, held between them, besides a wealth of information about several aspects of the sciences of the time, exact numbers

16 'Roger Babson often related how his ability as a financial analyst was based on his application of Newton's Third Law – the law of action and reaction – learned as part of his training' at MIT. www.babson.edu/about/news-events/babson-centennial/babsons-history/archives-and-collections/grace-k-babson-collection/

17 Youschkevitch, A. P. and Rosenfeld, B. A., 'al-Kāshī, (or Kāshānī), Ghiyāth al-Dīn Jamshīd Mas'ūd', Dictionary of Scientific Biography (DSB) 7 (1973), pp. 255–62. Vernet, J., 'Al-Kāshī or al- Kāshānī, Ghiyās al-Dīn DJamshīd b. Masud b. Mahmud', Encyclopedia of Islam (EI²), 4 (1976), pp. 702–3; Saliba, George. 'Kāši, Ĝiāṯ-al-Din', Encyclopedia Iranica (EIr), 6, 1 (2002), pp. 64–7. www.iranicaonline.org/articles/kasi. Schmidl, Petra G., 'Kāshī: Ghiyāth (al-Milla wa-) al-Dīn Jamshīd ibn Mas'ūd ibn Maḥmūd al-Kāshī [Kāshānī]', Biographical Encyclopedia of Astronomers (BEA) (2007), pp. 613–15. https://islamsci.mcgill.ca/RASI/BEA/Kashi_BEA.htm

18 Thackston, W. M. (sel, trans), A Century of Princes: Sources on Timurid History and Art (Cambridge, MA, 1989).

19 Kāshānī, Ghīyāth al-Dīn Jamshīd, 'A letter of Jamshīd al-Kāshī to his father: Scientific research and personalities at a fifteenth-century court', Kennedy, E. S. (tr), Orientalia, 29 (1960), pp. 191–213. Bagheri (ed), Az Samarqand bih Kāshān; (tr), 'Newly found letter'. Rosenfeld and Ihsanoğlu, Mathematicians, Astronomers, and Other Scholars, No. 802, p. 269: English and Turkish translations: Aydın Sayılı; Arabic translation: Damardash; Russian translation: Babayev, Sobirov and Yusupova, D.

and details that conflicted with the best 'pictures' and statistics of dominant treatments. The last decade of the 20th century had produced surveys with the number of manuscripts in Islamic languages in the millions, of scientific manuscripts in the tens of thousands, and of scientific instruments in the thousands, 'most of the manuscripts and instruments' being from 'after the most creative period, from the eighth to the fifteenth century'.[20] The statistics of the 'newly found' Kashi letter alone plotted all but a period of 'decline'. A conference on the life and work of that author would take him from Samarqand to his native Kashan[21] in the early twenty-first century, when an Archive in his name would be established in a nearby city. But it would be in faraway London, through a conference on the 'Timurid Century' when Kashi lived and worked, that discussions and publications involving the understudied premise of scientific 'decline' would be occasioned, and images of underexposed 'dark chambers' inverted by 'revisiting' a quartet of scientific traditions, 'from Maragha to Samarqand and beyond'.[22]

Leo remembered an assignment on that 'newly discovered letter' from halfway around the world inspiring creative historical writings by his classmates, from which one sat deep in his mind. Placed in the voice of the letter's author, Kashi, and his patron, Ulugh Beg, figures whose lives were cut far too short by imperfections of the human soul with impacts on developments in science as one of the most noble products of human spirit, the powerful words of that creative writing assignment stood out in the form of a historical poem with reaches beyond a specific time and place: 'The universe runs with perfect grace and dignity', had read its timeless verses, 'no star strikes another star; nor looks to expand its reign; the world of men, however, runs with uncertain, unpredictable rhythms'.[23]

One of Leo's favourite features of the Micromapping project was its linking of time and place records, 'time-links', linking the same time to different places, and 'place-links', the same place to different times. A time-link around the year 1000 was when the two scholars Buzjani and Biruni pre-arranged to observe a lunar eclipse in the year 997 from Baghdad and Khwarazm of Arab and Persian lands respectively;[24] a place-link around the year 1500 was when Isfahan was coming under Safavid rule about halfway between the Mongol and Afghan invasions before 1250s and 1750s respectively. Such time-place conjunctions could be generated electronically without any prior knowledge of such coincidences through multiple links of a database. To Leo, this meant multiple characters and events for his upcoming *Dialogue* sections could be generated through

20 Geoffrey, Roper (ed.), World Survey of Islamic Manuscripts, Vol. 4 (Leiden, 1994); King, David A., 'Some remarks on Islamic scientific manuscripts and instruments and past, present, and future research', in John Cooper (ed), The Significance of Islamic Manuscripts (London, 1992), pp. 115–43, p. 115.

21 Kashan: 'Scientific heritage of Kāshānī', Kashan, 3–4 Isfand, 1390 [22–23 February 2012], 600th anniversary of Kāshānī's death.

22 Kheirandish, 'From Maragha to Samarqand', Appendix: I–VI; Kāshī, Appendix: II, p. 174.

23 Rutter, Michael, 'Creative historical writing'; Kheirandish, 'Science in the Islamic Middle Ages', Harvard Extension, Fall 2006.

24 Bīrūnī, Abū Rayḥān, Kitāb Taḥdīd nihāyāt al-amākin li-taṣḥīḥi masāfāt al-masākin, Bulgakov, P. G. and Aḥmad, Imām Ibrāhīm (eds) (Cairo, 1964), p. 250; The Determination of the Coordinates of Positions for the Correction of Distances between Cities, Jamīl, ʿAlī (tr) (Beirut, 1967).

the time and place records of the evolving Micromapping project itself. For the four hundred years of his next section, from around the years 1350 to 1750, the first two centuries could turn up records beyond a 'Baghdadi' working in Isfahan of the 1350s or an 'Isfahani' in Baghdad of the 1450s: these could be through links to other key cities, from Damascus of the 1350s to Kashan of the 1450s, and from Istanbul of 1550s to Isfahan of 1650s. Such capabilities further offered Eastern cities beyond Baghdad and Isfahan to cross over to relevant cases in Western cities, from Rome and Florence to Paris and London of those same time slots. The evolving technologies were endless; so were the generation of histories around them, which would have remained uncreated or not the same without those technologies. All this led to the next stage of Leo's work as a co-curator of a multimedia timeline with micromaps and multi-links next to screening clips and travelling exhibits, setting a 'future' stage for generating parallel histories in early science. In what was the last school year and first post-college year of Leo's project, he would turn to the role of 'tools' in scientific development, focusing on mechanics as a 'sciences of devices', this time through a larger pool of historical cases. His much expanded narrative would now not only show the importance of tools when effective and consistent, as opposed to outdated or misdirected; he could increasingly add physical to textual sources, and viewable to archival items.

Accordingly, Leo turned from the 'dialogues' of Asadi forming the opening quotes of his earlier chapters – those between night and day, Muslim and Zoroastrian, Arab and Persian, and sky and earth – to a dialogue between two physical objects, one even more fitting for opening his next chapter than Asadi's dialogue of 'arrow and bow'.[25] He chose a dialogue between 'pen and sword', a rich subject of not only successive authors, but of different languages. Among multiple 'dispute poems and dialogues in the ancient and medieval Near East',[26] and 'literary debates' in several languages from Sumerian, Akkadian, Egyptian and Aramaic to Syriac, Middle Persian and Arabic, and their spreads to Greek, Latin and other European languages, was a 'conceit of pen and sword'.[27] He soon found a 'dialogue' on those two objects in Persian verse, fittingly from the period after the 1350s: an author of over 100 works[28] raising the worth of pen over sword, also spoke on subjects as current during his time as circles of celestial orbs being valid entities, however imaginary.[29]

25 Asadī Ṭūsī (attribution), Munāẓirih-i Ramḥ va Qaws (ca. 1000 CE), Khaleghi-Motlagh (ed), 'Asadī Ṭūsī', pp. 104–5.

26 Reinink, G. J. and Vanstiphout, H. L. J. (eds), Dispute Poems and Dialogues in The Ancient and Mediaeval Near East: Forms and Types of Literary Debates in Semitic and Related Literature (Leuven, 1991).

27 van Gelder, Geert Jan, 'The conceit of pen and sword: On an Arabic literary debate', Journal of Semitic Studies, 32, 2 (1987), pp. 329–60, p. 329.

28 Mīr Siyyid Sharīf [Jurjānī] (post-1350), 'Munāẓarah al-Sayf wa al-Qalam', pp. 702–3. Dhanani, Alnoor, 'Jurjānī: ʿAlī ibn Muḥammad ibn ʿAlī al-Ḥusaynī al-Jurjānī (al-Sayyid al-Sharīf)', Biographical Encyclopedia of Astronomers (BEA) (2007), pp. 603–4. https://islamsci.mcgill.ca/RASI/BEA/Jurjani_BEA.htm

29 Dhanani, 'Jurjānī, p. 604: on 'the reality of the celestial orbs, Al-Ījī had declared that they were imaginary, no more real than a "spider's web". But Jurjānī disagreed: Even though the circles have no external reality, being imaginary entities, they are still valid imaginary entities corresponding to what actually is the case. . .'.

Chapter 6: 'Dialogue' of Pen and Sword
Dark Half, Light Half – Tools
By Charles Leo Scribner, January 2011

[*Sword:*] *If your head does not bow to my dictate,*
I'll have it cut off, darken your stars [of fate]
[*Pen:*] *May the blade of will, fill your case [of steel]*
May the ink of reed, water the shrub of your years...

Mīr Siyyid Sharīf = Jurjānī, *'Dialogue of Sword and Pen'*, post-1350, Persian edition Dastgirdi, Vahid, 1934, English translation: Elaheh Kheirandish[30]

6.3 *An Arab City with a Treasure Box*

It was December circa 1350, and a man called ʿAlaʾ al-Din, later known as 'Ibn Shatir'[31] to mean 'son of a baker', was sitting in a mosque in Damascus where he had been a head 'timekeeper' for close to twenty years. The Baghdad of the century before he was born no longer being the centre of scientific activity in the lands ruled under the descendants of the Mongols capturing that city in the late 1250s, Damascus was rising as a prominent Arab city, with the Great Mosque of Damascus[32] considered to be 'unparalleled in any other period of Muslim rule'. The prayer room of that great mosque was a place where Ibn Shatir kept dear to his heart for the five times of prayer that would leave him pensive in a corner for hours at a time. But towards the end of that December day, in a drowsy winter afternoon when the dwellers in the mosque were waiting for the evening call to prayer, their caller was far from thinking about his duties until it was time to pray.

Ever since Ibn Shatir's father had left him to this world when he was very young, and throughout the period where his grandfather had bounced him between the households of a maternal aunt and a paternal uncle, where his training in the craft of inlaying ivory won him the title of an 'inlayer',[33] he had been drawn to working with various gadgets and puzzles. The travels of the years of his youth to places like Alexandria and Cairo,[34]

[30] Mīr Siyyid Sharīf, 'Munāẓarah al-Sayf wa al-Qalam', Dastgirdi (ed), pp. 702–3, Kheirandish, Elaheh (tr, excerpt)
'[*Sword:*] *Agar nah bar khaṭ-i ḥukm-am nah-ī sar-i taslīm,*
Sar-at zih tan bur-am u sāzam-at siāh-akhtar
[*Pen:*] *Darūn-i qabḍih-i ḥukm-i tu bād tīq-i murād,*
zih āb-i kilk-i tu bād-ā nahāl-i ʿumr-i tu tār...'.

[31] King, David. A., 'Ibn al-Shāṭir: ʿAlāʾ al-Dīn ... ʿAlī ibn Ibrāhīm', Dictionary of Scientific Biography (DSB), 12 (1975), pp. 357–64; Kennedy, E. S. and Ghanem, I. (eds), The Life and Work of Ibn al-Shatir (Aleppo, 1976), p. 13: 'muwaqqit' (timekeeper); King, David A., 'Ibn al-Shāṭir...', Biographical Encyclopedia of Astronomers (BEA), pp. 569–70, p. 569: 'muwaqqit' (timekeeper): 'astronomically defined'. https://islamsci.mcgill.ca/RASI/BEA/Ibn_al-Shatir_BEA.htm

[32] Flood, Finbarr Barry, The Great Mosque of Damascus: Studies on the Makings of an Umayyad Visual Culture (Boston, 2000).

[33] Charette, Francoise, Mathematical Instrumentation in Fourteenth-Century Egypt and Syria (Leiden, 2003).

[34] Kennedy-Ghanem, Life and Work of Ibn al-Shatir, p. 13, King, 'Ibn al-Shāṭir', DSB, p. 358; Charette, Mathematical Instrumentation, p. 16.

the centres of Greek and Arabic learning with a long heritage in various sciences, had given him firsthand exposure to the practical aspects of fields such as geometry and astronomy; and his mastered skills of using both hands and tools to make sophisticated constructions had long occupied his younger years. He had made astronomical instruments called astrolabes and quadrants in his twenties and thirties, which were to survive for centuries beyond his own life to enrich several sites beyond his own native lands. He had made an astrolabe with a driving mechanism reflecting the passage of time and used 'mechanics' of a different kind for making timekeeping devices kept in his native Syria long after, from a small portable sundial in the form of a treasure box called 'Ruby Chest' to reside in a school in nearby Aleppo, to a large sundial he would build a few years before his death. This work of his mature years was to sit at the top of the northern minaret of the great mosque in Damascus until duplicated over five hundred years later, while fragments of the original instrument would continue life in the garden of the city's National Museum.[35]

Ibn Shatir's handmade instruments and invented gadgets would have unexpected survival rates as compared to other cases known before or after them; and the various 'tools' passed down from his hands in the form of at least two sundials and three astrolabes were to have unexpected geographical fates starting with a split between cities to the east and west of Damascus[36] where their maker lived, inventively combining theory and practice. Of the sundials preserved in Ibn Shatir's native lands, the 'treasure box' containing one of the two surviving sundials would end up in Aleppo, to the north east of Damascus, no less at risk in that war-stricken city in Syria centuries later than the enduring capital of Damascus, where the original fragments and duplicates of the other surviving sundial would delicately reside. Of three surviving astrolabes, one would make it to Cairo, to the south west of Damascus, the other two parting ways in Paris, between that city's Observatory and National Library.

But on that December day of hundreds of years earlier, as the dusk was setting in on a cold winter afternoon, Ibn Shatir was not thinking about tools like his astronomical astrolabes and quadrants to reflect the map of the sky; or his mechanical and timekeeping devices to capture the passage of time. He was thinking about more active engagements with both the visible sky and invisible time, for both of which the best instrument was still the naked eye. For active engagement with the sky, he would use his naked eye looking up, as it would take another good few hundred years for astronomers of distant skies to make a 'spy-glass' to unravel the secrets of a common universe under the more lasting name of 'telescope'.[37] For active engagement with

[35] King, 'Ibn al-Shāṭir', DSB, pp. 361–2, and p. 363, n. 6: 'Ṣandūq al-yawāqīt (jewel box)'; Janin, Louis and King, David A., 'Ibn al-Shāṭir's Ṣandūq al-yawāqīt: An astronomical "compendium"', Journal for the History of Arabic Science, 1 (1977), pp. 187–256; King, 'Ibn al-Shāṭir', BEA, p. 569; Charette, Mathematical Instrumentation, p. 17, n. 75: 'a composite instrument (compendium) called Ṣandūq al-yawāqīt'.

[36] King, 'Ibn al-Shāṭir', DSB, pp. 361–2; Charette, Mathematical Instrumentation, p. 17, n. 74.

[37] van Helden, Albert. 'The invention of the telescope', Transactions of the American Philosophical Society, 67, 4 (1977), pp. 1–67; Ilardi, Vincent, Renaissance Vision from Spectacles to Telescopes (Philadelphia, 2007); Willach, Rolph, The Long Route to the Invention of the Telescope, in Transactions of the American Philosophical Society, 98, 5 (Philadelphia, 2008).

invisible time, he would use his naked eye looking down, as it would take a good hundred years for spectacles[38] of any kind to help his strained eyes from looking at what had taken hundreds of years for astronomers of his own native skies to pass down to him through astronomical books called configurations or hay'a, and handbooks called tables or 'Zij'es. But that day, all this had to wait for the moment when the last daily prayer relieved him from his day-long duties, and into the fast-flying hours released to him until the next prayer at dawn, when he could attend to any of his personal matters.

That moment would, of course, come every day when Ibn Shatir would eagerly start looking up and down through the patient records of the visible sky and invisible time, and straight into the puzzles that his sky-watching predecessors had wrestled with, day-in and day-out. He had everything he needed in the form of books. The astronomical works of the most recent scholars to be used in his book, *Final Inquiry*,[39] and to receive a mention in his own 'New Tables', were all familiar names by then: Ibn al-Haytham, from more than three hundred years before, with a name known mostly though his astronomy and 'Doubts on Ptolemy'; Ibn Rushd, from more than two hundred years before, with a name best known as the judge of Cordoba; Nasir al-Din Tusi from more than a hundred years before, with a name best known as the director of the Maragha Observatory; and others from the same period, from Tusi's student Qutb al-Din Shirazi from Eastern Islamic lands, to assistants like Yahya Maghribi, or 'John the Westerner', joining them from further west, all of whom had struggled with features in Ptolemy's planetary model which violated the cardinal principles of master Aristotle: uniform and circular motions. But one model, that of Tusi, was closest to what came to be signed and passed on along with that of Ibn Shatir in containing features too close to the work of a man who would become world famous under the name Nicholas Copernicus, features with which scholars close to seven hundred years later would compare them for indisputable transmissions from East to West.

Ibn Shatir was quite aware of the novelty of the ideas he was coming up with in matters of the sky. In describing his life's work, for whose inspiration and collection in a book he had spent many days and nights praying, he would come to write in its preface that his named predecessors 'took pains . . . were not granted success, however, and they admitted this in their writings' but 'this book should be a fundamental work for people to rely on, in which astronomical operations and problems are precisely formulated'. In modern times, Ibn Shatir's models, which still left out the critical part of

38 Dati, Carlo, 'On the invention of eyeglasses', Isis, 44, 1/2 (1953), pp. 4–10. Rosen, Edward, 'The invention of eyeglasses', Journal of the History of Medicine and Allied Sciences, 2, 1 (1956), pp. 13–47; 2, 2 (1956): 183–218; Glick, Thomas F., 'Eyeglasses', in Glick, T., Livesey, Steven and Wallis, F. (eds), Medieval Science, Technology, and Medicine: An Encyclopedia (London, 2005), pp. 167–8; Mazor, Amir and Abbou Hershkovits, Keren, 'Spectacles in the Muslim World: New evidence from the mid-fourteenth century', Early Science and Medicine, 18, 3 (2013), pp. 291–305. Benfeghoul, Farid, 'Through the lens of Islam: A note on Arabic sources on the use of rock crystals and other gems as vision aids', in Hahn, Cynthia and Shalem, Avinoam (eds), Seeking Transparency: Rock Crystals Across Medieval Mediterranean (Berlin, 2020), pp. 237–49.

39 King, 'Ibn al-Shāṭir', DSB, p. 358, and King, 'Ibn al-Shāṭir', BEA, p. 569, give the full titles of the Final Inquiry as Nihāyat al-sūl and New Tables as Zīj al-jadīd, the former entry has a passage from the Final Inquiry, including its preface, in English translation.

the Sun, not the Earth, being at the centre of the universe, and the Earth, not the Sun, being in orbital motion, as later done by Copernicus, had a mixed reception, though in the case of the Moon, his new configuration was noted as a correction of 'major defects in Ptolemaic lunar theory'.[40] His lunar model being discovered in comparable form in a Greek manuscript in the Vatican next to the diagram of the 'Tusi couple', it was to become part of the evidence 'piling up' to reformulate the 'question' of links to Copernicus as 'not whether, but when, where, and in what form'.[41]

But times being what they were, it was not to be a Persian Nasir al-Din, or an Arab ʿAlaʾ al-Din credited for the so-called 'Copernican Revolution' beyond 'pre-Copernican Copernican' models.[42] Neither was a European of any name, or a Nicholas with any last name: before Nicholas Copernicus,[43] a Nicholas surnamed Oresme, and a Nicholas surnamed Cusa,[44] the first a contemporary of ʿAlaʾ al-Din Ibn al-Shatir from Arab lands, and the second, a contemporary of a Ghiyath al-Din Kashi from Persian lands, were similarly invisible until later, despite works comparable to features of the upcoming astronomical 'revolution'. Nicholas Oresme, a French Roman Catholic bishop of high standing, was to write a Book on the *Sky and the World* in 1377, in which he was later evaluated as having 'brilliantly argued against any proof of the Aristotelian theory of a stationary Earth' and 'the possibility of a daily axial rotation', still 'finished by affirming his belief in a stationary Earth'; and Nicholas of Cusa, a German theologian, philosopher and astronomer, to be born a year after the Great Mosque of Damascus was to be sacked by Tamerlane in 1400, and presenting astronomical views throughout his long career, would be later evaluated as having 'complete independence of traditional doctrines' for holding nonstandard views, though as 'abstract speculations rather than observation':[45] one view that 'the earth is a star like other stars, not the centre of the universe, is not at rest, nor are its poles fixed; another, that 'celestial bodies are not strictly spherical, nor are their orbits circular'. Between the dominant scriptural dictates of a stationary, central Earth, and the philosophical dictums of uniform circular motion for planets including the Sun, the competing position of a stationary, central Sun, and uniform motion of planets including the Earth, while still supported by observable phenomena, was to wait until much later in time.

Up until then, many of the elements for groundbreaking theories were there, from founding 'roots' and transmitting 'routes', to supporting 'rules', and inspiring 'books': it would take some time for evolving 'tools' to be in place for further breaks with the past.

40 King, 'Ibn al-Shāṭir', BEA, p. 569–70. https://islamsci.mcgill.ca/RASI/BEA/Ibn_al-Shatir_BEA.htm
41 Ragep, Ṭūsī's Memoir on Astronomy, Vol. 1, pp. 57–8, n. 12, quoting Swerdlow and Neugebaur.
42 Roberts, 'The solar and lunar theory of Ibn al-Shāṭir', pp. 428–32. Kuhn, Copernicus Revolution.
43 Rosen, 'Nicolas Copernicus'; Clagett, Marshall, 'Nicole Oresme', Dictionary of Scientific Biography (DSB), 10 (1974), pp. 223–30.
44 Kirschner, Stefan, 'Nicholas Oresme: French bishop, scholar, and economist', Encyclopedia Britannica, 2019. www.britannica.com/biography/Nicholas-Oresme. Hofmann, J. E., 'Nicholas of Cusa', Dictionary of Scientific Biography (DSB), 3 (1971), pp. 512–16. Hagen, J., 'Nicholas of Cusa', The Catholic Encyclopedia, 11 (New York, 1911). www.newadvent.org/cathen/11060b.htm
45 Quotes: Kirshner, 'Nicholas Oresme'. www.britannica.com/biography/Nicholas-Oresme and Hagen, 'Nicholas of Cusa'. www.newadvent.org/cathen/11060b.htm

6.4 *A Persian City with a Tower Clock*

It was January circa 1450, and a man named Ghiyath al-Din whose last name, Kashani, shortened to Kashi,[46] recorded his origins in the Persian city of Kashan close to Isfahan, had suffered an early and unexplainable death close to twenty years before that date in Samarqand, a city won through the vast conquests of the fast expanding Persian lands. That particular year, which marked the first anniversary of the devastating death of Kashi's esteemed Patron, Ulugh Beg,[47] the 'great prince' that his name meant in Turkish, was an especially outstanding year. The death of Ulugh Beg, one who had risen from a governor of Samarkand to the ruler of that city only a few years before, and suffered a brutal death reportedly at the hands of his own son, was a serious blow to a lot of other great things. The mysterious death of the young prince's protégé, Kashi, whose own name was inseparable from the magnificent tiling[48] that went into the schools and observatory of Samarqand – one possibly involving a bloody hand from Ulugh Beg himself, as rumour had it – was decades before 1450; and the glowing brilliance of both Kashi and that 'student prince' assassinated the year before, was, by then, fully extinguished. A 'student prince' Ulugh Beg was, a student for attending classes and events, like any other student in that fine school regardless of his daily conquests or activities, from hunting and star watching to solving complex problems even on horseback; a prince, in a 'century of princes',[49] and a model for everything he stood for beyond a governor or ruler, from his stellar reputation for having a crystal-clear memory to his multi-lingual skills[50] in Arabic, Persian, Turkish, Mongolian, and even some Chinese. But a year into the flight of that larger-than-life ruler-astronomer away from all that went under his wings, activities including astronomical records for Samarqand, were prone to similar extinctions, as in the earlier case of Maragha.

But Samarqand of Kashi's time had long enjoyed glorious days as well, as lofty as those of the city's twin counterpart on the heights of Maragha in north west Persia during the time of residents like Tusi and Shirazi, whose names were similarly immortalised through their cities of origin. In the case of the Samarqand school and observatory, for whose constructions and establishment Kashi was known to have been recruited, its glories were long detailed by none other than Kashi himself, in not one but two surviving letters to his father: signing those letters with a short version of his first name as 'Ghiyath', he had written one letter shortly after his arrival in Samarqand, sent it through some merchants from the Persian city of Qum, then sent a similar one in case that one had not reached his father in nearby Kashan, an expected occurrence

46 Youschkevitch and Rosenfeld, 'al-Kāshī'; Vernet, 'Al-Kāshī'; Saliba, 'Kāši'; Schmidl, 'Kāshī'. https://islamsci.mcgill.ca/RASI/BEA/Kashi_BEA.htm. Saliba, 'Kāši. www.iranicaonline.org/articles/kasi Rosenfeld and Ihsanoğlu, Mathematicians, Astronomers, and Other Scholars, No. 802, pp. 269–72.

47 van Dalen, 'Ulugh Beg'.

48 Graves, Margaret S., 'Kashan vii. Kashan ware', Encyclopedia Iranica (EIr) (2014): 'site's name (kāši/kāšāni, or qāši/qāšāni) as the general designation for glazed tilework in Arabic and Persian sources'. www.iranicaonline.org/articles/kashan-vii-kashan-ware

49 Thackston, Century of Princes.

50 Bagheri, Az Samarqand bih Kāshān, p. 43 and p. 62; Bagheri, 'Newly found letter', p. 247.

in the days of piecemeal communication. In those letters, Kashi had not left out any details related to remarkable Samarqand, and numbers had occupied a markedly central place in many of the valuable details quantified by him as a mathematical whiz: he had written with exactness of 'His Royal Majesty's charitable gift of thirty thousand *kopakī*', a local currency of the time, of 'ten thousand given to students with their individual names', of 'about ten thousand-odd students steadily engaged and qualifying for the aid', of 'the same large number among the notables in their own home', of 'five-hundred persons who have begun to study mathematics', and 'of about sixty and seventy receiving him upon arrival'. Numbers also filled Kashi's other accounts of 'His Royal Majesty, the World-Conqueror', of him 'having himself been engaged in mathematic for twelve years', of 'this art taught at twenty places', and of 'twenty-four calculators, some astronomers, studying Euclid's *Elements*', all to say 'how the state of teaching and learning mathematics in Samarqand had no parallel in Persia and non-Arab 'Iraq'.[51] The name of Kashi's colleagues, and at times rivals, had also popped up in the letters, like one Qadizade Rumi with a last name connecting him to Byzantium, who directed the Samarqand school and observatory before his descendent 'Ali Qushji would assume that prominent role. All that would evaporate with the demise of the great 'Ulugh Beg', whose world of knowledge and culture would live long after him and his ill fate.

So would the heritage of Kashi. He would be known far beyond his birthplace of Kashan, his death bed of Samarqand, and cities he was associated with, including Isfahan.[52] His best known and most lasting heritage would be the discovery of the constant number later known as Pi, the constant ratio of a circle's circumference[53] to the size of its diameter, and of its area to the square of its radius. But Kashi had started as an avid observer, not calculator: in the court of his early patron in Isfahan, Iskandar Bahadur, he and at least two other 'observers of phenomena' like wandering and fixed stars had been subjects of a less known letter[54] where they were depicted as 'all secret-

51 Bagheri, Az Samarqand bih Kāshān, p. 38; 'Newly found letter', p. 243: has 'twelve' places for the number given for 'twenty' in the original; also 'Fārs [i.e., Persia, the southern province of Iran] and 'Irāq [i.e., the western part of modern Iran]' are given there in their modern senses. The historical meanings of the Persian terms 'Fārs and ʿIrāq' are 'Persia' and 'non-Arab ʿIraq (ʿajam)' respectively.

52 Iskandar Bahādur, a ruler of Isfahan and Fars. Youschkevitch and Rosenfeld 'al-Kāshī', p. 255; Kennedy, E. S., The Planetary Equatorium of Jamshīd Ghiyāth al-Dīn al-Kāshī (Princeton, 1960), p. 2; Bosworth, Islamic Dynasties, p. 168; Karamati, Younes, Kāshānī Shinākht: An Investigation of the Mathematical Works of Giyāth al-Dīn Jamshīd Kāshānī (Tehran, 1396 [2017]): 'Iskandar Bahādur as 'Taymūr's grandson'; Kāshī as 'serv[ing] in his court for a while'. Pike, Kathy, The Birth Horoscope of Iskandar Sultan: Astrology in the Service of Kingship (unpublished MA Thesis, Harvard Extension, 2006).

53 Kāshānī, Ghīyāth al-Dīn Jamshīd, al-Risālah al-Muḥītīyah: A Facsimile Edition of the Autograph Manuscript, Karamati, Younes (ed), Persian and English Introduction (Tehran, 1392 [2013].

54 Karamati, Kāshānī Shinākht, Introduction in Persian, mentions an anonymous letter in which Kāshī is named as 'one of the resident scientists in the court of Iskandar Bahādur Khān in Isfahan': originals for my translations of 'observers of phenomena' (āthār-i anẓār); 'wandering and fixed stars' (kavākib-i sayyārih va thābit), 'all secret-sharers of the company of stars' and 'spies of the kingdom of heavens' (hamih ham-rāz-i majlis-i anjum, hamih jāsūs-i kishvar-i aflāk); visit to 'old buildings' (ʿimārat qadīm) in Isfahan and muqarnas works (below).

sharers of the company of stars' and 'spies of the kingdom of heavens'. But later in time, far from the language and spirit of a 'spy-glass' whose invention would change everything for unveiling the secrets of the heavens, Kashi would get further from both theoretical astronomy and works patronised by Persian rulers or written in Persian. Once in the school and observatory of Samarqand, his aversion to his rivals would push him further from the books they taught in theoretical astronomy, works often composed by his pioneering predecessors in the Maragha school and observatory. The titles of Kashi's works in Samarqand, from the writings and instruments he proudly spoke of in the letters to his father from Samarqand to Kashan, to those recorded in and beyond his own writings, would well reflect his increasing tilt to the practical aspects of mathematics, those one day cleverly called 'practical practices of practical knowledge'[55] as distinct from their 'theoretical practices'. From the earlier titles of Kashi's works, like the theoretical bends of his *Compendium on Cosmography*, and *Stairway to Heaven*, on astronomical orbits and distances and sizes, to his last recorded compositions with the more famous titles, *Treatise on Circumference*, and *Key of Arithmetic*,[56] titles alone would be enough for the revelation of his tilts towards practical knowledge. Kashi's final work fittingly titled as a *Key* opened many unopened doors, from calculations involving domed or spherical structures, in both theoretical and practical contexts, to his related visit to what would soon become an architectural capital in nearby Isfahan. His calculations, from decimal fractions to constant ratios, went beyond applying simple rules of proportion like those in early algebra or mechanics, or calculating an unknown value from three known ones, even applying rules of inverse force and distance in mechanical branches called the sciences of 'devices' and 'weights'. His impressive work was to partly pass on through his colleagues in Samarqand, like 'Ali Qushji, who settled in Constantinople after Ulugh Beg's assassination, or a Byzantine collection brought to Vienna more than a century later. Kashi's short life of hardly fifty years would not allow for the completion of the 'fourth-degree equations he had discovered', nor his 'method for the determination of unknowns in . . . seventy problems' mentioned in the fifth book of his *Key* as not having 'been touched upon by either ancients or contemporaries'; but his heritage would still leave its most pronounced marks on all approximate values of the ratio of the circumference of a circle to its diameter, as detailed in his *Treatise on Circumference*. Pointing out 'his predecessors' great errors', he had 'posed the problem of calculating the said ratio with such precision' that it made 'the error in the circumference whose diameter is equal to 600,000 diameters of the earth' even 'smaller than the thickness of a horse's hair'.[57] What such accuracies would still leave out were comparable calculations

55 Taheri, Jafar, 'Mathematical knowledge of architecture in the works of Kâshânî', Nexus Network Journal, 11, 1 (2009), pp. 77–88, p. 77: Kāshī addresses 'the relation between architecture and mathematics in two areas of knowledge, theoretical and practical, the latter itself including theoretical practice and practical practice'.

56 Mukhtaṣar dar ʿilm-i hayʾa, Sullam al-samāʾ, al-Risālah al-Muḥīṭīyah and Miftāḥ al-ḥisāb: Youschkevitch and Rosenfeld, 'al-Kāshī', pp. 260–1, p. 261, nos. 2, 1, 6 and 8; Rosenfeld and Ihsanoğlu, Mathematicians, Astronomers, and Other Scholars, p. 271, no. 802, A14, A4, M3 and M1 respectively.

57 Youschkevitch and Rosenfeld, 'al-Kāshī, p. 257.

from not a predecessor or contemporary, but a closely dated successor of Kashi named Kubanani:[58] this was a man from southern Yazd and Kerman, whose letters containing excerpts from his own work on *Measurement* to approximate the ratio of the circle's circumference to its diameter would remain obscure, in favour of his discovered role in a different chapter in practical geometry including critical datings, partly based on his letters.

Questions would arise in modern times[59] about Kashi's practical innovations, outweighing theoretical achievements like those by Tusi and Shirazi in the Maragha school and observatory. Kashi's own writings would reveal a combination of explanations on that front, including the intolerant characters and counterproductive settings of the Samarqand complex as compared to not only that institution's earlier counterpart in Maragha, but also those in the later Istanbul and Isfahan observatories and schools. A century after Kashi's death, a native of Ray[60] would not simply accuse the Samarqand patron, Ulugh Beg, as being 'behind the death' of his protégé, Kashi; but by adding that 'because he had thought observation would not complete without Kashani's help, he was patient with him until he completed the royal *Tables* dedicated to Ulugh Beg', the author of those words would point Kashi's eyes mostly towards the sky. The earthbound Kashi, who started and ended his career as a skybound observer through record after record of lunar eclipse observations alone,[61] was seemingly expressive about subjects as earthbound as mechanics, as revealed by sources including his own little-known works. In one of these, where he described astronomical observations as the work of generations, he would be quoted[62] as saying: 'it is not a problem if there is only one [observer], who "should work more". This (the observation job) is not like a heavy rock that one cannot move, it is like a pile of wheat that a man can move [gradually]'.

Kashi would not live to see other scientific works still requiring generations, including a tower clock[63] in the Kashan of a century later where he could have combined his observations of time with those of the stars. Neither could he live to see the invention of visual aids from eye-glasses with lenses to eye-pieces on telescopes. Kashi's

58 Karamati, 'Abū Isḥāq al-Kūbunānī'; Kheirandish, 'An early tradition in practical geometry', pp. 106–12: works, letters, dating; p. 112: on Measurement (Misāḥa). https://brill.com/view/title/32181

59 Saliba, 'Kāšī', p. 67: '[Kāši] remain silent about a different field of Islamic astronomy . . . the treatment of planetary theories in a cosmological mathematical context'. www.iranicaonline.org/articles/kasi

60 Karamati, Kāshānī Shinākht, Introduction in English: 'according to Amīn Aḥmad Rāzī some people believed that "Ulugh Beg was behind his death. . . . But because he had thought observation would not be complete without Kāshānī's help, he was patient with his bitter words. He always said: "When this job was finished and I was set free from Jamshīd's rough postures and speech"'; Memon, M. U., 'Amīn Aḥmad Rāzī', Encyclopedia Iranica (EIr), 1, 9 (1989), p. 939. www.iranicaonline.org/articles/razi-amin-ahmad

61 Kennedy, Planetary Equatorium, p. 1, starts from Kāshī's first of a series of three lunar eclipses, 2 June 1406. Rosenfeld and Ihsanoğlu, Mathematicians, Astronomers, and Other Scholars, p. 271, No. 802, A17 has a title that includes the Moon (qamar) followed by 'eclipse observations' (arṣād al-khūsūfīyah).

62 Karamati, Kāshānī Shinākht, English Introduction.

63 Majdī, Zinat al-majālis, ca. 1004/1595: 'one of Ḥafiẓ Iṣfahānī's reproductions was fixed in the tower of a hospital in Kashan'; p.772, gives the clock-maker's name as Muḥammad Mukhtari' [Muḥammad Ḥafiẓ Iṣfahānī]: Kheirandish, 'From Maragha to Samarqand', p. 167, pp. 180–1, notes 29–30.

near contemporary, a philosopher-poet by the name of 'Abd al-Rahman Jami,[64] with close dates and links to Isfahan as well as Samarqand, had referred in a poem to eyeglasses as 'foreign glasses that make two eyes four'; but neither Kashi, nor even his later contemporaries in Europe, from Nicholas Copernicus to Leonardo da Vinci, were close to the wonders of 'spyglasses': that critical instrument, renamed the 'telescope', was one that would be used to dramatically change the course of science by Galileo, the first to turn the eye-piece of a telescope towards the sky.

Centuries later than the time of not just Kashi and Jami, but also da Vinci and Galileo, cities like Kashan and Isfahan were to become part of constellations named 'cities of stars'[65] next to Rome and Florence: constellations that would find conjunctions far beyond the skies spreading over them. There, a city to stand out not only halfway between such Persian and European cities, but between East and West as the juncture of Asia and Europe, would be Istanbul, a city named as such after centuries of being named Constantinople.

6.5 *An Eastern City and an 'End of Time'*

It was December circa 1550, and a young man named Taqi al-Din[66] had recently come from Damascus with his father, Maʿruf Afandi, to Istanbul,[67] a city that would one day represent the 'tale' of not two, but three cities in its historic moves from Byzantium to Constantinople to Istanbul. The young Taqi al-Din, whose last name Ibn Maʿruf meant son of someone famous, had started his day in a city as brilliant as a 'diamond mounted over sapphires and emeralds',[68] as Istanbul had been described about three centuries before him. But he was ending that day with a heart as dark as the waning light of that winter dusk due to a gloomy thought: that he could not uphold the fame of his father through his state of affairs at the time. Here he was, a hard-working young man who,

64 Jāmī, ʿAbd al-Raḥmān Nūr-al-din b. Neẓām al-Din Aḥmad-e Dašti. . .': Losensky, Paul, 'Jāmī i. Life and Works', Encyclopaedia Iranica (EIr), 14, 5 (2008), pp. 469–75, p. 469: links to Isfahan and Samarqand. www.iranicaonline.org/articles/jami-i. Jāmī's poem: Arberry, A. J., Fitzgerald's Salaman and Absal: A Study (Cambridge, 1956). Kheirandish, Elaheh (tr): '*Az du chashm-i man nayā-yad hīch kār, Az farangī shīshih tā gasht-ih chahār*': *From my two eyes comes no more work, Since European glass has made [eyes] four*. My translation above is more literal than that given in Mazor, Amir and Abbou Hershkovits, Keren, 'Spectacles in the Muslim World', 18, 3 (2013), pp. 291–305, p. 292, citing Arberry, pp. 42–3 and p. 146 for the verse's edition and translation.

65 Kheirandish, Elaheh, 'Cities of stars: The historical relations of optics and astronomy', Symposium for the History of Science in Islam, Istanbul, 15 June, 2019.

66 King, David A., 'Takī al-Dīn', Encyclopedia of Islam (EI^2), 10, 165–6 (1998), pp. 132–3; Tekeli, Sevim, 'Taqī al-Dīn', in Selin, Helaine (ed.), Encyclopaedia of the History of Science, Technology, and Medicine in Non-Western Cultures (Dordrecht, 1997), pp. 934–5 (Berlin, Heidelberg, New York, 2008); Rosenfeld and Ihsanoğlu, Mathematicians, Astronomers and Other Scholars, No. 1004, pp. 333–5; Fazlioğlu, İhsan, 'Taqī al-Dīn Abū Bakr Muhammad ibn Zayn al-Dīn Maʿrūf al-Dimashqī al-Hanafī', Biographical Encyclopedia of Astronomers (BEA), pp. 1122–4, p. 1122: father's name. https://islamsci.mcgill.ca/RASI/BEA/Taqi_al-Din_BEA.htm. Ayduz, Salim, 'Taqi al-Din Ibn Maʿruf: A bio-bibliographical essay', Muslim Heritage, 26 June 2008. https://muslimheritage.com/taqi-al-din-bio-essay/

67 Hughes, Tale of Three Cities, p. xxv: Byzantium, Constantinople, and Istanbul.

68 Hughes, Tale of Three Cities, p. xiii: epigraph, dated 'c. AD 1280'.

having studied and taught in various schools in his native city of Damascus,[69] had not much benefitted from the fruits of his long labours; and on that unsettled moment of a sunset on a cold and dark December day, the next stage of his life seemed no closer than an emerging warm and bright sunrise.

But Taqi al-Din had all it took to outshine everyone around him from an early age. As young as he was on that last month of the year 1550, he had stood out through his worldliness alone. The epithets of his name, 'Shami' and 'Misri',[70] already marked the place of his early life and education as Syria and Egypt, and his early career as a judge had taken him to places like Palestine. But the fame of Taqi al-Din was to come not through his family routes in Damascus, his theological studies in Cairo, or his legal activities in Nabulus: it would come through Constantinople, a city later called Istanbul, which, having fallen to the Ottoman Turks about a century before, was by then at the crossroads of a few civilizations. Taqi al-Din had travelled away from Istanbul for long stretches at a time, with links as far and wide as an 'Italian connection',[71] as revealed by his marginal notes on a manuscript discovered much later in time, about him learning about Ptolemy in the dictionary of a contemporary Italian. But at the time, Taqi al-Din was far from knowing that it was in Istanbul that his later profiles as a chief astronomer/astrologer, 'Munajjim Bashi', and astronomical observer, 'Rasid',[72] were to overshadow not only those of his other selves, but also of everyone else. Direct encounter with his immediate predecessors would come through a grandson of ʿAli Qushji,[73] who gave Taqi al-Din works by his grandfather as well as by Jamshid Kashi and Qadizade Rumi, all from the Samarqand school and observatory, along with observation instruments allowing Taqi al-Din to pursue serious scientific investigations. A trip back to Istanbul around 1550 was also crucial when he was exposed to the Grand Vizier ʿAli Pasha, and his private library and clock collection. Still, it would be about two decades from the year 1550 until the ruling Ottoman Sultan, Selim the second, would employ Taqi al-Din in the capacity of a court astronomer; then close to another decade before that eager observer of the sky would assume the title of the director of an important observatory comparable to those erected in Europe, under the Sultan's newly crowned son, Murad the third. It was only at that time that the name Ibn Maʿruf would become more than famous as one inseparable from that of an outstanding observatory named after a fast-developing city; and it would not be long before the name of Taqi al-Din himself would outshine the name of the Ottoman Sultan behind the construction of the Istanbul Observatory, and the commission of scientific works beyond astronomy. Soon the name of a middle-aged Taqi al-Din would travel with

69 King, 'Takī al-Dīn', p. 132; Fazlioğlu, 'Taqī al-Dīn', p. 1122.

70 Rosenfeld and Ihsanoğlu, Mathematicians, Astronomers and Other Scholars, p. 333: 'Shāmī'; Fezioğlu, 'Taqī al-Dīn', p. 1122; 'Damishqī' and 'Miṣrī'; King, 'Tak al-Din', p. 132, early education in Cairo, early career as a judge in Nabulus; Tekeli, 'Taqī al-Dīn', p. 934, and Fazlioglu, 'Taqī al-Dīn', p. 1122.

71 Ben Zaken, Avner, Cross-Cultural Scientific Exchanges in the Eastern Mediterranean, 1560–1660 (Baltimore, 2010), pp. 24–5: evidence for Italian connection; p. 178, n. 64: manuscript discovered.

72 King, 'Takī al-Dīn', p. 132: 'Munajjim-Bāshī'; Tekeli, 'Taqī al-Dīn': Rāṣid.

73 Fazlioğlu, 'Taqī al-Dīn, p. 1122. Period: Heidarzadeh, Tofigh, 'Patronage networks and migration: Turco-Persian scholarly exchanges in the 15th, 16th and 17th centuries', Archives Internationales d'Histoire des Sciences, 55, 2005, pp. 419–34.

enough resounding echo to reach from Ottoman Turkey to Safavid Persia; and about thirty years from that day in December 1550, a Persian poet from Shiraz named ʿAlaʾ al-Din Mansur would come to compose pages and pages of verse about Taqi al-Din, his last patron Sultan Murad the third, and their recently demolished institution, the Istanbul Observatory.[74] An unnamed manuscript illustrator would then supply ʿAlaʾ al-Din's verses with beautiful miniature folios, similar to those of its prototype title, in what was to be called, *The Book of King of Kings*, *Shahanshah-namih*[75] in the original Persian, though the book's subject was not limited to the Sultan inheriting that prestigious Persian title. ʿAlaʾ al-Din's versified story of the long construction and rushed destruction of the famous observatory of Istanbul were to rather centre around another name: key verses would start and end with the name Taqi al-Din,[76] the opening verses naming him a 'wise star-gazing astronomer', and the closing lines placing him behind the fateful abolishment of the observatory itself for the incorrect prediction of the victory of the Ottomans over Persia.

Whatever talent Taqi al-Din had, the gift of prediction was not among them. His inability to predict a political or astronomical event was nowhere as fateful to the course of events as his failure to foresee the course of his own fate. Had he predicted not just his rising fame and its scale, but also his most effective subjects and their most promising realms, things would have been different for both him and the sciences he so loved. Regarding fame, Taqi al-Din, would have never dreamt that the sound of his name would reach as far as across Arab and Persian lands; and had he foreseen the risk of planting the seeds of all his labours in a field like astronomy at a time of rivalries involving institutions like observatories, and controversies involving events like comets, he could have better impacted both the course of events in both Islamic and European lands, and the pivotal dynamics between them. Taqi al-Din would not even be conscious of how unique and critical his position could be in the crossroads between East and West. His own works would reveal his use of 'sources from other religions'. Others would also note his links to places such as Italy and Solonika through figures like a Jewish astronomer named Davud al-Riyadi, known as 'David the mathematician', or his patron, Sulan Murad the third, receiving European gifts like a terrestrial globe becoming subjects of future auctions; even himself as a captive in Rome as the servant of a mathematician, or having captured Christians to assist him in his later works.[77] But the most pronounced position of Taqi al-Din on the crossroads between East and West would emerge through a single folio in the book *Shahanshah-namih* completed about a year after that report, as well as the destruction of the Istanbul Observatory in 1580.

[74] Sayılı, Observatory in Islam, pp. 322–5, 337–42, and 368–78.

[75] Manṣūr, ʿAlāʾ al-Dīn, Shahanshāh-nāmih, F 1404, Istanbul University Library; Sayılı, Aydin ''ʿAlāʾ al-Dīn al-Manṣūr's poems on the Istanbul Observatory', Türk Tarīh Kurumu Belleten, 20, 79 (1956), pp. 429–84; Sayılı, Observatory in Islam, 1960, pp. 289–305. King, 'Some remarks on Islamic scientific manuscripts', p. 143: image.

[76] Sayılı, ''ʿAlāʾ al-Dīn al-Manṣūr's poems': pp. 449–544 (Persian); pp. 471–77 (English).

[77] Ben Zaken, Cross-Cultural Scientific Exchanges, respectively: pp. 18–19, 21–2; 14–16: Murad III Globes: auctioned on 30 October 1991: London: Christie, Manson & Woods; p. 24: from envoy to Istanbul in 1580.

An image of Taqi al-Din,[78] magnified next to a colleague above a number of observatory staff and scientific instruments, would have side by side Islamic and European representation, multiplied in various sources for centuries.

While the fame of Taqi al-Din would come from astronomy through the Istanbul Observatory, his name would impact science more in other fields. Under the patronage of Sultan Murad the third, he was to work on not one but a few important scientific fields. His book on optics, a field particularly close to astronomy for its age-old focus on vision for both near and far objects, was not to carry immediate promise, despite its author's claim of having made a crystal to improve seeing objects from a far distance.[79] As rich and resourceful as the Ottoman libraries were at a time as early as in the reign of Sultan Murad's ancestor, Bayazid the second, Taqi al-Din would not benefit from the masterpiece of his predecessors of half a millennium earlier, including the great *Optics* of Ibn al-Haytham recorded in the inventory of Sultan Bayazid the second's royal library, only through its important 'commentary', also recorded there.[80] But the case of mechanics, another 'mixed' mathematical-physical science[81] like optics and astronomy, was quite different. It was in the so-called science of devices or hiyal, as it was known in Arabic and Persian, that Taqi al-Din had excelled from an early age; and it was through concepts such as going 'beyond nature'[82] that a powerful 'control over nature', would soon take Europe by storm without any share of credit to him. This was an ancient concept that had made its first appearance in science by allowing production of great powers from little forces through devices such as levers and pulleys; and manipulation of nature[83] was a concept with which Taqi al-Din became intimately close, through his enduring passion for instrument making.

Taqi al-Din's first encounters with scientific instruments was in the library of a minister called ʿAli Pasha, where besides a wealth of books and manuscripts there were a few mechanical clocks.[84] In his early days of instrument making, he had played with

78 Sayılı, 'ʿAlāʾ al-Dīn al-Manṣūr's poems', p. 444; King, 'Some remarks', p. 143; Ben Zaken, Cross-Cultural Scientific Exchanges, p. 13.

79 Ibn Maʿrūf, Taqī al-Dīn, Kitāb Nūr hadaqat al-ibṣār wa-nūr haqīqat al-anẓār [The Book of Light of the Eye's Pupil and Light of the Sight's Veracity] (unpublished manuscript): www.wdl.org/en/item/2852/. Kheirandish, Elaheh, 'Optics: Highlights from Islamic lands', in The Different Aspects of Islamic Culture, Vol. 4, in al-Hassan, A. Y. et al. (eds.), Science and Technology in Islam, Part 1: The Exact and Natural Sciences (Beirut, 2001), pp. 337–57, p. 344 includes a facsimile of the manuscript folio in Oxford, Bodleian Library Marsh 119, 982 H [1574/75], fol. 82b–83a, containing the passage on ballūra. Topdemir, Hüseyin Gazi (tr, excerpt), 'Taqi al-Din ibn Maʿruf and the Science of Optics: The Nature of Light and the Mechanism of Vision', Muslim Heritage, 15 July 2008, citation of passage as 'folio 81b' is an error. https://muslimheritage.com/taqi-al-din-sci-optics-light-vision/. Benfeghoul, 'Through the lens of Islam', pp. 248–9, n. 96, citing Rashed, Roshdi, Geometry and Dioptrics in Classical Islam (London, 2005), pp. 1038–9, and Kheirandish, 'Optics: Highlights from Islamic lands', p. 344.

80 Sabra, Optics of Ibn al-Haytham, Vol. 2, p. lxxii, n. 116; Kheirandish, 'Books on mathematical and mixed-mathematical sciences', pp. 857–68.

81 Kheirandish, Elaheh, 'Organizing scientific knowledge', pp. 135–54; Kheirandish, 'Mixed mathematical sciences'.

82 Schiefsky, 'Art and nature in ancient mechanics', pp. 67–8.

83 Ben Zaken, Cross-Cultural Scientific Exchanges, p. 17: mechanics and 'manipulation of laws of nature'.

84 Fazlioğlu, 'Taqī al-Dīn'.

building machines anywhere from utilitarian waterwheels to entertaining shish-kebab makers, even lovers' beds.[85] But in his later years, he became the maker of an important scientific instrument: a mechanical clock. Centuries later, Taqi al-Din was to be credited as the first artisan from the East to make a mechanical clock with a second hand,[86] one even before its appearance in Europe a few years later. He was also to be credited for pointing out the importance of minutes and seconds, and the precision of mechanical clocks would bring astronomy beyond unfolding the secrets of nature. Not that European-style mechanical clocks were not constructed in the East before: an older contemporary of Taqi al-Din by the name of Hafiz Isfahani[87] had recently made a successful model comparable to European prototypes. Nor was it the case that patrons from the East were not actively seeking such scientific 'marvels' and 'wonders': Sultan Bayazid the second, an ancestor of Taqi al-Din's patron, Murad the third, had sent a messenger to Europe seeking a 'time piece' and clock, with initially unsuccessful attempts. This was reportedly perceived as the 'ancestral habits of Europeans to keep such matters to themselves' and not let them be taken to Islamic territory. The Ottoman Sultan would eventually acquire the remarkable device via the Persian King of the time sponsoring Isfahani with the expressed intention that the 'marvelous and wondrous device should become commonplace among Muslims'.[88]

A slightly later time than when Taqi al-Din lived and worked was a critical time for major scientific breakthroughs which were not so promising in his own setting. While Taqi al-Din's slightly earlier European contemporaries had privately funded observatories and constructed scientific instruments, by people like the Danish astronomer Tycho Brahe,[89] to pave the way for future discoveries, times were not on Taqi al-Din's side when it came to marked breakthroughs. Between the appearance of the 1577 comet under his watch, and the destruction of the observatory within three years, all so vividly put to verse by Taqi al-Din's slightly later Persian contemporary, 'Ala al-Din,[90] he would turn further and further from measurements and constructions including those involving time. He was to be associated in a more distant future with measures of the flow of time, and through it, conceptions of creation, and the 'end of time'.[91] Still, it would be 'control in timekeeping' that was to bring people like Taqi al-Din and the European clock-makers along with him closer to new conceptions of science. These were to be new, active *manipulations* of nature instead of the old, passive *understandings* of nature. If only 'tools' like mechanical clocks were enough to upgrade

[85] Ben Zaken, Cross-Cultural Scientific Exchanges, p. 17: 'sarīr al-ʿāshiq'.

[86] Ben Zaken, Cross-Cultural Scientific Exchanges, pp. 16–17, and 174: Taqī al-Dīn, Kitāb al-kawākib al-durrīyah fī bānkāmāt al-dawrīyah, and Kitāb al-ṭuruq al-samiyyah fī al-ālāt al-rūḥānīyyah, and the facsimile edition of al-Hassan, A. Y., Taqī al-Dīn wa al-handasah al-mīkānīkiyyah (Aleppo, 1976).

[87] Ḥāfiẓ-i Isfahānī, Natījat al-dawla: Kheirandish, 'From Maragha to Samarqand', pp. 166–70, Appendix: IV; pp. 175–6: Ḥāfiẓ-i Isfahānī's work on the European-style clock may be dated between ca. 1481 and 1501, and his Risāla describing its construction to after the death of Bāyazid II (ca. 1512) and before that of Dashtakī (ca. 1541), based on his citing them as deceased and living.

[88] Kheirandish, 'From Maragha to Samarqand', pp. 169, Appendix: IV, p. 175.

[89] Dreyer, J. L. E., Tycho Brahe: A Picture of Scientific Life and Work in the Sixteenth Century (New York, 1963).

[90] Sayılı, 'ʿAlāʾ al-Dīn al-Manṣūr's poems'.

[91] Ben Zaken, Cross-cultural Scientific Exchanges, p. 18: refers to the term 'ultimate' (muntah) in the opening title of Taqī al-Dīn's Tree of Ultimate Knowledge, as meaning 'both the end of time and the end of the world'.

conceptions of science, the name of Taqi al-Din would rise above many others through that route alone. But it would take much more than a combination of roots, routes, books, and schools next to tools to raise science of even the advancing age of Taqi al-Din to the status of a so-called 'science'. A single episode in the life of an Ottoman subject such as Taqi al-Din, versified by his Persian Safavid counterpart, ʿAla al-Din, whose detailed poem about the Istanbul Observatory may not have been accessible to him with all the obstacles of distance and communication, would point something to the future onlookers on the course of science about what was missing in the East at this critical time and place, a time like the late 1500s, so close to a 'Scientific Revolution' arising in the West, and a place like Istanbul, so close to the Asian-European divide of East and West. The Observatory poem, telling the story of its rise and fall in the chronological order of events, some with verifiable dates and details despite the occasional 'upper hand' of rhymes over facts,[92] would have revealing verses on at least seven items acting as indicators on the nature and sequence of developments. The one hundred and seventy six verses were not only specific about what was there, from the roots, routes, and rules of science to its books, schools and tools; they were also revealing, if only between the lines, about what was not there, regarding the most critical of them all: loops of communication. The Persian poem and its illustrations included references related to all seven items:[93] For 'roots', references to the ancient Greeks, Euclid and Ptolemy; for 'routes', Arab and Persian predecessors, from Tusi to Ibn Shatir and Kashi; for 'rules', patrons like Ottoman Sultan Murad the third, and his Grand Vizier; for 'books', texts like *Zij* of Ulugh Beg; for 'tools' instruments, like quadrants; and for 'schools', from buildings to activities. But for 'loops', they spoke of the limited nature of communications, including the destructive nature of a community through mostly personal competitions.

The historical poem revealed that while not as diverse as the Muslims, Christians, Jews and Zoroastrians of 9th-century Baghdad,[94] or Arab, Persian, Indian and Chinese scholars of 13th-century Maragha,[95] 16th-century Istanbul did involve a constructive community. With the inner competitions expressed in that poem as the 'heart of the foe twisted into coils',[96] its community was closer to 15th-century Samarqand than 17th-century Europe. The poem also revealed awareness of lost chances and hopes, those beyond isolated cases of ruling patrons impatient to get personal or self-serving predictions,[97] or religious communities fueled by other self-centred motives. The whole

92 Sayılı, 'ʿAlāʾ al-Dīn al-Manṣūr's poems', p. 430.
93 Sayılı, 'ʿAlāʾ al-Dīn al-Manṣūr's poems', pp. 429–84.
94 Gutas, Greek Thought, Arabic Science.
95 Sayılı, Observatory in Islam, pp. 187–223.
96 Sayılı, 'ʿAlāʾ al-Dīn al-Manṣūr's poems', lines 144–5: Persian, pp. 455; English, p. 482: '. . .Now through observation the tables have been corrected, And out of grief[,] the heart of the foe has writhed and twisted into coils From now on, order the abolishment of the Observatory, To the consternation of the ill-wishers and the jealous. . .'
'. . .*Kunūn shud zih tarṣid taṣḥīḥ-i zīj,*
Dil-i dushman az gham biz-ad mār-pīch
Az īn pas bi-farmāy rafʿ-i raṣad,
Bi raghm-i bad-andīsh u ahl-i ḥasad . . .'.
97 Sayılı, 'ʿAlāʾ al-Dīn al-Manṣūr's poems', p. 436: patrons named as impatient for the required thirty years of observational program include Mongol Hulaku and Safavid Shah Ismāʿil I. Sayılı, Observatory in Islam, p. 288: adds Safavid Shah Tahmasp I, all citing ʿAbd al-Mumʿin al-ʿĀmilī.

event, however limited to a single place and three short years, had a long-term effect on communities from 16th-century Istanbul to 17th-century Isfahan, diverting attention as well as ambition away from the effective transmission and direct communication that overpowered all else in Europe to mark a new age.

Nasir al-Din Tusi from about three centuries before Taqi al-Din had written: 'In no age which was without a great and world-conquering king, has it been possible to build observatories',[98] having been aware of the critical role of rules in the case of the Maragha observatory supported by his Mongol patron Hulaku. Taqi al-Din himself could have written, in no age which was without a great book had it been possible to build observatories, in his case, having been aware of illustrated constellation books in both Maragha and Samarqand observatories before Istanbul, where its director, Taqi al-Din would be credited with owning a fine illustrated *Book Constellations*,[99] next to other key resources needed to set up an institution like an observatory. But a line from the much earlier time of Tusi's close contemporary, Nizam al-Din Nishaburi,[100] that 'It is necessary to bring together wise men from all corners so that their experience and knowledge would be pulled together', had been furthest ahead of its time in underlining the indispensable role of 'loops', those of communication, this time for tapping into not just the roots, routes and rules behind the sciences, but also books, schools and tools pushing them forward.

6.6 *A Western City with a Turn of Tides*

It was January circa 1650, and a man named Baha' al-Din[101] living in an increasingly advancing age in science outside his native lands, had been dead for about three decades. Everything about him and his beloved city of Isfahan, a city of neither his birth nor grave, but of his work and fame throughout most of his active life, pointed to him and his resident city as earning high marks in the realm of science. The roots and routes having transmitted major scientific works from ancient Greece and the Islamic Middle Ages, the rules and schools having nurtured Baha' al-Din's cultured city through a superior Safavid patron, 'Shah 'Abbas the Great', and the various books and tools deeply engaging him through hundreds of his own works alone,[102] all pointed to a markedly

98 Sayılı, ''Alā' al-Dīn al-Manṣūr's poems', p. 442.

99 Caiozza, Anna, 'Iconography of the constellations', in Vesel, Živa, Tourkin, Serge and Porter, Eve (eds), in collaboration with Francis, Richard and Ghasemloo, Farid, Images of Islamic Science (Tehran, 2009), pp. 106–33, p. 121 and pp. 122–3: samples linked to Maragha and Samarqand respectively; p. 118: cites a manuscript in St Petersburgh, 9th/15th century, with ownership note of Taqī al-Dīn.

100 Sayılı, ''Alā' al-Dīn al-Manṣūr's poems', p. 442. On Nīsābūrī, see Morrison, Robert G., Islam and Science: The Intellectual Career of Niẓām al-Dīn al-Nīsābūrī (Abingdon, 2007).

101 Munshī, Iskandar Bayg, Tārīkh-i ʿālam-ārā-yi ʿabbāsī, Farīd Murādī (ed) (Tehran, 1390 [2011], pp. 155–7. Kohlberg, E., 'Bahā' al-Dīn ʿĀmilī', Encyclopedia Iranica (EIr), 3, 4 (1988), pp. 429–30. www.iranicaonline.org/articles/baha-al-din-ameli-shaikh-mohammad-b. Hashemipour, Behnaz, 'Bahā' al-Dīn al-ʿĀmilī', Biographical Encyclopedia of Astronomers (BEA) (2007), pp. 42–3. https://islamsci.mcgill.ca/RASI/BEA/Amili_BEA.htm

102 Bosworth, Islamic Dynasties, pp. 172–3: Shāh ʿAbbās; Rosenfeld and Ihsanoğlu, Mathematicians, Astronomers, and Other Scholars, no. 1058, pp. 348–50.

high place on the ladder of science. But as it turned out, the name Baha' al-Din would come to exemplify the opposite, a so-called scientific 'decline'[103] in his native lands, a time when 'the impetus of science in Islam came to an end'. What had been missing from the rich combination of all that it would take someone with the sources and resources of Baha' al-Din to have his name rise from a mere scholar or statesman to a first-rate scientist and mathematician, or for a city such as Isfahan of the 1600s to have its brilliance extended to the sciences of the time, was something else: external as well as internal communications. Despite frequent European visits to Safavid Persia, even Baha' al-Din's upholding of a positional rotation for the Earth,[104] based on insufficient proof to the contrary, would not carry the marks of European influences. Any travels Baha' al-Din had taken himself, from a pilgrimage to Mecca, and journeys from Arab speaking lands like Lebanon and Syria where he took his last name, ʿAmili after 'Jabal al-ʿAmil' of his ancestors, to Tabriz, Qazvin and Mashhad of Persian speaking lands, where he was known as 'Shaykh Baha'i', he had stayed within the confines of his neighbouring lands at best, including Ottoman territory,[105] well-known for the stories of the doomed Istanbul observatory. Baha' al-Din, having heard enough about the initial patron of the Istanbul observatory to have dedicated a work to the same Ottoman Sultan, had limited exchanges with such close neighbours, having stayed mostly within Persian lands after the year 1610.[106] That year, when Baha' al-Din's small world was closing in on him for the last decades of his life mostly in Isfahan, happened to be a year when the world of science was fast-opening elsewhere all around him.

Within the exponentially expanding world of science across Eastern and Western European lands, the Arab and Persian lands of Bahaʿ al-Din and a few other obscure contemporary scholars were not to be relevant to major scientific developments marked by a full-fledged 'Scientific Revolution'. Nor did the widening Sunni and Shiʿi divides of Arab and Persian lands matter to a Europe facing critical rifts not just between post-Reformation Catholics and Protestants, but between faith and reason at large. An age to be soon known as the 'Age of Reason' was not a fitting place for names like Baha' al-Din, which literally meant 'worth of faith'; and an era where reason was getting an upper hand over faith, not so fitting for a subject so submissive to faith that even his title 'Shaykh al-Islam'[107] reflected his position as chief jurisconsult. This was an age of scientific advancements beyond 'ʿilm' as knowledge that happened to develop largely outside Baha' al-Din's native lands. The year 1610, a decade before death would make his name fade within the realm of science, was a year when Galileo had published his historic and consequential astronomical observations of the year before. This was not only to be called an 'Age of Galileo',[108] an age coinciding with the expansion of

[103] Hartner, 'When and how'.
[104] Hashemipour, 'Bahāʾ al-Dīn al-ʿĀmilī', p. 42.
[105] Hashemipour, 'Bahāʾ al-Dīn ʿĀmilī', p. 43.
[106] Bosworth, Islamic Dynasties, pp. 136–7: Ottomans.
[107] Stewart, Devin J., 'A biographical notice on Bahāʾ al-Dīn Al-ʿĀmilī', Journal of the American Oriental Society, 111, 3 (1991), pp. 563–71, p. 563; Stewart, Devin J., 'The first Shaykh al-Islām of the Safavid capital Qazvin', Journal of the American Oriental Society, 116, 3 (1996), pp. 387–405, p. 387: father as shaykh al-Islam or chief jurisconsult of the Safavid capital, Qazvin.
[108] Langford, Jerome L., Galileo, Science and the Church, revised edition forwarded by Stillman Drake, (Ann Arbor, 1971): Chapter 1: 'The Age of Galileo'; quotes: pp. 3–4.

knowledge after the discovery of new worlds through sea and land, and the expansion of education from the elite to all classes, where Italy happened to 'lead the way'; it was also an age of massive communications, from the invention and expansion of the printing press, to the widening of channels of communication in a relatively confined Europe where scientific authors were benefitting from the works of each other even across nations: the Italian Galileo, getting inspired by the Polish Copernicus; the German Kepler, corresponding with the Italian Galileo; the Danish Tyco Brahe basing his observations on such knowledge; and the British Newton, reworking them all.

Any contributions to science from someone like Baha' al-Din, by contrast, would not even be known in his own time and place, as he himself was not much aware of earlier works. The single case of Hafiz-i Isfahani,[109] credited with the construction a European-style mechanical clock, one reportedly made in Kashan, so close to Isfahan, would one day show that such scientific activities had been largely isolated cases at the time; and the case of that clock alone would be enough to show that its Persian patron had looked in vain for someone to meet the challenge of its construction. The piece describing that construction, the only surviving text of Hafiz-i Isfahani, would further show the rarity of advanced scientific activities in the telling story of how the author had refused, then submitted to the will of a persistent patron unable to find fitting candidates for his open competition project.

The setting of Baha al-Din's slightly later time, and his high-profiled patron, the Safavid Shah ʿAbbas the first, were to be still more different. With the lost biography[110] of Baha al-Din written by one of his students, it would take a few centuries after his death for him to be written about as a scholar and statesman in the Safavid Court. The Safavid dynasty, assuming power half a century before Baha' al-Din's birth, and credited with making Persia 'a nation once again' after centuries of turbulence, was made especially impressive by 'Shah ʿAbbas the Great'. This was a visionary noted for stretching the Persian borders to that of the Sasanian Empire, and making his capital Isfahan, later called 'half of the world' or 'Medio mundo', particularly outstanding by the glory and diversity endowed upon it, despite some 'dark pages' in the records of his reign.[111] A near contemporary of famous rulers, from 'Elizabeth the first of England and Phillip the second of Spain to Ivan the Terrible of Russia, and Akbar, the Mughal Emperor', Shah ʿAbbas, the first would send envoys abroad, to Russia, Poland, Germany, France, Spain, England, Scotland, and Italy; and he moved his capital first from Tabriz to Qazvin to be further from the growing threat of the Ottoman Empire,[112] and later to Isfahan, a city visited and praised by many Europeans.

[109] Ḥāfiẓ-i Isfahānī, Natījat al-dawla: Kheirandish, 'From Maragha to Samarqand', pp. 166–70, and pp. 180–1, notes 29 and 30.

[110] Stewart, Devin J., 'The lost biography of Bahā' al-Dīn Al-ʿĀmilī and the reign of Shah Ismāʿil II in Safavid historiography', Iranian Studies, 31, 2, (1998), pp. 177–205.

[111] Browne, Literary History of Persia, Vol. 4, p. 4. and p. 107: 'his tolerant attitude towards non-Muslims'; p. 111: 'cruel murder of his son'. . . , 'blinding of another'; pp. 7–8: his putting on the throne a subject for three days, then having them killed to divert an astrological prediction from himself.

[112] Bosworth, Islamic Dynasties, p. 173; Browne, Literary History of Persia, Vol. 4, p. 5.

Despite scholarly circles as renowned as the 'School of Isfahan,'[113] to which Baha' al-Din belonged, there were no strictly 'scientific' centres in Isfahan at the time like the observatories of Maragha and Samarqand of Mongol and Timurid times centuries before, or that of Constantinople of the Ottomans more recently. No evidence would show that Safavid rulers ever seriously considered establishing an observatory, despite it being considered more than once: by the dynasty's founder, Shah Isma'il the first,[114] whose intended restoration of the Maragha Observatory had not materialised; by his son Shah Tahmasp the first,[115] whose similar impatience with a thirty-year observational program was reported by another ''Amili'; even by Shah 'Abbas the first,[116] whose name would be associated with astronomical instruments, from fine astrolabes made for him to instruments received from Italy. There was no shortage of Safavid patronage in related areas from architecture to decorative crafts, as in the beautifully executed and illustrated manuscript of a late Persian translation of Sufi's *Book of Constellations*,[117] commissioned by a rising governor in Mashhad associated with Isfahan through a constellation illustration. There was, however, still little sign of major scientific developments to increase chances of breakthroughs, like those brought about by such tools of instrumentation as the telescope of the Italian Galileo, British Harriot or Danish Brahe. No less crucial to any development, was the scarcity of libraries recorded in Arab and Persian lands of Baha' al-Din's time. He was privileged to have inherited, through marriage to the daughter of a scholar named Zayn-al-Din, a decent library by the time's standards. His own wife[118] had stood above other women of her time and place, not just as the uncommon only child and only wife of her father and husband respectively, but as a scholar and teacher herself accompanying Baha' al-Din on a trip on foot from Isfahan to Mashhad where her mathematically minded husband had measured the distance between those two cities through a rope stretched from house to house. Baha' al-Din was far from being scientifically inactive: in practical fields, his associations included a bathhouse,[119] with a famously undying flame heating the bath's water; in philosophy, his associates ranged from those in the 'Isfahan School'[120] like his

[113] Newman, Andrew, 'Towards a reconsideration of the Isfahān school of philosophy: Shaykh Bahā'ī and the role of the Safawid 'ulamā'', Studia Iranica, 15 (1986), pp. 83–99, pp. 84–97.

[114] Sayılı, ''Alā' al-Dīn al-Manṣūr's poems', p. 436.

[115] Sayılı, Observatory in Islam, p. 288: cites report by 'Abd al-Mum'in al-'Āmilī.

[116] Winter, H. J. J, 'Persian science in Safavid times' in Jackson, Peter and Lockhart, Laurence (eds), The Cambridge History of Iran, Vol. 6: The Timurid and Safavid Periods, Chap. 11: pp. 581–609, p. 597: 'fine astrolabe' made for Shāh 'Abbās I; Wilding, Nick, Galileo's Idol: Gianfrancesco Sagredo and the Politics of Knowledge (Chicago, 2014), p. 1: cites Galileo's 'closest friend, student and patron' Sagredo; p. 13, an 'entire collection of devices manufactured by his instrument maker' sent to Shah 'Abbās after 1611, with a rug promised by the Shah in return.

[117] Babaie, Sussan, Babayan, Kathryn, Baghdiantz McCabe, Ina, and Farhad, Massumeh, Slaves of the Shah: New Elites of Safavid Iran (London, New York, 2004), pp. 128–9: cites Manūchihr Khān, the grandson of Shāh 'Abbās's former slave and later military commander, as the governor of Mashhad, whose birth sign may have been the constellation Sagittarius, associated with Isfahan for its construction in corresponding months.

[118] 'Āmilī, Bahā' al-Dīn = Shaykh Bahā'ī, Fāl-nāmih in Vujdānī, Muḥammad (ed) (Tehran, 1322 [1943]), p. 52.

[119] Documentary film: Shaykh Bahā'ī House (my visit: Nov 2017). www.jadidonline.com/story/26022009/frnk/sheikh_bahai_eng

[120] Newman, 'Towards a Reconsideration', p. 84: cites Mirdāmād (d. 1631), and Mullā Ṣadrā (d. 1640).

colleague and student Mirdamad and Mulla Sadra, to his student and biographer Muzafar ʿAli; and in literature, his popular works, like *Kashkul*,[121] the *Bowl of Darwish*, included scientific subjects, however scattered.

Among Baha' al-Din's most substantial scientific works was an *Abridgement of Arithmetic, Khulasat al-Hisab*[122] in Arabic, a work with hundreds of manuscripts, and translations from Persian and Russian to French and German, besides an impressively rich manuscript that would one day make it to a modern exhibit and virtual gallery (Plate 6). But the *Abridgement*, being no more than a narrow bridge over a vast ocean of scientific knowledge with far too elementary content also showed the scientific isolation of its author. A man like Baha' al-Din could not benefit scientifically from a single person in a city as magnificent as Isfahan, one comparable to European cities otherwise, and standing far above many others in other times. The best its author could do in that unimpressive magnum opus, was dress it up with the works of impressive figures from a distant past, those as ancient as Euclid's *Elements* from two millenniums before that, while focused on geometry, included subjects later called 'algebra' after Arabic texts in the Euclidean tradition. His *Kashkul* included from the hand of his own father, a far too elementary problem based on a simple mathematical identity, and associated with the pre-Euclidean Greek 'Pythagoreans', one amounting to the equality of the area of a square on the hypotenuse of a right-angled triangle, to the sum of the squares on its sides.[123] The identity itself was called by him not by its historical names as the 'Pythagorean Theorem' or 'Euclidean Identity', but by the odd expression 'bride' proposition,[124] involving the right-angled triangle of sides 3, 4, 5. When Europeans of Baha' al-Din's own time, early modern authors like the French Francois Viète and René Descartes, were benefitting from the works of ancient Greek authors like Diophantus which had been translated into Arabic, to present unknown quantities with symbols translatable to x and y,[125] Baha' al-Din's was an outdated geometric entity in the form of unknown sides of figures like triangles or squares, called in Arabic and Persian a 'thing', or shay' by historical authors as early as Khwarizmi and Khayyam, the respective 'father of algebra' and 'mathematician-poet'.

Baha' al-Din found the subject of unknown quantities and extracting them from known entities particularly capturing because he was obsessed with puzzles. He was aware that it was science as a process of puzzle-solving, more than any one scientific

121 ʿĀmilī, Bahā' al-Dīn = Shaykh Bahāʾī, Kitāb al-Kashkūl (Dehli, 1296 [1879]). Bosworth, Clifford Edmund, Bahāʾ al-Dīn al-ʿĀmilī and His Literary Anthologies (Manchester, 1989), pp. 1–15: 'The Author and His Age'. Manuscripts in Rosenfeld and Ihsanoğlu, Mathematicians, Astronomers, and Other Scholars, No. 1058, p. 348: E1: Persian translation: Sāʿīdī Khurāsānī, Muḥammad Bāqir, Kitāb-i Kashkūl, 2 vols., (Tehran, 1358 [1979/1980]).

122 ʿĀmilī, Khulāṣat al-ḥisāb, pp. 1–43, bound with Qūshjī, Kitāb Fārisī Hayʾat, and Ṭūsī, Sī fasl. Harvard University, Houghton Library manuscript Arab SM4284, undated, completed in the hand of Muḥammad Hāshim; opening folio in 'Windows into early science', 2008, and its Virtual Gallery, 2009 (Plate 6). Rosenfeld and Ihsanoğlu, Mathematicians, Astronomers, and Other Scholars, p. 348–9, M1: excludes the Houghton manuscript exhibited.

123 Euclid, Elements, proposition I. 47; Berggren, Episodes, p. 128.

124 ʿʿarūs' [Uqlīdis/Euclid?], ʿĀmilī, Kashkūl, pp. 158–9; Sāʿīdī Khurāsānī (tr), Vol. 1, pp. 251–2.

125 Cohen, I. Bernard, Revolutions in Science (Cambridge MA, 1985); Kheirandish, Problems Corresponding to Quadratic Equations.

work or production, that was to move the train of human progress forward; and he tried hard to keep up with the vehicle of 'science', even if he and his fellow natives were to be left out of that fast-moving train. His passion for puzzles took him beyond mathematics to their extension to literary subjects, and a creative work that could immortalise his name was a so-called 'Fal-namih', a collection of fortune-telling poems requested by Shah ʿAbbas the first. This was an unmatched textual collection in Persian where letters, words, verses and rhymes uniquely merged together to respond to inquiries on over twenty subjects through one-line poems, to be one day printed as a pamphlet, then individual printed cards.[126] But Baha' al-Din busying himself with such games and riddles instead of more serious problems and puzzles of science occupying people in Europe was due to his lack of access to sources needed for such activities in Isfahan, a city he had not left since the year 1610.

That same year marked important breakthroughs elsewhere on the Earth Baha' al-Din stood on, an Earth by then proposed, but still not proved, to be moving, not in the form of a positional rotation as he himself suggested, but more radically around a stationary Sun. The year before 1610, in January of 1609, Galileo, a mathematics lover in faraway Italy, had looked into his self-made telescope, an instrument built almost simultaneously with those made by Dutch instrument makers, one even used by the British scientist, Thomas Harriot.[127] Galileo could make breakthroughs within the century-old Copernican astronomical theory he had closely followed through a much closer scientific community in Europe than Baha' al-Din could imagine, despite his exposure to various Europeans visiting the glorious Safavid capital. Galileo had seen through his so-called 'telescope'[128] that the Earth was not a perfectly smooth surface; that the heavenly bodies rotating around Jupiter, or the phases of Venus observable over time, meant that neither the Earth nor the Sun were unique entities; that other observable data fitted the model of a stationary Sun and rotating Earth just as well. Despite challenges to Galileo from religious, political and personal quarters, starting with scripture dictating a stationary Earth and rotating Sun, further advances would come through correspondences between Galileo and Kepler, observations of Tycho Brahe, and other transfers of knowledge to figures like Newton and others.

All this time, Baha' al-Din, who would one day be credited with 'advocating the feasibility of the Earth's rotation' in his *Anatomy of Celestial Spheres*,[129] was far from news or signs of such major scientific developments: he would be sitting in his private library, going over the limited manuscripts he had inherited from his father in law, or obtained otherwise. By then, the books authored by the likes of Copernicus and Galileo were published in Europe in hundreds and thousands. Copernicus's revolutionary *De Revolutionibus*, a book that turned around the revolutions of the heavens themselves, was produced in hundreds of copies in its early editions; and Galileo's controversial

[126] ʿĀmilī, Fāl-nāmih: Vujdānī, Fālnāmah-i Shaykh Bahāʾī [sic]. Introduction: composed in 1002 H [1593–94]; requested by Shāh ʿAbbās the first. Kheirandish, Asadollah, Fāl-nāmih-i Shaykh Bahāʾī (card edition) (Tehran, 1362 [1983]; 1374 [1995]).

[127] Cohen, 'Galileo and the telescope', in Birth of a New Physics, pp. 185–7, p. 186.

[128] Cohen, 'What Galileo "saw"', pp. 188–93.

[129] Hashemipour, 'Bahāʾ al-Dīn al-ʿĀmilī', p. 42: Original title: Tashrīḥ al-aflāk. Rosenfeld and Ihsanoğlu, Mathematicians, Astronomers, and Other Scholars, p. 349: A1: several manuscripts.

Dialogue of Two Chief World Systems[130] – one Ptolemaic and Earth-centred, and the other Copernican and Sun-centred – one thousand copies. While it still took about a year to finish printing all the copies of the four-hundred page book of Copernicus in the spring of 1543, the circulation was not only far and wide enough to reach all of Europe, but as long-lasting and far-reaching as the England of Newton's time 200 years later. The books that fell into the hands of Baha' al-Din or people like him were, by contrast, not just outdated, containing yet another version of a geocentric universe, through yet another non-Ptolemaic model; far from the prospects of a printing house, even in a 'craft' paradise such as Isfahan, Baha' al-Din's books were handwritten texts that in their much limited forms 'nobody read' for real, in contrast to Copernicus's highly annotated book.

In his final days in Isfahan, about three decades before that January of 1650, Baha' al-Din was sitting in the beautiful setting of his study, a refined and well-designed room in a house once owned by Shah ʿAbbas's aunt,[131] and offered to Baha' al-Din by the king after her death for its proximity to Isfahan's Jamiʿ Mosque where the privileged scholar taught. The room to the right of a beautiful courtyard, one above a basement known for the design of his famous bathhouse, was his bright study standing on a perfect height overlooking well-lined trees and flowers around a rectangular pool. In that room, under vaulted arches balancing the yard's angles and the roof's curves, Baha' al-Din was selecting his manuscripts and books for donation in preparation for his departure from Isfahan. He had been staring one moment on his books, another on the intricate designs of a room with the polygonal shapes of its walls, ornamental vaults of its ceiling, geometrical patterns of its floors, and coloured glasses of its windows. Of the four eye-opening geometrical designs surrounding him, the angled walls, vaulted ceiling, and patterned floor were directing him towards his books on geometry; while the fourth, the coloured windows across him, were drawing him to books on optics, the study of light and colour still considered by him a subdivision of geometry, five hundred years after the subject had become a physical and experimental science in Europe. On geometry, Baha' al-Din had taken out his manuscript of the only work written on the subject of *What Was Needed by Craftsmen from Geometrical Constructions*, a work in Arabic reporting the presence of geometers and craftsmen in the same gathering by the Persian Buzjani working in Baghdad, dedicating it to the Buyid Baha' al-Dawla.[132] Tied to that manuscript from centuries before were two other surviving manuscripts: an early Persian translation of that same work, both anonymous and undated; and an Arabic commentary, with a known author from three centuries later. A Persian commentary by another well known mathematician was still being written in the year of Baha' al-Din's death, so at the time, only two valuable manuscripts were endowed to the Shrine Library in Mashhad,[133] a city where Baha' al-Din's body would be taken from Isfahan for burial.[134]

[130] Galilei, Galileo, Dialogue Concerning the Two Chief World Systems.
[131] Documentary film on the House of Shaykh Bahāʾī. www.jadidonline.com/story/26022009/frnk/sheikh_bahai_eng
[132] Kheirandish, 'Early tradition in practical geometry', pp. 80–1 and 83–9; Bosworth, Islamic Dynasties, pp. 94–6, Mottahedeh, Roy P., 'The Idea of Iran in the Buyid dominions', in Herzig, Edmund and Stewart, Sarah (eds), Early Islamic Iran (London, 2012), pp. 153–60.
[133] Kheirandish, 'Early tradition in practical geometry', pp. 100–02; p. 132 n. 98.
[134] Hashemipour, 'Bahāʾ al-Dīn al-ʿĀmilī', p. 42.

As Baha' al-Din was thinking about the few works he felt fortunate to own singly, and gift generously, he also thought of those his private library did not own to donate, those as recent as works by a neighbouring 'Taqi al-Din' on optics and mechanics. And while his eyes moved from the geometries closing on him within the confines of his study, to the coloured-glass windows opening to him a world outside of it, a gem shining brightly at the forefront of his mind was an early work on optics, a subject that to a secluded scholar like Baha' al-Din was only reminiscent of subjects such as light and colour in front of his eyes. He had long known about that optical work in Arabic in seven books by a certain Ibn al-Haytham, through the 'preface' of an Arabic commentary on it by a Persian native, called Farisi about three centuries later, a work with bold teachings about effective 'combinations of' mathematical and natural sciences', spotted in two thick volumes in a Persian library by Farisi's mentor, Shirazi, another Persian native bringing those volumes from distant lands to help his student with the 'puzzle' of light reflection and refraction.[135] Baha al-Din had looked in vain for more hints about the likely site of those volumes in 'one of the libraries in Fars' during Shirazi's youth, or the place of that 'distant land', as part of his primitive forms of puzzle-solving. Baha' al-Din had also remained unaware of these and other related historical matters: of the European versions of that book by a Latinised Alhazen or Alhacen after the first name of its author, Al-Hasan, of its Latin and Italian translations and printed edition a century before his own time, of the so-called 'checkered history' of the book's 'underserved misfortune' in its native lands overlapping its 'unexpected good luck' in Europe; and of projects recording the work's footpaths centuries later[136] through an electronic revolution following scientific and industrial revolutions. The once so glamorous city of Isfahan, the residence choice for not just Baha' al-Din, but so many visitors from the West in the 17th century alone to bring it closest to a 'Western' city, would itself be isolated from all such events. Subject to another turning of the tide, the events before and after this time, from a fallen scientific program in Istanbul to the west of Isfahan of the 1570s, to a massive military invasion of Isfahan from its east in the 1720s, would involve various chance moments, some occurring against all odds.

Between the year 1610, when Baha' al-Din did not leave Isfahan, and 1629 when the reign of his great patron, Shah 'Abbas the first, ended with his death, there were some chance moments for scientific breakthroughs which were curiously and consequentially derailed. In lands to their west, the year 1610[137] coincided with the development of the single most important tool for one major cosmological breakthrough through Galileo's 'occhiale', coined as the 'telescope' by a Greek scholar from two Greek words, tele, meaning far away, and skopeo, meaning to look, within a year; and in lands to their

135 Sabra, Optics of Ibn al-Haytham; 'The physical and the mathematical'; Kheirandish, 'Puzzle of Ṭūsī's Optical Works'; 'Light and dark', pp. 74–5.

136 Kheirandish, 'Light and dark', p, 64, pp. 74–5, and pp. 78–9, includes maps with footpaths.

137 Kapoor, R. C., 'Nūr ud-dīn Jahangīr and Father Kirwitzer: The independent discovery of the great comets of November 1618 and the first astronomical use of the telescope in India', Journal of Astronomical History and Heritage, 19, 3 (2016), pp. 264–97, p. 280: Galileo's 'occhiale', and the Greek word, 'telescope' coined from tele (far away) and skopeo (to look).

east, the year 1618[138] coincided with the use of the Western 'telescope' in India, and the transport of one to China within another year, and its explanation published in 1629. Around or in between those dates there were a few missed chances for the effective use of one such game-changing instrument in the half-positioned lands of the Islamic Middle Ages: if in the year 1593–1594 of Shah Abbas's reign,[139] the chief astrologer had not 'foretold disaster to the occupant of the throne', or instead of having a 'subject' selected to rule for three days then executed to divert an astrological prediction, Isfahan's Persian King had not acted as destructively as Istanbul's Ottoman Sultan; if after the year 1611, coinciding with astronomical instruments sent to Shah ʿAbbas the first by Galileo's student, friend, and patron, Sagredo, they had included a 'telescope' to introduce the revolutionary findings of Europe; and if a letter dated 1624 by another Italian, the traveller Pietro de la Valle, to his Persian addressee, Zayn al-Din Lari, to describe Europeans models and findings, including the 'long-eyed instrument', worded as *alat-i chishmak-i diraz* for 'telescope',[140] had been effectively communicated, there would have been more chance of developments comparable to those in Europe, India and China, in the intermediary Islamic lands.

[138] Kapoor, 'Nūr ud-dīn Jahangīr', p. 282: 1618, telescope in India. Baichun, Zhang, 'The introduction of European astronomical instruments and the related technology into China during the seventeenth century', East Asian Science, Technology, and Medicine, 20 (2003), pp. 99–131, p. 100: 1619 and 1629, transportation and publication of the telescope in China.

[139] Browne, Literary History, Vol. 4, pp. 7–8.

[140] Wilding, Galileo's Idol, p. 13. Sayılı, Aydın, 'An early seventeenth century Persian manuscript on the Tychonic system', Anatolia, 3 (1958), pp. 84–7, p. 83: Latin original and Persian and Italian translations; p. 85. Brentjes, 'Early modern European travellers'.

7

Plan and Chance

1000 Years (ca. 750–1750): Full Phase

A chequered history in which undeserved misfortune overlapped with unexpected good luck.

A. I. Sabra, *Optics of Ibn al-Haytham*, 1989, Preface[1]

7.1 An Old Manuscript in a Game of Chance

What matters is a living trace...

It was the spring of 2017, and the manuscript of the *Dialogue of Baghdad and Isfahan* was going through the four seasons of a new life. With the recent discovery of a new record of a '*Munazirih-i Baghdad va Isfahan*' in an old library inventory, the *Dialogue* manuscript had assumed at least one more life through another possible transcription. A few years before, a set of sharp eyes had unexpectedly detected the trace of such a title in an Ottoman palace library inventory from Istanbul of the early 1500s, one whose unthinkable evidence of 'Treasures of Knowledge'[2] on any thinkable subject would publish in a few years. No one would have thought such an exhaustive royal library inventory existed, let alone be discovered; that a single handlist would preserve names, dates and details[3] of hundreds of years of history documented in that form for the first time; that such a unique manuscript collection would not end up in Western Europe, in Italy, Spain, Germany, France, or England, the safe haven of many oriental manuscripts and codices; that it would land, not just in Eastern Europe, but in a place as rarely associated with oriental manuscripts as Hungary; and above all, that it would move across the ocean to reach somewhere that would secure its place in history, not

1 Sabra, Optics of Ibn al-Haytham, Preface: Vol. 2, p. xi.

2 Necipoğlu, Kafadar, and Fleischer (eds), Treasures of Knowledge: The manuscript MS Török F. 59, Library of the Hungarian Academy of Sciences, Preface, Vol. 1, pp. xi–xiii, and notes; Vol. 2, pp. 1–365 in black ink, fols. 1–180, in red ink; Munāẓirih-i Baghdād va Iṣfahān, p. 328 [fol. 161r].

3 Names: Sulṭān 'Bāyezīd II' (patron); ''Atufī' (compiler): Necipoğlu, Kafadar, and Fleischer (eds), Treasures of Knowledge: Appendix V, Vol. 1, pp. 1079–80 (English), Vol. 2., fol. 11b (Arabic), Vol. 1, p. 1 (preface); dates: 908, 909 H (compilation): Vol. 1, p. xi (preface), Vol. 2, p. 5 (transliteration), and fol. 1b (Arabic); Ottoman Sultans: Bosworth, Islamic Dynasties, p. 136: 'Bayāzīd II'.

by a single 'orientalist' as was long the case, but in the collective hands of a team of international scholars with multidisciplinary specialties,[4] the least likely of all such chance moments.

While the *recorded* manuscript of a 'Dialogue between Baghdad and Isfahan' atypically listed among the 'science' entries of a library inventory once in Turkey, and now in Hungary,[5] had only a chance of having survived the course of time, the *existing* manuscript of that *Dialogue*, actually preserved within a literary collection once in India, and now in England,[6] was assuming a new life of its own. Up until then, the many lives of that singly known manuscript, from a composition and transcription to various forms and travels around the world, were all bound by a finite, textual, realm. But now, the *Dialogue* was surpassing the finite world of a manuscript as a 'manual script' altogether, to enter into more open-ended realms: there, a 'munazara' or eye to eye exchange between two timeless cities would find new expression, no longer as words on a page, but as entities with a 'living trace' in a new mix of physical and digital space.

With the arrival of spring on the first day of a solar year corresponding to the year 2017, Baghdad and Isfahan would first shine through the symbolic images of a 'universal spectrum',[7] representing a new era. Inside a travelling display case where seven symbols represented universal realms beyond a new solar year, symbols for the cities of Baghdad and Isfahan sat across one another, much like modern cities under their age-old seven skies. The display case featured not the seven 'S's of the traditional 'Haft Sin' spread of the Persian New Year,[8] but seven items starting with the letter 'S' that formed a 'universal spectrum' (Plate 7), never set in such terms before. Centre-staged within the display's midnight-blue background, symbols for the cities of Baghdad and Isfahan were shining through the astronomical sign 'Sagittarius', a sign that happened to symbolise both cities in historical sources next to other cities and regions assigned with birth signs.[9] Here, symbols for Baghdad and Isfahan stood out as hybrid half-horse, half-human 'centaurs' representing the zodiac sign Sagittarius, posing as two facing 'Archers' drawing their bows towards one another in a visual, not verbal, dialogue form encircled by five other universal symbols: 'Sun' and 'Stars', symbolised by a sun-face and star-reader known as an astrolabe; rolling dice representing the number 'Seven' through sums like four and three for the four seasons and their

[4] Necipoğlu, Kafadar, and Fleischer (eds), Treasures of Knowledge: Contents, Vol. 1, pp. vii–ix.

[5] Kheirandish, 'Books on mathematical and mixed-mathematical sciences', Vol. 1, pp. 857–68, List of Entries, pp. 869–90: Munāẓirih entry follows the astronomical text: Jahān-i Dānish fi al-hay'a.

[6] Manuscript BL Add 18, 411, codex colophon: Kanauj, India: presented by William Yule's sons, 1850. https://blogs.bl.uk/asian-and-african/2017/02/some-british-islamic-style-seals-in-persian-manuscripts-from-india.html

[7] Kheirandish, Elaheh, 'A universal spectrum of seven "S"s: Sun, Stars, Sipāhān, Sagittarius, Shāh-nāmih, Seven, Spectrum', production, script, narration, and coordination; slide presentation and display case at Harvard University, Hilles Library, 30 March 2017; Music: 'Piano, Piano': Dang Show. https://www.scholar.harvard.edu/ekheirandish/exhibits

[8] Haft Sīn (seven 'S's) of the Persian New Year (Nowrūz): apple (sīb), hyacinth (sunbul), garlic (sīr), coin (sikkih), vinegar (sirkih), jubba jubba (sinjid), and green (sabzih).

[9] Examples of place and birth sign correspondences: Babylon and Kufa: Aries and Aquarius; Kashan, Tabriz, Samarqand: Virgo, Scorpio and Pisces; Alexandria, Constantinople, Jerusalem, Kabul: Taurus, Caner, Leo Libra; Egypt and India: Gemini and Capricorn. Sources include Bīrūnī, Kitāb Tafhīm, Wright (ed), p. 365.

three-month cycles; an artistic adaptation of Firduwsi's *Shah-Namih* as a *Book of Kings* featuring seven portraits of differently timed kings and queens; and finally, a central *Calendar of Timekeeping*, symbolising the very concept of a 'Spectrum' in a display of weeks, days, hours and minutes, both from and beyond Arab and Persian lands. An audio-visual version of the physical display thus presented Baghdad and Isfahan in a new physical-digital mix where a voice recited verses over images of the two cities' universal icons. Twelve verses echoed over seven images, in successive rhyme:

In this solar year of 1396, A number with the magical sum of Nineteen,[10]
Nowruz, the new day of ancient Iranian spring, Has seven other 'S's, on its 'Haft Sin'
As the spread of Seven 'S's extends the Persian letter 'Sin'. . .,
A universal spectrum of seven S's, Spreads beyond a timeless screen. . .

Verses involving Baghdad and Isfahan followed through their common zodiac sign:

SagittariuS, with . . . 'S's at the both ends of its name,
A zodiac sign of a mighty realm, Linked to the Earth, through cities of fame.

First spoke Baghdad over an Archer's sign:

Salam, once named the 'city of peace', Posed as a half-man, half-horse split,
Hiding as Archer, named in disguise, Built in a month, with a rival on rise.

Next replied Isfahan over a facing Archer:

Sipahan, known as 'half of the world', With half of its world, yet to be known,
Its father and mother, heavenly spheres, Sipahan the child, better than the parent.[11]

The closing lines then underscored the timeless and boundless nature of them all:

As the spectrum of 'S's spreads its wings, The sky is no limit for higher spheres,
Timeless, the turns of year after year, Boundless, the rounds of spring after spring.[12]

On the first day of spring in that same solar year, a sequel to the 'universal spectrum of seven "S"s' followed as a historical dialogue in rotating voices, here with voices of Baghdad and Isfahan echoing their respective ages of science and craft over panoramic perspectives of those historic cities.[13]

10 Rosenthal, Franz, 'Nineteen', Analecia Biblica, 12 (1959), pp. 304–18. Historically important as a sum of 12 (year months) and 7 (week days).

11 'SagittariuS, with . . . "S"s written all over its name': presence of letter 'S' at both ends. Salām: Coke, Baghdad, the City of Peace: 'Madīnat al-salām', historically, Baghdad'; The rest of the verses are below
'A central city of Īrān-shahr, In one of the seven ancient zones,
A riding Archer is its symbol, East and West within its reach. . .'.

12 The full script involved more than the verses included here.

13 Welch, The Travels and Journal of Ambrosio Bembo, p. 119 and p. 322; panorama sketches: 7.2.

The 'round' city of Baghdad first addressed Isfahan, a city best known for its square-shaped 'square':

I am Baghdad, a city in ʿIraq, With a distance between it and Isfahan,
Round with no square set within my land, As is my rival's alternate plan[14]
If I don't have its 'plan of the world', Jewel of science sits within my soul,
Once 'house of wisdom' honoured my name, What is your honour, which is your fame?[15]
I was one day at science's core, How can you say, what honour is your's?
Kindi and Haytham, Nasir al-Din, Each of them matchless, wise and esteemed. . .[16]

Isfahan addressed Baghdad through the echo of its own voice, to complete their jointly composed twelve verses.

I, the renowned city of Isfahan, Renamed as 'half of the world',
Monuments on my 'plan of the world', Have so much beauty none fit in words[17]
Residents famed, from youngest to old, For arts and the crafts, from the oldest of times,
From one side, drawn to the arts and the crafts, From patterns in hand, to every design[18]
From another side, a magnet of minds, From inventors, to the experts and wise,
The lap of my land long nurtured the likes, Of figures as great as Bahaʾ, the Shaykh. . .[19]

The next voices of Baghdad and Isfahan would open a dialogue at a much later time: this time, the setting would be a historic site with a twelve-house 'Zodiac room' and seven-room 'Planets house', reminiscent of age-old 'palaces' and 'treasure-houses' long reported with associations with Baghdad and Isfahan.[20] In this new cosmological setting, Baghdad and Isfahan were not only two of the twelve cities linked to birth signs in the site's Zodiac room; they stood further out as the luminous Moon and Sun shining

[14] Kheirandish, Asadollah, Surūdih-hā (Compositions) (unpublished): Verses below composed for the present book, English translations: Elaheh Kheirandish. Baghdad addressing Isfahan:
'Man-am shahr-i Baghdād andar ʿIrāq, Kih bā Iṣfahān hast-am andar firāq,
Ma-rā nīst maydānī andar miyān, Bi-dān gūnih kū hast dar Iṣfahān'.
[15] *'Agar nīst maydān-i Naqshi-Jahān, Ma-rā guhar-i ʿilm dar naqsh-i jān,*
Bi-man Bayt-i Hikmat bidād-and nām, Tu-rā īn-chinīn fakhr būdih kudām?'
[16] *'Budam markaz-i ʿilm-i ān rūz-gār, Tu-rā bā chinīn iftikhār-ī chih kār?*
Zih Kindī u Haytham, bih Khwājih Naṣīr, Bas-ī ʿālim-ān, yik bi yik bī-naẓīr. . .'.
[17] Kheirandish, Surūdih-hā, Kheirandish, Elaheh (tr, excerpts). Isfahan addressing Baghdad:
'Man-am shahr-i nām-āvar-i Iṣfahān, Kih maʿrūf hast-am bih Niṣf-i Jahān,
Banā-hā-yi aṭrāf-i Naqsh-i Jahān, Nayā-yad zih zībāy-ī andar bayān'.
[18] *'Bih shiʿr u hunar shuhrih-and az qadīm, Ma-rā shahr-vandān zih pīr u javān,*
Zih yik sū bih ṣanʿat girāyīdih-am, Kih tarḥ-ī dar andāz-am andar miyān'.
[19] *'Zih sū-yi digar, jadhb-i nu-avāran, Yik-ī mukhtariʿ digar-ī kār-dān*
Bih dāman-ī khud parvarānīdih-am, Kisān-ī chu Shaykh-i Bahāʾ- ī dar ān'.
[20] Ibn al-Nadim, Fihrist, Dodge (tr), Vol. 2, p. 573; Pingree, Thousands, pp. 9–11.
[21] Reconstructed Zodiac room and Planet houses: 7.4.

silver and gold rays through rooms named after them in the Planets house:[21] facing each other between rooms dedicated to Mercury and Venus of the lower planets, and Mars, Jupiter and Saturn of the upper planets, they adopted their own historical colours and associations; twelve new verses would fill the site's Moon and Sun rooms through changing wall projections throwing different lights on their ongoing 'dialogue'.

In the first set of projections, Baghdad would be reflected through historical images of a Moon in verses from a book titled *Baghdad: The City in Verse*,[22] verses arranged in the same chronological order as the book reflecting the city's representations through time.

Projected on the walls of the Planets house's Moon room, verses on Baghdad composed in Arabic started with the earliest poets since the city's foundation:

Oh moon, dusk escaped from you, oh pearl that the shell cannot shelter. . .[23]
Will our earth revert to what it was, now that circumstances brought us to this pass[24]
Each night, the moon disappears but retains. . . full moon sits on the western horizon . . .[25]
The Tigris on the moon, a blue carpet, the moon over the river, a golden veil. . .[26]
When the moon is about to set, it is a golden sword unsheathed over the water. . .[27]
Two banks like pearls in a necklace. . .
Crown besides a crown, palace beside a palace. . .[28]

Isfahan would, in turn, reflect the historical image of a Sun through verses surviving on the walls of one of its lasting monuments, dating to the time of that building. Projected on the walls of the historic Sun room shone verses on Isfahan in Persian:

Its arch bends the back of heaven, (for) heaven's loftiness is too short for its height,[29]
If its lofty vault were the orbit of the sun, it would never set until the end of time. . .
The sky would appear as humble as the circle of a compass, if it were to reside [in it]. . .
Should the new moon find its way into its [palace's] winsome surroundings,
From the brightness of its [palace]'s mantle it will instantly turn into a [full moon]. . .
The never setting sun of its golden medallion, makes the mote disdain the sun rays.[30]

22 Snir, Baghdad: The City in Verse.
23 Snir, Baghdad: The City in Verse, pp. 64–5: 'Al-ʿAbbās ibn al-Aḥnāf (750–809)'.
24 Snir, Baghdad: The City in Verse, pp. 82–5: 'Isḥāq al-Khuraymī (?-829)'.
25 Snir, Baghdad: The City in Verse, p. 102: 'Ibn Dūst (ninth century)'.
26 Snir, Baghdad: The City in Verse, p. 125: 'ʿAlī ibn Muḥammad al-Tanūkhī (892–953)'.
27 Snir, Baghdad: The City in Verse, p. 126: 'Manṣūr ibn Kayaghlagh (?–960)'.
28 Snir, Baghdad: The City in Verse, p. 131: 'Al-Ṭāhir ibn al-Muẓaffar ibn Ṭāhir al-Khāzin (tenth century?)'.
29 Babaie, Safavid Palaces at Isfahan, pp. 319–20: Ṭāhir-i Vaḥīd (inscription: 1057 [1647]): *'Awj-i falak hast zi bālā-sh kam, Ṭāqa-ash az ān pusht nimuda-st kham'*.
30 Babaie, Safavid Palaces at Isfahan, pp. 321–6: 'Muhammad ʿAlī Ṣāʾib-i Tabrīzī Iṣfahānī'; p. 325, line 17: the translation of the term 'badr' as 'sun' is changed by me to the more literal 'full moon'.
'Gar shav-ad ṭāq-i buland-i ū madār-i āftāb, Az zavāl iman buv-ad tā dāman-i ākhar-zamān . . .
Dar naẓar chun ḥalqih-i pargār mī-āy-ad ḥaqīr, Dar faḍā-yi ū murabbaʿ gar nishīn-ad āsmān . . .
Māh-i nu gar rāh yāb-ad dar ḥarīm-i dil-kash-ash, Badr gardad az furūgh-i Shamsī-ash dar yik zamān
Āftāb-i bī-zavāl-i Shamsī-yi zarrīn-i ū, Dharrih rā dil-sard kard az mihr-i Khurshīd-i jahān'.

The next set of 'dialogues' would follow with projections and profiles, further and further away from words and lines limited to the manual scripts of a 'manuscript'.

7.2 A Young Player with a Change of Plans

His genius cast its shadow o'er the world . . . the Age's Sun was he. . .

It was the summer of 2018, and a young narrator reconstructing a lively history beyond the lifeless pages of a 'manuscript' was adopting new lenses and casts for the last stages of his project. Much had happened during the years of Leo's reach for his final 'dialogue' chapter, most of it not far from Istanbul, the city in which a rich royal library inventory had recently turned up a trace of a '*Dialogue*' manuscript. But whether the copy of the *Dialogue* manuscript long in Leo's hands was historically 'unique' as the only version ever produced, or at least one other handwritten copy was so far undetected in Istanbul or elsewhere, seemed immaterial: it placed each case in a game of chance that could not affect Leo's plans: what did, was the course of events starting with those occasioned by new visits to the city of Istanbul, and those to the east and west of that East-West frontier, in a grand tour leading to more than a change of plan.

The visits to Istanbul were not only repeated over and over again, but pivotal in each case. Since the opening of a Museum of history of science and technology[31] on the grounds of the Topkapi palace, the birth place of the Ottoman palace library inventory surfacing recently, Leo had spent a few summers as an assistant in workshops in that Museum's summer schools under themes as relevant to his project as 'history of science as a universal heritage', 'traveling sciences for teaching and education', and 'light and shadow through interdisciplinary approaches'[32] offered from 2013 to 2015. Of these, the theme of 'traveling sciences' had been especially critical to the closing of Leo's project through a workshop held by his mentor titled *Around the World with Early Science*, a title used in terms of both contributions *to* early science from around the world, and representations *of* early science itself around the world in venues like libraries and museums. The workshop had offered Leo experiences with both venues. A library as impressive as Istanbul's Süleymaniye library had been where his mentor and another assistant had arranged to display the earliest Arabic manuscripts of the first three books of Ibn al-Haytham's *Optics*.[33] And a museum as suitable as a history of science and technology devoted to the lands of Islam had been where Leo had been given the floor to stream a video clip where Ibn al-Haytham had been featured

[31] Sezgin, Fuat, The Istanbul Museum for the History of Science and Technology in Islam, Catalogue (Istanbul, 2010). www.ibtav.org

[32] Istanbul: International Summer School, Sezgin Foundation: 'History of Science in Islam as a Universal Heritage', 22–25 August 2013; 'Traveling Sciences: Applying the History of Sciences in Islam for Teaching and Education', 24–9 August 2014; 'Light and Shadow: Experimental Spirit and Interdisciplinary Approaches', 17–22 August 2015.

[33] Istanbul, Süleymaniye Library, 27 August 2014: display of the earliest Arabic manuscripts of the first three books of Ibn al-Haytham's *Optics* as part of the workshop: 'Traveling Sciences: Around the World'; Workshop presenter: Siddiqi, Maera, Early Science and Authority in the Medieval Islamic Empire (unpublished undergraduate thesis, Harvard Extension, 2010).

prominently by a charismatic astrophysicist visiting 'the golden age of Islam' in an episode titled 'Hiding In The Light' in the popular science TV show, Cosmos.[34] The combination had been key for capturing a story of transmission relevant to world knowledge, and the mixed physical-digital media used in it, for undertaking the exciting and challenging idea of transmitting knowledge about the transmission of knowledge itself. The theme 'Light and Shadow' of the next summer school had occasioned its own after effects by coinciding with the upcoming 'Year of Light',[35] and events surrounding the 'checkered history' of the *Optics* of Ibn al-Haytham as a lens for viewing, besides the bright and dark sides of the presence of that momentous work in Islamic and European lands and their effects, the role of plan and chance in the key developments involved.

Before an 'International Year of Light' was to outshine many events in the year 2015, Leo had attended two back to back events in Berlin and Paris focused on optics and the closely related subject of perspective, with a focus on practical as well as theoretical, matters.[36] The Berlin event had offered a brand new framework formed by four new angles, those of onsite presentations and a keynote address, followed by an offsite installation and a headquarter tour. The onsite presentations had offered the angle of a novel technique variously called invention, discovery, and rediscovery, to describe a groundbreaking method called 'Linear Perspective', one mostly associated with Renaissance Italy in applying geometrical rules and relations to the reductions and enlargements of near and far objects, and the reproduction of exact forms by what had kept coming up with expressions as visually captivating as a central 'vanishing point'.[37] The presentations had offered, one after another, novel methodologies that contrasted with those as outdated as distinctions between the 'Western window' and that of the East, where some 'great cultures of the world ... the Chinese, the Persian, Indian, Arab, and Byzantine civilizations', were named as seemingly not 'interested in this geometric-optical way of picture making'; a keynote address had then amplified, as late as the 21st century, essentialist overtones through blanket expressions from 'mindsets' and 'gazes' representing an Eastern Alhazen and his Western counterparts, to cities like Florence and Baghdad representing 'Renaissance Art versus Arab Science'.[38]

[34] Tyson, Neil deGrasse, 'The golden age of Islam: When Arabic was the language of science', in the 'Hiding In The Light' episode of Cosmos: A Spacetime Odyssey, Sunday, 6 April 2014. www.space.com/25366-cosmos-hidden-light-universe-preview-video.html. Presentation: Esam Goodarzy in Istanbul Summer School: 'Traveling Sciences', 26 August, 2014.

[35] 2015 International Year of Light (UNESCO). Presentations: Fourth International Summer School, Light and Shadow, 17–22, 2015; Conference: 'The Islamic golden age of science for today's knowledge-based society: The Ibn Al-Haytham example': 14–15 September 2015 (UNESCO: Paris). Publication: God Is the Light of the Heavens and the Earth, 2015.

[36] Dupré, Sven and Peiffer, Jeanne, Perspective as Practice: Berlin, Max Plank Institute, 12–13 October, 2012; and Paris, Centre Alexandre Koyré, 10–11 September, 2013; proceedings published in Dupré, Sven (ed), Perspective as Practice: Renaissance Cultures of Optics (Turnhout, 2019).

[37] Edgerton, Samuel Y., The Renaissance Rediscovery of Linear Perspective: Cartography and Astronomy (New York: Basic Books, 1975), p. xv–xvii: Chronological Outline; pp. 5–7: invention, discovery, rediscovery; Chap. 9: 'The discovery of the vanishing point', pp. 124–32.

[38] Edgerton, Renaissance Rediscovery, p. 3 and p. 5: quote; Belting, Florence and Baghdad. Keynote speaker at Berlin workshop: Perspective as Practice; a discussion of essentialist overtones is included in Kheirandish, 'Optics and perspective'.

Such expressions were not unfamiliar to Leo as uttered and repeated elsewhere, as if pre-and post-perspective practices could not be conceived of as a historical continuum with different forms and models explainable through transmissions, transformations and appropriations of books, concepts and methods, rather than religious, philosophical, or ethnic associations; as if the extension of Linear Perspective rules and drawings to pre-telescope devices of a Thomas Harriot,[39] or a Galileo, both directed at the Moon in the same year and continent with very different results, was linked to them being British and Italian; and as if inventions variously called 'perspective tube', 'perspicillum' and 'spy glass',[40] before the more familiar 'telescope', were linked to anything other than their sources or resources: sources like books, and resources like schools, all being part of the wider circle of 'loops' linking them all. No less startling had been the imaginary example of a 'time machine'[41] he had found in one modern treatment to 'dial' the place and time when a 'singular moment marks the realization of one of the most profound ideas in all of world history: the perceptual "truth" of linear perspective', there set at Florence, Italy of 1425. This was different from the rotating *Timekeeping Calendar* on the micromaps of Leo's class: it was one thing to dial specific times and places for localising events, another to start with an event and reduce it to a single time and place.

Next to the angle of invention, with buzzwords like linear perspective and vanishing points, and that of precaution, with those like essentialism to reductionism, two other angles had completed the framework offered by the 'Perspective as practice' event. In Berlin, Leo had also experienced the 'perspectives' of a rotating panorama through a physical installation on its last day of display, one resurrecting the ancient Roman city of Pergamon through a monumental round structure set up by a visionary artist whose very name translated into 'living memory'.[42] The panorama's round and round experience, one as slow as that of the sky and clouds to a viewing eye, created different perspectives of time and space through turns of dawn and dusk marked by changing visual and audible experiences; and the experience of a 360-Pergamon, one to be repeated years later with 3D add-ons through a museum whose displays were awarded as 'excellent landmarks in the land of ideas',[43] had planted a new idea in Leo's mind: that of panoramic perspectives of Baghdad and Isfahan to similarly 'step back in time' and 'shine light' on his subjects and their critical times and places. The lessons of that physical landmark had soon been followed by a 'virtual workbench' in recovering lost moments in history through a combination of physical and virtual reconstructions.

Soon after the 'Perspective as practice' event and its sequel in Paris, the upcoming 'Year of Light' had occasioned an event in nearby Italy on 'Light' from different perspectives, one exposing Leo to both the bright and dark sides of studies on light and

[39] Edgerton, Mirror, Window, and Telescope, p. 154: 'Hariot'.

[40] Edgerton, Mirror, Window, and Telescope, p. 151: perspective tube; p. 159: Alberti's 'newly made-up Latin word for the instrument was perspicillum'; later translation: 'spy glass'.

[41] Edgerton, Renaissance Rediscovery, pp. 124–5: 'time machine'.

[42] The panorama installation of the ancient city of Pergamon and its architecture around 129AD: visit 14 October 2012; installation by Yadegar Asisi and Berlin state museums; Yadegar: 'living memory' in Persian. www.asisi.de/en/panorama/pergamon/

[43] www.smb.museum/en/museums-institutions/pergamonmuseum/home.html. The Ancient Metropolis of Pergamon in 360° view, on display after museum's opening May 2020 until 2024.

vision, and to the 'footpaths and footprints'[44] of key optical works beyond Ibn al-Haytham's. The visit to that heartland of the Renaissance Linear Perspective would then provide the invaluable occasion of a trip to Rome to visit the headquarters of a project with the fitting name of 'Perspectiva +'.[45] This was a digital platform self-defined on the project's website at the time with a description that extended from 'the reception and appropriation of Alhacen's *De Aspectibus*, or *Perspectiva*, the Latinised title of the *Optics* of Hasan Ibn al-Haytham' to one that 'integrated Latin manuscripts, printed editions and translations of Alhacen's treatise with historical and modern comments in the manner of a virtual workbench, enabling interdisciplinary research and collaboration for and between historians of science and art historians'. Leo's own perspective was never the same after touring the site of that unforgettable place with the director of the Perspectiva + project up to the roof of the project's headquarters in Rome:[46] there, against the breathtaking view of that city, the towering figure of Ibn al-Haytham, his brainchild, *Optics*, and its Latinised *Perspectiva* had far and wide reaches in and beyond Europe at various distances.

The next few years offered occasions for extensions and distinctions of such subjects through two presentations that Leo would contribute to in different ways. The first presentation, delivered in 2015 at a local university, had opened with the cover page of a book directed to the 'turn of the first millennium', where 'the year 1000 as a moment in history'[47] was centre-staged on the podium to extend it to 'Eastern cities' like Baghdad, not mentioned once in that entire book. The second presentation, followed in 2016 during the 50th anniversary of an academic 'association' in an adjacent city, had extended the timeframe and context. To the first presentation, titled 'A history duet and a science quartet',[48] Leo had contributed by extending their project's timelines and intersections to new players: for the part 'history duet', to two early historians from close to the Baghdad of the year 1000; and for the part 'science quartet', to authors on four closely related subjects. Together, these highlighted distinctions within history and science, fields whose overlaps were limited to things like the inability to say that something *would* happen again, only that it *may*, if it has happened before. The historians and scientists of the past had thus been cast as playing different tunes, just like their modern counterparts, where historians were more likely to be mindful of individual cases than scientists.

The follow-up presentation was titled 'Checkered history recolored',[49] with an eye on not only 'changing fortunes and misfortunes' involving both Islamic and European

44 Palermo, Sicily: November 9–11, 2013: Bloom and Blair (eds), God Is the Light of the Heavens and the Earth. Kheirandish, 'Light and dark', pp. 78–9: footpaths of the *Optics* of Ibn al-Haytham, Euclid and Ptolemy.

45 https://www.mpiwg-berlin.mpg.de/research/projects/1566_FG_Dupre_Perspectiva

46 Werner, Klaus E.: Biblioteca Hertziana (Max Planck Institute for Art History), Rome, Italy.

47 Lacey, Robert and Danziger, Danny, 'The year 1000 as a moment in history', in What Life Was Like at the Turn of the First Millennium: The Year 1000 (Boston, 1999).

48 Kheirandish, Elaheh, 'A history duet and a science quartet', joint presentation with Maryam Kamali, MIT: Cambridge, MA, 17 April, 2015. http://iranianmedievalhistory.com/index.php/aboutus.html

49 Kheirandish, Elaheh, '"Checkered history" recolored: The changing fortunes and misfortunes of optical works in Islamic and European lands', Middle East Studies Association (MESA), Boston: 19 November 2016 (Session: 'The legacy of A. I. Sabra': New perspectives on the history of science in Islam).

lands, but also 'New perspectives' opening the title of the conference session itself. Here, side by side images in two different colours had opened the presentation from an exhibition titled 'Homage to al-Hasan Ibn al-Haytham', the changing nature of historical evidence and its interpretation being captured through the changing colours of the opening image fittingly titled 'Hidden [is] in the Evident'.[50] The presentation's take-off point had been the expression 'checkered history' as coined by a recently deceased scholar whose legacy had been honoured there; and the landing premise, about the meanings and distinctions of words like 'chance' and 'circumstance'. The scholar being honoured, well known for his life's work on the writings of Ibn al-Haytham – one whose death, likened to the extinguishing of 'lamps of knowledge' and darkening of 'surviving minds', now applied to the closing of his own eyes – [51] had a legacy beyond what met the eyes: he had been quoted from an unpublished interview for having used words like luck, fortune and chance differently: the word 'luck' by saying Ibn al-Haytham 'was lucky his book came to be known in the West' and inspire 'people all the way down to the seventeenth-century'; the word 'fortune', by saying Ibn al-Haytham's Eastern commentator, Farisi, 'fortunately came, well late, but he came, and he did what he did, without which nobody would have known much about Ibn al-Haytham in the Islamic World';[52] and the word 'chance', used most distinctly by saying the book's 'profound influence on thirteenth-century European thinkers . . . at a time when it had hardly made an impression among Arabic reading scholars in the Islamic world must have been largely due to chance'.[53] Leo had left that session with bigger pictures than ever before, from minute differences between outcomes to shades of meaning between concepts like uniqueness and chance, topped by the scholar's own *implicit* noting of the uniqueness of historical moments, circumstances and events, and his *explicit* references to elements of chance, fortune and misfortune.

In the following year, Leo's slow inching in such directions were to be accelerated by several major leaps. First, a publication in 2016 of Ibn al-Haytham's important *Shape of the Eclipse*[54] written by him shortly after his much better-known *Optics*, had sparked a few new ideas. The newly published book on a work called a 'key milestone' in merging branches of optics and catoptrics, and the 'first experimental study' of the camera obscura – both long associated with later developments in Europe in science and art – had great timing for Leo's final chapter. The book's content 'inverted' images long held of the underexposed 'dark chambers' of developments in Islamic lands much earlier than in Europe through the very imagery of the 'camera obscura', itself exemplary of concepts and terms in the East before the West; and the author's imaginative methods cleverly approximated the date and place of Ibn al-Haytham's *Eclipse* composition by a combination of historical analysis, astronomical data, image projection, even modern eclipse predictors, lifting historical studies to higher levels.

50 'Hidden [is] in the evident' (al-Khafī fī al-Jalī), was the title of a calligraphic piece from the Exhibit: Homage to al-Hasan Ibn al-Haytham by artist Kamal Boullata, Dubai 2009.

51 Sabra, Optics of Ibn al-Haytham, Preface: 'Chequered history'; Session: 'Legacy of A. I. Sabra'; Kheirandish, 'Eloge: A. I. Sabra', pp, 281–2, and n. 1.

52 Kheirandish, 'Eloge: A. I. Sabra', partly based on an unpublished interview in 1993, Harvard University, p. 285.

53 Sabra, Optics of Ibn al-Haytham, Preface: Vol. 2, p. xi.

54 Raynaud, Ibn al-Haytham's On the Shape of the Eclipse, pp. 163–5: combined historical method.

Another major leap had come in the month of March of that same year: an inspiring 'Museum of lost objects'[55] had been broadcast to millions of viewers in an effort to use advancing technologies to immortalise destroyed monuments in recent 'trouble areas' of the world. To Leo, finely tuned to both digital technologies in historical studies and the role of chance in historical developments, the idea of a 'Museum of lost objects' and its powerful ring would spark the idea of a 'Museum of chances' showcasing various historical scenarios including lost chances. He already had parallel histories on the 'quartet' of geometry, astronomy, mechanics and optics, and how missing components in their development could be identified and communicated as 'missed chances'; how some could be analysed as missing books (in the case of geometry), missing tools (in the case of astronomy), missing routes (in the case of mechanics), and in the most critical case of optics, missing loops; and most of all, how timely it could be to have displays on various subjects, including cities like Baghdad and Isfahan, next to displays on other cities and settings in a 'Museum of chances'.

A few months before that summer of 2018, Leo had attended a presentation titled 'Virtual realities: Mapping fictional spaces',[56] one introducing a project with multiple points of interest for his own. Held at the rare book library where Leo had once contributed to an 'Early science' exhibit, the presentation had been eye-opening on several fronts. Besides letting him stand as a viewer rather than exhibitor, and experiencing a cutting edge technology firsthand, he had been attracted to two features of that project that always won him over: to its subject as 'a virtual reality game' where a book is the main subject, and a city, a major character;[57] and to its method as an 'excursion' into extensions of 'digital humanities' by not only reconstructing places lost to time, but recreating combined virtual experiences in real time.[58] Leo could never forget the voice of the Project director, a literature professor in a nearby college chronicling his class's reconstruction of a virtual city from a classic book;[59] nor the demos of his students with virtual reality goggles from the school's 'lab' to expose new audiences to both the book and the city's virtual walking tours. But the presentation had been especially valuable to Leo in projecting a realistic picture of the infancy of such technologies, and their suitability for applications to his own two-city project: 'We are at the edge of VR', the presenter had been quoted as saying about virtual reality in a write-up:[60] 'There is no guidance for this. What we have produced has been purely out of our imagination'.

55 'Museum of Lost Objects is an attempt to preserve the memory of a few of the thousands of ancient treasures'. https://www.pri.org/stories/2016-03-04/welcome-museum-lost-objects-remembering-winged-bull-nineveh

56 Nugent, Joseph, 'Professor in Boston College', 'Landmarks: Maps as literary illustration': Harvard University Houghton Library, 27 February 2018. https://houghton75.org/?event=virtual-realities-mapping-fictional-spaces

57 The book is James Joyce's Ulysses, and the city, Dublin, Ireland.

58 'Grand and preposterous: Can gamification help you learn about "Ulysses"?: BC's "Joycestick" team is keen to find out', Humanities/Literature – Published: 17 January, 2017. www.bc.edu/bc-web/bcnews/humanities/literature/joycestick-ulysses-nugent.html

59 Wolters, Benjamin, 'Joycestick: BC professor and students take on virtual reality', BC News, 21 November 2016. www.bcgavel.com/2016/11/21/joycestick-bc-professor-students-take-virtual-reality

60 Marcelo, Philip, 'Turning James Joyce's "Ulysses" into a virtual reality game', Associated Press, 18 March 2017, quoting director Joseph Nugent about being 'at the edge of VR', with 'no guidance. . .'. www.telegram.com/news/20170317/turning-ulysses-into-virtual-reality-game-at-boston-college

Imagination, Leo had. But such sobering words tossing limitations at him in no uncertain terms were tilting him in directions where his finite time and resources could be saved for the most immediate opportunities and technologies at hand. At their forefront was a creative online course titled 'Prediction', with a caption-rich timeline called 'Path to Newton',[61] to which Leo had made contributions through his mentor's 'module' in that course. He had been asked to contribute to the coverage of the Islamic Middle Ages in that module with surprisingly little demand of his technical expertise or of the 'timelines' he had long helped develop. Picking premodern scholars in Arab and Persian lands to fit into a 'Path to Newton' had not been much of a challenge. But the question of a single theme binding those scholars to each other and to that 'Path' had taken precious time. A key theme to be singled out as such had oscillated in his mind, from celestial and terrestrial motion in astronomy and mechanics, to geometrical and experimental proof in geometry and optics. In an 'aha moment' rarely experienced by him as intensely, the idea had crystallised that the brightest moments of the sciences were all sparked by the 'critical thinking' of their practitioners in some form; how could his mind have missed such an idea? Once there, various forms of critical thinking were to line up one by one to be considered for the soon launching 'Path to Newton' link.

The earliest and best forms of critical thinking had first come to Leo from a quotation magnified on the walls of a museum meeting him literally in the eye as he had stood before it. The museum, which was the host of several summer schools in Istanbul participated in by Leo and a number of international students and junior scholars, had a catalogue which had caught Leo's attention for its statements about the museum's commitment to the history of science and technology for representing 'a common heritage of mankind'.[62] But it had been under the heading 'Emphasis on a critical attitude' in that catalogue that a statement about critical thinking from a so-called 'Ibn al-Haitham' rang a bell, however differently worded:[63] that 'whoever studies the works of science must . . . transform himself into a critic of everything he reads . . . question them from all angles and aspects . . . also observe himself with a critical eye'. That statement was so far ahead of its time that even with the insertion of the word 'critical' into the original, the 'thinking' behind that statement fit well into a 'Path to Newton', along with other cases picked by Leo for making it to that 'Path'.[64]

While searching for the historical senses and forms of critical thinking, Leo had found notable statements by other outstanding scholars: from scholars like Ibn Sina and Biruni, closer to Ibn al-Haytham's own time and place, statements in the form of 'educating oneself to find acceptable teachings',[65] and 'conducting fresh examinations

[61] Goodman, Alyssa A. 'The Prediction Project: The Past and Present of the Future' includes 'a set of modular "courses" on edX': https://predictionx.org/. And 'Path to Newton': https://path-to.org/newton.html

[62] Sezgin, Istanbul Museum, p. 15, opening: 'history of science and technology represents a common heritage of mankind'; exhibits reconstructed in Goethe University's Institute for the history of Arabic-Islamic science', based on historical sources.

[63] Sezgin, Istanbul Museum, p. 21, Heading: 'Ibn al-Haytham's emphasis on a critical attitude towards the use of the sources'; Wall: 'enemy of what he reads' translated there as 'critic of everything he reads'.

[64] Critical thinking selections submitted to the Path to Newton project.

[65] Ibn Sīnā: 'I would listen to them and comprehend what they were saying, but my soul would not accept it': 'Autobiography', in Gutas, Avicenna and the Aristotelian Tradition, p. 22.

and collaborations';[66] and from later scholars like Tusi and Farisi, statements in the form of 'cross-disciplinary principles yielding innovative work',[67] and 'contradictions to experience leading to controlled experimentation'.[68] But while all these reflected mostly methodological, rather than critical, thinking, an exception overshadowed them through a startling statement by a slightly later Qushji, one unthinkable to have come from a premodern scholar, namely rejecting the 'claim' that any one 'explanation represents the only possible one'.[69] Here, the context being the argument that 'nothing false follows from the assumption of a rotating Earth',[70] a 'path' had been directly drawn in Leo's mind not only to Newton working out the celestial and terrestrial motions for such assumptions in the Europe of post-1750s, but to points in common between Qushji and both the earlier Ibn al-Haytham and later Newton. These scholars had all made major breakthroughs through different forms of critical thinking, those away from feigned 'hypotheses', and towards verifiable theories: in the case of Ibn al-Haytham, away from the hypothesis of visual-rays; in the case of Qushji, of a stationary Earth; and in the case of Newton, an Earth-centred universe. They had also broken ground in changing focus from subjective to objective realms: Ibn al-Haytham's 'rays' originating not from a subject's eye, but from outside sources; Qushji's Earth, not being stationary as subjectively 'sensed', but rotating among other possibilities; and Newton's universe having a centre other than Earth regardless of anything being 'observed'. The more Leo had thought critically about such cases, the more progress he had made; and the more objective his thoughts had become, the further the centres of his own thoughts had moved away from himself.

Such thoughts and experiences were taken to the next stage of Leo's work in the form of contributions to a presentation titled 'Paths and chances in early science',[71] one to cast its reach beyond Baghdad and Isfahan to showcase early science in its bright and dark paths as well as their won and lost chances. The physical site of that presentation would be the birthplace of the previously launched 'Around the world' project in the Museum of history of science and technology in Istanbul, the city of all

[66] Bīrūnī, 'It is obligatory upon the servant of knowledge . . . to avoid whatever differs from established fact' . . . 'puzzle . . . is an incentive for a fresh examination and observations': Rosenthal, 'On some epistemological and methodological presuppositions of Al-Biruni', in Science and Medicine in Islam: A Collection of Essays, Vol. 12 (Aldershot, 1991), pp. 145–56.

[67] Ṭūsī: 'Every science has . . . principles, which are either self-evident, or obscure, in which case they are proved in another science . . . The solution to this doubt (in astronomy) has been put forward by none of the practitioners of this science': Ragep, Ṭūsī's Memoir on Astronomy, Vol. 1, p. 90.

[68] Fārisī: 'I read in the writings of more than one of the leading thinkers [premises] . . . was at a loss where these rules came from . . . contrary to experience': Sabra, '"Commentary" that saved the text', pp. 131–3.

[69] Qūshjī: we should 'have confidence that the heavens normally follow a regular pattern that we have the capacity to explain. We do not, however, need to make the further claim that our explanation represents the only possible one': Ragep, ''Alī Qushjī [sic.] and Regiomontanus', pp. 359–71 (includes full Arabic text).

[70] Qūshjī: 'it is not established that what has a principle of rectilinear inclination is prevented from [having] circular motion . . . Thus nothing false [fāsid] follows [from the assumption of a rotating Earth]': Ragep, 'Freeing Astronomy from Philosophy', p. 68.

[71] Kheirandish, Elaheh, 'Paths and chances in early science', Istanbul's Museum for the History of Science and Technology in Islam, venue: wing of the director, Detlev Quintern, 25 September 2018. https://www.scholar.harvard.edu/ekheirandish/projects

manuscripts of Ibn al-Haytham's *Optics*, and the critical years of Qushji.[72] With 'future' being at the forefront of Leo's mind, the displays being prepared were to be titled after some forward-looking works of the past. The presentation's subtitle, 'Forward into the past', was used before for a documentary short as the reversed title of the futuristic film 'Back to the Future'[73] based on the classic *Time Machine* by H. G. Wells.[74] Here, other 'Wells' titles took new turns as captions for images introducing the 'path and chance' displays: the opening display featured the 'traveling' exhibit 'Around the world with early science' through the image of the revolving *Calendar of Timekeeping* (Plate 9), captioned as *Wheels of Chance*[75] for dialing key times and places; six displays then followed with the acronyms of the title 'Around the world with early science', used for the displays' successive titles and supplied with well-matched images and Wells-inspired captions: *Tales of Space and Time*[76] captioned the *A*bout display for pointing to 'paths and chances' through parallel panoramas of Baghdad and Isfahan from an early modern European sketch (Plate 10); *A Vision of the Past*[77] captioned the *T*imeline display for transmitting knowledge about transmission of knowledge through historical micromaps from 750 through 1750 (Plate 11); *A Wonderful Visit*[78] captioned the *W*orldmap display, through a historical map with cities of Baghdad and Isfahan (Plate 12) representing footpaths of works; *The Rediscovery of the Unique*[79] captioned the *W*eblink display with the cover of the Latin *Perspectiva* (Plate 13) representing footprints of words; *Shape of Things to Come*[80] captioned the *E*vents display, through the image of twelve zodiac constellations (Plate 14) dating evidence-based events like an upcoming 'Cities of stars' presentation; and *Through a Window*[81] captioned the *S*ources display, through the image of a combined book and lens camera obscura (Plate 15) representing multiple outlooks.

The closing Wells title was *Meanwhile*, captioning open-ended 'Around the world' displays with Moon, Sun, Star and Timekeeping Calendar icons (Plate 16) to capture timeless ideas from the author of the *Time Machine*: that for 'the Great Age that comes … we ought to do all that we could to increase knowledge', as it were,

[72] On all manuscripts of Ibn al-Haytham's Optics in Istanbul libraries: Sabra, Optics of Ibn al-Haytham, Vol. 2, pp. lxxx–lxxxi; On Qushjī: Ragep, 'Freeing Astronomy from Philosophy', p. 61.

[73] 'The timeless classic original: A worldwide cultural phenomenon … Back to the Future launched one of the most successful franchises in Universal's history. . .' www.backtothefuture.com/

[74] Wells, H. G., Time Machine, 1895: Encyclopedia Britannica. https://www.britannica.com/biography/H-G-Wells

[75] Wells, H. G., The Wheels of Chance, 1897: a 'Cycling Romance', Jacqueline Banerjee, Associate Editor, Victorian Web: www.victorianweb.org/authors/wells/wheels.html

[76] Wells, H. G., Tales of Space and Time, 1899: Encyclopedia Britannica. https://www.britannica.com/biography/H-G-Wells

[77] Wells, H. G., A Vision of the Past, 1887: The Literary Elitist. http://literaryelitist.blogspot.com/2015/06/review-vision-of-past-by-h-g-wells.html

[78] Wells, H. G., A Wonderful Visit, 1895: Encyclopedia Britannica. https://www.britannica.com/biography/H-G-Wells

[79] Wells, H. G., The Rediscovery of the Unique, 1887: The Fortnightly Review. https://fortnightlyreview.co.uk/2017/08/the-rediscovery-of-the-unique/

[80] Wells, H. G., Shape of Things to Come, 1933: Project Gutenberg. http://gutenberg.net.au/ebooks03/0301391h.html

[81] Wells, H. G., Through a Window, 1934: Fantastic Fiction. www.fantasticfiction.com/w/h-g-wells/through-a-window.htm

'meanwhile'.[82] Such creative titles and words had made Leo mindful of various forms of critical thinking; but from that futuristic author of titles like the *Rediscovery of the Unique* had also come vital lines about concepts as ageless as 'uniqueness', that 'when a man speaks of a thousand years, the suspicion never crosses his mind that he is referring to a unique series of unique gyrations'; that he is hit with an 'arithmetical virus' when 'he lets a watch and a calendar blind him to the fact that every moment of his life is a miracle and a mystery'.[83]

For Leo, also mindful of verses as timeless as being 'involved with past and future', next to paths 'never taken', doors 'never opened',[84] the name of the game had long been continuity, and its path, technology. His project could now combine its fast-forward into the past, with the laser-focused demands of the future; and the seven wings of his 'traveling portal' could spread over time in exporting digital displays into more and more physical sites.

The physical, digital, textual, and visual displays of the 'Around the world' exhibit would combine to turn Leo's task from narrating the story of early science through a 'dialogue' between Baghdad and Isfahan into reconstructions beyond science and the city. While in Istanbul, Leo had visited an exhibit reproducing the contents of a book about that city's own recent history with various objects exhibited from that book to capture the many lost aspects of a city. The 'Museum of innocence',[85] as that exhibit and book were titled, had sparked Leo's imagination in the same way a 'Museum of lost objects' had done more recently, as the preserver of objects that for his project had both a much longer history and more than one lost city. The combination would inspire Leo to conceive of a 'Museum of chances' involving more than his two cities, one to showcase not only 'won and lost' chances, but also 'living and lasting chances' of cities themselves. The popular genre of 'pop-up' venues emerging in all forms and shapes around the world would then occasion the extension of the 'Around the world' exhibit to a 'pop-up' museum, one to make a once 'young student' and 'co-curator', along with viewers beyond his age, place and gender, more linked to matters ranging from the long reaches of history to the fast-forwards of technology.

If Leo's own past was mostly spent on piecing together bigger pictures from microscopic details, he wanted his future to be part of grander visions, both in and out of the academy. In promoting wider and wider exposures, onsite and online, in and beyond libraries and museums, across the country, and around the world, he had a

[82] Wells, H. G., Meanwhile (London: Ernest Benn Ltd., 1927). Kessinger; Project Gutenberg. http://gutenberg.ca/ebooks/wellshg-meanwhile/wellshg-meanwhile-00-h-dir/wellshg-meanwhile-00-h.html

[83] Wells, H. G., The Rediscovery of the Unique, 1887: The Fortnightly Review. https://fortnightlyreview.co.uk/2017/08/the-rediscovery-of-the-unique/

[84] Elliot, T. S., Four Quartets (New York, 1943): Burnt Norton (No. 1 of 'Four Quartets'):
'Time present and time past, are both perhaps present in time future,
And time future contained in time past, if all time is eternally present. . .
What might have been and what has been, point to one end, which is always present.
Footfalls echo in the memory, down the passage which we did not take
Towards the door we never opened'.
www.davidgorman.com/4quartets/1-norton.htm

[85] Pamuk, Orham, Museum of Innocence, 29 August, 2008: Kennedy, J. Michael, 'Turkish writer opens museum based on novel', New York Times, 29 April, 2012. www.nytimes.com/2012/04/30/books/orhan-pamuk-opens-museum-based-on-his-novel-in-istanbul.html

hope and a dream. His hope was to link the old and the new, the East and the West, and any other 'divides' from physical to digital. His dream was a common language for understanding and for strengthening not just the 'humanities', but 'humanity' itself. Leo thus gave voices to his two cities, to express his hopes and dreams.
Baghdad started with rhyming verses:

If the way to predict the future, Is 'invent', and not to foresee,
Should the story of our long history, Not be told by both you and me?
Are we not from the land of poets? The creators of 'perfect beings'?
Could we not enrich our stories, With a pair of 'perfecting' wings?
Like the wings of the guardian angel, In the Wonderful Life on the screens
What he wrote the past of life with, We could write, the future ones with.
Should we not erase, forever, The divide between all 'you' and 'me's?
Should we not bring, all attention, Not to hu'man's, but rather to 'being's?

Isfahan followed with matching verses:

Are we not from the land of hybrids? Where the she-sun meets the he-lion,
Are they not, at once, the she-he, With no walls, or shades in between?
Are we not from the land of weavers, From the 'thousand and one', to one dream?
Should we not have the threads of future, From the finest ones, ever to weave?
Should we weave, the name of all heroes, To the cover of our 'Book of Kings'?
Should the youth of the future centuries, Not be riding on 'East and West' wings?
Were we not to be blessed, as cities? With the scale of mountains and seas?
Should the story of our long history, Not be known to all 'you' and 'me's.[86]

Leo's final narrative of a thousand years would feature each city within the distinctions and fluctuations of their respective ages, to project more than one message: that in the story of the early sciences, no one indicator contributed to their highs or lows to the exclusion of others; that besides roots, routes, rules, and books next to schools, tools, and loops, there were 'outlooks' as another key indicator of outcomes; and that for cases in and beyond the cities on display, more was at play than bright and dark paths, and won and lost chances involving them all.

The seventh chapter of Leo's project would thus start with a dialogue between 'chess and backgammon', followed by a mediator to represent the constant interplay of plan and chance in the outcomes of early science. A contest between chess and backgammon, associated with ancient India and Persia,[87] had already been brought to life in a story in the *Book of Kings* of around the year 1000 (Plate 8); a historical dialogue between them was also placed by Leo next to chess and backgammon sets in their 'Early science' exhibit, where black and white pieces stood for day and night, their number at 30, for days of the month, and the combined sum of the dice from 7 to 12, for days of the week

[86] Kheirandish, Elaheh, 'Creature of the next century', composed at the turn of the twenty-first century.
[87] Brunner, Christopher J., 'The Middle Persian explanation of chess and invention of backgammon', The Journal of the Ancient Near Eastern Society of Columbia University, 11 (1979), pp. 43–51. Daryayee, T., 'Mind, body and the cosmos: Chess and backgammon in ancient Persia', Iranian Studies, 35, 4, pp. 281–312.

and months of the year. Through the confluence of such ideas Leo would invent a combined game called 'ancients', based on games in and beyond ancient chess and backgammon, and their respective lessons of plan and chance.[88] He would aim to direct skills like strategy to probability and randomness as subjects increasingly more important to the future, those already exposing him to concepts not just from university-linked platforms like the future of humanity, society, life or people with fast-forward challenges,[89] but to the future of history and historiography through applications of technology with their own forwards into the past. Through these, Leo would gather that a combination of plan and chance, as applied to the patterns of the past, could also be applied to the problems of the future; and that the greatest gifts of his generation were not only chance encounters of the past, but also planned ones of the future. His plans for his final chapter would accordingly change by representing Baghdad and Isfahan not just as figures and settings associated with each through time, but as cities next to others, from 'Cities of stars' to stars in a 'Museum of chances'.

Chapter 7: 'Dialogue' of Chess and Backgammon
Up and Down Bends – Loops
By Charles Leo Scribner, March 2016

[*Backgammon:*] *I am the game, named, 'nard',*
Who is unique, with the highest of ranks. . .
[*Chess:*] *I am that chess, who is the soother of hearts*
The eye of the wise and stretcher of minds.
Khwarazmi, S., 'Dialogue of Chess and Backgammon', ca. 1300s, Persian edition: Pourjavady, N., English translation: Elaheh Kheirandish[90]

[*Mediator:*] *Fate is like cubic dice, strategy, like the game,*
It is in your hands, yet, not in your hands.
Amuli, *Nafa'is al-Funun* (attribution), Tafadduli, A., *Takhtih Nard*, opening verse, English translation: Elaheh Kheirandish[91]

88 'Ancients' is a hybrid of chess, backgammon, and real time strategy games: it involves characters called heroes who navigate the chess board through a mixture of tactics and probabilities in order to increase their advantage; the game's digital version involves dice rolls, and the combination of strategy and chance helps players understand probabilistic risks and complex strategies; game description by Esam Goodarzy (inventor).

89 Future of Humanity Institute: Oxford University. www.fhi.ox.ac.uk/. Future Society: Harvard University. https://thefuturesociety.org/. Future of Life Institute: Massachusetts Institute of Technology. https://futureoflife.org/. Future of People: inaugural conference, MIT, 2016 included a 'FastForward Challenge' to build various scenarios in 40 to 50 years; audience award recipients: Esam Goodarzy and Marie-Therese Png.

90 Khwarazmī, 'Munāẓirih-i Shaṭranj va Nard', Pourjavady (ed), Kheirandish, Elaheh (tr, excerpts):
'Man gar-chih bih nām dar zabān-hā nard-am,
Dar avval-i bāzī az nishān-hā fard-am. . .
Shaṭranj man-am kih ranj-i dil-hā bibar-am,
Maḥbūb-i dil u dīdih-i ahl-i naẓar-am'.

91 Tafaḍḍulī, Aḥmad, Takhtih Nard: Taqdīr yā Tadbīr (Tehran, 1382 [2003]), reference: Khosrow Tousi; opening verse attribution: 'Muḥammad ibn Maḥmūd Āmulī, ṣāḥib-i [author of] Nafā'is al-Funūn', Kheirandish, Elaheh (tr, excerpt):
'Taqdīr chu ka'batayn u tadbīr chu nard,
Dar dast-i tu hast, līk dar dast-i tu nīst. . .'

7.3 *An Arab City with Living Traces*

Look, therefore, at our works when we are gone...

It was the fall of 2019, and Baghdad held a central place in a presentation titled 'Cities of stars' held at the beautiful historic palaces of Istanbul under a full moon at the turn of spring into summer,[92] where light shining over the surrounding domes and tiled ceilings kept many eyes half-fixed on the sky. Presented as part of a panel in an international symposium, 'Cities of stars' shared new findings about the historical relations, and changing relations, of astronomy and optics, the two sciences most directly involved with observations and experiments, leading to a so-called Scientific Revolution in early modern Europe. But despite the fixed focus of 'Cities of stars' on those two sciences through the lens of cities having either authors on both subjects, or links with observatories and observation sites, the study's coverage of time and place was far and wide: in time, a period of seven centuries separating the 1700s of the 'early modern' West from developments in the East as early as around the year 1000; and in place, seven cities qualified for such a title, with Baghdad next to six others from Isfahan, Maragha, and Tabriz of the first half of that period, to Samarqand, Istanbul and Padua of its second half. Within the seven-century, seven-city, time and place dials of the presentation's rotating displays, Baghdad stood at the centre of them all for a key role in not just developments, but also non-developments. Piece after piece of evidence showcased Baghdad in the relations between astronomy and optics, and the central role of that city and its authors in that relation through something as critical to both disciplines as the treatments of a single law: that of 'refraction'.

'Cities of stars' had proceeded with an atypical chronology for the occurrence of events, starting with Galileo in Padua of the early 1600s. Not because Galileo wrote on both astronomy and optics, nor because his consequential observations were first performed in Padua; but because of his explicit statements about the role of not just vision, but also vision through refraction in his novel combination of principle from optics and instrumentations from astronomy. Galileo's *Starry Messenger*, published in March 1610 shortly after his critical observations with a self-made telescope in Jan 1610, was the first to be quoted in that presentation for its discrete, yet revealing statements: that the 'theory of refraction' had been the basis of his 'invention of a spyglass' following a Flemish construction 'by means of which visible objects, though very distant from the eye ... were distinctly seen as if nearby'; and that 'observations repeated many times had 'led to opinions and convictions' through his 'own eyes',[93] in

[92] Kheirandish, 'Cities of Stars: The historical relations of optics and astronomy', International Symposium for the History of Science in Islam, Istanbul University, 15 June 2019. https://www.scholar.harvard.edu/ekheirandish/projects

[93] Galileo Galilei, Sidereus Nuncius (Starry Messenger) (Venice, 1610), Drake (tr), pp. 28–9: 'a report reached my ears that a certain Flemish had constructed a spyglass by means of which visible objects, though very distant from the eye ... were distinctly seen as if nearby ... which caused me to apply myself wholeheartedly to inquire into [how] I might arrive at the invention of a similar instrument. This I did shortly afterwards, my basis being the theory of refraction'. Galileo's observations: 7 Jan.–2 Mar., first in Padua.

this case, aided vision. Here, the display included the full text of Galileo's famous words that 'we have not just one planet, Moon, revolving around another, Earth, while both run around a great orbit around the Sun; our own eyes show us four stars that wander around Jupiter as does the Moon around the Earth'. What was highlighted next went beyond Galileo's use of an advanced instrument or repeated observation records, but the role of the city of Padua in this fascinating story. Another Italian city mentioned in this connection was Venice, where Galileo had first heard about the 'device to make distant objects appear closer' in his visit in July 1609, before the 'simultaneous arrival' of such a device in Padua making him rush back there to learn that the carrier of the device had left for Venice. Even before Galileo's own construction of such a device as a nine-power telescope by August 1609, and a thirty-power one by the end of that year before he turned his self-made telescope to the sky in January 1610, there was a strong Padua link. The next display shared new, eye-opening evidence about Galileo's optics-related training in that city as early as 1580s. This came from a modern specialist arguing against widespread assumptions about Galileo's limited interest and experience in optics-related fields, unveiling case after case to the contrary, and stressing the role of practical traditions in works published in the same year as that presentation.[94]

As a transition to other 'Cities of stars', and their earlier roles in developments and non-developments alike, the Galileo displays had closed with the historical observation that, had Galileo not understood rules of refraction, like some of his predecessors, the nature or order of events would have been different; and had authors in cities to the east of Padua had enough understanding of those rules and their applications, they may have been closer to reaching the stars in ways still more fitting for the designation 'Cities of stars'.

The story had started with the unusual case of how a simple optical principle like the 'reflection' of light at polished surfaces like mirrors had been mistranslated in the Arabic translation of the *Optics* of Euclid[95] by a term standard for 'refraction', a term only applicable to the principle of refraction of light through transparent mediums like water or glass, not polished surfaces. This translation had unintentionally produced an erroneous form of the 'law of refraction' in which the angle of refraction through water or glass was wrongly made 'equal to' the angle of incidence, instead of 'smaller than' it, through its bend inside a denser medium. Tusi's later *Recension of Euclid's Optics* had added that problematic principle to the definitions of his own widely circulated book and contributed to later 'puzzles', in the words of the observant corrector of that slip, Kamal al-Din Farisi.[96]

Farisi, working in Tabriz of the early 1300s, had used the word 'puzzled' for confusions over treatments of the equality of the angles of incidence and *refraction*, instead of *reflection*, terms with close transcriptions in Arabic and Persian. Farisi's words in that connection now projected on the screen of the 'Cities of stars' presentation had a hint at Tusi: that Farisi had 'read in the writings of more than one of the leading

94 Dupré, Sven, 'Ausonio's mirrors and Galileo's lenses: The telescope and sixteenth-century practical optical knowledge', Galilaeana, 2 (2005), pp. 145–80; 'How-to optics', in Sven Dupré (ed), Perspective as Practice: Renaissance Cultures of Optics (Turnhout, 2019), pp. 279–300.

95 Kheirandish, Arabic Version of Euclid's Optics, Vol. 2, p. 56 and n. 200; pp. 58–9 and the related notes.

96 Kheirandish, 'Puzzle of Ṭūsī's optical works'; 'Light and dark'.

thinkers' about the faulty premise of the equality of the angles of refraction and incidence, 'contrary to experience'; that he 'was at a loss to find where these rules came from'; and that his teacher, and Tusi's student Qutb Din Shirazi, brought Farisi from 'distant lands' a book attributed to Ibn al-Haytham on optics that Shirazi had seen 'in his youth in one of the libraries of Fars', Persia.

Here Baghdad of around the year 1000 was first highlighted for both developments and non-developments regarding the critically important 'law of refraction', based on which not only lenses but combinations of convex lenses and concave mirrors were key for later telescopic magnifications. Developments were through the treatment of the principle after the year 1000 in an *Optics* by Ibn al-Haytham widely transmitted to Europe; and non-developments through the non-transmission of the *Optics* of both Ptolemy and Ibn al-Haytham, as well as the non-standard treatment of that principle in a mistranslation of the earlier *Optics* of Euclid before the year 1000. Cases like Maragha and Tabriz of the 1200s and 1300s were next highlighted through authors like Tusi and Farisi who had not just worked in those cities with recorded observations, but written on both optics and astronomy, with documentations of the problematic treatments of refraction.

Then came cases from Samarqand to Istanbul of the 1400s and 1500s, cities endowed with observatories like the earlier Maragha, in addition to later authors on optics and astronomy, from Kashi in Samarqand to Qushji in both Samarqand and Istanbul. Through the evidence of Kashi's letter from Samarqand to Kashan,[97] one display captured his adherence to the 'visual ray issuing from the eyes' long-disproved by Ibn al-Haytham. The case of Qushji then followed, with a display on the problematic treatment of double vision by even that 'highest of scholars', as Qushji was described in a Persian anonymous treatise dateable to the early 1500s through its naming of the Ottoman Sultan Selim the first.

The 'Cities of stars' had next turned to the presentation's host city of Istanbul, a city where more than one author on optics and astronomy had worked till the late 1500s, before the unfortunate rise and fall of the city's impressive observatory around 1580. Here, questions included the role of concepts no less critical than that of refraction when it came to groundbreaking developments, concepts belonging to aspects of optics involving mirrors and lenses, respectively called catoptrics and dioptrics since Greek antiquity. The earliest of the three authors from Istanbul selected for display was Miram Čelebi, whose work on the rainbow referred to Ibn al-Haytham's treatises on that subject, but his tests with raindrops undergoing double refraction suggested access to Ibn al-Haytham's *Treatise on Rainbow*,[98] not to his *Book of Optics*. The displays on the next two authors contained statements related to catoptrics and dioptrics from the early and late parts of the 1500s respectively, which were not only revealing, but

[97] Bagheri, Az Samarqand bih Kāshān, p. 39: 'khaṭṭ-i shuʿāʿ-ī kih az baṣar-i ū khārij shav-ad'; Bagheri, 'Newly found letter', p. 244: 'the visual ray that issue from his eyes. . .'

[98] Fazlıoğlu, İhsan, 'Mīram Čelebī: Maḥmūd ibn Quṭb al-Dīn Muḥammad ibn Muḥammad ibn Mūsā Qāḍīzāde', The Biographical Encyclopedia of Astronomers (BEA) (2007), pp. 788–9. http://islamsci.mcgill.ca/RASI/BEA/Miram_BEA.htm. Čelebi, Mīram, Risāla fī Qaws Quzah wa al-Hāla; Ibn al-Haytham, al-Hāla wa Qaws Quzah, unpublished manuscript, Istanbul, details and folios: Kheirandish, 'Light and dark', p. 70.

astonishing. From the anonymous author of a text from the early 1500s, a display was presented with a puzzling passage from a Persian treatise titled *Vision of Objects through Constructed Mirrors*,[99] next to its Arabic version: there, the author 'saw a mirror in the hands of some travellers, one that if held close to one's face, the face would appear in its natural state; if held further away, as reflected or inverted; and if in an intermediate position, not appear at all'; given that such mirrors were stated to have been sent atypically from Europe further east for 'experiment and testing', the passage stood out for exchanges on practical knowledge and relevant works on catoptrics in particular, regardless of its unknown author and date. The next display followed on the subject of dioptrics, this time from a text by Taqi al-Din ibn Maʿruf on *Vision* where the closing folio included a no less startling passage: there, Taqi al-Din could be read in one of the manuscripts reportedly in his own hands, that he 'made a transparent glass'[100] through which one sees from far distances discrete objects like a thin new moon or hardly visible ship. A more interpretive translation of that same passage had it as Taqi-al-Din's 'construction of a crystal with two lenses displaying in detail the objects from long distances': that problematic translation was added to stress that regardless of a more correct, literal, translation of that passage, or understanding of its part about the tower of Alexandria, the relevance of the works of an author working in 16th-century Istanbul cannot be separated from either the activities of an observatory there, however short-lived, or comparable cases elsewhere, including 16th-century Europe.

The last displays before returning full circle to Padua in an increasingly rich period in Europe during the 16th and 17th centuries had presented the curious case of Isfahan as the last of the seven 'Cities of stars' covered in that presentation. The Isfahan displays had adopted a fittingly poetic tone by opening its case with a Persian verse from 17th-century Isfahan, one through which the problematic understanding of indirect or mediated vision could be captured and framed for broader audiences: six beautifully calligraphed and illuminated verses were projected with a magnification of a verse datable to the year 1057, for 1647, according to the closing hemistich inscribed on that 'most auspicious of the world's buildings', one named 'Forty Pillars' for doubling twenty reflected on water:

> *So high is its reach into the sphere of the stars,*
> *That the Pleiades appears as a pebble at the bottom of a stream.*[101]

[99] Persian treatise, Arabic title: Risālah fī sabab ruʾyat al-ashyāʾ wa bayān al-madhāhib fīhi wa bayān ruʾyat al-ashyāʾ fī'l-marāyā al-maṣnuʿah; Arabic treatise, Risālah fī al-manāẓir: Kheirandish, 'From Maragha to Samarqand', Appendix: V–VI, pp. 176–7.

[100] Ibn Maʿrūf, Taqī al-Dīn, Kitāb Nūr hadaqat al-ibṣār . . .: Oxford, Bodleian, Marsh 119, fol. 82b–83a, 982 H (unpublished): 'I made a crystal (billūra) through which we see discrete objects from a distance like a thin new moon or ships' tears . . . as Greek sages had made and placed in the tower of Alexandria'; a less literal translation is given in Topdemir, Hüseyin Gazi, 'Taqi al-Din ibn Ma̲ʿruf and the Science of Optics', Muslim Heritage, 15 July 2008, cites the same passage (folio 81b is an error): 'I made a crystal (billawr) that has two lenses displaying in details the objects from long distances. . .'. https://muslimheritage.com/taqi-al-din-sci-optics-light-vision/

[101] Babaie, Safavid Palaces at Isfahan, pp. 319–20: '*Mubārak tarīn-i banā-hā-yi dunyā*'; pp. 317–38: '*Zi bas rafʿat-ash bar sipihr-i kavākib, Namā-yad chu rīg-i tah-i jū thurayā*'. Chihil Sutūn (Forty Pillars) is a prominent historical monument in Isfahan in the 'Naqsh-i Jahān' square. https://archnet.org/sites/2711

These verses magnified on the first Isfahan display were selected to do more than capture the poor understanding of magnified appearances through transparent mediums, those like examples of a piece of grape in water[102] persisting as late as the 17th century, despite the earlier treatments of Ptolemy and Ibn al-Haytham. They were to highlight an especially notable time in the story of early science through the inscribed text and date of that poem on a monument embodying mediated appearances, in this case doubling the number of the pillars of the famous 'Chihil Sutun'. A piece of evidence exposed for the first time anywhere in that context then followed through a little known story.

As that story had been presented, three years before the inscription of those verses in 1647, a visitor from France, a Catholic named Raphaël du Mans,[103] had entered Isfahan as one of many Europeans visiting that prosperous city. In his visit, that Frenchman had recorded a list of books on early science present at the library of his Persian host, one that included a single title with a long and puzzling history few could have known about. The title of that book as given by the Frenchman was the 'perspective of Ebne al-heissen', to mean the *Optics* of Ibn al-Haytham, a title that created further puzzles for being given there not in its original Arabic, *Manazir*, but in the Latin form *Perspectiva*, the only form the French du Mans must have known. This was different from the earlier Isfahan visitor, Della Valle, the Italian who came there with his Christian wife from Baghdad and was fluent in Arabic, Persian and Turkish.[104] The next Isfahan displays were devoted to the puzzle of how and how long the 'Optics' book had been present in Isfahan, and how its recorded presence as late as the 17th-century in at least Persian lands had not affected better treatments of vision and refraction for scholars from Ibn Sina to Shaykh Baha᾽i; and most curiously, when Shirazi was bringing from 'distant lands' the 'two thick volumes' of Ibn al-Haytham's *Optics* that he had seen in Fars for his student Farisi,[105] was the book sitting in nearby Isfahan at the time? Regarding someone as late as Shaykh Baha᾽i living in early 17th-century Isfahan, a related puzzle was also how he or his rich library could have been unaffected by the presence of that book, and whether it had been there all along. The presentation being given in Istanbul, a question orchestrated with a reverence to that city, and the newly discovered record of the same work in 16th-century Istanbul,[106] had followed as to how long the recorded book, with all its manuscripts still in Istanbul, may have been in that city.

All such questions had been built up to close the presentation with a finale, about a limited relation in the Islamic lands of the Middle Ages and Early Modern periods, between not only theory and practice, including the 'long route to the invention of the telescope,[107] but also between astronomy and optics themselves; and that the two subjects, and their relation, had been as much affected by limited communications as

[102] Kheirandish, Arabic Version of Euclid's Optics, Vol. 2, p. 56 and n. 200.
[103] Brentjes, 'Early modern European travellers', p. 412: 'Raphaël du Mans, a French Capuchin, who came in 1644 arrived in Isfahan was a missionary'.[sic]
[104] Brentjes, 'Early modern European travellers', p. 413 and p. 406 respectively.
[105] Sabra, '"Commentary" that saved the text', pp. 131–3.
[106] Kheirandish, 'Books on mathematical and mixed-mathematical sciences', Vol. 1, pp. 861–2; Necipoğlu, Kafadar and Fleischer (eds), Treasures of Knowledge: p. 359 [fol.176v]: 'Manāẓir li-Ibn al-Haytham'.
[107] Sabra, 'Scientific enterprise', p. 47: 'curious lack of interaction between theory and observation'. Willach, Long Route to the Invention of the Telescope, pp. 4–10 and pp. 29–55.

other scientific areas. Examples from as early 10th-century Baghdad and as late as 17th-century Isfahan[108] had rolled one after another of the old and outdated language of 'visual rays' of a Buzjani or Shaykh Baha'i, despite its decisive refutation by Ibn al-Haytham with experimental demonstrations forming the starting points of developments in Europe of the Middle Ages and Early Modern periods. And lastly, that above all else, developments in and beyond optics and astronomy were advanced most effectively by critical thinking: whether 'making enemies'[109] of unexamined knowledge as applied to optics by Ibn al-Haytham, or rejecting the claim that 'our explanations represent the only possible one',[110] as applied to astronomy by another observer of the stars, Qushji, it was such critical 'outlooks' that were highlighted for having moved westward, some from Istanbul, and through more than one path.

7.4 *A Persian City with Lasting Places*

Seek for our place, not on the earth...

It was the winter of 2020, and Isfahan was being raised to new heights as a 'City of stars' by hosting a 'House of stars' inspired by the ancient planet and zodiac palaces and treasure houses of Baghdad and Isfahan.[111] The House of stars, located in the modern province of Isfahan's star-rich city of Kashan, was a restored historic site made up of a seven-room 'Planet house' and a twelve-house 'Zodiac room'. The space was being set up for a pop-up 'Museum of chances' curated for showcasing the lost chances of old cosmologies, and what the new technologies meant to living and lasting chances at large. The historic site on which this stood was in part of the Isfahan province placed among the oldest civilizations, a part that, besides naming an astronomer in the ranks of Kashani, shortened to Kashi, had famously star-lit skies and observation sites, including a modern observatory next to an ancient fire temple.[112]

The pop-up Museum of the historic House of stars was curated such that it could bridge knowledge and practice, as well as sciences and crafts, starting with architecture. But it did more than physically restore multiple spaces to capture lost and living traditions, theoretical and practical know-how, or Eastern and Western developments, all aided by imaginative selections of historical names, terms and concepts. This began with the given name of the House of stars as 'Thabit', a name with multiple connotations in Arabic and Persian, most directly through a historical figure from a community of star-worshippers associated with planet and zodiac houses.[113] The historical figure was Thabit ibn Qurra, a translator and scholar in early ʿAbbasid Baghdad, after leaving his

[108] Būzjānī, Qurbānī and Shaykhān, Būzjānī-nāma, facs, pp, 3–4: 'bi al-ʿayn ... al-shuʿāʿāt'. ʿĀmilī, Kashkūl, pp. 158–9; Sāʿīdī Khurāsānī (tr), Vol. 1, pp. 251–2.
[109] Sabra, 'Vita: Ibn al-Haytham', p. 55.
[110] Ragep, 'ʿAlī Qushjī [sic] and Regiomontanus', pp. 359–71.
[111] Ibn al-Nadim, Fihrist, Vol. 2, p. 573; Pingree, Thousands, pp. 9–11.
[112] The modern observatory and telescope belong to the university of Kashan. The adjacent ancient fire temple dates back to the Sasanid period, and is a registered monument. https://archnet.org/sites/5299
[113] Carra de Vaux, B., 'Al-Ṣābiʾa, the Sabaeans', First Encyclopedia of Islam (EI1), 7 (1987), pp. 21–2, p. 22: 'some Ṣabians were administrators of the seven planets, which were their temples'.

native Harran, a city after which the twelve and seven 'star' palaces were reportedly modelled.[114] The 'Thabit house', best named for the continuous presence given to it by the meaning of the term 'thabit' as permanent – besides still or fixed – had that term beam at its gate in a timeless verse calligraphed about 'the plan of the times' itself being 'in no state permanent'.[115]

The House's entry gate opened into an outdoor courtyard called 'biruni', a space referring to the public frontal architecture of historic houses, as distinct from their private indoor 'andaruni' spaces.[116] 'Biruni' happened to also match the name of the scholar whose *Book of Instructions* inspired many spaces and features of that historic house. The 'Biruni courtyard' exhibited two physical items to set off the 'chance' experiences of the Museum of chances among other things. Side by side in a glass case were a drawing of an elementary Galilean telescope transforming cosmological understanding in early modern times, and a magnifying lens placed over the title page of a work of Ibn al-Haytham with critical outlooks of over half a millennium before. The two items were placed on the right and left of their shelf in the same spirit and orientation of the images of Galileo and Alhazen on pedestals in an Early Modern frontispiece marking 'observation' and 'rational thought'.[117] The Galilean telescope drawing was of a simple two-lens 'spyglass' as it was called by Galileo, and 'long-eyed instrument'[118] by his Italian contemporary Della Valle, reporting new European concepts and instruments to his Eastern correspondent;[119] and the magnifying lens next to it was there for the message that the concept and technology of lenses came before that of telescopes.

But there were also messages about the discovery versus invention of each of those items. The story of the telescope was once attributed to the 'discoverer' of the principle behind it, holding by chance a convex and concave lens in a line with his eye while looking at a distance. But the birth of both lenses and telescopes having involved inventions as well as discoveries, the role of each, as well as chance in such stories, were much more complex. Ibn al-Haytham, credited in modern times with the optics of lenses,[120] could have possibly conceived of one, or of putting two together, if the technology of lens making and grinding was in place during his lifetime. His contemporary successors in the East and West, Farisi and Roger Bacon,[121] may have

114 Ruska, 'Thābit ibn Kurra', p. 733; Weir, T. H., 'Ḥarrān', p. 270: 'seat of Ṣabians . . . the moon-god Sin' and a 'list of men of science', Thābit ibn Kurra, his sons, grandsons. . .

115 Ḥafiẓ Shīrāzī, *'Chun nīst naqsh-i duwrān dar hīch hālī thābit'*
Literally: Since the plan of the times is in no state permanent . . .
Calligraphy by Muḥammad ʿAlī-Khānī.
The second hemistich not included is: *'Ḥafiẓ mak-un shikāyat; Tā may khur-īm ḥāl-ī'*

116 Djamalzadeh, M. A., 'Andarun', Encyclopedia Iranica (EIr), 2, 1 (1985), p. 11. www.iranicaonline.org/articles/andarun

117 Sabra, 'Vita: Ibn al-Haytham', p. 54: 'sensu' and 'ratione' (Plate 4).

118 'ālat-i chishmak-i dirāz'.

119 Brentjes, 'Early modern European travellers', pp. 409–12.

120 Marshall, O. S., 'Alhazen and the telescope', in Astronomical Society of the Pacific Leaflets, 6, 251 (1950), pp. 4–11. http://adsabs.harvard.edu/full/1950ASPL....6....4M, p. 11: from 'the writings and scientific contributions of Alhazen, it is evident that had he possessed the imagination of a Galileo and applied his knowledge of optics towards building a telescope, the story of telescopic astronomy might have started six hundred years ago'.

121 Marshall, 'Alhazen and the telescope', p. 5: 'Friar Bacon's *Opus Majus* contained some information on the subject, but it was not in a form suited for use by spectacle makers'.

gone further, if the glass technology of their later time had become mature enough. But Museum visitors would learn that these earlier figures all missed the chance of coming even close to any such developments in both theory and practice, chiefly for reasons of accessibility; that 'chance' for Galileo had a different meaning when he first missed the opportunity of meeting an early maker of a 'spyglass' in Venice and Padua before he made his own; or in Florence, where initial 'fortune' came with the patronage of the Medici court and tutorship of young Prince Cosimo, naming the four stars Galileo had observed 'wandering' around Jupiter as the 'Medicean Stars'.[122]

Such centrepieces in the Museum of chances, an elementary telescope fittingly named the 'greatest eye in the world',[123] and a magnifying lens, so critical to developments from eyeglasses to spyglasses, were enough to lend themselves to captions on lost and won chances in the form of simple questions; those like why any earlier observers or star-gazers did not conceive, let alone construct, a device for magnifying remote objects, and why any earlier potentials on that front did not materialise like those in early modern Europe: potentials from the joint observations of Biruni and Buzjani, and observational texts of Ibn Sina and Ibn al-Haytham, to later cases in observatories like Maragha, Samarqand, or Istanbul.[124] Such thought-provoking questions set the tone for these and other museum items, all selected, created, reproduced or projected, to point to historical questions including missed chances, and in the case of the Islamic Middle Ages, missed not once, but over and over again; lost chances along with many related advances, in not only astronomy and optics, but also theory and practice.

Captions for the museum items started with those on the glass case featuring the telescope and lens, and the first caption opened with a Persian verse from the 1400s, expressing both awareness of, and interest in, the presence of eyeglasses in Europe:

'*From my two eyes comes no more work, Since European glass has made [eyes] four*'.[125]

The caption followed that the technology of spectacles came before that of telescopes in Europe:[126] that there were two kinds of early spectacles, reading glasses using convex lenses, common after the early 1300s, and distance glasses adding concave lenses, common by the mid-1400s; that convex and concave lenses were worked on by glass makers and grinders by the late 1500s, and that these were used jointly in telescopes for magnifying distant objects, first three to four times, then twenty and thirty times, by Galileo in the early 1600s, and so on.

On the lower glass shelf there was a small portable modern telescope with a much higher resolution to view planets and constellations – the wandering and fixed stars of the old cosmology – in the clear nights of that star-rich city from the sky-watch corner of the 'Biruni courtyard'. In that corner, with a distant view of a cone-shaped turquoise

[122] Heilbron, J. L., Galileo (Oxford, New York, 2010). Gattei, Stefano (ed, tr), On the Life of Galileo: Viviani's Historical Account & Other Early Biographies (Princeton, 2019).
[123] 'From the ground up: Eye and telescope' © Smithsonian Institution. https://mo-www.cfa.harvard.edu/OWN/pdf/eyeScopeT.pdf
[124] Sayılı, Observatory in Islam, Chap. 6, p. 187, and Chap. 8, p. 259.
[125] '*Az du chashm-i man nayā-yad hīch kār, Az Farangī shīshih tā gasht-ih chahār*'.
Jāmī, Arberry (ed), Fitzgerald's Salaman and Absal, Kheirandish, Elaheh (tr, except).
[126] Long, Priscilla, 'Galileo's spyglass', The American Scholar, 19 December 2012. https://theamericanscholar.org/galileos-spyglass/#.XmkREBRKgcg

dome, stood an illustrated wall after Biruni's *Book of Instructions*, inscribing seven circles around a central Earth, and transcribing a versed *Explanation of the Heavens*[127] next to a fountain pool tiled with zodiac signs. The courtyard itself opened into a foyer named 'House of Leo', Asad Khanah, rhyming with the term Rasad Khanah, for observatory. The picturesque roof above the foyer's patterned floors was reachable through two sets of stairs with other calligraphed walls, one linking the seven planets to the twelve zodiac constellations,[128] the other, only to Leo,[129] all in Persian verse.

A cosmological setting where cities like Baghdad and Isfahan were represented as facing Archers in a Zodiac room, and as Moon and Sun rooms in a Planets house, now acted as stages for other Museum items to showcase lost and won chances for breakthroughs, from the outdated 'hypothesis' of an Earth-centred cosmology to the compromised model of a Sun-centred universe, holding on to a stationary Earth.[130] That led any Museum tour to the rooms in the Planets house, one by one, with rotating wall projections about how some 'lost chances' may have been avoided or reversed, with captioned images in each case. For the Moon room, Galileo's own drawings of the sky through his newly constructed telescope had a caption that read how for one man, a self-made 'spyglass' made him see bright and dark spots on its surface not visible to the naked eye before that; how his Sun-centred 'outlook' affected his thinking about a Moon with mountains and valleys as just like the Earth; and how the critical analogy of a Moon-like Earth took him, or anyone else looking upwards, away from a central Earth with a unique and special place. For the Sun room, the caption was about the same 'spyglass' making sunspots visible as another step away from the old cosmology of 'passing' planets blocking the Sun. For the Venus room, the caption was about its

[127] Mīr Nishānih Tomb in Kashan has a cone-shaped turquoise dome; Explanation of the Heavens (Bayān-i aflāk): Versed Introduction (Madkhal-i manẓūm) attributed to Ṭūsī, Naṣīr al-Dīn: full text in Kheirandish, 'Astronomical Poems from the "Four Corners" of Persia', pp. 83–4:
'On one is the Moon, and on the other, Mercury, then, the third, after Mercury, is Venus,
On the fourth orb is ever the Sun, as on the fifth one is Mars.
Know the sixth orb as Jupiter, the seventh is Saturn's abode,
On the eighth are the fixed stars, and above it the ninth, on which is everything else'.
'Bar yik-ī Māh u bar duvum Tīr ast, Bāz Nāhīd rā, siyum Tīr ast,
Shams bar charkh-i char-um ast mudām, Ham-chu bar charkh-i panjum-īn Bahrām
Shīshum-īn charkh Mushtarī rā dān, Haftum-īn ast manzil-i Kayvān,
Bāz hasht-um kih Thābitāt bar ū-st, Zibar-i ū nuh-um kih jumlih dar ū-st'.

[128] Kheirandish, '*Zodiacs of Paris: Verses, places, faces*', p. 151:
'The first and last of the zodiacs, this one called Aries, the other, Scorpio,
Both reside in the house of Mars, like Jupiter, housing Archer and Pisces
Taurus and Libra, housed in Venus, and as Leo in the Sun, and Cancer in the Moon,
Virgo and Gemini are housed in Mercury, Capricorn and Aquarius, in Saturn'.
'Avval-īn az burūj bā hasht-um, Nām-i īn Barrih nām-i ān Kazh-dum,
Har-du Mirrīkh rā shud-and buyūt, Ham-chu Birjīs rā Kamān bā Ḥūt
Zuhrih rā Khānih Thawr bā Mīzān, Shams rā Shīr u Māh rā Saraṭān,,
Tīr rā-Khānih Khūshih bā Jawzā, Mar Zuhal rā-st Judy u Sākib-i mā '.

[129] Firduwsī, Shāh-nāmih, Varjavand, Kavush-i Rasad-khanah-i Maragha, p. 13; Kheirandish, Elaheh (tr, excerpt).
'Whether [it is] Saturn, Jupiter Mars and Leo
Or the Sun and Moon, Venus and Mercury'
'Chih Kayvān, chih Hurmuz, chih Bahrām u Shīr
Chih Mihr u chih Māh u, chih Nāhīd u Tīr, . .'.

[130] Hellman, 'Tycho Brahe'.

'phases' only visible through aided eyes, and the effect of the one-year phase of Venus as compared to the one-month phases of the Moon; and for the Jupiter room, how four smaller wanderers, close to that largest of all planets, first appeared to move along with it, and eventually, circling around it. All these were major steps towards conceiving of the Moon as circling around the Earth, and of the Earth, Moon and the planets, as all circling around the Sun.[131] Room after room, image after image, and caption after caption, showed how all such cases involved successive chances lost by early and late scholars alike, including those discussing arguments for and against a moving Earth, from Tusi and Qushji to their European contemporaries.

The same seven rooms of the Planets house, acting as physical venues for displays of lost chances in reversing an old cosmology, simultaneously acted as living examples of won chances in other critical cases, this time showcasing constructive contributions to early science through outstanding examples in each case. Rooms named Moon and Sun, the two 'great luminaries',[132] showcased the roots and routes of early science through critical transmissions like cross-cultural transfers; and rooms for the five planets showcased examples through their own historical cases and associations.[133] The room named Mercury, the scribal planet, showcased books through critical concepts like experiments; Venus, the instrument planet, showcased tools through critical instruments like lenses; Mars, the warrior planet, showcased rules through critical laws like refraction; Jupiter, the leader planet, showcased schools through critical circles like communities; and Saturn, the ringed planet, showcased loops through critical communications like exchanges. The Museum tour came full circle to the Zodiac room where constellations showcased outlooks through critical thinking, the case contributing to science and history at once.

The House of stars hosting the Museum of chances was to fill through time with outlets to broadcast evolving cosmological and universal messages, starting with animated and audible outlets. The Moon room was to project old and new cosmologies through animated models of Earth-centred universes from Ptolemaic epicycles to the Tusi couple;[134] and its audible pieces were to range from the 'clear Moon' of our soul through music and poetry[135] to 'live connection' to a satellite orbiting the Moon in a

[131] Rosen, 'Copernicus'.

[132] Kheirandish, 'Astronomical poems', pp. 86–7: The Sun and Moon, the two great luminaries (nayyirayn aʿẓamayn): Kulliyāt of Shāh Niʿmatullāh Valī (d. ca. 835/1431).

[133] Bīrūnī, Kitāb al-Tafhīm (Book of Instruction), includes heavenly body associations.

[134] Crowe, Theories of the World, Ptolemy: 'A planet (P) moves with a constant speed in a small circle, called an epicycle. The centre of the epicycle (F) moves in a larger circle, called a deferent. The combined motions . . . results in . . . a "loop-the-loop" motion . . . between loops, west-to-east; within a loop, east-to-west. . .' www.polaris.iastate.edu/EveningStar/Unit2/unit2_sub1.htm Ṭūsī Couple: a device where a circle rolling inside a fixed circle twice its radius produces linear motion. https://mathworld.wolfram.com/TusiCouple.html

[135] 'Clear Moon': 'Claire de Lune' (Moonlight); music: Claude Debussy, composed in 1890 when he was 28, but not published until 15 years later; poem: Paul Verlaine, composed in 1869, depicting the soul as 'somewhere full of music . . . in a minor key': David, Elizabeth, 'Debussy's Clair de Lune: the romantic piano piece that even has a starring role in Twilight', Classic FM, 27 February 2019. www.classicfm.com/composers/debussy/clair-de-lune-piano-twilight/. Routledge, Chris, 'Featured poem: Clair de Lune by Paul Verlaine', The Reader, 30 March 2009. www.thereader.org.uk/featured-poem-3/
'Votre âme est un paysage choisi, Que vont charmant masques et bergamasques
Jouant du luth et dansant et quasi, Tristes sous leurs déguisements fantasques,

'music of the spheres for real';[136] the Sun room was to project animated Sun-centred models from a book of coincidences in the solar system,[137] with rotating musical pieces like a string quartet about the Sun;[138] and the Planet rooms were to project animated models of the dance of Venus around the Earth as it rotates around the Sun,[139] with audible sounds like the orchestral suite, *The Planets*.[140] As for the cities of Baghdad and Isfahan, featured in the Planet rooms through a facing Moon and Sun, and in the Zodiac room, through facing Archers, their living traces and lasting places in the universal stories of the early sciences were as 'Cities of stars' and 'aiming Archers' on the same side of history. They were to stand alongside cities within reach, from Alexandria and Cairo to Kashan and Istanbul, those further away, from Padua and Venice to Florence and Rome, and those all around the world, in both East and West.

In time, venues showcasing won and lost chances would turn into those of living and lasting chances; and the more venues, participants, contributors and communicators, the more chances for the evolvement of physical and virtual environments to transmit knowledge about the transmission of knowledge, and through it, exchange and understanding.

Tout en chantant sur le mode mineur . . .'.
'Your soul is a select landscape, Where charming masqueraders and bergamaskers go,
Playing the lute and dancing and almost, Sad beneath their fantastic disguises. All sing in a minor key. . .
See also Postscript.

136 Golub, Leon, 18 December, 2013: 'This link is a live connection to a satellite orbiting the Moon and detecting cosmic ray particles. The sounds that you hear are the incoming cosmic rays, detected one at a time, and the different tones tell you the energies of the individual detected particles. Music of the spheres for real'. http://prediccs.sr.unh.edu/craterweb/craterliveradio.html

137 Martineau, John, A Little Book of Coincidence (London, 2000; 2002).

138 Haydn, Joseph, 'Sun' Quartets, Op. 20 nos. 4–6 (Vol. 2), composed in 1772; 'establishing a high watermark to which every other subsequent composer of quartets has paid homage'. https://bis.se/orchestras-ensembles/chiaroscuro-quartet/haydn-sun-quartets-op-20-nos-4-6-vol-2

139 'The Dance of Venus': poster from Daniel Docherty at Prince's School of Traditional Arts, July 2019. https://princes-foundation.org/school-of-traditional-arts

140 Holst, Gustav, The Planets: Suite for large orchestra (1914–16), Wise Music Classical, London: 1) Mars, the Bringer of War 2) Venus, the Bringer of Peace 3) Mercury, the Winged Messenger 4) Jupiter, the Bringer of Jollity 5) Saturn, the Bringer of Old Age. . . . www.wisemusicclassical.com/work/13079/

Postscript

Now and Then[1]

A Leo by *Name*,
Wrote: 'A quest for the seeker . . .
A story of motion, on universe stage . . .

The mind that traverses,
The farthest in future
Can harness the promise,
Of treasure and goal

The one to look back to,
Primordial essence
Digs deep to the rootage,
To learn from below . . .

The past is the keeper of where to beware . . .
A future beholding which bringings to bear . . .
The motion is ceaseless regardless of when . . .
In wind or in motion, in Now or in Then . . .'

A Leo by *Sign*,
In the ranks of a 'sawai'
A word meaning a 'quarter',
Above all 'one's

Sat under a full moon and new solar year,
On the 19th of the month
The magic of seven plus twelve,
Making him equal to none

His fingers touching the keys,
Faster and faster

1 These verses were respectively composed and inspired by my sons, Asad and Esam Goodarzy, dating to a full moon on 19 February 2019, and new year on 19 March 2020 corresponding to the Persian solar year 1399. 'Clear Moon': 'Claire de Lune'; music and poem: Chapter Seven.

To create thoughts,
Finer and finer

While the stars echoed praise,
Louder and louder, than ever before
Until he pressed the last key,
Under the 'Clear Moon' of all our souls.

Moon and Sun[2]

In a dark night, bright from the 'Moon of ten and four',[3]
The sky's heaven, full-mooned, with union and outpour

Light stepped into the realm of darkness,[4]
Life met the eyes of loss, with full presence

[2] These verses are adapted from the poems 'Love and death' by Alfred Lord Tennyson, The Works of Alfred Lord Tennyson (London, 1893), and 'Moon of ten and four' by Rūmī, Muwlānā Jalāl al-Dīn (d. ca. 1273), Kulliyyāt-i Shams-i Tabrīzī, Furūzānfar, Badīʿ al-Zamān (ed) (Tehran, 1336 [1957], pp. 431–2; Kheirandish, 'Astronomical Poems', pp. 81–2; also Chapter 5.

[3] Rūmī, 'Moon of ten and four':
'For the stars, it is the night of union, giving and outpour,
As in the heavens, there is a wedding [lit] by the Moon of Ten and Four . . .'.
'Akhtarān rā shab-i vaṣl-ast u nithār ast u nithār,
Chun sūy-i charkh ʿarūsī-st zih Māh-i dah u chār. . .'.
'O' Shams of Tabrīz, on the morning that you receive it,
Bright day will become the dead of night – with your face as its moon'.
'Shams-i Tabrīz, dar ān ṣubḥ kih tu daryāb-ī,
Rūz-i ruwshan shav-ad az rūy-i chu māhat shab-i tār'

This Rūmī poem opens with the striking imagery of stars in a night of union, where the heavens are lit by the 'Moon of ten and four': the constellation of verses crowning the poem glow with varying radiance, from the opening lines where the full moon of the fourteenth night of the month emerges as a bright light on a festive night, to the closing lines where the sky's seven heavens and twelve constellations sparkle in historic rhyme from the distance of seven hundred years.

[4] Tennyson, 'Love and death':
'What time the mighty Moon was gathering light
Love paced the thymy plots of Paradise,
And all about him roll'd his lustrous eyes;
When, turning round a cassia, full in view,
Death, walking all alone beneath a yew,
And talking to himself, first met his sight:

You must begone, said Death, these walks are mine.
Love wept and spread his sheeny vans for flight;
Yet ere he parted said, This hour is thine:

Thou art the shadow of life, and as the tree
Stands in the Sun and shadows all beneath,
So in the light of great eternity
Life eminent creates the shade of death;
The shadow passeth when the tree shall fall,
But I shall reign forever over all'.

'Begone', said the dark, 'these walks are mine'
Your Sun is trapped by my star-less night

When light heard the hum of dark, so near
Wrote this, on the dome of hope, with tear:

If the hour of life is ever in your hands,
It is not forever, nor from an eternal past

Your life, is no more than a life-less shade,
The fall of a Sun-lit tree, and your shadow fades

The dark of night, if scarce, as a Moon in veil,
The light of day is a Sun, with a lasting reign.[5]

Elaheh Kheirandish
Spring 2020

5 Kheirandish, Elaheh, adaptation of Tennyson's 'Love and death', and Rūmī's 'Moon of ten and four':
'Dar tīrih shab-ī badr zih Māh-i dah u chār,
Firduws-i falak pur-qamar az vaṣl u nithār
Hastī guzar-ī bih ʿarṣih-i nīst nah-ād,
Hichī nigah-ash bar nigah-i zīst fit-ād

Guft-ā buru īn kūrih-rah-i gām-i man-ast,
Khurshīd-i tu dar band-i sīah-shām-i man-ast
Hastī chu navā-yi nīst-ī, pīsh shin-īd,
Bā ashk chinīn nivisht bar bām-i umīd:

Gar sāʿat-i ʿumr laḥẓih-ī dar kaf-i tu-st,
Nah tā bih abad buv-ad, nah az rūz-i nakhust
ʿUmr-i tu chu khud bih sāyih-ī bīsh namānd,
Chun shākhih fitād, sāyih-ī hīch namānd
Tārīkī-yi shab gar bih Mah-ī mīman-ād,
Tābandih chu Mihr-ī abadī mītāb-ad'.

Bibliography

Primary Sources

Alhazen. (1572). Opticae Thesaurus, Risner, Friedrich (ed) (Basel; repr. New York, Johnson, 1972). Harvard University, Houghton Library. f GC5 R4947 572i.

ʿĀmilī, Bahāʾ al-Dīn = Shaykh Bahāʾī. (1879). Kitāb al-Kashkūl (Dehli, s.n. [1296]); Sāʿidī Khurāsānī, Muḥammad Bāqir (Persian tr), 2 vols., (Tehran, Islāmīyah, 1979/1980 [1358]).

ʿĀmilī, Bahāʾ al-Dīn = Shaykh Bahāʾī. (1893). Khulāṣat al-ḥisāb (Tehran, s.n. [1311]).

ʿĀmilī, Bahāʾ al-Dīn = Shaykh Bahāʾī. (1943). Fāl-nāmih, Vujdānī, Muḥammad (ed) (Tehran, Firduwsī [1322]).

Amīrī, Fīrūz-kūhī (ed). (1954). Kulliyāt-i Ṣāʾib-i Tabrīzī (Tehran, Khayyām [1333]).

Amulī, Shams al-Dīn Muḥammad ibn Maḥmūd (1891/1892). Nafāʾis al-Funūn (Tehran, s.n. [1309]).

Andalusī, S.āʿid. (1991). Kitāb Ṭabaqāt al-umam, Salem, Semaʿan I. and Kumar, Alok (ed, tr) (Science in the Medieval World: Book of the Categories of Nations) (Austin, TX, University of Texas).

Archimedes. (1976). Kitāb Arishmīdis fīʿamal al-binkāmāt, Hill, Donald R. (ed, tr) (On the Construction of Water-Clocks) (London, Turner & Devereux).

Aristotle. (1971). On the Heavens, Guthrie, W. K. C. (tr) (Loeb Classical Library, No. 6) (Cambridge, MA, Harvard University Press).

Asʿad Gurgānī, Fakhr al-Dīn. (2008). Vīs va Rāmīn, Davis, Dick (tr) (Fakhraddīn Gorganī Vīs va Rāmīn) (Washington, DC, Mage).

Asadī Ṭūsī. (1978). Munāẓirāt (attribution), Khaleghi-Motlagh, Djalal (ed). 'Asadī Ṭūsī', Journal of the Department of Literature and Humanities, Firduwsī University, Mashhad, 1, 4, pp. 68–130.

Averroeana. (1695). Transcript of Several Letters from Averroes to Metrodorus, a Young Grecian Nobleman, Student at Athens (Athens and Cordoba, 1149 and 1150). (London, T. Sowle; accessed Harvard University, Houghton Library).

Averroes = Ibn Rushd. (1930). Tahāfut al-Tahafāt, Bouyges, M. (ed) (Beyrouth, Imprimerie Catholique), van den Bergh, Simon (tr) (The Incoherence of the Incoherence) (London, Luzac & Co., 1954).

Āvī, Ḥusayn ibn Muḥammad. (2006). Maḥāsin Iṣfahān, Iqbāl Āshtiyānī, ʿAbbās (ed) (Isfahan, Municipality [1385]).

Bayhaqī, ʿAlī. (1948). Tatimmat Ṣiwān al-ḥikma, Meyerhof, Max (tr), 'A biographical work on the learned men of Islam', Osiris, 8, pp. 122–216.

Bīrūnī, Abū Rayḥān. (1879). Āthār al-bāqiyah, Sachau, Edward (ed, tr) (The Chronology of Ancient Nations or Vestiges of the Past) (London, Oriental Translation Fund of Great Britain & Ireland).

Bīrūnī, Abū Rayḥān. (1925). Fī Taḥqīq mā lil-Hind: India, Sachau, Edward (ed, tr) (An Account of the Religion, Philosophy, Literature, Chronology, Astronomy, Customs, Laws and Astrology of India about A.D. 1030) (Leipzig, Otto Harrassowitz).

Bīrūnī, Abū Rayḥān. (1934). Kitāb al-Tafhīm li-awā'il ṣinā'at al-tanjīm, Wright, R. Ramsay (Arabic facs, tr) (The Book of Instruction in the Elements of the Art of Astrology) (London, Luzac & Co; repr., Frankfurt, 1998). Humā'ī, Jalāl al-Dīn (Persian ed) (Tehran, Vizārat-i Farhang, 1939 [1318]; repr. 1983–84 [1362]).

Bīrūnī, Abū Rayḥān. (1964). Kitāb Taḥdīd nihāyāt al-amākin li-taṣḥīḥ-i masāfāt al-masākin, Bulgakov, P. G. and Aḥmad, Imām Ibrāhīm (eds) (Cairo, Maṭba'at Lajnat).

Bīrūnī, Abū Rayḥān. (1967). The Determination of the Coordinates of Positions for the Correction of Distances between Cities, Jamīl, 'Alī (tr) (Beirut, American University).

Bīrūnī, Abū Rayḥān. (1974). Bīrūnī-nāmah. Qurbānī, Abū al-Qāsim (facs) (Tehran, Anjuman-i Āthār-i Millī [1353]).

Bodleian Library. (1965). An Islamic Book of Constellations (Bodleian MS. Marsh 144) (Bodleian Picture Books No. 13) (Oxford, Bodleian Library).

Borges, Jorge Luis. (1962). 'Averroes' search', in Irby, James E. and Yates, Donald A. (tr), Labyrinth: Selected Stories (New York, New Directions).

Borges, Jorge Luis. (1974). In Praise of Darkness, di Giovanni, Norman Thomas (ed, tr) (New York, Dutton).

Būzjānī, Abu al-wafā'. (1992). Fī Mā yaḥtāju ilayhi al-ṣāni' min a'māl al-handasa [On What is Needed by the Craftsman from Geometrical Constructions], Qurbanī, Abu al-Qāsim and Shaykhan, M. A. (facs), Būzjānī-nāma: sharḥ-i aḥvāl va āthār-i riyāḍī-i Abu al-vafā' Būzjānī, pizhūhish va nigārish-i (Tehran, Engelāb-e Islāmi [1371]).

Dawlatshāh-i Samarqandī. (1901). Tadhkiratu al-shu'ará, Browne, Edward G. (ed, tr) (Memoirs of the Poets) (London, Luzac).

Elliot, T. S. (1943). Four Quartets (New York, Harcourt).

Fārisī, Kamāl al-Dīn. (1928–30). Tanqīḥ al-Manāẓir li-dhawī al-abṣār wa al-baṣā'ir, 2 vols. (Hyderabad, 'Uthmāniyya [1347–48]; Cairo, Colecția Biblioteca arabă, 1984).

Firduwsī Ṭūsī, Abu al-Qāsim. (2005). Stories from the Shahnameh of Ferdowsi, Selections in English Davis, Dick (tr) (Washington, DC, Mage); Afshar, Iraj and Omidsalar, Mahmoud, Firdawsī, Shāhnāmah (facs) (Tehran, Ṭalāyah, 2005).

Galilei, Galileo. (1953). Dialogue Concerning the Two Chief World Systems, Ptolemaic & Copernican, Drake, Stillman (tr) (Berkeley, CA, University of California Press).

Galilei, Galileo. (1957). Starry Messenger, in Drake, Stillman (tr), Discoveries and Opinions of Galileo (Garden City, Doubleday).

Gattei, Stefano (ed, tr). (2019). On the Life of Galileo: Viviani's Historical Account & Other Early Biographies (Princeton, NJ, Woodstock, Oxfordshire).

Gilanentz, Petros di Sarkis. (1965). Suqūṭ-i Iṣfahān [Fall of Isfahan: The Reports of the Author about the Afghan Attack and the Surrender of Isfahan] Vol. 9 (Isfahan, Shahriyār [1344]).

Ḥāfiẓ-i Iṣfahānī, Muḥammad. (1971). Natījat al-dawla, in Binesh, Taqi (ed), Sih risālah dar ikhtirā'āt-i ṣan'atī: sā'at, āsīyā, dastgāh-i rūgan kashī (Tehran, Bunyād-i Farhang-i Īrān [1350]).

Ḥakīm Shifā'ī. (1830–1831). The Life of Sheikh Mohammed Ali Hazin, Belfour, F. C. (ed, tr) (Oriental Translation Fund No. 9) (London, J. Murray etc.).

Hanway, Jonas. (1753). An Historical Account of the British Trade Over the Caspian Sea: With a Journal of Travels from London through Russia into Persia, and Back through Russia, Germany and Holland (London, Dodsley etc.).

Heron of Alexandria. (1900). Mechanics, Nix, L. and Schmidt, W. (ed) (Heron von Alexandria Mechanik und Katoptrik) (Leipzig, Druck und Verlag von B. G. Teubner).

Hevelius, Johannes. (1647). Selenographia, Frontispiece: Harvard University. Houghton Library. Typ 620.47.452F.

Ibn Abī Uṣaybiʿa. (1884). ʿUyūn al-anbāʾ fī Ṭabaqāt al-aṭibbāʾ [Classes of Physicians], Müller, August (ed), 2 vols. (Köninsberg, Selbstverlag).
Ibn al-ʿArabī. (1911). Tarjumān al-Ashwāq, in Nicholson, Reynold A. (ed, tr), A Collection of Mystical Odes by Muhyiʾddīn ibn al-ʿArabī (London, Royal Asiatic Society).
Ibn al-Faqīh al-Hamadhānī. (1967). Mukhtaṣar Kitāb al-buldān, de Goeje, M. J. (ed) (Leiden, Brill; repr. 2014).
Ibn al-Haytham, al-Ḥasan. (1971). Ibn al-Haytham: Al-Shukūk ʿala Baṭlamyūs (Dubitationes in Ptolemaeum), Sabra, A. I. and Shehaby, N. (eds) (Aporias Against Ptolemy) (Cairo, The National Library Press).
Ibn al-Haytham, al-Ḥasan (ed). (1983). Kitāb al-Manāẓir, Books I–III: On Direct Vision, Sabra, A. I. (ed) (Kuwait, National Council for Culture, Arts and Letters).
Ibn al-Haytham, al-Ḥasan (tr, comm). (1989). The Optics of Ibn al-Haytham, Books I–III: On Direct Vision, Sabra, A. I. (ed), 2 vols., in J. B. Trapp (ed), Studies of the Warburg Institute (London, Warburg Institute).
Ibn al-Haytham, al-Ḥasan (ed). (2002). Kitāb al-Manāẓir, Books IV–V: On Reflection, Sabra, A. I. (ed), 2 vols. (Kuwait, National Council for Culture, Arts and Letters).
Ibn al-Haytham, al-Ḥasan. (2016). Maqāla fī ṣūrat al-kusūf, Raynaud, Dominique (ed, tr). A Critical Edition of Ibn al-Haytham's On the Shape of the Eclipse: The First Experimental Study of the Camera Obscura. (Cham, Springer).
Ibn Maʿrūf, Taqī al-Dīn. (1976). Al-Ṭuruq al-samiyyah fī al-ālāt al-rūḥānīyyah, al-Hasan, A. Y. (facs ed), Taqī al-Dīn wa al-handasah al-mīkānīkiyyah (Aleppo, University of Aleppo).
Ibn al-Nadīm. (1871–72). Fihrist, Flügel, G. (ed) (Leipzig, Vogel).
Ibn al-Nadīm. (1970). Fihrist, Dodge, B. (tr) (New York, London, Columbia University Press).
Ibn al-Qifṭī, Jamāl al-Dīn. (1903). Tāʾrīkh al-ḥukamāʾ, Lippert, Julius (ed) (Leipzig, Dietrich Verlag).
Ibn Sīnā. (1878). Al-Qānūn fī al-ṭibb (Bulaq, al-Maṭbaʿah al-ʿĀmirah [1294]).
Ibn Sīnā. (1952). Miʿyār al-ʿuqūl (attribution), Humāʾī, Jalāl al-Dīn (ed) (Tehran, Anjuman-i Āthār-i Millī [1331]).
Ibn Sīnā. (1953). Autobiography, Sar-gudhasht-i Ibn Sīnā, Nafīsī, Saʿīd (ed, Persian tr) (Tehran, Anjuman-i Dūstdārān-i Kitāb 3 [1332]).
Ibn Sīnā. (1974). Autobiography, The Life of Ibn Sīnā: A Critical Edition and Annotated Translation, Gohlman, William, E. (ed, tr) (Albany, NY, State University of New York).
Ibn Sīnā. (1983–). Al-Shifāʾ al-ṭabiʿīyāt, Ibrāhīm Madkūr (ed) (Cairo, Hayʾah al-Miṣrīyah al-ʿĀmmah lil-Kitāb).
Ibn Sīnā. (1988). Autobiography, Avicenna and the Aristotelian Tradition: Introduction to Reading Avicenna's Philosophical Works, Gutas, Dimitri (tr), in Hans Daiber (ed), Islamic Philosophy and Theology: Texts and Studies, Vol. 4 (Leiden, Brill), pp. 22–30.
Jazarī, Badīʿ al-Zamān. (1974). The Book of Knowledge of Ingenious Mechanical Devices, Hill, Donald K. (tr) (Dordrecht, Boston, Reidel).
Jazarī, Badīʿ al-Zamān. (1979). Al-Jāmiʿ bayn al-ʿilm wa al-ʿamal al-nāfiʿ fī ṣināʿat al- ḥiyal, [Compendium of Theory and Useful Practice in the Mechanical Arts], al-Ḥassan, A. Y. (ed) (Aleppo, University of Aleppo).
Jurjānī, Mīr Siyyid Sharīf ʿAllāmah. (1934). 'Munāẓarah al-Sayf va al-Qalam' (attribution), Dastgirdi, Vahid (ed), Armaghan, 15, 1, pp. 702–3 [1312].
Kāshānī, Ghīyāth al-Dīn Jamshīd. (1960). 'A letter of Jamshīd al-Kāshī to his father: Scientific research and personalities at a fifteenth-century court', Kennedy, E. S. (tr), Orientalia, 29, pp. 191–213.

Kāshānī, Ghīyāth al-Dīn Jamshīd. (1996). Az Samarqand bih Kāshān: Nāmih-hā-yi Ghīyāth al-Dīn Jamshīd Kāshānī bih pidar-ash, Bagheri, Mohammad (ed) (Tehran, Scientific & Cultural Publications Co. [1375]).

Kāshānī, Ghīyāth al-Dīn Jamshīd. (1997). 'A newly found letter of al-Kāshī on scientific life in Samarqand', Bagheri, Mohammad (tr), Historia Mathematica, 24, pp. 241–56.

Kāshānī, Ghīyāth al-Dīn Jamshīd. (2013). al-Risālah al-Muḥīṭīyah: A Facsimile Edition of the Autograph Manuscript, Karamati, Younes (ed, intro) (Tehran, Miras-e Maktoob [1392]).

Khaṭīb al-Baghdādī. (1970). Tārīkh Baghdād, Lassner, Jacob (tr) (The Topography of Baghdad in the Early Middle Ages: Text and Studies) (Detroit, MI, Wayne State University Press).

Khayyām, ʿUmar. (1947). Rubaiyat of Omar Khayyam, Fitzgerald, Edward (tr), Louis Untermeyer (ed, intro) (New York, Random House).

Khayyām, ʿUmar. (1964). Rubaiyat Hakim Omar Khayyam, Fitzgerald, Edward (tr), Sadegh Hedayat (intro), Ostovar, Mohammad Karim Ostovar (intro, tr) (Tehran, Tahrir).

Khwārazmī, Ḥisām Ṣarrāf. (2004). 'Munāẓirih-i Shaṭranj va Nard' (attribution), Pourjavady, Nasrollah (ed), Nāmih-i Farhangistān, 6, 1 (Series No. 24), pp. 16–29 [1383].

Krusinski, Tadeusz Jan. (1840). The Chronicles of a Traveller: or, A History of the Afghan Wars with Persia . . . 'Ta-reekh-i-Seeah', from the Latin of J. C. Clodius, by George Newnham Mitford, esq. (London, J. Ridgway).

Māfarrūkhī, al-Mufaḍḍal. (1933). Kitāb Maḥāsin Iṣfahān taʾlīf Mufaḍḍal ibn Saʿd ibn Ḥusayn al-Māfarrūkhī al-Iṣfahānī, Ṭihrānī, Jalāl al-Dīn al-Ḥusaynī (ed) (Tehran, Majlis).

Majdī, Majd al-Dīn Muḥamma al-Ḥusaynī. (1963). Zīnat al-majālis (Tehran, Kitābkhānah-i Sanāʾī [1342]).

Manṣūr, ʿAlāʾ al-Dīn. (1956). Shahanshāh-nāmih, F 1404, Istanbul University Library in Sayılı, Aydin ''Alāʾ al-Dīn al-Manṣūr's poems on the Istanbul Observatory', Türk Tarīh Kurumu Belleten 20, 79, pp. 429–84.

Munshī, Iskandar Bayg. (2011). Tārīkh-i ʿālam-ārā-yi ʿabbāsī, Farīd Murādī (ed) (Tehran, Nigāh [1390]).

Mustuwfī Qazvīnī, Ḥamd Allāh. (1983). Nuzhat al-qulūb (Tehran, Dunyā-yi Kitāb [1362]).

Newton, Isaac. (1730). Opticks, or, A Treatise of the Reflections, Refractions, Inflections & Colours of Light (London, New York, Dover, 1952, based on the original 4th edn).

Newton, Isaac. (1999). The Principia: Mathematical Principles of Natural Philosophy, Cohen, I. Bernard, and Whitman, Anne (tr), assisted by Julia Budenz (Berkeley, CA, University of California).

Niẓāmī ʿArūḍī Samarqandī. (1899). Chahār maqāla, Browne, Edward G. (tr) (Four Discourses) (Hertford, S. Austin and Sons; repr., Journal of the Royal Asiatic Society, July and October, 1899; London, Luzac & Co., 1900).

Ptolemy. (1984). The Almagest, Toomer, Gerald J. (tr, annot.) (Ptolemy's Almagest) (New York, Springer-Verlag).

Rāzī, Fakhr al-Dīn. (1967–68). Jāmiʿ al-ʿulūm (Kitāb-i Sittīnī), Tasbīḥī, Muḥammad Ḥusayn (ed, intro) (Tehran, Asadī [1346]).

Rūmī, Muwlānā Jalāl al-Dīn. (1957). Kulliyyāt-i Shams-i Tabrīzī, Furūzānfar, Badīʿ al-Zamān (ed) (Tehran, Tehran University [1336]; repr., Tehran, Amīr Kabīr, 1966 [1345]).

Saʿdī. (1911). Būstān, Hart, Edward, A. (tr) (Būstān of Saʿdī) (London, J. Murray).

Sa ʿdī. (2002). Ghazaliyāt-i Sa ʿdī, Arjang, Gh. (ed) (Tehran, Qatrah [1383]).
Sijzī, Zayn al-Dīn. (2006). 'Munāẓirih-i Khurshīd va Māh' (attribution), in Pourjavady, Nasrollah (ed), Zabān-i Ḥal dar ʿIrfān va Adabīyāt-i Fārsī (Tehran, Hermes [1385]), pp. 421–29.
Ṣūfī, ʿAbd al-Raḥmān. (1986). Kitāb Ṣuwar al-kawākib [Book of Constellations] (Frankfurt, Goethe University).
Ṭāshkubrī-zādah, Aḥmad ibn Muṣṭafa. (1985). Al-Shaqā ʾiq al-nu ʿmānīyah fī ʿulamā ʾ al-Dawlat al-ʿUthmānīyah, Ṣubḥī Furāt, Ahmad (ed) (Istanbul, Istanbul University).
Tennyson, Alfred Lord. (1893). The Works of Alfred Lord Tennyson (London, MacMillan and Co.).
Ṭūsī, Naṣīr al-Dīn. (1594). Recension of Euclid's Elements. [Arabic] (Rome), Harvard University, Houghton Library Typ 525.94.373F.
Ṭūsī, Naṣīr al-Dīn. (1868). Dhikr-i Daryā-yi Khazar (attribution), Melgunof, Gregory (Vienna Manuscript) (Kaspischen Meeres oder Die Nordprovinzen Persiens) (Leipzig: Leopold Voss).
Ṭūsī, Naṣīr al-Dīn. (1886). Taḥrīr al-Mutawassiṭāt (Tehran, Lithograph [1304]).
Ṭūsī, Naṣīr al-Dīn. (1956). Risālah-i Mu ʿīnīyah, Danish-Pazhuh, Muhmmad-Taqi (ed) (Tehran, Tehran University [1335]).
Ṭūsī, Naṣīr al-Dīn. (1956). Ḥall-i Mushkilāt-i Mu ʿīnīyah, Danish-Pazhuh, Muhammad-Taqi (ed) (Tehran, Tehran Univeristy [1335]).
Ṭūsī, Naṣīr al-Dīn. (1969). Tarjamah-i Ṣuwar al-kawākib [Translation of Book of Constellations] (facs) (Tehran, Bunyād-i Farhang-i Īrān [1348]; repr. Tehran, Bunyād-i Farhang-i Īrān 1972 [1351]).
Ṭūsī, Naṣīr al-Dīn. (1993). Naṣīr al-Dīn al-Ṭūsī's Memoir on Astronomy: Al-Tadhkira fī ʿilm al-hay ʾa, Ragep, F. Jamil (ed, tr, comm), 2 vols., in Toomer, G. J. (ed), Sources in the History of Mathematics and Physical Sciences, Vol. 12 (New York, Springer-Verlag).
Ṭūsī, Naṣīr al-Dīn. (1998). Sayr wa sulūk, Contemplation and Action: The Spiritual Autobiography of a Muslim Scholar, Badakhchani, S. J. (ed, tr) (London, New York, I.B. Tauris).
Whitman, Walt. (1975). The Complete Poems, Murphy, Francis (ed) (London, Penguin).

Secondary Sources

Abbott, Nabia. (1986). Two Queens of Baghdad: Mother and Wife of Hārūn al Rashīd (Chicago, IL, University of Chicago Press; London, Al-Saqi).
Abdullaeva, Firuza. (2009). 'The Bodleian manuscript of Asadī Ṭūsī's Munāẓara between an Arab and a Persian: Its place in the transition from ancient debate to classical panegyric', Iran, 47, pp. 69–95.
Abdullaeva, Firuza. (2012). 'The origins of the Munāẓara genre in new Persian literature', in Seyed-Gohrab, A. A. (ed), Metaphor and Imagery in Persian Poetry (Leiden, Boston, Brill), pp. 249–73.
Abdullaeva, Firuza and Melville, Charles (eds). (2010). Iranian Studies, 43, 1, Special Issue: Millennium of the Shahnama of Firdausi.
Adivar, A. Adnan. (1960). 'ʿAlī ibn Muḥammad al-Kūshdjī', Encyclopedia of Islam (EI[2]), Vol. 1, p. 393.
Adle, Kamran. (1992). Ānān kih khāk rā bi-naẓar kīmiyā kun-and (Tehran, Soroush [1371]).
Anawati, G. C. (1978a). 'Ibn Sīnā, Abū ʿAlī al-Ḥusayn Ibn ʿAbdallāh, also known as Avicenna', Dictionary of Scientific Biography (DSB), Vol. 15 (Supp. I), pp. 494–8.

Anawati, G. C. (1978b). 'Ḥunayn ibn Isḥāq al-ʿIbādī, Abū Zayd, known . . . as Johannitius', Dictionary of Scientific Biography (DSB), Vol. 15 (Supp. I), pp. 230–4.

Arberry, A. J. (1956). Fitzgerald's Salaman and Absal: A Study (Cambridge, Cambridge University Press).

Arnaldez, Roger. (1969). 'Ibn Rushd', Encyclopedia of Islam (EI²), Vol. 3, Facs. 55–6, pp. 909–20.

Arnaldez, Roger and Iskandar, Albert Z. (1975). 'Ibn Rushd: Abu al-Walid Muhammad ibn Ahmad ibn Muhammad, also known as Averroës', Dictionary of Scientific Biography (DSB), Vol. 12, pp. 1–9.

Ashraf, Assef. (2019). 'Pathways to the Persianate', in Abbas Amanat and Assef Ashraf (eds), The Persianate World: Rethinking a Shared Sphere (Leiden, Brill).

Associated Press (eds). (1998). 'Was supernova invisible in 1250?' Deseret News, 12 November.

Atiyeh, George N. (1966). Al-Kindi: The Philosopher of the Arabs (Rawalpandi, Islamic Research Institute).

Attiyeh, Jenny. (2003). 'Scholars resuscitate dead languages', Harvard Gazette, 13 November.

Axworthy, Michael. (2006). Sword of Persia: Nader Shah, from Tribal Warrior to Conquering Tyrant (London, New York, I.B. Tauris).

Babaie, Sussan. (1993). Safavid Palaces at Isfahan: Continuity and Change (1590–1666) (New York, New York University).

Babaie, Sussan, Babayan, Kathryn, Baghdiantz McCabe, Ina, and Farhad, Massumeh (eds). (2004). Slaves of the Shah: New Elites of Safavid Iran (London, New York, I.B. Tauris).

Bacharach, Jere L. (1974). A Near East Studies Handbook (Seattle and London, University of Washington Press; repr. 1976).

Baichun, Zhang. (2003). 'The introduction of European astronomical instruments and the related technology into China during the seventeenth century', East Asian Science, Technology, and Medicine, 20, pp. 99–131.

Baily, Francis. (1843). The Catalogues of Ptolemy, Ulugh Beg, Tycho Brahe, Halley, Hevelius: Memoirs of the Royal Astronomical Society (London, The Society).

Baldwin, John W. (1971). The Scholastic Culture of the Middle Ages (Lexington MA, D. C. Heath and Company).

Barker, Peter and Heidarzadeh, Tofigh. (2016). 'Copernicus, the Ṭūsī Couple and East-West exchange in the fifteenth century', in Miguel Á Granada, Patrick J. Boner and Dario Tessicini (eds), Unifying Heaven and Earth: Essays in the History of Early Modern Cosmology (Barcelona, Biblioteca Universitària), pp. 19–57.

Basinger, Jeanine, in Collaboration with the Trustees of the Frank Capra Archives. (1986). The It's A Wonderful Life Book (New York, Knopf).

Battles, Matthew. (2004). Widener: Biography of a Library (Cambridge, MA, Harvard College Library: Distributed by Harvard University Press).

Bayani, Shirin. (1998). Tīsfūn va Baghdād (Tehran, Jami [1377]).

Beach, Denison. (2002). 'Everyone's wild about Harry', Harvard Library Bulletin, 13, 1, pp. 3–4.

Bearman, P., Bianquis, Th., Bosworth, C. E., van Donzel, E. and Heinrichs, W. P. (eds). (1954–2005). Encyclopedia of Islam (EI²) (Leiden, Brill).

Beelaert, Anna Livia. (2010). 'Khāqānī Shīrvānī', Encyclopedia Iranica (EIr) Vol. 15, Facs. 5, pp. 522–3.

Begley, S. (1999). 'The power of big ideas', Newsweek, 11 Jan.

Belting, Hans. (2011). Florence and Baghdad: Renaissance Art and Arab Science, Lucas Schneider, Deborah (tr) (Cambridge, MA, Belknap Press of Harvard University Press).

Benfeghoul, Farid. (2020). 'Through the lens of Islam: A note on Arabic sources on the use of rock crystals and other gems as vision aids', in Hahn, Cynthia and Shalem, Avinoam (eds), Seeking Transparency: Rock Crystals Across Medieval Mediterranean (Berlin, Gebr, Mann Verlag), pp. 237–49.

Ben Zaken, Avner. (2010). Cross-Cultural Scientific Exchanges in the Eastern Mediterranean, 1560–1660 (Baltimore, MD, John Hopkins University Press).

Berggren, J. Len. (1986). Episodes in the Mathematics of Medieval Islam (New York, Springer-Verlag).

Berners-Lee, Tim with Fischetti, Mark. (1999). Weaving the Web: The Original Design and Ultimate Destiny of the World Wide Web by its Inventor (San Francisco, CA, Harper).

Bier, Carol. (2012). 'The decagonal tomb tower at Maragha and its architectural context: Lines of mathematical thought', Nexus Network Journal, 14, pp. 251–73.

Blair, Ann. (2010). Too Much to Know: Managing Scholarly Information before the Modern Age (New Haven, CT, Yale University Press).

Blake, Stephen P. (1999). Half the World: The Social Architecture of Safavid Isfahan, 1590–1722 (Costa Mesa, CA, Mazda).

Blochet, E. (1912). Catalogue des Manuscrits Persans de la Bibliothèque Nationale (Paris, Imprimerie Nationale).

Blodgett, E. D. and Mannani, Manijeh. (2014). Speak Only of the Moon: A New Translation of Rumi (Santa Monica, CA, Afshar publishing).

Bloom, Jonathan. (2001). Paper before Print: The History and Impact of Paper in the Islamic World (New Haven, CT, Yale University Press).

Bloom, Jonathan and Blair, Sheila (eds). (2002). Islam: A Thousand Years of Faith and Power (New Haven, CT, Yale University Press).

Blunt, Wilfrid. (1966). Isfahan Pearl of Persia (New York, Stein and Day; London, Elek; repr., 2009).

Bosworth, Clifford Edmund. (1967). The Islamic Dynasties: A Chronological and Genealogical Handbook. (Islamic Surveys No.5) (Edinburgh, Edinburgh University Press).

Bosworth, Clifford Edmund. (1989). Bahā᾽ al-Dīn al-ʿĀmilī and His Literary Anthologies, Journal of Semitic Studies (Monograph; no. 10) (Manchester, University of Manchester).

Bosworth, Clifford Edmund. (1995). 'E. G. Browne and his "A Year Amongst the Persians"', Iran, 33, pp. 115–22.

Brancaforte, Elio and Brentjes, Sonja. (2008). 'From rhubarb to rubies', Iranian Studies, 41, 4, Special Issue: Bier, Carol, Kheirandish, Elaheh and al-Din Yousefi, Najma (eds), Sciences, Crafts, and the Production of Knowledge: Iran and Eastern Islamic Lands (ca. 184–1153 AH/800–1740 CE), pp. 595–600.

Brentjes, Sonja. (2004). 'Early modern European travellers in the Middle East and their reports about the sciences', in Pourjavady, N. and Vesel, Ž. (eds), Sciences, techniques et instruments dans le monde iranien (Xe–XIXe siècle) (Tehran, Institut Français de Recherche en Iran (IFRI)), pp. 379–420.

Brentjes, Sonja. (2007). 'Khwārizmī: Muḥammad ibn Mūsā al-Khwārizmī', Biographical Encyclopedia of Astronomers (BEA) (New York, Springer Reference), pp. 631–3.

Brentjes, Sonja, van Dalen, Benno and Charette, François (eds). (2002). Early Science and Medicine (ed: Christoph Lüthy), 7, 3, Special Issue: Certainty, Doubt, Error: Aspects of the Practice of Pre- and Early Modern Science: In Honor of David A. King, pp. 173–8.

Brewster, David. (1855). Memoirs of the Life, Writings, and Discoveries of Sir Isaac Newton, 2 vols. (Edinburgh: Thomas Constable & Co.; repr. London and New York: Johnson Reprint Corp, 1965).

Browne, Edward G. (1893). A Year Amongst the Persians: Impressions as to the Life, Character, & Thought of the People of Persia, Received During Twelve Months' Residence in that Country in the Years 1887–1888 (London, A. and C. Black).

Browne, Edward G. (1896). A Catalogue of the Persian Manuscripts in the Library of the University of Cambridge (Cambridge, Cambridge University Library).

Browne, Edward G. (1901a). 'Baghdad During the ʿAbbásid Caliphate from Contemporary Arabic and Persian Sources by Guy Le Strange', The Journal of the Royal Asiatic Society of Great Britain and Ireland, April (Notice of Books), pp. 349–51.

Browne, Edward G. (1901b). 'Account of a rare manuscript [of] history of Iṣfahán, presented to the Royal Asiatic Society on May 19, 1827', in John Malcolm and Edward G. Browne (eds), The Journal of the Royal Asiatic Society of Great Britain and Ireland, July, pp. 411–47.

Browne, Edward G. (1902a). 'Obituary notices: Professor Charles Rieu Ph.D. M.A', The Journal of the Royal Asiatic Society of Great Britain and Ireland, June, pp. 718–21.

Browne, Edward G. (1902b–). A Literary History of Persia, 4 vols. (New York, Charles Scribner's Sons).

Brunner, Christopher J. (1979). 'The Middle Persian explanation of chess and invention of backgammon', The Journal of the Ancient Near Eastern Society of Columbia University, 11, pp. 43–51.

Buchwald, Jed Z., Cohen, I. Bernard and Smith, George E. (eds). (2001). Isaac Newton's Natural Philosophy (Cambridge, MA, MIT Press).

Burnett, Charles. (2002). 'The certitude of astrology: The scientific methodology of Al-Qābisī and Abū Maʿshar', Early Science and Medicine, 7, 3, pp. 198–213.

Caiozza, Anna. (2009). 'Iconography of the constellations', in Vesel, Živa, Tourkin, Serge and Porter, Eve (eds), in collaboration with Francis, Richard and Ghasemloo, Farid, Images of Islamic Science (Tehran, Institut Français de Recherche en Iran (IFRI)), pp. 106–33.

Campbell, Joseph. (1949). The Hero with a Thousand Faces (New York, Pantheon; Princeton, NJ, Princeton University Press, 1968; Novato, CA, New World Library, 2003).

Carling, Jennifer and Rosenberg, John S. (2017). 'An "enchanted palace": A humanistic "masterclass" for Houghton Library's seventy-fifth anniversary', Harvard Magazine, March–April, pp. 36–41.

Carra de Vaux, B. (1987). 'Al-Ṣābiʾa, the Sabaeans', First Encyclopedia of Islam (EI^1), Vol. 7, pp. 21–2.

Charette, Francoise. (2003). Mathematical Instrumentation in Fourteenth-Century Egypt and Syria: The Illustrated Treatsise of Najm al-Dīn al-Miṣrī (Leiden, Brill).

Clagett, Marshall. (1974). 'Nicole Oresme', Dictionary of Scientific Biography (DSB), Vol. 10, pp. 223–30.

Clark, Joseph T. (1984). 'Something old, something new, something borrowed, something blue: Copernicus, Galileo, and Newton', in Everett Mendelsohn (ed), Transformation and Tradition in the Sciences: Essays in Honor of I. Bernard Cohen (Cambridge, New York, Cambridge University Press).

Cohen, I. Bernard. (1974). 'Newton, Isaac', Dictionary of Scientific Biography (DSB), Vol. 10, pp. 42–101.

Cohen, I. Bernard. (1985a). The Birth of a New Physics (Ontario, Penguin books).

Cohen, I. Bernard. (1985b). Revolutions in Science (Cambridge MA, Harvard University Press).
Coke, Richard. (1927). Baghdad, the City of Peace (London, T. Butterworth).
Comes, Mercè. (2007). 'Ibn Abī al-Shukr: Muḥyī al-Milla wa-'l-Dīn Yaḥyā . . . al-Maghribī al-Andalūsī', Biographical Encyclopedia of Astronomers (BEA) (New York, Springer Reference), pp. 548–9.
Crombie, A. C. (1971). 'Descartes, René', Dictionary of Scientific Biography (DSB), Vol. 3, pp. 51–5.
Crowe, Michael. (1990). Theories of the World from Antiquity to the Copernican Revolution (New York, Dover).
Dabbagh, Al-, J. (1970). 'Banū Mūsā: Three brothers – Muḥammad, Aḥmad and Al-Ḥasan . . . "sons of Mūsā"', Dictionary of Scientific Biography (DSB), Vol. 1, pp. 443–6.
Daffa, Al-, Ali. (1976). 'Thābit ibn Qurra's extension of the Pythagorean Theorem', Proceedings of the First International Symposium for the History of Arabic Science (Aleppo, University of Aleppo), pp. 33–4.
Daiber, Hans. (1993). 'Science and technology versus Islam: A controversy from Renan and Afghani to Nasr and Needham and its historical background', JAMES: Annals of Japan Association for Middle East Studies, 8, pp. 169–87.
Daiber, Hans and Ragep, F. Jamil. (2000). 'Al-Ṭūsī, Naṣīr al-Dīn, Abū Dja'far Muḥammad . . . or Khwāja Naṣīr al-Dīn', Encyclopedia of Islam (EI^2), Vol. 10, Facs. 175–6, pp. 746–50.
Danish-Pazhuh, M. T. and Munzavi, A. N. (1962). Catalogue of Sipahsālār Library, Vol. 3 (Tehran, Tehran University [1341]).
Daryayee, T. (2002). 'Mind, body and the cosmos: Chess and backgammon in ancient Persia', Iranian Studies, 35, 4, pp. 281–312.
Dashti, 'Ali. (1965). Damī bā Khayyām (Tehran, Amīr Kabīr [1344]).
Dati, Carlo. (1953). 'On the invention of eyeglasses', Isis, 44, 1/2, pp. 4–10.
Davidson, Olga M. (1994). Poet and Hero in the Persian Book of Kings (Ithaca, NY, Cornell University Press).
Dhanani, Alnoor. (2007). 'Jurjānī: 'Alī ibn Muḥammad ibn 'Alī al-Ḥusaynī al-Jurjānī (al-Sayyid al-Sharīf)', Biographical Encyclopedia of Astronomers (BEA) (New York, Springer Reference), pp. 603–4.
Dickens, Charles. (1859). A Tale of Two Cities (London, Chapman and Hall).
Dirāyatī, Muṣṭafā. (2010). List of Manuscripts in Iran, Vol. 10 (Tehran, Majlis [1389]).
Djamalzadeh, M. A. (1985). 'Andarun', Encyclopedia Iranica (EIr), Vol. 2, Facs. 1, p. 11.
Dolnick, Edward. (1952). The Clockwork Universe: Isaac Newton, the Royal Society, and the Birth of the Modern World (New York, Harper Collins).
Drake, Stillman. (1972). 'Galilei, Galileo', Dictionary of Scientific Biography (DSB), Vol. 5, pp. 237–50.
Dreyer, J. L. E. (1963). Tycho Brahe: A Picture of Scientific Life and Work in the Sixteenth Century (New York, Dover).
Duhem, Pierre. (1969). To Save the Phenomena: An Essay on the Idea of Physical Theory from Plato to Galileo, Dolan, Edmund and Maschler, Chaninah (tr) (Chicago, IL, University of Chicago Press; repr., Midway Reprints, 1985).
Dupré, Sven. (2005). 'Ausonio's mirrors and Galileo's lenses: The telescope and sixteenth-century practical optical knowledge', Galilaeana, 2, pp. 145–80.
Dupré, Sven (ed). (2019a). Perspective as Practice: Renaissance Cultures of Optics (Turnhout, Brepols).
Dupré, Sven. (2019b). 'How-to optics', in Dupré, Sven (ed) Perspective as Practice: Renaissance Cultures of Optics (Turnhout, Brepols).

Duri, A. A. (1958). 'Baghdad', Encyclopedia of Islam (EI²), Vol. 1, Facs. 11–22, pp. 894–909.
Edgerton, Samuel Y. (1975). The Renaissance Rediscovery of Linear Perspective: Cartography and Astronomy (New York, Basic Books).
Edgerton, Samuel Y. (2009). The Mirror, the Window, and the Telescope: How Renaissance Linear Perspective Changed our Vision of the Universe (Itacha, NY, London, Cornell University Press).
Eisenstein, Elizabeth L. (1979). The Printing Press as an Agent of Change: Communications and Cultural Transformations in Early Modern Europe (Cambridge, New York, Cambridge University Press).
Elwell-Sutton, L. P. (1971). In Search of Omar Khayyam (London, G. Allen & Unwin; New York, Columbia University Press).
Emami, Farshid. (2016). 'Coffee houses, urban spaces, and the formation of a public sphere in Safavid Isfahan', in Necipoğlu, Gülru (ed), Muqarnas: An Annual of the Visual Culture of the Islamic World (Leiden, Brill).
Esposito, John L. (ed). (1990). 'Rayhana bint Zayd ibn Amr (d. 632)', Oxford Dictionary of Islam (New York, Oxford University Press).
Fazlıoğlu, İhsan. (2007a). 'Mīram Čelebī: Maḥmūd ibn Quṭb al-Dīn Muḥammad ibn Muḥammad ibn Mūsā Qāḍīzāde', Biographical Encyclopedia of Astronomers (BEA) (New York, Springer Reference), pp. 788–9.
Fazlıoğlu, İhsan. (2007b). 'Qūshjī: Abū al-Qāsim ʿAlāʾ al-Dīn ʿAlī ibn Muḥammad Qushči-zāde', Biographical Encyclopedia of Astronomers (BEA) (New York, Springer Reference), pp. 946–8.
Fazlıoğlu, İhsan. (2007c). 'Taqī al-Dīn Abū Bakr Muhammad ibn Zayn al-Dīn Maʿrūf al-Dimashqī al-Hanafī', Biographical Encyclopedia of Astronomers (BEA) (New York, Springer Reference), pp. 1122–4.
Flood, Finbarr Barry. (2000). The Great Mosque of Damascus: Studies on the Makings of an Umayyad Visual Culture (Boston, MA, Brill).
Forcada, Miquel. (2004–05). 'Astronomy and astrology and the sciences of the ancients in early al-Andalus (2nd/8th–3rd/9th centuries)', Zeitschrift für Geschichte der arabisch-islamischen Wissenschaften, 16, pp. 1–73.
Forcada, Miquel. (2007). 'Ibn Rushd: Abū al-Walīd Muḥammad ibn Aḥmad ibn Muḥammad ibn Rushd al-Ḥafīd', Biographical Encyclopedia of Astronomers (BEA) (New York, Springer Reference), pp. 564–5.
Frye, Richard N. (1967). Persia (London, George Allen and Unwin Ltd).
Galbraith, John Kenneth. (1990). A Tenured Professor (Boston, MA, Houghton Mifflin Harcourt).
Gharagozlou, Yahya. (2016). 1001: Persiranian Stories of Love and Revenge (Boston, MA, Blackeyes Press).
Gibb Memorial Series. (1915–). (Leyden, Brill; London, Luzac & Co.).
Gillispie, Charles C. (ed). (1970–1990). Dictionary of Scientific Biography (DSB), 18 vols.; Supplements and Index, Vols. 15–18 (New York, Charles Scribner's Sons).
Gingerich, Owen. (1973). 'Kepler, Johannes', Dictionary of Scientific Biography (DSB), Vol. 7, pp. 289–312.
Gingerich, Owen. (2004). The Book Nobody Read: Chasing the Revolutions of Nicolaus Copernicus (New York, Walker & Company).
Glick, Thomas F. (2005). 'Eyeglasses', in Glick, T., Livesey, Steven and Wallis, F. (eds). Medieval Science, Technology, and Medicine: An Encyclopedia (London, Routledge).

Gnoli, Gherardo and Panaino, Antonio (eds). (2009). Kayd: Studies in the History of Mathematics, Astronomy and Astrology in Memory of David Pingree (Roma, Istituto Italiano per l'Africa e l'Oriente).

Goitchon, A. M. (1969). 'Ibn Sīnā', Encyclopedia of Islam (EI[2]), Vol. 3, Facs. 55–6, pp. 941–7.

Goitein, S. D. (1963). 'Between Hellenism and Renaissance-Islam: The intermediate civilization', Islamic Studies, Journal of the Central Institute of Islamic Research, 2, 3, pp. 217–33.

Goldstein, Bernard R. (1967). 'The Arabic version of Ptolemy's Planetary Hypotheses', Transactions of the American Philosophical Society, 57, 4, pp. 3–55.

Golub, Leon and Pasachoff, Jay M. (2001). Nearest Star: The Surprising Science of Our Sun (Cambridge, MA, Harvard University Press).

Golub, Leon and Pasachoff, Jay M. (2017). The Sun (Kosmos) (London, Reaktion Books).

Goodman, Matthew. (2008). The Sun and the Moon: The Remarkable True Account of Hoaxers, Showmen, Dueling Journalists, and Lunar Man-Bats in Nineteenth-Century New York (New York, Basic Books).

Grant, Ethel Watts Mumford. (1904). The Hundred Songs of Kamal Ad-Din Isfahan (New York, Charles Scribner's Sons).

Grasshoff, Gerd. (1990). The History of Ptolemy's Star Catalogue (New York, Springer-Verlag).

Greco Josefowicz, Diane. (2019). 'Into the blue: Through the years with Jed Buchwald', in Cormos-Buchwald, Diana et al. (eds), Looking Back As We Move Forward: The Past, Present and Future of the History of Science – Liber Amicorum for Jed Z. Buchwald on his 70th Birthday (New York, Ink Inc.), pp. 167–73.

Gutas, Dimitri. (1987). 'Avicenna. ii. Biography', Encyclopedia Iranica (EIr), Vol. 3, Facs. 1, pp. 67–70.

Gutas, Dimitri. (1988). 'Autobiography', Avicenna and the Aristotelian Tradition: Introduction to Reading Avicenna's Philosophical Works, in Hans Daiber (ed), Islamic Philosophy and Theology Texts and Studies (Leiden, Brill), pp. 22–30 (repr., 2014, pp. 11–19).

Gutas, Dimitri. (1998). Greek Thought, Arabic Culture: The Graeco-Arabic Translation Movement in Baghdad and Early 'Abbāsid Society (2nd–4th/8th–10th centuries) (London, Routledge).

Gutas, Dimitri. (1999). 'The "Alexandria to Baghdad" complex of narratives: A contribution to the study of philosophical and medical historiography among the Arabs', Documenti e Studi Sulla Tradizione Filosofica Medievale, 10, pp. 155–93.

Hahn, Roger. (1971). The Anatomy of a Scientific Institution: The Paris Academy of Sciences, 1666–1803 (Berkeley, CA, University of California Press).

Hartner, Willy. (1966). 'When and how did the impetus of science in Islam come to an end?' in Introduction to the History of Science: Course Source Book, compiled by A. I. Sabra (1978) (Cambridge, MA, Harvard University, Department of History of Science), pp. 99–120.

Hartner, Willy. (1969). 'Naṣīr al-Dīn al-Ṭūsī's lunar theory', Physis, 11, pp. 287–304.

Hashemipour, Behnaz. (2007a). 'ʿĀmilī: Bahāʾ al-Dīn', Biographical Encyclopedia of Astronomers (BEA) (New York, Springer Reference), pp. 42–3.

Hashemipour, Behnaz. (2007b). 'Būzjānī: Abū al-Wafāʾ Muḥammad ibn Muḥammad ibn Yaḥyā al-Būzjānī', Biographical Encyclopedia of Astronomers (BEA) (New York, Springer Reference), pp. 188–9.

Hashemipour, Behnaz. (2007c). 'Khayyām: Ghiyāth al-Dīn Abū al-Fatḥ ʿUmar ibn Ibrāhīm al-Khayyāmī al-Nīshāpūrī', Biographical Encyclopedia of Astronomers (BEA) (New York, Springer Reference), pp. 627–8.

Hawking, Stephen. (2002). On the Shoulders of Giants: The Great Works of Physics and Astronomy (Philadelphia, PA, Running Press).

Hayes, John R. (ed). (1975). The Genius of Arab Civilization: Source of Renaissance (New York, New York University Press; repr., Cambridge, MA, MIT Press, 1978).

Heidarzadeh, Tofigh. (2005). 'Patronage networks and migration: Turco-Persian scholarly exchanges in the 15th, 16th and 17th centuries', Archives Internationales d'Histoire des Sciences, 55, pp. 419–34.

Heilbron, J. L. (2010). Galileo (Oxford, New York, Oxford University Press).

Hellman, C. Doris. (1970). 'Tycho Brahe', Dictionary of Scientific Biography (DSB), Vol. 2, pp. 401–16.

Hockey, Thomas et al. (eds). (2007). Biographical Encyclopedia of Astronomers (BEA) (New York, Springer Reference; repr. 2014).

Hofmann, J. E. (1971). 'Nicholas of Cusa', Dictionary of Scientific Biography (DSB), Vol. 3, pp. 512–16.

Hogendijk, Jan P. (1986). 'Discovery of an eleventh-century geometrical compilation: The Istikmal of Yusuf ibn Hud, King of Saragossa', Historia Mathematica, 13, pp. 43–52.

Hogendijk, Jan P. (2008). 'Ancient and modern secrets of Isfahan', Nieuw Archief voor Wis kunde, 5, 9, p. 121.

Hogendijk, Jan P. (2017). 'A mathematical classification of the contents of an Anonymous Persian Compendium on decorative patterns', in Necipoğlu, Gülru (ed), The Arts of Ornamental Geometry: A Persian Compendium on Similar and Complementary Interlocking Figures. Supplements to Muqarnas, Vol. 13 (Leiden/Boston, Brill), pp. 145–61.

Holod, Renata (ed). (1974). 'Studies on Isfahan, Proceedings of the Isfahan Colloquium, Harvard University', Iranian Studies, 7, 1–4.

Horton, Scott. (2009). 'Emerson's Saadi', Harper's Magazine, 21 June.

Hoskin, M. A. (1972). 'Herschel, William', Dictionary of Scientific Biography (DSB), Vol. 6, pp. 322–3.

Houtsma, M. Th., Arnold, T. W, Basset, R., Hartmann, R. (eds). (1913–36). Encyclopedia of Islam (EI^1) (Leiden, Brill; repr. 1987).

Huart, Cl. (1987). 'Iṣfahān, Sipāhān', Encyclopedia of Islam (EI^1), 3, pp. 528–30.

Hughes, Bettany. (2017). Istanbul: A Tale of Three Cities (London, Weidenfeld & Nicolson).

Huxley, George L. (1986). Why did the Byzantine Empire not fall to the Arabs? An Inaugural Lecture: American School of Classical Studies at Athens (Athens, [s.n.]).

Ilardi, Vincent. (2007). Renaissance Vision from Spectacles to Telescopes (Philadelphia, PA, American Philosophical Society).

Iqbal, Abbas. (1966). Khāndan Nawbakhtī (Tehran, Ṭahūrī [1345]).

Ireland, Corydon. (2008a). 'Houghton exhibit features Islamic sciences', Harvard Gazette, 22 April.

Ireland, Corydon. (2008b). 'Yes, it was a magical talk', Harvard Gazette, 5 June.

Ireland, Corydon. (2008c). 'Fair shows progress of humanities', Harvard Gazette, 18 December.

Ireland, Corydon. (2011). 'Treasure island', Harvard Gazette, 9 November.

Ireland, Corydon. (2012). 'A poem for Harvard', Harvard Gazette, 24 May.

Ireland, Corydon. (2015). '100 years of Widener', Harvard Gazette, 22 May.

Irving, Clive. (1979). 'Half of the world: 1450–1750', Crossroads of Civilization: 3000 Years of Persian History (London, Weidenfeld and Nicholson), pp. 147–81.
Janin, Louis and King, David A. (1977). 'Ibn al-Shāṭir's Ṣandūq al-yawāqīt: An astronomical "compendium"', Journal for the History of Arabic Science, 1, pp. 187–256.
Jolivet, Jean and Rashed, Roshdi. (1978). 'Al-Kindī, Abū Yūsuf Yaʿqūb ibn Isḥāq', Dictionary of Scientific Biography (DSB), Vol. 15 (Supp. I), pp. 261–7.
Kaplan, Robert. (2000). The Nothing That Is: A Natural History of Zero, Illustrations by Ellen Kaplan (Oxford, New York, Oxford University Press).
Kapoor, R. C. (2016). 'Nūr ud-dīn Jahangīr and Father Kirwitzer: The independent discovery of the great comets of November 1618 and the first astronomical use of the telescope in India', Journal of Astronomical History and Heritage, 19, 3, pp. 264–97.
Karamati, Younes. (2008–2009). 'Abū Isḥāq al-Kūbunānī', Negahban, Farzin (tr), in Madelung, Wilfred and Daftary, Farhad (eds), Encyclopedia Islamica (London, Brill).
Karamati, Younes. (2017). Kāshānī Shinākht: An Investigation of the Mathematical Works of Giyāth al-Dīn Jamshīd Kāshānī, English Introduction (Tehran, Miras-e Maktoob [1396]).
Kary-Niiazov, T. N. (1976). 'Ulugh Beg', Dictionary of Scientific Biography (DSB), Vol. 13, pp. 535–7.
Kennedy, E. S. (1957). 'Comets in Islamic astronomy and astrology', Journal of Near Eastern Studies, 16, 1, pp. 44–51.
Kennedy, E. S. (1960). The Planetary Equatorium of Jamshīd Ghiyāth al-Dīn al-Kāshī (Princeton, NJ, Princeton University Press).
Kennedy, E. S. (1966). 'Late medieval planetary theory', Isis, 57, 3, pp. 365–78.
Kennedy, E. S. (1970). 'Bīrūnī (or Berūnī) Abū Rayḥān (or Abu'l Rayḥān)' (Dictionary of Scientific Biography) (DSB), Vol. 2, pp. 147–58.
Kennedy, E. S. and Ghanem, I. (eds). (1976). The Life and Work of Ibn al-Shatir, an Arab Astronomer of the 14th Century (Aleppo, University of Aleppo).
Kennedy, Hugh N. (2004). The Court of the Caliphs: The Rise and Fall of Islam's Greatest Dynasty (London, Weidenfeld & Nicolson).
Kennedy, Hugh N. (2005). When Baghdad Ruled the Muslim World: The Rise and Fall of Islam's Greatest Dynasty (Cambridge, MA, Da Capo Press).
Khaleghi-Motlagh, Djalal. (1987). 'Asadī Ṭūsī', Encyclopedia Iranica (EIr), Vol. 2, Facs. 7, pp. 699–700.
Kheirandish, Asadollah. (1983). Fāl-nāmih-i Shaykh Bahāʾī (card edn) (Tehran, self-published [1362]; repr. 1995 [1374]).
Kheirandish, Asadollah. (1998). A Verse Amongst Thousands (Yik Bayt az Hizārān) (Tehran, Simin [1377]).
Kheirandish, Elaheh (ed, tr, comm). (1999). The Arabic Version of Euclid's Optics: Kitāb Uqlīdis fī Ikhtilāf al-manāẓir, 2 vols., in Toomer, Gerald J. (ed), Sources in the History of Mathematics and Physical Sciences, Vol. 16 (New York, Springer-Verlag).
Kheirandish, Elaheh. (2000). 'A report on Iran's "jewel" codices of Ṭūsī's Kutub al-Mutawassiṭāt', in Pourjavady, N. and Vesel, Ž. (eds), Naṣīr al-Dīn al-Ṭūsī: Philosophe et savant de xIIIe siècle (Tehran, Institut Français de Recherche en Iran (IFRI)), pp. 131–43.
Kheirandish, Elaheh. (2001a). 'Optics: Highlights from Islamic lands', in The Different Aspects of Islamic Culture, Vol. 4, in al-Hassan, A. Y. et al. (eds), Science and Technology in Islam, Part 1: The Exact and Natural Sciences (Beirut, UNESCO), pp. 337–57.
Kheirandish, Elaheh. (2001b). 'What "Euclid said" to his Arabic readers: The case of the optics', in De Diversis Artibus (Collection of Studies from the International Academy of the History of Science), Tome 55 (N.S. 18), Vol. 12, in Simon, Gérard and Débarbat,

Suzanne (eds), Proceedings of the XXth International Congress of History of Science (Turnhout, Brepols), pp. 17–28.

Kheirandish, Elaheh. (2003). 'The many aspects of appearances: Arabic optics to 950 AD', in Hogendijk, Jan P. and Sabra, Abdelhamid I. (eds), The Enterprise of Science in Islam: New Perspectives (Cambridge, MA, MIT Press), pp. 55–83.

Kheirandish, Elaheh. (2004). 'The Puzzle of Ṭūsī's optical works', in Pourjavady, N. and Vesel, Ž. (eds), Les sciences dans la monde iranien (Xe-XIXe siècle) (Tehran, Institut Français de Recherche en Iran (IFRI)), pp. 197–213.

Kheirandish, Elaheh. (2006a). 'Organizing scientific knowledge: The "mixed" sciences in early classifications', in Endress, Gerhard (ed), Organizing Knowledge: Encyclopaedic Activities in the Pre-Eighteenth Century Muslim World (Leiden, Brill), pp. 135–54.

Kheirandish, Elaheh. (2006b). 'The "fluctuating fortunes of scholarship": A very late review occasioned by a fallen book', Early Science and Medicine, 11, 2, pp. 207–22. (Review of Jackson, David E. P., 'Scholarship in Abbasid Baghdad with Special Reference to Greek Mechanics in Arabic', Quaderni di Studi Arabi (1987–88)).

Kheirandish, Elaheh. (2007). 'Qusṭā ibn Lūqā al-Ba῾labakkī', Biographical Encyclopedia of Astronomers (BEA) (New York, Springer Reference), pp. 948–9.

Kheirandish, Elaheh. (2008a). 'Science and "mithāl": Demonstrations in Arabic and Persian scientific traditions', Iranian Studies, 41, 4, Special Issue: Bier, Carol, Kheirandish, Elaheh and Yousefi, Najm al-Din (eds), Sciences, Crafts, and the Production of Knowledge: Iran and Eastern Islamic Lands (ca. 184–1153 AH/800–1740CE), pp. 465–89.

Kheirandish, Elaheh. (2008b). 'Windows into early science', Iranian Studies, 41, 4, Special Issue: Bier, Carol, Kheirandish, Elaheh and al-Din Yousefi, Najma (eds), Sciences, Crafts, and the Production of Knowledge: Iran and Eastern Islamic Lands (ca. 184–1153 AH/800–1740 CE), pp. 581–91.

Kheirandish, Elaheh. (2009). 'The footprints of "experiment" in early Arabic optics', Early Science and Medicine, 14, 1–3, Special Issue: Newman, William R. and Sylla, Edith Dudley (eds), Evidence and interpretation: Studies on early science and medicine in honor of John E. Murdoch, pp. 79–104.

Kheirandish, Elaheh. (2013). 'The mixed mathematical sciences: Optics and mechanics in the Islamic Middle Ages', in Lindberg, David C. and Shank, Michael H. (eds), The Cambridge History of Science, Vol. 2, Medieval Science (Cambridge, Cambridge University Press), pp. 84–108.

Kheirandish, Elaheh. (2014). 'Eloge: A. I. Sabra (8 June 1924–18 December 2013)', Early Science and Medicine, 19, 3, pp. 281–6.

Kheirandish, Elaheh. (2015). 'Light and dark: The "checkered history" of early optics', in Bloom, Jonathan and Blair, Sheila (eds), God Is the Light of the Heavens and the Earth: Light in Islamic Art and Culture (New Haven, CT, Yale University Press), pp. 61–85.

Kheirandish, Elaheh. (2016). 'Astronomical poems from the "four corners" of Persia (c. 1000–1500 CE)', in Korangy, Alireza, Thackston, Wheeler, Mottahedeh, Roy and Granara, William (eds), Essays in Islamic Philology, History, and Philosophy, in Heidemann, Stefan, Hagen, Gottfried, Kaplony, Andreas and Matthee, Rudi (eds), Studies in the History and Culture of the Middle East, Vol. 31 (Berlin/Boston, De Walter de Gruyter), pp. 51–90.

Kheirandish, Elaheh. (2017). 'An early tradition in practical geometry: The telling lines of unique Arabic and Persian sources', in Necipoğlu, Gülru (ed), The Arts of Ornamental Geometry: A Persian Compendium on Similar and Complementary Interlocking Figures. Supplements to Muqarnas, Vol. 13 (Leiden/Boston, Brill), pp. 79–144.

Kheirandish, Elaheh. (2019a). 'Books on mathematical and mixed-mathematical sciences: Arithmetic, geometry, optics and mechanics', in Necipoğlu, Gülru, Kafadar, Cemal, and Fleischer, Cornell, H. (eds), Treasures of Knowledge: An Inventory of the Ottoman Palace Library Commissioned by Sultan Bayezid II from his Librarian ʿAtufi, 2 vols., Supplements to Muqarnas Vol. 14/1 (Leiden/Boston, Brill), pp. 857–68.

Kheirandish, Elaheh. (2019b). 'Optics and perspective in and beyond the Islamic Middle Ages: A study of transmission through multidisciplinary sources in Arabic and Persian', in Dupré, Sven (ed), Renaissance Cultures of Optics and Practices of Perspective (Turnhout, Brepols), pp. 205–39.

Kheirandish, Elaheh. (2019c). 'Zodiacs of Paris: Verses, places, faces', in Cormos-Buchwald, Diana et al. (eds), Looking Back As We Move Forward: The Past, Present, and Future of the History of Science (New York, Ink Inc.), pp. 142–53.

Kheirandish, Elaheh. (2020). 'From Maragha to Samarqand and beyond: Revisiting a quartet of scientific traditions in Greater Persia (ca. 1300–1500s)', in Melville, Charles (ed), The Timurid Century: The Idea of Iran, Vol. 9 (London, I.B. Tauris/Bloomsbury), pp. 161–87.

King, David A. (1975). 'Ibn al-Shāṭir: ʿAlāʾ al-Dīn … ʿAlī ibn Ibrāhīm', Dictionary of Scientific Biography (DSB), Vol. 12, pp. 357–64.

King, David A. (1992). 'Some remarks on Islamic scientific manuscripts and instruments and past, present, and future research', in Cooper, John (ed), The Significance of Islamic Manuscripts (London, Al-Furgan), pp. 115–43.

King, David A. (1998). 'Takī al-Dīn', Encyclopedia of Islam (EI^2), Vol. 10, Facs. 165–6, pp. 132–3.

King, David A. (2004). 'A Hellenistic astrological table deemed worthy of being penned in gold ink: The Arabic tradition of Vettius Valens' auxiliary function for finding the length of life', in Burnett, Charles, Hogendijk, Jan P., Plofker, Kim and Yano, Michio (eds), Studies in the History of the Exact Sciences in Honour of David Pingree (Leiden, Boston, Brill).

King, David A. (2004–05). In Synchrony with the Heavens: Studies in Astronomical Timekeeping and Instrumentation in Medieval Islamic Civilization, 2 vols. (Leiden, Brill).

King, David A. (2007a). 'Henry C. King (1915–2005)', Journal for the History of Astronomy, 38, 4, pp. 526–7.

King, David A. (2007b). 'Ibn al- Shāṭir. . .', The Biographical Encyclopedia of Astronomy (BEA), pp. 569–70.

King, David A. and Samso, Julio. (2002). 'Zīdj, in Islamic Science an astronomical handbook with tables', Encyclopedia of Islam (EI^2), Vol. 11, pp. 496–508.

Knobel, Edward Ball. (1917). Ulugh Beg's Catalogue of Stars: Revised from all Persian Manuscripts Existing in Great Britain, with a Vocabulary of Persian and Arabic Words (Washington, DC, Carnegie Institution).

Kohlberg, E. (1988). 'Bahāʾ al-Dīn ʿĀmilī', Encyclopedia Iranica (EIr), Vol. 3, Facs. 4, pp. 429–30.

Koyré, Alexander. (1957). From the Closed World to the Infinite Universe (Baltimore, MD: Johns Hopkins Press; New York, Harper Torchbooks 31, 1958).

Krause, Max. (1936). 'Stambuler handschriften islamischer mathematiker', Quellen und Studien zur Geschichte der Mathematik, Astronomie und Physik, 3 (Abt. B), pp. 437–532.

Kuhn, Thomas S. (1957). The Copernican Revolution: Planetary Astronomy in the Development of Western Thought (Cambridge, MA, Harvard University Press).

Kuhn, Thomas S. (1968). 'Science: The history of science', International Encyclopedia of the History of the Social Sciences, Vol. 14 (New York, Macmillan Co. and Free Press), pp. 74–82.
Kunitzsch, Paul. (1982). 'Description of the night in Gurgānī's Vīs u Rāmīn', Der Islam, 59, pp. 93–110.
Kunitzsch, Paul. (1992). 'Al-Nudjūm, the stars', Encyclopedia of Islam (EI²), Vol. 8, Facs. 131–2, pp. 97–105.
Lacey, Robert and Danziger, Danny. (1999). What Life Was Like at the Turn of the First Millennium: The Year 1000 (Boston, MA, Little Brown).
Lambton, A. K. S. (1973). 'Iṣfahān: History', Encyclopedia of Islam (EI²), Vol. 4, Facs. 61–2, pp. 97–105.
Langermann, Y. Tzvi. (2007). 'Ibn al-Haytham: Abū ʿAlī al-Ḥasan ibn al-Ḥasan', Biographical Encyclopedia of Astronomers (BEA) (New York, Springer Reference), pp. 556–7.
Langford, Jerome L. (1971). Galileo, Science and the Church (Ann Arbor, MI, The University of Michigan Press).
Le Strange, Guy (ed). (1915–19). The Geographical Part of the Nuzhat-al-qulūb Composed by Ḥamd-Allāh Mustawfī of Qazwīn in 740 (1340) (Gibb Memorial Series) (Leyden, Brill; London, Luzac & Co.).
Le Strange, Guy. (1924). Baghdad During the Abbasid Caliphate from Contemporary Arabic and Persian Sources, with Eight Plans (London, Oxford University Press, H. Milford).
Levy, Reuben. (1929). A Baghdad Chronicle (Studies in Islamic History, No. 17) (Cambridge, Cambridge University Press; repr., 2011).
Levy, R., Bosworth, C. E. and Freeman-Greenville, G. S. P. (1992). 'Nawrūz (P.), New (Year's) Day', Encyclopedia of Islam (EI²), Vol. 7, Facs. 129–30, p. 1047.
Lewis, Bernard. (2002). What Went Wrong: Western Impact and Middle Eastern Response (Oxford, New York, Oxford University Press).
Lincoln, Rose. (2014). 'Hidden spaces: Secret garden', Harvard Gazette, 2 September.
Lincoln, Rose. (2003). What Went Wrong: The Clash between Islam and Modernity in the Middle East (New York, Perennial).
Lindberg, David C. (1975). A Catalogue of Medieval and Renaissance Optical Manuscripts (Toronto, Pontifical Institute of Mediaeval Studies).
Lindberg, David C. (1976). Theories of Vision from Al-Kindi to Kepler (Chicago, IL, University of Chicago Press).
Lindberg, David C. (1978). 'The intromission-extramission controversy in Islamic visual theory: Alkindi versus Avicenna', in Machamer, Peter K. and Turnbull, Robert C. (eds), Studies in Perception: Interrelations in the History and Philosophy of Science (Columbus, OH, Ohio State University Press).
Lockhart, Laurence. (1939). Famous Cities of Iran (Brentford, W. Pearce and Co.).
Lockhart, Laurence. (1960). Persian Cities (London, Luzac & Company Ltd).
Long, Priscilla. (2012). 'Galileo's spyglass', The American Scholar, 19 December.
Losensky, Paul. (2008). 'Jāmī. i. Life and Works', Encyclopedia Iranica (EIr), Vol. 14, Facs. 5, pp. 469–75.
Maalouf, Amin. (2004). Samarkand, Russell, Harris (tr) (Northampton, MA, Interlink Publishing Group Inc.).
Mahdavi, Yahya. (1954). Catalogue of Manuscripts of the Compositions of Ibn Sīnā (Tehran, Tehran University [1333]), pp. 1–255, 259–304.
Manz, Beatrice F. (2000). 'Ulugh Beg', Encyclopedia of Islam (EI²), Vol. 10, pp. 812–14.

Maróth, Miklós. (2003). 'The library of Sultan Bayazit II', in Jeremiás, Éva M. (ed), Irano-Turkic Cultural Contact in the 11th–17th Centuries (Piliscsaba, Avicenna Institute of Middle Eastern Studies).
Marshall, O. S. (1950). 'Alhazen and the telescope', in Astronomical Society of the Pacific Leaflets, Vol. 6, Facs. 251, pp. 4–11.
Martineau, John. (2000). A Little Book of Coincidence (London, Walker Books; repr. 2002).
Masood, Ehsan. (2009). Science and Islam: A History (London, Icon).
Masoumi Hamedani, Hossein. (2000). 'Ustād-i bashar' [Teacher of Mankind], in Pourjavady, N. and Vesel, Ž. (eds), Naṣīr al-Dīn al-Ṭūsī: philosophe et savant de XIIIe siécle (Tehran, Institut Francais de Recherche en Iran (IFRI)), pp. 1–38.
Massé, H. (1958). 'Asadi', Encyclopedia of Islam (EI²) Vol. 1, Facs. 11, pp. 685–6.
Massignon, Louis. (1913–16/1987). 'Nawbakht', Encyclopedia of Islam (EI²), Vol. 6, p. 887.
Mazor, Amir and Abbou Hershkovits, Keren. (2013). 'Spectacles in the Muslim World: New evidence from the mid-fourteenth century', Early Science and Medicine, 18, 3, pp. 291–305.
McGinnis, Jon. (2010). Avicenna (Oxford, New York, Oxford University Press).
Melikian-Chirvani, A. S. (2000). 'Khwāje and the Iranian past', in Pourjavady, N. and Vesel, Ž. (eds), Naṣīr al-Dīn al-Ṭūsī: Philosophe et savant du XIIIe siècle (Tehran, Institut Francais de Recherche en Iran (IFRI)), pp. 69–104.
Melville, Charles. (1997). 'Ebn al-Fowaṭī, Kamāl al-Dīn ʿAbd al-Razzāq', Encyclopedia Iranica (EIr), Vol. 8, Facs. 1, pp. 25–6.
Melville, Charles. (2002) 'Great Britain x. Iranian Studies in Britain, the Islamic period', Encyclopedia Iranica (EIr), Vol. 11, Facs. 3, pp. 260–7.
Melville, Charles. (2008). 'Obituary: Persian scholar Peter Avery', The Times, 16 October.
Melville, Charles. (2016). 'New light on Shah ʿAbbas and the construction of Isfahan', in Necipoğlu, Gülru (ed), Muqarnas: An Annual of the Visual Culture of the Islamic World (Leiden, Brill), pp. 155–76.
Memon, M. U. (1989). 'Amīn Aḥmad Rāzī', Encyclopedia Iranica (EIr), Vol. 1, Facs. 9, p. 939.
Ménage, V. L. (1964). 'Firdawsi' (Ferdosi)', Encyclopedia of Islam (EI²), Vol. 2, Facs. 37, pp. 918–21.
Mendelsohn, Everett (ed). (1984). Transformation and Tradition in the Sciences: Essays in Honor of I. Bernard Cohen (Cambridge, New York, Cambridge University Press).
Menocal, María Rosa. (2002). The Ornament of the World: How Muslims, Jews, and Christians Created a Culture of Tolerance in Medieval Spain (Boston, MA, Little Brown).
Merton, Robert K. (1965). On the Shoulders of Giants: A Shandean Postscript (New York, Free Press; San Diego, CA, Harcourt Brace Jovanovich, 1985; Chicago, IL: University of Chicago Press, 1993).
Metz, Rachel. (2017). 'Second Life is back for a third life, this time in virtual reality', MIT Technology Review, 27 January.
Meyerhof, Max. (1930). From Alexandria to Baghdad: A Study of the History of Philosophical and Medical Teaching among the Arabs, Heinen, Anton (tr), in Introduction to the History of Science: Course Source Book, compiled by A. I. Sabra (1978) (Cambridge, MA, Harvard University, Department of History of Science).
Meyerhof, Max. (1948). 'ʿAlī Bayhaqī's Tatimmat Ṣiwān al-ḥikma. A biographical work on the learned men of Islam', Osiris, 8, pp. 122–216.

Morrison, Robert G. (2007). Islam and Science: The Intellectual Career of Niẓām al-Dīn al-Nīsābūrī (Abingdon, Routledge).
Morrison, Robert G. (2014). 'A scholarly intermediary between the Ottoman Empire and Renaissance Europe', Isis, 105, pp. 32–57.
Mottahedeh, Roy P. (1967). 'Sources for the study of Iran', Iranian Studies, 1, 1, pp. 4–7.
Mottahedeh, Roy P. (2012). 'The Idea of Iran in the Buyid dominions', in Herzig, Edmund and Stewart, Sarah (eds), Early Islamic Iran (London, I.B. Tauris), pp. 153–60.
Muʿaẓẓamah Iqbālī (aʿẓam). (2000). Shiʿr va Shāʿirī dar āthār-i Khwājah Naṣīr al-Dīn Ṭūsī (Tehran, Cultural Ministry [1379]).
Mudarris-i Raḍavī, Muḥammad Taqī. (1976). Aḥvāl va athār-i Khwāja Naṣīr al-Dīn Ṭūsī (Tehran, Tehran University [1355]).
Mudarrisī (Zanjānī), Muḥammad. (1984). Sar-gudhasht va ʿaqāʾid-i falsafī-yi Khwāja Naṣīr al-Dīn Ṭūsī: bih inḍimām-i baʿdī az rasāʾil va mukātibāt-i vay (Tehran, Amīr Kabīr [1363]).
Murdoch, John E. (1971). 'Euclid: Transmission of the Elements', Dictionary of Scientific Biography (DSB), Vol. 4, pp. 437–59.
Murdoch, John E. (1984). Album of Science: Antiquity and the Middle Ages, I. Bernard Cohen (ed) (New York, Charles Scribner's Sons).
Nafīsī, Saʿīd. (1954). Zindigī va kār va andīshah va rūzgār-i Pūr Sīnā (Tehran [1333]).
Nagy, Gregory. (2005). 'The epic hero', in Foley, J. M. (ed), A Companion to Ancient Epic (Malden, MA and Oxford: Blackwell), pp. 71–89.
Nasr, Seyyed Hossein. (1976a). Islamic Science: An Illustrated Study (London, World of Islam Festival Pub. Co.).
Nasr, Seyyed Hossein. (1976b). 'Al-Ṭūsī, Muḥammad ibn Muḥammad ibn al-Ḥasan . . . Naṣīr al-Dīn', Dictionary of Scientific Biography (DSB), Vol. 13, pp. 508–14.
Nasr, Seyyed Hossein. (1996). 'Bīrūnī versus Ibn Sīnā on the nature of the universe', in Nasr, S. H. and Amin Razavi, Mehdi (eds), The Islamic Intellectual Tradition in Persia, Vol. 9 (Richmond, Curzon Press), pp. 100–2.
Naẓīf, Muṣṭafā. (1942–1943). Al-Ḥasan ibn al-Haytham: buḥūthuhu wa-kushūfuhu al-Baṣariyya [al-Ḥasan ibn al-Haytham, His Researches and Discoveries in Optics], 2 vols. (Cairo, Maṭbaʿat Nūrī).
Necipoğlu, Gülru (ed). (2017). The Arts of Ornamental Geometry: A Persian Compendium on Similar and Complementary Interlocking Figures. Studies and Sources in Islamic Art and Architecture. Supplements to Muqarnas: An Annual on the Visual Cultures of the Islamic World, Vol. 13 (Leiden/Boston, Brill).
Necipoğlu, Gülru, Kafadar, Cemal and Fleischer, Cornell H. (eds). (2019). Treasures of Knowledge: An Inventory of the Ottoman Palace Library (1502/3–1503/4), 2 vols. Studies and Sources in Islamic Art and Architecture. Supplements to Muqarnas: An Annual on the Visual Cultures of the Islamic World, Vol. 14 (Leiden and Boston, Brill).
Needham, Joseph. (1954–). Science and Civilization in China (Cambridge, Cambridge University Press).
Neugebauer, Otto. (1982). 'The date of the "horoscope" in Gurgānī's poem', Islam, 59, pp. 297–301.
Newman, Andrew. (1986). 'Towards a reconsideration of the Isfahān school of philosophy: Shaykh Bahāʾī and the role of the Safawid ʿulamāʾ', Studia Iranica, 15, pp. 83–99.
Overbye, Dennis. (2001). 'How Islam won and lost the lead in science', The New York Times, 30 Oct.

Owen, G. E. L. (1970). 'Aristotle', Dictionary of Scientific Biography (DSB), Vol. 1, pp. 250–8.

Özdural, Alpay. (1998). 'A mathematical sonata for architecture: Omar Khayyam and the Friday Mosque of Isfahan', Technology and Culture, 39, 4, pp. 699–715.

Palmeri, JoAnn. (2007). 'Thābit ibn Qurra', Biographical Encyclopedia of Astronomers (BEA) (New York, Springer Reference), pp. 1129–30.

Pedersen, Johannes. (1984). The Arabic Book, French, Geoffrey (tr), Robert Hillenbrand (ed, intro) (Princeton, NJ, Princeton University Press).

Pellat, Charles. (1985). 'Alf layla wa-layla', Encyclopedia Iranica (EIr), Vol. 1, Facs. 8, pp. 831–5.

Pines, Shlomo. (1974). 'Maimonides, Rabbi Moses Ben Maimon . . .', Dictionary of Scientific Biography (DSB), Vol. 9, pp. 27–32.

Pingree, David. (1968). The Thousands of Abū Ma'shar (London, Warburg Institute).

Pingree, David. (1970a). ''Ilm al-hay'a, the science of the figure of the heavens or astronomy', Encyclopedia of Islam (EI^2), Vol. 3, Facs. 57–8, pp. 1135–8.

Pingree, David. (1970b). 'The fragments of the works of Al-Fazārī', Journal of Near Eastern Studies (JNES), 29, 2, pp. 103–23.

Pingree, David. (1971). 'Fazārī: Muḥammad ibn Ibrāhīm', Dictionary of Scientific Biography (DSB), Vol. 4, pp. 555–6.

Pingree, David. (1975). 'Al-Kamar (A.), the moon, I. Astronomy', Encyclopedia of Islam (EI^2), Vol. 4, Facs. 69–70, pp. 517–18.

Pingree, David. (1983a). 'Abu'l-Fatḥ Esfahanī', Encyclopedia Iranica (EIr), Vol. 1, Facs. 3, pp. 284–5.

Pingree, David. (1983b). 'Abū Sahl B. Nawbaḵt', Encyclopedia Iranica (EIr), Vol. 1, Facs. 4, p. 369.

Pingree, David. (1983c). 'Abu'l-Wafā Būzjānī', Encyclopedia Iranica (EIr), Vol. 1, Facs. 4, pp. 392–4.

Pingree, David. (2000). 'Indian reception of Muslim versions of Ptolemaic astronomy', in Ragep, F. Jamil and Ragep, Sally P., with Livesey, Steven (eds), Tradition, Transmission, Transformation (Leiden, Brill), pp. 471–85.

Pingree, David. (2001). 'From Alexandria to Baghdad and Byzantium: The transmission of astrology', International Journal of Classical Traditions, 8, 1, pp. 3–37.

Pingree, David. (2009). Eastern Astrolabes, Vol. 2, Kheirandish, Elaheh (ed), in Bruce Chandler (ed), Historic Scientific Instruments of the Adler Planetarium (Chicago, IL, Adler Planetarium, Astronomy).

Pingree, Isabelle and Steele, John M. (eds). (2014). Pathways into the Study of Ancient Sciences: Selected Essays by David Pingree (Philadelphia, PA, American Philosophical Society).

Plofker, Kim. (2007). 'Fazārī: Muḥammad ibn Ibrāhīm al-Fazārī', Biographical Encyclopedia of Astronomers (BEA) (New York, Springer Reference), pp. 362–3.

Powers, Richard. (1999). 'Eyes wide open', The New York Times Magazine, 18 April.

Ragep, F. Jamil. (2000). 'The Persian context of the Tūsī Couple', in Pourjavady, N. and Vesel, Ž. (eds), Naṣīr al-Dīn al-Ṭūsī: Philosophe et savant du XIIIe siècle (Tehran, Institut Français de Recherche en Iran (IFRI)), pp. 113–30.

Ragep, F. Jamil. (2001a). 'Freeing astronomy from philosophy: An aspect of Islamic influence on science' (includes text), Osiris, Science in Theistic Contexts: Cognitive Dimensions, 16, pp. 49–71.

Ragep, F. Jamil. (2001b). 'Ṭūsī and Copernicus: The earth's motion in context', Science in Context, 14 (1/2), pp. 145–63.

Ragep, F. Jamil. (2005). ''Alī Qushī [sic] and Regiomontanus: Eccentric transformations and Copernican revolutions', Journal of History of Astronomy, 36, pp. 359–71.
Ragep, F. Jamil. (2007a). 'Copernicus and his Islamic predecessors: Some historical remarks', History of Science, 45, pp. 65–81.
Ragep, F. Jamil. (2007b). 'Ṭūsī: Abū Jaʿfar Muḥammad ibn Muḥammad ibn al-Ḥasan Naṣīr al-Dīn al-Ṭūsī', Biographical Encyclopedia of Astronomers (BEA) (New York, Springer Reference), pp. 1153–5.
Ragep, F. Jamil. (2017). 'From Tūn to Torun: The twists and turns of the Ṭūsī Couple', in Feldhay, Rivka and Ragep, F. Jamil (eds), Before Copernicus: The Cultures and Contexts of Scientific Learning in the Fifteenth Century (Montreal, McGill-Queen's University), pp. 161–97.
Ragep, F. Jamil and Ragep, Sally P. (2004). 'The astronomical and cosmological works of Ibn Sīnā: Some preliminary remarks', in Pourjavady, N. and Vesel, Ž. (eds), Sciences, techniques et instruments dans le monde iranien (Xe-XIXe siècle) (Tehran, Institut Français de Recherche en Iran (IFRI)), pp. 3–15.
Ragep, F. Jamil and Ragep, Sally P. with Livesey, Steven (eds). (2000). Tradition, Transmission, Transformation: Proceedings of Two Conferences on Pre-Modern Science Held at the University of Oklahoma (Leiden, Brill).
Ragep, Sally P. (2007). 'Ibn Sīnā: Abū ʿAlī al-Ḥusayn ibn ʿAbdallāh ibn Sīnā', Biographical Encyclopedia of Astronomers (BEA) (New York, Springer Reference), pp. 570–2.
Rashed, Roshdi. (1993). Géométrie et dioptrique au Xe siècle: Ibn Sahl, al-Qūhī, et Ibn al-Haytham (Paris, Les Belles Lettres).
Rashed, Roshdi. (2005). Geometry and Dioptrics in Classical Islam (London, Al-Furqan).
Rashed, Roshdi. (2009). Thābit ibn Qurra: Science and Philosophy in Ninth-Century Baghdad (Berlin, Walter de Gruyter).
Rashed, Roshdi. (2013). Ibn al-Haytham's Theory of Conics, Geometrical Constructions and Practical Geometry, Field, J. V. (tr), Vol. 3, in El-Bizri, Nader (ed), A History of Arabic Sciences and Mathematics, 4 vols. (London, New York, Routledge).
Reeves, Eileen. (1999). Painting the Heavens: Art and Science in the Age of Galileo (Princeton, NJ, Princeton University).
Reinink, G. J. and Vanstiphout, H. L. J. (eds). (1991). Dispute Poems and Dialogues in The Ancient and Mediaeval Near East: Forms and Types of Literary Debates in Semitic and Related Literature (Leuven, Uitgeveru Peeters).
Rice, D. S. (1959). 'The oldest illustrated Arabic manuscript', Bulletin of the School of Oriental and African Studies, 2, 1/3, pp. 207–20.
Richard, Alain. (2003). 'L'astronomie et l'astrologie dans la poésie persane', Luqmān: Annales des Presses Universitaires d'Iran Revue Semestrielle, 20, 1, pp. 81–101.
Rieu, Charles. (1881). Catalogue of the Persian Manuscripts in the British Museum, 3 vols. (London, British Museum).
Ritter, Hellmut. (1953). 'Autographs in Turkish libraries', Oriens, 6, 1, pp. 63–90.
Roberts, Victor. (1957). 'The solar and lunar theory of Ibn al-Shāṭir: A pre-Copernican Copernican model', Isis, 48, pp. 428–32.
Robinson, Francis (ed). (1996). The Cambridge Illustrated History of the Islamic World (Cambridge, Cambridge University Press).
Robson, J. (1971). 'Hadith', Encyclopedia of Islam (EI^2), Vol. 3, Facs. 41–2, pp. 23–8.
Roemer, Hans Robert. (1975). 'Research on al-Biruni in Germany', in Chelkowski, Peter J. (ed), Scholar and the Saint: Studies in Commemoration of Abu'l-Rayhan al-Biruni and Jalal al-Din al-Rumi (New York, New York University Press), pp. 95–102.
Roper Geoffrey (ed). (1994). World Survey of Islamic Manuscripts, Vol. 4 (Leiden, Brill).

Rosen, Edward. (1956). 'The invention of eyeglasses', Journal of the History of Medicine and Allied Sciences, 2, 1, pp. 13–47; 2, 2, pp. 183–218.
Rosen, Edward. (1971). 'Copernicus, Nicolas', Dictionary of Scientific Biography (DSB), Vol. 3, pp. 401–11.
Rosenfeld, B. A. and Grigorian, A. T. (1976). 'Thābit ibn Qurra, Al-Ṣābi Al-Ḥarrānī', Dictionary of Scientific Biography (DSB), Vol. 13, pp. 288–95.
Rosenfeld, Boris A. and Ihsanoğlu, Ekmeleddin. (2003). Mathematicians, Astronomers, and Other Scholars of Islamic Civilization and their Works (7th–19th c.) (Istanbul, Research Center for Islamic History, Art and Culture (IRCICA)).
Rosenthal, Franz. (1947). The Technique and Approach of Muslim Scholarship (Rome, Pontificium Institutum Biblicum).
Rosenthal, Franz. (1959). 'Nineteen', Analecia Biblica, 12, pp. 304–18.
Rosenthal, Franz. (1974). 'On some epistemological and methodological presuppositions of Al-Biruni', in Science and Medicine in Islam: A Collection of Essays, Vol. 12 (Aldershot, Variorum, 1991), pp. 145–56.
Rosenthal, Franz. (1975). The Classical Heritage in Islam, Marmorstein, Emile and Marmorstein, Jenny (tr) (London and New York, Routledge).
Rosenthal, Franz. (1976). 'Al-Biruni between Greece and India', in Yarshatir, E. (ed), Biruni Symposium (Persian Studies Series No. 7) (New York, 1976; repr., Science and Medicine in Islam: A Collection of Essays, Vol. 11 (Aldershot, Variorum, 1991), pp. 1–12).
Rosenthal, Franz. (2014). Man versus Society in Medieval Islam, Dimitri Gutas (ed) (Leiden, Brill).
Ruska, J. (1987). 'Thābit ibn Kurra', First Encyclopedia of Islam (EI^1), Vol. 8, p. 733.
Russel, Gül A. (2015). 'In Memoriam: A. I. Sabra (June 8, 1924–December 18, 2013)', Journal of the History of the Neurosciences, 24, 2, pp. 193–8.
Sabra, A. I. (1966). 'Ibn al-Haytham's criticisms of Ptolemy's *Optics*', Journal of the History of Philosophy, 4, 2, pp. 145–9.
Sabra, A. I. (1971). 'The astronomical origin of Ibn al-Haytham's concept of experiment', Actes XIIe Congrès International d'Histoire des Science (Paris, Albert Blanchard), pp. 133–36 (repr., Optics, Astronomy and Logic (Aldershot, Variorum, 1994)).
Sabra, A. I. (1972). 'Ibn al-Haytham', Abū 'Alī al-Ḥasan Ibn al-Ḥasan . . . also known as Alhazen', Dictionary of Scientific Biography (DSB), Vol. 6, pp. 189–210 (repr., Optics, Astronomy and Logic (Aldershot, Variorum, 1994)).
Sabra, A. I. (1976a). 'The physical and the mathematical in Ibn al-Haytham's theory of light and vision', The Commemoration Volume of Biruni International Congress in Tehran (Tehran, Tehran University), pp. 439–78 (repr., Optics, Astronomy and Logic (Aldershot, Variorum, 1994)).
Sabra, A. I. (1976b). 'The scientific enterprise: Islamic contributions to the development of science', in Lewis, Bernard (ed), The World of Islam: Faith, People, Culture (London, Thames and Hudson), pp. 181–99.
Sabra, A. I. (1984). 'The Andalusian revolt against Ptolemaic astronomy: Averroes and al-Bitrūjī', in Mendelsohn, Everett (ed), Transformation and Tradition in the Sciences: Essays in Honor of I. Bernard Cohen (Cambridge, Cambridge University Press), pp. 133–53 (repr., Optics, Astronomy and Logic (Aldershot, Variorum, 1994)).
Sabra, A. I. (1987a). 'The appropriation and subsequent naturalization of Greek Science in Medieval Islam: A preliminary statement', History of Science, 25, 3, pp. 223–43 (repr., in Ragep, F. Jamil and Ragep, Sally P., with Livesey, Steven (eds), Tradition, Transmission, Transformation, (Leiden, Brill, 1996, pp. 3–27).

Sabra, A. I. (1987b). 'Manāẓir, or ʿIlm al-Manāẓir', Encyclopedia of Islam (EI[2]), Vol. 6, Facs. 103–4, pp. 376–7.

Sabra, A. I. (1994). Optics, Astronomy and Logic (Aldershot, Variorum).

Sabra, A. I. (1996). 'Situating Arabic science: Locality versus essence', Isis, 87, pp. 654–70.

Sabra, A. I. (1998, 2002–03). 'One Ibn al-Haytham or two: An exercise in reading bio-bibliographical sources', Zeitschrift für Geschichte der arabisch-islamischen Wissenschaften, 12, pp. 1–50; 15, pp. 95–108.

Sabra, A. I. (2003). 'Vita: Ibn al-Haytham: Brief life of an Arab mathematician, died circa 1040', Harvard Magazine, October, pp. 54–5.

Sabra, A. I. (2007). 'The "commentary" that saved the text: The hazardous journey of Ibn al-Haytham's Arabic optics', Early Science and Medicine, 12, pp. 117–33.

Saliba, George. (1972–73). 'The meaning of Al-Jabr wa al-Muqabalah', Centaurus, 17, pp. 189–204.

Saliba, George. (1993). 'Qushjī's [sic.] reform of the Ptolemaic model for Mercury' (includes text), Arabic Sciences and Philosophy, 3, pp. 161–203.

Saliba, George. (1994). 'An observational notebook of a thirteenth-century astronomer', in A History of Arabic Astronomy: Planetary Theories During the Golden Age of Islam (New York, New York University), pp. 163–76.

Saliba, George. (2002). 'Giāṯ-al-Din', Encyclopedia Iranica (EIr), Vol. 6, Facs. 1, pp. 64–7.

Saliba, George. (2007). Islamic Science and the Making of the European Renaissance (Cambridge, MA, The MIT Press).

Sarton, George. (1917). 'An institute for the history of science and civilization', Science, 45, 1160, pp. 284–6.

Sarton, George. (1927–1948). Introduction to the History of Science, 3 vols. (Baltimore, MD, Williams & Wilkins Co.; repr., 1962).

Sarton, George. (1956). 'Arabic science and learning in the fifteenth century, their decadence and fall', in Homenaje a Millas-Vallicrosa (Barcelona, Consejo Superior de Investigaciones Científicas), pp. 303–24.

Saunders, J. J. (1968). 'Problem of Islamic decadence', Journal of World History, 7, pp. 701–20.

Savage-Smith, Emily. (2013). 'The most authoritative copy of ʿAbd al-Rahmān al-Ṣūfī's tenth-century Guide to the Constellations', in Bloom, Jonathan and Blair, Sheila (eds), God Is Beautiful and Loves Beauty: The Object in Islamic Art and Culture (New Haven, CT, Yale University Press), pp. 123–56.

Sayılı, Aydın. (1956). 'ʿAlāʾ al-Dīn al-Manṣūr's poems on the Istanbul Observatory', Türk Tarīh Kurumu Belleten, 20, 79, pp. 429–84.

Sayılı, Aydın. (1958). 'An early seventeenth century Persian manuscript on the Tychonic system', Anatolia, 3, pp. 84–7.

Sayılı, Aydın. (1960a). The Observatory in Islam and its Place in the General History of the Observatory (Ankara, Türk Tarih Kurumu Basımevi; repr. 1988).

Sayılı, Aydın. (1960b). 'Thâbit ibn Qurra's generalization of the Pythagorean Theorem', Isis, 51, 1, pp. 35–7.

Schiefsky, Mark J. (2007). 'Art and nature in ancient mechanics', in Bensaude-Vincent, Bernadette and Newman, William R. (eds), The Artificial and the Natural: An Evolving Polarity (Cambridge, MA, MIT Press), pp, 67–108.

Schmidl, Petra G. (2007). 'Kāshī: Ghiyāth (al-Milla wa-) al-Dīn Jamshīd ibn Masʿūd ibn Maḥmūd al-Kāshī [Kāshānī]', Biographical Encyclopedia of Astronomers (BEA) (New York, Springer Reference), pp. 613–15.

Schramm, Matthias. (1963). Ibn al-Haytham Weg zur Physik (Weisbaden: F. Steiner).

Seherr-Thoss, Sonia P. (1968). Design and Color in Islamic Architecture (Washington DC, Smithsonian Institution Press).
Sezign, Fuat. (2010). The Istanbul Museum for the History of Science and Technology in Islam (Catalogue) (Istanbul, Metropolitan Municipality).
Shah, Mir Hussein. (1955). 'Athār-ī mansūb bih Shaykh al-Raʾīs' (A work attributed to Shaykh al-Raʾīs = Ibn Sinā), Indo-Iranica, 8, 3, pp. 1–14.
Shinagel, Michael. (2009). The Gates Unbarred: A History of University Extension at Harvard, 1910–2009 (Cambridge, MA, and London, Distributed by Harvard University Press).
Shoja, Mohammadali M., Agutter, Paul S. and Tubbs, R. Shane. (2015). 'Rhazes doubting Galen: Ancient and medieval theories of vision', International Journal of History and Philosophy of Medicine, 5, pp. 1–6.
Sidoli, Nathan and van Brummelen, Glen (eds). (2014). From Alexandria, Through Baghdad: Surveys and Studies in the Ancient Greek and Medieval Islamic Mathematical Sciences in Honor of J. L. Berggren (Berlin, Heidelberg, Springer-Verlag).
Sivin, Nathan. (1982). 'Why the Scientific Revolution did not take place in China – or didn't it', Chinese Science, 5, pp. 45–66.
Snir, Reuven (ed, tr). (2013). Baghdad: The City in Verse (Cambridge, MA, Harvard University Press).
Sobel, Dava. (1995). Longitude: The True Story of a Lone Genius Who Solved the Greatest Scientific Problem of his Time (New York, Walker; repr. 2005).
Sobel, Dava. (1999). Galileo's Daughter: A Historical Memoir of Science, Faith, and Love (New York, Penguin).
Sobel, Dava. (2005). The Planets (New York, Viking).
Sobel, Dava. (2007). 'The shadow knows: Why a leading expert on the history of timekeeping set out to create a sundial unlike anything the world has ever seen', Smithsonian Magazine, January.
Sobel, Dava. (2011). A More Perfect Heaven: How Copernicus Revolutionized the Cosmos (New York, Walker).
Sobel, Dava. (2016a). And the Sun Stood Still (New York, Bloomsbury).
Sobel, Dava. (2016b). The Glass Universe: How the Ladies of the Harvard Observatory Took the Measure of the Stars (New York, Viking).
Soudavar, Abolala. (1999). 'The concepts of "al-aqdamo aṣaḥḥ" and "yaqīn-e sābeq", and the problem of semi-fakes', Studia Iranica, 28, 2, pp. 255–73.
Sourdel-Thomine. (1973). 'Iṣfahān: Monuments', Encyclopedia of Islam (EI²), Vol. 4, Facs. 61–2, pp. 105–7.
Spuler, Bertold. (1994). The Mongol Period, Bagley, F. R. C. (tr) (Princeton, NJ, M. Wiener).
Sripada, Kam. (2005). 'David Pingree obituary', The Brown Daily Herald, Campus News, 18 November.
Steele, Philip. (2007). Isaac Newton: The Scientist Who Changed Everything (Washington DC, National Geographic Society).
Stevens, Sir Roger. (1974). 'European visitors to the Safavid court', Iranian Studies, 7, Special Issue: Holod, Renata (ed), Studies on Isfahan, Proceedings of The Isfahan Colloquium, Harvard University, pp. 421–49.
Stewart, Devin J. (1991). 'A biographical notice on Bahāʾ al-Dīn Al-ʿĀmilī', Journal of the American Oriental Society, 111, 3, pp. 563–71.
Stewart, Devin J. (1996a). 'The first Shaykh al-Islām of the Safavid capital Qazvin', Journal of the American Oriental Society, 116, 3, pp. 387–405.

Stewart, Devin J. (1998). 'The lost biography of Bahā' al-Dīn Al-ʿĀmilī and the reign of Shah Ismāʿil II in Safavid historiography', Iranian Studies, 31, 2, pp. 177–205.

Storey, Charles Ambrose. (1927). Persian Literature: A Bio-Bibliographical Survey, Vol. 2, Part 1: A. Mathematics, B. Weights and Measures, C. Astronomy and Astrology, D. Geography (London, Luzac & Co.).

Streck, M. (1987). 'Baghdad', Encyclopedia of Islam (EI¹), Vol. 2, pp. 563–6.

Tafaḍḍulī, Aḥmad. (2003). Takhtih Nard: Taqdīr yā Tadbīr (Tehran, Atāʾī [1382]).

Taheri, Jafar. (2009). 'Mathematical knowledge of architecture in the works of Kâshânî', Nexus Network Journal, 11, 1, pp. 77–88.

Taub, Liba. (2006). 'The "grand" orrery: Explore Whipple collections', Whipple Museum of the History of Science (Cambridge, University of Cambridge).

Tekeli, Sevim. (1974). 'Muḥyi 'l-Dīn al-Maghribī . . . Yaḥyā . . . al-Maghribī al-Andalūsī', Dictionary of Scientific Biography (DSB), Vol. 9, pp. 555–7.

Tekeli, Sevim. (1997). 'Taqī al-Dīn', in Selin, Helaine (ed), Encyclopedia of the History of Science, Technology, and Medicine in Non-Western Cultures (Dordrecht, Kluwer publishers; Berlin, Heidelberg, New York, Springer-Verlag, 2008).

Thackston, Wheeler M. (sel, tr). (1989). A Century of Princes: Sources on Timurid History and Art (Cambridge, MA, Agha Khan Program in Islamic Architecture).

Titley, Norah. (1983). Persian Miniature Painting (London, British Library; repr. Austin, University of Texas Press, 2009).

Toomer, Gerald J. (1970). 'Ptolemy (Claudius Ptolemaeus)', Dictionary of Scientific Biography (DSB), Vol. 11, pp. 186–206.

Toomer, Gerald J. (1973). 'Al-Khwārizmī, Abū Jaʿfar Muḥammad ibn Mūsā', Dictionary of Scientific Biography (DSB), Vol. 7, pp. 358–65.

Toomer, Gerald J. (tr). (1984). Ptolemy's Almagest (New York, Springer-Verlag).

van Dalen, Benno. (1996). 'Al-Shams (A.), the sun (f.), 2. In Astronomy', Encyclopedia of Islam (EI²), Vol. 9, Facs. 151–2, pp. 291–4.

van Dalen, Benno. (2007). 'Ulugh Beg: Muḥammad Ṭaraghāy ibn Shāhrukh ibn Tīmūr', Biographical Encyclopedia of Astronomers (BEA) (New York, Springer Reference), pp. 1157–9.

van Gelder, Geert Jan. (1987). 'The conceit of pen and sword: On an Arabic literary debate', Journal of Semitic Studies, 32, 2, pp. 329–60.

van Helden, Albert. (1977). 'The invention of the telescope', Transactions of the American Philosophical Society, 67, 4, pp. 1–67.

Varjavand, Parviz. (1987). Kāvush-i raṣad-khānah-i Marāgha (Tehran, Amīr Kabīr [1366]).

Verba, Sydney. (1998). 'Speaking volumes', Harvard Gazette, 26 February.

Vernet, J. (1976). 'Al-Kāshī or al-Kāshānī, Ghiyās al-Dīn DJamshīd b. Masud b. Mahmud', Encyclopedia of Islam (EI²), Vol. 4, pp. 702–3.

von Grunebaum, Gustave E. (1946). Medieval Islam: A Study in Cultural Orientation (Chicago, IL, University of Chicago Press).

Walsh, Colleen. (2010a). 'What's possible', Harvard Gazette, 30 November.

Walsh, Colleen. (2010b). 'Digital drive', Harvard Gazette, 16 December.

Walsh, Colleen. (2014). 'Harry's books', Harvard Gazette, 15 April.

Weir, T. H. (1987). 'Ḥarrān', First Encyclopedia of Islam (EI¹), Vol. 3, Facs. 19, p. 270.

Welch, Anthony. (2003). 'Safavi Iran as seen through Venetian eyes', in Newman, Andrew J. (ed), Society and Culture in the Early Modern Middle East (Leiden, Boston, Brill), pp. 97–119.

Welch, Anthony (ed). (2007). The Travels and Journal of Ambrosio Bembo (1671–1675). Bargellini, Clara (tr) (Berkeley, CA, University of California Press).

Westfall, Richard S. (1993). The Life of Isaac Newton (Cambridge, Cambridge University Press).

Wickens, G. Michael (ed). (1952). Avicenna: Scientist and Philosopher: A Millenary Symposium (London, Luzac).

Wickens, G. Michael. (1989). 'Browne, Edward Granville', Encyclopedia Iranica (EIr), Vol. 4, Facs. 5, pp. 483–8.

Wilding, Nick. (2014). Galileo's Idol: Gianfrancesco Sagredo and the Politics of Knowledge (Chicago, IL: University of Chicago Press).

Willach, Rolph (ed). (2008). The Long Route to the Invention of the Telescope, in Transactions of the American Philosophical Society, Vol. 98, Part 5 (Philadelphia, PA, American Philosophical Society).

Winter, H. J. J. (1960). 'Persian science in Safavid times', in Peter Jackson and Laurence Lockhart (eds), The Cambridge History of Iran, Vol. 6: The Timurid and Safavid Periods, pp. 581–609.

Wisnovsky, Robert. (ed). (2001). Aspects of Avicenna (Princeton, NJ, Markus Wiener).

Woods, John E. (1977). 'A note on the Mongol capture of Iṣfahān', Journal of Near Eastern Studies, 36, 1, pp. 49–51.

Yano, Michio. (2007). 'Bīrūnī: Abū al-Rayḥān Muḥammad ibn Aḥmad al-Bīrūnī', Biographical Encyclopedia of Astronomers (BEA) (New York, Springer Reference), pp. 131–3.

Yarshater, Ehsan (ed). (1982). Encyclopedia Iranica (EIr) (vols. 1–4: London and Boston, MA, Routledge and Kegan Paul; later vols.: Mazda Publishers; Bibliotecha Persica Press; Encyclopaedia Iranica Foundation).

Youschkevitch, A. P. and Rosenfeld, B. A. (1973a). 'al-Kāshī (or Kāshānī), Ghiyāth al-Dīn Jamshīd Masʿūd', Dictionary of Scientific Biography (DSB), Vol. 7, pp. 255–62.

Youschkevitch, A. P. and Rosenfeld, B. A. (1973b). 'Khayyāmī (or Khayyām), Ghiyāth al-Dīn . . . al-Nisābūrī (or Al-Naysāburī), also known as "Omar Khayyām"', Dictionary of Scientific Biography (DSB), Vol. 7, pp. 323–34.

Name Index

A selection of historical and modern names for authors, works, rulers, and figures cited

I. Historical

ʿAbbāsīds
Caliphate x, 5, 5 n.40, 28, 29, 29 n.50, 32, 32 n.65, 37, 59, 59 n.80, 60, 60 n.84, 61, 101, 109, 148, 203
Caliphs 28, 29, 30, 32, 37, 60, 61, 61 nn.89–90, 65, 65 n.109, 88, 90, 91, 92, 94, 95, 121
Capital city 22, 29, 32, 32 n.65
Viziers 91, 91 n.74
Afghāns
Invasion 29, 32 n.65, 37, 39 n.93, 40, 44, 156
Rulers 29, 29 n.50, 32, 32 n.65
Afshārs
Dynasty 44 n.4
Nādir Shāh 39, 44, 44 nn.4–5, 144
Alhacen/Alhazen (= Ibn al-Haytham)
Alhazen and Galileo viii, 112, 112 n.74, 131, 131 n.32, 132, 204
'Alhazen and the telescope . . .' 204 nn.120–1
Opticae thesaurus viii, 50, 102 n.15, 104, 109, 111 n.69, 179
Perspectiva 110, 154, 179, 189, 189 n.45, 202
Timeline 13
Almohāds
Dynasty 137, 137 n.68
ʿĀmilī, ʿAbd al-Mumʿin
On observatories 171 n.97, 175 n.115
ʿĀmilī, Bahāʾ al-Dīn (= Shaykh Bahāʾī)
Author 127 n.12, 135, 135 n.56, n.60, 172 n.101, 173 nn.103–7, 174 n.110, 175 n.113, nn.119–20, 176, 176 n.121, 178 n.131, 202, 203
Fāl-nāmih (Fortune-telling book) 175 n.118, 177, 177 n.126
House in Isfahan 135 n.60
Kashkūl (*Bowl of Darwīsh*) 176 n.121, n.124, 176, 202 n.108
Khulāṣat al-ḥisāb (*Summary of Arithmetic*) viii, 102 n.14, 127 n.12, 176, 176 n.122
Profile 172–80
Tashrīḥ al-aflāk (*Anatomy of Celestial Spheres*) 177, 177 n.129
Timeline 13
Āmulī, Muḥammad ibn Maḥmūd
Nafāʾis al-Funūn (verse attribution) 197, 197 n.91
Archimedes
Author 121
Bathtub 18, 18 n.4
'Death ray' 50, 50 n.35, 51
'Eureka' 50, 50 n.36
Fī ʿamal al-binkāmāt (*On the Construction of Water-Clocks*) 68 n.120
Project 50, 50 n.36
Aristotle
Author 69, 69 n.133, 75, 84 n.41, 114, 116, 119–20, 137, 140–1
First teacher 138–9, 143
Metaphysics 140
Posterior Analytics 17 n.3
Poem on 37, 37 n.87, 40, 40 n.98
Saving appearances 69, 142
Asadī Ṭūsī
Author 7 n.47, 35, 35 n.78, 80, 80 n 21, 83, 84, 84 n.40, 129 n.22
'*Dialogues*' (English titles) 80, 84, 85, 157
'*Munāẓirih*' (Persian titles) 7 n.47, 85, 85 n.43
ʿArab va ʿAjam (Arab and Non-Arab/ Persian) 7 n.47, 85, 110, 110 n 61, 157
Āsmān va Zamīn (Sky and Earth) 7 n.47, 85, 137, 137 n.66

Musalmān va Gabr (*Muslim and Zoroastrian*), 7 n.47, 90, 90 n.66, 157
Ramḥ va Qaws (Arrow and Bow) 129 n.22, 157 n.25, 157
Shab va Rūz (*Night and Day*) 7 n.47, 58, 58 n.76, 66, 66 n.110, 84, 84 n.40, 105, 157
Asʿad Gurgānī, Fakhr al-Dīn
Painting on poem 65 n.104
Vīs va Rāmīn 57 n.72, 64, 64 n.103, 65, 65 n.105, 148–9
Ayyūbids
Rulers 67, 67 n.116
Averroes (= Ibn Rushd)
Author 48 n.24, 76 n.169, 84 n.42, 137, 137 n.67, 139 nn.74–5, n.80, 140 n.81, 160
Averroes play 4, 4 n.26, 48, 48 n.25
'Averroes' search' 3 n.22, 4 n.26, 48, 48 n.25, 125, 125 n.1, 140 n.83, 141 n.84
Commentary on 'poem on medicine' 139, 139 n.75
Letters (attribution) 138 n.70, 140 n.82
Profile 137–43
Statue 131 n.130, 132
Tahāfut al-Tahāfut (*Incoherence of the Incoherence*) 139, 139 n.74
Timeline 13
Titles 141
Āvī, Ḥusayn ibn Muḥammad
Maḥāsin Iṣfahān (Persian) 30 n.56, n.58, 36 n.82

Bacon, Roger
Author 204, 204 n.121
Timeline 13
Banū Mūsā
Brothers 59, 59 n.82
Bayhaqī, ʿAlī
Tatimmat Ṣiwān al- ḥikma 111 n.72, 113, 113 nn.81–2
Bembo, Ambrosio
Author 39, 39 n.95, 183 n.13
Display in 'From rhubarb to rubies' 101 nn.10–11
Panoramas of Baghdad and Isfahan viii, 25, 25 n.34, 39, 39 n.95, 183 n.13
Bīrūnī, Abū Rayḥān
Āthār al-bāqiyah (*Chronology/Vestiges . . .*) 56, 56 n.69
Author 56, 57, 57 n.71, 64, 108, 192–3, 193 n.66
'Al-Biruni between Greece and India' 55 n.70
Bīrūnī courtyard 204
'Bīrūnī in the 15th/21st Century' 55 n.64
Bīrūnī's death date 57, 57 n.72
'Bīrūnī versus Ibn Sīnā . . .' 56, 56 n.67
'Maqālīd ʿilm al-hayʾa' 133 n.42
Tafhīm (*[Book of] Instructions*) viii, 3 n.15, 55 n.62–3, 56, 56 n.66, 57, 108, 108 n.49, 129 n.22, 130, 133, 138 n.72, 182 n.9, 204–6, 207 n.133
Taḥdīd al-amākin (*Geographical Coordinates*) 56 n.67, 156 n.24
Taḥqīq mā lil-Hind (*India*) 56, 56 n.69
'Research on al-Biruni in Germany' 55 n.70
Treatise on Shadows 93
Timeline 13
Brahe, Tycho
Author 72 n.154, 170, 170 n.89, 174–5, 177, 206 n.130
Kennedy, E. S., remarks 23, 23 n.20
Būyīds
'Idea of Iran in the Buyid dominions' . . . 178 n.132
Rulers 178, 178 n.132
Būzjānī, Abu al-Wafāʾ
Aʿmāl al-handasa (*Geometrical Constructions*) 106, 107, 107 n.40, n.48, 133, 133 n.46, 178, 178 n.132–3, 203, 203 n.108, 203
Author 108
Būzjānī-nāma 107 n.48, 202 n.108
Calendar attribution 101, 101 n.12, 105, 105 n.29, 106
Timeline 13

Čelebī, Mīram
Author 200, 200 n.98
Qaws Quzaḥ wa al-Hāla (*Rainbow and Halo*) 200, 200 n.98
Timeline 13

Copernicus, Nicolas
Author 41 n.99, 64, 68, 69, 75, 75 n.164, 160–1, 161 n.43, 166, 174, 177–8, 207 n.131
Commentariolus 75, 75 n.168
De Revolutionibus 45, 50, 74, 75, 75 n.168, 177–8
'observation tower' 76 n.170
Sculpture 49 n.29
Timeline 13
Cusa, Nicholas of
Author 161, 161 n.44

Da Vinci, Leonardo
Author 50,166
Biblioteca Ambrosiana 54, 54 n.57
Codex Atlanticus 54 n.57
Drawing 'Man' 49, 49 n.30
Exhibit 54, 54 n.56, n.57
Sculpture 50
Timeline 13
de la Valle, Pietro
Correspondence with Zayn al-Dīn Lārī 180, 180 n.140, 202
Descartes, René
Algebra 176, 176 n.125
Author 41, 41 n.99
Timeline 13
Dibner, Bern
Burndy Library 49, 49 n.28, 49 nn.31–2, 50 n.34
Dibner Institute 49, 49 nn.28–31
Du Mans, Raphaël
List of Books 202, 202 n.103

Euclid
Author 48, 104, 114, 116–17, 154, 171
Elements 10, 49–50, 96, 97, 105, 120, 146, 163, 176, 176 nn.123–4
Optics 189 n.44, 199, 199 n.95, 200
Propositions 176, 176 n.124
Uqlidis (= Uqlīdis) 49

Fārābī, Abū Naṣr
Film academy named after 111, 112 n.73
Second teacher after Aristotle 138–9, 143
Fārisī, Kamāl al-Dīn
Author 134, 134 n.49, 150, 179, 190, 193, 193 n.68, 199
Student of Quṭb al-Dīn Shīrāzi, a student of Ṭūsī 150, 179, 200, 202
Tanqiḥ al-Manāẓir (*Revision of Optics*) 134 n.49, 150, 179, 199
Timeline 13
Fātimīds
Dynasty 112
Rulers 112, 112 n.75, 113
Fazārī, Muḥammad ibn Ibrāhīm
Astronomical poem 91, 91 n.72
Author 88, 88 n.62, 89, 148
On the Measurement on Noon 91, 91 n.72
Profile 90–3
Timeline 13
Use of Armillary Spheres and Astrolabes 91, 91 n.72
Firduwsī Ṭūsī, Abu al-Qāsim
Author 80, 80 n.20
Shahnama/*Shāh-Nāmih* (*Book of Kings*) viii, 79, 80, 80 n.18, 83, 94, 129, 129 n.20, n.22, 148, 149, 149 n.129, 182 n.7, 206 n.129
Statue 85 n.44

Galen
Author 48, 114, 116
Jalinus (= Jālinūs) 49
Galileo, Galileo
Alhazen and Galileo viii, 112, 112 n.74, 131, 131 n.32, 132, 204
Author 2, 41, 41 n.99, 54–5, 64, 75, 166, 173, 173 n.108, 174, 175 n.116, 177, 179–80, 180 n.140, 198, 201, 204 n.120, 205, 205 n.122, 206
Conference on 131, 131 n.28
Dialogue . . . 45, 45 n.13, 178, 178 n.130
'Galileo and the Moon' 131 n.31
'Museo Galileo' 3, 3 n.20, 54 nn.55–6
Starry Messenger (*Sidereus Nuncius*) . . . 54, 54 n.52, 131 n.27, 198, 198 n.93, 199
Student Sagredo 180, 180 n.140
Telescope 3, 3 n.20, 54, 76, 76 n.170, 177 n.127, 179, 179 n.137, 204, 205, 205 n.126
Timeline 13

Ghazzālī, Muḥammad (= Algazel)
Incoherence of the Philosophers 139

Ḥāfiẓ-i Iṣfahānī, Muḥammad
Author/Inventor [Mukhtari'] 165 n.63
Clock in Kashan 136, 136 n.65, 165, 165 n.63
Natījat al-dawla 133, 133 n.46, 136, 170, 170 n.87, 174, 174 n.109
Work on Clocks 170, 170 n.87
Ḥafiz-ị Shīrāzī, Shams al-Dīn
Poem 204 n.115
Ḥakīm Shifā'ī
Poem 37 n.87, 40 n.98, 77, 77 n.2
Portrait 24 n.32
Poet-physician 37
Hanway, Jonas
Historical Account 39, 39 n.93
Harriot, Thomas
Author 175, 177, 177 n.127, 188 n.39: 'Hariot'
Harvard, John
University named after 19 n.10
Ḥazīn-i Lāhījī, Muḥammed 'Alī
Author 38 n.88, 77 n.2
Quoting poem 37 n.87, 40 n.98, 77 n.2
Herschel Family
John, William, Caroline 53, 53 n.45
Heron of Alexandria
Author 120, 121 n.129

Ibn al-'Arabī, Muḥyi al-Dīn
Tarjumān al-Ashwāq 31 n.61
Poem involving Isfahan 31, 31 n.61
Ibn al-Haytham, al-Ḥasan (= Alhacen/ Alhazen)
'Alhazen and the telescope . . .' 204 nn.120–1
Author 48, 65, 65 nn.106–8, 70, 102, 104, 104 n.88, 106–9, 139, 139 n.77, 147, 154, 179, 200, 202–5
Book of Optics (Kitāb al-Manāẓir) 2 n.12, 50, 104, 104 n.26, 107, 109–10, 114–117, 134, 134 n.49, 169, 179, 181, 186 n.33, 187, 189, 190, 193–4, 200, 202, 204
Critical thinking 192 nn.63–4
Doubts on/Aporias Against (*Shukūk*) *Ptolemy* 70 n.135, 99, 99 n.1, 113, 113 n.85, 160
Exhibit on 102
Footpaths 189 n.44
Halo and Rainbow (*al-Hāla wa Qaws Quzah*) 200, 200 n.98
Historical report on 65 n.106
Named by Ṭūsī 147, 147 n.114
No knowledge of Greek 48
On the Light of the Moon 84 n.42
On the Quality of Shadows 84 n.42
On the Shape of the Eclipse 114 n.89, 190 n.54
Profile 110–18
Timeline 13
Year of Light presentations 111 nn.67–8, 187 n.35
Ibn Khaldūn
Historical record 61, 61 n.90
Ibn Ma'rūf, Taqī al-Dīn
Author 167 nn.69–73, 168 nn.74–7, 169 n.84, 201, 201 n.100
Nūr ḥadaqat al-ibṣār (*Light of the Eye's Pupil*) 169 n.79, 201 n.100
Ownership of Constellation manuscript 172, 172 n.99
Profile 166–72
Timeline 13
Works 170 n.86, n.91
Ibn Maymūn (= Maimonides)
Author 113, 113 n.80, 139
Guide to the Perplexed 142
Ibn al-Nadīm
Fihrist 87, 88 n.59, 90 n.69, 91 n.73, 94, 94 n.90, 96 n.104, 184 n.20, 203 n.111
Ibn Nawbakht, Abū Sahl
Author 88, 88 n.60, 89, 92, 93
Book of Nativities 92, 92 n.80, 94, 95 nn.95–6
Profile 94–8
Timeline 13
Ibn Qurra, Thābit
Author 75 n.169, 96, 96 nn.100–5, 97, 106, 203, 204 n.114
Pythagorean Theorem 97, 98 n.109
Timeline 13
Ibn al-Shāṭir, 'Alā' al-Dīn

Author 139–40, 139 n.79, 158 n.31, n.34, 161 n.42, 171
Nihāyat al-sūl (*Final Inquiry*) 159, 159 n.39
Profile 158–61
Timeline 13
Zīj al-jadīd (*New Tables*) 160 n.39
Ibn Sīnā (= Avicenna)
Author 68, 68 n.125, 104–5, 107–8, 118 nn.106–7, 119, nn.110–15, nn.117–18, 122, 122 nn.136–7, 123 n.140, 138–9, 205
Autobiography 99, 99 n.2, 104 n.27, 118 nn.106–7, n.115, 117–18, 192 n.65
'Bīrūnī versus Ibn Sīnā . . .' 56, 56 n.67
Dome of Ibn Sīnā 135
Qānūn fī al-ṭibb (*Canon of Medicine*) 40, 101, 102 n.13, 119, 119 n.113, 127
Miʿyār al-ʿuqūl (*Rational Measures*) (attribution) 102 n.13, 107 n.41, n.47, 121, 121 n.130, 122, 122 n.134
Poem on 37, 37 n.87, 40, 40 n.98
Profile 118–23
Shifāʾ 37, 40, 119 n.112
Timeline 13
Ṭūl Jurjān (Longitude of Jurjān) 56 n.67
Work manuscripts 107 n.46
Ismāʿīlī
Patrons 146–7

Jāmī, ʿAbd al-Raḥmān
Author 166, 166 n.64, 205 n.125
Poem on 'European glass' 166 n.64, 205, 205 n.125
Jazarī, Badīʿ al-Zamān
Compendium of Theory and Useful Practice . . . viii, 81 n.24
Jurjānī, Mīr Siyyid Sharīf (ʿAllāmah)
Munāẓarah al-Sayf va al-Qalam (*Sword and Pen*) 7 n.48, 157 n.28, 158, 158 n.30

Kamāl-i Iṣfahānī
Munāẓirāt-i Baghdād va Iṣfahān (*Dialogues of Baghdad and Isfahan*) viii, x, xi, 2 n.11, 6, 21–2, 25, 26 n.39, 27, 27 n.41, 28, 32, 33, 33 nn.68–70, 34 nn.71–4, 35 n.77, 36, 38, 38 n.89, n.91, 43, 77, 79, 99, 101, 102, 125–6, 126 n.4, 127–8, 181 n.2 and 182 n.5 ('*Munāẓirih* . . .': unnamed author), 182 n.6
Pen name 28
Kamāl-i Iṣfahānī, Ismāʿīl
Poem 29 n.52
Poet 6, 6 n.42, 28, 29, 29 n.52
Kāshānī/Kāshī, Ghīyāth al-Dīn Jamshīd
Author 73 n.143, 155, 155 n.17, n.19, 161, 162 n.46, 167, 171, 200, 203
Conference 156 n.21
Letters 3 n.18, 155 n.19, 161–2
Profile 162–6
al-*Risālah al-Muḥīṭīyah* 163 n.53, 164 n.56
Timeline 13
Works 164, 164 n.56
Kepler, Johannes
Author 41, 41 n.99, 154, 174, 177
Timeline 13
Khaṭīb al-Baghdādī
Tārīkh Baghdād 27 n.42
Khayyām, ʿUmar
Algebra 176
Author 58, 58 n.75, 62–6, 62 nn.91–4, 63, 63 n.95–8, 64, 64 nn.99–101, 85, 176
Calendar 35 n.76
Profile 62–6
Timeline 13
Khwārazmī, Ḥisām Ṣarrāf
Munāẓirih-i Shaṭranj va Nard (*Dialogue of Chess and Backgammon*) 7 n.49, 197 n.90
Khwārizmī, Mummad ibn Mūsā
Al-Jabr (Algebra) 59, 59 n.77, 97, 176
Author 58, 58 n.75, 59 nn.77–9, n.82, 64, 85, 97, 106, 176
Epithet 'Majūsī' 61, 61 n.87
Profile 59–61
Taʾrīkh (*Chronology*) 59, 59 n.79
Timeline 13
Kindī, Yaʿqūb ibn Isḥāq
Conjecture 61, 61 n.90, 139
Kirmānī, Awḥad al-Dīn
Date reference 6, 39 n.92
Kūbanānī, Abū Isḥāq
Letters 106 n.35, 165, 165 n.58

Measurement 165

Larī, Zayn al-Dīn
Correspondence with Pietro de la Valle 180, 180 n.140

Māfarrūkhī, al-Mufaḍḍal
Maḥāsin Iṣfahān 30 n.55
Maghribī, Muḥyi al-Dīn Yaḥyā
Author 58, 58 n.75, 66, 66 n.112, 67, 67 nn.114–16, 70, 85, 101, 101 n.12, 147 nn.118–19, 147, 160
Profile 66–70
Timeline 13
Majdī, Majd al-Dīn
Zīnat al-majālis 130 n.23, 165 n.63
Manṣūr, ʿAlāʾ al-Dīn
Poem on observatory 168, 168 nn.75–6, 169 n.78, 170, 170 n.90, 171, 171 nn.92–3, nn.96–7, 172, 172 n.98, n.100, 175 n.114
Mīrdāmād
Author 176
Mongols
Invasion 29, 29 n.51, 30, 32, 32 n.65, 36, 37, 65, 65 n.109, 66, 66 n.114, 144, 146–7, 149–50, 156, 158
Rulers 147–8, 171 n.97, 172, 174
War costumes 64 n.109
Mughāls
Awrangzib (Pād-Shāh Ghāzī; ʿĀlamgīr) 6, 6 n.41, 39 n.92
Relations with Safavīds 6 n.43
Rulers 174
Mullā Ṣādra
Author 176
Mustuwfī, Ḥamd Allāh
Nuzhat al-qulūb 31 n.62, 77, 77 n.1
Poem (attribution) 31 n.62, 148 n.123

Nawbakht
Family 94, 94 nn.86–9
Newton, Isaac
Aphorism 41 n.99; 75, 75 n.167
Author 2, 41, 41 nn.99–100, 45, 45 nn.10–11, n.14, 46, 46 n.15, 75, 75 nn.164–8, 154–6, 174, 177–8
Burndy Library and Huntington collection 49 n.32
Coloured Spectrum 52, 52 n.44
Figure on orrery 52
Large and ancient spots 76 n.170
'Letter to Robert Hooke . . .' 75 n.165
London residence 3 n.21, 45, 45 n.9
Newton Project 75 n.165
Newtonia Collection 154 n.15, 155 n.16
Notebook 52 n.44
Opticks . . . 52 n.44
Principia 45, 45 n.14, 50
Statue 44, 44 nn.7–8, 45, 79
Three Laws 45
Timeline 13
Nīsābūrī, Niẓām al-Dīn
Profile 172, 172 n.100
Nīẓāmī ʿArūḍī Samarqandī
Chahār maqāla (*Four Discourses*) 63, 63 n.97

Oresme, Nicholas
Author 161, 161 nn.43–5
Ottomans
Bayezid II 3 n, 19, 109 n.57, 144, 169, 170 n.87, 181 n.3
Rulers 32 n.65, 71, 71 n.147, 107, 144, 167–9, 168 n.77, 171, 173, 173 n.106, 174, 180, 181 n.3
Royal library 2, 3 n.19, 108, 108 n.57, 181, 181 nn.2–3

Pappus of Alexandria
Author 120
Pāshā-zādah, Kemāl
Turkish poem 15, 15 n.2
Plato
Poem on 37, 37 n.87, 40, 40 n.98
Saving appearances 69, 142
Pseudo-Galen
Kitāb al-Diryāq (*Book of Antidotes*) viii
Ptolemy
The Almagest 40, 57 n.73, 64, 68, 91, 120, 139, 139 n.80, 142, 142 n.87, 146
Astronomical models 141, 207, 207 n.134
Author 74, 104, 114–17, 154, 171, 200, 202

Optics 189 n.44, 200
Planetary Hypotheses 142, 142 n.87
Poem on 37, 37 n.87, 40, 40 n.98
Saving appearances 69, 142
Star Catalogue 57 n.73, 108
Tetrabiblos 68
Pythagorean
Theorem 176

Qūshjī, ʿAlī
Author 58, 58 n.75, 70, 70 n.140, 71, 71 n.142, n.144, n.147, 72, 72 nn.148–53, 73, 73 nn.156–9, 74, 74 n.161–3, 85, 139, 164, 167, 193, 193 nn.69–70, 200, 203, 207
Commentary on Epitome of Belief 72, 72 n.148, 73–6
Commentary on Zīj Ulugh Beg 2 n.152
Moon Treatise (*Ḥall Ashkāl-Qamar*) 72 n.151
Poem 74 n.160
Profile 70–6
Risāla dar ʿilm al-hayʾa 72 n.153
Timeline 13

Rāzī, Amīn Aḥmad
Kāshānī/Kāshī's death 165 n.60
Rāzī, Fakhr al-Dīn
Jāmiʿ al-ʿulūm (*Kitāb-i Sittīnī*) 130 n.25
'Science/craft of war instruments' 129 n.22, 130
Rāzī, 'Zakariyā (= Rhazes)
Doubts Against Galen 114, 114 n.86, 130 n.26
Riyāḍī, Davud (David the mathematician)
Author 168
Rūmī, Muwlānā Jalāl al-Dīn
Poems 16, 16 n.4, 148, 149, 149 n.132, 210 nn.2–3, 210 n.5
Speak Only of the Moon 149 n.132
Rūmī, Qāḍīzāda
Author 163, 167

Saʿdī, Muṣlih al-Dīn
Author 35, 36, 36 n.81
'Banī Ādam' (Children of Adam) 35, 36 n.80
Būstān (*Orchard*) 35, 35 n.78, 36 n.83, 37 nn.84–6
Ghazaliyāt (*Odes*) 36 n.79
Gulistān (*Flower Garden*) 35 n.78
Lament on the Fall of Baghdad . . . 35 n.79, 37, 37 nn.84–6
'Soldier in Isfahan' 36 n.83
Safavīds
Capital city 22, 29, 39, 39 nn.93–5, 40 nn.96–7, 119, 135
Dynasty x, 5, 5 n.40, 25 n.34, 29, 29 n.50, 35 n.75, 39 nn.94–5, 174, 175 n.116
Rulers 35 n.75, 122, 122 n.138, 135, 168, 171 n.97, 172, 173 n.102, 174, 174 n.111, 175, 175 nn.114–16, 177, 177 n.126, 178–80
Sagredo
Galileo's student and patron 175 n.116, 180
Contacts with Safavīd Shāh ʿAbbās I 175 n.116, 180 n.140
Ṣāʿid al-Andalusī
Kitāb Ṭabaqāt al-umam 138, 138 n.71
Sasānids
Dynasty 174, 203 n.112
Fire temple 203 n.112
Rulers 88, 118
Seljūqs
Capital city 32, 32 n.65
Dynasty 32 n.65, 64, 64 n.102
Malik-Shāh I 35 n.76, 63–4
Niẓām al-Mulk 63
Shaykh Jamāl
Copyist 6, 35 n.77, 38, 38 n.89
Shaykh Wafāʾ
Rūz-nāma . . . mīqāt (*Calendar of Timekeeping*) viii, ix, 101 n.12, 105, 106, 106 n.39, 127 nn.13–14, 127–8, 128 n.15, 154
Shīrāzi, Quṭb al-Dīn
Author 160, 179, 202
Student of Ṭūsī 150, 160, 165, 200
Sijzī, Zayn al-Dīn
Munāẓirih-i Khurshīd va Māh (*Dialogue of Sun and Moon*) 7 n.50
Ṣūfī, ʿAbd al-Raḥmān
Ṣuwar al-kawākib ([Book of] Constellations) 3 n.16, 55, 55 n.61, 108, 108 n.50, 129 n.22, 144–5, 145 n.103, n.155, 175

Timūrīds
Rulers 4 n.33, 50 n.34, 71, 72, 144, 155 n.18, 155 n.18, 156, 161, 162 n.49, 175, 175 n.116
Ṭūsī, Naṣīr al-Dīn
Alamūt 132, 132 n.36, 144, 147
Author 67, 67 n.117, 68, 69, 70, 102, 129 n.22, 139, 143 n.91, n.93, 145 n.104, 148 nn.124–5, 165, 172, 207
Chronology of life 132 n.35, 133
Dhikr Daryā-yi Khazar [commemorating the *Caspian Sea*] (attribution) 145 n.108
'Epitome of Belief . . .' 72, 72 n.148, 73
Exhibit on 102
Ḥall-i Mushkilāt-i Muʿīnīyah 146, 146 n.112
'Ikhtiyārāt-i qamar' 135 n.56
'lunar theory' 69 n.128
Madkhal-i manẓūm (*Versed Introduction*) 206 n.127
Maragha Observatory 67, 67 n.118, 68, 70, 130, 130 n.23, 132, 132 n.35, 147, 160
Naming Ibn al-Haytham 146
Naṣīr al-Dīn al-Ṭūsī volume . . . 67 n.117
Non-Ptolemaic models 70, 70 n.136
Poems (attribution) 108, 125, 125 n.2, 148 nn.120–2, n.125
Poems on 148 nn.123–4
Profile 143–50
Risālah-i Muʿīnīyah 70 n.136, 146 n.112
Recension of Euclid's Elements 102 n.15
Recension of Euclid's Optics 199
Recension of Intermediate/Middle Books 133 n.40, n.43
Sayr wa sulūk (*Contemplation and Action*) 145 n.109
Sons 145
Tadhkira 69, 69 n.129, n.131, 70 n.136, 145–6
Taḥrīr al-Mutawassiṭāt (Middle/ Intermediate Books) 133, 133 n.40, n.43, 134, 134 n.54, 135 n.55, 145
'Taḥrīr-i Maʿrifat-I Masāḥat' 135 n.56
Tarjamah-i Ṣuwar al-kawākib (*Translation of Book of Constellations*) 3 n.16, 108 nn.51–2, 129 n.22, 130, 130 n.24, 143 n.94, nn.96–7, 144 n.99, 144, 144 n.100, n.102, 143, 146
Titles 143
Ṭūsī Couple, 145, 146 n.113, 161, 207, 207 n.134

Ulugh Beg
Author 71, 71 n.141, nn.143–4, 73, 108, 144, 156, 162–5, 171
Dedication to 72 n.151
Kāshānī/Kāshī's death connection 165 n.60
Star Catalogue 72, 72 n.152
Timeline 13
Umāyyāds
Caliphate 32, 101, 158 n.32
Spanish Umayyads 137, 137 n.69
Visual Culture 158 n.32

Viéte, Francois
Algebra 176, 176 n.125
Vitruvius
De Architectura 49 n.30

II. Modern

Abbott, Nabia
Two Queens of Baghdad . . . 32 n.66, 60, 60 n.83, n.86, 87 nn.53–4
Abdullaeva [-Melville], Firuza
'The Bodleian manuscript of Asadī . . .' 78 n.10, 85 n.45
'The origins of the Munāẓara genre . . .' 78 n.10, 85 n.45
Shahnameh Centre (research director) 78 n.10
Abdullaeva [-Melville], Firuza and Melville, Charles (eds)
Millennium of the Shahnama 129 n.20
Adle, Kamran
Ānān kih khāk rā bī-naẓar kīmiyā kun-and 135 n.63
Afraz, Arash
Exhibit caption 102 n.18

Afshar, Arash
Speak only of the Moon (reference source) 149 n.139
Afshar, Iraj
Obituary of 134 n.48
Shahnama/Shāh-Nāmih (*Book of Kings*) (facs) (with Omidsalar, Mahmud) 80 n.18
Akchoti-Shahbazi, Artemis
Painting on poem 65 n.104
Amanat, Abbas and Assef, Ashraf (eds)
The Persianate World ... 78 n.11
Andrewes, William
Guest Lecturer 82, 82 n.31
Harvard, Collection of Historical Scientific Instruments (former director) 81 n.26
Instrument construction 81 n.29, 82 n.32
Ashraf, Assef
'Pathways to the Persianate' 78 n.11
The Persianate World ... (ed) (*see* Amanat, Abbas) 78 n.11
Asisi, Yadegar
Pergamon installation 188 n.42
Attiyeh, Jenny
'Scholars resuscitate dead languages ...' 50 n.36, 121 n.128

Babaie, Sussan
Safavid Palaces at Isfahan ... 185 nn.29–30, 201 n.101
Babaie, Sussan, Babayan, Kathryn, Baghdiantz McCabe, Ina, and Farhad, Massumeh
Slaves of the Shah 175 n.117
Bagheri, Mohammad
'A newly found letter' 3 n.18, 5 n.37, 71 n.143, 155 n.19, 162 n.50, 163 n.51, 200 n.97
Az Samarqand bih Kāshān 3 n.18, 5 n.37, 71 n.143, 155 n.19, 162 n.50, 163 n.51, 200 n.97
Bagherzade, Iradj
Acknowledgements xi
Barker, Peter and Heidarzadeh, Tofigh
'Copernicus and the Ṭūsī Couple' 69 n.130, 70 n.139, 71 n.142, 72 n.150, 73 n.156, n.158
Bayani, Shirin
Tīsfūn [Ctesphon] va Baghdād 28 n.43, 31 n.62, 77 n.1
Belting, Hans
Florence and Baghdad ... 112 n.73, 187 n.38
Bensaude-Vincent, Bernadette and Newman, William R. (eds)
The Artificial and the Natural ... (ed) 121 n.131
Berggren, J. Len
Episodes 59 n.78, nn.81–2, 61 n.89, 97 n.108, 176 n.123
Volume in honour 103 n.21
Berners-Lee, Tim with Fischetti, Mark
Weaving the Web ... 25 n.37
Bier, Carol
'The decagonal tomb tower at Maragha ...' 132 n.36
'Patterning knowledge' 47, 47 n.20
Bier, Carol, Kheirandish, Elaheh and Yousefi, Najm al-Din (eds)
Sciences, Crafts, and the Production of Knowledge ... 101 n.10, 130 n.125
Blair, Ann
Too Much to Know ... 38 n.90
Bloom, Jonathan
Paper before Print ... 38 n.90
Bloom, Jonathan and Blair, Sheila (eds)
God Is Beautiful ... 55 n.61
God Is the Light ... 110 n.62, 187 n.35, 189 n.44
Islam: A Thousand Years ... 47 n.20
Borges, Jorge Luis
'Averroes' search' 3 n.22, 48, 48 n.25, 125, 125 n.1, 140 n.83, 141 n.84
'Cambridge' poem 22, 22 n.13, 48
Boullata, Kamal
'Homage to al-Hasan Ibn al-Haytham' 112 n.73, 190 n.50
Bremmer, John
'Understanding Geometry' 47, 47 n.20
Brancaforte, Elio
'From rhubarb to rubies ...' (ed) (*see* Brentjes, Sonja) 101, 101 nn.10–11
Brazelton, Mary
Exhibit caption 102 n.17

Brennan, Patrick
Student (academic years) 7 n.45
Student quoted 4 n.28
Exhibit caption 102 n.17
Brentjes, Sonja
'Early modern European travellers . . .' 39 n.94, 180 n.140, 202 nn.103–4, 204 n.119
'Khwārizmī . . .' 59 n.77
Brentjes, Sonja and Brancaforte, Elio
'From rhubarb to rubies . . .' 101 nn.10–11
Brentjes, Sonja, van Dalen, Benno and Charette, François (eds)
Certainty, Doubt, Error . . . 53 n.50
Brown, Timothy
'Tokyo, Beijing, Cairo, Isfahan' 47, 47 n.12
Browne, Edward G.
'Account of a rare manuscript . . .' 30 n.56, n.58, 36 n.82
'Baghdad During the ʿAbbasid Caliphate . . .' 30 n.59
Catalogue of Persian Manuscripts, University of Cambridge 78 n.6
Chahār maqāla (*Four Discourses*) (tr) 63 n.97
Profile 78, 78 n.5
Journal of the Royal Asiatic Society (ed) (with Malcolm, John) 30 n.56
Literary History of Persia 25 n.32, 29 nn.51–2, 35 n.76, 36 n.79, 37 n.85, 57, 58, 58 n.76, n.78, 60, nn.84–5, 65 n.109, 66, 66 n.110, 72 n.149, 77 nn.1–2, 78, 78 n.4, 80 nn.20–1, 83 nn.35–6, nn.38–9, 84 n.40, 118 nn.108–9, 119 n.110, nn.117–18, 144 n.98, 174 nn.111–12, 180 n.139
'Obituary' of 78 n.3, n.5
'Obituary' of Charles Rieu 21 n.14, 24, 24 n.29, 78, 78 n.3
Statue 78 n.5
Tadhkiratu al-shuʿará (*Memoirs of the Poets*) (ed, tr) 83, 83 n.37, 84, 105 n.28
Year Amongst the Persians 78, 78 nn.4–5
Buchwald, Jed Z.
Looking Back as We Move Forward, Cormos-Buchwald et al. (ed), 2 n.9
Buchwald, Jed Z., Cohen, I. Bernard, and Smith, George E. (eds)
Isaac Newton's Natural Philosophy (eds) 45 n.14
Burnett, Charles
'The certitude of astrology . . .' 68 nn.126–7
Burnett, Charles, Hogendijk, Jan P., Plofker, Kim and Yano, Michio (eds)
Studies in the History of the Exact Sciences . . . 86 n.48

Capobianco James
'Treasure Room' of Widener Library 18 n.5
Carlsfield, Carla
'roses of Isphahan' 2 n.4
Cavicchi, Elizabeth
Contribution to 'Windows' exhibits 100 n.4, 102 n.16
Dibner Institute visit 49 n.31
'Recreate Historic Experiments' 81 n.25
Chandler, Bruce
Eastern Astrolabes . . . (ed) 51 n.40
Charette, François
Certainty, Doubt, Error . . . (ed) (*see* Brentjes) 53 n.50
Mathematical Instrumentation 158 n.33, 159 n.35
Cohen, I. Bernard
Album of Science (ed) 2 n.7
Interview with 2 n.4
Birth of a New Physics 45 n.10, 177 n.127
'Galileo and the telescope' 177 n.127
Isaac Newton's Natural Philosophy (ed) (*see* Buchwald) 45 n.14
Manuscript gift 50 n.34
'Newton, Isaac' 41, 41 n.99, 46 n.15
Revolutions in Science 176 n.125
Volume in honour 70 n.137
'What Galileo "Saw" in the Heavens . . .' 54, 54 n.54, 76 n.170, 177 n.128
Comes, Mercè
'Ibn Abī al-Shukr . . .' 66 n.112, 67 n.114, 68 n.121

Cormos-Buchwald, Diana
Looking Back as We Move Forward (ed) 2 n.9, 148 n.126
Corsi, Pietro
Intervieww with 2 n.8
Crook, Lester
Acknowledgements xi

Darby, Abigail
Exhibit caption 102 n.17
Daryayee, T.
'Mind, body and the cosmos . . .' 197 n.87
Davenport, Anne
Acknowledgements xi
'Personal vocation' 47, 47 n.21
Davidson, Olga M.
'Poet and Hero . . .' 80 n.19
Davis, Dick
Vīs va Rāmīn (tr) 56 n.57
Stories from the Shahnameh . . . 80 n.18
Dhanani, Alnoor
'Jurjānī . . .' 157 nn.28–9, 158, 158 n.30
Dickens, Charles
'All Year Round' xi
Tale of Two Cities xi, 22 n.15, 25, 43, 43 n.1, 151, 151 n.1
Docherty, Daniel
'Dance of Venus' 208, 208 n.139
Donovan, Colin
Exhibit caption 102 p. 17
Dupré, Sven
'Ausonio's mirrors and Galileo's lenses . . .' 199 n.94
'How-to optics' 199 n.94
Perspective as Practice . . . (ed) 187 n.36, n.38, 199 n.94
Renaissance Cultures of Optics (ed) 150 n.138

Ecademics
ecademic.org Inc., Non-Profit organization 79 n.14
Einstein, Albert
Crater on the Moon 111, 111 n.66
'Shoulders of Giants' 75, 75 n.168
Eisenstein, Elizabeth L.
The Printing Press . . . 38 n.90
Elliot, T. S.
Four Quartets 195 n.84
Emami, Farshid
'Coffee houses, urban spaces . . .' 35 n.75
Endress, Gerhard
Organizing Knowledge . . . (ed) 120 n.123
Ettehadieh, Mansoureh
Nashr-i Tārikh-i Iran (founder) 106 n.33

Fazlıoğlu, İhsan
'Qūshjī . . .' 70 n.140, 71 n.144, 72 nn.152–3
'Taqī al-Dīn . . .' 165 n.66, 166 nn.69–70, 167 n.73
'Mīram Čelebī . . .' 200 n.98
Feldhay, Rivka and Ragep, F. Jamil (eds)
Before Copernicus (ed) 73 n.157
Frye, Richard N.
Persia 79 n.13

Galison, Peter
Harvard, Collection of Historical Scientific Instruments (director) 51 n.38
Galluzzi, Paolo
'Museo Galileo' (director) 54, 54 nn.55–6
Garcha, Yasmin
Acknowledgements xi
Ghanbari, Vahid
'. . . Abū Isḥāq Kūbanānī' 106 n.35
Gharagozlou, Yahya
1001: Persiranian Stories . . . 79 n.15
Gingerich, Owen
The Book Nobody Read . . . 45 n.12
'Kepler, Johannes' 41 n.99
Golub, Leon
'How the Sun teaches us patience . . .' 52 n.43
Moon orbit satellite 208 n.136
'Need for collaboration' 47, 47 n.21
Satellite orbiting the Moon 207–8, 208 n.136
Golub, Leon and Pasachoff, Jay M.
Nearest Star . . . 52 n.43
The Sun (*Kosmos*) 52 n.43

Goodarzy, Asad
Exhibit caption 102 n.18
'honour's thesis: Heroes in Fiction, Heroes in Action' 80 n.17
Postscript verses 209 n.1
Student (academic years) 7 n.45
Goodarzy, Esam
'Ancients' game inventor 197 n.88
Istanbul Summer School 187 nn. 34–5
Future of People: Audience award recipient (with Marie-Therese Png) 197 n.89
Postscript verses 209 n.1
Student (academic years) 7 n.45
Goodarzy, Hormoz
Acknowledgements xii
'Unweaving the web' 47, 47 n.21
Goodman, Alyssa A.
'Path to Newton' 192 n.61, n.64
'Prediction Project . . .' 192 n.61
Gormley, Anthony
Planets 45 n.9
Gormley, Rory
Acknowledgements xi
Grasshoff, Gerd
The History of Ptolemy's Star Catalogue 57 n.73
Greco Josefowicz, Diane
'Into the blue' 2 n.9
Gutas, Dimitri
'The "Alexandria to Baghdad" complex of narratives' 103 n.20
'Avicenna . . .' 68 n.125
Autobiography, Avicenna and the Aristotelian Tradition . . . 99, 99 n.2, 119 n.112, n.115, nn.117–18, 192 n.65
'The "Alexandria to Baghdad" complex of narratives' 103 n.20
Greek Thought, Arabic Culture . . . 5 n.34, 59 n.81, 61 n.88, 87, 87 nn.57–8, 88, 88 n.60, 90 n.69, 91 n.74, 92 n.77, n.80, 93 n.85, 94 n.91, 95 n.96, 97 n.107, 112 n.76, 171 n.94
Man versus Society in Medieval Islam (ed) 87 n.56

Hashemipour, Behnaz
'Bahā' al-Dīn al-ʿĀmilī' 172 n.101, 173 nn.104–5, 177 n.129, 178 n.134
'Būzjānī . . .' 105 n.29
'Khayyām . . .' 62 n.91
Hawking, Stephen
On the Shoulders of Giants . . . 75 nn.166–8, 76 n.170
Heaney, Seamus 46 n.17
Heidarzadeh, Tofigh
Astronomical Works of ʿAlī Qūshjī . . . 70 n.140
'Patronage networks and migration . . .' 167 n.73
'Copernicus and the Ṭūsī Couple' (see Barker, Peter) 69 n.130, 70 n.139, 71 n.142, 72 n.150, 73 n. 156, n.158
Helbig, Daniela
Averroes play 4 n.26, 48 n.25
Exhibit caption 102 n.17
Student (academic years) 7 n.45
Hoffman, Roald
'Entertaining Science/Science Cabaret' 3 n.22, 4 n.33, 47 n.23
Hogendijk, Jan P.
'Abū Rayḥān Bīrūnī in the 15th/21st Century' 55 n.64
'Ancient and modern secrets of Isfahan', 135 n.57, 136 n.64
'Discovery of an eleventh-century geometrical compilation . . .' 117 n.100
'A mathematical classification' 3 n.14
Studies in the History of the Exact Sciences . . . (ed) (*see* Burnett, Charles) 86 n.48
Hogendijk, Jan P. and Sabra, A. I. (eds), *Enterprise of Science in Islam . . .* 120 n.120
Holod, Renata (ed)
Studies on Isfahan . . . 26 n.33, 87 n.52
Hopper, Michael
Identification of Calendar of Timekeeping 101 n.12

Ireland, Corydon
Acknowledgements xii

'Fair shows progress . . .' 125 n.3, 126 n.4, n.8, n.10, 127 n.10, 151 n.4
'100 years of Widener' 18 n.4
'Houghton exhibit features Islamic sciences' 3 n.24, 99 n.3, 100 n.6, 117 n.101
'Poem for Harvard . . .' 46 n.17
'Treasure island . . .' 100 n.5
'Yes, it was a magical talk . . .' 109 n.59

Isberg, Kristine
Student (academic years) 7 n.45

Jordan
Samuel Jordan Center for Persian Studies and Culture 79 n.14

Kaplan, Robert
The Nothing That Is 15, 25, 25 n.36

Karamati, Younes
'Abū Isḥāq al-Kūbunānī' 106 n.35, 165 n.58
Kāshānī Shinākht . . . 163 n.52, 165 n.60, n.62
Kāshānī, al-Risālah al-Muḥīṭīyah 163 n.53

Karimian, Adele
Acknowledgements xii

Kasica, Christina
'Lessons in communication' 47, 47 n.21

Kennedy, Alicia
Acknowledgements xii

Kennedy, E. S.
'Bīrūnī . . .' 56 n.65, 57 n.71, 89 n.63
'Comets in Islamic astronomy and astrology' 67 n.115, 68 n.123
'Late medieval planetary theory' 70 n.138, 113 n.85, 139 n.78
Planetary Equatorium 163 n.52, 165 n.61
Remarks 23 n.20

Kheirandish, Asadollah
Acknowledgements xii
A Verse Amongst Thousands xii
Exhibit caption 102 n.18
Fāl-nāmih-i Shaykh Bahāʾī 177 n.126
Surūdih-hā (Compositions) 184 nn.14–19

Kheirandish, Elaheh
The Arabic Version of Euclid's Optics . . . 74 n.161, 125 n.2, 133 n.43, 135 n.55, 150 n.140, 199 n.95, 202 n.102
'Astronomical poems . . .' 57 n.72, 65 n.104, 148 n.125, n.127, 149 n.131, 206 n.127, 207 n.132
'Books on mathematical and mixed-mathematical sciences' 3 n.19, 169 n.80, 182 n.5, 202 n.106
'An early tradition in practical geometry . . .' 106 nn.33–5, n.38, 107 n.40, n.48, 133 n.46, 136 n.64, 165 n.58, 178 nn.132–3
'Classical Library of Islam', Packard Humanities Institute (Coordinator) 57 n.74
Eastern Astrolabes . . . (ed) (*see* Pingree) 51 n.40
'Elogue' 2 n.3, 190 nn.51–2
'The "fluctuating fortunes of scholarship" . . .' 121 n.127
'The footprints of "experiment" in early Arabic optics' 98 n.110, 115 n.92
'From Maragha to Samarqand and beyond . . .' 4 n.33, 133 n.46, 136 n.65, 156 n.22, 165 n.63, 170 nn.87–8, 174 n.109, 200 n.99
'Light and dark . . .' 110 n.62, 150 n.136, 179 nn.135–6, 189 n.44, 199 n.96, 200 n.98
'The many aspects of appearances . . .' 120 n.120
'Mixed mathematical sciences . . .' 120 n.119, n.121, n.124, n.126, 121 n.132, 169 n.81
'Optics and perspective' 150 n.138, 187 n.38
'Optics: Highlights from Islamic lands' 169 n.79
'Optics, History of' 114 n.91
'Organizing scientific knowledge . . .' 120 nn.122–3, 169 n.81
'The puzzle of Ṭūsī's optical works' 150 n.135, n.137, 179 n.135, 199 n.96
'Qusṭā ibn Lūqā al-Baʿlabakkī' 121 n.127

'A report on Iran's "jewel" codices . . .' 133 n.43, 134, 134 n.54, 135
'Science and "mithāl" . . .' 130 n.25
Sciences, Crafts, and the Production of Knowledge . . . (*see* Bier) 101 n.10, 130 n.125
What "Euclid said" to his Arabic readers . . .' 115 n.95
'Windows into early science . . .' 3 n.24
'Zodiacs of Paris . . .' 148 n.126, 206 n.128
Courses
'From Alexandria to Baghdad . . .' 3 n.23, 4, 4 n.26, 46, 46 n.16, 47, 47 n.23, 49, 49 n.31, 50 n.35, 100 n.8
'From Baghdad to Isfahan . . .' 3 n.23, 4, 100 n.8
'The age of Rūmī . . .' 4 n.27, 149 n.130, n.134
'Historical dialogues from the Near East . . .' 4, 4 n.25, n.28, 80 nn.22–3, 82 n.31, 100 n.8
'Science in the Islamic Middle Ages' 4, 4 n.25, n.29, 22 n.18, 46, 47 nn.20–1, 126 n.23, 156 n.23
Exhibits
'A universal spectrum of seven "S"s . . .' 182, 182 n.7
'From Baghdad to Isfahan and Beyond' (Virtual Gallery) 125 n.3
'The spread of science . . .' 111 n.69, 117 n.102
'Windows into early science . . .' 3 n.24, 99 n.3, 101 n.10, 102 n.17, 100, 102, 117 n.101, 125 n.3, 128 n.16
'Windows into early science and craft . . .' 3 n.24, 102, 102 n.16, n.18, 126 n.16, 129, 129 n.17
'When astrology was part of astronomy' 65 n.104
Films
'An Early Science Quartet' 153, 153 n.8
'When optics was more than physics' 153, 153 n.9
Presentations
'"Checkered history" recolored . . .' 189 n.49
'Cities of stars . . .' 166, 166 n.65, 198, 198 n.92
'Historical relationship between astronomy and optics' 131 n.31
'A history duet and a science quartet.' (with Maryam Kamali) 189 n.48
'Paths and chances in early science . . .' 189 n.71
'A quartet of Persian scientific traditions' 153 n.8, n.10
'Two-culture problems . . .' 47 n.21
Projects
Archimedes 50 n.36
Historical play 4 n.26, 48, 48 n.25
'Micromapping early science' 82 n.34, 151 n.2, 152, 156–7
Unpublished
Catalogue of the Persian manuscripts of the Minassian Collection . . . 129 n.19
'Creature of the next century' 196 n.86
Interviews 2 n.3, n.4, n.6, n.8
Problems Corresponding to Quadratic Equations . . . 64 n.99, 176 n.125
King, David A.
'A Hellenistic astrological table . . .' 86 n.48
'Henry C. King . . .' 53 n.46
'Ibn al-Shāṭir . . .' 158 n.31, n.34, 159 n.35, n.36, 160 n.39, 161 n.40
Interview with 2 n.6
'Instruments of mass calculation' 53, 53 nn.47–8
In Synchrony with the Heavens . . . 53, 53 nn.47–8
Poem in honour 53, 54 n.51
'Some remarks . . .' 156 n.20, 169 n.78
'Takī al-Dīn' 166 n.66, n.72
Volume in honour 53 n.50
'When the night-sky over Qandahar was lit only by stars' 53, 53 nn.47–8
King, David A. and Samso, Julio
'Zīdj . . .' 67 n.119
King, Henry
Biography 53 n.46
Exploration of the Universe . . . 53 n.49
Geared to the Stars . . . 53 n.49
Residence at William Herschel's 'Observatory House' 53
Two Sketches 53

Kingsdale, Julia
Exhibit caption 102 n.17
Korangy, Alireza, Thackston, Wheeler, Mottahedeh, Roy and Granara, William (eds)
Essays in Islamic Philology, History, and Philosophy . . . 57 n.72
Koyré, Alexander
From the Closed World to the Infinite Universe 130 n.27
Kuhn, Thomas
The Copernican Revolution . . . 72 n.155, 161 n.42
'Science: The history of science', 1 n.1
Kunitzsch, Paul
'Description of the night . . .' 57 n.72, 64 n.103, 65 n.104
'Al-Nudjūm, the stars' 66 n.111

Langermann, Y. Tzvi
'Ibn al-Haytham . . .' 70 n.135, 110 n.62
Lewis, Bernard
What Went Wrong . . . 23 n.22
Lindberg, David C.
A Catalogue of Medieval and Renaissance Optical Manuscripts 117 n.100
'The intromission-extramission controversy . . .' 104 n.23, 118 n.105
Theories of Vision from Al-Kindi to Kepler 104 n.23, 113 n.87, 114 n.91, 116 n.96, 117 n.103, 118 n.105
Lopes, Cecily
Exhibit caption 102 n.17
Lüthy, Christoph
Early Science and Medicine (ed) 53 n.50

McCarthy, Timothy
'Public service' 47, 47 n.21
McGinnis, Jon
Avicenna 122 n.136
Mahdavi, Asqar
manuscript and map collections 122 n.135, 134, 134 n.50
Mahdavi, Yahya
Catalogue of Manuscripts of the Compositions of Ibn Sīnā 122 n.133, n.135, 134 n.50
Ibn Sīnā Library 122 n.135
Malek-Soudavar, Ezzat-Malek
Malek Library and Museum 133 n.45
Masoumi Hamedani, Hossein
'Galileo and the Moon' 131 n.31
'Ustād-i bashar' (Teacher of Mankind) 67 n.117, 143 n.91, n.93, 145 n.107
Mathew, John
Averroes play 4 n.26, 48 n.25
Student (academic years) 7 n.45
Melikian-Chirvani, A. S.
'Khwāje and the Iranian past' 145 n.106
Melville, Charles
'Ebn al-Fowaṭī..' 68 n.121, 147 n.119
'. . . Iranian Studies in Britain . . . 78 n.8, 79 n.12
'New light on Shah ʿAbbas . . .' 5 n.39, 35 n.75
'Obituary' of Peter Avery' 79, 79 n.12
Project Shahnama (director) 78 n.9, 79
Shahnama Centre for Persian Studies (director) 78, 78 n.9, 80, 80 n.16
The Timurid Century (ed) 4 n.33, 156
Millennium of the Shahnama (ed) (*see* Abdullaeva [-Melville], Firuza) 129 n.20
Mendelsohn, Everett
Transformation and Tradition in the Sciences . . . (ed) 70 n.137, 75 n.164
Menocal, María Rosa
The Ornament of the World 5 n.35, 32 n.64, 131 n.29, 137 n.69
Merton, Robert K.
On the Shoulders of Giants . . . 41 n.99, 75 nn.165–7
Molavi, Parvin-Dokht
Acknowledgements xii
Morrison, Robert
Islam and Science 172 n.100
'A scholarly intermediary . . .' 73 n.157
Mottahedeh, Roy
Acknowledgements xi
'Classical Library of Islam', Packard Humanities Institute (director) 57 n.74
'The Idea of Iran in the Buyid dominions' 178 n.132
'Sources for the study of Iran' 79 n.13

Murdoch, John E.
Album of Science 2 n.7
'Euclid: Transmission of the Elements' 97, 97 n.106
Volume in honour 98 n.110

Nagy, Gregory
'The epic hero . . .' 80 n.19
Nasr, S. H.
'Bīrūnī versus Ibn Sīnā . . .' 56 n.67
Islamic Science: An Illustrated Study 133, 133 n.44
'Al-Ṭūsī . . .' 67 n.117
Nasr, S. H. and Amin Razavi, Mehdi (eds)
The Islamic Intellectual Tradition in Persia 56 n.67
Necipoğlu, Gülru
The Arts of Ornamental Geometry (ed) 3 n.14, 105 n.32, 106 n.33, n.36, 135 n.59
Muqarnas (ed) 5 n.39, 35 n.75
Necipoğlu, Gülru, Kafadar, Cemal and Fleischer, Cornell H.(eds)
Treasures of Knowledge . . . 3 n.19, 109 n.57, 181 nn.2–3, 182 n.4, 202 n.106
Newman, William R.
The Artificial and the Natural . . . (ed) (*see* Bensaude-Vincent) 121 n.131
Newman, William R. and Sylla, Edith Dudley (eds)
Evidence and interpretation . . . 98 n.110
Noy, Avigail
Exhibit caption 102 n.17

Ogunnaike, Ayodeji
Exhibit caption 102 n.17

Packard
Packard Humanities Institute (PHI) (founder: David Packard) 57 n.74
Pamuk, Orham
Museum of Innocence 195 n.85
Pasachoff, Jay M.
Nearest Star . . . (*see* Golub, Leon) 52 n.43
The Sun (*Kosmos*): (*see* Golub, Leon) 52 n.43

Pike, Kathy
The Birth Horoscope of Iskandar Sultan 163 n.52
Pingree, David
'Abu'l-Fatḥ Esfahanī' 105 n.30
'Abu'l-Wafā Būzjānī' 105 n.29
'Abū Sahl B. Nawbakt' 88 n.62, 90 n.68, 92, nn.75–6, n.79, 94, nn.86–7, n.90
Eastern Astrolabes . . . 51 n.40, 86 n.47
'Fazārī . . .' 88 n.62, 90 nn.67–8, 91 n.71, p. 95 n.94
'The fragments of the works of Al-Fazārī' 90 n.67, 91 nn.70–1, n.73, 92 n.81, 93, nn.82–5
'From Alexandria to Baghdad and Byzantium . . .' 89, 89 n.64
Exhibit in honour of 102 n.16
'Hakim extraordinaire' title 86, 86 n.46, 129 n.21
''Ilm al-hay'a . . .' 66 n.111
'Indian reception of Muslim versions of Ptolemaic astronomy' 72 n.153
Minassian Catalogue supervision 129 n.19
Obituary of 86 n.49, 88 n.61
The Thousands of Abū Maʿshar 89 n.63, 90 n.69, 93 n.85, 94 n.91, 95 n.98, 96 n.104, 184 n.20, 203 n.111
Volume in honour of 86 n.48
Pingree, Isabelle and Steele, John M. (eds)
Pathways into the Study of Ancient Sciences . . . 87 n.50
Plofker, Kim
'Fazārī . . .' 88 n.62, 90 n.67, 91 n.70, n.72
Pingree obituary quote 86 n.49, 88 n.61
Studies in the History of the Exact Sciences . . . (ed) (*see* Burnett, Charles) 86 n.48
Png Marie-Therese
Future of People: Audience award recipient (with Esam Goodarzy) 197 n.89
Porter, Eve (eds) (*see* Vesel, Živa)
Images of Islamic Science 172 n.99
Pourdavoud
Center for the Study of the Iranian World 79 n.14

Pourjavady, Nasrollah
'*Munāẓirih-i Khurshīd va Māh*' (ed) 7 n.50.
'*Munāẓirih-i Shaṭranj va nard*' (ed) 7 n.49, 197 n.90
Zabān-i Ḥāl ... (ed) 7 n.50
Pourjavady, Nasrollah and Vesel, Živa (eds)
Naṣīr al-Dīn al-Ṭūsī ... 67 n.117, 69 129, 133 n.43, 145 n.66
Les sciences dans la monde iranien ... 150 n.135
Sciences, techniques et instruments ... 39 n.94, 119 n.114

Quintern, Detlev
Istanbul Museum (director) 193 n.71

Rabbat, Nasser
Identification of Maghribī on manuscript 101 n.12
Ragep, F. Jamil
"'Alī Qushjī [sic] and Regiomontanus ...' 71 n.142, 73 n.58, 193 n.69, 203 n.110
'Copernicus and his Islamic predecessors ...' 71 n.142, 73 n.157, 76 n.169
'From Tūn to Torun ...' 73 n.157
'Freeing astronomy from philosophy ...' 71 n.142, n.146, 72 n.153, 73 n.156, nn.158–9, 74 nn.162–3, 75, 193 n.70, 194 n.72
'The Persian context of the Ṭūsī Couple' 69 n.129, 143 n.92, 144 n.98, 145 n.107, 147 n.114
'Ṭūsī ...' 67 n.117
'Ṭūsī and Copernicus ...' 69 n.130, 70 n.139
Ṭūsī's *Tadhkira* (*Memoir on Astronomy*) 2 n.5, 69, 69 n.129, n.131, 86 n.46, 129 n.21, 132 n.35, 133 n.43, 143 n.95, 145, 146 nn.110–11, 147 nn.115–18, 150 n.139, 161 n.41, 193 n.67
Ragep, F. Jamil (ed) (*see* Feldhay, Rivka)
Before Copernicus (ed) 73 n.157
Ragep, F. Jamil and Ragep, Sally P. with Livesey, S. (eds)
Tradition, Transmission, Transformation ... (ed) 72 n.153
'The astronomical and cosmological works of Ibn Sīnā' 119 n.114
Ragep, Sally P.
'The astronomical and cosmological works of Ibn Sīnā' (*see* Ragep, F. Jamil) 119 n.114
'Ibn Sīnā ...' 56, 56 n.67, 118 n.106
Tradition, Transmission, Transformation ... (ed) (*see* Ragep, F. Jamil) 72 n.153
Rashed, Roshdi
Geometry and Dioptrics in Classical Islam 169 n.79
Ibn al-Haytham's Theory of Conics ... 106 n.37
'Mathematics and Science' 104 n.24
Thābit ibn Qurra ... 96 n.102, n.108
Raynaud, Dominique
A Critical Edition of Ibn al-Haytham's On the Shape of the Eclipse 114 n.89, 190 n.54
Rieu, Charles
Catalogue of the Persian Manuscripts 6, nn.41–3, 17, 17 n.1, 20, 22, 26, 29, 29 n.49, 39 n.92
'Obituary notice' 21, 21 n.14, 24, 24 n.29
Positions 21, 77, 78
Rosenthal, Franz
'Al-Biruni between Greece and India' 56 n.70
The Classical Heritage in Islam 58 n.81, 87, 87 n.55, 88 n.59
Man versus Society in Medieval Islam (*see* Gutas, Dimitri) 87 n.56
'Nineteen' 183 n.10
'On some epistemological and methodological presuppositions of Al-Biruni' 193 n.66
The Technique and Approach of Muslim Scholarship 23 n.25
Rowling, J. K.
Harvard graduation speaker ... 109 n.59

Russel, Gül A.
'In Memoriam: A. I. Sabra . . .' 113 n.84
Rutter, Michael
Student poem 4 n.29, 156 n.23

Sabra, A. I.
'The "Commentary" that saved the text' 65 n.106, 107 n.45, 110 n.62, 118 n.104, 150 nn.135–6, 193 n.68, 202 n.105
'The Andalusian revolt . . .' 70 n.137, 132 n.33, 138 n.73, 139 n.76, 140 n.81, 141 n.85, 143 n.90
'The Appropriation and subsequent naturalization . . .' 23 n.20, n.23, 65 n.107
'The astronomical origin of Ibn al-Haytham's concept of experiment' 115 n.93 116 n.98, 132 n.34
'Eloge' of 190 nn.51–2
The Enterprise of Science in Islam . . . (*see* Hogendijk, Jan P.) 120 n.120
'The European Journey of Ibn al-Haytham's MSS . . .' 104 n.25
'Ibn al-Haytham . . .' 65 n.108, 112 n.75, 113 n.84, 123 n.139
'Ibn al-Haytham's criticisms of Ptolemy's *Optics*' 115 n.94
Interview with 2 n.3
Legacy session 189 n.49, 190 n.51
'Manāẓir, or ʿIlm al-Manāẓir' 120 n.120
'One Ibn al-Haytham or two . . .' 104, 104 n.25, 111 n.70
The Optics of Ibn al-Haytham 2 n.12, 3 n.13, 84 n.42, 98 n.110, 104 n.26, 107 n.45, 110 n.62, 111 n.72, 113 n.82, 114 n.88, n.90, 116, 116 n.97, 117, 117 nn.99–100, 119 n.116, 134 n.49, 150 n 135, 169 n.80, 179 n.135, 181, 181 n.1, 190 n.51, n.53, 194 n.72, 200, 202–3
'The physical and the mathematical . . .' 139 n.77, 179 n.135
'Sarton Medal Award Acceptance Speech . . .' 113 n.84
'The scientific enterprise . . .', 68 n.124, 120 n.125, 202 n.107
'Situating Arabic science' 23 n.23
Sourcebook 23 nn.20–1
'Vita: Ibn al-Haytham . . .' 65 n.108, 99 n.1, 111 n.71, 112 n.78, 115 n.94, 131 n.32, 203 n.109, 204 n.117
Sabra, A. I. and Shehaby, N. (eds)
Aporias Against Ptolemy . . . 70 n.135, 99, 99 n.1
Sabra, Adam
'What is wrong with What Went Wrong' 23 n.22
Saliba, George
'An observational notebook . . .' 66 n.112, 67 n.114, n.116, 68, nn.121–2
Islamic Science and the Making of the European Renaissance 73 n.157
'Kāši . . .' 155 n.17, 165 n.59
'The meaning of al-Jabr . . .' 59 n.77
'Qushjī's [sic] reform' 71 n.142, 72 n.148, 73 nn.156–8, 74 n.160, n.163
Samso, Julio
'Zīdj . . .' (*see* King, David A.) 67 n.119
Sarton, George
'An institute for the history of science and civilization' 1 n.1
'Arabic science and learning in the fifteenth century' . . . 24, 24 n.27
Harvard office 25 n.35
Introduction to the History of Science 24, 24 n.27
Savage-Smith, Emily
'The most authoritative copy . . .' 55 n.61, 145 n.103
Schechner, Sara
Harvard, Collection of Historical Scientific Instruments (curator) 51 n.38
Schiefsky, Mark J.
'Art and nature in ancient mechanics' 121 n.131, 169 n.82
Schmidl, Petra G.
'Kāshī . . .' 155 n.17
Sezgin, Fuat
Foundation Summer School 186 n.32
Istanbul Museum 186 n.31, 192 nn.62–3, 193 n.71
Shinagel, Michael
The Gates Unbarred . . . 46, 46 n.19

Siddiqi, Maera
Acknowledgements xii
Early Science and Authority ... 186 n.33
Films and productions 153 n.7
Student (academic years) 7 n.45
Workshops 186 n.33
Siddiqi, Maham
Exhibit caption 102 n.17
Sidoli, Nathan and van Brummelen, Glen (eds)
From Alexandria, Through Baghdad ... 103 n.21
Sobel, Dava
A More Perfect Heaven ... 81 n.27
And the Sun Stood Still 81 n.27
Galileo's Daughter ... 54 n.53
The Glass Universe ... 81 n.27
Longitude 52 n.42
The Planets 52 n.42, 81
'The shadow knows ...' 81 n.28, n.30
Soudavar, Abolala
'...the problem of semi-fakes' 145 n.103
Soudavar, Fatema
Soudavar Memorial Foundation 79 n.14
Steele, John M.
Pathways into the Study of Ancient Sciences ... (ed) (*see* Pingree, Isabelle) 87 n.50
Storey, Charles Ambrose
Persian Literature ... 78, 78 n.7
Sylla, Edith Dudley
Evidence and interpretation ... (ed) (*see* Newman, William) 98 n.110
Swerdlow, Noel M.
The Renaissance of Astronomy 2 n.10

Taheri, Jafar
'Mathematical knowledge of architecture ...' 164 n.55
Taskomur, Himmet
Turkish poem (transliteration) 15 n.2
Taub, Liba
Acknowledgements xi
'The "grand" orrery ...' 55 n.60
Whipple Museum (director) 54 n.58, 55 nn.59–60
Tennyson, Alfred Lord
'Love and death' 210 n.2, n.4, 211 n.5
Ulysses 24 n.28
Thackston, Wheeler M.
A Century of Princes (sel, trans) 155, 155 n.18, 162, 162 n.49
Toomer, G. J.
'Al-Khwārizmī ...' 59 n.77, n.79, 61 n.87
'The mathematical sciences ...' 48 n.26
'Ptolemy ...' 69 n.133
Ptolemy's Almagest 57 n.73, 64, 139 n.80, 142 n.87
Sources (ed) 2 n.5, 74 n.161
Tourkin, Serge (ed) (*see* Vesel, Živa)
Images of Islamic Science 172 n.99
Tousi, Khosrow
Takhtih Nard (Backgammon) (reference source) 197 n.91
Tyson, Neil deGrasse
'The golden age of Islam ...' 187 n.34

Vafa, Farzan
Exhibit caption 102 n.18
van Brummelen, Glen
From Alexandria, Through Baghdad ... (ed) (with Nathan, Sidoli) 103 n.21
van Dalen, Benno
Certainty, Doubt, Error ... (ed) (*see* Brentjes, Sonja) 53 n.50
'Al-Shams ...' 28 n.47
'Ulugh Beg ...' 71 n.141, n.144, 72 n.154, 162, 162 n.47
van Zuylen, Marina
'Philosophy in everyday life' 47, 47 n.12
Velani, Sonam
Exhibit caption 102 n.17
Vesel, Živa, Tourkin, Serge and Porter, Eve (eds) (with Francis, Richard and Ghasemloo, Farid) *Images of Islamic Science* 172 n.99

Walker, Stephen
'Joker in the Pack' 17 n.3
Walsh, Colleen
'Digital drive' 152 n.5, 153 n.6
'What's possible' 151 nn.3–4
Wells, H. G.
Meanwhile 195 n.82

Rediscovery of the Unique 194 n.79, 195 n.83
Shape of Things to Come 194 n.80
Tales of Space and Time 194 n.76
Through a Window 194 n.81
Time Machine 194 n.74
A Vision of the Past 194 n.77
A Wonderful Visit 194 n.78
Wheels of Chance 194 n.75

Werner, Klaus E.
Biblioteca Hertziana (director) 189 nn.45–6

Whitman, Walt
'Vocalism' 1 n.2

Wisnovsky, Robert
Aspects of Avicenna . . . (ed) 122 n.136

Yang, Yan
Student astronomer 3 n.27

Yano, Michio
'Bīrūnī . . .' 56 n.57
Studies in the History of the Exact Sciences . . . (ed) (*see* Burnett, Charles) 86 n.48

Yarshater, Ehsan
Encyclopedia Iranica (*EIr*) 89 n.65
'Iraj Afshar (1925–2011)' 134 n.48

Subject Index

Scientific disciplines, key components and concepts in historical context

Algebra
- Discipline 59–66, 59, 59 nn.77–9, 97, 164, 176
- Identity 97, 98, 98 n.108
- Inheritance algebra 59, 59 n.82
- Latinised 'Algorithm' 59
- Unknown 64, 64 n.99, 176, 176 n.125

Architecture/Architectural sites
- Alamūt, fortress 132, 132 n.36, 144, 146
- Amīnī-hā house, Qazvīn 132, 132 n.39
- Ancient Fire Temple, Kashan 203, 203 n.112
- Ayasofya complex, Istanbul 72, 107
- Azhar mosque, Cairo 2, 112
- British Library, London 43, 43 n.3, 79
- Cambridge University Library 52, 52 n.44
- Chihil Sutūn (Forty Pillars), Isfahan 30, 30 n.57, 201, 201 n.101, 202
- 'Clock tower', Isfahan 40, 40 n.96, 135, 135 n.62, 136
- Discipline 132 n.36, 164 n.55
- Great mosque of Damascus 158, 158 n.32
- Houghton Library, Cambridge, US 47 n.22, 100, 100 n.7
- Library of Alexandria (Bibliotheca Alexandrina) 103, 103 n.19, nn.21–2
- Mahdavī Library and Map Collection, Tehran 122, 122 n.135, 134 n.50
- Malik National Library and Museum, Tehran 133 n.45
- Maragha Observatory site, Maragha 132, 132 n.36
- Maragha Tomb Tower, Maragha, 132 n.36
- Markazī (Central) Library and Documentation center 134 n.47
- Millī (National) Library and Museum, Tehran 134 n.49
- Mīr Nishānih Tomb, Kashan 205–6, 206 n.127
- Museum for the History of Science and Technology in Islam, Istanbul 186, 186 n.31
- Museum of Innocence, Istanbul 195, 195 n.85
- Muṭahharī/Sipahsālār School and Library complex, Tehran 133, 133 n.41, n.43, 134, 134 n.53, 135, 135 n.56
- Naqsh-i Jahān square, Isfahan 30, 30 n.57, 35, 35 n.75, 135, 135 n.61, 201 n.101
- Old (ʿAtīq)/Congregational (Jāmiʿ)/ Friday (Jumʿa)/ mosque, Isfahan 3, 3 n.14, 15 n.1, 63, 63 n.95, 95 n.98, 135 nn.57–8, 136, 178
- Pergamon Museum and Installation, Berlin 188, 188 nn.42–3
- Shaykh Bahāʾī House, Isfahan 135, 135 n.60, 178, 178 n.131
- Shrine Library, Mashhad 178, 178 n.133
- Soltaniyeh dome, Zanjan province 132, 132 n.37
- Süleymaniye school complex, Istanbul 107, 107 n.43, 108 n.53, 134, 186 n.33
- Thābit house/House of stars, Kashan 203–4
- Topkapi palace complex, Istanbul 107, 107 n.44
- Widener Library, Cambridge, US 17 n.2, 18 nn.4–6, 19, 19 n.7, n.9, 25 n.35, 101 n.12, 108, 108 n.54, 109, 109 n.60, 126 n.7

Arithmetic
Discipline 3 n.19, 56, 97, 102, 102 n.14, 119, 119 n.18, 127, 164, 164 n.56, 176, 176 n.122, 195, 195 n.83
Numbers 7, 15, 15 n.0, 25, 25 n.36, 54, 56, 85, 89, 93, 100–1, 109, 129, 129 n.22, 138, 149, 149 n.129, 153–4, 163–4, 171, 182, 182 nn.7–8, 183, 183 nn.10–11, 184, 195, 195 n.4, 198, 201, 203, 203 n.113, 204, 206–7, 209, 210 n.3
Pi (concept) 163, 163 n.53, 165, 165 n.58
Astronomy/Astrology
Astrolabe/Usṭurlāb 51, 51 n.40, 53 n.49, 91, 159, 175 n.116, 182
Astrophysicists 66, 187, 187 n.34
Calendars, lunar/solar x, 6, 27, 28, 28 nn.45–7, 35, 35 n.76, 47, 63, 64, 75, 82, 84, 143
Comets 65, 67, 67 n.115, 68, 68 n.123, 170, 179 n.137
Constellations/Zodiacs viii, 3, 7, 55, 55 n.62, 57, 64–5, 130, 130 n.32, 132, 132 n.38, 143–5, 148, 148 n.125, 149, 149 n.33, 172, 172 n.99, 175, 175 n.117, 182, 182 n.7, n.9, 183 n.11, 184 n.21, 203, 203 n.113, 206, 206 nn.128–9, 207, 209
Cosmology 7, 22, 58, 69, 69 n.130, 80, 100, 119, 119 n.114, 128, 129, 142, 149, 150, 165 n.59, 179, 184, 203, 204, 205, 206, 207
Discipline 11, 55, 55 n.60, 56, 58, 59, 64, 65, 65 n.104, 66–70, 66, 66 n.111, 67 nn.114–19, 68, 68 nn.121–3, nn.126–7, 69 n.33, 70, 70 n.137, 71, 71 n.142, n.146, 72, 72 n.153, n.155, 73, 73 n.156, nn.158–9, 74 nn.162–3, 75, 75 n.66, 86, 88, 89, 95, 107 n.40, 115, 115 n.93, 130, 131, 131 n.31, 133, 133 n.43, 134, 136, 139–40, 144–6, 148, 153, 153 n.8, n.13, 159, 164, 166 n.65, 167, 169, 170, 177, 191, 192, 193 n.67, n.70, 194 n.72, 198, 198 n.92, 200, 202, 203, 205
Earth-/Sun-centered models 44–5, 45 n.9, 49, 54, 64, 69, 70, 74–6, 131 n.27, 137, 141, 161, 178, 193, 206–8
Eclipses 73, 114, 114 n.89, 156, 165, 165 n.61, 190, 190 n.54
Instruments 3, 3 n.20, 51, 51 n.38, nn.40–1, 54, 76 n.170, 81, 81 nn.25–30, 82 n.32, 131, 132, 158 n.33, 159, 159 nn.35–7, 164, 166–7, 169–71, 175, 175 n.116, 177, 179, 179 n.137, 180, 180 n.138, 188 nn.39–40, 198, 198 n.93, 199, 202, 202 n.107, 203 n.112, 204, 204 n.118, 205, 205 n.123, n.126, 206
Motion 69–71, 73–6, 120, 141–2, 146–7, 154, 160, 161, 192, 207 n.134, 209
Observatories 3, 3 n.17, 4 n.27, 5 n.36, 53, 53 nn.46–7, 67, 67 n.118, 68, 71, 76 n.170, 81 n.27, 130, 130 n.23, 132, 132 nn.35–6, 147, 148, 148 n.28, 155, 159, 160, 162–5, 167–72, 168 nn.74–6, 171 nn.95–7, 173, 175, 198, 200, 201, 203, 203 n.112, 205, 205 n.124, 206
Planets 44–5, 52, 52 n.42, 53, 54, 54 n.52, 69, 141, 184, 184 n.24, 199, 203, 203 n.113, 206, 206 nn.127–9, 207, 207 n.134, 208 n.137, nn.139–40, 209–10
Prognostications 61, 61 nn.89–90, 149
Ptolemaic/non-Ptolemaic Models 11, 45, 45 n.13, 68–70, 70 n.137, 73, 76, 132, 137, 139–40, 141–2, 145, 161, 178, 207, 207 n.134
Retrograde/loop-the-loop motion 141–2, 207 n.134
Royal New Day (Nowruz/Nuwrūz-i Sulṭānī) 128
Spring equinox/Persian New Year/ New Day (Nowruz/Nuwrūz) 28
Supernova 66, 66 n.113
Tables/handbooks 67 n.119, 68, 86 n.48, 91, 160, 160 n.39, 165, 171 n.96
Telescope 110, 159–60, 164, 166, 177, 179–80, 188, 199, 202–3, 204–6

Geometry/Practical Geometry
Discipline 3 n.14, n.19, 10, 47, 47 n.20, 56, 59, 89, 105, 105 n.32, 106,

106 nn.33–8, 107, 107 n.40, n.48, 117, 120, 120 nn.122–3, 133, 133 n.36, 134, 135, 135 n.59, 136, 136 n.64, 145–6, 153, 153 n.8, n.13, 159, 165, 165 n.58, 169 n.79, 178, 178 nn.132–3, 191, 192
- Patterns/Shapes 3, 21, 26, 85–6, 106, 106 nn.33–8, nn.135–6
- Proof/Identity 96–8, 106, 176, 176 nn.123–4, 192
- Theorems/Propositions 97, 98 n.109, 135 n.55, n.59

History/History of Science
- Discipline xi, 1, 1 n.1, 2, 2 n.9, 5, 9, 10–12, 22, 24, 24 n.27, 25–7, 41, 49 n.30, 50, 54 n.54, n.58, 55 n.60, 59, 61, 147, 148 n.126, 186, 186 nn.31–2, 188, 192, 192 n.62, 193, 193 n.71, 195
- Premodern historians/biographers 22, 61, 61 n.87, 93, 113, 176, 189, 189 n.48
- *Taʾrīkh* (*Chronology*) 59, 59 n.79

Mechanics
- Beyond nature 21, 21 n.131, 169, 169 n.82
- Clocks/Water-clocks 40, 68, 68 n.120, 135, 136, 165, 165 n.63, 167, 169, 169 n.84, 170, 170 n.87, 174
- Discipline 3 n.19, 12, 75, 97, 107, 118–23, 120, 120 n.119, 121, 122, 123, 130, 136, 153, 153 n.8, n.13, 169, 169 n.83, 179, 191
- Moving devices 120, 120 n.119
- Simple machines 121, 121 n.129
- Weights 121, 121 n.132

Medicine
- Discipline 95
- Ibn Sīnā/Avicenna (practitioner) 118, 122 n.137
- Poem on 139, 139 n.75
- Physician/Physicians 48, 65, 137, 138

Optics
- Camera obscura 114, 114 n.89
- Discipline 3 n.19, 11, 110–18, 120, 120 nn.119–20, 123, 131, 131 n.31, 153, 153 nn.8–9, n.13, 154, 154 n.14, 166 n.65, 169 n.79, 179, 179 nn.136–7, 187, 187 nn.36–8, 188, 189, 189 n.45, 191, 198, 198 n.92, 202–3
- Extramission/Intromission 104 n.23 114, 118 n.105
- Lenses 49, 110, 110 nn.63–5, 117, 117 n.103, 160, 160 n.38, 165, 199 n.94, 200, 201, 201 n.100, 204, 204 nn.120–1, 205, 205 n.123, n.126, 207
- Light 52 n.44, 66, 66 n.115, 73, 84, 84 n.42, 93, 106, 110, 110 nn.62–3, 111, 111 nn.66–8, 115, 120, 139 n.77, 154
- Light Reflection/Refraction 150, 150 nn.135–7, 153, 153 n.9, 154, 154 n.14, 179, 198, 201 -2
- Perception 114–5, 117, 154, 154 n.14
- Rainbow 52, 52 n.44, 120, 200, 200 n.9
- Shadow 29, 82, 84 n.42, 93
- Vision 106, 111, 139 n.77, 201, 202
- Visual rays 114, 114 n.91, 115, 115 n.120, 154, 154 n.14, 193, 200, 200 n.97, 203
- Visual cone 114

Perspective/Surveying
- Linear Perspective, 187, 187 nn.37–8, 188, 189
- Measurement 106, 106 n.37, 154, 165, 165 n.58
- Perspective/Perspectiva 110, 154, 187, 188, 189, 189 nn.45–6, 199 n.94, 202
- Pre-perspective practices 117, 150, 150 n.138
- Vanishing point 187, 187 n.37

General Index

Additional items including terms, titles and transliterations in original languages

Cities/Regions

Alamut (Alamūt) 132, 132 nn.35–6, 144, 146, 147
Aleppo (Ḥalab) 159
Alexandria (Iskandarīyah) 48, 96, 101, 103, 103 n.19, n.21, 104, 121 n.129, 154, 158, 182 n.9, 201 n.100, 208
Andalusia (Andalus) 31, 32, 58, 138, 138 n.72
Armenia 39
Asia 5, 23, 26, 44, 56, 58, 107, 138, 166, 171
Athens 30, 48, 138, 138 n.70, 140
Azarbaijan (Azarbāyjān/Azarbāygān) 31, 31 n.63, 39

Babylon (Bābil) 182 n.9
Baghdad (Baghdād) viii, x–xiii, 1–7, 17, 21, 22, 25, 25 nn.30–1, 26, 27–35, 36, 36 n.82, 37, 39, 39 n.92, n.95, 40, 41, 46, 47, 48, 50 n.34, 55, 55 n.61, 57, 59, 60, 60 n.83, n.86, 61, 65–8, 70, 77, 77 n.1, 80, 82, 84, 85–6, 87, 87 nn.52–4, 88, 89, 90, 91, 92, 93, 95, 96, 96 n.102, 97, 100–2, 104–7, 109, 110, 112, 121, 123, 126 n.4, 127, 130, 130 nn.23–4, 131, 136, 137, 139, 141, 144, 144 n.99, 147, 148, 148 nn.123–4, 150, 152, 154, 157, 158, 171, 178, 181, 182, 183, 183 n.11, 184–6, 188, 189, 191, 193–8, 200, 201–3, 206, 208
  and Alexandria 3 n.23, 4, 4 n.26, 46, 46 n.16, 47, 47 n.23, 48, 49, 49 n.31, 50 n.35, 89, 89 n.64, 100 n.8, 103, 103 nn.20–1
  and Cordoba 4, 4 n.33, 46, 47 n.20
  and Florence 112 n.73, 187, 187 n.38
  and Isfahan x, 1, 2, 2 n.11, 3 n.23, 4, 100 n.8, 17, 21, 25, 26, 26 n.39, 35 n.77, 38, 38 n.89, n.91, 43, 79, 85, 99, 101, 102, 104, 125 n.3, 126 n.4, 127, 181–2; *see also* 'Dialogue of Baghdad and Isfahan'
  as a capital x, 5, 5 n.40, 22, 25, 27, 29, 32, 36, 61, 90
  as a 'city of peace' 25, 25 n.31, 27, 27 n.42, 29 n.54, 30, 30 n.59, 183, 183 n.11
  as a 'city in verse' 29 n.53, 185, 185 nn.22–8
  diversity of 5, 61
  foundation horoscope 88, 88 n.62, 90, 91, 93, 95
  historical maps and sources viii, 22, 22 n.18, 25, 25 n.31, 87, 87 nn.52–4
  House of Wisdom 59, 59 n.81, 90, 90 n.69, 92, 112, 112 n.76, 184, 184 n.15
  Mongol Invasion of 29, 29 n.51, 30, 32, 36, 36 n.79, 37, 37 n.84, 39, 65, 65 n.109, 82, 147
  mosque, as made by the Persians 40
  navel of the universe/navel of the world 27, 28, 28 n.44, 35
  panorama sketch viii, 25, 25 n.34, 183
  Persian roots 28, 32
  as a 'round city' 25, 25 n.31, 27, 90, 95, 184
  translation and scientific movement 5, 5 n.34, 87, 88, 92 n.77, 97
  travel accounts 39–40
  zodiac sign of 3, 130, 130 n.23, 182–3
Balkh (Balkh) 63 n.97, 150
Basra (Baṣrah/Baṣrih) xi, 2 n.12, 36, 36 n.82, 107, 111, 112, 117
Beijing 47, 47 n.22
Berlin 187, 187 n.36, n.38, 188, 188 n.42
Bologna 41, 41 n.100

Boston viii, 3, 19 n.8, 21, 21 n.12, 26, 51, 55 n.63, 100 n.4, 189 n.49
Britain 78, 78 n.8, 79, 79 n.12
Buzjan (Būzjān) 106
Byzantium (Rūm) 36, 36 n.82, 88, 89, 89 n.64, 103 n.20, 138, 149, 163, 166, 166 n.67

Cairo (Qāhirah/Qāhirih) xi, 3, 47, 47 n.22, 101, 112, 113, 137, 139, 141, 158, 159, 167, 208
Cambridge UK 20, 21, 41, 41 n.100, 52, 54, 54 n.58, 55, 77–8, 79, 82, 85
Cambridge US 12, 17 n.2, 19, 19 n.19, 20, 21, 21 nn.12–13, 47 nn.21–1, 48, 49 n.28, 51, 52, 55, 57 n.74, 79, 79 n.14, 80
Central Asia 56, 59, 138
China (Ṣīn/Chīn) 4, 23 n.19, 33, 41, 49, 67, 88, 90, 138, 147, 180, 180 n.138
Constantinople (Qustanṭanīyah/Qustanṭanīyih) 30, 58, 72, 144, 164, 166, 166 n.67, 167, 175, 182 n.9
see also Istanbul
Cordoba/Cordova (Qurṭubah/Qurṭubih) xi, 5, 11, 32, 48, 131, 131 n.30, 132, 137, 138 n.70, 141, 160
Ctesphon (Tīsfūn) 28 n.43, 31 n.62, 77 n.1

Damascus (Damishq) xi, 32, 58, 60, 67, 67 n.116, 136, 139, 147, 157, 158, 158 n.32, 159, 161, 166, 167, 167 n.70
Dublin 191 n.57

Egypt (Miṣr) 65, 103, 113, 138, 158 n.33, 167, 182 n.9
England 20, 41, 44, 46 n.15, 49 n.32, 52, 79, 82, 85, 174, 178, 181, 182
Ethiopia (Ḥabash) 138 n.72
Europe 4, 5, 23, 38, 38 n.90, 39, 41, 64, 68, 69, 70, 72, 73 n.157, 74–6, 82, 100–2, 104, 104 n.25, 105, 107, 110, 114, 117, 118, 122–3, 131, 132, 135–6, 139, 146, 150, 154–5, 157, 161, 166, 166 n.64, 167–70, 170 n.87, 171–4, 176–80

Florence 3, 54, 54 n.55, 112 n.73, 131, 157, 166, 187, 187 n.38, 188, 205, 208

France viii, ix, 41, 105, 111 n.68, 174, 181, 202

Germany 41, 174, 181
Greece (Yūnān) 41, 103, 111, 137, 138–41, 154, 172
Gurgan (Jurjān/Gurgān) 56 n.67, 149

Harran (Ḥarrān) 96, 96 n.100, 204, 204 n.114
Herat (Hirāt) 72, 73
Hungary 181, 182

India (Hind) 4, 6, 35, 41, 44, 44 n.4, 56, 88, 91, 92, 147, 180, 182, 182 n.9, 196
Iran (Īrān) xi, 25 n.34, 78 n.5, 145 n.106
see also Persia
Iraq (Īrāq) xi, 39, 90, 91, 106, 111, 117, 138, 163, 163 n.53, 184, 184 n.14
see also Mesopotamia
Ireland 21 n.14, 30 n.56, 191 n.57
Isfahan (Iṣbahān/Iṣfahān) viii, x–xii, 1–7, 17, 21–2, 25, 25 nn.31–3, 27–41, 47, 47 n.21, 95–6, 163, 163 n.52, n.54, 164, 166, 166 n.64, n.67, 172–80, 183–4, 185, 185 n.29–30, 188, 191, 193, 194, 196, 197, 198, 201, 202, 202 n.103, 203, 206, 208
Afghan Invasion 25, 25 n.32, 29, 29 n.50, 32, 32 n.65, 37, 39, 39 n.93, 40, 156
Bazaars 40, 136
as a capital x, 5, 22, 29, 32, 32 n.65, 119, 174, 177
coffee houses 35 n.75
diversity 5
Fall 37, 39, 39 n.93
Forty pillars (Chihil Sutūn) 30, 30 n.57, 201, 201 n.101, 202
'Half the world' (Niṣf-i Jahān) 25, 25 n.32, 28, 30, 50
historical descriptions 29–31, 30 n.60
historical map viii, 22, 22 n.18, 25, 25 n.32
Mongol Invasion 29, 29 n.51, 32, 36, 144, 144 n.98
Old (ʿAtīq)/Congregational (Jāmiʿ)/Fri (Jumʿa)/mosque 3, 3 n.14, 15 n.1, 63, 63 n.95, 135 nn.57–8, 136, 178

Panorama sketch viii, 25, 25 n.34, 183
'Plan of the World' (Naqsh-i Jahān)
square 30, 30 n.57, 35, 35 n.75, 95 n.98, 135, 135 n.61, 184, 184 n.15, n.17, 201 n.101
Sa'dī on 36, 36 n.83, 37, 37 n.84
scholarly circles 175–6
as second Baghdad 29–30
rare manuscript on history of 30 n.56, n.58, 36 n.82
travel accounts 39–40, 39, 39 nn.93–5
zodiac sign of 3, 130, 130 n.23, 182–3
Istanbul (Istānbul) xi, 3, 5, 5 n.38, 55 n.64, 72, 72 n.150, 107, 107 n.46, n.48, 108, 108 nn.49–51, 109, 111, 111 n.68, 127, 127 n.13, 134, 134 n.52, 136, 144, 144 n.100, 157, 165, 166, 166 n.65, n.67, 167, 168, 168 n.77, 171, 172, 179, 180, 181, 186, 186 n.31–3, 187 nn.34–5, 192, 192 n.62–3, 193, 193 n.71, 194 n.72, 195, 195 n.85, 198, 200, 200 n.98, 201, 203, 208
Observatory, 167, 168, 168 n.75, 169, 171, 173, 205
see also Constantinople
Italy 43, 54 n.57, 85 n.44, 111 n.68, 131, 168, 174, 175, 177, 181, 187, 188, 189 n.46

Japan 24
Jerusalem (Bayt al-Muqaddas/Urshalīm) 182 n.9

Kabul (Kābul) 182 n.9
Kanauj (Qunūj/Qunūch) 35, 35 n.77, 38, 38 n.89, n.91, 182 n.6
Kashan (Qāsān/Kāshān) xi, 5 n.37, 96 n.104, 136, 155, 156, 156 n.21, 157, 157 n.48, 162, 163, 164, 165, 165 n.63, 166, 174, 182 n.9, 200, 203, 206 n.127, 208
Kerman (Kirmān) 31, 31 n.63, 71, 72 n.148, 165
Khurasan (Khurāsān) 144, 144 n.98, 147
Khwrazm (Khwārizm/Khwārazm) 58, 156, 156 n.24
Kubanan (Kubanān) 106 n.35, 165
Kufa (Kūfah/Kūfih) 90, 182 n.9
Kunya (Qūnīyāh/Qūnīyih) 150

Lebanon (Lubnān) 173
London xi, 3, 3 n.21, 21, 26, 30, 39, 43, 44, 46 n.15, 53, 55, 72, 77, 78, 79, 79 n.14, 102, 105, 140, 154, 154 n.15, 156, 157, 168 n.77
Los Angeles ix

Maragha (Marāghah/Marāghih) 5, 11, 67, 68, 70, 101, 132 nn.35–6, 133, 139, 162, 165, 171, 172, 172 n.99, 175, 198
Observatory/Complex 3, 3 n.17, 5, 67, 68, 70, 130, 130 n.23, 132, 139, 147, 160, 164, 165, 171 n.95, 172, 175, 205
Mashhad (Mashhad) 7, n.47, 58, 85, 85 n.43, 133 n.45, 144, 144 n.100, 173, 175, 175 n.117, 178
Mecca (Makkah/Makkih) 28, 34, 72, 92, 128, 128 n.15, 173
Medina (Madīnah/Madīnih) 28
Mesopotamia (Bayn al-nahrayn/Mīyān rūdān) 7, 58, 153
see also Iraq
Middle East xi, 18 n.5, 39 n.94, 49, 65, 82 n.34, 100–1
see also Near East
Minneapolis/Minnesota viii, 113 n.84
Morocco (Maghrib/Marākish) 138, 138 n.72

Nabulus (Nābulus) 167, 167 n.70
Najaf (Najaf) 90
Nayshabur (Nisābūr/Nisāpūr) 63, 63 n.97
Near East viii, xi, 4, 4 n.28, n.30, 80, 80 n.22, 82, 157, 157 n.26
see also Middle East
New Haven 111
New York viii, 3 n.22, 47, 47 n.23, 111
North America 4, 20 n.11

Oxford 41, 41 n.100, 83, 85, 105, 145 n.103, 169 n.49, 201 n.100

Padua 41, 41 n.100, 198, 198 n.93, 199, 201
Palermo 111, 111 n.68, 189 n.44
Palestine (Philisṭīn) 167

Paris viii, xi, 3, 21, 41, 41 n.100, 51, 102, 105–6, 111, 111 n.68, 122, 135, 135 n.59, 136, 148 n.126, 157, 159, 187, 187 n.36, 188 , 206 n.128
Pergamon (Birjāmun/Pirgāmun) 188, 188 n.42–3
Persia (Fārs) 4 n.33, 7, 25 n.32, 29 n.50, 31, 35 n.75, 36, 38, 39, 39 n.93, 40, 41, 44, 44 nn.4–5, 56 n.67, 57 n.72, 58, 62, 73, 73 n.158, 78, 78 n.4, 79, 79 n.13, 83, 88, 88 n.60, 90, 91, 93, 95, 118, 136, 138, 144, 148, 149, 153, 163 n.51, 168, 173, 174, 174 nn.111–12, 196, 196 n.87, 200, 206 n.127
see also Iran
Poland 41, 174

Qandahar (Qandahār/Qandihār) 53
Qazvin (Qavīn) 132, 132 n.38, 173, 174
Quhistan (Quhistān) 144
Qum (Qum) 132, 132 n.59, 133

Ray (Ray/Riy) 31, 31 n.63, 132
see also Tehran
Rome 30, 85, 85 n.44, 131, 157, 166, 168, 189, 189 n.46, 208
Russia 39, 39 n.93, 174

Samarqand (Samarqand) 3 n.18, 5, 11, 62, 70, 71, 72, 73, 101, 108, 136, 139, 144, 155, 156, 162, 163, 164, 166, 166 n.64, 167, 171, 172, 172 n.99, 175, 182 n.9, 198, 200, 205
Observatory/Complex 3, 71, 162, 163, 167
Saudi Arabia 128 n.15
Scotland 174
Seville 137
Shiraz (Shīrāz) 31, 31 n.63, 36, 153 n.11, 168
Sicily 131, 137, 189 n.44
Soltaniyeh (Sulṭānīyah) 132, 132 n.37
Spain 2 n.6, 5 n.35, 31, 48, 67, 117, 131, 131 n.30, 132, 137, 174, 181
see also Andalusia
Syria (Shām/Sūrīyah) 36, 113, 138, 158 n.33, 159, 167, 173

Tabriz (Tabrīz) 72, 72 n.150, 173, 174, 182 n.9, 198, 199, 200, 210 n.3
Tehran (Ṭihrān/Tihrān) 78 n.5, 106 n.35, 112 n.73, 122, 132, 132 n.36, 133, 134, nn.47–8, n.52, 135, 139 n.77, 165
see also Ray
Tokyo 47, 47 n.22
Toledo 131, 137
Turkey 109, 111 n.68, 134 n.51, 168, 182
Tus (Ṭūs) 67, 80, 83, 149–50

Ulm 111
Uzbakistan (Uzbakistān) 62

Washington 111

Venice 73 n.158, 135, 199, 205, 208
Vienna viii, 83 n.35, 145 n.108, 164

Yazd (Yazd) 165

Zanjan (Zanjān) 131, 131 n.28

Events

'A history duet and a science quartet' (Presentation) 189, 189 n.48
'A quartet of early scientific traditions' (Film) 153, 153 n.10
'Age of Rūmī' (Course) 4 n.27, 149 n.130, n.134
'Around the World with Early Science' (Workshop/Exhibit) 186–7, 186 n.33, 193–5
'Astronomy and Science before and after Galileo (Conference) 131, 131 n.28
'Averroes's search' (Play), 48–9, 140 n.83, 141, 141 n.84

'Checkered history recolored' (Presentation) 189, n.49, 190
'Cities of stars' (Presentation), 166, 166 n.65, 194, 197, 198–201, 198 n.92, 208
'Cosmos: Hiding in the light' (TV Show) 187, 187 n.34

'Digital Humanities Fair' (Exhibit) 125 n.3, 126–7, 126 n.9, 127 n.10

'European travelers to Safavid Iran' (Exhibit) 101, 101 n.11

'From Alexandria to Baghdad' (Course, Exhibit) 3 n.23, 4, 4 n.26, 46, 46 n.16, 47, 47 n.23, 48, 49, 49 n.31, 50 n.35, 89, 89 n.64, 100 n.8
'From Baghdad to Cordoba' (Presentation) 4 n.33
'From Baghdad to Isfahan' (Course, Exhibit) 3 n.23, 4, 100 n.8, 125, n.3, 126 n.4, 127
'From Maragha to Samaqand' (Presentation) 4, 4 n.33, 46, 47 n.20

'Galileo and the Moon' (Presentation) 131, 131 n.31

'Harvard Film Archives' (Production) 153, 153 n.7
'Historical Dialogues from the Near East' (Course) 4 n.28, 80–2, 80 n.22, 82 n.31
'Historical relationship between astronomy and optics' (Presentation) 131 n.31
'History of Science in Islam as a Universal Heritage' (Workshop) 186, 186 n.32

'Importance of imagination' (Presentation) 109 n.59
'International year of astronomy' (Conference) 131–2
'International Year of Physics' (Conference) 111

'The Keeper: Legend of Omar Khayyam' (Film) 64, 64 n.100

'Light and Shadow: Experimental Spirit and Interdisciplinary Approaches' (Workshop) 186, 186 n.32
'Lost and embedded manuscripts' (Conference) 103–4, 103 n.22

'Micromapping Early Science' (Presentation) 82 n.34, 151–2, 151 n.2
'Multimedia timeline (Presentation) 101 n.9, 157

'Paths and chances in early science' (Presentation) 193–5, 193 n.71
'Pergamon Installation' (Exhibit) 188, 188 n.42–3
'Personal Enrichment Series' (Presentation) 47, 47 n.21
'Perspectiva +' (Displays), 189, 189 n.45
'Perspective as practice' (Workshop) 187–8, 187 n.36

'Science in the Islamic Middle Ages' (Course) 4, 4 n.25, n.29, 22 n.18, 46, 47 n.20–1, 156 n.23
'Science of stars and craft of wars instruments' (Exhibit) 129 n.17, n.22
'Scientific heritage of Kāshānī' (Conference) 156 n.21
'Spread of science. . .' (Exhibit) 111 n.69, 117 n.102

'The Physician' (Film) 122 n.137
'Traveling Sciences: Applying the History of Sciences' (Workshop) 186 nn.32–3, 187 n.34

'Virtual realities: Mapping fictional spaces' (Presentation) 191–2, 191 n.56, nn.59–60

'When astrology was part of astronomy' (Exhibit) 65 n.104
'When optics was more than physics' (Film) 153, 153 n.9
'Windows into Early Science' (Exhibit) viii, 99–102, 99 n.3, 100 n.6, 102–3, 102 n.16, 117 n.101, 125 n.3, 126, 128–9, 128 n.16, 130, 176 n.122
'Windows into Early Science and Craft' (Exhibit) 3 n.24, 4, 128 n.16, 129–31, 129 n.17

'Year of Light' (Conference) 111 nn.67–8, 187 n.35, 188–9

Heavenly bodies
General 51, 51 n.37, 129, 142, 177

Jupiter (Mushtarī/Birjīs/Hurmuz) 45, 54, 69, 95, 149 n.133, 177, 185, 199, 205, 206 nn.127–9, 207, 208 n.140

Mercury (ʿAṭarud/Tīr) 44, 54, 69, 71 n.142, 72 n.151, 74, 149 n.133, 185, 206 nn.127–9, 207, 208 n.140
Mars (Mirrīkh/Bahrām) 45, 54, 69, 149 n.133, 185, 206 nn.127–9, 207, 208 n.140
Moon (Qamar/Māh) ix, x, xii, 7, 7 n.50, 10, 27, 28, 28 n.47, 43, 44, 47, 47 n.22, 51–2, 52 n.42, 53, 53 n.45, 54, 57, 58, 59, 61, 64–5, 69, 72 n.151, 73, 73 n.159, 76, 76 n.170, 84, 84 nn.41–2, 90, 92–5, 111, 128, 131, 131 nn.31–2, 142, 149 nn.132–3, 161, 165 n.63, 184, 185, 185 n.30, 188, 194, 199, 206, 206 nn.127–9, 207, 207 n.132, n.135, 208, 108 n.136, 209 n.1, 210, 210 nn.2–4, 211, 211 n.5

Neptune 54

Pluto 54

Saturn (Zuḥal/Kayvān) 45, 53, 54, 69, 149 n.133, 185, 206 nn.127–9, 207, 208 n.140
Sun (Shams/Mihr/Khurshīd) ix, x, xii, 7, 7 n.50, 10, 27, 28, 28 n.47, 43, 45, 47, 47 n.22, 51–2, 52 n.42, 53 n.45, 54, 57, 58, 64–6, 69, 76, 76 n.170, 84, 84 n.41–2, 90, 92–5, 128, 139, 141, 142, 149 n.133, 161, 167, 177, 178, 182, 182 n.7, 184–6, 194, 196, 199, 201, 201 n.100, 204 n.114, 206, 206 nn.127–8, 207–8, 207 n.132, 208, 208 n.138, 210, 210 n.4, 211

Uranus 53, 54

Venus (Zuhrih/Nāhid) 44, 54, 69, 149 n.133, 177, 185, 206, 206 nn.127–9, 207, 208 n.139–40

Institutions

Boston College xi, 191 n.56, n.60
Boston University 21 n.12, 49 n.28
Boston University Academy 21 n.12, 80 n.17
Brandeis University 49 n.28

Cambridge Shahnameh/Persian Studies Centre 78, 78 n.10, 79, 80 n.16
Cambridge University xi, 52, 55 n.59, 78, 78 nn.9–10, 79, 80 n.16
Cambridge University Library 52, 52 n.44, 77, 79, 83, 83 n.37, 85

Dibner Institute 49–50, 49 nn.28–31

Ecademics.org Inc. 79 n.14

French Academy of Sciences 41 n.100

Getty Research Institute ix

Harvard University viii, vi, xi, xii, 2 nn.3–4, n.8, 3 nn.22–4, 4 nn.25–33, 17 nn.2–3, 19, 19 n.10, 21 nn.12–13, 25 n.33, 47 nn.22–3, 51 nn.38–9, 46, 46 nn.16–19, 65 n.104, 80 n.23, 82 n.34, 99 n.3, 101 n.9, 102 nn.13–15, 109 n.60, 112 n.74, 126 n.9, 131 n.32, 138 n.70, 151 nn.2–3, 176 n.122, 182 n.7, 190 n.52, 191 n.56, 197 n.89

Istanbul University 70 n.140, 168 n.75, 198 n.92

Kashan University 203 n.112

London University 153 n.10

Massachusetts Institute of Technology 20, 21 n.12, 49 nn.28–9, 50 n.35, 51, 81 n.25, 100 n.4, 127 n.11, 155 n.16, 189 n.45, 197 n.89

Oxford University 105 n.31, 175 n.165, 197 n.89

Packard Humanities Institute 57 n.74
Pembroke College 78 n.9
Pourdavoud Centre 79 n.14

Nashr-i Tārikh-i Iran 106 n.35

Royal Astronomical Society 72, 72 n.154
Royal Society of London 41 n.100

Samuel Jordan Centre 79 n.14
Soudavar Memorial Foundation 79 n.14, 153 n.10

Tehran University, 134, 134 n.47

Year Up 47 n.21, 52 n.43

Languages

Akkadian 157
Arabic x, 1, 3, 3 n.15, 5 n.34, 7, 10, 11, 16, 16 n.3, 20, 21, 25 n.31, 26, 28, 28 n.48, 29, 30, 30 n.59, 31, 31 n.61, 32, 32 n.67, 36, 38, 43, 46, 47 n.20, n.22, 48, 51, 51 n.40, 55, 59, 64, 65 n.106, 66, 66 n.112, 70, 72 nn.153–4, 73, 73 n.158, 74 n.161, 77, 78, 79, 80, 85 n.45, 86 n.48, 87, 88, 89, 91, 92, 93, 94, 95, 96, 97 98 n.110, 101, 102 n.15, 103, 104, 105, 106, 106 n.33, 107, 107 n.42, 108, 109, 110, 113, 115, 115 n.95, 119 n.116, 120 n.120, 121, 125, 125 n.2, 127, 128, 129, 130 n.25, 133, 133 n.46, 137, 138, 140, 141, 142, 142 n.87, 143, 144, 145, 145 n.105, 146, 147, 150 n.138, 154, 154 n.14, 155 n.19, 157 n.27, 159, 160 n.38, 162, 162 n.48, 169, 176, 178, 179, 181 n.3, 185, 186, 186 n.33, 187 n.34, 190, 193 n.69, 199, 199 n.95, 201, 201 n.99, 202, 203
Aramaic 157

Babylonian 64

Chinese 88, 162

Dutch 101

Egyptian, ancient 157

French 56 n.67, 101, 107 n.42, 114 n.88, 122, 176

German 101, 108, 108 n.55, 114 n.88, 176
Greek 5 n.34, 7, 10, 11, 21, 48, 50, 61, 64, 81, 86, 88, 95, 97, 101, 104, 110, 115, 120, 121, 125, 129, 140, 141, 142, 144, 154, 154 n.14, 157, 159, 161, 179

Hebrew x, 7, 101

Indian 82
Italian 101, 117, 179, 180 n.140

Latin x, 7, 21, 39, 46, 47 n.20, 48, 56, 57, 59, 69, 70, 73, 73 n.158, 86, 101, 102 n.15, 104, 105, 109, 110, 113, 114 n.86, 115, 117, 118, 132, 137, 139, 142, 154, 157, 179, 180 n.140, 188 n.40, 189, 194, 202

Mongolian 162

Pahlavi/Middle Persian x, 86, 92, 94, 95, 101, 157, 196 n.87
Persian x, 1, 3, 6 nn.41–3, 7, 16, 16 n.4, 17, 20, 21, 25 n.31, 26, 28, 29–30, 29 n.56, n.59, 32, 32 n.67, 36, 38, 39, 43, 50 n.34, 51, 53, 55, 57, 57 n.74, 63 n.96, 66, 68, 69 n.129, 70, 72, 72 n.153, 77, 78, 78 nn.7–10, 79, 80, 83–5, 88, 89, 92, 94, 95, 95 n.98, 101, 102 n.13, 104 n.27, 105, 106, 106 n.33, 107–9, 118, 120, 121, 122, 122 n.133, 128, 129, 129 n.17, n.19, n.22, 130, 130 n.25, 133, 133 n.40, n.43, n.46, 134, 137 n.66, 138 n.72, 143, 144, 145, 146, 147, 149 n.132, 150 n.138, 153 n.10, 157, 158, 162, 162 n.48, 163 nn.52–4, 164, 168, 168 n.77, 169, 171, 175, 175 n.116, 176, 176 n.121, 177, 178, 180 n.140, 185, 188 n.42, 197, 197 n.91, 199, 200, 201, 201 n.99, 202, 203, 205, 206, 206 n.127–9

Russian 155 n.19, 176

Sanskrit 7, 72, 72 n.153, 86, 91
Sumerian 157
Syriac 48, 86, 96, 97, 125, 140, 157

Turkish x, 7, 15, 15 n.2, 23, 23 n.20, 71, 72, 72 n.153, 101, 108, 127, 129, 155 n.19, 162, 202

Libraries

Alexandria/Bibliotheca Alexandrina 103, 103 n.19, nn.21–2
Āstān Quds Library 133 n.45, 144 n.100

Bibliothèque nationale de France viii, 105–7, 107 n.41
Bodleian Library 55 n.61, 78 n.10, 83 n.37, 85, 85 n.45, 105, 105 n.31, 145 n.105, 169 n.79, 201 n.100
British Library viii, 2 n.11, 6 n.41, 43, 43 n.3, 44 n.7, 45, 55, 77, 79, 120 n.23
Burndy Library 49, 49 n.28, nn.31–2, 50, 50 n.34

Cambridge University Library 52, 52 n.44, 77, 79, 83, 83, 83 n.37, 85, 89
Classical Library of Islam 57–8, 57 n.54

Getty Library ix

History of Science Library, Harvard University 25 n.35
Houghton Library viii–ix, 3 n.24, 4 n.28, 18 n.5, 19 n.7, 47 n.22, 51 n.41, 99 n.3, 100 nn.5–7, 101 n.12, 102 n.13–15, 109 n.60, 112 n.74, 117 n.101, 125 n.3, 131 n.32, 138 n.70, 176 n.122, 191 n.56
Huntington Library 49 n.30, n.32, 50 n.33

Istanbul University Library 168 n.75

James Ford Bell Library viii
John Hay Library 3 n.24, 102 n.16

Mahdavī Library/Collections 122 n.135, 134, 134 n.50
Majlis Library 133
Malik/Malek Library 133, 133 n.45
Millī/National Library 134, 134 n.49
Markazī Library 134, 134 n.47
Muṭahharī/Sipahsālār Library 133, 133 n.41, n.43, 134, 134 n.53, 135, 135 n.56

Pusey Library viii, 82 n.34

Süleymaniye Library 107, n.43, n.46, 108 n.51, n.53, 134, 186

Topkapi Library 107 n.44, 186

Vienna National Library/ Nationalbibliothek viii, 83 n.35, 145 n.108

Widener Library 17 n.2, 18 nn.4–6, 19, 19 n.7, n.9, 25 n.35, 101 n.12, 108, 108 n.54, 109 n.60, 126 n.7

Museums

Ambrosiana Museum 54 n.57
Arthur M. Sackler Museum viii

Boston Museum of Fine Arts viii
British Museum 6 n.41, 25 n.32, 43

Collection of Historical Scientific Instruments 51–2, 51 n.38, 81, 81 n.26

Harvard Art Museums viii
History of Science and Technology in Islam 186, 186 n.31

Malek Museum 133 n.45
Metropolitan Museum of Art viii
Museum of Chances 191, 195, 197, 203–8
Museum of Innocence 195, 195 n.85
Museum of Lost Objects 191, 191 n.55
Museo Galileo 54, 54 nn.55–6

Pergamon Museum 188, 188 n.3

Whipple Museum 54–6, 54, 54 n.58, 55, 55 n.59–60

Poems

'Astronomical poem' (Fazārī) 91, 91 n.72
'Astronomical Poems' (Collection: Kheirandish, E.) 57, n.72, 65 n.104, 147–9, 148 n.127, 149 n.131–3, 206 nn.127–9, 210 n.2–3

Backgammon/Nard poem (ʿĀmulī: attribution) 197, 197 n.91
Backgammon/Nard poem (Firduwsī) 196, 196 n.87
Baghdad poem (Anvarī) 29, 29 n.54
Baghdad poem (Ibn ʿAqīl) 29, 29 n.53
Baghdad poem (Mustuwfī) 31, 31 n.62, 77, 77 n.1
Baghdad poem (Saʿdī) 35, n.79, 37, 37 nn.84–6
Baghdad poems (Collection) 29 n.53, 185, 185 nn.22–8
Baghdad: The City in Verse (Collection: Snir) 29 n.53, 185, 185 nn.22–8
Book of Kings/Shāh-Nāmih (Firduwsī) 80, 80 n.18–19, 83, 129 n.22, 206 n.129

Cambridge Poem 21, 21 nn.13, 48
Chihil Sutūn/Forty Pillars (Ṭāḥir-i Vaḥīd) 201, 201 n.101
Claire de Lune (Verlaine) 207–8, n.135
Creature of the next century (Kheirandish, E.) 196, 196 n.86

Description of the Night (Gurgānī): *Vis and Ramin/Vīs va Ramīn* 57, 57 n.72, 64, 64 n.103, 65, 65 n.105, 149
Description of the Night (Niẓāmī Ganjavī): Layli and Majnun/Laylī va Majnūn 129 n.22
Dialogue of Arab and Persian/Munāẓirih-i ʿArab va ʿAjam (Asadī Ṭūsī) 110, 110 n.61
Dialogue of Arrow and Bow/Munāẓirih-i Ramḥ va Qaws (Asadī Ṭūsī) 129 n.22, 157, 157 n.25
Dialogue(s) of Baghdad and Isfahan/ Munāẓirāt-i Baghdad va Iṣfahān (Kamāl-i Iṣfahānī) 27, 27 n.41, 28, 33, 33 n.69–70, 34 n.71–2
Dialogue of Baghdad and Isfahan/ Munāẓirih-i Baghdad va Iṣfahān (Kheirandish, A.) 184, 184 nn.14–19
Dialogue of Chess and Backgammon/ Munāẓirih-i Shaṭranj va Nard (Khwārazmī, Ḥisām) 197, 197 n.90
Dialogue of Muslim and Zoroastrian/ Munāẓirih-i Musalmān va Gabr (Asadī Ṭūsī) 90, 90 n.66
Dialogue of Night and Day/ Munāẓirih-i Shab va Rūz (Asadī Ṭūsī) 58, 58 n.76, 66, 66 n.110, 84, 84 n.40
Dialogue of Pen and Sword (Various) 7, 60, 60 n.85
Dialogue of Sky and Earth/Munāẓirih-i Āsmān va Zamīn (Asadī Ṭūsī) 136–7, 137 n.66
Dialogue of Sword and Pen/'Munāẓarah al-Sayf va al-Qalam' (Jurjānī) 157 n.28, 158, 158 n.30

Explanation of the Heavens/Bayān-i aflāk: Versed Introduction/Madkhal-i manẓūm (Ṭūsī, Naṣīr al-Dīn: attribution) 206 n.127

Four Quartets (Elliot, T. S.) 195, 195 n.84

His genius cast its shadow o'er the world. . . (Pāshā-zādah, Kemāl) 15, 15 n.2

Isfahan poem (Hakīm Shifāʾī) 37, 37 n.87, 77 n.2
Isfahan poem (Ibn ʿArabī) 31, 31 n.61
Isfahan poem (Kamāl-i Iṣfahānī) 29, 29 n.52
Isfahan poem (Sāʾib-i Tabrīzī) 30, 30 n.57, 185, 185 n.30
Istanbul Observatory poem: *Book of King of Kings/Shahanshāh-Nāmih* (ʿAlaʾ al-Dīn Manṣūr) 168, 168 nn.75–6, 169 n.78, 170, 170 n.90, 171, 171 n.92–3, nn.96–7, 172, 172 n.98, n.100, 175 n.114; verses: 171 n.96

Land of Iran ... Ray and Azarbaijan, its arms (Haravī) 31, 31 n.63
Love and Death (Tennyson, A.) 210 n.4

Moon and Sun (Kheirandish, E.) 210–11, 211 n.5
Moon of Ten and Four (Muwlānā Rūmī) 149 n.131, 210 nn.2–3
Mutawakkil Poem (Ibn Kushājim) 60, 60 n.84

No star strikes another star ... unpredictable rhythms (Rutter, M.) 156, 156 n.23
Not Eastern or Western... or objects turning above (Muwlānā Rūmī) 149 n.132
Now and Then (Leo by Name) 209, 209, n.1
Now and Then (Leo by Sign) 209–10, 209, n.1

Planets and Leo (Firduwsī) 206 n.129
Planets and Zodiacs poem (Ṭūsī, Naṣīr al-Dīn: attribution) 206 n.128

O' King/Khusru-vā: Qaṣīdih-i muṣanna' (Qavāmī Ganjavī) 53–4, 54 n.51

Quatrains/Rubā'iyāt 62, 62 n.93–4, 63 n.96
Since the plan of the times is in no state permanent ... (Hāfiẓ) 204, 204 n.115

That Group of People...so they passed (Ṭūsī, Naṣīr al-Dīn: attribution) 125, 125 n.2
These are our works which prove what we have done... (Anonymous) 16, 16 n.3

Universal spectrum of seven S's (Kheirandish, E.) 183, 183 nn.11–12

'Vocalism' (Whitman, Walt) 1, 1 n.2

What matters in life is a lasting trace... (Anonymous) 15, 15 n.1
When we are dead, seek for our resting-place... (Rūmī, Muwlānā) 16, 16 n.4

Titles

Abridgement or Summary of Arithmetic/ Khulāṣat al-ḥisāb ('Āmilī, Bahā' al-Dīn) viii, 102 n.14, 127 n.12, 176, 176 n.122
Almagest/Syntaxis (Ptolemy) 40, 57 n.73, 64, 68, 91, 120, 139, 139 n.80, 142, 142 n.87, 146
Anatomy of Celestial Spheres/Tashrīḥ al-aflāk ('Āmilī, Bahā' al-Dīn) 177, 177 n.129

Book of Chronology of Ancient Nations/Āthār al-bāqiyah (Bīrūnī) 56, 56 n.69
Book of Constellations of Stars, Persian translation/Tarjamah-i Ṣuwar al-kawākib (Ṭūsī, Naṣīr al-Dīn) 3 n.16, 130, 130 n.24, 143–6, 144 nn.99–100
Book of Constellations of Stars/Ṣuwar al-kawākib (Ṣūfī, 'Abd al-Raḥmān) 3 n.16, 55, 55 n.61, 57, 107–8, 129 n.22, 130, 144–5, 175
Book of Geometrical Constructions/A'māl al-handasa (Būzjanī) 106, 107, 107 n.40, n.48, 133, 133 n.46, 178, 178 nn.132–3, 203, 203 n.108, 203
Book of Healing/Shīfā' (Ibn Sīnā) 37, 40, 119, 119 n.112
Book of India/Hind (Bīrūnī) 56, 56 n.69
Book of Instruction/Tafhīm (Bīrūnī) viii, 3 n.15, 55 n.62–3, 56, 56 n.66, 57, 108, 108 n.49, 129 n.22, 130, 133, 138 n.72, 182 n.9, 204–6, 207 n.133
Book of Kings/Shāh-Nāmih (Firduwsī) viii, 79, 80, 80 n.18, 83, 94, 129, 129 n.20, n.22, 148, 149, 149 n.129, 182 n.7, 206 n.129
Book on Measurement Principles/Uṣūl al-miṣāḥa (Ibn al-Haytham) 106, 106 n.37
Book on Measurement/Misāḥa (Kubanānī) 165, 165 n.58

Book of Nativities/Nahmaṭān/Nahmuṭān (Ibn Nawbakht) 92, 92 n.80, 94, 95 nn.95–6
Book of Optics/Optika (Euclid) 189 n.44, 199, 199 n.95, 200
Book of Optics/Optika (Ptolemy) 189 n.44, 200
Book of Optics/Manāẓir (Ibn al-Haytham) 2 n.12, 50, 104, 104 n.26, 107, 109–10, 114–17, 134, 134 n.49, 169, 179, 181, 186 n.33, 187, 189, 190, 193–4, 200, 202, 204

Calendar of Timekeeping/Rūz-nāma… mīqāt (Shaykh Wafā᾽) viii, ix, 101 n.12, 105, 106, 106 n.39, 127 nn.13–14, 127–8, 128 n.15, 154
Canon of Medicine/Qānūn fi-ṭibb (Ibn Sīnā) 40, 101, 102 n.13, 119, 119 n.113, 127
Category of Nations/Ṭabaqāt al-umam (Ṣā῾id al-Andalusī) 138, 138 n.71
Chronology/Ta᾽rīkh (Khwārizmī) 59, 59 n.79
Commentary on the Epitome of Belief/ Sharḥ Tajrīd al-aqā῾id (Qūshjī) 72, 72 n.148, 73–6
Commentary on Motion of the Heavens/ Commentariolus (Copernicus) 75, 75 n.168
Compendium on Cosmography/Mukhtaṣar dar ῾ilm-i hay᾽a (Kāshānī/Kāshī) 164, 164 n.56
Compendium on the Sciences/Jāmi῾ al-῾ulūm (Rāzī, Fakhr al-Dīn) 130 n.25

Dialogue(s) of Baghdad and Isfahan/Munāẓirāt-i/Munāẓirih-i Baghdād va Iṣfahān (Kamāl-i Iṣfahānī)
- catalogue entry 17, 22, 25
- colophon 38 n.89, n.91, 182 n.6
- colour scans viii, 99–100
- companion, of author 33–4
- comparisons 32–5
- competitions 32–3
- composition 6, 17, 27–9, 29 n.49
- dating x, 6, 27–9, 39
- digital 125–6, 126 n.4, 127–8, 151–2
- discovery x, xi, 1, 17–22, 17 n.1
- ending 34–5, 38
- languages 26, 43
- manuscript viii (Plate 1), xi, 21–2, 26–7, 26, 26, n.39, 35, 43–6, 186
- microfilm 17, 26, 77, 79
- new manuscript record 181–2, 181 n.2
- opening 32–3
- science not mentioned x, 45–6
- second life 125, 125 n.3
- transcription 6, 26–7, 35–6, 38, 38 n.89, n.91
- virtual 125–8
- 'Windows' manuscript exhibit viii, 99–102, 99 n.3, 100 n.6. 102–3, 102 n.16, 117 n.101, 125 n.3, 126, 128–9, 128 n.16, 130, 176 n.122

Dialogue of Two Chief World Systems/ Dialogo (Galileo) 45, 45 n.13, 178, 178 n.130
Doubts on/Aporias Against Ptolemy/ Shukūk ῾ala Baṭlamyūs (Ibn al-Haytham) 70 n.135, 99, 99 n.1, 113, 113 n.85, 160

Elements of Geometry/Stoicheia (Euclid) 10, 49–50, 96, 97, 105, 120, 146, 163, 176, 176 nn.123–4

Final Inquiry/Nihāyat al-sūl (Ibn Shāṭir) 159, 159 n.39
Fortune-telling book/Fāl-nāmih (῾Āmilī, Bahā᾽ al-Dīn) 175 n.118, 177, 177 n.126
Four Discourses/Chahār Maqāla (Nīẓāmī ῾Arūḍī) 63, 63 n.97

Guide for the Perplexed/Dalālat al-ḥā'irīn (Maimonides) 142

History of Philosophers/Tā᾽rīkh al-ḥukamā᾽ (Ibn al-Qifṭī) 113, 113 n.79

Incoherence of the Incoherence/Tahāfut al-Tahāfut (Averroes) 139, 139 n.74
Incoherence of the Philosophers/Tahāfut al-Falāsifa (Ghazzālī) 139

Intermediate Books, Recension/Taḥrīr al-Mutawassiṭāt (Ṭūsī, Naṣīr al-Dīn) 133, 133 n.40, n.43, 134, 134 n.54, 135 n.55, 145

Journey and Conduct/Sayr wa sulūk (Ṭūsī, Naṣīr al-Dīn) 145, 145 n.109

Key of Arithmetic/Miftāḥ al-ḥisāb (Kāshānī/Kāshī) 164, 164 n.56

Memoir on Astronomy/Tadhkira fī ʿilm al-hayʾa (Ṭūsī, Naṣīr al-Dīn) 69, 69 n.129, n.131, 70 n.136, 145–6
Memoir of the Poets/Tadhkiratu al-shuʿarā (Dawlatshāh) 83 n.37, 84

Perspectiva (Alhazen) 110, 154, 179, 189, 189 n.45, 202
Planetary Hypotheses/Manshūrāt (Ptolemy) 142, 142 n.87

Quatrains/Rubāʿiyāt (Khayyām) 62, 62 nn.93–4

Rational Measures/Miʿyār al-ʿuqūl (Ibn Sīnā: attribution) 121–3
Recension of Euclid's Optics/Taḥrir al-Manāẓir (Ṭūsī, Naṣīr al-Dīn) 199
Revolution of the Heavenly Spheres/De Revolutionibus (Copernicus) 45, 50, 74, 75, 75 n.168, 177–8

Shape of the Eclipse/Ṣurat al-kusūf (Ibn al-Haytham) 114 n.89, 190 n.54
Sky and the World (Oresme) 161
Solutions to the Difficulties of Muʿīnīyah/Ḥall-i Mushkilāt-i Muʿīnīyah (Ṭūsī, Naṣīr al-Dīn) 146, 146 n.112
Stairway to Heaven/Sullam al-samāʾ (Kāshānī/Kāshī Kashī) 164, 164 n.56
Star Catalogue/Zīj (Ulugh Beg) 72
Starry Messenger/Sidereus Nuncius (Galileo) 54, 198–9
Summary of Arithmetic/Khulāṣat al-ḥisāb viii, 102 n.14, 127 n.12, 176, 176 n.122

Thousand and One Nights/Alf layl wa al-layla 22, 22 n.16, 60
Treatise on Circumference/al-Risālah al-Muḥīṭīyah (Kāshānī/Kashī) 163 n.53, 164 n.56
Treatise on Halo andRainbow/Al-Hālah wa Qaws Quzah (Ibn al-Haytham) 200, 200 n.98
Treatise of Muʿīnīyah/Risālah-i Muʿīnīyah (Ṭūsī, Naṣīr al-Dīn) 70 n.136, 146 n.112
Treatise on Shadows/Aẓlāl (Bīrūnī) 93

Vision of Objects through Constructed Mirrors/ruʾyat al-ashyāʾ . . . fī al-marāyā al-maṣnūʿa (Anonymous) 200–1

Various

Critical thinking 114, 192–3, 192 n.63, 195, 203, 203 n.109, 207

Essentialism/Essentialist 23, 23 n.23, 187, 187 n.38, 188
Experimentation 115, 115 nn.92–3, 116, 120, 132, 154, 154 n.14, 178, 186 n.32, 190, 192, 193, 193 n.68, 198, 201, 203, 207

Generalisations/generalities 23, 24, 97, 98, 98 n.109–10, 116, 132

Historical experiments 3, 50–1, 50 n.35, 81 n.25, 128
Historical explanations 22–4
Historical maps viii, 22, 22 n.18, 25, 25 nn.31–2, 82, 82 nn.32–4, 101, 101 n.9, 102, 104 n.27, 105–6, 106 n.33, 122, 122 n.135, 134, 134 n.50, 151, 151 n.2, 152, 152 n.5, 154–7, 179 n.136, 188, 191, 191 n.56, 194
Historical plays xi, 3, 3 n.22, 4 n.26, 47, 47 n.23, 48, 48 n.25, 50
Historical reconstructions x, 6, 65 n.104, 105, 125–6, 136, 188, 191, 195
Historical travelogues 25, 25 n.34, 38–40

Historical understanding xi, 3, 9, 12, 26, 196, 208

Inspiration, sources of xi, xii, 1, 1 n.2, 2, 2 nn.3–10, 24–6, 25 nn.36–8, 46, 50, 52–3, 55, 58, 101, 104, 107, 113, 152, 152 n.5, 156, 156 n.23, 160
Intermediate civilization 23, 23 n.24
Irreducible factors 23–4

Knowledge/knowledge transmission viii, 4 n.27, 5, 6 n.43, 9–12, 17, 18, 18 n.6, 24, 24 n.28, 33, 41, 44, 65, 70, 73, 73 n.158, 84, 86, 88, 89, 90, 92–6, 97 n.106, 100, 101 n.10, 109 n.57, 112, 120 nn.122–3, 122, 137, 150, 150 n.138, 164 n.55, 172, 172 n.153, 174, 177, 181 n.2, 187–8, 193 n.66, 194, 200, 201, 203, 208
Knowledge exchange 5, 12, 32–3, 32 n.64, 69 n.130, 73, 167 n.71, n.73, 173, 201, 208

Microscopic studies 82

Precursorism/Reductionism 23, 188
Preset mentalities 23
Puzzles/puzzle-solving 5, 48, 55, 67, 72, 76, 84, 101–8, 122, 135–6, 150, 150 n.137, 158, 160, 176–7, 179, 193 n.66, 199, 202

Scientific authority 22, 54, 84 n.41, 86, 89, 100, 103, 115, 142, 186 n.33
Scientific classification 119, 120 n.122, 130
Scientific concepts 47, 63–4, 84, 87, 89, 96–8, 115, 115 n.93, 137, 141, 169, 197, 200, 204, 207
Scientific decline 24, 24 n.27, 65, 65 n.107, 74, 156, 173, 173 n.103
Scientific education 119, 119 n.115, nn.117–18
Scientific method, rise 110, 110 n.63
Scientific patronage x, 4 n.27, 67, 89, 91–2, 145, 154, 162–3, 167 n.73, 169, 172, 174, 175
Scientific Revolution 23, 23 n.19, 74, 171, 173, 198
Scientific traditions 4 n.33, 48, 92, 130 n.25, 149, 153, 153 n.8, n.10, 156
Strategy Games
- Ancients 197, 197 n.88
- Backgammon 7, 81, 100, 196, 196 n.87, 197, 197 n.88
- Chess viii, 7, 7 n.49, 81, 96, 96 n.103, 100, 196, 196 n.87, 197, 197 n.88

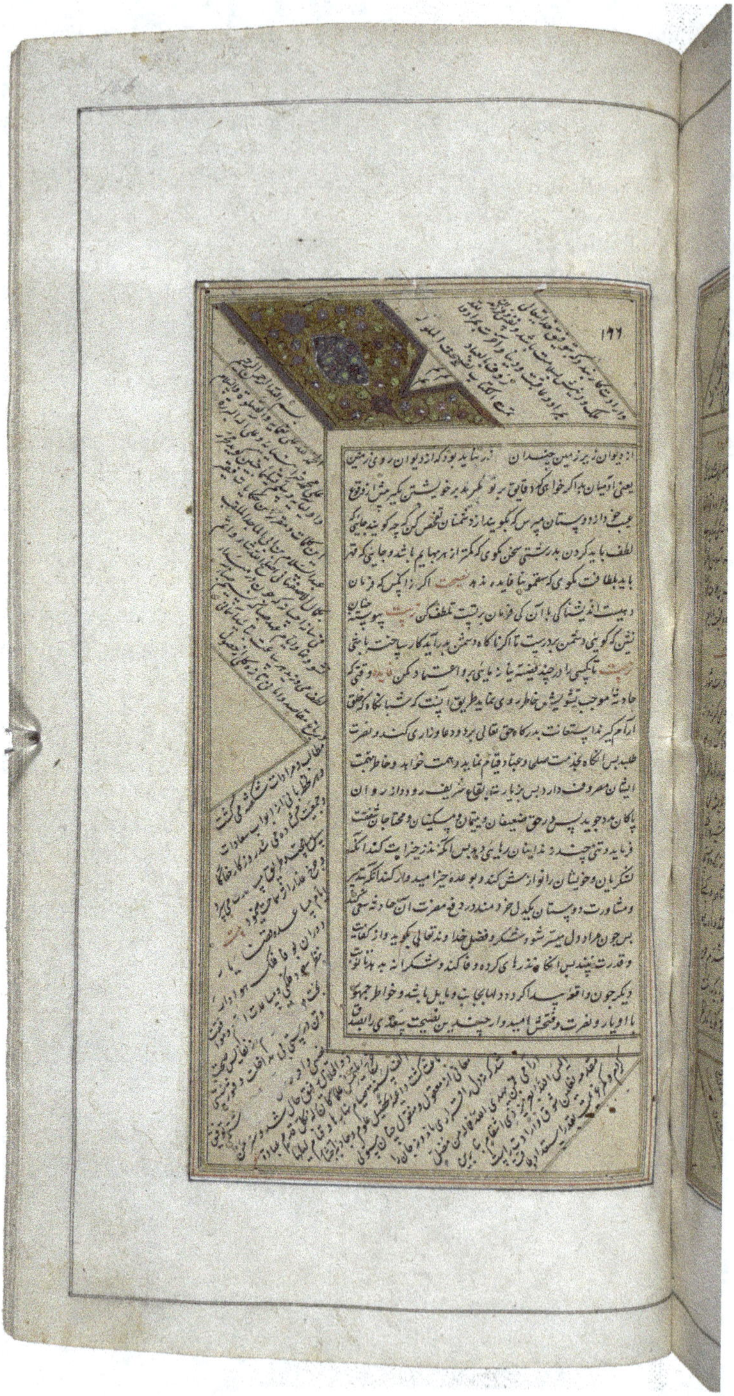

Plate 1 *Dialogues of Baghdad and Isfahan: Munāẓirāt-i Baghdād va Iṣfahān*
© The British Library Board. MS Add 18, 411, fol. 166a

Plate 2 *Pseudo-Galen Book of Antidotes: Kitāb al-Diryāq*
Nationalbibliothek, Vienna. MS AF. 10 fol. 157

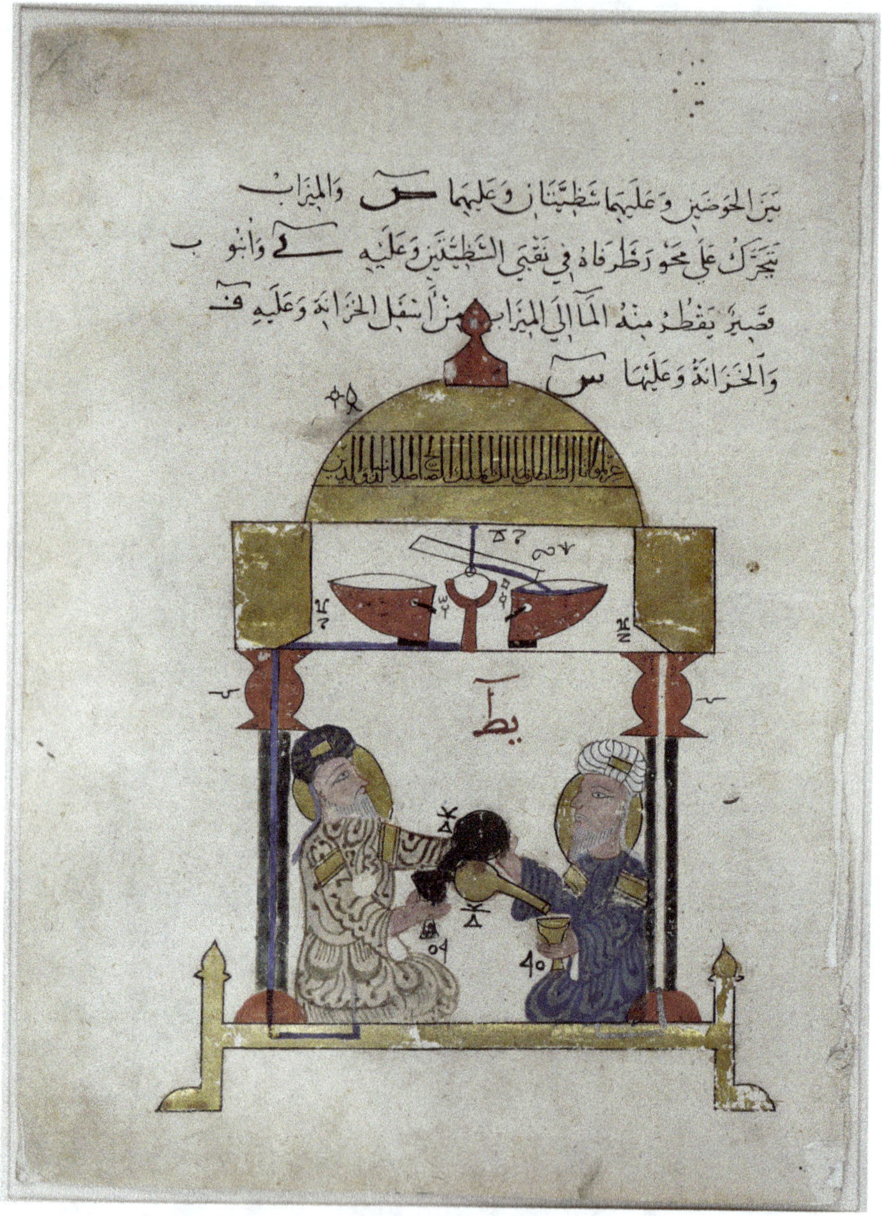

Plate 3 Jazarī, *Compendium of Theory and Useful Practice in the Mechanical Arts*
Boston Museum of Fine Arts. MS 15.114

Plate 4 Frontispiece. Alhazen and Galileo: *Selenographia*, Johannes Hevelius, 1647
Harvard University. Houghton Library. Typ 620.47.452F

Plate 5 Sagitarrius, Bīrūnī, *Book of Instructions*: *Kitāb al-Tafhīm* (adaptation)
© The British Library Board. MS Sup 7697

Plate 6 ʿĀmilī, *Summary of Arithmetic*: *Khulāṣat al-ḥisāb*
Harvard University, Houghton Library. MS Arab SM4284 (above)
Manuscript display: 'Windows into early science', Virtual Gallery (below)

Plate 7 *Timekeeping Calendar* (centre): Plate 9 Close up. Other: Private Collection © Elaheh Kheirandish https://www.scholar.harvard.edu/ekheirandish/exhibits

Plate 8 '*First Small Shahnama* : *Buzurgmihr masters the game of chess*'
Metropolitan Museum of Art, New York. MS 34.24.1b

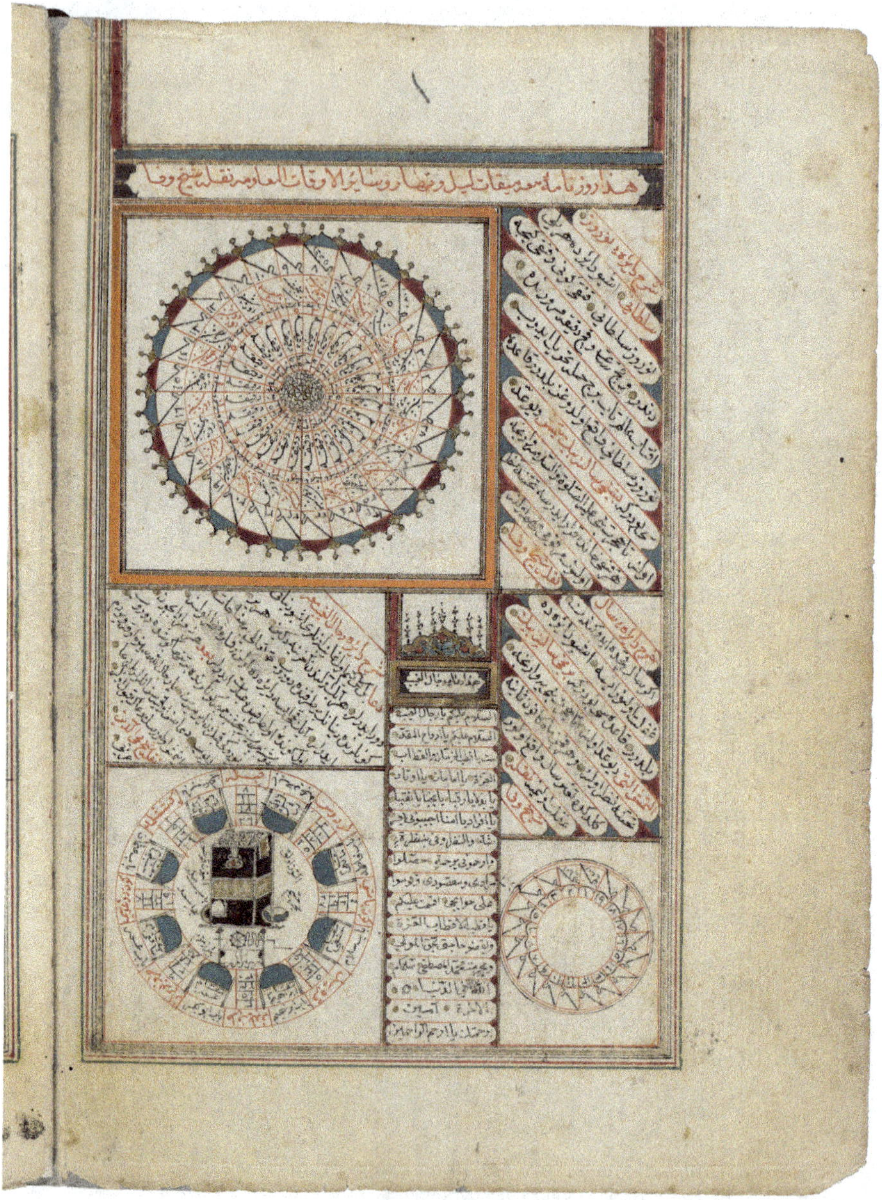

Plate 9 Shaykh Wafāʾ, *Calendar of Timekeeping*: *Rūz-nāma . . . mīqāt*
Harvard University, Houghton Library. MS Arab 397, opening folio

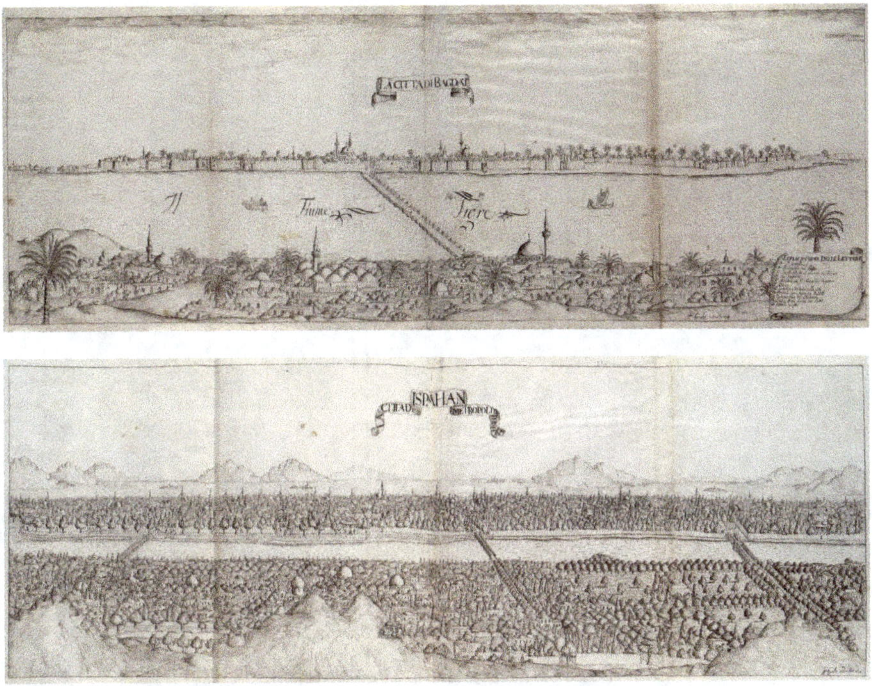

Plate 10 *Panoramas of Baghdad and Isfahan: Travels and Journal of Ambrosio Bembo*
The James Ford Bell Library, University of Minnesota. 1676 fBe

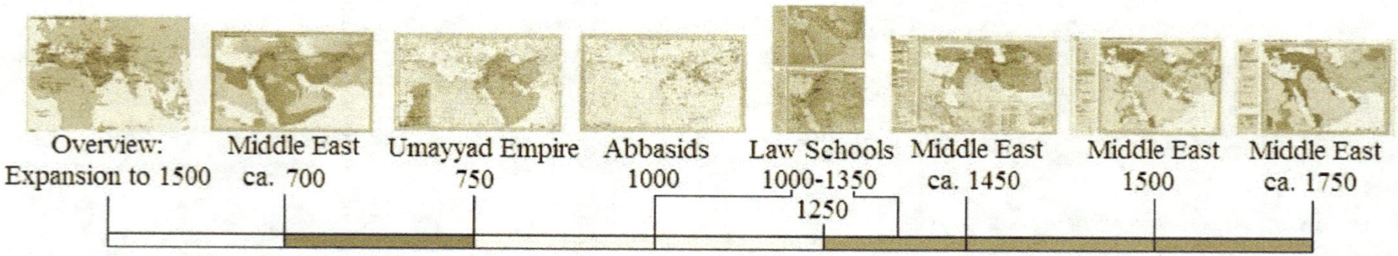

Plate 11 Maps from Tübingen Atlas of the Near East: ca. 750–1750
Harvard University, Pusey Library

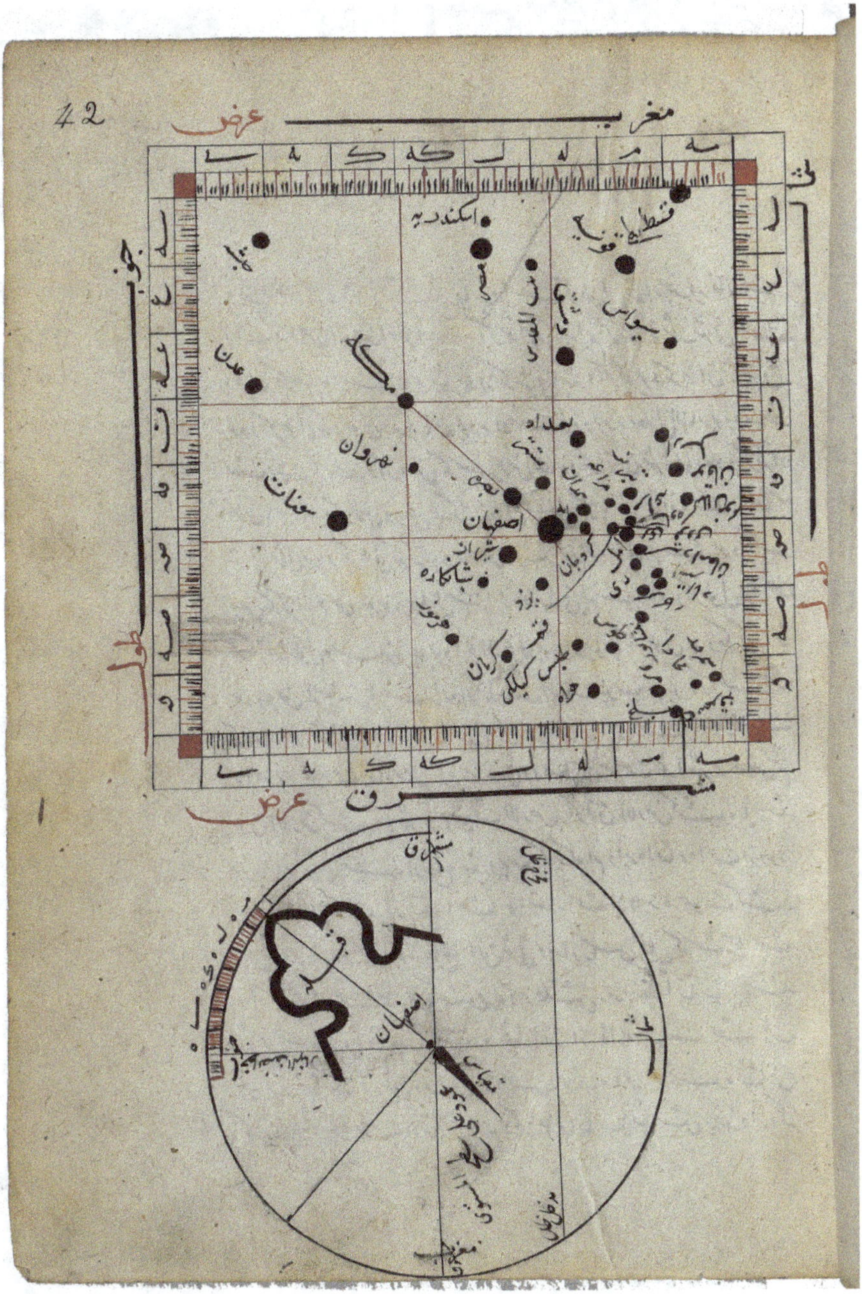

Plate 12 Map from a treatise on Determining the Direction of the Qibla
Bibliothèque nationale de France. BNF Paris: MS Persan 169, 6, fol. 42a

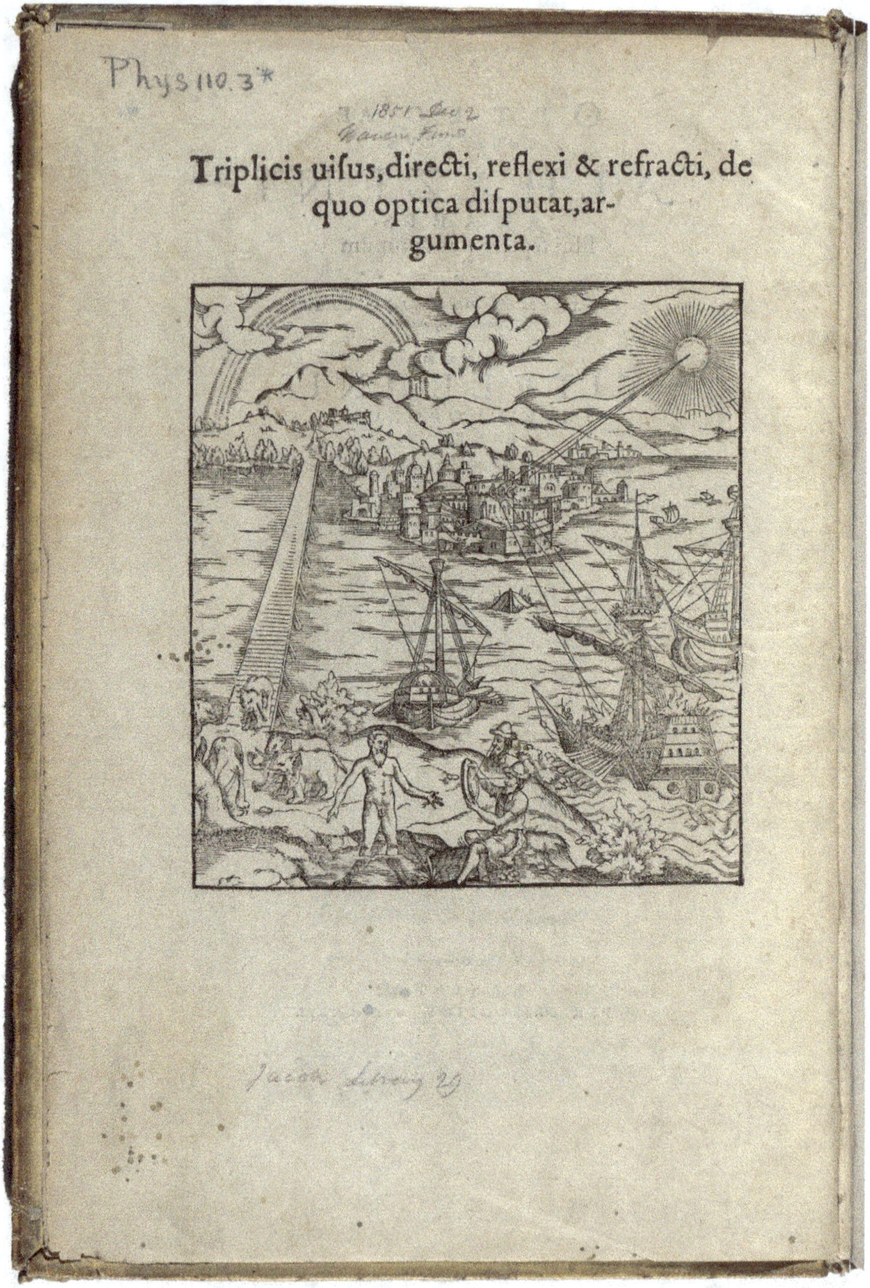
Triplicis uiſus, directi, reflexi & refracti, de quo optica diſputat, argumenta.

Plate 13 Frontispiece: Alhazen, *Opticae Thesaurus*, Risner, Friedrich (ed), 1572 Harvard University, Houghton Library. f GC5 R4947 572i

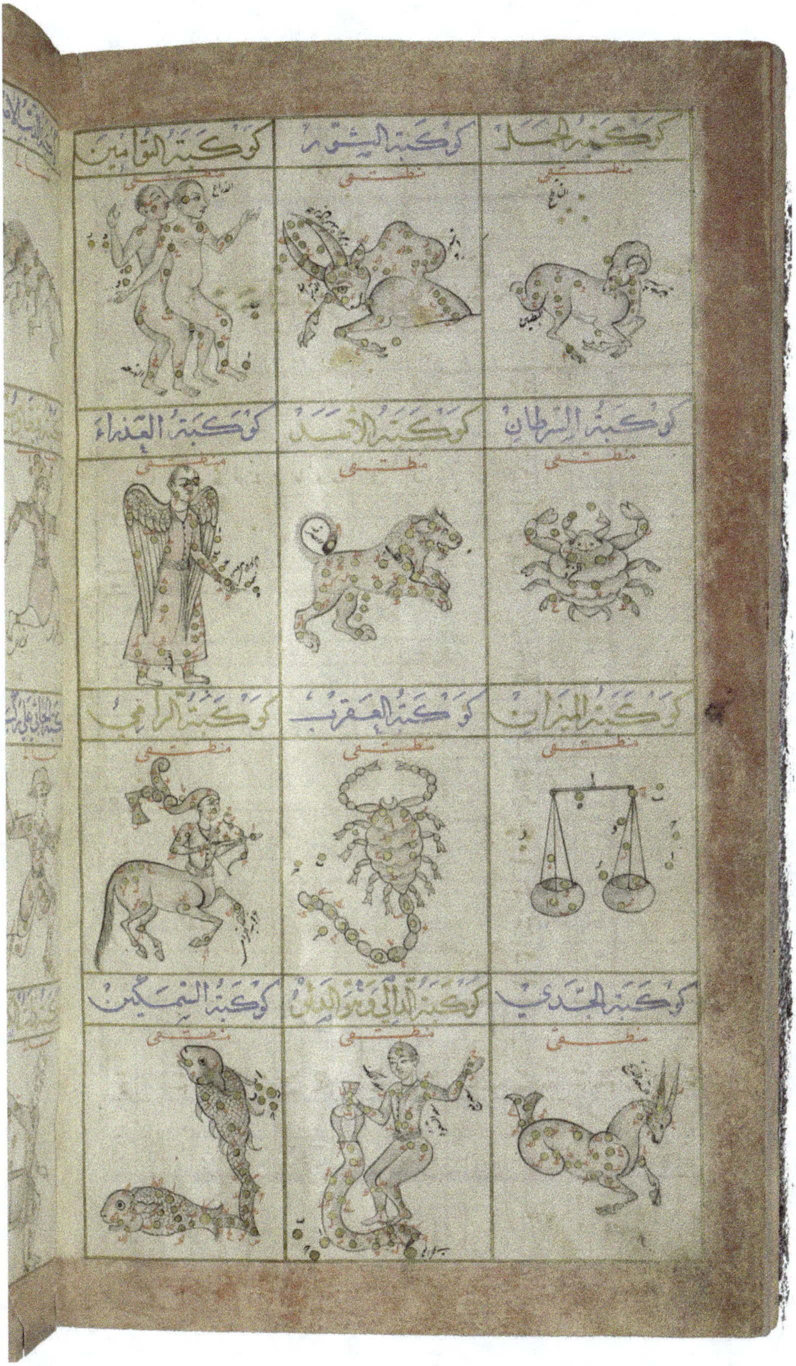

Plate 14 Zodiac Constellations, *Compendium of Knowledge* (Jung)
Harvard Art Museums/Arthur M. Sackler Museum, Gift of
Philip Hofer. Photo: © President and Fellows of Harvard College.
MS 1984.463, fol. 131b

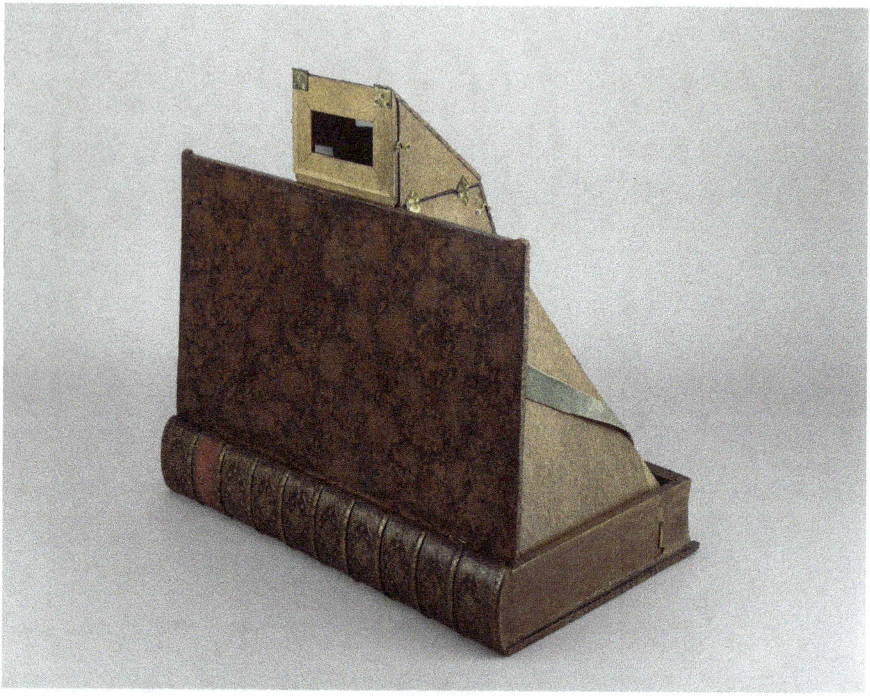

Plate 15 Photo: Book Camera Obscura, France about 1750
Getty Library and Research Institute, Los Angeles, Nekes collection 93.R.118

Plate 16 Shaykh Wafā', *Calendar of Timekeeping: Rūz-nāma . . . mīqāt*
Harvard University, Houghton Library. MS Arab 397, opening folio, close up (centre).
Other: Moon, Sun and Star icons © Adele Karimian

www.ingramcontent.com/pod-product-compliance
Lightning Source LLC
Chambersburg PA
CBHW052152300426
44115CB00011B/1638